# HANDBOOK OF DEVELOPMENT ECONOMICS
## VOLUME IIIB

# HANDBOOKS IN ECONOMICS

## 9

*Series Editors*

**KENNETH J. ARROW**

**MICHAEL D. INTRILIGATOR**

**ELSEVIER**
AMSTERDAM • LAUSANNE • NEW YORK • OXFORD • SHANNON • TOKYO

# HANDBOOK OF DEVELOPMENT ECONOMICS

## VOLUME IIIB

*Edited by*

**JERE BEHRMAN**
*University of Pennsylvania*

and

**T.N. SRINIVASAN**
*Yale University*

1995

**ELSEVIER**

**AMSTERDAM ● LAUSANNE ● NEW YORK ● OXFORD ● SHANNON ● TOKYO**

ELSEVIER SCIENCE B.V.
Sara Burgerhartstraat 25
P.O. Box 211, 1000 AE Amsterdam, The Netherlands


**Library of Congress Cataloging-in-Publication Data**
(Revised for volume 3)

Handbook of development economics.

(Handbooks in economics; 9)
Vol. 3 edited by Jere Behrman and T.N. Srinivasan.
Includes bibliographical references and index.
1. Economic development—Handbooks, manuals, etc.
2. Development economics. I.  Chenery, Hollis Burnley.
II. Srinivasan, T. N., 1933–     . III.  Handbooks in
economics; bk. 9.
HD82.H275  1988     338.9     87-34960
ISBN 0-444-70339-X (U.S.: set; jacket)
ISBN 0-444-70337-3 (U.S.: v. 1.: jacket)
ISBN 0-444-70338-1 (U.S.: v. 2)
ISBN 0-444-82301-8 (U.S.: v.3A)
ISBN 0-444-82302-6 (U.S.: v.3B)
ISBN 0-444-88481-5 (U.S.: set)


ISBN volume 3A: 0 444 82301 8
ISBN volume 3B: 0 444 82302 6
ISBN set: 0 444 88481 5

This book is printed on acid-free paper.

PRINTED IN THE NETHERLANDS

# INTRODUCTION TO THE SERIES

The aim of the *Handbooks in Economics* series is to produce Handbooks for various branches of economics, each of which is a definitive source, reference, and teaching supplement for use by professional researchers and advanced graduate students. Each Handbook provides self-contained surveys of the current state of a branch of economics in the form of chapters prepared by leading specialists on various aspects of this branch of economics. These surveys summarize not only received results but also newer developments, from recent journal articles and discussion papers. Some original material is also included, but the main goal is to provide comprehensive and accessible surveys. The Handbooks are intended to provide not only useful reference volumes for professional collections but also possible supplementary readings for advanced courses for graduate students in economics.

# Dedication to HOLLIS CHENERY

Hollis Chenery was a coeditor of the first two volumes of the Handbook of Development Economics. As the present volume was in press, Professor Chenery passed away after a long illness. He was among the pioneers of development economics whose well-known work on Patterns of Development based on an analysis of time series data on a cross section of developing countries was a landmark in policy relevant, and analytically-coherent, though eclectic, empirical analysis of the development process. Both of us knew him well personally and professionally and will miss his wise counsel. We dedicate this volume to Hollis Chenery's memory.

Jere Behrman
T.N. Srinivasan

# CONTENTS OF THE HANDBOOK

## VOLUME I

### PART 1: ECONOMIC DEVELOPMENT – CONCEPTS AND APPROACHES

### PART 2: STRUCTURAL TRANSFORMATION

# PREFACE

The first two volumes of the *Handbook of Development Economics* were published in 1988 and 1989 respectively. However, the analysis in various chapters of the two volumes, particularly those relating to debt, capital flows and the analytics of structural adjustment programs initiated by many developing countries in the early eighties, was completed in effect two years or so before publication. By that time the debt crisis had not been resolved and enough data on the experience with structural adjustment programs had not accumulated to allow a serious evaluation of their impact.

More importantly, the collapse of the centrally planned economies of Eastern Europe was in the future. Although the outstanding success of the Chinese reforms abandoning collectivized agriculture in favour of small peasant agriculture based on the household responsibility system was already evident, the rapid growth of Chinese foreign trade, the huge inflow of external capital into China (particularly in the special coastal economic zones), and the phenomenal growth of GDP at annual rates exceeding 10 percent were in the future. Finally and most importantly, the dismal failure of the dominant paradigm of development focusing on state-directed, inward-oriented, import-substituting industrialization on which the development strategies of most developing countries was based, and equally, the outstanding success of East Asian countries that departed early on from the dominant paradigm by emphasizing outward-orientation, was yet to be clearly perceived by policy makers in many, though not all, developing countries.

In part as a result of the mounting evidence against the dominant paradigm, many countries initiated economic reforms in the eighties by reducing state-involvement in the economy through privatization, opening up the economy to a much greater extent to foreign trade and investment and, above all, allowing market forces and the private sector to guide resource allocation to a much greater extent. Many of the reform efforts were undertaken in the context of a less favorable external environment for commodity exports, diminished capital flows (particularly from commercial banks) and a generally unfavorable macro-economic environment. Issues of credibility, sustainability, pace (gradual versus rapid), sequencing (for example, of the liberalization of external capital and current accounts), the response of individual agents to changes in incentives and political economy of reforms came to the fore. A substantial body of new analytical and empirical work on these issues based on the experience with structural stabilization and economic reforms has since become available. Several chapters of the present volume are devoted to this research.

Some significant developments in theoretical and empirical analyses of growth and development were either covered too briefly in the first two volumes or came after their publication. First, it has become possible to apply some relatively new tools of econometric analysis (e.g. kernel estimation of densities, non-parametric regression, ways of controlling for unobserved heterogeneities, cointegration, to mention just a few) for essentially two reasons: a vast increase in computing capability accompanied by a steep fall in computing costs, and the availability of sizeable data sets, particularly data from household surveys (a few of which surveyed the same set of households over a number of periods), and a new data set on real product for 130 countries over the period 1950–1985, put together by Summers and Heston (1988). Second, the applied general equilibrium models discussed in Chapter 18 of Volume 2 have since been generalized and used widely in development policy analyses. Many of these applications have involved extending the analytical scope of the model not only to cover scale economics and non-competitive and incomplete market structures, but also to incorporate macroeconomic aspects arising from the introduction of nominal assets and expectations. Third, interest in growth theory revived with the publication of the pioneering papers of Lucas (1988) and Romer (1986). Since then, a still growing literature variously described as "endogenous growth theory" or "new growth theory" has emerged, which formalizes the externalities from human capital accumulation and learning by doing, and endogenizes technical progress through the profit-seeking actions of agents operating in an imperfectly competitive market which enables them to appropriate the gains from their innovations, at least temporarily. The revived interest in growth theory has also stimulated empirical research on testing the implications of the theory using the Summers–Heston data set. One chapter has been devoted in the present volume to each of the above areas: data and econometric tools, applied general and equilibrium models, and endogenous growth theory.

Some topics which received only a brief attention or none at all in the first two volumes called for a more extensive treatment. For example, even though poverty has been endemic in many developing countries and, understandably, the eradication of poverty has long been, and continues to be, the overarching objective of most development strategies, the first two volumes discussed poverty only briefly. A chapter was devoted to the closely related, but distinct, concept of inequality and there was an extended discussion in it of the Kuznets hypothesis that income inequality will widen during the initial stages of development. But the analytics of poverty measurement, the determinants, correlates and trends in poverty, or the debates as to whether there was an unavoidable trade-off, at least in the short run, between rapid development and poverty alleviation, or whether rapid growth is the most effective strategy to eliminate poverty, were not covered. A second issue, which has become increasingly a matter of public concern around the world, is the need to prevent environmental degradation and to preserve bio-diversity. This concern has led to the search for a balance between the legitimate needs of poor countries to grow rapidly out of their poverty and the possible draft their rapid growth might make on global environmental endowments.

A third issue, which the difficulties experienced by the successor states of the former Soviet Union and its satellites in transforming themselves into market economies has highlighted, is the importance of the existence and effective functioning of appropriate institutions (social, political, legal, administrative and economic) for successful development as well as transition to a market economy. Although institutional economics is an ancient subdiscipline within economics, a rigorous analytical foundation for it is of recent origin. Institutional features of developing economics such as share-cropping, interlinking of land, labor, credit and product markets, etc., which were once thought to be inefficient semi-feudal relics, are now seen in a different light, as possibly efficient contractual arrangements in the absence of a complete set of contingent markets and in the presence of asymmetric information, moral hazard and adverse selection.

One of the crucial processes in development is the process of technological transformation. Kuznets (1966) viewed the epoch of modern economic growth as distinguished by the systematic application of science and technology to production. However, the process through which a technologically backward economy transforms itself not only by adapting and adopting available knowledge from elsewhere but also by beginning to generate new knowledge, is neither simple nor well understood. The first two volumes did not cover this process. Again, a chapter is devoted in the present volume to each of these four topics: poverty, environment, institutions, and technological transformation. Institutions relating to land use are discussed in a fifth chapter.

From early on development economists recognized that lack of infrastructure (then called social overhead capital) constrained development, and saw an important role for state action in ensuring adequate infrastructural investment because of scale economies due to lumpiness of such investment and externalities it generates. For example, Rosenstein-Rodan (1964) argued

"Because of these indivisibilities and because services of social overhead capital cannot be imported, a high initial investment in social overhead capital must either precede or be known to be certainly available in order to pave the way for additional more quickly yielding directly productive investments. This indivisibility of social overhead capital constitutes one of the main obstacles to development of under-developed countries". (p. 435)

In the earlier volumes there was no extended discussion of the role of the state in the development process and infrastructural activities figured primarily in the chapter on project evaluation, and briefly in that on Primary Exporting Countries. The present volume repairs this omission with a chapter devoted to infrastructure. Also, the role of the state in development process figures prominently in the chapter reviewing development experience.

Finally, the present volume also extends and updates the discussion in the earlier volumes on savings and human resource investments and household behavior. There have been recent theoretical developments on intertemporal allocation of resources and risk sharing and distribution in a context where the structure of financial markets is incomplete, existing markets are segmented and imperfect, and when relevant information is asymmetrically distributed among agents. These have major implications of savings and financial inter-mediation. Besides developments in institutional economics offer new insights on the role of informal savings and credit institutions that are ubiquitous in developing countries in all parts of the world. Formally, transferring resources over time through savings and investment, as well as borrowing and lending, is analogous to transferring resources across uncertain states of nature. Besides, given that future states of nature are often uncertain, intertemporal transfers simultaneously involve transfers across states of nature as well. Thus access to credit could influence an agent's ability to smooth her consumption against fluctuations in income over time as well as across states of nature. Many of these issues were not fully addressed in the earlier volumes and are covered in the present.

Part 3 of the first volume was devoted to Human Resources and Labor Markets. Again, since its publication there have been significant developments in tools of empirical analysis. Further, with the increased availability of micro data from household surveys, there have been several applications of these tools, which in particular pay careful attention to the implications for econo-metric estimation of the unobserved heterogeneities among individuals and households. The chapter on Human Resources in the present volume covers these recent developments and updates the discussion in the first volume.

**Acknowledgements**

We owe a deep debt of gratitude to the authors of this volume for their diligent efforts, for commenting on each others' chapters, and responding in their revision to the comments of their fellow authors and editors. We thank the Asian Development Bank for generous support in inviting the authors to present the first drafts of their chapters at the Bank's first Development Economics Conference during October 12–15, 1992. We are grateful to Dr.

S.C. Jha, Chief Economist, and Dr. M.G. Quibria, Head of the Economics and Development Resource Center of the Asian Development Bank, for their hospitality and unstinting cooperation. It is impossible to thank adequately the assistance of Louise Danishevsky of the Economic Growth Center at Yale University in ensuring that the drafts of each chapter were received on time and preparing them for the publishers.

JERE BEHRMAN
*University of Pennsylvania*


T.N. SRINIVASAN
*Yale University*

## References

Kuznets, S. (1966) *Modern economic growth: Rate, structure and spread*. New Haven: Yale University Press.

Lucas, R. (1988) 'On the Mechanics of Economic Development', *Journal of Monetary Economics*, 22:3–42.

Romer, P. (1986) 'Increasing returns and long-run growth', *Journal of Political Economy*, 94:1002–1037.

Rosenstein-Rodan, P. (1964) 'The "Big-Push" argument', in: G. Meier, ed., *Leading issues in development economics*, New York: Oxford University Press, 431–440.

Summers, R. and Heston, A. (1988) 'A new set of international comparisons of real product and price levels: Estimates for 130 countries', *Review of Income and Wealth*, 34:1–25.

# CONTENTS OF VOLUME IIIB

*Chapter 42*
Power, Distortions, Revolt and Reform in Agricultural Land Relations
HANS P. BINSWANGER, KLAUS DEININGER, and GERSHON FEDER                    2659

# PART 9

# POLICY REFORM, STABILIZATION, STRUCTURAL ADJUSTMENT AND GROWTH

# PART 9: POLICY REFORM, STABILIZATION, STRUCTURAL ADJUSTMENT AND GROWTH

## Introduction

We noted in our preface that since the publication of the first two volumes of the *Handbook of Development Economics*, the paradigm of development that was dominant for a long time after the Second World War and which emphasized a state-directed, inward-oriented, import-substituting industrialization as the appropriate strategy of development was finally dethroned with many countries undertaking reforms aimed at liberalizing their economies from the shackles of state control. Enough data and experience with structural adjustment and stabilization in several countries have since become available to permit a serious evaluation of their impact. We noted also that interest in theories of long-run growth revived in the late eighties and a burgeoning theoretical and empirical literature on growth has since emerged.

The chapters that follow examine, from an analytical and empirical perspective, the important issues thrown up by the experience of developing countries, particularly since 1980, but also earlier. These include: a comparison of alternative development strategies, macroeconomic stabilization and microeconomic structural adjustment, poverty and the poor during the process of development, stabilization and adjustment, credibility, sequencing and the political economy of reforms. Also an assessment of recent contributions to the literature on growth theory and empirics from the perspective of the economics of development is included. The chapters are:

Chapter 40. Anne Krueger: Policy Lessons from Development Experience Since the Second World War

Chapter 41. Michael Lipton and Martin Ravallion: Poverty and Policy

Chapter 42. Hans Binswanger, Klaus Deininger and Gershon Feder: Power, Distortions, Revolt and Reform in Agricultural Land Relations

Chapter 43. Emmanuel Jimenez: Human and Physical Infrastructure: Investment and Pricing Policies in Developing Countries

*Handbook of Development Economics, Volume III, Edited by J. Behrman and T.N. Srinivasan*
© *Elsevier Science B.V., 1995*

Chapter 44. Vittorio Corbo and Stanley Fischer: Structural Adjustment, Stabilization and Policy Reform: Domestic and International Finance

Chapter 45: Dani Rodrik: Trade and Industrial Policy Reform

Chapter 46: Pranab Bardhan, "The Contribution of Endogenous Growth Theory to the Analysis of Development Problems: An Assessment"

The dethronement of the dominant paradigm and the elevation to a higher status, if not enthronement, of openness, competition and the market in development is best illustrated by India, the earliest articulator and adopter of, and the last among major developing countries to abandon, the dominant paradigm. The Indian case is worth stating in some detail not only because of India's large share of the population and of the poor in the developing world, but also, as Krueger (Chapter 40) points out, because of the significant influence of Indian thought and experience on development. Further, Indian experience also illustrates and confirms some of the analytical results presented in some of the chapters about the reform process.

The foundations of post-independence Indian planning for economic development were laid in the late thirties and early forties, predominantly by the National Planning Committee of the Indian National Congress constituted in 1938 under the chairmanship of Jawaharlal Nehru. Also, other groups spanning the entire political spectrum including businessmen, labor unions and followers of Mahatma Gandhi put forward their own development plans in the early forties. Remarkably all groups agreed not only on the overarching objective of poverty eradication, but also on the dominant role the state had to play in achieving the objective. Indeed, that the strategy for economic development should be articulated through a national development plan and implemented through state-directed planning was also widely accepted.

The National Planning Committee completed most of its work prior to the arrest in 1940 of Nehru by the colonial government. Nehru (1946) provides a fascinating account of the committee's plan. It clearly shows that many, though not all, post-war debates among development economists and in international organizations about objectives, strategy, roles of industrialization, the state and foreign trade were anticipated by the committee.

The committee declared the overarching objective of development was

   ... to insure an adequate standard of living for the masses; in other words, to get rid of the appalling poverty of the people. There was lack of food, of clothing, of housing, and of every other essential requirement of human existence. To remove this lack and insure an irreducible minimum standard for everybody, the national income had to be greatly increased, and in addition to this increased production there had to be a more equitable distribution of wealth.[1]

We fixed a ten-year period for the plan, with control figures for different periods and different sectors of economic life. Certain objective tests were also suggested:

(1) The improvement of nutrition – a balanced diet having a calorific value of 2400 to 2800 units for an adult worker.

(2) Improvement in clothing from the then consumption of about 15 years to at least 30 yards per capita per annum.

(3) Housing standards to reach at least 100 square feet per capita. Further, certain indices of progress had to be kept in mind:
    (a) Increase in agricultural production
    (b) Increase in industrial production
    (c) Diminution of unemployment
    (d) Increase in per capita income
    (e) Liquidation of illiteracy
    (f) Increase in public utility services
    (g) Provision of medical aid on the basis of one unit for 100 population
    (h) Increase in the average expectation of life [Nehru (1946), pp. 402–403]

The committee deemed industrialization to be the primary instrument of development and asserted that the problems of poverty and unemployment, of national defence and of economic regeneration in general, cannot be solved without industrialization. Promotion of large scale manufacturing, heavy industries, electric power and scientific research were thought to be essential: "The three fundamental requirements of India, if she is to develop industrially and otherwise, are: a heavy engineering and machine-making industry, scientific research institutes, and electric power . . . an attempt to build up a country's economy largely on the basis of cottage and small-scale industries is doomed to failure". (p. 416)

The committee assigned a dominant role for state ownership and regulation in the development of industrial, agricultural and financial sectors:

---

[1] Disquiet expressed in the post-independence Parliament about the distribution of the income growth in the first two five-year plans was to lead Nehru to appoint a committee in 1960 under the chairmanship of the eminent statistician and planner, Professor P. C. Mahalanobis, to study the Distribution of Income and Levels of Living. The committee reported in 1964 long before the World Bank woke up to distributional issues.

"The very essence of this planning was a large measure of regulation and co-ordination. Thus while free enterprise was not ruled out as such, its scope was severely restricted. In regard to defense industries it was decided that they must be owned and controlled by the state. Regarding other key industries, the majority were of opinion that they should be state-owned, but a substantial majority of the committee considered that state control would be sufficient. Such control of these industries, however, had to be rigid". (p. 403)

"Agricultural land, mines, quarries, rivers and forests are forms of national wealth, ownership of which must vest absolutely in the people of India collectively . . . We, or some of us at any rate, hoped to evolve a socialized system of credit. If banks, insurance, etc. were not to be nationalized, they should at least be under the control of the state, thus leading to a state regulation of capital and credit. It was also desirable to control the export and import trade. By these various means a considerable measure of state control would be established in regard to land as well as in industry as a whole, though varying in particular instances, and allowing private initiative to continue in a restricted sphere". (p. 404)

Last, but not the least, foreign trade was viewed, not as an engine of growth, but of economic imperialism and autarkic development was extolled:

"The objective for the country as a whole was the attainment, as far as possible, of national self-sufficiency. International trade was certainly not excluded, but we were anxious to avoid being drawn into the whirlpool of economic imperialism. We wanted neither to be victims of an imperialist power nor to develop such tendencies ourselves". (p. 403)

The development thought and strategy as formulated by Nehru's pre-independence committee governed India's development plans and policies in the first four and a half decades (1947–1991) since independence. An elaborate regulatory framework was instituted to implement the plans. The regulations covered the whole spectrum: the scale, technology, and location of any investment project other than relatively small ones were regulated; permission was needed to expand, relocate, change the output or input mixes of operating plants; critical inputs, particularly imported ones, were allocated; access to domestic equity markets and debt finance was controlled; some vital consumption goods were subject to complete or partial price controls; almost automatic and made-to-measure protection from import competition was granted to domestic producers in many "priority" industries, including in particular the equipment producers.

The crucial aspect of all these regulations was that they were essentially discretionary rather than rule-based and automatic. Although some principles and priorities were to govern the exercise of these regulatory powers, these were largely non-operational for two reasons. *First*, it was impossible, even in theory, to devise a set of principles or rules for all the myriad categories of regulations that were mutually consistent and in consonance with the multiple goals of the industrial policy framework, which in themselves were not entirely consistent. *Second*, the problem of translating whatever rules there were into operational decisions was a problem of Orwellian dimensions. The allocative mechanism was largely in the form of quantitative restrictions unrelated to market realities. A chaotic incentive structure and the unleashing of rapacious rent-seeking and political corruption were the inevitable outcomes.

The achievements under more than four decades of planning and inward-oriented development were modest: incidence of poverty (with a very modest poverty line) went down from over 50 percent of the population in the mid-fifties to about a third in the late eighties; real GDP grew at an average rate of less than 4 percent between 1950–1951 and 1992–1993; self-sufficiency was achieved in a number of commodities, including notably foodgrains, but at very modest levels of per capita consumption; life expectancy at birth increased from 32 years in 1951 to 61 years in 1992 and infant mortality fell from around 150 per 1000 live births to 79 during the same period; a diversified, but internationally uncompetitive, industrial structure was established, but the share of industry in GDP rose only modestly from about a sixth in 1950–1951 to a fifth in 1992–1993, and its share in employment rose far less; gross domestic saving and investment as a share of GDP more than doubled from about 10 percent in 1950–1951 to about 25 percent in 1992–1993; public sector became dominant in several industries, accounting for over 25 percent of GDP and 25 percent of capital stock; India's share in world exports fell from 2 percent in the late forties to about 0.6 percent in the nineties.

Even though the systemic failures of the Indian development strategy was already evident in the mid-sixties and were documented by, among others, Bhagwati and Desai (1970), Bhagwati and Srinivasan (1975) and more recently Bhagwati (1992), their arguments in favour of reforms were largely ignored by the government until a major macroeconomic (fiscal and balance of payments) crisis hit the economy in the wake of the Gulf War and brought it close to default on external debt in June 1991. The government of Prime Minister Rao that took power on June 21, 1991 recognized the *systemic and long-term* failures of India's development strategy and embarked on major reforms by dismantling the strangulating regulatory apparatus governing investment, foreign trade and the financial sector.

The Indian experience brings out, in an especially clear way, the reluctance to abandon cherished beliefs about the virtues of and the need for the state to assume a dominant role in the economy long after their failures had become evident. It also suggests that while macrostability (such as that India enjoyed until the eighties) in itself is not sufficient to generate sustained and rapid growth if micro distortions are massive, a severe macroeconomic crisis could trigger overdue systemic reforms. While the Indian development strategy needed drastic revision, its overarching objective, viz. poverty eradication, still remains as valid as it was in 1938 when the National Planning Committee began its work. Achieving credibility of a reform programme that drastically changes the development strategy pursued for over four decades and challenges long-held beliefs shared across the political spectrum is not easy.

Krueger examines the evolution of thought on development policy, the experience with the application of policies that challenged received wisdom and thought, and the two-way interaction between thought and policy. With this background, she examines a number of studies with individual aspects of economic policy and experience as their focus. She begins with the ideas that were part of the dominant paradigm described above, since, in her view, the experience with the policies that followed from it is still a factor affecting policies and thinking about development. She then reviews the few sustained successes (largely in East Asia), and many aborted successes and outright failures, from a policy perspective. This review leads her to argue that the association of outward-orientation with the successes and inward-orientation with failures was seen by policy makers in countries that failed as calling for policy reform. She concludes her chapter with a review of the theory of and evidence on alternative approaches to policy reform and of the crucial considerations of political economy in policy formulation, reform and execution.

Krueger's discussion of early ideas on development recapitulates the dominant paradigm, in particular its distrust of the private sector, markets and foreign trade and investment, and its exaggerated notions of what state interventions in the economy could achieve. She points out that the outcome of these ideas "was a fairly tightly interconnected set of economic policies. In country after country, an "economic plan" was drawn up (p. 2506). The plan set targets for investment to generate desired growth of income, estimated likely domestic savings, with the difference between required investment and available savings being the required external capital inflow. The analytical framework for deriving investment was the one-sector Harrod–Domar model and a simple Keynesian aggregate savings function for estimating available savings. Often the plan set detailed targets for the output of and investment in individual sectors, these being derived using input–output tables and simple capital–output ratios. Plans also included proposals to extend public sector involvement in economic activities, either by nationalization of private enterprises or creation of new public enterprises, particularly for producing import substitutes including intermediates. The financial sector was repressed to ensure credit was available at low cost to finance the public sector activities and favored private sector enterprises. Krueger points out that "there does not appear to have been very much thought given to the question either of how governments would ensure that the public sector activities specified in plans would be carried out or how private sector output and investment targets would be met" (pp. 2506–2507). Thus, the policy instruments to achieve plan targets (which, to begin with, were based on optimistic technical assumptions) were rarely fully specified and, unsurprisingly, achievements fell short of targets in plan after plan.

Yet, as Krueger points out, many countries achieved rapid rates of growth in the 50's and 60's, in part because of the favorable external environment of rapid growth of the global economy and in part because initial import substituting investments were in light consumer industries in which developing countries were not at a comparative disadvantage. But this growth could not be sustained for several reasons: import substitution was extended at high cost in many countries into activities in which they had no comparative advantage; interventions in and biases against agriculture created an excess demand for food and adversely affected the supply of export crops; the resort to monetary expansion to finance the growing public sector led to inflation; and the growth in import intensity of production in the face of slowly growing export earnings and other foreign exchange receipts resulted in periodic balance of payments crises. Interestingly enough, the problems and periodic crises did not, until the eighties, lead to rethinking of the policies and government control of the economy but rather to intensification of controls.

Krueger contrasts the above dismal experience with the success story of East Asia. Initially East Asian rapid growth was attributed to their special circumstances including massive foreign aid to Korea and Taiwan. As their growth was not only sustained but accelerated even after aid flows diminished, it became clear that good policies, particularly with respect to the external sector, rather than peculiar circumstances, explained East Asian success in achieving rapid growth, equitable sharing of the fruits of such growth, and the flexibility of the economy to withstand external shocks (e.g. the two oil shocks) without having to sacrifice growth to any significant extent. By the same token, inappropriate policies with respect to foreign trade and exchange rate, macroeconomy, agriculture and the financial sectors individually and in combination, explain the stalled growth of many other developing countries in the late seventies and eighties, according to Krueger.

The reform processes initiated in the eighties are briefly discussed by Krueger. Since the other chapters go more deeply and extensively into them (see below), it is worth focusing instead on her analysis of the political economy. As a prelude she briefly touches on the hoary topic of the proper role of government in development. She distinguishes three types of government actions: first, the things governments *must do* because the private sector cannot (e.g. maintenance of law and order, a system of property rights and contract laws and a stable macroeconomic framework); second, additional activities that governments *should* do that may enhance development efforts (e.g. provision of public health services, education and physical infrastructure such as roads, ports, railway and communication); third, the role of government in "picking winners".

While there is a consensus on the need for the first two types of government action, the third is very controversial. Some see the third role as explaining the success of East Asia (other than Hong Kong) through purposive government action in choosing industries and exports and ensuring their success through industry-specific interventions. Others, while acknowledging extensive government intervention in East Asia, nonetheless attribute the success to the uniformity of the exchange rate, combined with the discipline international markets provided in an outward-oriented economy. This discipline "severely constrained the scope of bureaucratic intervention and provided strong signals when policy mistakes were made" (p. 2542). This is in contrast to the inward-oriented economy of India where industry-specific protection was granted on a made-to-measure and permanent basis. Mistakes in investment that resulted in unprofitable operation of firms, instead of being corrected by letting them go bankrupt, were allowed to continue through budgetary support of losses. She quotes a study by Lee (1992) that government's attempt to "pick winners" was not that successful in Korea: those industries that had received less government support had experienced more growth in total factor productivity than those that did. The debate on the contribution of industry-specific government intervention per se in contrast to that of the provision of an environment conducive to growth by way of an excellent human and physical infrastructure and a roughly uniform set of incentives across activities in explaining East Asian success is still open.

Krueger raises two important aspects of the political economy of reform. First are the set of "circumstances in which policy reform is undertaken, the factors that appear to result in a higher probability of sustained reform, and ways in which reforms can be undertaken that reduce the likelihood of strengthening the opposition" (p. 2543). The second is "the extent to which it is appropriate to regard political reactions and pressures as exogenous, and the extent to which political-economic interactions render economic policies partially endogenous". (p. 2543)

Research on the first aspect focused on the role of potential gainers and losers from the reforms and on finding ways in which their balance could be tilted in favour of reforms. Although such a traditional interest-group analysis is useful, Krueger finds that it underplays four important features of policy reform. First, the policies to be reformed because of their adverse impact on growth were adopted in the first place for idealistic motives and in fact enjoyed broad support rather than that of narrow interest groups. This is best seen in the evolution of the Indian development strategy described earlier. Second, once certain policies are in place, those benefitting from them form a group with a vested interest in their continuation. The opposition to privatization of inefficient and loss-making public enterprises in India and elsewhere amply illustrates this. And even those who recognize that the policies have adverse effects often cling to the belief that it is not the policies that are at fault but particular ways of implementing them. Until recently this was common in India. Third, a crisis of major proportions can realign the power of various interest groups and thus provide a window of opportunity for introducing reforms. The initiation of far-reaching reforms in India after a major macroeconomic crisis in 1991 illustrates this. Fourth, it is simplistic to view the government as a Platonic guardian intent on maximizing social welfare. The nature of the state and the extent of its autonomy from interest group pressures would influence whether any reforms are undertaken, and if they are, the types of reform attempted and their outcomes. Bardhan (1984) provides an illuminating analysis of this phenomenon in India.

Endogeneity of policy is an area of active research. Krueger draws attention to the well-known and understandable phenomena that

> "once a political decision is made to undertake a particular economic policy or set of policies, market forces are set in motion which can thwart the policy or make it operate in ways which were not initially intended. The effects of the policy can also influence the alignment of political forces supporting and opposing the policy. Those interactions can then lead to changes in the initial policy, further market reactions, and so on". (p. 2544)

Indeed, this way of posing the problem at once suggests a sequential-game-theoretic approach to its analysis, as indeed some have attempted. Rodrik (Chapter 45) presents illustrative examples of such attempts. Krueger concludes, correctly, that

> "While analysis of the political economy of policy determination is still in its infancy, lessons already learned are sufficient to indicate that one cannot regard the political factors determining the choice of economic policies as entirely exogenous, nor can all economic policies be treated as stable steady states; interactions between political and economic markets are an important part of the process of policy formulation and execution". (p. 2546)

It should cause no surprise that eradication of mass poverty has been the overarching objective of development (at least in the rhetoric, if not in practice) of many developing countries from early on. As was noted earlier, India's National Planning Committee declared this objective more than five decades ago. What is surprising of course is the late discovery of the poor and poverty by multilateral development institutions such as the World Bank! Lipton and Ravallion (Chapter 41) trace the history of ideas about mass poverty and the realization that poverty is not an immutable human condition but one amenable to change through secular economic growth and through social and economic policy. They point out that until about 1750 in contemporary industrialized countries (and until the end of the Second World War in developing countries) there was hardly any growth in output per person and, as such, "moves to reduce poverty by peaceful redistribution proved politically inviable. In such a world poverty did not seem curable" (p. 2555). Adam Smith (1937) was aware of this. After pointing out that "No society can surely be flourishing and happy, of which the far greater part of the members are poor and miserable" (p. 79), he concludes that

> "... it is in the progressive state, while the society is advancing to the further acquisition, rather than when it has acquired its full complement of riches, that the condition of the laboring poor, of the great body of the people, seems to be the happiest and the most comfortable. It is hard in the stationary, and miserable in the declining state". (p. 81)

Thus, Smith did not think in terms of either equity versus growth or even equity with growth along the lines of the rather sterile discussion among development economists of recent vintage, but in terms of growth as a necessary dynamic force towards poverty alleviation.

The suggestions of Lipton and Ravallion that the Western European transition from poverty "drove the colonization process ... (that) reproduced European progressive economies, and associated changes in poverty problems, led to important experiments in anti-poverty policy ... relevant to poor countries today" and that it is precursor to a transition in less developed countries in the past half century, "to a stronger civil society, to a progressive economy, to modern demography and to more consensual states" (p. 2559) seem rather hyperbolic. But they are not entirely without foundation.

Lipton and Ravallion argue that import-substituting "forced draft planned industrialization offered little for the poor. Growth was often retarded; even when not, it brought few gains for the poor" (p. 2634), and it was financed in large part by extracting an agricultural surplus at the expense of the poor. They see a turn away from this towards rural development and investment in physical and human infrastructure in the 70's. They find that "many of the arguments that adjustment – relative to non-adjustment – had unambiguously hurt the poor were implausible. But so were some of the high expectations of supply-side response to adjustment, and hence to a rapid transition to a more favorable growth path". (p. 2634)

Lipton and Ravallion see a more balanced and realistic consensus emerging in the late 1980's as to how poverty can be most effectively reduced.

"In this view, the main role of the state is to facilitate provision of privately under-supplied goods (infrastructure, but also social equity itself) in an otherwise market driven economy. With neutral incentives, growth in such an economy is seen as being in the best interests of the poor, who are intensive suppliers of the main factor of production likely to benefit, labor. Growth in private-sector economic activity is a key part of this story, both as an instrument for income poverty reduction, and as one of the means of financing public support where it is needed. But it is only a part. As much emphasis is given to successful public action, in the areas where it is called for". (p. 2635)

They suggest that the enduring topics of poverty research include

". . . the political economy of poverty reduction; country-incentive issues in pro-poor aid policies; the costs and benefits to the poor of asset redistribution; the ways initial distribution affects the type of growth, and hence final distribution; the extent to which poverty considerations should influence macroeconomic and trade policies; complementarities between fighting chronic poverty and fighting vulnerability to poverty; the status of the so-called "special poverty groups" (women, children, remote areas); environmental effects (positive and negative) of poverty and its reduction; the impacts of developed country policies on distribution within developing countries". (p. 2635)

They also identify two important roles for public action:

"One involves fostering the conditions for pro-poor growth, particularly in providing wide access to the necessary physical and human assets, including public infrastructure. The other entails helping those who cannot participate fully in the benefits of such growth, or who do so with continued exposure to unacceptable risks. Here there is an important role for interventions aiming by various means to improve the distribution of the benefits of public expenditures on social services and safety nets in LDCs". (pp. 2637–2638)

Lipton and Ravallion's comprehensive discussion of poverty measurement, dimensions and characteristics of the poor and the interaction among growth, inequality and poverty ably summarizes a rich literature to which the two authors themselves have contributed significantly.

One of the robust features of the development process is the transformation of the economy from a structure in which the share of value added by agriculture in gross domestic product exceeds 50 percent and the share of the labour force dependent on agriculture for gainful activity exceeds two thirds, to one in which the two shares fall below 10 percent. Thus at early stages of development not only agriculture looms large in value added and gainful employment but also it shelters a disproportionate share of the poor consisting of landless agricultural laborers and marginal farmers. Arable land is obviously the crucial input in agricultural and livestock activities. Until cost of transporting agricultural commodities over long distances and storing them for extended periods of time fell, historically domestic (even local) agriculture supplied the food and fibre needs of most populations. It is not surprising therefore that the terms and conditions under which a right to owner cultivate land and the organization of agricultural production have been crucial in determining the pace and character of the above-mentioned structural transformation and progress towards alleviation of poverty. For example, the egalitarian character of the growth process in Japan, Korea and Taiwan has been attributed to their having had a thorough-going land reform, albeit imposed on them by "outsiders", soon after the end of the Second World War.

Binswanger et al. (Chapter 42) offer a fascinating account of the evolution of land rights and modes of production (e.g. slash and burn cultivation, communal ownership, manorial estate, junker estate, family farms) from the pre-Christian era to the present. They argue that it is much too simplistic and ahistorical to suggest that increasing land scarcity (in part driven by the increasing population relative to arable land) "leads to better definition of rights, which are then traded in sales and rental markets that are equally accessible to all players. The outcome should be the allocation of land to the most efficient use and users" (p. 2664) In their view:

> "rights over land and the concentration of ownership observed in most developing countries at the end of World War II are outgrowths of power relationships. Landowning groups used coercion and distortions in land, labor, credit, and commodity markets to extract economic rents from the land, from peasants and workers, and more recently from urban consumer groups or taxpayers. Such rent-seeking activities reduced the efficiency of resource use, retarded growth, and increased the poverty of the rural population". (p. 2664)

Land reforms are necessary, they suggest, to ensure that efficient small family farmers cultivate most of the land, since land markets are unlikely to bring this about. They describe the vicissitudes of land reforms in market and non-market economies and the subversion of the ideal of small family farms into large commercial farms in the former and large collectives in the latter. They establish that small farms are indeed efficient by examining the case for scale economies in agriculture and finding that such economies are exceptions. They attribute the failure of the land market to bring about an efficient distribution of land to a number of factors including covariance of risks, imperfections in credit markets, distortions in commodity markets and government subsidization of large farms. They review the theoretical and empirical literature on land lease arrangements and reiterate that tenancy and share cropping are not as inefficient as a naive Marshallian analysis would suggest. In fact they are optimal responses to incomplete or distorted markets for labour, credit and risk sharing and spending. Clearly government regulation of tenancy or banning it outright would have perverse efficiency and equity effects.

Binswanger et al. provide a thorough discussion of land policy. While recognizing that clear land titles and registration provide the necessary institutional framework for an efficient land market, they warn that in practice titling can lead to greater concentration of land ownership and dispossession of groups that have enjoyed land rights under a customary system. They then suggest a number of steps that could be taken to avoid these undesirable effects and reduce the cost of titling programs.

Although since the days of Henry George the virtues of a land tax have been recognized, in the absence of up-to-date land records indicating the size, value and ownership status of each tract of land, its productive capacity and profitability, designing and administering an efficient land tax is virtually impossible. Even where reasonably complete and up-to-date land record system and a tax structure based on it once existed, as in parts of British India, the political economy of post-independence India ensured that the taxes were repealed or allowed to be inflated away. Nonetheless Binswanger et al. find it useful to have flat or mildly progressive land taxes based on rough classification of land.

Regulations on land sales by imposing ceilings and floors on land holdings on balance are found to be inefficient. At the same time, even if the absence of a floor results in fragmentation of holdings, Binswanger et al. do not think land consolidation programs are likely to be cost-effective. As mentioned earlier, Binswanger et al. are against restrictions on land rents on grounds of efficiency and equity. They argue that unless the distortions that drive land prices above the capitalized value of profits from cultivation are removed, redistributive land reforms would fail since small farmers will have an incentive to sell out to large farmers and the environment would continue to favour large ownership holdings. The decidedly mixed experience with redistributive land reforms around the world confirms their assessment.

It was almost an article of faith in the early literature on development that investment in creating physical infrastructure (or in social overhead capital as it was called then) was lumpy (and hence subject to scale economies) and its supply and use had external effects. For both these reasons it was argued that less than socially optimal investment in infrastructural services would come about unless the government intervened. Given the rudimentary fiscal system of most developing countries, public subsidization of private investment in infrasturctural services was deemed infeasible so that the government itself had to invest and produce.

Jimenez (Chapter 43) analyzes issues relating both to physical infrastructure (services that enhance the productivity of physical capital) and human infrastructure (i.e. health, education and nutrition that enhance the productivity of labour). His survey of recent studies confirm the continuing critical importance of infrastructure for economic growth and for poverty alleviation. He finds that the positive link between measures of infrastructure and development is fairly robust across studies and methodologies. Micro level studies, despite problems with data and methodology, broadly confirm the aggregate results. The key role of government in financing and the supply of infrastructure is reemphasized by the recent literature, for the same reasons as in the early literature, viz. externalities, scale economies and public goods characteristics, are significant in infrastructure. However, Jimenez finds that in practice infrastructure investment has been inefficiently allocated in that projects with high social returns do not always get priority over those with low returns; services that are being provided are not often provided at the least cost; inappropriately priced; and their distribution is inequitable (i.e. the poor do not get an adequate share). Jimenez suggests that infrastructural investments are subject to "capture" by special interest groups and this is in part why projects that have higher social returns do not always receive funding. Examples are larger investments in lower yielding tertiary education than in higher yielding primary education, relative neglect of rural infrastructure, underinvestment in operations and maintenance and underspending in non-wage categories.

Jimenez reviews the analytics as well as the practice of pricing of publicly provided infrastructure. While properly cautioning against deriving general conclusions from studies with disparate and problematic methods and data of varying quality, he finds increasing empirical support for the conceptual arguments for increasing prices of infrastructural services. Empirical evidence strongly suggests that subsidies currently being offered could be directed more towards the poor and moderate increases in user fees are feasible and desirable. However, more research is needed to assess the feasibility of measures to protect the poor and for operationalizing the idea of raising user fees. Jimenez's analysis supports the broad conclusion reached by the World Bank (1994) in its report on infrastructure:

> "The potential for improving performance in infrastructure provision and investment is substantial, as is the quantity of resources devoted to infrastructure. Thus, both the need and the broad direction for reform are clear. Additional investment will obviously be needed – but more investment will not in itself avoid wasteful inefficiencies, improve maintenance, or increase user satisfaction. Achieving these improvements will require three broad actions: applying commercial principles to infrastructure operations, encouraging competition from appropriately regulated private sector providers,

and increasing the involvement of users and other stakeholders in planning, providing, and monitoring infrastructure services. These adjustments call not only for policy changes, but also for fundamental institutional changes in the way that the 'business' of infrastructure is conducted". (p. 109)

The report also discusses the strengths and weaknesses (as well as measures to augment strengths and reduce the weaknesses) of four broad options regarding infrastructure: (a) public ownership and public operation, (b) public ownership and private operation, (c) private ownership and private operation, and (d) community and user provision. It concludes, correctly, that the choice among these options will depend on what is needed and what is possible in each country.

Chapter 44 by Corbo and Fischer is devoted to an analysis of structural adjustment and stabilization (SAS) programs. They point out that

"In the 1980s many developing countries faced a combination of severe balance of payments problems, high and variable inflation, slow growth, and high unemployment. These problems emerged from the cumulative effects of weak national policies and institutions that combined with a drastic and unfavorable change in external conditions (terms of trade shocks, interest rate shocks, a worldwide recession, and a severe reduction in commercial bank lending) to lead to the debt crisis". (p. 2846)

Their definition of structural adjustment is rather broad

*"Structural adjustment is a process of market-oriented reform in policies and institutions, with the goals of restoring a sustainable balance of payments, reducing inflation, and creating the conditions for sustainable growth in per capita income"*. (p. 2847, emphasis in original)

While concentrating on the experience since the early eighties, they briefly discuss earlier adjustment programs as well, even though they were not called as such: the term "structural adjustment" came into common use only in the 1980's after the World Bank proposed lending for structural adjustment. This new form of lending introduced in 1979, was to

"support a program of specific policy changes and institutional reforms designed to reduce the current account deficit to sustainable levels; assist a country in meeting the transitional costs of structural changes in industry and agriculture by augmenting the supply of freely usable foreign exchange; act as a catalyst for the inflow of other external capital to help ease the balance of payments situation". (Ernest Stern, then Senior Vice President of the World Bank, as quoted by Corbo and Fischer, p. 2851)

Structural Adjustment Loans (SAL's) were complemented by Sectoral Adjustment Loans (SECALS) to support reforms in particular sectors. The International Monetary Fund introduced its own lending programs for structural adjustment in the 1980's by creating the Structural Adjustment Facility and the Extended Structural Adjustment Facility.

Corbo and Fischer point out

"Adjustment programs were not confined to developing countries: New Zealand undertook a radical adjustment program starting in the 1980s; and the OECD increasingly laid stress on efficiency-oriented reforms in its member countries ... Nor was structural adjustment in the developing countries confined to those receiving financial support from the IFIs: China pursued its reform program with strong World Bank intellectual and financial support, but without the benefit of Bank adjustment lending until late in its adjustment process". (p. 2852)

They suggest that typically countries enter into an SAS programme after experiencing a severe balance of payments crisis. The crisis usually arises from one of two sources: unfavorable external shocks and pursuit of unsustainable policies. As they point out, correctly, countries would have to adjust in *some way* to the crisis, whether or not funding from the World Bank, IMF or other sources is available. The question then is whether such funding delays the adjustment process and makes it more expensive to undertake in the future, or whether it reduces the burden of adjustment by providing funds to countries at a lower cost than the cost at which they themselves would have been able to acquire the funds. The lowered cost presumably arises, not from subsidization by the international financial institutions, but from imperfections in the international capital market. But the argument based on capital market imperfections is relevant for lending for *any* project earning the relevant social rate of return and not just to adjustment lending. Lending for policy reform raises another difficult issue of its rationale in the case of a country that would not have undertaken such reform in the absence of such lending or, alternatively, that of a country that would have undertaken the reform even in the absence of such lending.

A policy is defined as unsustainable by Corbo and Fischer "when it cannot continue forever" (p. 2858). They distinguish between *economic* unsustainability (arising from the infeasibility to meet government's intertemporal budget constraint if policies do not change) and *political* unsustainability because of political infeasibility to continue with the policies. They also analyze economic unsustainability in the context of debt dynamics. They discuss issues relating to the *timing* of the crisis, i.e. when it will occur given unsustainable policies, and the political economy of the *timing* of the response to the crisis, i.e. whether stabilization will be delayed. They (also Srinivasan (1993a)) illustrate the economics of stabilization using the well-known dependent economy model of Salter (1959). This analysis demonstrates the need for two instruments, expenditure reduction and expenditure switching away from traded to non-traded goods, for restoring equilibrium once financing the external deficits is no longer possible. Thus a reduction in absorption and a real devaluation are needed.

Their model of the dynamics of disinflation in high inflation countries (such as those in Latin America) enables them to sort out the differences between the orthodox stabilization programs that focus on absorption and real devaluation and heterodox programs that in addition have wage-price controls as parts of the policy package.

Corbo and Fischer provide an illuminating discussion of the credibility and the optimal speed of implementing an adjustment and reforms package (e.g. big bang versus gradualism, to use the popular terminology). They correctly point out that if the package is fully credible and this is common knowledge to all participants, then the first-best solution is to implement it immediately. But if administrative constraints or political feasibility of removing particular distortions is not established, then either the package is no longer credible or one enters the realm of the second best so that no general recommendation can be made.

Their analysis of evaluations of structural adjustment programs (according to Corbo and Fischer, the World Bank committed as much as $41 billion to 258 adjustment loans between 1980 and 1991) is again very insightful. They reiterate an important and difficult to solve methodological issue in such evaluations, an issue that has been often recognized but less frequently acted upon in the literature. An *ex ante* evaluation of any proposed programme is difficult, if not impossible, given the multiplicity of its objectives, some of which are often vaguely defined at best, and the difficulty of controlling for myriad other factors besides the adjustment programme that would influence the course of the economy. An *ex post* evaluation that limits itself to the question whether the economy was performing better in some well defined sense after adjustment is difficult, if not altogether infeasible, primarily because the relevant comparison, namely, with a counterfactual scenario of a continuation pre-adjustment disequilibria, distortions and weaknesses without adjustment is not easy to construct (Srinivasan, 1988, 1993a).

A simplistic but common "before and after" approach (e.g. Cornia et al. (1987)) that compares the pre-and post-adjustment path of the economy can reveal nothing about the effect of an adjustment programme. Corbo and Fischer discuss results from the so-called "control group" and modified control group approaches. In the control group approach one proxies the relevant counterfactual for an adjusting country with the performance of a "control group" of countries which are similar but did not undertake adjustment. However, it is not easy to ensure that the "control group" is appropriate in the sense that they did not undertake adjustment but had pre-adjustment situations comparable to that of the country that undertook adjustment and experienced similar trends, as the adjusting countries did, during and after the period of adjustment, in exogenous variables, including in particular those relating to foreign trade and payments. On the other hand, counterfactual simulations from an econometric model of the adjusting country are not free of problems either unless the model tracks the pre-adjustment unsustainable disequilibrium path well and the methodology of comparison adequately captures the fact that the single *realized* actual path of the economy during adjustment and beyond has to be compared with a *distribution* of counterfactual paths.

Some might consider the conclusion of Corbo and Fischer that "The statistical cross-sectional studies provide an aggregate and reasonably consistent picture of the effectiveness of adjustment programs" (pp. 2889–2890) as somewhat stronger than warranted, given the above methodological problems. On the other hand, they are right in their conclusions that the research on evaluation "has not empirically evaluated the economics behind the programs; nor has it taken the extent of compliance into account with any care" (p. 2890) and

"The absence of agreed-upon analytic or econometric models to analyze some of the basic problems of adjustment is striking. For instance, the analysis of sequencing problems is still underdeveloped. The important issue of the distributional impact of adjustment has received attention in computable general equilibrium models . . . but it is fair to say that this work has not yet had a wide impact. It is also striking how few empirical generalizations are yet widely accepted. In part this is because of the difficulty of constructing counterfactuals, a problem that lies at the heart of the econometric issues . . . In part it reflects the very broad and imprecise questions often asked in the analysis of adjustment, e.g. should the financial sector be deregulated before the trade sector. Almost surely the answer is "it depends", but we do not as yet have sufficient evidence or analytics to know precisely on what it depends. One thing we do know is that it depends also on political factors . . . That of course adds both interest and complexity to the analysis of adjustment". (p. 2917)

Rodrik (Chapter 45) also focuses on structural adjustment. He uses the term *structural adjustment* more narrowly than Corbo and Fischer to denote *policies* "aimed at improving an economy's efficiency and its long-term growth" (p. 7), thereby excluding the macroeconomic stabilization policies covered by Corbo and Fischer from his discussion, while recognizing the importance of the latter for the success of the former.

He identifies two common features of the 1980's from the perspective of developing countries:

"First, much of the developing world, including a majority of countries in Latin America and Africa, became engulfed in a debt and macroeconomic crisis of major proportions. Per capita income scarcely grew, and, in many countries, declined over the course of the decade. It became commonplace to call this the 'lost decade' for development.

But maybe not all was lost. For the second major feature of the decade was that in scores of countries, the inward-oriented, import-substituting policies of the past came under critical scrutiny from policy makers – often from the same government leaders who had enthusiastically espoused and implemented the older policies. By the end of the decade, the anti-export and anti-private enterprise bias of the prevailing policy regimes was largely discredited. Public enterprise, industrial promotion, and trade protection were out; privatization, industrial deregulation, and free trade were in". (p. 2927)

His chapter presents the theory (particularly from the recent literature), evidence, and their interplay in reviewing the available knowledge about the consequences of these reforms. His focus is confined to trade and industrial policies since the chapter by Corbo and Fischer covers macroeconomic stabilization issues; although, as he notes, it is not always easy to draw clear distinctions between stabilization and structural measures.

Rodrik, following Thomas et al. (1991, p. 11), terms structural adjustment as "changes in relative prices and institutions designed to make the economy more efficient, more flexible, and better able to use resources and so to engineer sustainable long-term growth" (p. 2929) and structural adjustment policies as those aimed at improving an economy's efficiency and its long-term growth.

The trade policies to be reformed "were directed at licensing and other quantitative restrictions, high and extremely differentiated tariff rates, export taxes, and burdensome bureaucratic requirements and paperwork" (p. 2930). The targets of reform in industrial policy were "inefficient and loss-making public enterprises, entry and exit restrictions on private enterprise, price controls, discretionary tax and subsidy policies, and soft-budget constraints" (p. 2930).

Rodrik identifies "four basic arguments in favour of "market-oriented policy reform: (i) economic liberalization reduces static inefficiencies arising from resource misallocation and waste; (ii) economic liberalization enhances learning, technological change, and economic growth; (iii) outward-oriented economies are better able to cope with adverse external shocks; (iv) market-based economic systems are less prone to wasteful rent-seeking activities. While all four of these arguments are used widely, it is the last three that have dominated the discussion on structural adjustment policies" (p. 2932).

It is hard to disagree with his statement that no compelling case has been made regarding the *magnitude* of static resource misallocation costs, even though the *qualitative* "theoretical and empirical arguments for the resource misallocation costs of the import-substitution syndrome are strong" (p. 2932). He identifies a number of problems that plague the empirical studies of the *dynamic* costs of distortion. These include:

> (i) the trade-regime indicator used is typically measured very badly, and is often an endogenous variable itself; (ii) the direction of causality is not always clear, even when a policy variable is used as the trade indicator: governments may choose to relax trade restrictions when economic performance is good; (iii) openness in the sense of lack of trade restrictions is often confused with macroeconomic aspects of the policy regime, notably the exchange-rate stance; (iv) the causal mechanisms that link openness to beneficial dynamic effects are rarely laid out carefully and subjected to test themselves; this makes it very difficult for policy conclusions to be drawn". (p. 2941)

He is equally dismissive of studies that purport to show that export-oriented countries are better positioned to deal with negative external shocks than inward-oriented countries. He argues that while the informal evidence is consistent with the view "that outward oriented countries have greater flexibility in responding to shocks, or that their political economy more easily allows (and accommodates) a change in macro policies" (p. 2943), still "we lack a good understanding of how and why certain configurations of economic policy render the economy more resilient to external shocks than others" (p. 2943).

Rodrik examines the mainstream (liberalizers') and heterodox (revisionists') interpretations of the success of East Asia. He identifies the following core set of conclusions on which the two groups might agree:

> "(i) there has been a lot of government intervention and an active trade and industrial policy; (ii) but intervention has taken place above all in the context of stable macroeconomic policies in the form of small budget deficits and realistic exchange-rate management; (iii) equally important, the governments' emphasis on and unmitigated commitment to exports has helped minimize the resource costs and incentive problems that would have otherwise arisen from heavy intervention; (iv) also, intervention has taken place in an institutional setting characterized by a "hard" state and strong government discipline over the private sector; (v) furthermore, such a setting is lacking in most other developing countries. What one then does with these conclusions depends on one's predilections. Some would argue that it is possible to engineer local versions of the institutions that have made Korea's

or Taiwan's policies so successful . . . Others would conclude that weaker governments should economize on their scarcest resource, administrative competence, and restrict their involvement in the micro-management of the economy . . . Yet others would call for an entirely hands-off approach". (p. 2948)

Rodrik then looks at the East Asian experience in light of recent developments in trade and growth theories that emphasize scale economies, imperfect competition, externalities associated with human capital, endogenous technical progress, and so on. While these theories are elegant and insightful, and are indeed seen by some enthusiasts as rationalizing the interventions of the Korean, Japanese and Taiwanese governments, which, endowed with the uncanny ability to pick winners among industries, created comparative advantage for them, Rodrik is certainly right in suggesting that "Informal case studies like these aside, there are as yet practically no direct empirical tests of the specific trade-growth linkages identified above. We need such tests to close the large gap that presently exists between the empirical work . . . and the theoretical models . . . The former is informative but largely devoid of policy content, while the latter are stimulating, but remain empirically untested". (p. 2958)

Rodrik offers an incisive summary of theoretical models of the strategy of reform, and in particular, of aspects of political economy. Though he does not say it, his comment about the applicability of recent theoretical models of trade and growth in analyzing actual experience applies to these models as well. They are suggestive, but hardly conclusive, as descriptions of the actual reform strategy or the political economy of real countries.

Rodrik is again critical of available studies of the consequences of reform as "too often sloppy in identifying precise cause-and-effect relationships". But this criticism will apply to a large number of empirical studies in economics! Nonetheless, he finds that the evidence on the supply response to price changes (on which the argument for getting prices right is predicated) with respect to exports is clear: "a credible, and lasting effort to increase the supply-price of exportables is rewarded by a large, often very quick export response" (p. 2967), and that "export performance is subject to strong hysteresis effects: it may take a big push (i.e., sizable change in incentives) to get exports out, but by the same token, once the transition is made, not much may be required to keep them going". (p. 2968)

On the static and dynamic efficiency consequences of policy reforms, Rodrik is once again critical of the methodology of most studies for the same reason as Corbo and Fischer (Chapter 44) and Srinivasan (1993a):

"One needs a counterfactual regarding what would have happened in the absence of reform, and to disentangle the effects of the reform under consideration from the effects of other changes in the environment. To render a welfare judgment, one needs in addition a set of shadow prices to value the change in the quantities of outputs and inputs. Even if all these obstacles are surmounted, there is the difficulty of figuring out exactly what has happened". (p. 2969)

The one study that Rodrik finds the most systematic is that of Tybout (1992) who asks: "(i) has trade liberalization led to reduced price-cost margins in import-competing sectors? (ii) has it resulted in firms taking better advantage of scale economies through industry rationalization? (iii) has it led to improvements in technical efficiency?" (p. 2970). The first question is answered affirmatively in the studies reported by Tybout, the results regarding the second question are ambiguous, but are generally favorable to the third.
Rodrik's cautious conclusions are worth reproducing:

"the benefits of price reform remain small in relation to developmental objectives, and tend to be linked to economic growth through uncertain and unreliable channels . . . relative-price distortions, and the analysis thereof, are vastly over-emphasized relative to the institutional dimensions of reform . . . South Korean and Taiwanese economies have prospered in policy environments characterized by quantitative trade restrictions, selective subsidies, and discretionary incentives bearing more than a passing superficial resemblance to those in other developing countries. What has differed, of course, is the discipline exerted by the East Asian state over private-sector groups . . . (however) countries like Mexico, Argentina, Chile, and Bolivia have travelled recently much faster and further on the road to price reform and trade liberalization than South Korea, Taiwan, and Japan before they ever did . . . So a minimal conclusion for policy makers from the available evidence would be: get prices right if you can, but don't be deluded into thinking that reform ends there. Genuine reform requires the creation of a new set of interactions between government and the private sector, one that provides for an environment of policy stability and predictability, that discourages rent-seeking activities, and that improves on the governments' ability to discipline the private sector. In other words, the change that is needed is not only in policy, but also in policy *making*. The East Asian experience is full of clues as to what the end-product should look like. But we know much less about how to get there". (p. 2972)

Scholarly interest in the theory of long-run growth revived after a hiatus of two decades or so with the publication of the very influential papers of Lucas (1988) and Romer (1986). Lucas motivated his approach by arguing that neo-classical growth theory cannot account for the observed differences in growth across countries over time and its prediction that international trade should induce rapid movements toward equality in capital–labor ratios and factor prices is evidently counter-factual. Romer also looked for alternative theories to escape from what he viewed as a strong implication of the neoclassical growth model that in the absence of technical change, there can be no sustained growth in per capita output in the long run.

In Lucas's (1988) model each individual acquires productivity-enhancing skills by devoting time to such acquisition and away from paying work. The acquisition of skills by a worker not only increases that worker's productivity but by increasing the average level of skills in the economy as a whole, it has a spill-over effect on the productivity of <u>all</u> workers. In fact sustained growth in per capita output occurs in the Lucas model even if there is no spill-over effect because the marginal return to time devoted to skill accumulation is constant and not diminishing. In Romer (1986) long-run growth is driven by the accumulation of knowledge by forward-looking profit-maximizing agents, with the creation of knowledge by one firm having a positive external effect on the production possibilities of other firms. Thus in the aggregate the marginal product of knowledge does not diminish.

Readers of the still growing literature spawned by the papers of Lucas and Romer might be misled into thinking that indefinite scale economies, and positive externalities to human capital, knowledge capital and so forth postulated in most recent growth models, are essential to generating sustained-growth in per capita output in the long run and for endogenizing such growth. In fact, as was well understood by earlier growth theorists, in the neoclassical constant returns to scale model, sustained growth in the long run is possible if the marginal product of capital is bounded away from zero as the capital-labour ratio grows indefinitely. Indeed, as noted earlier, the models of Lucas and Romer in effect ensure this in different ways. Further it can be shown that increasing scale economies are neither necessary nor sufficient for generating sustained growth [Srinivasan (1993b)].

Bardhan points out that many of the growth models of the 1950's and 1960's endogenized technical progress in significant ways. Kaldor and Mirrlees (1962) endogenized technical progress (and hence the rate of growth of output) by relating productivity of workers operating newly produced equipment to the rate of growth of investment per worker. And there was the celebrated model of Arrow (1962) of "learning by doing" in which factor productivity was an increasing function of cumulated output or investment. Uzawa (1965) also endogenized technical progress by postulating that the rate of growth of labor augmenting technical progress was a concave function of the ratio of labor employed in the education sector to total employment. The education sector was assumed to use labor as the only input. Lucas (1988) in fact based his human capital accumulation process on Uzawa's model. Besides in the literature on induced innovation [Ahmad (1966), Boserup (1965), Kennedy (1964)] technical change was, by definition, endogenous.

Bardhan correctly argues that the contribution of recent authors is therefore neither in building models that generate sustained growth in per capita output nor in endogenizing technical progress. It is in the formalization of technical progress "in terms of a tractable imperfect-competition framework in which temporary monopoly power acts as a motivating force for private innovators. The leading work in this area (is) what has been called neo-Schumpeterian growth theory ... Growth theory has now been liberated from the confines of the competitive market framework of earlier endogenous growth models in which dynamic externalities played the central role (even considering the models of Kaldor who repeatedly emphasized the importance of imperfect competition in the context of endogenous technical progress, the current models drawing upon the advances in industrial organization theory are more satisfactory). In particular, the emphasis on new goods and the fixed costs in introducing them provides valuable new insights. The major impact of this literature on development theory has been in the area of trade and technological diffusion...". (pp. 2985–2986)

This impact is best seen by contrasting the effect of trade liberalization in a standard Heckscher–Ohlin type constant-return-to-scale-neo-classical model of international trade with that from other models. In such a model, if all markets are competitive and trade restrictions take the form of tariffs (so that the economy operates on its production possibility frontier), the removal of tariffs yields a once-and-for-all real income (welfare) gains. These gains would accrue even if resources do not move freely across production activities in response to changed incentives, but would obviously be greater if they do. There would be no effect on *long-run growth* even if part or all of the gains in real income is invested, again under the assumption that the marginal product of capital diminishes to zero as capital accumulates indefinitely relative to other inputs. This is not to say of course that there would be no growth effect in the short to medium run, particularly if there are frictions in resource movements across sectors. Of course, if the marginal product of capital does not diminish to zero, say, if it is constant as in the one-sector Harrod–Domar or two-sector Mahalanobis–Fel'dman models, trade liberalization could affect long-run growth [Srinivasan (1993c)]. In the models of new growth theory the mechanism in which long-run growth is influenced by openness to foreign trade and investment is different.

Bardhan points out:

"A major result in the new literature is to show how economic integration in the world market, compared to isolation, helps long-run growth by avoiding unnecessary duplication of research and thus increases aggregate productivity of resources employed in the R & D sector (characterized by economies of scale). World market competition gives incentives to entrepreneurs in each of these countries to invent products that are unique in the world economy". (p. 2986)

Further

". . . the new models of trade and growth bring into sharp focus the features of monopolistic competition particularly in the sector producing intermediate products and, in some models, the Schumpeterian process of costly R and D races with the prospect of temporary monopoly power for the winner – aspects which were missing in most of the earlier macroeconomic growth models...". (p. 2990).

In Bardhan's assessment

"probably the most important contribution of the new growth theory is to formally draw our attention to the process of introduction of an ever-expanding set of new goods and technologies (in the case of developing countries, often imports of new types of produced inputs) and the large fixed costs usually associated with it. These fixed costs underline the fundamental importance of nonconvexities and imperfect competition in economic analysis". (p. 2992)

We noted in our Introduction to Part 7 that the representation of imperfect competition in applied general equilibrium models is limited. Its representation in endogenous growth theory is similarly simple or even simplisitic. Also, as Bardhan points out,

"The new literature in some ways diverts our attention from the abiding concern of development economists with the problems of structural transformation and with those of reallocation of resources from traditional sectors to other sectors with different organizational and technological dynamics. But it does serve a purpose in focusing attention on the serious nonconvexities involved in the process of diffusion and adoption of new goods and technologies in a developing country". (p. 2992)

Non-convexities in growth models often generate multiple long-run equilibria, some of which are unstable, and the possibility arises that initial conditions determine to which equilibrium the economy converges, if it does converge, in the long run. These facts were well-known to and discussed by earlier growth and development theorists. Recent literature goes further in recognizing that in such a set up, temporary shocks instead of having only transitory effects could have permanent or long-run effects (so-called hysteresis). In the early development literature, it used to be argued that a poor economy is caught in a "low-income-equilibrium trap" while a high-income-equilibrium is feasible. The task of the development state was seen as to institute appropriate policies to enable the economy to break out of the trap. The recent literature points out that this is a simplistic view: just because there are many equilibria that can be ranked in terms of welfare, does not necessarily mean that there is room for government action to steer the economy away from a "bad" equilibrium to a "good" one. How a particular equilibrium gets established, whether through a "historical" accident or through self-fulfilling expectations of economic agents, is not a simple matter. As Bardhan points out

"This 'history versus expectations' dichotomy in the dynamic process of how a particular equilibrium gets established has been further analyzed by Krugman (1991) and Matsuyama (1991) and the relative importance of the past and expected future is shown to depend on some parameters of the economy (like the discount rate and the speed of adjustment)". (p. 2994)

Xavier Sala-i-Martin (1994), a major contributor to the recent empirical growth literature, has provided an admirably short, though naturally sympathetic, survey of it. He points out that the early contributions to the literature tested an implication of the neoclassical growth model, viz. given diminishing returns to capital, other things being equal, countries with low amounts of capital per worker will grow faster, so that a negative relation should exist between the growth rate and the initial level of income. The hypothesized negative relation (the so-called convergence hypothesis) was not found in the Summers–Heston set used to test it. This rejection was taken as evidence against the neoclassical model.

Later researchers viewed this rejection, not as that of the neo-classical model, but a restricted version of it in which all countries had the same steady state growth path. The neo-classical model in fact suggests only that the growth rate of an economy will be inversely related to how far it is from its own steady state. The more general hypothesis, namely that of *conditional convergence* (each economy converges to its own steady state) was tested in two ways: by confining the test to a sample of economies which a priori could be deemed to have the same steady state (e.g. regions within a country), or by controlling for differences in steady states by including variables in the model to proxy the steady state of each economy. Tests, again with Summers–Heston data or with data on regions such as states of the United States, did not reject the conditional convergence hypothesis. The speed of convergence as estimated by many of the studies was found to be remarkably similar, around 2 percent per year, which is *slow* relative to a six percent rate associated with a neo-classical model with a plausible share of capital of 30 percent or less. The slow speed of convergence also implies that the effects of exogenous shocks or of policy shifts, even though they eventually wear out, could take very long to do so.

A second strand of empirical research [Barro (1991), Barro and Lee (1994)] regressed growth rates not only on initial income levels but in addition on a grab bag of explanatory variables "such as primary and secondary school enrollments, number of political assassinations, investment rates, and measures of distortions in capital markets" [Sala-i-Martin (1994), p. 741]. Barro and Lee found:

"Differences in growth rates across economies are large and relate systematically to a set of quantifiable explanatory variables. One element of this set is a net convergence term, the positive effect on growth when initial real GDP per capita is low in relation to the starting levels of secondary school attainment and life expectancy. Growth depends negatively on a group of variables that reflect distortions and the size of government: the ratio of government consumption to GDP, the black-market premium on foreign exchange, and the frequency of revolutions. Growth depends positively on the ratio of gross investment to GDP but not as strongly as in some previous studies". (p. 294)

They were properly cautious about jumping to "reality from regression results to policy proposals" (p. 295).

How seriously should the growth regression results be taken? Unfortunately there are very serious data and econometric problems associated with the regressions. First, although Summers and Heston are careful to list the problems with their data, including in particular in identifying commodities that are close to being identical in different countries so that they can be priced out using a common set of prices, the users pay scant attention to their cautionary warnings. It is one thing to adjust for international differences in *price* structures as Summers and Heston do. But what they do not adjust for, and what in many cases is more serious, are *biases* in measurement of quantities [Srinivasan (1994)]. Indeed Summers and Heston (1991) themselves assign a quality rating of D + or D to the data of 66 out of their 138 countries, most of which are less developed countries, 37 of them being African countries. Data on investment are particularly unreliable. Biases as well as measurement-errors might vary in an unknown fashion over time and across countries and obviously such variations have implications for growth regressions.

Second, in their critique of the regressions, Levine and Renelt (1992) find that small changes in the right-hand side variables produce different conclusions about the links between individual policies and growth in cross-country studies. Sala-i-Martin reads their critique, not as an indictment of the non-robustness of their results, but as implying that some group of policy variables always matters. However, since policies are highly correlated with each other, he argues that data cannot tell them apart. But he does not note that this also means that it is impossible to tell which policy matters and which does not!

Third, policy indicators as well as some of the other variables often included in cross-country regressions are *endogenous*. As such, the problem of simultaneity bias arises. This is not just a technical quibble – simultaneity bias may change drastically the interpretation of the parameter estimates. Fourth, in studies involving cross-sections repeated over time, sometimes country-specific effects (fixed or random) are included. Since the other explanatory variables (particularly policy variables) might plausibly correlate with country-specific effects, as Deaton's chapter in this volume points out, the random effects estimator will be inconsistent. On the other hand, if these effects are treated as *fixed*, removing fixed effects by differencing introduces a correlation between the disturbance term in the differenced regression and its explanatory variables, if the latter include lagged values of the dependent variable. If the number of time periods over which the cross-sections are repeated is small relative to the number of countries included in each cross section, the fixed effect estimate will also be inconsistent.

Finally, whatever other insights cross-country regressions testing some version or the other of the convergence hypothesis relating to *aggregate* growth have yielded about the growth process, by their very nature, they have little to say about the microeconomic forces that together generate the aggregate outcome or about effectiveness of policies. Here again the observations of Lucas (1993) are pertinent:

> "I do not intend these conjectures about the implications of a learning spillover technology for small countries facing given world prices to be a substitute for the actual construction of such a theory. . . . What is the nature of human capital accumulation decision problems faced by workers, capitalists and managers? What are the external consequences of the decisions they take? The purpose cited here considers a variety of possible assumptions on these economic issues, but it must be said that little is known, and without such knowledge there is little we can say about the way policies that affect incentives can be expected to influence economic growth" [Lucas (1993), p. 270].

Even if one were to ignore their lack of a solid microeconomic foundations and their uncritical use of aggregate data with serious measurement errors and biases, the inference drawn from many convergence regressions could be questioned on econometric grounds as Quah (1993a, 1993b and 1994) has done. He suggests that these studies "do not at all shed light on the important, original question: Are poor economies catching up with those richer" (Quah (1994), p. 52). This is indeed the fundamental question of development and it is yet to be answered satisfactorily.

JERE BEHRMAN
T.N. SRINIVASAN

## References

Ahmad, Syed. (1966) 'On the theory of induced innovation'. *Economic Journal*, 76:344–357.
Arrow, K.J. (1962) 'The economic implications of learning by doing'. *Review of Economic Studies*, 29:155–173.

Bardhan, P. (1984) *The political economy of development in India*, Oxford.

Barro, R. (1991) 'Economic growth in a cross section of countries', *Quarterly Journal of Economics*, 106:407–501.

Barro, R. and Lee, J.-W. (1994) 'Losers and winners in economic growth', in: *Proceedings of the World Bank Annual Conference on Development Economics 1993*, Supplement to the *World Bank Economic Review* and *World Bank Research Observer*. Washington, DC: The World Bank, 267–297.

Bhagwati, J. and Desai, P. (1970) *India: Planning for industrialization*. London: Oxford University Press.

Bhagwati, J. and Srinivasan, T.N. (1975) *Foreign trade regimes & economic development: India*. New York: Columbia University Press.

Bhagwati, J. (1992) *India's economy: The shackled giant*. Oxford: Clarendon Press.

Boserup, E. (1965) *The conditions of agricultural growth*. Chicago: Aldine.

Cornia, A.G., Jolly, R. and Stewart, F., eds., (1987) *Adjustment with a human face*, A study by UNICEF, Vol. I, Oxford: Clarendon Press.

Kaldor, N. and Mirrlees, J. (1962) 'A new model of economic growth', *Review of Economic Studies*, 29(3):174–192.

Kennedy, C. (1964) 'Induced bias in innovation and the theory of distribution', *Economic Journal*, 74(298):541–547.

Krugman, P. (1991), 'History versus Expectations', *Quarterly Journal of Economics*, 106:651–667.

Lee, J.H. (1992) 'Government interventions and productivity growth in Korean manufacturing industries', Paper presented at NBER Conference on Economic Growth, October, Cambridge, MA.

Levine, R. and Renelt, D. (1992) 'A sensitivity analysis of cross-country growth regressions', *American Economic Review*, 824, 942–963.

Lucas, R. (1988) 'On the mechanics of economic development', *Journal of Monetary Economics*, 22:3–42.

Lucas, R.E. (1993) 'Making a miracle', *Econometrica*, 61(2):251–272.

Matsuyama, K. (1991) 'Increasing returns, industrialization and indeterminacy of equilibrium', *Quarterly Journal of Economics*, 106:616–650.

Nehru, J. (1946) *The discovery of India*, New York: The John Day Company.

Quah, D. (1993a) 'Empirical cross-section dynamics in economic growth', *European Economic Review*, 37(2/3), (April)426–434.

Quah, D. (1993b) 'Galton's fallacy and tests of the convergence hypothesis', *The Scandinavian Journal of Economics* 95(4), (December)427–443.

Quah, D. (1994) 'Convergence empirics across economies with (some) capital mobility', London School of Economics and Political Science, Suntory-Toyota International Centre for Economics and Related Disciplines, Discussion Paper No. EM/94/275.

Romer, P. (1986) 'Increasing returns and long-run growth', *Journal of Political Economy*, 94:1002–1037.

Sala-i-Martin, X. (1994) 'Cross-sectional regressions and the empirics of economic growth', *European Economic Review*, 38, 739–747.

Salter (1959) 'Internal and external balance: The role of price and expenditure effects', *Economic Record*, 35 (August), 226–238.

Smith, A. (1937) *The wealth of nations*, New York: Random House, Inc.

Srinivasan, T.N. (1988) 'Structural adjustment, stabilization, and the poor', Working Paper, Economic Development Institute, Washington, DC: The World Bank.

Srinivasan, T.N. (1993a) 'Adjustment lending: Some analytical and policy issues', Yale University, processed.

Srinivasan, T.N. (1993b), 'Long-run growth theories and empirics: Anything new?'', in: T. Ito and A. Krueger, eds., *Lessons from east Asian growth*, Chicago: University of Chicago Press, forthcoming.

Srinivasan, T.N. (1993c), 'Comments on Paul Romer: Two strategies for economic development: Using ideas vs. producing ideas', *Proceedings of the World Bank Annual Conference on Development Economics, 1992*, Supplement to the *World Bank Economic Review* and *World Bank Research Observer*, Washington, DC: The World Bank, 103–109.

Srinivasan, T.N. (1994) 'Data base for development analysis: An overview', *Journal of Develop-ment Economics* 44, June 1994, pp. 3–27.
Thomas, V., Chhibber, A., Dailami, M. and de Melo, J., eds. (1991) *Restructuring economies in distress: Policy reform and the World Bank*, Oxford and New York: Oxford University Press.
Tybout, J.R. (1992) 'Linking trade and productivity', *The World Bank Economic Review* 6, 189–211.
Uzawa, H. (1965) 'Optimum technical change in an aggregative model of economic growth'. *International Economic Review*, 6:18–31.
World Bank (1994) *World Development Report 1994*, Oxford University Press.

*Chapter 40*

# POLICY LESSONS FROM DEVELOPMENT EXPERIENCE SINCE THE SECOND WORLD WAR

ANNE O. KRUEGER[1]

*Stanford University*

## Contents

[1] I am indebted to Jere R. Behrman, T.N. Srinivasan, and participants in the Asian Development Bank seminar for helpful comments on earlier drafts of this paper. Nakil Choi provided research assistance in preparation of this manuscript. Han-Young Lie also assisted with analysis of East Asian growth. The Institute for Policy Reform provided research support for delving into development thought in the 1950s, reported in Krueger (1991) .

*Handbook of Development Economics, Volume III, Edited by J. Behrman and T.N. Srinivasan*

## 1. Introduction

Prior to the Second World War, many governments undertook policies that influenced economic growth, but only a few governments (most notably the Soviet Union) regarded economic growth as their direct responsibility and adopted policies for which economic growth was the primary stated objective. It may fairly be said that development economics was not a separate field of study, nor was there much interest – outside central planning – in development policy as such prior to that time.[2]

After 1945, the emergence of previous colonies as newly independent states in Asia and the Middle East, and later in Africa, was accompanied by strong nationalist sentiments. These movements, and the fact that living standards in all the former colonies were very low contrasted with those of the industrialized countries, resulted in a political imperative for governments to undertake policies to foster economic growth. In poor countries which had been independent, identification with other developing countries (underdeveloped, as they were then called) was natural, and the political mandate equally impelling. For a variety of reasons, the policies adopted in an effort to achieve development were much the same in most developing countries.

Since then, the history of the field of economic development has been an interesting one as experience with, and empirical evidence regarding, the effects of a variety of policies has led to increased understanding of the development process. That understanding, and frustration with outcomes, have in turn resulted in altered policies. Further experience has then resulted in still more research and additional insights, and still further refinement of economic policies for development. As time has passed, not only has experience accumulated, but research has become increasingly well grounded with solid empirical techniques and improved bodies of data. Early insights were based on interpretation of available evidence, although that evidence was usually less than systematic. Over time, available data and empirical techniques have

---

[2] Indeed, most observers credit Rosenstein-Rodan (1943) and Mandelbaum (1945) as having been the first writers on the problems of underdeveloped countries (as they were then called). Clark (1940) was seminal and early and clearly influenced thought about development policy, but his analysis itself tended to be more positive than normative in nature. Leaders of the Indian independence movement spent considerable time discussing economic policies for development. Indeed, the Congress Party had even published a "plan" prior to the Second World War. Nehru's thinking, quoted below, was the predominant influence in newly-independent India, dominating the Ghandian pleas for reliance upon cottage industry and small-scale traditional activities for development. See Srinivasan (forthcoming) for a discussion.

enabled much more systematic analyses and underpinning of policy conclusions.

Understanding behavior of people in developing countries, and their response to policies, become more crucial than ever in the 1980s. By the late 1980s, there was widespread agreement that many of the earlier policies that had been adopted with the express intention of fostering development had been counterproductive, at least when carried out over a long period. Interest in economic policies, their effects, and the policy reform process has thus become a central issue in developing countries and in the development community more generally.

In this chapter, the evolution of thought regarding development policy and the evidence which challenged development thinking are examined. Focus is especially on the interaction between experience with development policy and development thought, as a prelude to the more detailed studies of individual aspects of economic policy and experience that follow.

The first section of this chapter starts with the ideas and thinking that underlay the initial formulation of development policy. The overriding influence of the experience with early development policies is still a major factor affecting policies and thinking about development, and as such is important in its own right. Thereafter, the experience of developing countries, both the success stories (primarily in East Asia), and the stories of those countries whose growth stalled in the 1980s, is reviewed with respect to the influence of success or failure on policy formulation. Next, attention turns to the difficulties that confronted many developing countries in the 1980s. The lessons learned from the combination of successful outer-orientation and difficulties with inner-oriented policies convinced most policy makers of the need for policy reform. The theory and evidence regarding alternative strategies to undertake policy reform are then reviewed in Section 4. Finally, the coherence of policy and the political economy of economic policy formulation and execution are addressed in Section 5.

## 2. Initial postwar development strategies

Any analysis of the evolution of thought regarding development strategy must start with an examination of the ideas that underlay policy in the euphoric days after independence, or after development became a conscious goal, in the late 1940s and 1950s. One of the striking phenomena of that era, especially in light of the absence of an inherited body of knowledge regarding development and development policy, is the degree to which there was virtual unanimity among policy makers, academics, and others regarding the ideas that underlay development policy.[3] In part because of the idealism of many nationalist leaders in the 1940s and 1950s,[4] and in part because of the unanimity of view, the early experience of most developing countries was much the same. Indeed, it might be said that the greatest distinguishing characteristic of individual developing countries in the 1990s is the rate at which lessons from early development experience have been learned and led to changed policies!

It should be recalled that the early postwar years were ones in which memories of the Great Depression were still vivid, the economies of the allies had been run as command economies during the war time years, belief in the economic success of the Soviet Union was still strong, and Keynesian ideas were in full sway. Combined, these factors resulted in a strong distrust of markets, even in developed countries. The fact that there had been a Great Depression was widely taken to imply that markets had failed, and that governments had a major responsibility for guiding the economy, at a minimum with respect to macroeconomic polices. In developing countries, memories of colonialism and the sharp deterioration in the terms of trade for primary commodities during the Great Depression also resulted in a deep-seated suspicion of the international economy.

The apparent economic success of the Soviet Union led many to conclude, following such authors as Lange and Taylor (1938), that there was little difference between public and private ownership and control of economic activity.[5] And, while private markets were suspect, little attention was given to any problems that might arise in public ownership and management of economic activities. Indeed, there was what in hindsight appears as a blind faith in the efficacy of government controls over economic activity.

Keynesian economics itself contributed to the distrust of markets, as most economists took the central idea to be that, in the absence of government

---

[3] T.N. Srinivasan has suggested that one might distinguish between "development strategy", and development policies. Certainly, the fact that the policy set was so similar across many countries tempts that conclusion. To conclude, however, that a "strategy" is something different from a set of policies seems unjustified unless it can be shown that the entire policy set sprang from the same underlying considerations. It is not clear that this must have been the case. One could, for example, have had import-substitution as a policy, consistent with reliance either on state owned enterprises or private enterprise for producing import-substituting goods. Likewise, there is no obvious reason why expansionary fiscal policies, fixed nominal exchange rates, and credit rationing were logically connected to other elements of the policy set. While all of these policies had as part of their analytical underpinning a suspicion of markets, many of them are also followed, albeit usually to a lesser extent, by other countries.

[4] Perhaps the most articulate statement of these views by a nationalist leader is that of Nehru (1941).

[5] See Tinbergen (1984) for a statement of this view as recently as the early 1980s.

intervention, a low – and Pareto inferior – level equilibrium might result. In addition, the Keynesian emphasis on investment also contributed to development thought as will be seen below.[6]

In an environment in which private economic activity was in any event suspect, it is small wonder that leaders in developing countries viewed their governments as responsible for undertaking measures to achieve rapid economic growth, and expected governments to take a leading role in the economy while controlling private economic activity.

To a remarkable extent, the new field of development economics generated the ideas, ideology, and rationale for the policies that were in fact adopted in country after country. There were several prevalent and dominant strands to that thought: 1) the desire and drive for "modernization"; 2) the interpretation of industrialization as *the* route to modernization; 3) the belief in "import substitution" as a necessary policy to provide protection for new "infant" industries; 4) the distrust of the private sector and the market and the belief that government, as a paternalistic benevolent guardian, should take the leading role in development; and 5) related to (4), a distrust of the international economy and pessimism that exports from developing countries could grow.

The desire for "modernization" itself is understandable. The policies undertaken with respect to the remaining four ideas were the crucial ones. Industrialization was taken to be synonymous with "manufacturing".[7] Combining the proposition that manufacturing needed to be the "leading engine of growth" with the deeply-held view that protection was essential for manufacturing to expand inevitably led to policies promoting import substitution and discriminating against agriculture.

A quote from Nehru, whose own thought was influential not only for India

---

[6] There were even some who interpreted the Keynesian message as meaning that developing countries were poor because of inadequate aggregate demand. Most analysts, however, knew better. T.N. Srinivasan has pointed out in correspondence that V.R.V.K. Rao (1952) of India was one of the first to point out that Keynesian ideas of inadequate demand had nothing to do with India's problems. The Keynesian emphasis on investment, however, was doubtless one of the factors that led economists and policy makers initially to neglect the role of other factors of production in development.

[7] An interpretation more in accord with economic theory would have been that industrialization was synonymous with mechanization. Indeed, the notion of increasing capital per man that underlay much of development policy was far more consistent with the idea of mechanization than of increasing manufacturing activities. In addition, modern development economics would tend to regard an increasing fraction of the labor force engaged in nonagricultural activities as a symptom of successful development. Early development thought emphasized the importance of increasing manufacturing output *even to the neglect of agriculture* whereas modern development thought would regard successful expansion of agricultural output as a necessary and strongly facilitating factor in encouraging industrial development.

but for all concerned with development, aptly provides an idea of the tenor of the discussion:

"No modern nation can exist without certain essential articles which can be produced only by big industry. Not to produce these is to rely on imports from abroad and thus to be subservient to the economy of foreign countries. It means economic bondage and probably also political subjugation... Big industry must be encouraged and developed as rapidly as possible, but the type of industry thus encouraged should be chosen with care. It should be heavy and basic industry, which is the foundation of a nation's economic strength and on which other industries can gradually be built up. The development of electric power is the prerequisite for industrial growth. Machine-making, ship-building, chemicals, locomotives, automobiles and the like should follow..."[8]

Simple observation was sufficient to convince any observer in the 1950s that existing manufacturing capacity in developing countries was extremely small, and that successful development would entail, as Arthur Lewis pointed out, a shift from a population 70 percent rural to one with at least that proportion urban. However, there is a difference between knowing that successful growth will entail such a shift and concluding that such a shift will necessarily generate the desired growth, no matter how attained. In most developing countries, it was thought that a very high proportion of increased investment levels should be directed toward manufacturing activities and those infrastructure investments that would be needed to support them. That such an allocation would not be sustainable without growth in agricultural output and productivity was not initially widely noted, although it would appear that it was thought that small investments in fertilizer subsidies, irrigation, and agricultural extension services would induce desired increases in agricultural output.[9]

Given the desire for industrialization, it seemed evident to those formulating policy that the only way to achieve a rapid increase in capacity to produce and output of manufactures was through "import substitution". Because most manufactured commodities consumed in developing countries were imported,

---

[8] Quoted in Srinivasan (forthcoming). Robert Bates (1981, p. 11) reflects a similar sentiment: "Common sense, the evidence of history, and economic doctrine all communicate a single message: that these [developing countries'] objectives can best be secured by shifting from economies based on the production of agricultural commodities to economies based on industry and manufacturing".

[9] Most developing countries in the 1950s were net exporters of agricultural commodities, the only exceptions being a few mineral exporters. The fact that there was an agricultural surplus, combined with the assumption that world markets for agricultural commodities would be stagnant, also contributed to the neglect of agriculture.

policy makers concluded that domestic producers would not enter without protection[10]. However, with protection from imports, it was thought that rapid growth of new industries could take place as domestic production replaced imports: hence, the term import substitution. Little or no thought was given to the possibility of industrialization through establishment of manufacturing enterprises which would export their products. Whether this was because policy makers believed that exports would automatically follow at a later stage or that their fledgling industries would be unable to compete with producers in developed countries is not entirely clear. What is evident is that rapid expansion of manufacturing production was expected to be the "leading growth sector", and that this would take place through import substitution.[11]

As has already been alluded to, there was a tendency to emphasize the role of low endowments of capital per worker in explaining low per capita incomes and low manufacturing capacity, and to focus therefore on the potential for investments in physical capital in manufacturing to accelerate growth. Thus, capital-output ratios were estimated for a variety of activities, and planning consisted largely of estimating levels of investment and outputs of each activity.

While it would be wrong to say that it was believed that there was no missing factor of production other than physical capital, many discussions of development, and development plans, came very close to that position. In the Indian Five Year Plans, for example, incremental capital-output ratios were estimated and used in projecting growth of industrial sectors. The overall incremental capital-output ratio so derived was then used to estimate the rate of growth of the entire economy, based on a simple Harrod–Domar model. (Government of India, 1957 and 1962). Implicitly, use of incremental-capital output ratios suggested that increased supplies of factors other than physical capital would not lead to increases in output.[12] Certainly it was not thought that, e.g. a lack

---

[10] Little or no attention was given to the alternative of subsidizing production (which trade theory suggests would be first best). This was apparently in part because it was assumed that developing countries could not raise revenues, or, to the extent that they could, that those revenues should be used for increasing investment. While reading of the literature of the times conveys this interpretation, it fails to explain why non-revenue raising quantitative restrictions on imports were relied upon, rather than revenue-raising tariffs.

[11] Even such a leading trade theorist as Ragnar Nurkse concluded that there should be "balanced growth", in which the rate of expansion of output of each commodity would be equal to the rate of growth of income times the income elasticity of demand for the commodity. Such a rule would be appropriate in a closed economy if there were no change in commodity or factor prices; it completely overlooks the possibility of international trade, however. See Nurkse (1958, especially pp. 11 ff.).

[12] The two-gap model of Chenery and Bruno (1962) and Chenery and Strout (1966) augmented the "physical capital only" model by positing a "foreign exchange constraint" in addition to the "capital constraint" on growth.

of skills in the labor force would or could constitute an overriding bottleneck to growth.[13]

For policy makers and others concerned with the conformity of policy to the precepts of economic efficiency, the infant industry argument was usually evoked to defend import substitution in manufacturing industries. As is well known, there is a case for *temporary* assistance to some new activities *if* those activities generate sufficient externalities and exhibit dynamic "learning by doing" or other properties that imply that they will eventually become sufficiently competitive to provide a return both for the initial costs to society of the losses during the start up period and for the investments made in the industry[14].

Distrust of markets and of private producers was another pillar of policy and pervaded virtually every aspect of development thinking. The view was widely held that private agents, and especially peasants, were economically irrational, and that there was little response to incentives on the part of most poor people. Rural moneylenders, landlords and traders who bought farmers' crops and sold them their inputs, were all viewed as rapacious profiteers serving little if any economically useful function or, if they did serve it, doing so only at great profit to themselves and "exploiting" the uninformed and ignorant poor. Urban employers were thought to exploit their workers, so that stringent laws would be necessary to protect workers. The Government of India went so far as to regard new investment by any of the twenty largest industrial houses as requiring permission, and being permissible only when the investment could not be carried out by others! Price controls, rationing, direct government ownership and operation, investment licensing, and other mechanisms were all developed to thwart the presumed tendencies of private entrepreneurs to profit at the expense of society.

This suspicion of private economic activity meant that not only were there controls and government direction of economic activity, but that there was a neglect of incentives that might have elicited improved economic performance. The opposite side of the coin, as already noted, was a belief in the ability of governments effortlessly to ascertain how the social good could be achieved and costlessly to undertake whatever measures were necessary to attain it.

It is arguable that the sway of these ideas over policy formulation would in

---

[13] This is not to say that development economists did not recognize that education and training would have to increase. Rather, it was implicitly assumed that expansion of the educational and training capacity of developing countries could readily be accomplished as additional employment opportunities became available for skilled workers.

[14] For an analysis of the practical difficulties with the infant industry argument, see Krueger (1991).

and of itself have been sufficient for those policies which emerged to have done so in the way they did. However, the prevailing views about the international economy, and the "export pessimism" of the time regarding the possibility of primary commodity exports undoubtedly reinforced the other ideas. In sharp contrast to the implications of Malthusian doctrine, economists in the late 1940s and 1950s were convinced that the demand for primary commodities would grow only slowly, at best. From this, they concluded that prices of primary commodities would either be stagnant or falling, and that developing countries could not rapidly increase their export earnings through increased quantities of primary commodity exports. Raul Prebisch's (1950) analysis, which was highly influential especially in Latin America, started from the premise that foreign exchange earnings from primary commodities could not grow rapidly enough to permit a growth of imports sufficient to allow satisfactory growth.[15] He therefore initially advocated import substituting industrialization; when he perceived the difficulties of carrying out that strategy in small domestic markets, he began advocating preferential trading arrangements among developing countries, again in the belief that they could not penetrate developed countries' markets.[16] Prebisch also believed that all of the gains from productivity increases accrued to manufacturing industries in the center (developed) countries, and presented the case for industrialization based upon import-substitution as the only feasible means of capturing income and productivity gains for developing countries.[17]

It is also necessary to note that the belief in the unimportance of incentives in inducing a supply response was influential in the subsequent willingness of policy makers to maintain fixed nominal exchange rates in the face of domestic inflation rates well above world rates. The potential for increasing exportables from expanding agricultural production was therefore diminished by the low

[15] It is also possible that a misinterpretation of the $2 \times 2$ statement of comparative advantage reinforced the commitment to import substitution in manufacturing. If one interpreted the $2 \times 2$ model to mean that one country would specialize in manufactures and one in agriculture, the conclusion seemed to be that developing countries *were* following their comparative advantage in exporting primary commodities and that such specialization would inevitably continue. That there are many manufactured goods and many agricultural commodities, and that there is comparative advantage within manufacturing and agriculture, does not seem to have been widely recognized.

[16] See Arndt (1978), p. 12ff. for a discussion.

[17] Prebisch's analysis was not entirely logically coherent. See Flanders (1964) for an analysis. It is often pointed out that Prebisch (1964) was among the first to spot the difficulties with import substitution strategies, and that is certainly true. It is significant, however, that he believed that developing countries could not develop export markets for nontraditional exports in developed countries, and he advocated regional common markets (such as the Latin American Free Trade Area) as a means for achieving sufficiently large markets to make development of manufacturing industry – still his first priority – economically more beneficial.

real returns to producers, while that in manufacturing was largely obviated by the huge rewards for those investing their resources in new import-competing activities.

The outcome of these ideas was a fairly tightly interconnected set of economic policies. In country after country, an "economic plan" was drawn up. The "plan" set forth levels of investment and savings deemed appropriate, given the conflicting tensions of low savings rates and the imperative for stepped-up rates of investment, for the next several, usually five, years. The level of private savings was estimated consistent with the marginal savings rate and the anticipated rate of growth, and that estimate, along with anticipated or hoped-for aid levels and the indicated rate of investment led to a target level of public savings that would be necessary.

While estimates were made of what some key variables would be – the incremental capital-output ratio, agricultural output and exports, for example – targets were established for others. For industrial activities, a large proportion of the target increases was to be achieved through government investments in electricity, transport, communications, and through parastatal activities in large-scale and visible manufacturing activities.[18] Individual targets were often set for outputs of such items as bicycles, yards of cloth, motorcycles and scooters, fertilizers by type, vegetable oils, and so on.

Most governments' plans included numbers indicating what aggregate investment should be, and then estimated the public and private savings that would be forthcoming to achieve it, in some cases closing the "gap" by indicating required levels of foreign savings. Estimates were made of the demand for imports that would accompany the (usually ambitious) investment program and income growth, and of export earnings and other sources of foreign exchange that would finance them. However, in most cases investment expenditures and import demands were normally underestimated, while public and private savings and export growth were usually overestimated.[19]

There does not appear to have been very much thought given to the questions either of how governments would insure that the public sector activities specified in plans would be carried out or of how private sector output

---

[18] State-owned enterprises often went well beyond large-scale activities. In many countries, hotels and other tourist facilities were publicly financed and operated by parastatal enterprises. In some, even retail stores, especially for the sale of food at controlled prices, were government owned and operated.

[19] See, for example, the review in the Indian *Third Five Year Plan* or the Turkish *Second Five Year Plan* of performance contrasted with targets for the preceding five years. At the end of the Indian Third Plan Period, the draft of the fourth plan had to be set aside and a series of three annual plans was substituted because of difficulties associated with plan implementation. A balance of payments crisis in the middle of Turkey's Second Plan resulted in substantial changes.

and investment targets would be met. In many countries, nominal interest rates were well below market-clearing levels (often with negative real interest rates) and credit rationing in the absence of developed financial markets proved a policy instrument for attempting to insure consistency of private investment with plans.[20]

In addition, many economic activities that had previously been private or nonexistent were taken over or undertaken by the state. Parastatal enterprises were established to manufacture new import-substitution commodities, while existing Agricultural Marketing Boards were given monopoly and monopsony powers for the distribution of agricultural inputs and the collection of outputs.

## 3. Initial feedbacks

The 1950s and 1960s witnessed rates of economic growth[21] even more rapid than had been hoped.[22] In part, this performance reflected the buoyancy of the international economy, which created a favorable environment for the growth of all countries. Growth was also facilitated by initial conditions in which many countries had held large sterling balances or other foreign exchange reserves as an outcome of the Second World War.

Equally important, there appears to have been large scope for gains in a number of areas. Increased expenditures on health and education yielded large dividends. Although reliable statistics are scarce, the data suggest

---

[20] This mechanism, of course, was far more successful in preventing investments that the planners did not want than it was in inducing privately unprofitable investments that the planners did want. However, the implicit subsidy entailed in low or negative real interest rates, combined with the incentives that rapidly developed through quantitative controls on imports, normally made those activities, especially in manufacturing, decided upon by the planners privately profitable. There was more difficulty in agriculture, where peasants shifted away from those export crops whose relative price had dropped significantly.

[21] It was certainly recognized that the objective of economic policy was to improve the lot of individual citizens, and that the rate of economic growth was only an indicator of welfare. Nonetheless, with real incomes as low as they were in many countries, it was generally thought that significant reductions in poverty would not be feasible without sustained growth in real per capita income. That other measures of well being, such as infant mortality, literacy, and life expectancy, were highly correlated with per capita income reinforced this belief. See Srinivasan (forthcoming, pp. 3ff.) for a discussion.

[22] See Morawetz (1978) for an analysis of early forecasts of growth and actual outcomes. Although overall growth of developing countries was more satisfactory than had been anticipated, forecasts of growth rates for individual countries varied greatly from outcomes. In general, the countries expected to perform best (most prominently India) did relatively less well, and countries expected to do poorly (including notably Korea) greatly exceeded expectations.

large increases in life expectancy and other health and well-being indicators.[23]

Almost certainly, there was also a significant backlog of worthwhile investments which had not been possible during the Second World War when ocean transport was almost entirely allocated to wartime needs and when in any event supplies of investment goods and other imports to developing countries were largely diverted to military uses of the belligerents. Thus, it may be that in the late 1940s and early 1950s, *any* economic policies that did not entirely thwart these investments would have generated rates of economic growth significantly above long-term trends.

With respect to import substitution policies, first investments were usually in relatively labor-using consumer goods. These investments appear, for the most part, to have yielded satisfactory, if not high, social and private real returns, as fairly large markets for those consumer goods existed, and factor proportions were reasonably well suited to most developing countries' factor endowments.[24]

Even so, with the benefit of hindsight, it is evident that symptoms of difficulty were already appearing. Four types may be distinguished. First, many countries encountered severe problems in administering Agricultural Marketing Boards and other parastatal agencies. Second, many countries experienced chronic or acute problems associated with much sharper increases in demand than in supply of food. Third, a number of countries encountered inflationary difficulties, often associated with problems in their balance of payments. Fourth, some countries experienced chronic "foreign exchange shortages" and/or "balance of payments crises".

Difficulties in administering parastatal enterprises presented major economic and political problems in many countries. Agricultural marketing was typical. The challenges associated with collecting crops, paying farmers, and distributing agricultural commodities appropriately were often more than fledgling bureaucracies could handle. Reports of fertilizers delivered too late to be useful in the current crop year and too soon to be usable in the following crop year were frequent. Inability to collect the crop at farmgate, or requirements that farmers bring their crops long distances, were frequent. So, too, were

---

[23] See Birdsall (1989) and World Bank (1993) for an analysis. See also Srinivasan (forthcoming), p. 6–7 for a skeptical view of the reliability of statistics on life expectancy and other indicators of well being. While there is no doubt that the indicators are poor, the available evidence from countries where data is believed somewhat better, such as India, casual observation, and the order of magnitude of the estimated improvement all suggest that there have been distinct improvements in these measures.

[24] Fei and Ranis (1964), among others, have argued that the difference between the East Asian NICs (see Section 3 below) and the other developing countries is that the East Asian NICs changed their development strategy after this "easy" import substitution phase had ended. On this interpretation, early development strategy was appropriate, but usually persisted long after it was no longer so productive. For consideration of the reasons for the early East Asian policy changes, see Section 3 below.

difficulties associated with pricing, quality grading, and transport. Panterritorial pricing resulted in uneconomic locations of crops and compounded transport and storage problems.[25] Efforts to provide incentives for, e.g. use of domestic wheat in flour milling in Brazil, resulted in "paper wheat" as individual millers obtained receipts from scores of domestic farmers in order to be eligible to receive their subsidies. [See Carvalho and Haddad (1981)]. Suppression of producer prices of export crops resulted in smuggling commodities across borders, with loss of official foreign exchange earnings and attendant difficulties in financing imports purchased for investment in the public, or large-scale private, sector.

These, and related, problems led the authorities to intensify controls, as scrutiny of applications and licensing procedures was stepped up. New regulations increased the economic costs of carrying out economic activities. Even so, administrative difficulties and regulations resulted in shortages of goods, loss of commodities (as when inadequate storage facilities resulted in losses of crops to mildew, rotting, or rodents), or reduced prices received for exportables (as when quality deteriorated or delivery dates became uncertain).

However, most problems of this type emerged in individual units and sections of bureaucracies; there was little reason for those coping with, e.g. the deterioration in the quality of Turkish tea, to learn of similar problems in Sri Lanka. Thus, they were largely regarded as one-off, sui generis to each individual situation, and not seen as indicative of larger or more systemic problems.

The second symptomatic difficulty was associated with apparent food shortages. This problem emerged most acutely and visibly in India in the late 1950s,[26] but was experienced elsewhere as well. Essentially, as urban populations and incomes were increasing rapidly, demand for food was rising commensurately. However, supplies of food to the cities did not grow at the same rate. Although increased imports would have mitigated the result, little consideration was given to importing food.[27] Instead, increased imports were largely eschewed except for emergency supplies for near-famine or short-term conditions, and food prices rose sharply. Policy makers then became concerned that either the real wages of urban workers would decline, resulting in urban

---

[25] See Krueger (1992b), Chapter 3, for a fuller description. See also Fernando (1987) for a fascinating account of difficulties in Sri Lanka, and Jansen (1988) for an account of Zambian problems.

[26] See Government of India (1959).

[27] This possibility appears to have been ignored for two reasons. On one hand, policy makers believed that their countries' comparative advantages lay in agriculture, and hence did not think (perhaps correctly) that it made sense for them to import food instead of the manufactured commodities that predominated among their imports. On the other hand, as discussed below, foreign exchange "shortages" rapidly emerged in most developing countries, which led further to the presumption that food should not usually be imported.

unrest, or rising real wages would choke off industrial development.[28] Either outcome was deemed unsatisfactory. Some countries adopted price controls on staple foods or food rationing, which gave rise in many instances to further administrative difficulties. In many instances, policies were adopted which were intended to enhance the rate of growth of production of major food crops, although many were at best partial offsets to the enormous bias against agriculture that had been created by the combination of trade, exchange rate, agricultural pricing, and other policies that had been adopted.

By current standards, inflation rates in the 1950s and 1960s appear to have been relatively low. But by standards of the time, especially when the dollar price level of internationally traded goods was stable, accelerating inflation constituted a significant policy problem in a number of developing countries. Policy makers in Chile in 1956, Brazil on several occasions but especially in 1964, Korea and Turkey each in 1958, and in a number of other developing countries all felt impelled to put development plans and programs aside in an effort to stabilize their economies and halt inflation. However, because these countries were adhering to systems of fixed nominal exchange rates,[29] these inflationary problems were closely associated with balance of payments difficulties. Failure to adjust nominal exchange rates had led to real appreciation, with consequent pressures on the balance of payments.

There were other countries such as India which, without major inflation problems, also encountered balance of payments difficulties. These difficulties arose for a number of reasons. Excess demand in the domestic economy was generated by increased public expenditures for development purposes without sufficient additional savings or government revenue. Development expenditures seemed to have higher import contents than was expected. Finally, import regimes, appreciated real exchange rates, and buoyant domestic demand constituted far more significant disincentives for exporters than had been anticipated.

Regardless of whether inflation led to real exchange rate appreciation, excess domestic demand, and balance of payments difficulties or whether instead failure of exports to grow resulted from disincentives associated with heavy protection of domestic industry and an appreciated real exchange rate, there were two consequences. On one hand, chronic balance-of-payments difficulties

---

[28] This set of issues was modelled by a number of economists in variants of a "dual economy" literature. Perhaps the best-known paper was that of Jorgenson (1962).

[29] It was official policy of the Bretton Woods charter for the International Monetary Fund that nominal exchange rates should be fixed, and adjusted only after consultation with the Fund. However, many countries in the 1950s had multiple exchange rate systems, and in many instances, the more important reasons for maintaining fixed nominal exchange rates were either national pride or concern over the potential effects of devaluation on the rate of inflation, the price of imported investment goods, or on other variables. For an analysis of one of these lines of concern, see Diaz Alejandro (1963).

were experienced in virtually all developing countries, and came to be seen as a key bottleneck to growth.[30] In a sense, the "elasticity pessimism" viewpoint had been a self-fulfilling prophesy, and little attention was given to the possibility that domestic policies had brought about the very consequence that had been feared. It took the experience of East Asian countries to demonstrate that this latter possibility deserved serious consideration.

The second consequence of inflation and balance-of-payments difficulties was the nature of the policy responses to these problems. They were of two kinds. The first was an intensification of controls over economic activity, and the second was the resort to IMF stabilization programs.

Turning first to the intensification of controls, countries which had initially had fairly simple trade regimes, with protection accorded to domestic industry but relatively free importation of other commodities, rapidly adopted exchange controls to restrict imports in line with foreign exchange availability. The intention, of course, was to use "scarce" foreign exchange for those uses deemed most conducive to development. The Philippines, for example, evolved a complicated trade regime which distinguished between consumer goods, producer intermediate goods and raw materials, and capital goods. Within each category, there were "essential" commodities, "semi-essentials", and luxuries.[31] In Turkey, import licenses were granted only after long delays as officials decided among applicants until an IMF Stabilization program was accompanied by a regime in which some commodities were divided into three "Lists": "liberalized" and importable with a fairly-freely issued license, "quota" with only a limited amount permissible, and "bilateral", which were importable only from countries with whom Turkey had a bilateral trading arrangement. Commodities not listed were ineligible for receipt of import licenses and therefore for importation. When this system started in the early 1960s, there were 215 separate quota categories of which 69 were for $25,000 or less. By 1970, there were 474 quota categories, of which 115 were for $25,000 or less (Krueger, 1974, pp. 166–168). In addition to the quotas, imported goods were regulated through complex systems of import duties, surcharges, guarantee deposits, and delays in issuances of foreign exchange.

With this increasing complexity, administration became more difficult and simultaneously opportunities for profiting by evading (or taking advantage of profitable legal loopholes) the system increased. As efforts were made to prevent evasion, the costs of the system rose both in terms of enforcement efforts and in terms of costs of obtaining needed licenses and permits.

The final phenomenon that requires attention, in light of subsequent events, was the incidence of economic policy reform programs in which policy makers

---

[30] See below, for a description of the "two-gap" model of this phenomenon.
[31] See Baldwin (1975) for a fuller account.

adopted Stabilization Programs.[32] Starting in 1956 with Argentina, a large number of developing countries encountered difficulties of sufficient magnitude either in financing their existing obligations or in financing imports deemed essential that they undertook significant policy changes. These changes varied from country to country, but almost always included reductions in excess demand through cutbacks in projected public expenditures and nominal devaluations. Depending on circumstances, additional measures included: raising nominal interest rates, simplifying highly complex import regimes, raising of prices of output of parastatal enterprises (to reduce the public sector deficit), removal of export taxes, simplifying tariff structures, and so on. When domestic authorities had reached agreement with Fund officials on a set of policy changes, the Fund usually lent to the country in question after receiving a Letter of Intent from the authorities indicating their intended course of action under the Stabilization Program.[33] In many instances, loan proceeds financed a resumption of imports and thus ameliorated the "import shortage" which was perceived to have been the bottleneck to increased economic activity.

Since inflation was often a significant part of the macroeconomic imbalance leading up to a Stabilization Program, reduction of ex-ante excess demand was usually an important part of Stabilization Programs. That, in turn, often led to a slowdown in domestic economic activity, with attendant political reactions.[34] Although many developing countries underwent Stabilization Programs at various points in the thirty years leading up to the 1980s, each was seen as a consequence of particular circumstances. Criticisms focussed on the resulting slowdown in economic activity or presumed tendency for accelerated inflation; in the former case it was thought that that was detrimental to growth, whereas in the latter, the argument was that these programs were ineffective. Little, if any, consideration before the 1980s, was given to the proposition that Fund stabilization programs did not go far enough in addressing the underlying policies adopted by most developing countries.

During the period when these policies were being pursued by most developing countries, economic understanding was also advancing, as research focussed on a variety of issues arising out of development experience. One line of

---

[32] Stabilization Program was the formal name adopted by the International Monetary Fund for programs supported by the Fund that normally entailed a reduction in the public sector deficit, a change in the nominal exchange rate, and other measures designed to reduce the inefficiencies of economic policy. In a few instances, countries followed Stabilization-like programs without Fund support. For ease of exposition here, the discussion will cover those programs – the vast majority – that were Fund-supported.

[33] Letters of Intent were not and are not made public by the Fund. A government wishing to make the Letter of Intent public is free to do so, but that does not frequently happen.

[34] See Carlos Diaz Alejandro (1981) for an analysis of some Fund programs. Diaz Alejandro concluded that Fund programs had been highly successful in righting payments imbalances, but much less so in achieving other objectives.

research attempted to improve the quality and usefulness of input-output data, and techniques for optimizing based on them, for development planning. [See, for example, Chenery and Clark (1959)]. Another line was addressed at analyzing the balance of payments constraint and the role of foreign capital in development. Most notable in this line was the "two-gap" model, initially exposited by Chenery and Bruno (1962). In that model, export growth was exogenous, while domestic savings was a function of domestic income. Domestic investment required both savings (domestic or foreign) and imports. To the extent that exogenous export growth was insufficiently rapid to absorb all of domestic savings, foreign capital could provide a powerful stimulus to development by breaking the foreign exchange bottleneck.[35]

Other lines of research challenged some of the fundamental tenets of the early development policy paradigm. T.W. Schultz (1964) argued convincingly the general responsiveness of people to incentives, especially poor people in agriculture. A large number of subsequent empirical studies confirmed that view in a variety of country settings.[36] Dual economy models, already mentioned, were developed showing the infeasibility, in a closed economy model, of sustained growth of manufacturing at a rate in excess of the rate of growth of the urban demand for food.

A second line of research, also focussing on human behavior, challenged the view that investment in physical capital was all-important in development. Again pioneered by T.W. Schultz (1961) and then followed by work by Gary Becker (1964), the role of human capital as an important factor of production came to be better understood. That was followed by research on investments in education, nutrition, health, and migration, which demonstrated conclusively that there were high real returns for these investments, and that neglect of them could seriously impair the productivity of physical capital accumulation.[37]

Meanwhile, cost-benefit analysis was being developed and utilized in assessing public-sector investment projects. Questions as to appropriate pricing, when controlled prices failed to reflect opportunity cost, were analyzed. It

---

[35] The "two-gap" model took export, savings, investment-output, and import coefficients as given functions of income or entirely exogenous. Other researchers attempted to analyze the causes of balance of payments difficulties. Diaz Alejandro (1965), for example, focussed on the "import intensity" of import substitution, noting the higher imports of capital goods associated with investment in import-competing sectors than in other sectors of the economy. That India was losing her share of world markets (and thus could not simply be a victim to slowly growing world demand) was noted by Bhagwati and Srinivasan (1975).

[36] See Timmer (1988) for further discussion of the evolution in thinking regarding the role of agriculture.

[37] To be sure, investment had to be productive, and there was some evidence that investments in e.g. education, were not efficient, focussing too many resources on the few university students, contrasted with enabling more students to complete primary school and extending low-quality education to too many students (as contrasted with providing higher quality education to fewer students). See Behrman (1983). See Psacharopoulos (1988) for a recent statement. For an earlier analysis of imbalances in real rates of return to physical and human capital, see Harberger (1965).

came to be increasingly recognized that appropriate pricing of public sector services, such as water and electricity, was a sine qua non both for the efficient allocation of those services and for the financing of maintenance and further investment expenditures (see Little and Mirrlees 1968).

Those sorts of studies began gradually to undermine the underpinnings of the earlier, simplistic, paradigm. Foreign exchange difficulties also prompted research, and led to efforts challenging the trade and exchange rate policies of developing countries. Bhagwati and Desai (1970) and then Bhagwati and Srinivasan (1975) showed that Indian economic plans had not lived up to their promise, and provided convincing evidence of the inefficacy of the Indian trade regime. Krueger (1966) provided estimates of the domestic resource costs of import-substituting industry in Turkey. Studies of other countries, organized as comparative studies by Little, Scitovsky, and Scott (1970) on industrialization and by Bhagwati (1978) and Krueger (1978) on trade regimes and exchange controls associated with import-substitution development strategies, and other evidence all pointed to the inefficacy of highly restrictive trade and exchange rate policies.

## 4. Experience in East Asia

Despite all the research and evidence, however, it took the experience of the East Asian countries to begin to persuade policy makers that there was a feasible and desirable alternative set of policies. By the 1960s, some East Asian countries were already breaking away from the import-substitution, government-control model of development. Taiwan had begun increasing incentives for exports and reducing reliance on government controls as early as the mid-1950s, and Hong Kong had a virtual laissez-faire economy. Korea reversed the earlier import-substitution policies in the early 1960s and Singapore began her impressive growth after breaking away from Malaya in the mid-1960's.[38]

Efforts to understand why East Asian NICs were the first to change policies have provided descriptive accounts, rather than convincing analyses of why countries decide to undertake policy reform. Hong Kong was a colony, and alternative policies were not a viable alternative. Korea was highly raw-

---

[38] For accounts of growth in these countries, see the works by Frank, Kim and Westphal (1975), Mason et al. (1980), and Kim (1991) on Korea; Kuo (1983) on Taiwan; Lim and Lloyd (1986) on Singapore; and Findlay and Wellisz (forthcoming) on Singapore and Hong Kong. See also the papers in the symposium edited by Tang and Worley (1988) and the contrast between Korea's and Turkey's performance in Krueger (1987).

material dependent, was incurring current account deficits of around 10 percent of GDP, financed by US foreign aid, and faced the prospect of a reduction in aid; without altered policies growth was virtually inconceivable. Singapore, too, as a city-state was, import-dependent. Taiwan, whose policies changed first, seems to have been heavily influenced by S.C. Tsiang.

Table 40.1 gives some data on their impressive performance. As can be seen, per capita incomes grew so rapidly that they were four to five times higher in 1990 than they had been in 1965. Whereas in the mid 1960s the East Asian countries had been among the poorest in Asia and regarded as having the bleakest growth prospects,[39] they had living standards among Asian countries second only to Japan by 1990.

At first, East Asian growth was little noticed or thought to be attributable to special circumstances, such as U.S. aid to Korea and Taiwan.[40] However, as growth accelerated, it gradually became clear that the East Asian economic performance was not a fluke: not only did exports, real GDP, and living standards grow more rapidly than in other developing countries, but impressive economic performance was sustained in the late 1970s after the first oil crisis. Even in the debt-and-recession years of the early 1980s, the East Asian NICs resumed growth rapidly.

Table 40.2 presents evidence on their growth rates contrasted with those of

Table 40.1
Economic growth of East Asian NICs

|  | GDP Per Capita | | Average annual rate of growth |
|  | 1965 | 1990 | of per capita income 1965–1990 |
| --- | --- | --- | --- |
|  | (1990 U.S. dollars) | | |
| Hong Kong | 2,544 | 11,490 | 6.2 |
| Korea | 970 | 5,400 | 7.1 |
| Singapore | 2,312 | 11,160 | 6.5 |
| Taiwan | 995a | 8,800b | 8.1 |

*Sources*: For Hong Kong, Korea and Singapore: World Bank, *World Development Report, 1992*. World development indicators, Table 1.
a. 1965 per capita income for Taiwan derived from International Monetary Fund, *International Financial Statistics*, May 1976 China page. Converted to 1990 prices by using the IMF Index of Dollar Export Unit Values.
b. Per capita income for Taiwan is in current dollars for 1991 from *Economist* survey, October 19, 1992, p. 5.

---

[39] See Hicks (1989) for a review of projections at that time.
[40] George Hicks concludes that: "The problem of explaining rapid East Asian economic growth had not arisen in the 1960s as the growth had not been noticed". (Hicks, 1989, p. 37). He notes that as late as 1968, the success stories were listed as Japan, Mexico and India, and that projections put Indian growth prospects well ahead of those of East Asian countries. Sri Lanka's per capita income was projected to be 20 percent higher than that of Korea.

Table 40.2
Growth rates of real GDP of East Asian NICs and selected other developing countries, 1960–1988
(percent per annum)

|  | 1960–1973 | 1973–1980 | 1980–1988 |
|---|---|---|---|
| *Asian NICs* | | | |
| Hong Kong | 9.6 | 8.8 | 7.6 |
| Korea | 9.3 | 6.9 | 8.3 |
| Singapore | 8.8 | 7.6 | 6.1 |
| Taiwan | 10.5 | 8.4 | 6.7 |
| *Other* | | | |
| Algeria | 4.3 | 8.7 | 1.8 |
| Argentina | 3.9 | 1.8 | −0.3 |
| Brazil | 10.0 | 6.5 | 2.0 |
| China | 4.6 | 5.3 | 9.2 |
| Colombia | 5.9 | 4.8 | 2.7 |
| Egypt | 5.9 | 11.1 | 4.3 |
| Ghana | 2.6 | 0.9 | 1.8 |
| India | 2.5 | 2.3 | 5.0 |
| Kenya | 6.7 | 4.2 | 3.4 |
| Mali | 0.3 | 5.3 | 1.5 |
| Nigeria | 4.4 | 3.6 | −2.2 |
| Pakistan | 4.9 | 4.4 | 7.3 |
| Philippines | 5.5 | 6.0 | 1.9 |
| Sri Lanka | 2.0 | 3.9 | 4.6 |
| Sudan | 1.6 | 5.9 | 0.5 |
| Thailand | 7.0 | 6.8 | 5.9 |
| Turkey | 6.1 | 4.4 | 4.6 |
| Zambia | 4.0 | −2.6 | 0.6 |

*Source*: Summers and Heston (1991), Table III.

other developing countries.[41] As can be seen, among the countries adopting the then-more conventional economic policies, only Brazil is estimated to have grown as rapidly as the East Asian NICs, and many countries' real GDP

[41] No effort was made to choose a "representative" list of other developing countries. The countries included in the table are among the more prominent of the developing countries, and ones whose experience influenced the thinking of development economists.

The estimates of rates of growth of real GNP are based on Summers and Heston, rather than official national income accounts. Data from developing countries are judged to be much less reliable than those from developed countries, both because so much larger a proportion of economic activity takes place in rural areas and small shops whose activities are difficult to estimate, and because statistical services are weaker. See the Summers–Heston (1991) quality ratings in their Appendix A.2. Only two African countries (Kenya and Botswana) received a quality rating as high as C, as the other countries' statistics were judged to be worse than that.

See the chapter by Deaton in this volume for a discussion of the defects of national accounts (and other) statistics in developing countries, and also the Symposium in the *Journal of Development Economics* on data availability and reliability, 1994.

growth was well below the rate of population growth. The contrast in performance became even sharper in the 1973–1980 period, after the first oil price increase. Egypt's rapid growth was attributable largely to the discovery of oil and the huge increase in foreign aid after the Camp David accord. If account is taken of the shifts in terms of trade (with Algeria and Egypt exporting oil and the East Asian NICs all being heavily dependent on oil imports), the difference in economic performance was even more striking. By the 1980s, even those countries (such as Brazil, Kenya and the Philippines) adopting import-substitution that had earlier achieved fairly rapid growth were experiencing sharp slowdowns in growth rates and the differences in performance became more evident still.

When the phenomenal growth rates of the East Asian countries were sustained, the first lessons that were learned pertained to the foreign trade regime. Whatever else was evident about the rapid growth of the East Asian NICs, it was clear that all of them had altered their foreign trade regimes and abandoned policies of import substitution in favor of an outer-oriented trade strategy. Exporters were enabled to import needed inputs fairly freely. At first, incentives were provided for exporting over and above those entailed in the nominal exchange rate. This led economists to begin calculating effective exchange rates, adding the value of these incentives to the nominal exchange rate. The effective exchange rate estimates were fairly uniform and across the board applying to all categories of exports, in comparison with highly variable effective exchange rates for various categories of imports and import competing goods.[42] Analysis demonstrated that the real effective exchange rate for exporters was maintained fairly constant over time, although reliance shifted from export subsidies and tax credits to use of the exchange rate itself to provide export incentives.

That exports responded to these incentives was and remains unquestioned. Moreover, the structure of the East Asian economies shifted, as the share of both exports *and* imports in GNP rose dramatically. Table 40.3 gives some data for Korea: the experience of the other NICs was very similar. As can be seen, export and import growth rates were almost incredible. The shares of exports and imports in real output increased continuously from 1960 to 1980. Although real output grew at an average annual rate of almost ten percent over three decades, export and import growth significantly outpaced the growth of GNP.[43]

---

[42] See Frank, Kim and Westphal (1975) for these calculations for Korea.

[43] The export growth rate somewhat overstates both the importance of exports in GNP and the rate of growth of value added in exporting, because imports of intermediate goods that were reexported constituted almost half of the value of Korean exports, which is higher than that for most economies, although it may be noted that Singaporean exports equal more than 100 percent of GNP! Prior to the early 1960s, it is likely that the value added component of exports was considerably higher. However, that 50 percent figure was reached by the late 1960s, and the rate of growth of exports thereafter is probably an accurate reflection of the rate of growth of value added in exporting.

Table 40.3
Evolution of Korean exports and imports, 1960 to 1990

|  | Exports | Imports | Percent share of GNP of: | |
| --- | --- | --- | --- | --- |
|  | (millions of U.S.$) | | Exports | Imports |
| 1960 | 33 | 306 | 3.3 | 13.3 |
| 1965 | 175 | 416 | 8.5 | 15.8 |
| 1970 | 882 | 1,804 | 13.9 | 23.5 |
| 1975 | 5,003 | 6,674 | 28.3 | 37.0 |
| 1980 | 17,214 | 21,598 | 35.2 | 42.9 |
| 1985 | 26,442 | 26,461 | 35.8 | 34.5 |
| 1990 | 63,123 | 65,127 | 31.8 | 32.3 |

*Source*: International Monetary Fund, *International Financial Statistics*, 1990 and 1991 Yearbooks, Korea pages.
*Note*: Both exports and imports are reported f.o.b. and are from balance of payments data. Exports and imports cover both goods and nonfactor services. Shares of GNP were calculated from the national income accounts.

There was little question but that the shift to the outer-oriented trade strategy was a significant factor in bringing about the spectacular growth of exports, and that that in turn had contributed in a major way to the accelerated growth rate of GNP.

It was further noted that, while there were export subsidies and other incentives, these were specified in terms of the rate of incentive per dollar of exports received, and generally were not commodity-specific. While there were many debates about the lessons for policy arising from the East Asian experience,[44] there was no question that the reorientation of the trade regime had played a significant role. Research[45] on the effects of highly restrictive trade regimes in a number of countries, and of the experience of countries that had reoriented their trade regimes, even partially, confirmed the importance of an outer-oriented trade regime.[46] By the 1980s, few could dismiss the East Asian experience; instead, the questions were focussed on an analysis of the

[44] See Section 5 below, where the role of government is discussed. It is in this context that the East Asian experience has been most subject to analysis and debate.

[45] See Balassa (1971), Bhagwati (1978), Krueger (1978), Little et al. (1970), for syntheses of comparative studies across countries. Econometric estimates by, among others, Balassa (1978) and Michaely (1977) reached the same conclusions.

[46] The terms "outer-oriented", or "outward-oriented" are used synonymously to mean that the overall bias of incentives, relative to that which would prevail at free trade, is at least neutral as between production of goods for export and goods for the domestic market. The term is owed to Keesing (1967). A laissez-faire regime is an outer-oriented regime, in this terminology, but a regime in which imports are subject to a duty of $x$ percent, while exports are subject to incentives, over and above the exchange rate, of $x$ percent or more, would also be regarded as outer-oriented. The key distinction in practice is that outer-oriented regimes seem to provide fairly uniform incentives for exports regardless of the individual commodities exported, whereas import-substitution regimes tend (automatically, in the case of prohibitive barriers to trade) to confer highly variable effective rates of protection on different categories of goods.

factors underlying that experience that accounted for such rapid growth. A first and clear lesson, agreed to by all, was that the rapid export growth in East Asian countries was an important factor in their overall performance. The role of the real exchange rate as a mechanism for efficient resource allocation (or more accurately, the role of an inappropriate real exchange rate as a misallocator of resources) was evident, and few could doubt its importance. This meant that incentives for exporting were fairly uniform across commodity groups as there was little in the incentive structure that differentiated between exports by type of commodity. The dramatic response of exports in each of the East Asian countries also showed that the allocative signals and incentives given by the overall macroeconomic framework were crucially important and could not be overlooked if other countries were to attempt to achieve similar results.

One question that arose related to whether in East Asia "export-substitution" had replaced "import-substitution" as a trade-development policy. Although researchers were able to identify some aspects of governmental policies which favored exports, it was clear that there were other, residual, elements of the policy regime that were biassed toward import substitution. Overall, the evidence seemed to be that an "outer-oriented" economy was the result of a trade regime which was not heavily biassed toward import-substitution.[47] Small, labor-abundant countries without many natural resources were ones that would find themselves producing a large fraction of their output for export, and importing many other commodities. This understanding was reinforced as Korea, Taiwan, Hong Kong and Singapore continued to grow: their commodity composition of trade altered toward goods which were less labor-intensive in production.[48]

Uniformity of incentives for exporting in small countries (relative to the international market) also meant that, when attempts were made to encourage the development of economic activities without comparative advantage, feedback was fairly rapid.[49] The Korean authorities, for example, concluded that their economy was ready for the development of heavy and chemical industries in the late 1970s. Imbalances in the economy rapidly became evident, however, and the effort was rapidly scaled back [see Yoo (1990)].

Other factors that derived from rapid export growth and contributed to rapid overall growth in the East Asian countries were the ability of firms with comparative advantage to expand rapidly, and to take advantage of indivisibilities and economies to scale, as well as the spur to productivity growth

---

[47] See the comparative data in Krueger (1978), Chapter 6. For estimates of the effective rates of protection to imports and exports [see Frank, Kim and Westphal (1975)].

[48] See Hong (1981) for an analysis of the Korean case.

[49] See Lee (1992) for a demonstration that total factor productivity growth was less rapid in those industries receiving direct support from the Korean government.

provided by competition in the international market. The upshot was rapid rates of total factor productivity growth [see Nishimizu and Robinson (1984)]. The significance of the trade and payments regime was thereafter not in doubt.[50] Even by the late 1970s, there was a discernible, albeit not overwhelming, drift toward somewhat less overvalued exchange rates, reduced reliance on exchange controls, and somewhat more attention to the incentives for exporting on the part of other developing countries.

There were, to be sure, many other factors that contributed to growth in the East Asian economies. In all, infrastructure was rapidly improved, as the capacity and efficiency of ports, telephones, domestic transport, and other facilities was expanded and improved to facilitate exports. Fiscal reforms had drastically reduced fiscal deficits, and inflation rates were very low by the mid-1980s. Protection to domestic industries, where it had been present, was lowered and the payments regime liberalized.

One other feature of the East Asian experience deserves note. That is: real wages rose rapidly [see Krueger (1987)], and there is little evidence, apart from the period of short-lived heavy and chemical industry drive in Korea, of any deterioration in the income distribution. Indeed, most estimates suggest that income distribution in East Asia was and remained significantly less unequal [see Chenery, Ahluwalia, et al. (1974)] than that in many developing countries where the stated purpose of import-substitution and related policies was to improve the relative and absolute living standards of the poor.

Thus, there is now a fairly wide consensus that the East Asian economies were highly successful, that there were reasonably uniform incentives for exporting and importing, that rapid export growth was a central component of their growth experience and, in that regard, that there was little bias of the East Asian trade regimes toward import substitution. That the real exchange rate and other export incentives were available across the board to virtually any who could export is not in doubt. Precisely how policies interacted and the relative importance of each is still a question on which there is ongoing research. Questions remain, also, as to the role of government in the development of the East Asian economies. Some of these are addressed in Section 5, where issues of political economy and the role of government are considered.

---

[50] There were some, however, who questioned whether a developing country in the 1980s could succeed by emulating East Asian policies with respect to the trade and payments regime. The stated basis for skepticism was a question as to whether markets in industrialized countries were sufficiently open to permit a newcomer's exports to grow as rapidly as had those of East Asian countries. The experience of Turkey in liberalizing her trade regime at the onset of the severe recession of 1980–1988 belies this argument.

## 5. Stalled growth and lessons of the 1980s: Interconnected policies and sustainability

The combined impact of the worldwide recession and other events of the 1980s on many developing countries is well known. In country after country, growth rates plummeted, and in many, real per capita incomes in fact fell for much or all of the decade.[51]

After Mexico had signalled her inability to service her debt in mid-1982, commercial banks became extremely reluctant to lend to developing countries. The sharp reduction in private capital inflows, combined with high nominal and real interest rates and very low prices of primary commodities, represented a massive change in the external environment.

As development economists began analyzing these phenomena, however, it became evident that some countries – especially those in East Asia – were able to adjust and resume growth rather rapidly, while others were not. By the mid-1980s, moreover, it became clear that the magnitudes of debt-servicing obligations were not in themselves sufficient to account for the severity of the impact on growth rates. Comparison of East Asian debt-servicing obligations as a percentage of GDP to those of heavily-indebted Latin American countries, for instance, showed little difference. It was only when examining the relationship of debt-servicing obligations to exports that it became clear that the import-substitution strategy of earlier years was itself part of the problem of the heavily indebted countries.[52]

It was out of the experience of the 1980s that the lessons for policy, which have transformed thinking about development strategy from that which had prevailed in earlier years, were learned. As was seen in Table 40.1, relatively rapid growth had been experienced over the 1950–1980 period in many countries whose development strategies centered on import substitution and controls over private economic activity. That had led even the critics of those policies to conclude that they were not sufficiently important to be basically inimical to growth. The traditional analysis of welfare-cost triangles simply did not show orders of magnitude large enough to suggest that growth rates were seriously affected by policies that departed from static economic efficiency

---

[51] The events of the 1980s discussed here dominated the attention of the development community and occupied much of the attention of those undertaking research on development. Certainly, the debt crisis and related issues characterized Latin America (except for Colombia), sub-Saharan Africa, and many countries in North Africa and the Middle East. China, India, the NICs, and Southeast Asian countries (except the Philippines) fared relatively better during the decade. Thus, to say that the 1980s were a lost decade for all developing countries is far too sweeping a generalization.

[52] See, for example, Sachs (1985).

considerations.[53] Even though rent-seeking costs were recognized to be sizeable, they did not seem to be large enough to thwart development efforts. Combining theory with the fact that growth rates were rapid by any historical standard, criticism of economic policies had been muted.[54]

To a considerable degree, earlier research on the effects of sectoral policies provided an important underpinning for the new focus of research on policy. But whereas critics had earlier viewed, e.g. agricultural pricing policies as having at most static resource misallocation consequences, the rethinking of the 1980s focussed on the linkages between agricultural pricing policies, large and inefficient parastatal sectors, trade and exchange rate policies, on the one hand, and macroeconomic difficulties, on the other. Recognition of the similarity of the policy set across countries led to focus on the linkages between policies, their cumulative effects over time, and the political economy of policy formulation and implementation.

By the early 1990s, research and analysis had resulted in a broad consensus about those facets of policy that had been detrimental to growth, and the desirable directions in which policy reforms should go. In this section, attention is devoted to these policies sector by sector, with focus on linkages between them: in-depth analyses of sectoral policies is contained in other chapters in this volume. In the next section, attention turns to the problems of economic policy reform, where the number of issues still subject to question is considerably greater. Even after those issues are addressed, there remains the broader and still relatively unexplored set of issues surrounding the political economy of policy formulation and evolution, which is addressed in the final section.

*Macroeconomic policies and debt.*[55] The countries whose real incomes were most dramatically affected by the debt crisis were those that had previously 1) borrowed heavily; 2) been experiencing high inflation rates; and 3) had sizeable fiscal deficits. Table 40.4 gives some illustrative data.

---

[53] For the classic analysis of traditional welfare costs of policy see Harberger (1959).

[54] This is not to say that economists had not advocated changes in policies. As already mentioned, analyses of trade and exchange regimes had been highly critical of inward-looking policies and the role of human capital had already been stressed. Moreover, individual policies were subject to scrutiny on country-specific bases in many instances. The critical distinction in the 1980s was that the policies which had earlier been seen as minor detractors from reasonably rapid overall growth rates came in the 1980s to be viewed as major obstacles to resumption of growth.

With hindsight, some if not most of the growth performance of the 1970s in countries following import substitution policies was unsustainable, and percentage points of GDP growth were, in effect, "borrowed" and had to be repaid in the 1980s. Seen in that light, the slowdown in growth rates in the 1980s is much less puzzling and dramatic than it is if it is assumed that the growth rates of the 1970s were sustainable.

[55] See Corbo and Fischer (this volume) for an analysis of macroeconomic issues in development policy.

Table 40.4
Fiscal deficits, inflation rates and debt-service obligations

| Country | Fiscal deficit | Inflation rate | Debt/GNP | Debt/GNP |
|---|---|---|---|---|
| | (% of GDP 1982) | (% 1982) | 1982 | 1988 |
| Argentina | −12.7 | 184 | .84 | .66 |
| Bolivia | −19.0 | 179 | 1.06 | 1.34 |
| Ghana | −6.1 | 28 | .35 | .61 |
| Jamaica | −14.5 | 9 | 1.01 | 1.54 |
| Kenya | −8.1 | 14 | .57 | .71 |
| Mexico | −15.4 | 61 | .53 | .61 |
| Panama | −11.3 | 5 | .99 | 1.38 |
| Philippines | −4.2 | 9 | .62 | .75 |
| Uruguay | −9.1 | 16 | .30 | .50 |
| Zambia | −18.6 | 6 | 1.02 | 1.91 |
| Korea | −3.0 | 7 | .52 | .21 |
| Singapore | +1.8 | 4 | .09 | a |

*Sources*: Fiscal deficits and inflation rates from International Monetary Fund, *International Financial Statistics Yearbook*, 1991, pp. 154–5 (for fiscal deficits) and l65–7 (for GDP deflators). World Bank, *World Debt Tables*, 1990–91 for debt data. Estimates for each country are from country tables.

The first three columns give estimates of the fiscal deficit and the inflation rate as of 1982. It is not possible to choose one year to characterize the difficulties of a single country, much less a group of countries. Ghana, for example, was using extensive price controls in 1982 and the rate of inflation estimated for that year is much lower than that for earlier or later periods. Panama was using the dollar as a currency and thus could not record very much inflation; borrowing, however, was large. Ghana's situation was the opposite as borrowing was low because Ghana was not creditworthy. Despite these, and other, necessary qualifications, the data in the first three columns of Table 40.4 are all illustrative of the proposition that the countries with large fiscal deficits also experienced rapid inflation and had large accumulated debt.

The final column of Table 40.4 gives the debt/GNP ratios in 1988. As can be seen, in most of the countries listed in the top portion of the table, the debt/GNP ratio in 1988 was higher than in 1983, indicating that countries had continued to accumulate debt at rates in excess of GNP growth[56] (with new

[56] Debt is denominated in foreign currency and GNP in domestic currency. When countries' exchange rates are significantly overvalued (as Ghana's was in the early 1980s), the debt/GNP ratio is greatly understated. When the exchange rate is adjusted to a more realistic level, the recorded debt/GNP ratio rises. In the countries in question, however, the ratios rose because of increased debt as well as, in some cases, because of an altered real exchange rate. The decline in the Argentine debt/GNP ratio reflects the opposite phenomenon, as the exchange rate changed between 1982 and 1988 by less than the price level; in 1989, after devaluation, the Argentine debt/GNP ratio rose to 1.19.

lending taking place "involuntarily" under the auspices of IMF programs and country committees) during the 1980s.

The last two rows of Table 40.4 give comparable data for Korea and Singapore. By the early 1990s, Singapore was no longer listed by the World Bank as a debtor country. But as can readily be seen, Korea's debt-GNP ratio fell sharply during the 1982–1988 interval.[57]

In contrast to many lines of research where empirical work provided most insights, a considerable body of analytical research focussed on the issues surrounding debt and macroeconomic imbalances. Initial analysis focussed on the debt problem itself.[58] Analysts concentrated on issues surrounding countries' abilities to finance their debt-service obligations. One line of analysis centered on whether the problem was one of "liquidity or solvency".[59] Another approach examined the relationship between "debt overhang" and growth, arguing that there could be circumstances in which few would find it profitable to invest in a heavily indebted country because of the tax on new earnings streams necessary to finance debt-service of old ones, which in turn might imply that existing debt-servicing obligations could not be met. In such circumstances, there could be partial debt-forgiveness schemes which would benefit both debtor and creditor, as new investments could then become profitable and the actual proportion of debt servicing obligations that was paid might rise.[60]

However, as inflation rates soared and growth rates plummeted despite debt reschedulings, research began more and more to focus on the macroeconomic imbalances that had underlain the debt crisis. Here, there was little or no analytical challenge: excesses of government expenditures over government revenues that could not be financed by foreign borrowing were inevitably financed by domestic credit creation.[61] In most instances, the authorities recognized that sufficient increases in the real interest rate to finance public sector deficits in relatively noninflationary ways would result in sharp reduc-

---

[57] Hong Kong is not an independent state and does not incur sovereign debt. Taiwan's debt is not reported by the World Bank. Even for Southeast Asian countries such as Malaysia and Thailand which grew rapidly in the 1980s, debt-service ratios in the late 1980s were not more than 10 percentage points above those in 1982, and there had been no debt rescheduling.

[58] The debt crisis generated a huge literature. There are several collections of papers which appeared in the late 1980s, which contain references to most of that literature. See Frenkel, Dooley and Wickham (1989), Husain and Diwan (1989) and Sachs (1989a), and the symposium on New Institutions for Developing Country Debt in *Journal of Economic Perspectives*, Vol. 4, No. 1, Winter, 1990.

[59] See, for example, Cline (1983). The official U.S. position, as reflected in the 1983 *Economic Report of the President* was that the debt problem was a liquidity problem. For a brief history of economic policies toward heavily indebted countries, see Krueger (1993b).

[60] The leading proponent of this viewpoint was Sachs (1986).

[61] See the next section, in which the linkage between rising expenditures, foreign borrowing, domestic borrowing, and acceleration of the inflation rate is analyzed in attempting to come to grips with the notion of the sustainability of the growth rate.

tions in private sector investment, and hence in growth rates. Instead, therefore, the choice was to finance public sector deficits by expanding the domestic credit base.

Moreover, as inflation rates rose to triple, and even occasionally quadruple-digits, there was no longer any question that inflation itself negatively affected growth.[62] Not only was uncertainty about future relative prices, the real interest rate, and other variables greatly increased with attendant resource misallocation, but the inevitable measures taken to attempt to reduce inflation rates from those levels often led to declines in output.

Many of the questions that arose therefore concerned means of reducing fiscal deficits. Further examination showed that large and growing fiscal deficits were normally the result not of one or two excesses of expenditures or shortfalls of receipts, but rather of the tendency for the various sectoral policies which had previously been demonstrated to have negative consequences to become increasingly costly and ineffective over time, so that government expenditures had tended to grow with diminishing returns and rising costs. The consequent inflation itself then further raised these costs and lowered returns, thus increasing the fiscal deficit.

This vicious circle can best be understood by turning attention to the interactions between inflation, exchange rate policy, credit ceilings, and sectoral policies in several arenas. Thereafter, the notion of sustainable growth is considered.[63]

*Agricultural policies.* Agricultural pricing policies well illustrate the findings of research during the 1980s. Among the many policies adopted in developing countries, perhaps none was more frequently encountered than the discrimination against agriculture. As seen earlier, focus on industrialization and a belief that peasants were not responsive to incentives had combined to lead policy

---

[62] The experience of highly-visible India may have obscured the underlying linkage between sectoral policies, growth of fiscal deficits, and inflation. Those countries had been relatively fiscally conservative, with inflation rates well below those of most African and Latin American countries, despite similar sectoral policies. Earlier, it had been tempting to conclude that India's economic policies resulted in slow but steady growth. By the early 1990s, however, India had accumulated large foreign debt and it was becoming evident that India's economic policies, too, were unsustainable unless negative per capita income growth were to be accepted.

[63] Attention here focuses on the ways in which interactions among policies may intensify the negative consequences of each for resource allocation and growth over time. There are some offsetting mechanisms. For example, in the absence of indexation, more rapid inflation may mitigate some of the incentives of minimum wage legislation to employ capital rather than labor, and thus reduce the resource misallocation effects of that legislation. Although further research is needed on these sorts of offsets, the experience of the heavily indebted developing countries suggests that the negative interactions outlined in the text far outweigh those positive interactions that do exist. In the case of minimum wage legislation, the reason is obvious: as inflation rates rise, pressures for wage indexation increase and prevent the erosion of the real wage that might otherwise take place.

makers, both deliberately and through their emphasis on other objectives, to take measures that resulted in agricultural producers receiving prices for their outputs that were usually well below those they would have received under policies in which prices reflected relative returns to various factors.

Agricultural output had almost always been neglected, with the attention of government planners and others focussed much more on finding ways of encouraging industrial production. In addition to this "neglect" of agriculture, producer prices were often suppressed as governments were attempting to collect revenues for their own purposes or to provide cheap foodgrains to urban dwellers without major fiscal costs. Moreover, agricultural economists had thought that some of the negative effects of low producer prices might be offset by expenditures on infrastructure in agriculture.

As already mentioned, T.W. Schultz had pioneered in arguing that peasants were responsive to incentives, and that the neglect of agriculture, and suppression of producer prices was detrimental to agricultural output and increases in agricultural productivity. Low producer prices were recognized to be a disincentive in agriculture, and in some countries they had already been raised, with positive effects on the production of some agricultural commodities.[64]

But reexamination of agricultural pricing policies in the 1980s demonstrated several additional propositions. First, suppression of prices to agricultural producers was much greater than comparison of the border price with the domestic price to farmers indicated. Moreover, the reduction in agricultural producers' incomes was considerably greater than had been thought.

The suppression of prices was greater for two reasons. First, overvaluation of the exchange rate, already noted as a salient characteristic of most trade and payments regimes, fed through into a low domestic price for agricultural outputs: had nominal exchange rates been at more realistic levels, prices to producers would have been higher. This avenue of discrimination against agricultural producers, although recognized earlier, had not been systematically analyzed. Estimates indicated that, in many countries, discrimination through the exchange rate was proportionately greater than that through domestic pricing policies.[65]

There was a second source of additional discrimination, however. The protection accorded to domestic import-competing production of consumer goods and of other protected goods purchased by farmers discriminated against

---

[64] See also the work of Behrman (1968) on producer supply response in Thailand, which provided systematic empirical evidence indicating reasonable supply responses in agriculture in developing countries in response to changes in relative prices.

[65] See Krueger, Schiff and Valdes (1988) for a brief summary, and Krueger, Schiff and Valdes, editors, (1991a, 1991b, and 1991c) for the analysis for individual countries.

agriculture.[66] Not only were the prices farmers received for their products low due to direct suppression and to exchange rate policies, but in addition, prices paid for consumer goods and for the inputs farmers used in production were artificially high.

Combining these three sources of discrimination against agricultural producers indicated much larger suppression of producer prices than had previously been recognized. Efforts to estimate the value of the "offsets" provided through government expenditures on infrastructure and on other expenditures directed to the agricultural sector clearly indicated that there was no way these could provide a major offset to the income losses resulting from direct discrimination.[67]

It should also be noted that parastatal enterprises also contributed to inefficiencies in many cases. The rising costs of Agricultural Marketing Boards in many developing countries contributed either to rising fiscal deficits or to even further reductions in prices paid to farmers for their outputs and increases in prices they were charged for their inputs.

Taken altogether, the findings indicated several points. Discrimination against agriculture was significantly greater than had been earlier realized, and was the consequence not only of policies which were oriented toward agriculture, but also was the outcome of overall trade, payments, and macroeconomic policies. A lesson that is valid for all sectoral policies, and not only those pertaining to agriculture, is that the overall thrust of macroeconomic policy significantly affects the incentives and responses of each segment of economic activity, while the losses incurred in e.g. attempting to maintain cheap food to urban workers and operate Agricultural Marketing Boards contribute to increasingly large fiscal deficits.

*Financial policies.* A second illustration of the ways in which inappropriate policies with respect to one set of economic activities spill over and intensify

---

[66] Interestingly, it also became evident that, despite the belief that developing countries' policies always discriminated against agricultural producers, in fact they discriminated against agricultural export commodities. For import-competing agricultural commodities, producer prices were not directly suppressed. However, the impact of the exchange rate and high prices for consumer goods and inputs discussed below usually more than offset the price increases resulting from protection against imports.

[67] The one occasional exception to this generalization was with regard to subsidized credits, which became very large in some cases. (See for example Carvalho and Haddad in Krueger, Schiff and Valdes 1991a for an estimate of the extremely high value of these subsidies in Brazil). However, those subsidies, as well as most other subsidies on agricultural inputs, seem to have been received disproportionately by large landholders. When they were that large, they also resulted in sizeable distortions and resource misallocation. See Binswanger (1990) for a statement of the case for more infrastructure investment in agriculture. It is evident that both realistic agricultural pricing and adequate infrastructure investment are necessary conditions for sustained growth of agricultural output at satisfactory rates.

distortions in other sectors is provided by financial policies. Earlier analyses of trade and payments regimes oriented toward import substitution had suggested that most of those regimes provided incentives for using capital-intensive methods of production, at least for those producers able to obtain import licenses.[68] Combined with the tendency in most developing countries to impose requirements on private producers either for high minimum wages and social insurance payments, or for other benefits (such as immunity from layoffs) to labor, the incentives for capital – using methods of production were greater than would have been the case if efficiency pricing had been used.

However, in most developing countries ceilings were imposed on bank lending rates, in circumstances where banks were for many the only source of finance. When these ceilings were below market clearing prices (and they were often well below those prices), the resulting real rates of interest were low, and often became negative as the rate of inflation rose. To be sure, the total amount of available credit was limited, and to the extent that those receiving cheap credit used more capital-using methods of production or produced more capital-intensive goods than they would have at realistic prices, other producers (usually in the informal sector) used less capital-using methods and produced more labor-intensive commodities.

Once again, the linkages between policies became evident: higher inflation rates were more injurious than they would have been had interest rate ceilings been higher, and interest rate ceilings were potentially more costly, the higher the rate of inflation. The lower cost of borrowing for those with access to credit, moreover, increased the incentives for capital-intensive techniques of production. Since capital-intensive industries were seldom those in which developing countries had a comparative advantage, all of these policies combined to shift resources away from the production of exportable commodities. Whether resources were allocated to capital-using import substitution industries, or whether instead they were used in rent-seeking activities because of the increased profitability of scarce credit or imports, they yielded lower real rates of return than they would have with an incentive structure more accurately reflecting tradeoffs.

The increased incentives for capital-intensive production also intensified the excess demand for foreign exchange at the existing nominal exchange rate. It may be noted that the foreign exchange shortage in turn was used to justify even more incentives for import substitution, and to intensify the restrictiveness of the trade and payments regime. As that happened, agriculture and

---

[68] See, for example, the analysis in Krueger (1978), synthesizing the findings from the individual countries in the comparative project on foreign trade regimes and economic development. For an estimate of the extent to which low real interest rates, labor market regulation, and the trade regime combined to provide incentives for capital-intensive techniques of production, see the estimates in Krueger (1983).

labor-intensive manufacturing industries were even further discriminated against, as policies interacted in their effects.

*Parastatal enterprises.* It was already stated that one of the widely-held views in the early years of development was that there was little, if any, difference between the quality of management in public and private sector enterprises. In many developing countries, government enterprises were established or expanded to produce import-substituting commodities and for many other purposes.[69]

In India, for example, 62.1 percent of total "productive capital" and 26.7 percent of total labor in industry was in the public sector by 1978–1979. Parastatal enterprises, which produced heavy engineered goods, chemicals, fertilizer, steel, machine tools, textiles, and almost everything else, were major features of the economic landscape.

There is reason to believe that parastatal enterprises in India were more economically efficient than their counterparts in many other developing countries. Yet those enterprises accounted for only 29.5 percent of value added in manufacturing, while private entities, with 32 percent of capital and 68 percent of employment accounted for 64.6 percent of value added in manufacturing.[70]

A variety of factors seem to explain why parastatal enterprises were not usually able to be cost effective. These include the political constraints that were imposed upon them, including the necessity to hire politicians' relatives and friends, to increase employment before elections, and to locate in places determined by political, rather than economic, considerations.

But for present purposes, the important consideration is the ways in which the existence of parastatals intensified other policy inefficiencies. There were many. Parastatal enterprises often received preference in the allocation of scarce foreign exchange, thus raising the shadow price of import licenses to everyone else, and increasing the inefficiencies resulting from the trade and payments regimes. Often, too, parastatal enterprises were accorded monopoly positions within the domestic market, and their high costs and poor quality increased the costs of production in the private sector. Parastatal enterprises were often required to employ additional workers to avert unemployment, and, in addition to provide housing, health, and education facilities that were

---

[69] In addition to parastatal enterprises for manufacturing, parastatal enterprises operated agricultural marketing boards, hotels, wholesale and retail stores, importing and exporting, financial institutions, and other activities. The attributes discussed for manufacturing parastatals apply equally to other enterprises. Focus on those enterprises simplifies exposition.

[70] Bardhan (1984), p. 102. In Turkey, Baran Tuncer and I estimated that State Economic Enterprises used on average more than 3 times more labor and capital per unit of value added than did firms in the private sector producing comparable commodities. [See Krueger and Tuncer (1982)].

not included in the computation of wages and that increased their costs significantly. In many instances, parastatal enterprises were also subject to price controls (by governments desirous of repressing inflation). When those controls were effective, parastatals financed their resulting deficits from the central government budget, while private sector firms were unable to produce and compete at the controlled prices.

For these and other reasons, increasing parastatal enterprise deficits were themselves a major contributing factor to fiscal deficits and money creation, as the financing of their deficits constituted a drain on the government budget. Parastatal enterprise deficits as a percentage of GNP reached, and even exceeded, 10 percent by the early 1980s in some countries. As such, their inefficiencies constituted a drain on resources directly, but also contributed to fiscal deficits and thus accelerating inflation, which made credit rationing, import licensing, agricultural pricing policies and other measures even more distortive.

*Trade and exchange rate policies.* Many of the inefficiencies resulting from highly restrictive trade and payments regimes have already been noted. Here, the purpose is to note some of the mechanisms through which the trade and payments regimes interacted with other policies to intensify the economic costs of those policies.

First and perhaps most important, holding a given nominal exchange rate fixed was obviously more distortive the higher the rate of inflation. As domestic excess demand increased, the implicit premium on import licenses rose, and with it the potential for misallocation of such foreign exchange as was earned. Simultaneously, the incentive for producing and selling on the export market decreased still further, thus shifting exportables to extralegal channels or to the home market and decreasing the supply of legal foreign exchange.

Thus, in countries where nominal exchange rates were fixed, or at least adjusted only after foreign exchange difficulties had mounted to near-crisis proportions, accelerating inflation increased the costs of these policies. Meanwhile, foreign exchange difficulties also tended to result in upward shifts in demand for home goods, given the unavailability of imports, and thus contributed to further increases in the price level.

It may be noted that these same mechanisms implied that preferential treatment in foreign exchange allocations for parastatal enterprises became potentially more distortive as inflation resulted in greater restrictiveness of import licensing mechanisms. The consequent disincentives for private producers increased. Increased foreign exchange shortage also led the authorities to increase protection for import-competing agricultural commodities, with attendant shifts of resources away from exportable agricultural goods. Simultaneously, the greater real appreciation of the exchange rate provided more disincentives for production of exportable crops, again exacerbating the foreign exchange difficulties which triggered the process.

A more restrictive trade and payments regime was also distortive through a variety of other interactions. For example, as foreign exchange became scarcer, authorities were increasingly reluctant to grant import permits; that gave domestic producers increased monopoly power in domestic markets. That, in turn, usually led to further deteriorations in quality with attendant cost increases for other producers.

In addition to interactions of the trade regime with other policy instruments, interaction went from realistic exchange rate policy to other policies. That is, many observers of the success of the East Asian countries pointed to the necessity for other policies to have been appropriate in order for the NICs to be able to achieve the growth rates that they did. For example, many pointed to the absence of significant labor market interventions as a necessary condition for the successful initiation of the outer-oriented trade strategy.[71] Likewise, the fact that a very high percentage of the labor force had at least eight years of schooling was noted as a contributing factor to the ability of the NICs to grow rapidly.[72]

*Sustainability of policies.* For these and other reasons, an overriding lesson of the 1980s was the interconnectedness of policies in a number of markets. Not only was this interrelationship evident among various sectoral policies, but it applied with even more force to the large fiscal deficits which underlay the inflations and debt difficulties which focussed attention on the issue. Fiscal deficits did not typically emerge full-blown. Rather, analysis suggested that the deficits themselves were usually the consequence, often cumulative, of policy failures in individual markets, including loss-making parastatal enterprises, rising costs of food subsidies and increasing rates of subsidies to particular industries, to name just a few.

These insights led inevitably to the notion of the sustainability of economic growth. Clearly, many of the developing countries whose growth rates had appeared so satisfactory in the 1960s and 1970s had been pursuing policies which could not indefinitely be maintained with sustained economic growth. While the linkages between micro- and macroeconomic policies are still imperfectly understood, there is increasing recognition that some policies may

---

[71] See Hong (1981).
[72] There were, however, other countries (perhaps most notably Sri Lanka) where educational attainments exceeded those of the NICs and where growth rates were not high.

apparently deliver economic growth in the short run, but have within them self-destruct mechanisms.[73]

Seen in this light, there is an important distinction between sustainable policies and policies which generate current increases in GNP but build in necessary future growth-retarding adjustments. Rapid inflation, for example, may be consistent with continued growth this year, but at some point, may require a cessation of growth, or even a decline in GNP, in order to avoid acceleration into hyperinflation.[74] Any assessment of the net impact of inflation on growth must take into account these longer-term ramifications, as well as its short-term impact.

At a macroeconomic level, the question of sustainability is critical, as the debt crisis vividly illustrated. A stylized caricature of the growth process in many developing countries in the 1960s and 1970s might be that the rate of savings and investment was raised, but with increasing microeconomic inefficiencies that greatly lowered real rates of return on investment.[75] To sustain growth rates, therefore, governments[76] had to raise the rate of investment continuously. At first, this could be done by foreign borrowing. But as debt-servicing obligations mounted while real rates of return were declining, difficulties were encountered in continuing borrowing from abroad.[77] At some point, it became infeasible to continue borrowing from abroad. Sometimes, this led to a crisis atmosphere in which the authorities decided to alter their policies. In other instances, in order to sustain the rate of growth, the next resort was to domestic borrowing. As this happened, domestic inflation

[73] It is not clear whether politicians knowingly adopted unsustainable policies because of high discount rates or because they did not appreciate the future consequences. It is possible, of course, that there might be a sufficiently high societal discount rate so that it became efficient to have rapid economic growth in the short run with reduced future living standards and lower future growth rates in consequence. For most of the developing countries, however, poverty levels are so large, and the political imperative for development so great, that it seems implausible that policies were adopted in spite of the fact that they were known to be unsustainable!

[74] The example of Peru under Alain Garcia is frequently cited. In that country, real GDP is estimated to have increased by 8.9 and 8.2 percent in 1986 and 1987, but to have fallen thereafter by 8.5, 11.7 and 4.4 percent in the following three years. By 1990, real GDP was 9 percent below its 1985 level. Data are from International Monetary Fund, *International Financial Statistics Yearbook*, 1991, p. 603.

[75] See World Bank, *World Development Report*, 1983 for documentation of rising investment rates with no increase in growth rates. Incremental capital-output ratios therefore rose sharply, implying a decline in total factor productivity growth.

[76] An important question is *why* governments had to sustain growth rates. The answer clearly lies in political economy, a subject discussed in the final section of this survey.

[77] It may be noted that, quite aside from the fact that indebtedness cannot mount indefinitely, borrowing itself had to be at an increasing rate, both to cover the rising debt-service difficulties and to finance widening fiscal deficits.

accelerated. At some point, a rising rate of inflation became sufficiently intolerable so that measures were undertaken to reduce it.

Regardless of whether foreign exchange difficulties or concerns about accelerating inflation triggered efforts to adjust, those changes almost invariably resulted in a period, sometimes prolonged, of slow growth or even declining real GNP. To the extent that these were inevitable outcomes of the earlier process, it is natural to recognize that incremental growth may be achieved by more borrowing from abroad or more deficit finance at the expense of slower growth, or even declines in income, at later dates. It is also this fact which makes analysis of reform programs so difficult, since comparison with the counterfactual is inherently difficult: one cannot assume that the status quo ante would have persisted!

It is in that sense that sustainable growth must be distinguished from the several-year change in real GNP achieved by, for example, heavy foreign borrowing. Sustainability considerations, although not entirely understood, also provide the linkage between macroeconomic and microeconomic policies, as it is largely inefficient microeconomic policies that generate pressures for increasingly large macroeconomic imbalances.

## 6. Efforts at policy reform[78]

It was noted above that, prior to the 1980s, many developing countries following policies of import substitution had encountered balance of payments difficulties and adopted "stabilization programs". Those programs were designed to restore a sustainable balance of payments position, and usually included measures to reduce inflationary pressures as well as changes in the exchange rate and in the trade and payments regime.[79]

To be sure, the East Asian NICs had earlier reversed their policies on a much more far-reaching basis and that experience had been subject to some scrutiny, but mostly on the part of those concerned with the individual countries. Likewise, some other countries were in the process of changing their development stance, most notably Chile and Turkey.

However, as it became increasingly evident that policy reform was essential

---

[78] See the chapter by Rodrik, this volume, for a discussion of research findings with respect to experiences with policy reform.

[79] For an analyses of these programs and their results, see the collections of essays in Williamson (1983) and in Cline and Weintraub (1981). For a statement of the rationale for Fund programs as of the early 1980s, see Guitian (1981).

to resume growth in the heavily indebted developing countries, a number of new policy questions requiring research arose. These centered on various aspects of the policy reform process: whether reforms had to cover all markets at once or focus on a limited number; whether reforms should be accomplished quickly or spread out over time;[80] which were the key elements of reform; and so on.[81]

As these issues came to be addressed in both the policy and the research communities, the World Bank began lending in support of "structural adjustment", by which was meant the process of altering economic policies so that sustainable growth could be achieved. By the late 1980s, Fund programs also were no longer addressed primarily to restoration of a viable balance of payments position, and the Bank and Fund were issuing joint position papers on issues for individual countries.[82]

Corbo and Fischer (this volume) address the macroeconomic aspects of policy reform programs, while Rodrik (this volume) covers a number of sectoral issues. Attention can therefore be confined here to a few key issues: 1) trade and exchange rate policy reforms; 2) reforms in agricultural pricing; 3) interconnectedness of reforms; and 4) the role of government in the development process. Section 6 then addresses the difficult issues associated with the political economy of policy reform.

*Trade and exchange rate policy reform.* Although earlier studies had covered experience with a number of IMF and other programs which centered on reforms of the trade regime and exchange rate policy,[83] questions surrounding reforms of the trade and payments regime reemerged in the 1980s. One reason for this was that the three "Southern Cone" countries, Argentina, Brazil and Chile, had all embarked upon reforms to change their trade and payments regimes in the 1970s. These programs had all aimed at currency convertibility, and had in various ways attempted to reduce the bias of the trade regime toward import substitution. In all three cases, initial reforms were far-reaching,

---

[80] These two issues have come to be known as the problem of "timing and sequencing" of policy reforms.

[81] Underlying all of these questions there were issues as to how to tailor reform programs to avoid unnecessary costs of adjustment, how much the poor are adversely affected by reform programs (and how they are affected by the counterfactual continuation of failed policies) and techniques that can be used to buffer them without undermining the necessary budgetary stringency of reform efforts. See the paper by Lipton (this volume) for further analysis.

[82] To be sure, many in both the World Bank and the IMF would insist that earlier programs were regarded as consistent with long-term growth. See the papers in Corbo, Goldstein, and Khan (1987).

[83] See especially Bhagwati (1978) and Krueger (1978) and the individual country studies which those volumes synthesized.

but subsequent events forced abandonment of the programs.[84] Important questions arose as to why these efforts had failed.

A second reason, not unrelated to the first, was that by the late 1970s and early 1980s, international capital mobility was substantially higher than it had been in earlier years. That changed the constraints and possibilities with respect to changes in the trade and payments regime. Once it was recognized that private short-term capital would respond to opportunities in developing countries, questions concerning the trade and payments regime had to be reconsidered. One important question was whether full currency convertibility, which necessarily implies freedom of capital flows, was desirable initially, at a later time, or not at all, in a policy reform program. A third reason for attention to reform programs was that the urgency of reform greatly increased during the 1980s, as did the number of countries whose experience appeared relevant for analyzing the process. All of these factors combined to bring focus once again on the issue.

Analyses of the Southern Cone experience[85] pointed to several key conclusions. First, there had been considerable water in the tariff when tariff-rate reductions were announced, so that reductions even of 100 percentage points sometimes did not affect domestic prices. Second, maintaining a realistic exchange rate was important if the effort was to succeed, and the three southern cone countries had "prefixed" their exchange rates so that when domestic inflation did not decelerate as rapidly as anticipated, speculation against the currencies mounted, while exports were discouraged. Third, and related to the first two, when the "prefixes" of the exchange rate were announced, foreigners were able to buy domestic currency to hold in assets bearing nominal interest rates well above the rate at which currency depreciation was announced under the prefix, and assured that, as long as the prefix schedule was adhered to, they could earn a high real return on their assets. Speculation against the currency and capital flight (when it became apparent that policies were unsustainable) combined to force changes in each of the reform programs.

In the wake of analyses of the Southern Cone experience and that of other

---

[84] See below for a fuller description. See Corbo and de Melo (1987) for an analysis. Essentially, all three countries adopted a "tablita" of scheduled adjustments in their nominal exchange rates. These scheduled adjustments were below the rate of inflation (in an attempt to use the exchange rate as a nominal anchor). Domestically, nominal interest rates exceeded the rate of inflation. This provided foreigners with an opportunity to buy short-term debt instruments in the three countries with a very high dollar real rate of return. The capital inflow at first permitted the real exchange rate appreciation to continue, but that in turn discouraged exports and induced larger import flows. When it became apparent that the tablita could not be sustained, huge capital outflows forced abandonment of the policy and the reform program.

[85] See Corbo and de Melo (1987) and the huge literature cited therein for further analysis.

countries, a World Bank Comparative Study focussed on trade policy reform and its consequences in 19 countries.[86] Questions under investigation included who tried to liberalize and who did not; the influence of initial circumstances on outcomes; the impact of trade liberalization on domestic variables and especially production and unemployment; the factors influencing the sustainability of liberalization; impact of trade reforms on exports and the balance of payments; and the role of the exchange rate, monetary and fiscal policies; the sequencing of liberalizations in the goods and capital markets; and patterns of tariff reductions.

Based on the experience of the countries studied, Michaely, Papageorgiou and Choksi concluded that trade liberalization should not await macroeconomic stabilization, although in situations where inflation is high or rising, appropriate macroeconomic policies have to accompany trade policy reforms; trade liberalization need not take place all at once but can be phased in over a few years; however, a strong initial move toward liberalization (including both removal of quantitative restrictions and tariff reductions) is much more promising than a very gradual start; an exchange rate adjustment needs to be carried out at the start of the trade reform process in a way that assures decision makers that the real exchange rate will be sustained; removal of import barriers provides a major benefit to exporters and no further export stimulus beyond that provided by the exchange rate and liberalization of the trade regime appears necessary; and capital market liberalization should not take place until the process of trade liberalization is well advanced.[87]

One important issue that arises with respect to reforms of all aspects of economic policy, including especially the trade and payments regime, is that of credibility. Whether people will respond to the new price signals in desirable ways depends to a considerable extent on whether they believe the new policies are permanent. In the case of a devaluation and liberalization of the trade regime, for example, producers may not respond if they believe the new relative prices are temporary, that the real exchange rate will rapidly appreciate, and that restrictions on imports will be reimposed. Indeed, they may believe it profitable to increase imports in the window of opportunity while trade is liberalized. Likewise, they will not believe it profitable to shift resources toward exportables if the shift in incentives is temporary.

Making reform programs credible is clearly important, but defining what is credible is difficult. Incredible policies include major inconsistencies, such as

---

[86] See Michaely, Papageorgiou and Choksi (1991), and the individual country works cited therein. Countries whose experience with trade liberalization was analyzed in depth prior to the synthesis volume were: Argentina, Brazil, Chile, Colombia, Greece, Indonesia, Israel, Korea, New Zealand, Pakistan, Peru, the Philippines, Portugal, Singapore, Spain, Sri Lanka, Turkey, Uruguay and Yugoslavia.

[87] Michaely et al., pp. 270–284.

when there is a fixed nominal exchange rate and a large fiscal deficit. Achieving credibility may entail different policies in different situations, however, depending on such variables as whether there is a past history of failed reform efforts, the political strength and determination of policy makers, and so on. Clearly, further research is needed to increase understanding of credibility, making the concept operational in measurable ways.

*Reform of agricultural pricing policies.* As seen above, it became evident as early as the late 1950s that agricultural production would have to increase if development efforts were to be successful. This necessity arose in part because it was not possible to contemplate successful development where a majority of the population remained in agricultural activities with no productivity growth; in part because populations were growing and it was evident that not even the most successful of development programs could result in enough additional productive jobs outside agriculture to absorb the population; and in part because increased urban populations would result in rising demand for agricultural commodities, and it was unthinkable that these demands, as well as demands for manufactured goods, could be met out of imports.

Already in the 1960s and 1970s, a great deal had been learned about agricultural research and extension, development of appropriate infrastructure, and a variety of other aspects of policy toward agriculture. Indeed, even the strong tendency to suppress prices paid to agricultural producers had been subject to scrutiny after the many demonstrations of producer responsiveness to incentives.[88] While it was recognized that "getting the prices right" was not the only policy measure conducive to increasing agricultural productivity and output, it seemed clear that when producer prices were sufficiently suppressed, provision of infrastructure and other measures could not counteract the adverse effects of low prices on incentives, and hence production.

By the mid-1980s, other questions arose. Reports from many countries suggested that where agricultural producer prices were suppressed, agricultural research and extension services, and provision of agricultural infrastructure were weak. A World Bank comparative study was launched, analyzing the political economy of agricultural pricing policies. In the course of that project, experience with those policies in 18 countries was analyzed.[89] Focus was on the economic and political origins and evolutions of policies and their effects, as well as on efforts at policy reform. The relationship between lower producer

---

[88] See Ruttan (1989) and Timmer (1988) for good analyses.

[89] Countries covered were: Argentina, Brazil, Chile, Colombia, Côte d'Ivoire, Dominican Republic, Egypt, Ghana, Republic of Korea, Malaysia, Morocco, Pakistan, Philippines, Portugal, Sri Lanka, Thailand, Turkey and Zambia. See Schiff and Valdes (1992) and Krueger (1992b) for syntheses of the results. Three other volumes [Krueger, Schiff and Valdes (1991a, 1991b) and (1991c)] contain results of the individual country studies.

prices and poorer provision of other agricultural services was confirmed. It was also noted that most developing countries tended to discriminate more strongly against export agriculture than against domestic food crops, and even to provide some protection to import-competing agricultural production which partially, and in a few cases, entirely offset the negative effects of overvalued exchange rates and high prices for goods produced by farmers.[90]

It was these studies that demonstrated that "indirect" discrimination, discussed above, against agriculture through the exchange rate and through protection accorded to industrialized goods was at least as important in affecting farmers' real incomes as was direct price discrimination. They went further, however, and examined circumstances under which policy reform did or did not occur and the reasons for it.

Interestingly, almost all efforts to reform agricultural pricing in the countries covered in the research project were associated with changes in government. Typically, agricultural pricing policy reforms were part of a broader package of policy changes, including the exchange rate, the trade regime, and other issues. Agricultural interests had, to a considerable degree, exercised whatever influence they had to try to secure more favorable direct policies, such as increased input subsidies or higher farm prices for outputs.[91] However, when there were significant reforms that materially reduced discrimination against agriculture, reform was usually a part of an overall change in economic policy.

A significant and important result was that the impetus for reform was usually associated with pressures to reduce drains on the government budget. Typically, agricultural pricing policies had started with the dual and inconsistent objectives of keeping food prices low for urban residents while simultaneously encouraging agricultural production. When input subsidies and other piecemeal measures failed, and especially in the context of inflation, pressures intensified to increase the prices paid to farmers. But increasing those prices had budgetary costs. Often, governments had increased prices (but by less than the amount that would have reflected world prices) to farmers to a degree, but encountered resistance in raising urban food prices, with the predictable consequences for the fiscal deficit. When reducing the fiscal deficit was a prerequisite for IMF and World Bank support for policy reform, discrimination against agriculture decreased because of exchange rate changes, because of reduced protection to domestic import-competing goods, and because farmgate prices of agricultural commodities were directly increased. Concurrently, food prices to consumers were often raised.

---

[90] See Schiff and Valdes (1992) for a summary of these findings.

[91] Whether agricultural interests were silent on overall exchange rate, trade regime, and macropolicy issues because they were unaware of their interests or because they felt incapable of influencing outcomes remains an open question. [See Krueger (1992b), Chapter 7, for a discussion].

These reforms were often accompanied by removal of monopoly power for agricultural marketing boards and other institutional changes designed to bring about the desired structural adjustment and resumption of growth. Input subsidies were also greatly reduced, if not eliminated.

Thus, in the case of agricultural pricing policies, the measures that must be undertaken are fairly well understood. The difficulties that are encountered are twofold: 1) much of the discrimination against agriculture is embedded in policies outside the purview of the Agriculture Ministry and can be changed only when the overall policy regime is changed; and 2) political resistance to making the changes can be very great, especially when prices of staple foods to urban consumers have been kept at artificially low levels for long periods.

*Fiscal and monetary restraint.* Corbo and Fischer (this volume) discuss structural adjustment in considerable depth. Here, focus is once again on the linkages between the necessity for fiscal and monetary restraint and other policy reform measures.

The reasons why fiscal deficits need to be reduced as part of policy reform programs are evident. What is not so evident is that these deficits emerge, more often than not, not because a particular government has sharply increased spending or experienced reduced revenues, although those events can influence the timing of crises, but because policy inefficiencies often require increases in expenditures over time (or reductions in revenue) to prevent deterioration in performance.

To a degree, this phenomenon is the result of the push for economic growth: as the productivity of public sector investment falls, the level of investment must increase in order to maintain a given growth rate. It was already seen that urban consumers resist increases in subsidized food prices. Over time even with moderate inflation, therefore, the cost to the government (or the reduced production of the commodities whose producer prices remain low) rises. There is equal resistance to increased prices of energy, to changing the nominal exchange rate, and to other policy measures that would be required simply to keep matters from getting worse.[92]

Thus, at the time fiscal deficits must be reduced, changes in policies across a whole variety of sectors are called for, all of which are difficult politically. Yet a sustained reduction in the fiscal deficit is not possible unless policy measures are taken which address the underlying issues. Indeed, one sure means for insuring that policy reform will not achieve its stated objectives is for government expenditure cuts to consist largely of once-only measures, such as postponement of civil servants' pay, deferring maintenance expenditures, and

---

[92] Resistance to elimination of subsidies and other government expenditures is not confined to developing countries, of course.

cutting back expenditures across the board on all public sector investment projects. It is arguable that it is this politically painful aspect of government expenditure reduction, rather than the short term costs of "austerity" programs, which are the real reason why they are so unpopular.

This set of considerations leads directly to issues of political economy of policy reform. Before addressing them, however, the crucial questions surrounding the role of government in development must be addressed.

*What is the proper role of government in development?* As already indicated, the experience of the East Asian NICs convinced virtually all observers that an outer-oriented trade strategy had been an important contributing factor to rapid economic growth. Certainly, high savings and investment rates and a variety of other factors had also contributed, but the rapid growth of exports was held to be key. Reaching consensus on that issue, however, did not resolve a major policy question which arose as that experience was considered. Some observers tended to attribute the success to government policies which relied on markets. Others, however, pointed to what they believed was a more pro-active role taken by governments, and especially Korea, in promoting exports.[93]

The issues are several, and can only be briefly addressed here. It is to be expected that additional research and experience over the next decade will increase understanding of these issues considerably.

Here, questions are discussed in order of increasing contentiousness. First, there is the question of what things governments must do because the private sector cannot. Second, there is the question of the additional activities the government *should* do that may enhance development efforts. Third, there is the question of whether, having done those things, there is a potentially positive role for governments in "picking winners".

Turning first to those activities that only the government can undertake, the list is virtually universally agreed to but its importance, and the resources required for undertaking them, often underestimated. Clearly, law, order, and provision of a predictable and reasonable commercial code with clearly defined property rights are essential for well-functioning economic activities, and are a function the state must fulfill. In addition, provision of a stable macroeconomic framework, and insuring that incentives to private producers appropriately reflect tradeoffs (especially those available internationally) are key government functions, and require little discussion.

The second group of items is hardly more in dispute. Provision of public

---

[93] See, for example, Findlay's (1981) discussion of the issue.

health services and education are deemed to be important.[94] Likewise, physical infrastructure – roads, ports, railways, and communications – must function adequately if incentives are to spur the desired responses. In this regard, the interesting questions center more on why governments which have been so active with regard to the third set of activities, discussed below, have failed so dramatically to provide infrastructure services.[95] One of the hallmarks of government policy in all the East Asian NICs has been the provision of economically efficient infrastructure, and the high quality of the labor force. All available evidence points to the efficiency of the East Asian governments in increasing both the quality of the human capital stock and value of services of publicly-provided infrastructure goods.

Where controversy enters really surrounds the third set of issues: to what extent in East Asia was export performance, and presumably industrial composition more generally, a consequence of a market response to price signals, and to what extent was it the result of the intervention of very competent civil servants? Even on this issue, there is some agreement. Certainly the degree to which governments have engaged in industry-specific interventions has fallen over time, and reliance on market signals has greatly increased. There is little question that the long-run trend has been toward liberalization of financial, trade, credit, and other markets.

The question that seems to arouse most disagreement centers on the role of government officials in "picking the winners" in the first two decades of rapid development. Analyses ranged all the way from viewing the East Asian experience as the outcome of the unleashing of market forces to those who believed that government officials had guided selection of industries and exports.

Little (1981, p. 43) was among the first to argue cogently for the role of markets:

"The major lesson is that labor-intensive export-oriented policies, which amounted to almost free trade conditions for exporters, were the prime cause of an extremely rapid and labor-intensive industrialization which revolutionized in a decade the lives of more than fifty million people, including the poorest among them... Nothing else can account for it... Planning, in my opinion,

---

[94] Most observers would agree that, despite unreliability and unavailability of data, one of the major successes of development efforts since 1945 have been the dramatic rise in life expectancies and other indicators of health and the increase in literacy and other indicators of educational attainment. [See Birdsall (1989) for a discussion]. Even in government programs that should provide increased human capital and social services for the poor, there is considerable evidence that governments have in fact allocated resources inefficiently. [See Birdsall and James (1992) and Psacharopoulos (1985) for some arguments].

[95] See the discussion in Krueger (1992a).

has not played a key role. . . Luck has played little part in their development. Aid was. . . not important during the high growth period. . . I think it can be concluded that everything can be attributed to good policies and the people".

Others have acknowledged that industry-specific intervention did occur, but argued that the uniformity of the exchange rate, combined with the discipline that the international market provided to bureaucrats in the context of an export-oriented economy, severely constrained the scope of bureaucratic intervention and provided strong signals when policy mistakes had been made.[96] The evidence that incentives were considerably more uniform in Korea than in most import-substitution countries is not seriously challenged.

However, some believe that there was an even more activist role of government, including the choice of industries for development.[97] That government officials at least on occasion tried to determine the next set of industries to be developed is not questioned.[98] The question is how important this intervention was relative to the market and relative to other activities of the government.[99] Recently, Lee (1992) attempted to address this question by examining the relationship between the height of government intervention and the rate of productivity growth in various Korean manufacturing industries. He found that industries that had received less government support (in the form of tariff protection, tax credits, rationed credit, and other industry-specific incentives) had experienced more rapid growth of total factor productivity than had those receiving more support. He concluded that Korean success was in spite of, rather than because of, governmental sector-specific interventions, and that growth would have been even faster in their absence.

The issue as to how much intervention there was by government in industry-specific resource allocation, and the effects it had on the economic performance of the East Asian countries, will probably continue to be debated. What seems clear is that the East Asian governments provided excellent infrastructure and a reasonable incentive framework, including a reasonably uniform real effective exchange rate for exporting. When activities were unprofitable, there was quick feedback, and policy makers were willing to revise those decisions that turned out to have been mistaken. How much scope

---

[96] See Krueger (1990a) for an exposition of the argument.

[97] See especially Amsden (1987) and Wade (1990).

[98] See Park (1990) and Yoo (1990) for evidence in support of this.

[99] A great deal of controversy surrounds the episode during the 1970s when it was decided to push the "heavy and chemical industries" (HCI). There is no doubt that government officials increased incentives and virtually directed the start of these industries; there is also no doubt that there were a large number of deleterious effects on the entire economy. By the early 1980s, the effort was abandoned. Those believing that the Korean economy was market driven cite the HCI case as an instance in which market signals were sufficiently strong to reverse a policy. Those believing that the government intervened in direct resource allocation decisions also cite that case. See Yoo (1990) for an analysis.

there is for activist intervention within such a framework, and conditions under which any such intervention is likely to move the economy in the appropriate direction, are not yet completely understood.

## 7. Political economy of policy formulation and evolution

Once it became evident that inappropriate policies had been in large part responsible for many of the difficulties encountered by the inner-oriented developing countries, efforts at policy reform multiplied. In many cases, these efforts encountered serious resistance. Sometimes, political resistance within governments prevented the adoption of reform programs even in circumstances when most observers and participants believed that a crisis situation demanded action. In other cases, reforms were started but political resistance and opposition led to their reversal.

These events led to two interrelated lines of inquiry. One was analysis of the political economy of policy reform. The other was the extent to which it is appropriate to regard political reactions and pressures as exogenous, and the extent to which political-economic interactions render economic policies partially endogenous. Both of these lines of inquiry are little more than in their infancy, but nonetheless warrant mention here.

Focus on the political economy of reform efforts has led to investigations of the circumstances in which policy reform is undertaken, the factors that appear to result in a higher probability of sustained reform, and ways in which reforms can be undertaken that reduce the likelihood of strengthening the opposition.[100] Given the immense complexity of politics and the variety of circumstances in which policy reform is undertaken and carried out, it is hardly surprising that hard and fast conclusions are difficult to reach.

Much of the analysis is appropriately focussed on identifying potential gainers and losers from policy changes, and analyzing their roles in formulating, implementing, and supporting policy reform programs. For example, when the party in power in the government has as part of its coalition influential representatives of agriculture, the likelihood that reforms of agricultural pricing policies will be undertaken rises sharply.[101] It is to be expected that, as research proceeds, analysts will be able to analyze the role of the gainers and losers in supporting reform efforts, and perhaps to find ways in which potential gainers from reform can increase their voice in the political process.

Despite the importance of the gainer/loser analysis, however, there are

---

[100] See Nelson (1990), Meier (1991) and Bates and Krueger (1993) for analyses of this first type.

[101] See Hansen's (1992) analysis of the contrast between policies in Egypt and Turkey for one such analysis. [See also Bates (1982)].

other important insights.[102] First, many of the policies that eventually became so inimical to growth appear to have been adopted for idealistic motives, and not for the narrow self-interest of the groups in the ruling coalition. Second, the adoption of virtually any economic policies is likely to result in the development of vested interest supporting those policies. In the case of failed policies undertaken for idealistic motives, for example, by the time that the limitations of these policies became evident, those benefitting from the policies had been able to organize to protect their interests. As such, policy reversal was not simply a matter of the ruling group reversing its position: new interest groups had sprung up (including the bureaucrats administering the policies) to defend the new status quo. Third, and important for economists, very often a crisis situation breaks down the power of the various interest groups that can normally block policy changes; as such, a crisis may create the political conditions necessary to permit policy reform. In part, this may be because the costs of earlier policies are more apparent; in part, however, the usual political interest groups have less influence. Fourth and finally, it is certainly wrong to analyze all governmental behavior as if a benevolent social guardian were maximizing social welfare. Lal and Myint (forthcoming) have attempted a five-way classification of governmental behavior (whether authoritarian or democratic; if authoritarian, whether behaving as a predator and maximizing the rents to be extracted from the populace or as a benevolent social guardian; if democratic whether a factional weak state or whether representing a dominant interest, and so on). In their analysis, the nature of the state interacts with the country's factor endowments in determining behavior, and the outcome of reform efforts.

These sorts of findings lead directly to the second line of inquiry: the endogeneity of economic and political factors. Once a political decision is made to undertake a particular economic policy or set of policies, market forces are set in motion which can thwart the policy or make it operate in ways which were not initially intended. The effects of the policy can also influence the alignment of political forces supporting and opposing the policy. Those interactions can then lead to changes in the initial policy, further market reactions, and so on.

For example, in the case of agricultural marketing boards, an initial decision to keep producer prices somewhat low in order to obtain revenue for the government often meant that smuggling increased; it often also meant that there were major difficulties in collection, storage, and payment to farmers for their crops. Political reactions and efforts to correct these problems resulted in

---

[102] See Krueger (1993a) and Chapters 1 and 10 of Bates and Krueger (1993) for an extended discussion of these issues.

increased costs of administration, with tension between the policy choices of a further lowering of producer prices or reduced budgetary revenues. Meanwhile, increased employment in marketing boards created a constituency for them, despite evidence of inefficiencies.[103]

As prices paid to producers fall relative to border prices, smuggling increases. That then leads to bureaucratic efforts to "crack down" on the evaders, with attendant increases in regulations and the costs of enforcement and evasion. Often, the end result is further modification of the system, as political and bureaucratic objections to smuggling and other forms of evasion prompt yet another round of changes.

The analysis can be applied to the entire process by which developing countries initially adopted their development strategies of state-led import substitution and the evolution of economic policy and the political process thereafter. In most developing countries policies of import substitution and government direction of the economy were initiated by idealistic nationalists behaving as benevolent social guardians. These policy makers appear genuinely to have had the well being of their fellow citizens in mind, and to have regarded the attainment of rapid economic development as being virtually synonymous with maximizing a social welfare function.[104]

Once these policies were in place, however, beneficiaries of those policies became political forces lobbying for their continuation. The number of civil servants increased rapidly, and they became a potent political force for further controls. Industrialists who had established import-substitution enterprises, and the workers employed in them (and benefitting from laws regulating wages and working conditions) became advocates of restrictive trade policies.

Moreover, economic reactions to policies led to further policy measures. For example, efforts to thwart restrictive trade regimes by smuggling and under- and overinvoicing of exports and imports led the authorities to adopt additional measures to attempt to prevent these efforts. Additional policies resulted in additional or larger constituencies and hence led to further political support for a continuation of the interventionist regimes.

However, market responses to the incentives created by the regime resulted in the foreign exchange crises discussed above. Those crises eroded the political power of some groups, and thus changed the political equilibrium. When reform measures were undertaken, they, too, changed the political

---

[103] In circumstances such as these, another line of research analyzes alternative institutional arrangements that may reduce the economic costs of alternative arrangements. In the case of marketing boards, permission for private traders to compete may spur a change in behavior. So, too, may imposition of restrictions on the abilities of these agencies, and other parastatals, to borrow from the central government.

[104] See Krueger (1993) for a fuller discussion.

constellation of forces. In some circumstances, new groups (including especially exporters) sprang up or were sufficiently strengthened that incentives for production of tradeable goods over time became more uniform.

Thus, not only did political pressures influence the formation of economic policies, but market reactions to policies resulted in further policy change, and economic policies changed political constellations. While analysis of the political economy of policy determination is still in its infancy, lessons already learned are sufficient to indicate that one cannot regard the political factors determining the choice of economic policies as entirely exogenous, nor can all economic policies be treated as stable steady states; interactions between political and economic markets are an important part of the process of policy formulation and execution.

## References

Amsden, A. (1987) *Growth and stabilization in Korea*, 1962–1984. Helsinki: World Institute for Development Economics Research.

Arndt, H. (1978) *The rise and fall of economic growth. A study in contemporary thought.* Melbourne: Longman Cheshire.

Balassa, B. (1978) 'Exports and economic growth: Further evidence', *Journal of Development Economics*, 2:181–189.

Balassa, B. (1971) *The structure of protection in developing countries*. Baltimore: Johns Hopkins University Press.

Baldwin, R.E. (1975) *Foreign trade regimes and economic development. The Philippines*. New York: Columbia University Press for the National Bureau of Economic Research.

Bardhan, P. (1984) *The political economy of development in India*. Oxford: Basil Blackwell.

Bates, R.H. (1982) *Essays on the political economy of rural Africa*. Berkeley: University of California Press.

Bates, R.H. (1981) *States and markets in tropical Africa: The political basis of agricultural policy*. Berkeley: University of California Press.

Bates, R.H. and Krueger, A.O., eds. (1993) *Political economy of policy reform programs: Experience in eight countries*. Oxford: Basil Blackwell.

Becker, G. (1964) *Human capital*. New York: Columbia University Press.

Behrman, J.R. and Birdsall, N. (1983) 'The quality of schooling: Quantity alone is misleading', *American Economic Review*, 73, pp. 928–946.

Behrman, J.R. and Schneider, R. (1993) 'An international perspective on schooling investments in the last quarter century in some fast-growing east and southeast Asian countries', University of Pennsylvania, mimeo.

Bhagwati, J.N. and Desai, P. (1970). *Planning for industrialization. India*. Oxford: Oxford University Press for the OECD.

Bhagwati, J.N. and Srinivasan, T.N. (1975) *Foreign trade regimes and economic development. India*. New York: Columbia University Press.

Bhagwati, J.N. (1978). *Foreign trade regimes and economic development: Anatomy and consequences of exchange control regimes*. Lexington, MA: Ballinger Press for the National Bureau of Economic Research.

Binswanger, H. (1990) 'The policy response of agriculture', *Proceedings of the World Bank Annual Conference on Development Economics 1989*, (Supplement to the *World Bank Economic Review* and the *World Bank Research Observer*, 231–258.

Birdsall, N. (1989). 'Thoughts on good health and good government', *Daedalus*, 118:89–124.

Birdsall, N. and James, E. (1992) 'Efficiency and equity in social spending: How and why governments misbehave', Fifth Annual Interamerican Seminar on Economics, May 8 and 9, 1992, Buenos Aires.

Brandao, S. and Carvalho, J. (1991) 'Brazil', in: A.O. Krueger, M. Schiff and A. Valdes, eds., *The political economy of agricultural pricing policy. Vol. 1 Latin America*. Baltimore: Johns Hopkins University Press.

Carvalho, J.L. and Haddad, C.L.S. (1981) 'Foreign trade strategies and employment in Brazil', in: A.O. Krueger, H.B. Lary and N. Akrasanee, eds., *Trade and employment in developing countries. 1. Individual studies*. Chicago: University of Chicago Press for the National Bureau of Economic Research.

Chenery, H., Ahluwalia, M.S., Bell, C.L.G., Duloy, J.H. and Jolly, R. (1974). *Redistribution with growth: Policies to improve income distribution in developing countries in the context of economic growth*. Oxford: Oxford University Press.

Chenery, H.B. and Bruno, M. (1962) 'Development alternatives in an open economy', *Economic Journal*, 72:79–103.

Chenery, H.B. and Clark, P. (1959) *Interindustry economics*. New York: John Wiley.

Chenery, H.B. and Strout, A.M. (1966) 'Foreign assistance and economic development', *American Economic Review*, 56:679–733.

Clark, C. (1940) *The conditions of economic progress*. London: Macmillan.

Cline, W.R. (1983). *International debt and the stability of the world economy*. Washington, DC: Institute for International Economics.

Cline, W.R. and Weintraub, S. (1981). *Economic stabilization in developing countries*. Washington, DC: The Brookings Institution.

Corbo, V. (1992) *Development strategies and policies in Latin America*, International Center for Economic Growth, Occasional Papers No. 22. San Francisco: ICS Press.

Corbo, V. and de Melo, J. (1987) 'Lessons from the Southern Cone policy reforms', *World Bank Research Observer*, 2:111–142.

Corbo, V. and Fischer, S., this volume.

Corbo, V., Goldstein, M. and Khan, M., eds. (1987). *Growth-oriented adjustment programs*. Washington, DC: International Monetary Fund and World Bank.

Deaton, A. This volume.

Diaz Alejandro, C.F. (1963) 'A note on the impact of devaluation and the redistributive effect', *Journal of Political Economy*, 71:577–580.

Diaz Alejandro, C.F. (1965) 'On the import intensity of import substitution', *Kyklos*, 18:495–509.

Diaz Alejandro, C.F. (1981) 'Southern Cone stabilization plans', in: W.R. Cline and S. Weintraub, eds., *Economic stabilization in developing countries*. Washington, DC: The Brookings Institution.

*Economic report of the President*. (1983). Washington, DC: U.S. Government Printing Office.

Fernando, N. (1987) 'The political economy of Mahaweli', mimeo. World Bank.

Fei, J.C.H. and Ranis, G. (1964). *Development of the labor surplus economy: Theory and policy*. Homewood, Illinois: Richard D. Irwin, Inc.

Findlay, R. (1981) 'Comment', in: W. Hong and L.B. Krause, eds., *Trade and growth of the advanced developing countries in the Pacific basin*. Seoul: Korea Development Institute.

Findlay, R. and Wellisz, S. (forthcoming) *The political economy of poverty, equity and growth: Five small open economies*, A World Bank Comparative Study. Oxford: Oxford University Press.

Flanders, J. (1964) 'Prebisch on protectionism: An evaluation', *Economic Journal*, 64:305–326.

Frank, Jr., C.R. Kim, K.S. and Westphal, L.E. (1975) *Foreign trade regimes and economic development. South Korea*. New York: Columbia University Press for the National Bureau of Economic Research.

Frenkel, J.A., Dooley, M.P. and Wickham, P., eds. (1989) *Analytical issues in debt*. Washington, DC: International Monetary Fund.

Government of India, Planning Commission. (1962) *Third Five Year Plan, 1961–1966*, New Delhi.

Government of India, Planning Commission. (1957) *Second Five Year Plan, 1956–1961*, New Delhi.

Government of India, Ministry of Food and Agriculture and Ministry of Community Development and Cooperation. (1959) *Report on India's food crisis and steps to meet it*. New York: Ford Foundation.

Guitian, M. (1981) 'Fund conditionality: Evolution of principles and practice', Occasional Paper No. 38. Washington, DC: IMF.

Hansen, B. (1992) *The political economy of poverty, equity and growth. Egypt and Turkey.* Oxford: Oxford University Press.

Harberger, A.C. (1959) 'Using the resources at hand more effectively', *American Economic Review, Proceedings*, 49:134–146.

Harberger, A.C. (1965) 'Investment in men versus investment in machines: The case of India', in: C.A. Anderson and M.J. Bowman, eds., *Education and economic development*. Chicago: Aldine Publishing Co.

Hicks, G. (1989) 'The four little dragons: An enthusiast's reading guide', *Asian-Pacific Economic Literature*, 3:35–49.

Hong, W. (1981) 'Trade and employment in Korea', in A.O. Krueger, H.B. Lary and N. Akrasanee, eds., *Trade and employment in developing countries*, Vol. 1. Chicago: University of Chicago Press.

Husain, I. and Diwan, I. (1989) *Dealing with the debt crisis*. Washington, DC: The World Bank.

Jansen, D. (1988) *Trade, exchange rate, and agricultural pricing policies in Zambia*, World Bank Comparative Studies. Washington, DC: The World Bank.

Jorgenson, D.W. (1962) 'The development of a dual economy', *Economic Journal*, 71:309–331.

Keesing, D. (1967) 'Outward-looking trade policies and economic development', *Economic Journal*, 88:303–320.

Kim, K.S. (1991). 'Korea', in: D. Papageorgiou, M. Michaely and A.M. Choksi, eds., *Liberalizing foreign trade. Vol. 2: Korea, the Philippines, and Singapore*. Oxford: Basil Blackwell.

Krueger, A.O. (1966) 'Some economic costs of exchange control: The Turkish case', *Journal of Political Economy*, 74:466–480.

Krueger, A.O. (1974) *Foreign trade regimes and economic development. Turkey*. New York: Columbia University Press for the National Bureau of Economic Research.

Krueger, A.O. (1978) *Foreign trade regimes and economic development: liberalization attempts and consequences*. Lexington, MA: Ballinger Press for the National Bureau of Economic Research.

Krueger, A.O. (1983) *Trade and employment in developing countries. Vol. 3: Synthesis and conclusions*. Chicago: University of Chicago Press for the National Bureau of Economic Research.

Krueger, A.O. (1987) 'The importance of economic policies: Contrasts between Korea and Turkey', in: H. Kierzkowski, ed., *Protection and competition in international trade*. Oxford: Basil Blackwell.

Krueger, A.O. (1990a) 'Asian trade and growth lessons', *American Economic Review Papers and Proceedings*, May, pp. 108–112.

Krueger, A.O. (1990b) 'Economists' changing perceptions of government', *Weltwirtschaftliches Archiv*, 126:417–431.

Krueger, A.O. (1991) 'Ideas underlying development policy', Paper prepared for Institute for Policy Reform, Washington.

Krueger, A.O. (1992a) *Economic policy reform in developing countries*. Oxford: Basil Blackwell.

Krueger, A.O. (1992b) *The political economy of agricultural pricing policies: Volume 5. Synthesis of the political economy in developing countries*. Baltimore: Johns Hopkins Press.

Krueger, A.O. (1993a) *The political economy of policy reform in developing countries*. Cambridge, MA: MIT Press.

Krueger, A.O. (1993b) *Policy at cross purposes: U.S. international economic policies toward developing countries*. Washington, DC: The Brookings Institution.

Krueger, A.O. and Aktan, O.H. (1993) *Swimming against the tide: Turkish trade reforms in the 1980s*. San Francisco: ICS Press.

Krueger, A.O., Ruttan, V. and Michalopoulos, C. (1989) *Aid and development*, Johns Hopkins Press, Baltimore.

Krueger, A.O., Schiff, M. and Valdés, A. (1988) 'Agricultural incentives in developing countries: Measuring the effect of sectoral and economywide policies', *World Bank Economic Review*, 2:255–271.

Krueger, A.O., Schiff, M. and Valdes, A, eds. (1991a) *The political economy of agricultural pricing policy. Volume 1. Latin America*, A World Bank Comparative Study. Baltimore: Johns Hopkins Press.

Krueger, A.O., Schiff, M. and Valdes, A., eds. (1991b) *The political economy of agricultural pricing policy. Volume 2. Asia*. A World Bank Comparative Study. Baltimore: Johns Hopkins Press.

Krueger, A.O., Schiff, M. and Valdes, A., eds. (1991c) *The political economy of agricultural pricing policy. Volume 3. Africa and the Mediterranean*. A World Bank Comparative Study. Baltimore: Johns Hopkins University Press.

Krueger, A.O. and Tuncer, B. (1982) 'Growth of factor productivity in Turkish manufacturing industries', *Journal of Development Economics*, 11:307–325.

Kuo, S. (1983) *The TaiwaN economy in transition*. Boulder, CO: Westview Press.

Lal, D. and Myint, H. (forthcoming) *The political economy of poverty, equity and growth: A comparative study*. Oxford: Oxford University Press.

Lange, O. and Taylor, F.M. (1938) *On the economic theory of socialism*, B.E. Lippincott, ed. Minneapolis: University of Minnesota Press.

Lewis, W.A. (1954) 'Economic development with unlimited supplies of labour', *Manchester School of Economic and Social Studies*, 22:139–191.

Lee, J.-H. (1992) 'Government interventions and productivity growth in Korean manufacturing industries', Paper presented at NBER Conference on Economic Growth, Cambridge, MA, October.

Lim, C.-Y. and Lloyd, P.J., eds. (1986) *Singapore resources and growth*. Oxford: Oxford University Press.

Little, I.M.D. (1981) 'The experience and causes of rapid labour-intensive development in Korea, Taiwan Province, Hong Kong and Singapore and the possibilities of emulation', in: E. Lee, ed., *Export-led industrialization and development*. Geneva: International Labour Organization.

Little, I.M.D. and Mirrlees, J.A. (1968) *Social cost-benefit analysis*. Paris: Organization for Economic Cooperation and Development.

Little, I.M.D., Scitovsky, T. and Scott, M. (1970) *Industry and trade in some developing countries*. Oxford: Oxford University Press.

Mandelbaum, K. 1945. *Industrialization of backward areas*, Oxford University Institute of Statistics Monograph No. 2. Oxford: Basil Blackwell.

Mason, E.S., Je, K.M., Perkins, D., Suk, K.K. and Cole, D. (1980) *The economic and social modernization of Korea*. Cambridge, MA: Harvard University Press.

Meier, G.M., ed. (1991) *Politics and policy making in developing countries*. San Francisco: International Center for Economic Growth.

Michaely, M. (1977) 'Exports and growth: An empirical investigation', *Journal of Development Economics*, 4:49–53.

Michaely, M., Papageorgiou, D. and Choksi, A.M. (1991) *Lessons of experience in the developing world*, Volume 7 of D. Papageorgiou, M. Michaely and A.M. Choksi, eds., *Liberalizing foreign trade*. Oxford: Basil Blackwell.

Morawetz, D. (1978) *Twenty five years of economic development, 1950–1975*, Baltimore: Johns Hopkins University Press.

Nehru, J. (1941) *Toward freedom. The autobiography of Jawaharlal Nehru*. Boston: Beacon Press.

Nelson, J.M., ed. (1990) *Economic crisis and policy choice. The politics of adjustment in the Third World*. Princeton: Princeton University Press.

Nishimizu, M. and Robinson, S. (1984) 'Trade policies and productivity change in semi-industrialized countries', *Journal of Development Economics*, 16:177–206.

Nurkse, R. (1958) *Problems of capital formation in underdeveloped countries*. Oxford: Basil Blackwell.

Park, Y.C. (1990) 'Development lessons from Asia: The role of government in South Korea and Taiwan', *American Economic Review Papers and Proceedings*, May, pp. 118–121.

Prebisch, R. (1950) 'The economic development of Latin America and its principal problems', New York: The United Nations.

Prebisch, R. (1964) 'Towards a new trade policy for development', UNCTAD Conference E/Conf.AG13, United Nations.

Psacharopoulos, G. (1988) 'Education and development: A review', *World Bank Research Observer*, 3:99–116.

Republic of Turkey, *Second five year plan, 1968–1973*, Ankara.

Rao, V.R.V.K., 1952. 'Investment, income and the multiplier in an underdeveloped economy', *The Indian Economic Review*, February.

Rodrik, D. This volume.

Rosenstein-Rodan, P.N. (1943) 'Problems of industrialization of Eastern and South-Eastern Europe', *Economic Journal*, 53:202–211.

Ruttan, V.W. (1989) 'Improving the quality of life in rural areas', in: A.O. Krueger, C. Michalopoulos and V.W. Ruttan, *Aid and development*. Baltimore: Johns Hopkins University Press.

Sachs, J.D. (1984) 'Theoretical issues in international borrowing', Princeton Studies in International Finance No. 54, Princeton, July.

Sachs, J.D. (1985) 'External debt and macroeconomic performance in Latin America and East Asia', *Brookings Papers on Economic Activity*, 2:523–573.

Sachs, J.D. (1989a) 'The debt overhang of developing countries', in: G. Calvo, R. Findlay, P. Kouri and J. Braga de Macedo, eds., *Debt, stabilization and development: Essays in memory of Carlos Dias-Alejandro*. Oxford: Basil Blackwell.

Sachs, J.D., ed. (1989b) *Developing country debt and economic performance*, 3 Volumes. Chicago: University of Chicago Press for the National Bureau of Economic Research.

Sachs, J. (1986) 'Managing the LDC debt crisis', *Brookings Papers on Economic Activity*, 2:397–432.

Schiff, M. and Valdes, A. (1992) *The political economy of agricultural pricing policies: Economic consequences*. Baltimore: Johns Hopkins Press.

Schultz, T.W. (1961) 'Investment in human capital', *American Economic Review*, 51:1–17.

Schultz, T.W. (1964) *Transforming traditional agriculture*. New Haven: Yale University Press.

Srinivasan, T.N. (forthcoming) 'Development economics, then and now', in: *Trade, aid and development. Essays in honour of Hans Linneman*. Macmillan Press.

Summers, R. and Heston, A. (1991) 'The Penn world table (Mark 5): An expanded set of international comparisons, 1950–1988', *Quarterly Journal of Economics*, 106:327–368.

Symposium on new institutions for developing country debt. (1990) *Journal of Economic Perspectives*, 4.

Tang, A.M. and Worley, J.S., eds. (1988) 'Why does overcrowded, resource-poor East Asia succeed – Lessons for the LDCs?', *Economic development and Cultural Change*, 36: April supplement.

Timmer, C.P. (1988) 'The agricultural transformation', in: H.B. Chenery and T. N. Srinivasan, eds., *Handbook of Development Economics*, Vol. 1. Amsterdam: North‑Holland.

Tinbergen, J. (1984) 'Development cooperation as a learning process', in: G.M. Meier and D. Seers, eds., *Pioneers in Development*. Oxford: Oxford University Press.

Tun Wai, U. (1959) 'The relation between inflation and economic development: A statistical inductive study', *International Monetary Fund Staff Papers*, Vol. 7, October, pp. 302–3l7.

Wade, R. (1990) *Governing the market: Economic theory and the role of government in East Asian industrialization*. Princeton: Princeton University Press.

Williamson, J., ed. (1983) *IMF conditionality*. Washington, DC: Institute for International Economics.

World Bank (1992) *World development report, 1992: Development and the environment*. Oxford: Oxford University Press.

World Bank (1993) *World development report, 1993*. Oxford: Oxford University Press.

Yoo, J.-H. (1990) 'The industrial policy of the 1970s and the evolution of the manufacturing sector in Korea', KDI Working Paper No. 9017, October.

*Chapter 41*

# POVERTY AND POLICY

MICHAEL LIPTON

*University of Sussex*

MARTIN RAVALLION*

*The World Bank*

## Contents

* For their comments we are grateful to Harold Alderman, Jere Behrman, Tim Besley, Hans Binswanger, Gaurav Datt, Shanta Devarajan, Jean Drèze, Aly Ercelawn, Paul Glewwe, Bruce Herrick, Glenn Jones, Peter Lanjouw, Lant Pritchett, Elizabeth Savage, Lyn Squire, T.N. Srinivasan, Paul Streeten, Dominique van de Walle, Donald Winch and participants at the First Asian Development Bank Conference on Development Economics, Manila. We also thank Rupert Baber and Kirsty McNay for research assistance. Responsibility remains ours alone.

*Handbook of Development Economics, Volume III, Edited by J. Behrman and T.N. Srinivasan*
© *Elsevier Science B.V., 1995*

**Contents** (continued)

# 1. Introduction

By common usage, "poverty" exists when one or more persons fall short of a level of economic welfare deemed to constitute a reasonable minimum, either in some absolute sense or by the standards of a specific society. The literature on poverty in developing countries has often taken "economic welfare" to refer to a person's consumption of goods and services, and the "reasonable minimum" is then defined by pre-determined "basic consumption needs". This definition of "economic welfare" can be made more or less comprehensive (in the goods and services embraced), but it is intrinsically limited. It may reveal nothing about the disutility of work, the length or health of the life over which consumption is expected, risk and variability etc. While recognizing the limitations of the concept of "economic welfare" as "command over commodities", we will largely confine ourselves to that definition, in order to review the many important issues in the literature that has evolved around it. Even this narrow definition poses serious measurement problems, such as how to aggregate across commodities, across persons within households, and over time. We will return to some of these issues. However, it is not controversial that inadequate command over commodities is the most important dimension of poverty, and a key determinant of other aspects of welfare, such as health, longevity, and self-esteem. And it has been a powerful motive for policy.

"Economics is, in essence, the study of poverty" [Hartwell (1972, p. 3)]. The structure, efficiency and growth of production affect – and are affected by – the distribution of consumption. Poverty analysis has three tasks: i) to define and describe "poverty", ii) to understand its causes, and iii) to inform policy. Each task overlaps with other branches of economics; when a topic is well covered elsewhere we shall simply refer readers to that source. In Section 2 we sketch the history of economic thought on poverty since the mercantilists, concentrating on relevance to current economic analysis and policy. Section 3 examines how poverty is defined and measured. These two sections – history and measurement – lay the foundations for the subsequent discussion, which moves from the "grand" (the dimensions of global poverty) to the "small" (the farm-household). In Section 4 we provide a "snapshot" of poverty in the developing world today, looking first at the global picture, and then turning to the village and household levels. Evidence from modern household surveys has allowed us to examine the interactions between demographic, nutritional and labor-force characteristics of poverty groups; in this process, modern economics is developing some of the central insights of the classical economists, though with measurement and modeling methods not available to them. New knowledge about poor households has also greatly informed our understanding of how the economy and policy impinge on the poor, the topics of Sections 5 and 6. In Section 5 we look at the classic development issue of the effect of growth on poverty and inequality, and (the recent classic) macroeconomic adjustment and the poor. From this base, and the evidence of Section 4, we can then explore several issues that arise in governmental attempts to reduce poverty through direct interventions. Section 6 takes up these issues. Our conclusions in Section 7 suggest some directions for future research.

## 2. The history of ideas about the poor

### 2.1. The first transition

Most cultures have sought to explain poverty, and to devise a moral approach to it [Illiffe (1987)]. However, a transition in thought and policy about poverty emerged in Europe around 1750–1850. This transition can help us understand a similar transition since 1945 in the LDCs. Before about 1750 in Europe[1] – and before about 1945 in Asia, Africa and Latin America – poverty showed little if any secular trend; subsequently, its reduction, by economic growth and by public action, became a widely-held expectation. Both transitions had similar correlates: accelerated investment in human and physical capital; faster technical progress in food production and disease limitation; some degree of demographic transition; diversification out of food-growing agriculture; and some political empowerment of the poor. The 18th century transition from mercantilist to classical economic analysis of poverty is also paralleled in the economics of LDCs since 1945. And both the economics and economies of LDCs were linked to Western models by emulation, colonialism, advice with strings, and world markets.

Today's underdeveloped world is heterogeneous, and faces different problems to those confronting the initiators of modern economic growth. Nevertheless, the insights of the founders of modern economics, as they analyzed the impact on poverty of the first "great transition", help us to understand the second. In responding to Smith (1776), Malthus (1798) asked a key question: to what extent is poverty a consequence of the impact of demographic change on real wages? While modern economics rejects Malthus's answers (mainly because he does not adequately endogenize either fertility or technical progress), his and other "classical" questions have influenced the modern economics of poverty.

---

[1] "Anyone, before the middle of the eighteenth century, who expected a progressive improvement in material welfare . . . would have been thought eccentric. There was little variation in the lot of the unskilled [European] laborer in the two thousand years . . . to the France of Louis XIV" [Keynes (1923, p. vii)].

Before about 1750, there was little durable growth of world product per person. Partly for this reason, moves to reduce poverty by peaceful redistribution – from the land reforms of the Gracchi [Tuma (1965, pp. 31–36)] to the proposals of radicals within Cromwell's army [C. Hill (1972)] – proved politically unviable. In such a world, poverty did not seem curable. There were four approaches to poverty: acceptance, palliation, insurance, or theft. Poverty might be accepted: "embraced as a sacred vow [or] tolerated (or railed against) as an unhappy fact of life" [Himmelfarb (1984, pp. 2–3)]. Poverty might be palliated, by private charity: normally by the works of the devout, financed by alms-giving, which most religions saw as a pious duty. Poverty might be socially insured against: exceptionally by the state (as with England's relatively comprehensive Poor Law of 1597); sometimes by implicit informal contract among members of a group or tribe [compare Platteau (1988)]; but usually by a lord or chief, providing insurance to free or serf laborers because of his interest in maintaining their military or productive power and loyalty in bad times as well as good [compare Bardhan and Rudra (1981)].

In the absence of palliation or insurance, theft was an ethically accepted cure for life-threatening poverty. A person "in imminent danger [who] cannot be helped in any other way . . . may legitimately supply his own wants out of another's property" [Aquinas, ed. Gilby (1975, pp. 2a. 2ae.q. 66.a.7)]. This view dominated jurisprudential and ethical theory from Aquinas to Locke and his successors. The safety, as well as the morality, of capital required its owners "to provide with shelter and to refresh with food any and every man, but only when a poor man's misfortune calls for our alms and our property supplies means for charity" [Locke, cited in Hont and Ignatieff (1983, p. 37)].

This was normative economics, recognizing constraints, but concerned with rights and duties, not allocations and utilities. Although production was secularly static, proto-economics recognized: a right to assistance in extreme deprivation, and a corresponding duty to work; a duty of the well-off to provide such assistance, and a corresponding right to the security of property. Long before Smith, several major problems with achieving these rights and duties were recognized. For example, legislators sought to avoid disincentives to work for the able-bodied poor (the "sturdy beggars" denied relief in England's 1597 Poor Law). Means such as tithing or poor-rates were used to avoid free-riding by those rich people who chose to leave the duty of charity to others.

However, any duty to succor the poor created a deep problem for the first attempt to construct a rigorous economics of means and ends: mercantilism. The end was to maximize a nation's export surplus. A strengthening currency, and hence import capacity, could then permit one country to grow, but at the expense of the rest of the world. The means to maximize the export surplus was cheap, and therefore poor, labor. Mandeville's epigram that "the surest was cheap, and therefore poor, labor. Mandeville's epigram that "the surest wealth consists in a multitude of laborious poor" outraged fellow-economists [Home (1978, pp. 68–69)], but followed from his and their assumptions.

Into this dark world of necessarily low real wages, zero economic progress (at least for the poor), and (for extremists such as Mandeville) the belief that even basic education would do the poor and the economy more harm than good, came twin beams of light. First, from around 1740–1780 in England and somewhat later elsewhere, technical progress rapidly accelerated. Second, at the level of supportive economic theory, the light came from the Hume-Smith view of a progressive economy. The gains from specialization, rising demand for labor, and technical progress (embodied in rising rates of capital accumulation) would increase both the money-wage and the availability of corn for it to buy. Instead of low real wages to build up an export surplus, countries would trade freely at home and abroad, would experience rising real wages, and would balance their foreign accounts.

The view that economic development is feasible, that it can reduce poverty, and that such reduction is the main theme of economics, is thus quite recent. It stems from Smith's deeply anti-mercantilist observation that "no society can surely be flourishing and happy, of which the far greater part of the members are poor and miserable" [Smith (1776: bk.I, Chapter 8), (1884, p. 33)]. Torrens epitomized classical economists' rejection of any "plan of financial and commercial improvement . . . unless it raises the real wage rate" [1839: cited by Coats (1972, p. 160)].

It remained controversial to what extent a route through free-market growth to the reduction of poverty was feasible. Even for the first-comer (Britain 1740–1850), there were two important objections at the time. Malthus (1798) argued that not only free-market growth, but also policies such as poor-laws to underpin or increase real wage-rates, would self-destruct by inducing earlier marriage and therefore greater fertility, ". . thus at once driving up the price of food while forcing down the price of labor" [Himmelfarb (1984, p. 129)] until the living standards of the burgeoning poor had been reduced to subsistence level. However, in the second (1803) edition of his *Essay*, Malthus conceded that technical progress might raise wage rates and reduce poverty, provided "moral restraint" – delayed marriage and abstinence – prevented excessive fertility [Winch (1991, p. 42)]. By 1824, he was citing Swiss and other data to show how higher incomes, lower mortality, and better education could reduce fertility.[2]

Malthus himself destroyed the arguments for his earlier radical pessimism

---

[2] On editions of the *Essay* see Himmelfarb [(1984, pp. 114–117)]. On the 1824 article, which prefigures the "substituting quality for quantity" approach in Becker and Lewis (1974), see Lipton (1990).

about policies to reduce poverty. This pessimism (unlike Nassau Senior's view that a disincentive to work would arise if poor-relief were insufficiently stigmatizing and unpleasant) played no part in the increasingly restrictive application of English poor relief after 1834 [O'Brien (1975, pp. 281–282), Williamson (1991)]. Nor did Malthusian fears about the fertility consequences deter European governments (notably Bismarck's in Germany) from attempting pro-poor policies [Ahmad et al. (1991)]. The fears became even more remote with the spread of contraception – opposed by Malthus, but expected and vigorously advocated by the high priest of mid-century classical economics, J.S. Mill [Himmelfarb (1984, p. 115)]. This further de-linked the reduction of poverty from any subsequent increases in population. All this anticipates modern theory of the demographic impact both of poverty and of its remedies.

The second objection to the Smithian view – that poverty reduction was at once the aim of policy and the outcome of growth in a now normally progressive economy – came from Ricardo. He came to accept [Coats (1972, pp. 152–153)] that mechanization, induced inter alia by higher real wage-rates, could permanently displace workers. Yet he did not advocate stopping it, or doubt its contribution to the embodiment of technical progress, ultimately enhancing national and labor income. Hence serious economics, building on Ricardo's concerns, did not relate to the Luddite (or Ruskinian) view that machinery was damaging, but to Marxist and Owenite advocacy of working-class action to own and manage the machines, and later to neoclassical and underconsumptionist/Keynesian accounts of the paths to full employment whatever the capital/labor ratio.

Economics, from Adam Smith, generally saw the accumulation of physical capital (especially if it embodied technical progress) as reducing poverty. What of "human capital", both as a long-term preventer of poverty and as a short-term insurance for the poor? Better health was seen by Smith [(1776: bk. I, Chapter 8), (1884, p. 34)] as a consequence, and subsequently a cause, of greater working capacity, higher wages, and improved living standards. We do not know if the classical economists advocated publicly mediated health provision. Yet institutional care in old age and chronic infirmity was available to the poorest in many countries, long before the industrial revolution. In England even after 1834, workhouses offered the infirm pauper a refuge "more agreeable than life outside" [Himmelfarb (1984, pp. 164–165)].[3] Bismarck's reforms of the 1880s brought some security to the aged and infirm in Germany.

Public and/or subsidized "mass" basic education was strongly advocated by the classical economists, partly because it was expected to reduce total fertility rates [Himmelfarb 1984, pp. 120–121]. But human development was the main

---

[3] Public relief was only part of the reason; the growth of friendly societies was massive [Hanson (1972, pp. 118–127)].

argument [Smith (1776: bk. V, Chapter 1), (1884, pp. 327–328)]. The classical economists saw that education could well enhance the labor-productivity and hence living standards of the poor. But that outcome, and possible effects on growth, was viewed as a desirable but incidental by-product. Recent work on the returns to education in LDCs [Schultz (1975), Welch (1970), Jamison and Lau (1982)] provides some support for the classical insight here: that the transition to a progressive economy is what permits education to provide substantial income benefits for the poor as a whole.[4]

The demonstration by the classical economists that this transition could complement rising real wage-rates, and a healthier and better-educated workforce, was accompanied by a shift in moral and political philosophy. This took the view that, as capitalist civil society emerged, public institutions should accept responsibility not only for mass education, but also for poverty prevention and/or reduction [Wood (1991, p. xix)]. For this shift, Hegel was partly responsible. Hegel (1821/1991, paras. 238, 241) saw competitive political and economic action, by individuals and groups, to achieve both private and public goals as characterizing the emerging "civil society", which

> . . tears the individual away from family ties [so that] he has rights and claims in relation to it, just as he had in relation to his family. For the *poor*, the universal power [State] takes over the role of the family. The contingent character of alms-giving . . . is supplemented by public poorhouses, hospitals, street lighting, etc.

Smith had argued that (i) the modern economy requires division of labor; (ii) this risks deskilling the working poor; (iii) hence the State should provide means to educate them. Analogously, Hegel argued that (i) the modern progressive economy is associated with a stronger civil society; (ii) this endangers the kinship links that had previously protected the poor; (iii) hence the State should provide new safety-nets.

## 2.2. The second transition

The ethical and economic thinkers at the dawn of European industrialization were tackling many of the issues of poverty theory and policy that are central to development economics today. This is because, in some respects, the European transition that inspired the analysis of Hegel, Smith and their

---

[4] This is in marked contrast to Mandeville's denial – so shocking to his contemporaries – that, in a stationary economy, charity schools could raise the income (or the well-being) of workers, rather than merely delaying their earnings, in an epoch when there was no technical progress to complement the extra literacy or numeracy of, or add to the wage-bill for, labor as a whole. See Home (1978).

successors – and the effect of the transition on the poor – have close parallels in Africa, Asia and Latin America today. There too, civil society is gaining at the expense of familial society. Progressive (accumulating, specializing, innovating) economies are replacing stationary economies. There is temporary, but apparently alarming, population acceleration. And, on the whole, States are becoming less patrimonial, more dependent on consensual legitimacy. The first transition (so central in Europe after 1750) also had effects on the economics of poverty and of anti-poverty policy in developing countries since 1945. Three effects can be identified.

First, the Western transition drove the colonization process. To some extent, though less than envisaged by Marx (1853/1951, pp. 312–324), that process reproduced European progressive economies, and the associated changes in poverty problems, in the Third World. Colonization helped to form the institutions, power-structures and intellectual climates for LDCs' post-colonial poverty policy.

Second, the first transition led to important experiments in anti-poverty policy. These ranged from the 1834 Poor Laws and the Factory Acts in Britain, via the more comprehensive social insurance pioneered in Bismarck's Germany in the 1880s, to the US "war on poverty" in the 1960s. These experiments are relevant to poor countries today [Ahmad et al. (1991)].

Third, the transition in the Europe of 1750–1850 – to a stronger civil society, to a progressive economy, to "modern" demographics, and to more consensual States – was a precursor of the second transition in LDCs during the past half-century. This is not to support the crude, self-satisfied analogies of modernization theory and cultural evolutionism.[5] Yet there are similarities (alongside the differences) in processes and power-structures – and hence in changes in, and policies towards, poverty – as between the Europe of Smith, Hegel and their successors, and the post-colonial Third World.

## 2.2.1. Awakenings

One should not confuse a belief in what were to become (with the benefit of hindsight) failed theories and policies with a lack of poverty-orientation in policy design. It is sometimes said that economics underlying early development policy in the "ex-colonies" paid little regard to poverty. This is doubtful even as a judgement of the theorizing of western development pioneers, whether in the Clark-Kuznets or in the Rodan-Lewis-Nurkse schools. More seriously, the judgement slights the poverty concerns of economists and

---

[5] In political science, "modernization theory" suggests that, as developing countries progress economically, they approach the forms of political organization of developed Western countries. In anthropology, "cultural evolutionism" is the view that ways of domestic, economic and social organization follow an evolutionary sequence from lower to higher forms.

politicians in the "ex-colonies" themselves [Quibria and Srinivasan (1992)]. *Effective* anti-poverty actions (even in some fast-growing ex-colonies) proved elusive in the early post-colonial period. However, this was not a result of a lack of concern for the poor in policymaking, but of the structures of power, technology, factor-intensity, and the "soft state" [Myrdal (1968, pp. 895–900)]. These structures often diverted, captured or frustrated those who (whether through markets or through public action) sought to enhance the prospects of the poor. This process led to "the distribution of public largesse to the not-so-poor" [Minhas (1972, p. 26)], as in the Indian case, which is instructive.

The Indian elite that took power in 1947 was trained in the school of Gandhi, but also of Macaulay, J.S. Mill and (much less) Marx. It was certainly concerned with poverty. Both Indian nationalists and establishment intellectuals had long focused the debate on "Poverty and un-British Rule in India" [Naoroji (1901)]. Mann's still classic village study of 1909 in Pimpla Saudagar [Thorner (1968, p. xxiii), Mann (1916/1968, pp. 82–103), consciously modelled on Rowntree (1901)], like many others in the next few decades, was centered upon identifying and counting the poor and explaining their poverty.

Thus not only Gandhian (and earlier) traditions of religious and social service enquiry, but also socio-economic research emphases, had long prepared India for poverty-oriented policies. As Nehru (1946, pp. 399–403) emphasized, the National Planning Committee put higher priority on the reduction of poverty and unemployment than on economic growth per se. The trouble was not lack of concern for the poor, but rather the specific policies pursued. After Independence, the First Five-Year Plan explicitly rejected growth maximization, in favor of anti-poverty planning. So did some other plans of the time, notably Sri Lanka's Ten Year Plan. The indigenous traditions documented by Iliffe (1987) demonstrate similar concerns about poverty in Africa.

Many of the anti-poverty intentions of early development planning were frustrated, as with land reform (Section 6.4). Many plans were shelved. In most of Asia, and in some of Africa and Latin America, schemes for land reform, mass education, health, "community development", and rural credit directed at the poor, burgeoned from the moment of independence. Many such schemes were ill-considered or ill-implemented; most, perhaps, were not incentive-compatible. But the post-independence intellectual climate was explicitly sympathetic to the poor.

### 2.2.2. A diversion: Forced-draft industrialization

Yet the early industrialization plans of the post-colonial era largely failed the poor. They aimed at capital-intensive, somewhat autarkic, growth. They turned out to be over-hopeful of the capacity of such industrialization to raise the demand for labor, and so enrich the poor. Anti-trade biases did not help;

the poor (more, as a rule, than the non-poor) tend to earn their living by converting non-tradeable inputs, especially labor, into tradeable outputs (Section 4.3). Also, the poor tended to lose to the extent that accelerated industrialization is financed by extracting a surplus from agriculture, which provides most of their income, and produces their food (Section 5.2). Agriculturally extractive and/or trade-restrictive paths to industrialization not only slow growth down; they reduce its benefits to the poor.

Some of these criticisms were made at the time [e.g., Vakil and Brahmanand (1956) on India's Second Plan]. But, by and large, they appeared to carry little weight with the theorists of industrialization via the "big push", balanced growth, and above all labor transfer, such as Rosenstein-Rodan (1943), Nurkse (1963), and Lewis (1954) respectively. These theorists shared the classical optimism about "trickle-down", but not the classical worries about real wage trends. Yet these worries should have loomed large; population growth since 1950 has been much faster than during the first transition.

The impact of closed-economy assumptions on the poor was also little discussed in the 1960s. Indian approaches to industrialization – Nehru, Mahalanobis (1963), Pant – were heavily influenced by Preobrazhensky's (1924) model of the extraction of a surplus from agriculture via the intersectoral terms of trade (the "price scissors") and closely related to Fel'dman's model of the impact on growth of accelerated savings and investment [Domar (1957, pp. 223–261)]. These were essentially closed-economy models, and were based on the then heavily protected economy of the USSR.

The costs to the poor of an industrializing "big push" were unexpectedly heavy. Compared to the predictions of the planning models, forced-draft industrialization demanded less unskilled labor, supplies of unskilled labor grew faster, and the supply of food staples (typically 50–60 percent of poor people's spending) grew more slowly. This last problem arose partly because, as Hansen (1969) and others showed, the marginal agricultural product (lost when unskilled laborers were attracted to industry) was far from zero. Contrary to Lewis's (1954) model, when labor moved from farms to factories (and there was no "green revolution") capital moved as well, and food output per person declined. Also, industry proved unexpectedly capital-intensive as it grew. Hence unskilled wage rates, but not food prices, were sluggish. The poor fared worse than expected, and to little industrializing effect.

### 2.2.3. Counterblasts to planned industrialization

The policy approach of the Second and Third Indian Plans, and of many other (usually less operational) LDC planning documents prior to the mid-1970s, was in one key respect classical. Growth was to be achieved via accelerated capital accumulation and industrialization, thereby bidding up the demand for labor and the capacity to import; that was to be the main weapon against poverty.[6] Not at all classical were central planning itself; anti-trade-biased policies on quotas, tariffs and exchange-rates; and, above all, neglect of Smith's warning that food supply would constrain urban growth [Lipton (1977, pp. 94–95)]. These elements combined to discredit closed-economy, forced-draft industrialization.

Taiwan and South Korea [Fei et al. (1983), Kuo (1983), Wade (1991)] were outstanding exceptions both in the success of their industrializations and in their management of poverty. Yet they too had directive planning processes, "distorting" domestic relative prices and foreign trade, and extractive from agriculture. The key difference was that in these countries current-account rural *extraction* was offset by capital-account rural *recirculation*. This comprised (i) public investment in infrastructure for agricultural production (especially irrigation and crop research); (ii) public support to human capital formation (health and education); (iii) support, including subsidy, for rural non-farm enterprise. Probably essential to the big, fast response of food output to such stimuli had been prior, radically redistributive, land reform. Although imposed from abroad, it led to productive and dynamic owner-farmed smallholdings, along late-classical lines [Mill (1848–1871/1965, pp. 142–52, 342–36)]. There are similarities to China's experience [World Bank (1992d)].

Some developing countries made less full-blooded efforts at land redistributions, investment in education and health, and irrigation and agricultural research. Such countries – often despite anti-agricultural and anti-employment policies on exchange rates, protection and prices – avoided the extremes of retarded industrial growth (strangled for want of wage-goods and/or human capital) and of deepening rural poverty as agricultural employment and output failed to keep up with unexpectedly high population growth. However, these countries typically achieved only modest growth in real income per person – India at only 1–1.5 percent yearly in 1950–1973 – *and* little decline in poverty incidence, despite poverty-orientated "add-ons" to the inadequate macro-policies [for India, see Datt (1994)].

From the mid-1960s to the early 1970s, counterblasts to the failed consensus around poverty reduction by planned industrialization came from a number of sources.

- Seers (1972), Usher (1963), Bauer (1965) and others (from diverse ideological stances) denied either that GNP was correctly measured by LDC statistics, or that (if it was) it could itself correctly measure changes in welfare. Seers questioned that an economy in which GNP per person,

---

[6] Though not the only weapon; Indian and other LDC governments did subsidize and protect (via restrictions on big firms) craft, village, and cottage industry.

unemployment, and inequality were all increasing, could be counted as "developing" at all.

- The model in which the poor largely comprised underemployed persons – to be absorbed productively in a labor-intensive (and probably industrializing) process of planned modern-sector growth – also came under attack. Following Hansen (1969), a succession of studies confirmed that farm labor had non-zero (albeit seasonally fluctuating) marginal product; and that overt and prolonged urban unemployment was largely confined to the educated and better-off, in search of "a good job" and able to afford to wait for it. The ILO missions to Colombia, Kenya and Sri Lanka confirmed that the urban and rural poor were more seldom "underemployed" than overworked, especially as casual laborers and in the informal sector (Section 4.3). From the rural end, it became clear that the poorest seldom migrated successfully towards durable, adequately earning urban employment [Connell et al. (1976)].

- The celebrated "Nairobi speech" [McNamara (1973)] signalled a shift in donor priorities, away from the heavy (and largely urban) infrastructural lending of the 1960s, toward rural development designed to benefit the "poorest 40 percent", seen then as mostly "small farmers" rather than as landless laborers. "Urban bias" was increasingly recognized as bad for growth as well as for poverty reduction, though rooted in political structures in much of the developing world [Mamalakis (1970), Lipton (1968, 1977), Bates (1981)]. Apart from past disappointments, two facts supported the hope that a new, rural emphasis could accelerate growth *and* reduce poverty. First, the "green revolution" was seen, from the late 1960s, as potentially able to enrich even very "small" farmers [Lipton with Longhurst (1989, Chapter 2)]. Second, there was increasing evidence that farm size was inversely related to both employment and annual output per hectare [Berry and Cline (1979), Binswanger et al. this volume]. Thus an emphasis on small farms would reconcile anti-poverty and pro-growth policies within the rural sector. This process was to be supported, in attacking poverty, by investments in rural health, education, roads etc. However, there was no clear evidence that a given outlay would have most impact on poverty or growth if divided among several sectors, let alone if also managed as multi-sectoral "integrated rural development projects".[7] These projects – at least while conceived as localized exercises in central

---

[7] See Birgegaard (1987), Lipton (1987a). Most "rural development" spending of governments such as India's, and of agencies such as the World Bank, went mainly to sector-specific investments, not to "integrated" projects. The arguments against such projects in Asia, however, have been exaggerated, especially for second-generation, less top-down projects that invested in technology and institution-building before costly infrastructures [*ibid.*; Limcaoco and Hulme (1990)].

planning – also overstretched the administrative capabilities of agencies and governments.[8] As regards agricultural spending (and rural anti-poverty emphasis) itself, the donors' new initiative from the mid-1970s, and much domestic spending too, suffered from two weaknesses. It depended heavily on the efficiency – and genuine poverty-orientation – of bureaucratically directed credit labelled "For the Poor" (Section 6.4). And it carried no insurance against fungibility, i.e. against extra agro-rural aid being offset by reduced domestic agro-rural investment [Singer (1965)].

- Policies to increase the earned incomes of the urban poor had been neglected in the swings of intellectual fashion. But one set of urban anti-poverty policies did emerge in the 1970s. The urban poor, it was argued, lived largely in slums or near-slums. They would thus be helped by a shift of investment away from publicly built, so-called "low-cost" housing for middle-class civil servants, towards loans for private site-and-service hut building (with provision of water and electricity), and for slum upgrading.

- The earlier emphasis on forced-draft industrialization had been partly driven by the fact that the rate of growth is given by the share of national income invested in physical capital relative to the incremental capital-output ratio. This identity was interpreted as explaining growth in terms of savings embodied in physical capital. The resulting neglect of the social sectors led to a counterblast in both thinking and policy. Leibenstein (1957), Berg (1973) and others argued that better nutrition could be instrumental in raising the productivity of the poor. The role of human-resource development in equitable growth was emphasized by Adelman and Morris (1973). Schultz (1981a) summarized his earlier evidence for the importance of investment in human capital for growth; others, in analyses based on production or earnings functions, had established high private and social returns to education, especially primary [Psacharopoulos (1981)].[9]

- The tilt towards poverty-orientation in the mid-1970s was informed by a view of public objectives summarized in the words "redistribution with growth" (RWG) [Chenery et al. (1974)]. RWG reflected disillusionment with the poverty-reducing potential of trickle-down industrialization, *and* with radical redistribution of income or land, in view of the interlocking power and self-interest of the rich and the bureaucracy. It has become

[8] The fault may lie with inappropriate planning methods, not with integrated area development as such. Recent area projects such as Solidaridad in Mexico, which offer fiscal incentives instead of dictates from area authorities, appear to work better (personal communication with Hans Binswanger).
[9] Many of these estimates were almost certainly biased upwards. The main problem is that few of the estimates of the earnings-gain from extra schooling controlled for differences in ability, family environment, and school quality. On these and related issues see the surveys by Schultz (1988), Behrman (1990), and also the chapters by Jimenez and Strauss/Thomas in this volume.

fashionable to dismiss the poverty emphases of RWG, and of the 1970s as a whole, as unsophisticatedly reliant on the notion that the State is a benevolent "Platonic guardian" of the public interest, when in reality the state is permeated by rent-seeking and pressures to achieve political stability by distributing the fruits of growth to its friends. However, this is a caricature of RWG, which was quite explicit about such obstacles [Bell (1974, pp. 52–61)], but argued that some redistribution towards the poor could still be induced out of a growing GNP. First, there were pro-poor islands – whether idealistic or self-interested – within the power-structure of most countries. Second, RWG envisaged donor support, foreshadowing "poverty conditionality" [compare World Bank (1991a) and World Bank (1975)]. The severe slowdown of growth after the mid-1970s meant a harsher climate for both aid and redistribution. When RWG was written, however, this could not be foreseen.

- Data and analytic capabilities responded to the growing focus on poverty. While the collection of data on poor households had been used to generate social awareness and motivate policy since the 19th century, nationally representative surveys of household living standards are relatively new. From 1951, India's National Sample Survey had been tracking household expenditures. Using these and other data, Bardhan (1970) and Dandekar and Rath (1971) were instrumental in setting in motion ongoing monitoring of poverty data in India [Kadekodi and Murty (1992), Datt (1994)]. Bell and Duloy (1974, Chapter 12) helped to advance reorientations of statistical services, in order to track the performance of particular countries, groups, projects and policy interventions. A succession of experiments with the prediction of policy impacts on the poor using Social Accounting Matrices [Pyatt and Round (1980)] and computable general equilibrium models [Dervis et al. (1982)] offered promise, particularly in LDCs with relatively advanced basic data. A number of new initiatives for gathering data on poor households arose initiated in the 1970s. The UN National Household Capability Programme [UN (1989)] helped put household surveys on a sounder and more consistent basis. The World Bank began its efforts to collect high-quality household and community data on a wide range of welfare indicators and their correlates [Chander et al. (1980), Glewwe (1990), Grootaert and Kanbur (1990)]. The collection of panel data, even for small samples [Walker and Ryan (1990)], has proved of great value in illuminating the dynamics and causation of poverty. Such initiatives in household-level data collection facilitated both more systematic poverty monitoring and more sophisticated – and progressively more convincing – empirical analyses of the determinants of poverty and impacts of policies and projects [Ravallion (1993a), Deaton (1994), Strauss/Thomas and Deaton in this volume].

However, these data initiatives have not yet spanned a wide range of countries. Also, there has been concern that, in some data-poor settings, national statistical systems have been diverted from other poverty-oriented data needs, such as reliable smallholder food production data. Furthermore, the development of data and analytic capabilities has been slow to permeate policy analysis; for example, despite well-founded critiques from Sen (1976, 1981a) and others, uninformative and potentially misleading "head-counts" of poverty have tended to dominate policymakers' attention.

### 2.2.4. "Basic needs" and "capabilities"

Almost all these arguments concentrated on what McNamara termed "the productivity of the poor": income corresponding to retained value added. However, many poor people earn no such income: children and the sick are heavily over-represented among the poor; old people are currently under-represented, but this may be changing in Asia and Latin America (Section 4.2). The "basic needs" (BN) approach instead stresses ". . . human needs in terms of health, food, education, water, shelter, transport" [Streeten et al. (1981, p. 7), Richards and Leonor (1982)]. Two main arguments were advanced for tracking poverty reduction by observing BN, rather than incomes. First, increases in real income may be unable to command better health care, education, safe drinking water, sanitation, police protection, etc. Second, households vary greatly in their capacity to convert commodities into well-being. For example, there is notable "positive deviance" in the capacity of some poor households to convert income into adequate nutrition [Zeitlin et al. (1987)].

Closely related to the BN approach in motivation, but entailing a more fundamental re-definition of "poverty", is Sen's subsequent "capabilities" approach. Its roots lie in the rejection of the "welfarist" paradigm in which individual utility is taken to be the sole metric of welfare, and the sole basis for social choice [Sen (1979, 1985, 1987)]. Here commodities matter as one determinant of people's capabilities to function (rather than as a source of "utility"). The strength of this view is its emphasis on commodities not as ends, but as means to desired activities. This explicitly recognizes the contingent nature of benefits conferred by any claim over commodities: what these do for well-being depends on a host of factors, including the circumstances – personal and environmental – of an individual.

Unfortunately, focusing on capabilities is not devoid of its own problems. We rarely observe capabilities, but rather certain "achievements". The mapping from the latter to the former is not unique, but depends on factors such as preferences. For example, to conclude that a person was not capable of living a long life we must know more than just how long she lived; perhaps she preferred a short but merry life. The role ascribed to preferences in BN and capabilities approaches is still unclear; it is one thing to reject the strict welfarist view that *only* utilities matter, and quite another to claim that utilities are not at least a part of the objective. For a great many choices, people do know what is best for themselves.[10] If so, one should be cautious in forming judgements about poverty which are demonstrably inconsistent with those choices. The capabilities approach has not established why higher consumption – especially for the poor – should not remain an objective of policy, even if it does nothing for capabilities. There is also the unresolved issue of how one should aggregate over capabilities or basic needs. Single BN measures, such as the "physical quality of life index" or PQLI [Morris (1979)], are arbitrary in what they include, and in the weights attached to the included items.

The 1990s have seen attempts at operationalizing the capabilities approach, by measuring "human development". In the 1990s, the UNDP's "Human Development Reports" sought to explore the impact of the economic vicissitudes and adjustments of the 1980s on measures of human development. However, it is even more difficult to infer the effect of adjustment policies, over a decade or less, on outcome variables (such as health or literacy) than on incomes (Section 5.3). There are various reasons, including: weak and out-of-date numbers; long (and varying) time-lags between policies and BN outcomes; and reciprocal causation (simultaneity). Even the effect of adjustment on public spending for health care, education, etc. is controversial.[11] And the aggregation problem bites once again: the UNDP's attempt (1990) to finesse these problems via a single indicator of human development is subject to insuperable objections [Kanbur (1990b), Anand (1991), McGillivray and White (1993)].

The surviving lesson from these approaches is: recognize the limitations of a commodities-centered conceptualization of well-being. It is agreed that command over commodities matters – at some level – to well-being. Where these approaches differ is in the view they take on *why* incomes matter. On the most simplistic commodities-centered approach, aggregate affluence drives attainments of BN, or capabilities. This seems consistent with cross-country comparisons; there is a quite good correlation (after appropriate transformations to reflect the non-linearities) of a country's average real income with the main indicators of BN satisfaction in nutrition, health, education, shelter, etc. [Preston (1975), Sen (1981b), Isenman (1980)], and indeed in social and

---

[10] Gulati (1977) showed that in Trivandrum (Kerala), India, mothers sold food stamps to purchase better health care, even though in Kerala State free basic health was widely available. A BN approach appears to claim that planners know better than peasants how to allocate income.
[11] See Cornia et al. (1988), Pinstrup-Andersen (1989), Maasland and van der Gaag (1992), Lenaghan (1992), and Kakwani et al. (1993).

political rights [Dasgupta (1992, 1993)]. However, this correlation may well be spurious, in that it reflects other omitted variables correlated with average incomes, such as the incidence of absolute poverty, and access to key social services; on controlling for these, average incomes may matter far less than is often thought. There is evidence for that view: when public health spending and the incidence of poverty are held constant in cross-country regressions, the formerly strong relationship between a country's income-per-person and its health outcomes disappears [Anand and Ravallion (1993)]. There is other evidence that capacity for both private and public spending is required to achieve BN in health.[12] The message here is not that affluence is unimportant to well-being, but that we must be careful in identifying the precise ways in which affluence matters. Ipso facto, this approach can also throw light on what can be done to enhance well-being at low levels of average income: China, Costa Rica, Cuba and Sri Lanka show much better levels (or improvements) in BN than are predicted by income per head (or its growth) – sometimes even allowing for other variables such as poverty measures [Sen (1981b), Drèze and Sen (1989)].[13]

The pressures that emerged [Cornia et al. (1987)] to give adjustment a more human face – spurred by the BN approaches – probably helped the poor. In the early 1980s, it was almost impossible to persuade donors to design adjustment assistance with a view to improving its impact on the poor. By the late-1980s, add-on programs to "compensate the losers from adjustment" were common, though often focusing on the articulate and somewhat poor, rather than the inarticulate and very poor. Today it is increasingly recognized that poverty mitigation has to be designed into adjustment programs initially – not added as a tranquillizer later on – if otherwise desirable reforms in food pricing, foreign trade and exchange, public expenditure and employment are not to harm the poor in the short term.

It would be flattering to economists if these pro-poor "adjustments to adjustment" had resulted mainly from theory (such as Sen on capabilities) and/or major advances in empirical methods and measurement (such as the new household surveys and econometric tools). These did illuminate the social dimensions of adjustment. But a more important source of pressure to protect the poor during adjustment came from the less sophisticated analyses of

---

[12] It is not clear under what circumstances private poverty reduction and public health activities are substitutes, as opposed to complements, in the production of health. Substitutability is suggested by the fact that health outcomes are much better in Kerala, with widespread public health provision, than in many Indian States with far lower levels of poverty. Complementarity is suggested by a large study in the Narangwal area of the Indian Punjab; there a given outlay had much more impact on child health if divided between (private) food supplementation and (public) health provision than if used exclusively for either [Taylor et al. (1978)].

[13] Outliers also include countries with much *worse* than expected outcomes on BN indicators, notably "rich" oil-producing nations.

various international and non-governmental organizations. Though honest, these analyses were often dubious. Keynes has taught us that such "essays in persuasion" can do more to shift a stubborn policy than better theory and evidence – but also that these are needed as well, if policies are to be durably improved.

### 2.2.5. States, markets and poverty

In the 1980s there were strong reactions against state involvement in development policies and processes. It was widely seen as rent-creating, price-distorting, protectionist, inherently corrupt, and destructive of enterprise – and as preventing the state, with its limited resources, from providing the privately under-supplied goods (roads, education, health, etc.) that comprised its potentially useful contribution to development. Much state intervention was also deemed to harm the poor directly, by turning the terms of trade against poor producers of tradeables, and by creating discretionary access to inputs, subsidies, licenses and credit. These, even if labelled "for the poor", often went to the wealthy – partly as rents, shared between powerful bureaucrats and their private clients. A smaller state would, it was claimed, accelerate growth and help the poor.

Some aspects of this "neo-liberal" position are better developed than others. The policies it led to entailed a *partial* removal of distortions, implying ambiguous effects on efficiency [Lipsey and Lancaster (1956)]. Evidence that the new (less-distorted) policy set would do what is promised has often been either lacking or unconvincing.[14] While the wasteful rent-seeking behavior of elites was emphasized, the power structures which created those elites were typically ignored.

The last point may well be the most important. Shifting the boundaries between state and market may matter little to the poor while the balance of power is unaltered. Suppose that the poor are rural, dispersed and weak, but that "the state" is induced to desist from turning the terms of trade against the rural sector. On its own this is likely to help the poor. But, if the power-structure is unaltered, such a change will presumably be offset, due to the continuing power of non-poor groups. Hence the state will be pressured to make concessions to the non-poor, e.g. by increasing the share of public

---

[14] Agarwala's (1983) work stimulated much enthusiasm at the time, but the robustness of some of the conclusions has been questioned [Aghazadeh and Evans (1988), Taylor and Arida (1988)]. World Bank (1988) shows that countries receiving conditional adjustment loans – especially if repeated over several years – outperformed comparators on most indicators, but with rather important exceptions: low-income countries, heavily indebted countries, and sub-Saharan Africa! World Bank (1991c, Chapter 4) argues that trade restrictions reduce rates of return to Bank projects, though Taylor (1993) points to the possibility of spurious correlation. More rigorous empirical work is needed.

investments and expenditures in non-agricultural activities. Perhaps this is why, alongside the reduction of domestic terms-of-trade distortions against agriculture, its share in government spending (in oil-importing LDCs) fell from 7.9 percent in 1975 to 4.5 in 1988, registering a fall every year [Lipton (1992a: 232)].

The neo-liberal critique provided a valuable corrective to past statist excesses and errors, but was probably "a reaction too far" [Killick (1991: 1)], requiring correction by a more balanced view of the developmental "comparative advantage" of states and markets, and of how citizens in civil society can control abuses of each [Bardhan (1990), Colclough and Manor (1991), Wade (1991), Streeten (1993)].

## 2.2.6. A new consensus?

In the mid-1980s, it was widely alleged that poverty reduction had lost salience for LDC governments and donors. Pressures for fiscal stabilization and market liberalization would raise food prices, reduce public expenditure and employment, and curtail poverty programs. Even primary education and health were exposed to cuts and user charges. The poor would be the main losers, and the most defenseless. The counter-arguments were that non-adjustment would be worse. The "poverty programs" and social services had often missed the poor. The poor would gain most, as governments switched towards a more efficient, labor-intensive, pro-rural, tradeables-orientated, and non-interventionist policy set. The pain from public-sector cutbacks, food price rises, etc. would prove a brief evil.

The evidence is mixed. There was mass poverty long before adjustment – indeed, long before the imbalances and distortions that adjustment seeks to reduce. So it is not likely that either adjustment or its absence causes or cures most poverty. Neither theory nor evidence is conclusive on the impacts of adjustment on the poor (Section 5.3). They gained where adjustment was not needed, or worked. They lost where adjustment was needed but not tried, or was tried but failed.

Early claims, that relaxing trade and other distortions *alone* could greatly stimulate poverty-reducing growth, have given way to more sober assessments. The emerging consensus is that successful adjustment, while it can help reduce poverty, is harder than had once been thought. It requires a large and not too slow aggregate supply response. Markets may achieve this best where states do *more* – by providing infrastructural, public, or merit goods – to enable the poor to be part of that response.

Where does this leave the poor? The World Bank (1990, 1991a), UNDP (1990), the Asian Development Bank (1992), IFAD (1992), and other agencies have published criteria for anti-poverty lending or spending. Several have been followed up. For example, the World Bank (1992a) has set operational guidelines for supportive analysis and lending; implementation is completed or under way for most countries to which the Bank lends. These documents help us evaluate the current consensus on poverty [Lipton and Maxwell (1992)].

Central to the consensus is the World Bank's (1990) two-pronged strategy of labor-demanding growth combined with investment in poor people's human capital. The growth is to be based on private production, released in part by the removal of state-imposed market distortions that discriminate against agriculture and exports, and fostered by state-facilitated physical infrastructure. The human capital is to be expanded through primary education and basic health care, largely provided (though not necessarily produced) publicly. Additionally there is a perceived need for well-targeted social safety nets, provided by the state, to guard the poor and vulnerable against food and other insecurities. While there are differences in emphasis, there now appears to be broad agreement on these basic elements of a poverty reduction strategy. But some unsettled issues – only some of which we shall address in this chapter – still disturb the waters of consensus:

- If all distortions are removed, but many of the poor can find work only by accepting a return insufficient to prevent poverty, are further incentive or expansionary measures toward "labor-intensive growth" justified – or are the risks of inflation, new distortions, or logrolling too great?
- What is the role of asset redistribution in reducing poverty? The consensus is uneasy about unearned rents, but also about unstable regimes of property rights, and is somewhat evasive on this question (however, see the chapter by Binswanger et al.). Asset redistribution may be essential for a reasonable rate of poverty reduction in some circumstances: when initial inequality is so great that distribution-neutral growth brings few gains to the poor; when poverty is so severe that growth and redistribution are both needed; or when rapid growth is for some reason unattainable.
- Should some safety nets (guaranteeing food or work) *always* be available, while protection against extreme or localized hardships is provided on an ad hoc basis? Under what circumstances do private insurance markets, informal insurance arrangements, or even public investments such as irrigation which help stabilize incomes, provide more cost-effective risk reduction for the poor than formal safety nets?
- Although poverty often induces its victims to degrade natural resources, so do some of its remedies [Barbier (1988), Dasgupta and Maler (1990), Leach and Mearns (1991), Vosti et al. (1992), Leonard (1989)]. Is there a trade-off between reducing poverty and protecting the environment, and how should it be handled?
- The "country strategies" [World Bank (1991a)] seek to reduce poverty

mainly through economy-wide *policies*. Does this divert resources from, or does it stimulate, efforts to improve the poverty impact of major public-sector *projects* at each stage of the project cycle, from identification through post-evaluation? Or are such efforts useless because of fungibility [Singer (1965)]?

*   What is the economics of international non-aid actions? If a given amount of trade liberalization or debt restructuring is on offer, how (if at all) should it be allocated to favor the poor?

The smoke has cleared in the state-market battle. The extreme positions are deserted. A consensus about some key issues of anti-poverty policy has emerged. Yet this consensus still contains omissions and obscurities. Economic analysis and testing can help improve the position.

## 3. Measurement

Assumptions made in measuring poverty can matter to policy. We give two examples:

i) Will a development strategy which transfers income from the rural (agricultural) sector to the urban (manufacturing) sector increase or decrease poverty? The answer depends in part on the economy's poverty profile; is poverty incidence, depth, and/or severity higher in rural than urban areas? That is actually a difficult question to answer convincingly, and some common methodologies (discussed further below) can be deceptive.

ii) Should a poverty reduction scheme aim to reach the poorest, even if no beneficiary gains enough to escape poverty, or should it concentrate on those closer to the poverty line? The answer depends on the poverty measure used. The most common measure found in practice – the percentage of the population deemed poor – would suggest that one should only be concerned about getting people over the poverty line. Other measures will put little or no weight on this, and will instead indicate the need to raise the living standards of the poorest first. The choice of measure inevitably makes a value judgement, and can have considerable bearing on policy choices.

### 3.1. Living standards

The generally preferred indicator of household living standards is a suitably comprehensive measure of current real consumption, given by a price-weighted aggregate over all marketed commodities consumed by the household from all sources (purchases, gifts and own production).[15] There are two reasons why this is often preferred over current income. First, current consumption is often taken to be a better indicator than current income of *current* standard of living; it is assumed that within-period utility depends directly on within-period consumption. Second, current consumption may also be a good indicator of *long-term* average well-being, as it will reveal information about incomes at other dates, in the past and future. This is because incomes often vary over time in fairly predictable ways – particularly in agrarian economies. In such circumstances, there are typically consumption smoothing opportunities available to the poor, such as through saving, borrowing, and community-based risk-sharing; for recent surveys see Alderman and Paxson (1992), Deaton (1992), and Besley's chapter.

A number of factors do, however, make current household consumption a noisy welfare indicator. First, people will not in general prefer constant consumption over the life-cycle (even with unrestricted opportunities for smoothing). Two households with different lifetime wealth, but one younger than the other, may have the same consumption at the survey date. Second, different households may face different constraints on their consumption smoothing. The chronic poor tend to be more constrained than the non-poor in their borrowing options, so that not only lifetime wealth but its distribution over the life-cycle affect lifetime welfare. Third, even if current consumption varies less around long-term well-being than current income for a given household, it may not be the best *ordinal* indicator of who is poor in terms of typical long-term living standards. That also depends on how the various living-standards indicators rank different households; one cross-sectional indicator may vary less around long-term living standards than another, but cause more re-ranking across households and, hence, perform less well in identifying the chronically poor [Chaudhuri and Ravallion (1994)]. Fourth, we rarely have data on the differences in living standards *within* households. Usual practice is to measure household consumption and assume arbitrarily that it is divided equally or according to some concept of need (discussed further below). However, in reality a change in total household consumption may affect the welfare of different household members in different ways, and even in different directions. This has implications for both measurement and policy [Haddad and Kanbur (1990, 1993); Nelson (1993)].[16]

---

[15] Household surveys are the single most important source of data for measuring consumption and/or income, as they are the only data source which can tell us directly about their *distribution* in a society. See Ravallion (1993a) for a survey of the issues that the analyst should be aware of in using such data.

[16] For example, in Morocco, animal husbandry is intensive in child labor. While a poor farm *household* will enjoy higher total consumption from higher meat prices, the behavioral responses may involve longer-term losses to poor *children*, taken out of school to tend livestock [de Janvry et al. (1991)].

Comparisons between households pose a number of problems. Household size and demographic composition vary, as do prices and access to publicly supplied goods. So the same total expenditure might leave one household poor, and another comfortably off. Welfarist approaches to this problem exist, based on demand analysis; these include "equivalence scales", "true cost-of-living indices", and "equivalent income measures" [for a survey of the theory see Deaton and Muellbauer (1980)]. These methods assume that demand patterns reveal consumer preferences over market goods; the consumer maximizes utility, and a utility function is derived which is consistent with observed demand behavior, relating consumption to prices, incomes, household size and demographic composition.[17] In all such behavioral welfare measures, the problem arises that one cannot (in general) deduce preferences over both market and non-market goods from preferences over market goods alone [Pollak and Wales (1979), Deaton (1980), Deaton and Muellbauer (1980, 1986), Pollak (1991), Browning (1992)]. Observed behavior in the marketplace may be consistent with infinitely many reasonable ways of making interpersonal welfare comparisons; it is a big step to assume that a particular utility function which supports observed behavior as an optimum is also the one which should be used in measuring well-being. This is an important problem because some non-market goods will always determine well-being: children, many publicly provided goods and services, and common property resources.[18]

One should look critically at the assumptions used in demand-based welfare measurement; for example, models of unequal bargaining power can yield quite different interpretations of empirical equivalence scales to the more common assumption of equality within households, with implications for anti-poverty policy [Ravallion (1993a)]. What looks like a difference in "consumption needs" may well be due to discrimination based on unequal power.

Consider household size. The demographic profile of the poor can have implications for (inter alia) population policy and the targeting of transfers (such as family allowances). But whether one deems larger and younger households to be poorer than others can depend crucially on untestable assumptions made in welfare measurement. In developed countries, even poor people consume commodities with economies of scale in consumption; two can

---

[17] This assumes that the parameters of the empirical demand model satisfy the theoretical conditions of utility maximization [see, for example, Deaton and Muellbauer (1980)]. The utility function is derived from the estimated demand model either as an explicit functional form [as in, for example, Rosen (1978), King (1983), Jorgenson and Slesnick (1984)] or by more flexible numerical methods [Vartia (1983)].

[18] The latter are often very important to poor people's welfare, yet they are typically not valued in budget surveys. Access to common property resources appears to have been declining in India [Jodha (1986)]; hence market-based valuations of consumption tend to underestimate the level, but over-estimate the rate of growth, in poor people's living standards.

live less than twice as expensively as one [Lazear and Michael (1980), Nelson (1988)]. In LDCs, such commodities pay little part in the budgets of the poor – their consumption bundle is dominated by goods such as food and clothing for which few scale economies exist. For this reason, the developing country literature on poverty has tended to use a "flat" equivalence scale; the most common practice is simply to divide household consumption or income by household size. As a first-order approximation this is defensible, though it almost certainly understates the extent of the scale economies in consumption even for the poor [Lanjouw and Ravallion (1994)]. However, that is not the only consideration. Welfare measurement may also be influenced by the purpose for which a measure is used. For example, recognizing the likelihood, but unobservability, of larger intra-household inequalities in larger households, a policy-maker may want to put higher weight on household size than implied by scale economies in consumption alone. The welfare concept matters here; Lanjouw and Ravallion (1994) show that a utility-based measure (under standard identifying assumptions) implies a very different equivalence scale to a capability-based approach in which child stunting is the welfare indicator, and the latter is more likely to deem large households to be poorer.

In view of the difficulties in choosing an indicator, one should know how much the choice matters. A strand of recent research has compared how different indicators at the individual or household level identify different individuals as poor [Anand and Harris (1991), Glewwe and van der Gaag (1990), Haddad and Kanbur (1990), Lanjouw and Stern (1991)]. For example, surveys of individuals in a household can indicate whether an indicator of "household poverty", derived from the more common one-shot household survey, correctly identifies poor individuals. Panel surveys can similarly indicate to what extent a one-shot survey reveals chronic poverty [Chaudhuri and Ravallion (1994)]. The tools of dominance testing also allow analysts to assess the robustness of poverty orderings (Section 3.3.3).

## 3.2. Poverty lines

There exist consumptions of various goods below which survival is threatened. It is not clear what these levels are for any individual. Furthermore, in most societies – including some of the poorest – the notion of what constitutes "poverty" goes beyond the attainment of the absolute minimum needed for survival. Hence views differ on the location of poverty lines.[19]

However, for many policy purposes, what matters most is not the precise

---

[19] The following draws in part on Ravallion (1993a), which elaborates on these issues. Other surveys (though more from a developed country perspective) include Hagenaars and de Vos (1988), and Hagenaars and van Praag (1985).

location of some poverty line, but rather the poverty comparison that is implied across dates, sub-groups, or policies. A concern here is that the comparison should be consistent; two individuals deemed to enjoy the same standard of living should not be deemed to be at different levels of poverty. If they are then measurement may seriously misinform policy. How do existing methods perform?

The most common approach in defining a poverty line is to estimate the cost of a bundle of goods deemed to assure that basic consumption needs are met [Rowntree (1901), Atkinson (1975, Chapter 10)]. The difficulty is in identifying what constitutes "basic needs". For developing countries, the most important component of a basic needs poverty line is generally the food expenditure necessary to attain some recommended food energy intake. This is then augmented by a modest allowance for non-food.

The first problem is setting food energy requirements. There is little direct evidence on energy requirements.[20] The most widely used "official" estimates [FAO/WHO/UNU (1985)], give energy requirements relative to alternative levels of activity and body weight. Activity levels are, however, endogenous socio-economic variables rather than exogenous physiological ones, and are jointly chosen (under constraints) together with income and diet [Osmani (1987), Anand and Harris (1992), Payne and Lipton (1993), Bhargava (1994)]. A normative judgement must be made about desirable activity levels, and these then determine energy requirements beyond those needed to maintain the human body's metabolic rate at rest.

The second problem arises in measuring the cost of the normative nutritional requirement, and in making an allowance for non-food consumption. A popular method is to find the consumption expenditure at which a person is expected to attain the food energy requirement [Dandekar and Rath (1971), Reutlinger and Selowsky (1976), Osmani (1982, Chapter 6), Greer and Thorbecke (1986), Paul (1991), Anand and Harris (1992)]. This can be readily estimated from a graph or (parametric or non-parametric) regression.[21] Price data are not needed, and the method automatically includes an allowance for non-food consumption. However, while fine for a single national poverty line, this method can yield inconsistent poverty comparisons across sub-groups or over time since people with the same command over basic consumption needs will not in general be treated the same way. The problem is that the

---

[20] After forty years and endless sterile controversy, the Dunn team's work on pregnant and lactating women [Nestlé (1987–1990)], and a few good papers on specific work tasks under laboratory conditions, comprise almost all the LDC exceptions.

[21] Some versions of this method of setting poverty lines regress intake against income and invert the function, while others regress income on intake. These will not give the same answer, though the difference is not relevant to our present discussion.

relationship between food energy intake and consumption or income is not going to be the same across sub-groups or dates, but will shift according to differences in affluence, tastes, activity levels, relative prices, and publicly provided goods. And there is nothing to guarantee that these differences are ones which would be considered relevant to poverty comparisons. For example, poverty lines constructed by this method will tend to be higher in richer regions, where households choose to buy more expensive calories (such as by consuming "luxury" foods). The differences can be large enough to cause a rank reversal in measured poverty levels across sectors or regions of an economy.[22] This can be worrying when there is mobility across groups in the poverty profile, such as migration from rural to urban areas. In an inconsistent poverty profile it is possible for aggregate measured poverty to increase (decrease) even though no person is worse (better) off in terms of real consumption.

There are other methods. These aim to directly measure the local cost of a normative food and non-food consumption bundle. The food bundle can be anchored to the nutritional requirement, consistent with tastes of the poor, and data on food prices used for valuation. However, setting the non-food component is more difficult. When (as is common) non-food prices are unavailable, a defensible choice for the non-food component of the poverty line is the expected non-food spending of those who are capable of reaching the food component [Ravallion (1993a), Ravallion and Bidani (1994)]. Clearly normative judgements are still needed, but their consistency is less problematic for this method.

Recognizing that a certain amount of arbitrariness is unavoidable in defining any poverty line in practice, one should be careful about how the choices made affect the poverty comparisons, for these are generally what matter most to the policy implications. Given the uncertainties in setting poverty lines, the danger of focusing on a single line is evident. Certainly a lower poverty line should also be considered; Lipton (1983b, 1989) argues for focusing on the "ultra-poor", identified as that sub-set of the poor who are at serious nutritional risk.[23] The robustness of poverty comparisons over a (potentially wide) range of poverty lines is discussed further in the next Section.

---

[22] For example, Ravallion and Bidani (1994) show that rank reversals in Indonesia's regional poverty profile are quite common when comparing different methods of setting poverty lines, even when starting from the same specification of food energy needs. Also see Ravallion and Sen (1994a) on urban-rural poverty comparisons for Bangladesh.

[23] This may be revealed by "thresholds" in behavior, such as at income levels where the income-elasticity of the age- and sex-specific participation rate is not significantly different from zero, where the food-share does not fall as income rises, or where the income elasticity of demand for food is unity.

*3.3. Poverty measures*

Suppose now that a measure of individual well-being has been chosen, and estimated for each person in a sample, and that the poverty line is known. How do we aggregate this information into a measure of poverty for each of the distributions being compared?

*3.3.1. Alternative measures*

There a number of good surveys of the literature on poverty measurement [Foster (1984), Atkinson (1987)]. Here we focus on the main issues with bearing on policy analysis.

Let $y$ denote the living standard indicator, which has density function $f(y)$, and a cumulative distribution function (CDF) $F(y) = \int_0^y f(x)\,dx$. The poverty line is denoted $z$.[24] All values of $y$ and $z$ are associated with a measure of poverty $p(y, z)$, and this function is non-increasing in $y$ and non-decreasing in $z$. An important class of measures have the property that $p(y, z)$ is homogeneous of degree zero in $y$ and $z$, i.e. they are "invariant to scale" [Blackorby and Donaldson (1980)]. Various ways of aggregating the $p(y, z)$'s have been proposed in the literature.[25] Following Atkinson (1987) we consider the class of additive poverty measures; the value of aggregate poverty is then given by:

$$P(z) = \int_0^z p(y, z)f(y)\,dy \tag{1}$$

Additive measures satisfy sub-group consistency, as defined by Foster and Shorrocks (1991). This requires that when poverty increases in any sub-group of the population (such as rural areas) without a decrease in poverty elsewhere, then aggregate poverty must also increase. Sub-group inconsistent measures may mislead policy analysis; a well-targeted poverty reduction scheme, in which poverty is reduced in a target region, say, may not then show up in a reduction in national poverty.[26]

The widely used *head-count index* (H) is simply the proportion of the

---

[24] If $y$ has not been normalized for differences in the cost of living then one will need multiple poverty lines; but the results are the same and the exposition is simpler if we assume that the normalization has already been done at the individual level.

[25] One issue we do not discuss here is the relationship between such aggregations and other "social welfare functions" which put positive weight on the entire distribution; [see Ravallion (1994a)].

[26] Sen (1976, 1981) offers an otherwise attractive measure of the severity of poverty which is not, however, sub-group consistent; this is also true of the measures that have been proposed as generalizations of Sen's measure [Thon (1979), Anand (1983), and Kakwani (1980b)].

population for whom consumption (or another suitable measure of living standard) $y$ is less than the poverty line; this is simply $F(z)$, obtained by setting $p(y, z) = 1$ in equation (1). H is easily understood and communicated, but for some purposes (including analyses of the impacts on the poor of specific policies) it has the serious drawback that it is totally insensitive to differences in the depth of poverty.

The *poverty gap index* (PG) is obtained by setting $p(y, z) = 1 - y/z$ (the proportionate poverty gap). This reflects the depth of poverty, in that it depends on the distances of the poor below the poverty line as well as the number of poor. PG indicates the potential for eliminating poverty by targeting transfers to the poor (whether that potential can be realized or not will be taken up in Section 6).[27] The widely used *income gap ratio* is $I = 1 - \mu^p/z = $ PG/H, where $\mu^p$ is the mean $y$ of the poor; this measures the average proportionate shortfall below the poverty line. However, it can be a deceptive measure. If a poor person with a standard of living above $\mu^p$ escapes poverty then the income gap ratio will *rise*, yet no-one is worse off, and one of the poor is actually better off. PG is a better measure.

A drawback of PG and I is that they neglect inequality among the poor; they may not capture differences in the *severity* of poverty. For example, consider two distributions of consumption for four persons; the A distribution is $(1, 2, 3, 4)$ and the B is $(2, 2, 2, 4)$. For a poverty line $z = 3$, A and B have the same value of PG $= .25$ $(=[(3-1)/3 + (3-2)/3]/4$ for A). However, the poorest person in A has only half the consumption of the poorest in B. The poverty gap will be unaffected by a transfer from a poor person to someone who is less poor [Sen (1976) (1981a)]. This will require that the poverty measure is not only decreasing in $y$, but is strictly convex from below (PG is only weakly convex). The squared poverty gap (SPG) index of Foster–Greer–Thorbecke (FGT) (1984) has $p(y, z) = (1 - y/z)^2$ which is strictly convex. In the above example of A and B distributions, SPG is $[(2/3)^2 + (1/3)^2]/4 = 0.14$ for A and 0.08 for B, indicating the greater severity of poverty in A. The general class of FGT measures $P_\alpha$ is obtained when $p(y, z) = (1 - y/z)^\alpha (\alpha \geq 0)$. Other convex measures include that of Watts (1968), $p(y, z) = \log(z/y)$, and Clark et al. (1981), $p(y, z) = (1 - (y/z)^\beta)/\beta$ $(\beta \leq 1)$.

Poverty measures are normally calculated from samples, and so they have sampling distributions. Like any sample estimate of a population proportion, H has the standard error $\sqrt{[H.(1 - H)/n]}$ in a simple random sample of size $n$. Kakwani (1993) has derived the standard errors of other common poverty measures; for example, the standard error of the $P_\alpha$ measure is $\sqrt{[(P_{2\alpha} - P_\alpha^2)/n]}$.

---

[27] In particular, PG can be interpreted as ratio of the minimum cost of eliminating poverty with perfect targeting to the maximum cost with no targeting [Ravallion (1993a)].

Thus one can test whether (for example) a measured increase in poverty is statistically significant.[28]

A long-standing poorly resolved issue is whether there is a jump in well-being as one crosses the poverty line. The answer determines the effects of risk on expected poverty [Ravallion (1988)], and the properties of optimal poverty reduction policies [Bourguignon and Fields (1990), Ravallion (1991b)]. For SPG (and others in the FGT class for $\alpha > 1$), the individual poverty measure vanishes smoothly at the poverty line, $p(z, z) = p_y(z, z) = 0$. This does not hold for all distribution-sensitive measures [exceptions are the Watts (1968) and Sen (1976) indices]. Should poverty measures embody such kinks? There clearly are consumption thresholds below which health and survival are threatened. However, the poverty lines found in practice are typically well above such thresholds (Section 3.2). Also, the uncertainty about the location of thresholds, and their inter-personal variability, can make it hazardous for some purposes to rely on poverty measures which are not smooth at the poverty line.

### 3.3.2. Decompositions

"*Poverty profiles*" are decompositions of an aggregate poverty measure, showing how the measure varies across sub-groups of society, such as region of residence or sector of employment. A consistent poverty profile can be useful in assessing how the pattern of economic change is likely to affect aggregate poverty. For example, suppose that a transfer in equal amount to all residents of region A is financed by a lump-sum tax on each resident of B, and that their populations are constant. If the poverty profile shows that there is higher poverty incidence in region A than B, then such a transfer will reduce the aggregate poverty gap index; more generally, the relevant poverty indicator is $P_{\alpha-1}$ for allocating additively absorbed transfers (whereby each income, within a given sub-group, changes by the same amount) to minimize the aggregate value of the FGT measure $P_\alpha$ [Kanbur (1987a)]. To see why, consider regions A and B with population shares $n_i$ $(i = A, B)$ each resident of which receives a transfer $x_i$ $(i = A, B)$, and $n_A x_A + n_B x_B$ is fixed. The aggregate value of $P_\alpha$ is given by

$$P_\alpha = n_A P_{\alpha A} + n_B P_{\alpha B} \tag{2}$$

---

[28] The Kakwani formulae for this test assume independent random samples; for longitudinal data, or for comparing actual and simulated poverty measures in a single sample, one must also factor in the covariance of the two distributions. Cluster effects due to sample design should also be incorporated.

where

$$P_{\alpha i} = \int_0^{z-x_i} (1 - (y + x_i)/z)^{\alpha} f_i(y)\, dy \tag{3}$$

for $i$ = A, B. Consider the marginal impact of an increase in $x_A$ (at the expense of B). On differentiating equation (2) one finds that (for $\alpha \geq 1$):

$$dP_{\alpha} = [P_{\alpha-1B} - P_{\alpha-1A}]\alpha n_A\, dx_A/z \tag{4}$$

Poverty will fall if (and only if) region A has the higher value of the $\alpha - 1$ poverty index. Taking this argument further, it is also instructive to characterize the poverty minimizing allocation of a given budget across sub-groups. For example, consider again the additively absorbed transfer between two groups which minimizes the aggregate value of SPG. With unrestricted powers of redistribution between groups, SPG will be minimized when PG is equalized across groups.[29]

Similarly, the poverty indicator for allocating multiplicative transfers (whereby all incomes increase by the same proportion) is $(P_{\alpha-1} - P_{\alpha})/\mu$ where $\mu$ is the subgroup mean [Kanbur (1987a)].[30] Since multiplicatively absorbed transfers leave the Lorenz curve unchanged, this result also implies that the elasticity of $P_{\alpha}$ with respect to the mean holding the Lorenz curve constant is $\alpha(1 - P_{\alpha-1}/P_{\alpha})$ for $\alpha \geq 1$ [Kakwani (1994)]. In the case of the head-count index ($\alpha = 0$), that elasticity is (minus one times) the elasticity of the cumulative distribution function of living standards when evaluated at the poverty line.

More elaborate specifications of the constraints facing policy-makers can be included [see, for example, Thorbecke and Berrian (1992) and Thorbecke and Jung (1994) on general equilibrium effects]. But even without building in all real-world constraints, a partial analysis under simple budgetary and informational constraints can often provide a revealing indication of the upper bound to realizable benefits from targeting under more realistic conditions (Section 6.2).

Changes in poverty measures can also be decomposed. It is of interest to ask: how much of a change in poverty is due to changes in *distribution*, as distinct from *growth* in average living standards? The usual inequality mea-

---

[29] Ravallion and Chao (1989) show how the optimal allocation can be calculated.

[30] This is readily proved by differentiating through (1) w.r.t. $z$ and using the fact that for the FGT measures $p(y,z)$ is homogeneous of degree zero in $z$ and $y$.

sures, such as the Gini index, can be misleading in this context. One cannot conclude that a change in any measure of inequality will change, in the same direction, any measure of poverty (e.g., H *rises* if people just above the poverty line lose income to the poorest). Even when it does, the change in the inequality measure can be a poor guide to the quantitative impact on poverty. A simple decomposition is possible which allows one to quantify the relative importance of growth versus redistribution to the measured change in poverty [Ravallion and Huppi (1991), Datt and Ravallion (1992)]. When analyzing the sources of reductions in poverty, it can also be useful to decompose a change in aggregate poverty into changes *within* sectors versus changes *between* them, such as due to inter-sectoral population or work-force shifts [Ravallion and Huppi (1991)].

### 3.3.3. Assessing robustness

We have seen that there is pervasive uncertainty in poverty measurement. There are likely to be errors in our living-standards data, unknown differences in needs between households at similar consumption levels, uncertainty and arbitrariness about both the poverty line and precise poverty measure. Given these problems, how robust are our poverty comparisons? Would they alter if we made alternative assumptions? A recent strand of research in poverty analysis has shown how we can answer such questions, drawing on and developing results from the theory of stochastic dominance.[31]

Suppose we do not know the poverty line $z$, but we can be sure that it does not exceed $z^{max}$. Nor do we know the precise poverty measure. Then it can be shown that poverty cannot have risen between two dates if the CDF for the latter date lies nowhere above that for the former date, up to $z^{max}$ [Atkinson (1987)]. And poverty must have fallen if the new $F(z)$ is everywhere below the old one. This holds no matter what the poverty line or precise poverty measure. If the CDFs cross each other (and they may intersect more than once), then the ranking is ambiguous. Then we know that some poverty lines and some poverty measures will rank the distributions differently to others. We need more information. One can restrict the range of poverty lines, or one can impose more structure on the poverty measure. For example, if one restricts attention to weakly convex measures such as PG and SPG (but excluding H)

---

[31] We shall give an elementary exposition of the approach. For a fuller introduction see Ravallion (1993a). On the use of dominance conditions in ranking distributions in terms of measures of inequality see Atkinson (1970); on rankings in terms of poverty see Atkinson (1987), Foster and Shorrocks (1988), and Howes (1993). Our exposition will be confined to single dimensions of welfare, though the approach can be generalized to multiple dimensions (though, naturally, unambiguous poverty orderings become more illusive); on the multi-dimensional approach see Atkinson and Bourguignon (1982, 1987).

then poverty cannot have risen if the area under the new CDF is nowhere greater than that under the old one.[32] If this test is inconclusive, one can further restrict the range of measures [Atkinson (1987, 1989) and Foster and Shorrocks (1988)]. Such tests can also allow robust poverty comparisons in the presence of certain sorts of measurement errors in the welfare indicator. Suppose that there is a random measurement error in the indicator, and that the error distribution is the same for the two (or more) situations being compared. Then non-intersecting CDFs imply an unambiguous poverty ranking in terms of the true (but unknown) distribution of welfare [Ravallion (1994c)]. Methods also exist for making at least partial rankings when there are multiple dimensions of welfare but the precise welfare function is unknown [Atkinson and Bourguignon (1982, 1987)].

## 4. Dimensions and characteristics

This section will try to provide a "snapshot" of poverty in the developing world from recent available data. We will begin with a broad regional overview, and move on to a summary of what we know about the characteristics of the poor.

### 4.1. A global "snapshot"

International comparisons of poverty statistics are plagued with both conceptual and practical problems. It is not clear what meaning can be attached to comparisons across countries in which the real value of the poverty line varies. But then whose poverty line should be used? Poverty lines appropriate to the poorest countries, such as India, have been a popular choice in past work [Ahluwalia et al. (1979), Kakwani (1980a), World Bank (1980a, 1990), Ravallion et al. (1991)]. There are also comparability problems across the underlying household surveys (Deaton in this volume), though survey methodologies have both improved and become more standardized over the last decade or so. An equally worrying problem is converting currencies, for which official exchange rates can be a poor guide in making poverty comparisons across countries. The International Comparisons Project of the U.N. has helped here, by facilitating the construction of Purchasing Power Parity (PPP) exchange rates [Kravis et al. (1982), Summers and Heston (1988) (1991)].

---

[32] This can also be tested (equivalently) using the generalized Lorenz curve, obtained by scaling up the ordinary Lorenz curve by the mean. If the generalized Lorenz curve (ordinary Lorenz curve scaled up by the mean) of distribution A is everywhere above that of B then the area under A's cumulative frequency distribution must be everywhere lower than B's. On the generalized Lorenz curve see Shorrocks (1983).

Though these are not ideal for international poverty comparisons (not being anchored to poor people's consumptions), they appear to be the best available method for setting internationally comparable poverty lines, and have been used for this purpose by Ahluwalia et al. (1979), Kakwani (1980a), World Bank (1990), Ravallion et al. (1991) and Chen et al. (1994).

Recent estimates following this methodology indicate that about one-fifth of the population of the developing world in the mid-1980s had a real consumption level less than India's poverty line of about $23 per month in 1985 US prices (adjusted for cost-of-living differences between countries).[33] At a more generous poverty line of $31 per month – one dollar per day – the head-count index of poverty increases to about one in three. There are no strictly comparable earlier estimates, but the proportion of people poor has probably fallen since the mid-1970s, while the absolute number of poor has probably increased.[34] However, these aggregates hide great regional diversity; for example, while the proportion who are consumption-poor has declined in much of Asia it has probably increased in sub-Saharan Africa and Latin America during the 1980s [World Bank (1990, 1992b), Chen et al. (1994)].

Though the incidence of poverty by Indian standards is large, the aggregate poverty gap in the developing world is actually quite small. The aggregate poverty gap of the poorest fifth of the population of the developing world is about one percent of total consumption by the developing world in 1985; for the poorest third, the corresponding figure is about three percent [Ravallion et al. (1991)]. This suggests that only modest aid to LDCs would be needed to eliminate poverty, though this assumes perfect targeting without disincentive effects; that would be very difficult in real life (Section 6.2).

Properties of the static consumption distribution in the developing world can help us understand how poverty is affected by growth and redistribution. First, the aggregate CDF of persons by consumption per person is quite elastic to changes in the poverty line or mean, reflecting a high density of observations around commonly assumed poverty lines. This suggests that poverty will fall quite rapidly with distributionally neutral growth in mean consumption; around typical poverty lines for low-income countries, the elasticity of the head-count

---

[33] See World Bank (1990) and Ravallion et al. (1991); the latter paper describes the assumptions and data used. The estimate is based on distributions of persons ranked by household consumption or income per person, as derived from household surveys for the mid-1980s covering 76 percent of the population of developing countries, and on econometric extrapolations based on national accounts and social indicators for the remainder. Currency conversions use the Summers and Heston (1988) exchange rates adjusted for differences in purchasing power.

[34] See World Bank (1990, Chapter 3). Using comparable estimation methods, an earlier study at the World Bank estimated that 38 percent of the population of 36 low income countries in 1975 did not reach the consumption per capita of the 46th percentile of the Indian distribution [Ahluwalia et al. (1979)]. This implies a poverty line close to the lower one used by World Bank (1990) and Ravallion et al. (1991). Note that the earlier study did not include China.

index with respect to the mean consumption is about two, holding constant all relative inequalities. At the average rate of population growth in the developing countries, the total number of poor will decline as long as future growth and distributional shifts are equivalent to a distributionally neutral growth rate in mean consumption of about one percent per year [Ravallion et al. (1991)]. The steepness of the CDF also implies that aggregate estimates of the number of poor will be sensitive to the choice of the poverty line.

Second, aggregate prospects for poverty alleviation through growth are sensitive to changes in relative inequalities. Suppose that the Lorenz curve shifts by a constant proportion of the difference between each income group's actual share of total consumption and equal-shares allocation.[35] One then finds that poverty would respond very elastically to shifts in the Gini index of inequality among all persons in the developing world; for the $23 poverty line, PG for the developing world would respond to the Gini index with an elasticity of over 13 [Ravallion et al. (1991)]. Thus, while poverty in the developing world would fall fairly rapidly with distributionally neutral growth, it would take only small deviations from neutrality to wipe out those gains. Consider a one percent rate of increase in mean consumption from 1985 until 2000. It would take only a 0.25 percent per year increase in the aggregate Gini index to eliminate the total effect of such growth on the poverty gap index of the developing world.

As for trends over time, the World Bank (1990, Table 3.2) compares H, roughly from the mid-1960s to the mid-1980s, using a constant real poverty line over time, in each of 11 developing countries (none of them in SSA). In every case the incidence of poverty fell, and numbers of poor fell in most cases. Chen et al. (1994) compare poverty measures for 18 countries with survey data for two dates in the 1980s. Their methodology is consistent across time, and the poverty line is fixed (in terms of purchasing power parity) across time and countries. The estimates used available household consumption data sets from nationally representative surveys. The results show negligible change in the aggregate poverty measures between 1985 and 1990.

Poverty measures have fallen in the 1980s in both South and East Asia, but have risen in sub-Saharan Africa (SSA), Middle East and North Africa (MENA), and in Latin America and the Caribbean (LAC), though the extent of worsening varies by poverty measure and poverty line, and there have been improvements in some countries [Chen et al. (1994)]. SSA is now roughly level with SA in the percentage of persons living on less than $1 per day, but (during the late 1980s) SSA appears to have overtaken SA as the region with the

---

[35] This is an analytically convenient assumption [Kakwani (1990a)], but it also accords well with the observed pattern of shifts over time in the world Lorenz curves [Ravallion et al. (1991)]. Kakwani (1990a) gives formulae for the elasticities of various poverty measures w.r.t. the Gini index under this assumption about how the Lorenz curve shifts.

greatest depth and severity of poverty, as measured by PG and SPG.[36] Only in East Asia is there good evidence of falling poverty, and progress has been impressive.


## 4.2. Demographic characteristics of the poor

Much of our current empirical knowledge about specific characteristics of the poor is in the form of bivariate correlations; we know far less about the joint interrelationships with other characteristics of poverty, and attempts to infer causality are clouded in problems of simultaneity.[37] While we shall try to cast some light on these issues, better data and testing are needed.

### 4.2.1. Poverty and family size

Larger household size is associated with greater incidence of poverty, as measured by household consumption or income per person [Birdsall (1979, p. 132), Meesook (1979), Musgrove (1980), Visaria (1980, pp. 47–49), Lipton (1983a), House (1989), World Bank (1991b,d), Lanjouw and Ravallion (1994)]. However, few studies have tested the sensitivity of this relationship to measurement assumptions – notably the properties of the equivalence scale used in comparing households of different size and demographic composition (Section 3.1). One test finds that the conclusion that large households tend to be poorer is not particularly robust to changes in measurement assumptions [Lanjouw and Ravallion (1994)].

Children appear more likely to be poor than adults [Birdsall (1980, p. 39), Musgrove (1980), Lipton (1983a)]. This need not be because households underfeed children [Schofield (1979)]; child/adult ratios are larger in poor households. Child stunting in Pakistan is more likely in larger households [Lanjouw and Ravallion (1994)]. Also, heavy female burdens and child poverty often go hand in hand.

Households with low consumption or income per person are thus typically larger and younger, and their members – particularly the youngest – are less likely to live as long as others. Most mortality differences between rich and poor in LDCs arise in the first five years of life. In Asia and Africa, infant and child mortality increase steeply with poverty [Lipton (1983a, pp. 15–18)].

---

[36] Thus low poverty lines indicate higher poverty in SSA, while at sufficiently higher lines the ranking reverses [see Chen et al. (1993)].

[37] While the methodology of bivariate poverty profiles remains popular, there are alternatives, based on multi-variate models of the distribution of the poverty indicator which allow straight-forward dominance tests; see Ravallion (1992).

Often, poverty is linked to high child death-rates partly because it proxies the impact of low maternal education [Hull and Hull (1977, pp. 8,15), Caldwell (1979), Hill (1981, p. 35), Ruzicka (1984, Table 9), Roth and Kurup (1989)];[38] of inadequate housing or water supply [ibid., Mitra (1978, p. 210)]; of farm labor or insecure tenancy [ibid., p. 21; Natrajan, n.d., p. 12]; or above all of rural residence [ibid., p. 7; Hill (1981, p. 35), Mitra (1978, p. 223), Ruzicka (1984, Tables 5–6), Irfan (1989)]. However, poverty is causally related to this whole group of other correlates of high mortality [Flegg (1982)]. So the fact that poverty "proxies" the other correlates need not devalue its bivariate link to mortality.

Mortality is clearly a non-linear function of income. Under certain restrictions on the properties of the distribution of personal constitutions and the household production function for health one can derive a relationship between survival chance and consumption which is concave above some point [Ravallion (1987, Chapter 2)]. At high levels of income, nutrition and health care, further reductions in already low death rates are not easily attainable, nor strongly linked to further income gains. There is supportive evidence for a concave relationship between survival chances and incomes. In cross-country comparisons, Preston (1975) finds that the income-slope of mortality is greater at the low end of the income range, though low income may be proxying for other variables such as low education, poor health services etc. [Heston (1992), Anand and Ravallion (1993)]. Farah and Preston (1982) for the urban Sudan, and Irfan (1989) for Pakistan, show a strong link of poverty to mortality rates for the poorest few deciles. Clear discontinuities are shown in death-rates between the landless and others; for Bihar, India [Rodgers et al. (1989)] and Pakistan [Irfan (1989)]; and between those of low status and others [Mukhopadhyay (1989) for caste in West Bengal in 1983–1984].

If desired family size is to be maintained then clearly child deaths will have to be replaced. There is some evidence that child deaths stimulate *excess* replacement births, especially in rural areas [Schultz (1981b, pp. 137–140)]. This appears to be due partly to lifetime earnings patterns due to lower education, especially female [Birdsall (1980, p. 52)]. Over-replacement is probably correlated with poverty, and with the associated "felt need" to insure against high risk of further infant and child death. In Guatemala [Pebley et al. (1979)], desired family size was positively correlated with previous child deaths, holding several other variables – but not poverty – constant. However, if the effect of poor people's higher mortality is actually to increase their household size, then the fertility response must involve enough over-replace-

---

[38] These data may overstate the impact of maternal education, because they do not control for ability, family background, etc. [Behrman (1990)].

ment to outweigh the positive effect of sibling crowding on death risks. This is a substantial effect for the poor; in India the mortality of infants born within one year of a previous birth was twice as high as that of children born two or more years after a birth [Bennett (1991, p. 9.62); and cf. Ghosh (1987)].

Many data sets reveal an inverted-U relationship between poverty and overall fertility [Birdsall (1974, pp. 5–7), (1980, pp. 53–56), Hull and Hull (1976, p. 9), Schultz (1981b, p. 177)]. As income and its correlates (farming status, housing type, education, etc.) increase from zero to a very low level, perhaps near the "ultra-poverty line", total fertility rate (TFR) and its components (especially age-specific fertility) initially also increase slightly: extra income from very low levels is associated, via better nutrition, with earlier menarche [Huffman et al. (1987), Bhalla and Srivastava (1976)] and more generally with higher fecund-ability [Frisch (1978, 1980, 1982), Easterlin and Crimmins (1985)]; the ultra-poor are somewhat more exposed to marital disruption and interruption than the moderately poor [Hull and Hull (1976)]; and rising child wage-rates accompany increased fertility [Schultz (1981b, pp. 50–51)]. Fertility decreases as the level of living rises above ultra-poverty: women's time becomes valuable, and it becomes increasingly feasible to delay family income by educating one or two children, instead of using income from the wage labor of several [Becker and Lewis (1974), World Bank (1984), Birdsall (1988)]. The entire inverse-U relationship has been demonstrated for Pakistan in 1979 [Irfan (1989)]; for urban Juba, Sudan, in the mid-1980s [House (1989)]; and (to the extent that husband's education proxies income) for rural Bangladesh in 1968–1970 [Stoeckel and Chowdhury (1980)] and Indonesia in the early 1970s [Hull and Hull (1977)]. This is an asymmetric inverted-U. Fertility indicators rise initially, reach a peak – though still at a low standard of living – then fall steadily to far below their initial level as income continues to rise. Thus fertility differences do explain part of the size-poverty link.

Given the circumstances and risks in developing countries, one should not be surprised that poor couples often choose earlier marriage, and higher marital fertility, than rich couples [Cassen (1978), Schultz (1981b)]. First, to achieve a given completed family size, the poor require more births, due to higher child mortality. Second, the poor are likelier to need support from children in old age than are the rich, yet those children will face lower income, higher time-rates of unemployment (Section 4.3.1), and fewer incentives to remit in order to inherit. Third, the poor face worse prospects of education (which would allow them to substitute quality for quantity), and especially of female education (which raises the opportunity-cost of motherhood). Fourth, capital and environmental inputs are scarce (particularly for the poor) and so children are often needed as supplementary labor [Dasgupta (1993)].

## 4.2.2. Gender and poverty

Is there widespread "feminization of poverty"? In some parts of Asia and elsewhere, young females are often exposed to excess poverty-induced nutritional and health risk within households,[39] and this appears to be one factor explaining the "missing millions" of women [Drèze and Sen (1989)]. However, females are not generally over-represented in consumption-poor households; nor are female-headed households more likely to be poor as a rule. Evidence against widespread feminization of income or consumption poverty appears in Visaria (1977, 1980) for Asia; Drèze (1990) on India; H. Standing (1985) on Calcutta; Svedberg (1991) for Africa; Haddad (1991) and Lloyd and Brandon (1991) on Ghana; Louat et al. (1993) for Jamaica; and earlier sources cited in Lipton (1983a: 48–53). Lack of data on intra-household distribution limits such studies; but, even if it were true that consumption-poverty incidence is on average no greater amongst women, they are severe victims of poverty in other respects.

First, women work longer than men to achieve the same level of living. The burden of both parts of the "double day" – market labor and domestic labor – is more severe for poor women. Except among the very poor, female age-specific participation rates increase sharply as income falls; yet so do the ratios of children to adult women [Visaria (1977, 1980), Lipton (1983a: 43–45)]. There is evidence that, as women participate more in market work under pressure of poverty, their domestic labor is not substantially reassigned to men [K. Bardhan (1985), G. Standing (1985)].[40]

Second, women face lower chances of independent escape from poverty, in part because women's large share of domestic commitments prevents them from seizing new and profitable work opportunities as readily as men [Haddad (1991) for Ghana, Birdsall and Behrman (1991) for urban Brazil]. Many LDC job markets appear contain "progressive" (poverty-escaping, and usually male) and "static" (poverty-confirming and often female) segments.[41] Even more important than the domestic burden, in explaining this poverty trap, may be cultural discrimination against females in both education and job assignments.

---

[39] This has been found for some subsets of girls under 5 in North India [Levinson (1974), Bardhan (1982), Dasgupta (1987)] and in Bangladesh [Chen et al. (1981), Muhuvi and Preston (1991)].

[40] In Peru, the excess female burden was even more severe for *single-earner* households, where female heads even had to work 39 percent more "market" hours than male heads; even in multiple-earner households, market plus domestic work occupied female heads for 18 hours per week more than male heads [Rosenhouse 1989].

[41] See H. Standing (1985), Anker and Hein (1985), on silk-weaving work in South India; von Braun, Puetz and Webb (1989) on irrigated rice-farming in the Gambia; Telles (1993) on urban labor markets in Brazil.

In Taiwan, in some ways a model of "growth with equity", a 1978–1980 survey showed that 25 percent of sons, but only 4 percent of daughters, had been apprenticed; and that, in the poorest 80 percent of families, as the number of sisters rose from 0 to 4, the mean schooling per brother rose from 6.8 to 11.4 years, indicating that girls are sacrificing prospects of independent escape from poverty to pay for brothers' prospects via education [Greenhalgh (1985)]. In Ghana, much lower female literacy and numeracy after age 15 greatly reduce female access to good jobs [Haddad (1991)]. In Bangladesh, non-formal and technical/vocational training – far from correcting the big gender disparities in schooling – generally makes *no* provision for female enrolment [Safilios-Rothschild (1991)]. In rural India in 1981, the gender gap in adult literacy was higher among the far poorer scheduled castes (22 percent–6 percent) and scheduled tribes (28 percent–8 percent), than among the population as a whole (40 percent–18 percent) [Bennett (1991)].

Third, in some cultures widows face effective barriers against employment or remarriage, and are treated as second-class citizens within the home, leading to high risks of poverty. One of the few systematic studies [Drèze (1990b)] shows that nuclear, widow-headed households in India are by far the poorest (even average expenditure per person is 70 percent below the overall average). The younger the oldest male in such households, the deeper their poverty. Age-specific mortality for rural North Indian widows is also higher than for otherwise comparable wives [Chen and Drèze (1992)].

Thus an important way in which poverty is feminized is that male-dominated societies make the escape from poverty harder for women. This suggests that poverty is more likely to be chronic for women, and transient for men; individual, panel data are needed to test this, though such data are rare.

### 4.2.3. Poverty and old age

Poverty is juvenizing and may be feminizing; is it greying? The over-65s comprised 3.8 percent of South Asians in 1980, but are projected at 4.8 percent in 2000 and 8.2 percent in 2025; in other developing regions the expansion is as rapid, except in Africa where even by 2025 the proportion is projected at only 3.9 percent [Deaton and Paxson (1991, p. 2)]. In Côte d'Ivoire, average income within rural and urban areas is no lower for the elderly, but they are worse off on a national basis because of rural concentration. In Thailand, older Thais do not have lower average income [ibid., pp. 22–27]. That does not tell us whether proportions in poverty are higher for the old. This was not so in Nigeria and India in the 1970s [Gaiha and Kazmi (1982, p. 56), P. Hill (1982, pp. 187–188)]. Given their greater dependence on the variable and uncertain support of others, we hypothesize that inequality among the old is greater than among those of prime age. If so, similar average levels of living in these two groups would probably mean higher poverty among the elderly. With the ageing of LDC populations, these issues merit further research.

## 4.3. Labor and poverty

### 4.3.1. Participation and employment

Poor households depend heavily on labor income. Its quantum depends on their age-structure; their age- and sex-specific participation rates (ASPRs); prospects of employment (or self-employment) when they participate; and their wage-rates (or net daily rewards on own account) when employed.

The age-structure of poor households implies high dependency ratios [Visaria (1977), Lipton (1983 a,b)]. Even if reflecting privately optimal couple fertility decisions, this can be a horrendous drag on their overall participation in work. The drag appears to increase with early development and associated urbanization. The rich-poor gap in the dependency ratio is greater in cities than in villages, and in more than in less developed countries and regions [Lipton (1983a)].

It is to be expected that the poor will seek high ASPRs. First, assuming leisure is a normal good, poor people will work more, ceteris paribus. Second, with fewer assets (and often lower wage rates) the poor will have to work longer to reach any given income. Third, poor people's high dependency ratios increase the marginal utility of income-per-worker relative to leisure [Chayanov (1966)].

Among men aged 14–60, ASPRs – except in the agricultural slack season – are seldom much below 95 percent for any income group [Visaria (1980, pp. 76–77); Lipton (1983a, pp. 7,16)]. Therefore, if the poor are to raise ASPRs significantly, it must be mainly among the under-14s, the over-60s, or women. All we can say with confidence about child ASPRs is that they are understated by large official surveys; child labor is much more prevalent among the poor [Lipton (1983a, pp. 17–18)]. Many studies [Lipton (1983a, pp. 16–17)] confirm that women's ASPRs increase, but only modestly, with falling household income per person. However, the poorest 5–15 percent of households typically show female ASPRs no more than the moderately poor. Also, female ASPRs decline, given mean income, with rising household ratios of under-fives to women and older children [Dasgupta (1977, p. 153)].[42] Urbanization appears to cut female ASPRs, even for the poor [Lipton (1983a, pp. 23–25), Visaria (1981, p. 13), World Bank (1989)].

---

[42] Since child/adult ratios rise sharply with falling living standards, this partly explains why the increase of female ASPRs fades out among the ultra-poor.

Unemployment – as a usual status – rises with income [Udall and Sinclair (1982)]. However, the time-rate of unemployment (TRU) – the proportion of time in workforce spent in job search – is generally higher among workers from poor households, often sharply so among the poorest. The linkage operates via casual labor and is thus stronger for the assetless and landless, than for those who can fall back on asset-based self-employment [Sundaram and Tendulkar (1988)]. Also, unemployment is concentrated among the assetless and in areas, age-groups, etc. likely to over-represent the poor [Lipton (1983a, pp. 42–54)].[43] One explanation for this can be found in the general equilibrium theory of unemployment under the efficiency wage hypothesis [Dasgupta and Ray (1986), Dasgupta (1993)]. This explains higher unemployment amongst those with fewest assets as the competitive equilibrium of a labor market in which the cost of labor per efficiency hour is high for those with few assets, who are thus priced out of the market.[44] There is another explanation. Quasi-cooperative behavior amongst workers (arising from repeated interaction in a village labor market) can support a wage rate above market clearing levels without formal trade unions or binding minimum wages [Drèze and Mukherjee (1989), Osmani (1991)]. The employment available at that wage will then be rationed through hiring decisions which (presumably) favor those who are more productive; many of the poor will be unable to compete.

### 4.4.2. Wages

Given the heavy dependence of the poor on unskilled labor, one would expect the real wage rate for such labor to be an important determinant of poverty. The evidence on the co-movement of rural poverty incidence and real agricultural wage rates is mixed; poverty has often fallen without rising real wage rates for unskilled labor.[45] However, the lesson from these experiences is not that poverty incidence is unaffected by the real wage rate for unskilled labor, ceteris paribus, but rather that other variables can also matter to the outcome for the poor. Skilling, sectoral shifts,[46] increased cereal yields even on handkerchief-sized farms, rising employment, and remittance incomes, have

---

[43] For theories and evidence on unemployment in LDCs see Rosenzweig's (1988) survey.

[44] For a critical discussion of this theory see Lipton (1994).

[45] Though rural poverty clearly fell in Indonesia, Egypt, and Kenya in 1950–1975 or so, real farm wage-rates showed no clear uptrend [Lipton (1983a: 86–87)]. Real wage rates showed little gain – and by some accounts fell – during the 1980s in Java, while poverty measures fell markedly [Ravallion and Huppi (1991), World Bank (1991b)].

[46] Schooling is associated with higher productivity even for farm laborers [Chaudhri (1979), Jamison and Lau (1982), Otsuka et al. (1992)], and can help people to escape from low real wage-rates in unskilled agriculture by shifting or diversifying sector, or place, of work. In Malaysia, Thailand and Korea, this process eventually "turned round" the rising trend of farm labor supply; female education also helps this process in the long run by inducing lower fertility.

been important in explaining falling rural poverty in most poor Asian countries. And it is critical whether or not a real wage rate increase comes at the cost of higher unemployment; it cannot be presumed that an exogenously imposed wage increase will be pro-poor. Certainly Kerala's persistent (and genuine) 25 percent unemployment rate – thrice the Indian rural average – alongside a uniquely enforced statutory minimum farm wage, does not suggest that the latter is very helpful.[47] Only for India are there adequate time-series data to test the strength of the empirical link between real agricultural wage rate and rural poverty incidence controlling for at least some of these other determinants; on doing so there is evidence that higher real wages have resulted in lower poverty measures [van de Walle (1985), Ravallion and Datt (1994b)]. Household cross-sectional data for West Bengal suggest the same conclusion [Bardhan (1984, Chapter 14]. For India, the unskilled labor market is an important channel through which economic growth and contraction impacts on the poor [Ravallion and Datt (1994b)].

There is controversy about wage-discrimination, and the issues are far from settled. Task-specific earnings differentials between genders, castes or ethnic groups reflect (at least in part) differences in productivity (due to education and experience) or in work period [Lipton (1983a, pp. 69–72, 83–84), Ashenfelter and Oaxaca (1991), Birdsall and Sabot (1991)]. However, such earnings differentials testify to inferior access to better-paid skills and productive tasks; such access may well be depressed by prior forms of discrimination. This is harmful, not least because, where it most reduces women's earning opportunities, there appears to be greater neglect of (and death-rates among) little girls [Rosenzweig and Schultz (1982)]. Though *wage* discrimination has been observed in a few careful studies [Bardhan and Rudra (1981), Lluch and Mazumdar (1981)], *access* discrimination may well be more serious.

### 4.4. Nutrition and poverty

### 4.4.1. The income elasticity of nutrient intakes

The link between poverty and nutrition has been looked at mainly in terms of dietary food energy deficiency, relative to requirements. Energy deficiency can be measured directly, by recording energy intakes relative to supposed requirements (Section 3.2), or via its anthropometric correlates: upper arm circumference, and body mass index (BMI: $kg/m^2$) in adults, and height-for-age (or, as an acute indicator, weight-for-age) in children. Except where roots

---

[47] For a stark example of how the poor can lose from statutory minimum wage rates imposed on public employment see Ravallion, Datt and Chaudhuri, (1993).

and tubers are main staples, protein deficiency is rare in the absence of energy deficiency. However, micronutrient deficiencies are widespread, often occur without energy deficiency, and may or may not be closely linked to poverty.[48]

The poverty-nutrition link is conditioned by other variables (behavioral and/or biological), and involves simultaneity. From household resources, the link runs to expenditures (conditional on prices and tastes); thence to calories; to intra-family distribution; and to the level, variability, and adaptability of the adequacy of individual intake for normal "requirements" of resting metabolic rate (RMR), work, growth, etc. This last linkage is mediated by health-affected capacity to ingest, absorb, and use energy.[49] Even given all this, energy absorbed (given requirements, health, etc.) is related in highly variable ways to health-nutrition outcomes such as survival, physical and mental performance, and wellness. Each link can be modelled as "health-seeking behavior" [Alderman (1993)]. Furthermore, some of these linkages are likely to have feedback effects; nutritional outcomes may affect (in turn) productivity and hence household resources [Strauss (1986), Deolalikar (1988), Behrman (1993)].

While the income elasticity of food expenditure in poor populations is often close to unity [Bhanoji Rao (1981), Lipton (1983c), Edirisinghe and Poleman (1983), Pitt (1983)], several papers report low income- or expenditure-elasticities of calorie intake (CIEs) or of anthropometry [for a survey see Bouis and Haddad (1992)]. The ICRISAT nutrition observations for South Indian villages, used by Behrman and Deolalikar (1987), Bhargava (1991) and others, cannot be properly matched with the times of the consumption and income observations. That is not true of other studies, such as Behrman and Wolfe (1984) on Nicaragua, and Bouis and Haddad's (1992) Philippines data (which suggest a CIE of 0.05), and the Ivorian data of Thomas et al. (1992, p. 27) showing that most child anthropometry did not respond to extra income (though adult BMI, and urban child height, did).

To believe that very poor, hungry and underfed people raise *caloric adequacy* – as distinct from *energy intakes* – by only 1 percent or so when income rises 10–20 percent does seem contrary to common sense. There is evidence for several possibilities, not mutually exclusive:

- Food energy intakes were not inadequate at the mean (where the elasticity is typically measured) to begin with, so that income rises could be devoted to food quality improvement, as Behrman, Bouis and others emphasize. Mean adult weights in most tropical rural places – and hence approximate

---

[48] In a sample of Philippine farm households, Bouis (1991) finds that the incidence of certain micronutrient deficiencies (iron, calcium, thiamin) tends to be greatest amongst the poor.

[49] See Schiff and Valdès (1990); on Ivorian evidence, such capacity depends on *local* endowments of quite precisely specifiable health inputs [Thomas et al. (1992, p. 32)].

energy requirements – typically lie 15–30 percent below reference weights used in estimating energy requirements [Lipton (1983c, pp. 14–20), (1989, p. 12)].

- There are strong non-linearities in the calorie-income function [Ravallion (1990c), Holleman (1991), Garcia (1991, p. 118), Thomas (1990)]. For example, in Java the CIE rises from 0.15 at the mean to 0.33 at half a standard deviation below the mean [Ravallion (1990c)]. Also, income gains may have more impact on nutritional *adequacy* – as measured by the proportion of undernourished say – than on calorie intake per se, because the poor are clustered around a critical threshold of caloric adequacy [Ravallion (1990c)]. Food energy adequacy may thus be much more elastic to income than is energy quantum. For Java in the early 1980s, a low CIE (0.15 at the mean) still implied an income elasticity of the incidence of undernutrition – relative to caloric requirements – close to unity [Ravallion (1990c)]. To the extent that income rises are achieved in a way that reduces (increases) food energy requirements this will boost (diminish) the income effect on undernutrition [Lipton (1989, p. 11)].
- In unhealthy environments, using extra income solely for extra calories may do little for health status. A health-seeking person should then spend extra income on health improvements (sanitation or even leisure) rather than nutrition. Similarly, low levels of public inputs, complementary with incomes in their impact on such outcomes [Taylor et al. (1978), Thomas et al. (1992, p. 25), Anand and Ravallion (1993), Bidani and Ravallion (1994)] may entail that extra income is wasted on nutrition.
- The value of the CIE is contingent. Female-headed households show a higher CIE than equally poor male-headed ones [Garcia (1991) for the Philippines], perhaps due to smaller household size [Greer and Thorbecke (1986) for Kenya]. The effect appears to be stronger in poor households, in Kenya and Malawi, where extra incomes going to household members (men) with lower marginal propensities to purchase food implied a lower response of food energy intake [Kennedy and Peters (1992)].

### 4.4.2. Adaptation

A low CIE may indicate effective – though seldom costless – adaptation. In some environments, poverty is associated with smaller stature, harder work, and therefore worse health; in other environments, moderately small persons select work requiring body translation (rather than heavy lifting), in which they have a comparative advantage over people who are taller or with higher BMI. Some doubtful use has been made of an excellent Norwegian study by Waaler (1984), showing sharp rises in mortality if BMI falls below levels as high as 20–23; but this appears to be synergistic with smoking, and in any event, it need not apply in warm LDCs [Payne and Lipton (1993)]. In India, agricultural laborers with BMI as low as 16 appear healthy and hard-working [Shetty (1984)]. In a study of 199 men in Bangladesh, risk of illness rose sharply when BMI fell, but only below 17 [Pryer (1990)].

The discussion of adaptation to dietary energy stress has emphasized two biological paths: child growth reduction and adult downward adaptation of RMR/kg. The latter is considerable in semi-starvation [Keys et al. (1950)], but in response to milder stress may reduce RMR/kg by only 2–5 percent. Most important, such biological adaptation (i) happens only if victims choose to maintain "voluntary" (work or leisure) energy expenditure when intake falls, or intake when expenditure rises, yet do not fully compensate by weight loss; (ii) is an unknown quantity for children, the most seriously affected by a given proportionate energy shortfall; (iii) is much smaller than interpersonal variation in RMR/kg; given income, persons with lower RMR/kg select lower calorie intakes per day.[50]

More important is the question of child growth faltering, and of possible consequent higher mortality or lower mental or physical performance. For extreme states – the anthropometries of the 5–7 percent of LDC populations classified as severely undernourished – there is no disagreement: these people are at substantial risk of increased infant and child mortality, and of physical (and perhaps mental) impairment in adulthood.[51] What about the effects of "mild to moderate" anthropometric shortfalls?

Pelletier (1991) claims that a continuous positive relationship exists between sub-standard anthropometry and child mortality. However, his graphs show a greatly weakened or absent relationship once weight-for-age is at or above 65–70 percent of the US (NCHS) median, height-for-age 85–90 percent, or mid-upper arm circumference 105–115 mm [ibid., pp. 12–14]. A large bulk of evidence, and some supporting (immunological) theory, now shows clear turning-points, well below NCHS medians, above which few or no health impacts for stunting can be demonstrated. Further, we can find no evidence for claims [ibid., p. xii] that 25–50 percent of "child deaths are statistically attributable to anthropometric deficits" and that "33–80 percent of these deaths are associated with mild-to-moderate PEM". In any event, most non-genetic "anthropometric shortfalls", and much PEM, are due to infection, and may not be readily, if at all, prevented by pumping in calories (let alone income), rather than, say, by sanitation, clean water, and good primary health care [Payne and Lipton (1993), Lipton (1983c)].

---

[50] See Payne and Lipton (1993); for more enthusiasm about RMR adaptation, see Sukhatme (1981); for less, see Dasgupta and Ray (1990).

[51] Despite the controversies about calorie-income elasticities we have not seen, and would not readily believe, data showing high incidences of severe undernutrition well *above* an ultra-poverty line.

In adults, much the most important adaptations of poor people to energy stress are weight loss and work adjustment. This ranges from rescheduling arduous tasks towards periods of greater food availability, to improving ergonomic efficiency at the cost of discomfort or inconvenience. Bhargava (1994) finds that reduced energy intakes force poor Rwandese households to spend more time resting and sleeping. Little has been done to study, to assist via price and technology policy, or to lower the costs of, these and other behavioral or biological adaptations. The intellectually fascinating but quantitatively unimportant issue of intra-personal RMR adaptation, and the important but oversimplified issue of child growth faltering, have blinded students of poverty to the many, but currently constrained, adaptations to food energy shortage by poor people, and their communities and institutions.

*4.5. Income variability*

Income variability has been a concern of many direct interventions against poverty (Section 6.3). Clearly poorer people face higher disutility, and higher risks to infant life, from a fall in consumption. Policy has often assumed that intertemporal consumption smoothing possibilities are limited, or costly, for the poor. Various informal credit and insurance arrangements are common, though it is more contentious how well they perform.[52] Even if surrogates for state-contingent commodity markets exist, they may exclude some of the poor and/or involve high cost to longer-term poverty reduction (e.g. if savings are shifted from productive investment to grain storage). Then programs to reduce poverty may be more cost-effective if they steer some resources into reducing income downturns (Section 6.3).

There is evidence of adverse nutritional and other impacts of agricultural fluctuations on the rural poor.[53] Evidence from several countries indicates that poor households discriminate against vulnerable members in seasons of energy stress than at other times [Sahn (1989, p. 6)]. Worse still, bad outcomes go together. The second half of the wet season frequently brings heavier work, dearer food, and more infections [Schofield (1974, 1979)]. Times and places of low employment, wage-rates and participation, tend to overlap strongly, especially for the poorest [Lipton (1983, pp. 33–37, 56–60, 84–85)]. Also, the

---

[52] See Schofield (1974), Bardhan and Rudra (1981), Platteau (1988), Ravallion and Dearden (1989), Rosenzweig and Stark (1989), Walker and Ryan (1990), Townsend (1993), Ravallion and Chaudhuri (1992), Fafchamps (1992), Coate and Ravallion (1993), Saha (1993), and Besley's chapter in this volume.

[53] See, for example, Anderson and Hazell (1989), Chambers et al. (1981), Sahn, (1989), Ravallion (1987, 1988), World Bank (1990, Chapter 2), Walker and Ryan (1990), and Morduch (1990, 1991).

rural poor are more dependent on casual labor (which is much likelier to be laid off when the harvest is bad). Hence many of the rural poor are likelier to lose income, in bad seasons or years, than the rural non-poor, and they appear less well protected from any given income shortfall.

Of the peak-to-trough quarterly fluctuations in ASPRs in India in 1977–1978, changes among workers whose main activity is "casual labor" – a group that overlaps strongly with the poor – accounted for almost 70 percent for rural men, and about 100 percent for rural women. Where the time rate of unemployment is high on average, further seasonal rises produce "discouraged worker effects", so that periods with a higher TRU also feature a lower ASPR, especially among women. Nigerian and Indian village data confirm that seasonal variability in gainful worktime is greatest for the poorest [Lipton 1983a, pp. 34–36]. Moreover, the Javanese village in which the poorest workers were most driven to raise the proportion of workforce participation spent in job search [Hart (1980)] may well typify places where casual labor is a major source of income for the poor. In villages of West Bengal where uncertainty is greatest, employers provide a search-free work fallback for poor locals in slack times, thereby ensuring fealty during peaks [Bardhan and Rudra (1981)]; this transfers instability (and search costs) to poor non-locals.

Domestic tasks and cattle care expand in slack seasons [Hopper (1955)]. Yet unirrigated rural places with little non-farm employment continue to suffer great fluctuations in labor use. Hired labor shows much greater seasonal – and, more seriously because less predictably, annual – variability in employment [Lipton (1983a, pp. 54–59)]. Since rural poverty is associated with casual labor and low access to non-farm employment [e.g. Singh (1990)], the impact of agricultural fluctuations on not very mobile poor people appears large. Poor urban populations are also characterized by surprisingly high dependence on (unstable) *agricultural* work [Visaria (1977, Table 34) for Maharashtra, India].

Unemployment and ASPRs tend to fluctuate inversely, and so the harmful effects on labor income are covariant. This is serious because the variability of both employment and ASPRs increases with poverty, as does dependence on labor income, lack of reserves, and non-creditworthiness. Matters would improve if falls in ASPRs in slack seasons, or bad years, were large enough (compared with falls in demand for employees) to bid *up* wage-rates, given elasticities and plasticities of labor supply and demand. Unfortunately, evidence [Bardhan (1984), Ravallion (1987, Chapter 5)] confirms common sense: in bad times many poor people must work for whatever they can get, so that (because ASPRs fall proportionately far less than demand for labor) wage-rates fall too, possibly associated with a break-down in the wage setting arrangements on the supply side in village labor markets. Since this often happens when food is dearest and disease is most rampant [Chambers et al. (1981)], we can see the importance to the poor of safety nets in bad times.

## 4.6. *Sectoral and locational characteristics*

LDC settlement patterns usually concentrate the large majority of people into clearly rural or urban places. Around 1980 "intermediate" localities – with 5,000–20,000 persons – comprised only small proportions of population in most LDCs.[54] The contrast is usually sharp. Typically the rural places (<5,000) are sparsely settled, and employment is mainly agricultural; the towns (>20,000) are densely settled, and employment is 85–95 percent non-agricultural.[55]

Poverty comparisons between urban and rural areas pose a number of problems. This is partly because "urban" can mean different things.[56] National "poverty lines" also vary greatly, though this is less worrying for comparisons of rural-to-urban poverty incidence ratios (RUPIRs) than of absolute levels. Cost-of-living adjustments pose a more worrying problem, as spatial cost-of-living indices are far less common than inter-temporal indices, such as the CPI. Urban poverty lines are sometimes set at a higher real level than rural poverty lines, thus clouding inferences (Section 3.2).

Data based on consumption or income per person, allowing for rural-urban price differences, from thirteen LDCs for the 1980s, suggest the following RUPIRs:[57] Kenya 6.0; Côte d'Ivoire 4.6; Ghana 2.2; Indonesia 3.7; Malaysia 2.5; Thailand 1.7; Philippines 1.4; Panama, Peru, Venezuela, each 1.4; Guatemala, Mexico, each 1.3; India 1.1 [World Bank (1990: 31)].[58] Similar differences were found in the (fewer) studies that estimate higher-order poverty measures (such as PG and SPG); see Bidani and Ravallion (1993) for Indonesia, Boateng et al. (1991) for Ghana, Datt (1994) for India, World Bank (1992) for China. Even in a country such as India with a RUPIR near unity, the vast majority of the poor still live in rural areas.[59]

[54] 4.7 percent in Cameroon, 7.1 percent in Peru, 0.3 percent in Bangladesh, 3.0 percent in India, 4.8 percent in Sri Lanka and 2.2 percent in Thailand. They were slightly more significant in Turkey (9.7 percent), Syria (14.7 percent) and Paraguay (16.0 percent). Only in two of the ten countries with substantial populations and available data (Ecuador, Nepal) did over 30 percent of people live in "intermediate" settlements. See UN (1983, pp. 896–907) and (1988, pp. 711–718).

[55] Exceptions do exist. In parts of Kerala (India) and SW Sri Lanka, rural areas are not much less densely settled than are small towns.

[56] Official definitions of "urban" (as opposed to "rural") do not refer to comparable (or sometimes to any) population sizes of settlements. In Africa, five of the available (1980s) national data sets give no definition; ten give political definitions (e.g. "municipalities"); for five, the main criterion is ">5000"; for one, ">3000"; and for three, ">2000". In Asia, the respective numbers are 4 (including China), 15, 2 (including India), zero and 1. In South America, they are 1, 6, 0, 0 and 2, plus one country each using ">2500" and ">100 dwellings". In Asia a further two countries use ">10,000", and one each ">9000" and (Japan) ">50,000". See UN (1988, pp. 205–206).

[57] For example, an RUPIR of 3 means that a randomly selected person living in rural areas is three times more likely to be poor than one living in urban areas.

[58] Different methods of adjusting for cost-of-living differences can yield different results. For example, the India figure is 1.3 using the Minhas et al. (1991) deflators.

[59] Datt finds signs of convergence in poverty incidence around 1990, though 72 percent of the poor still live in rural areas.

Do RUPIRs understate or overstate the rural-urban differences in poverty? They allow only for price-deflated private income per person. The capacity of poor people to convert such income into well-being is probably lower in rural areas than in towns, due to worse rural public services, notably health care and sanitation. While the physical quality of life index (PQLI) has its limitations (Section 2), it is telling that India's urban PQLI in 1971 was 61, as against a rural PQLI of 35 [Morris and McAlpin (1982, p. 62)]. Infant mortality in rural India in the 1980s was 105, as against 57 in urban areas [World Bank (1990, p. 31); for Africa, see A. Hill (1981, p. 35)].[60] This, together with comparable gaps in adult literacy rates, suggests that urban/rural ratios between poverty measures based only on private real consumption or income are considerably lower than the urban/rural ratios of other indicators of human development. The health gaps are in sharp contrast to the development process in nineteenth-century Britain, where urban death-rates substantially exceeded rural rates [Williamson (1991, p. 127)].

Rural poverty is marked by its common connection to agriculture and land, whereas urban poverty is more heterogeneous in how incomes are generated. A comparative study of seven Asian developing countries in the late 1980s showed that the rural poor depended more on agriculture than the rural non-poor [Quibria and Srinivasan (1991)]; this has also been observed in West Africa [P. Hill (1972); Reardon et al. (1992)]. It remains important that one-third of rural income, and one-quarter of employment, typically derive from non-farm activities [Chuta and Liedholm (1981)], but their prosperity depends substantially on forward and backward production linkages – and even more [Hazell and Haggblade (1993), Hazell and Ramasamy (1991)] on consumption linkages – from farmers. Especially in view of agriculture's high labor-intensity and relevance to local food availability and price, an anti-rural poverty strategy for production activities should be based substantially on agriculture.

No such even moderately homogeneous base for anti-poverty policy is usually available in towns, with their normally much more diverse pattern of activities and problems. It is possible to focus rural anti-poverty policy on improving the amount, productivity, stability, and distribution of farm inputs, employment, and output, and their social and physical infrastructures. This is why – despite the urban bias of public spending and personnel allocation in most LDCs – there is a much clearer and more production-oriented menu of anti-poverty policies for rural areas than for towns.[61]

The urban informal sector (UIS) has traditionally been perceived as a

---

[60] Large excess rural mortality exists in India for both sexes at all ages; for under-fives, the gap appears to have widened since 1961 [Mitra (1978, p. 223), Ruzicka (1984, Tables 5–6)]. Rural infant mortality typically exceeds urban [World Bank (1990, p. 31)].

[61] However, even the urban poor, especially female casual workers, depend significantly on agricultural and allied employment and income.

residual category, made up of those who have not obtained employment in the "formal" urban sector, and their fortunes are linked to those of both the rural sector and the urban formal sector through migration and remittances. In contrast to the urban formal sector, the stylized view of the UIS is of a sub-sector with easy entry, little unionization, no legal minimum wages, weak safety standards at work, low physical capital inputs, low returns to labor, and mainly small (often family-based) enterprise units, typically producing non-traded goods, disproportionately consumed by the poor. However, views of the UIS have changed somewhat in the light of new data. There is greater recognition of its diversity, associated with the heterogeneity of products, and the wide range of skills. Large income inequalities are often found within the UIS, with some UIS workers earning far more than some formal sector workers [Telles (1993)]. In explaining poverty in the UIS, current thinking puts greater emphasis on individual characteristics such as human capital endowments than on the "structural" features of the economy arising out of a Todaro (1969) migration equilibrium with a fixed urban sector wage. Poverty in the rural sector tends to be explained more by low access to physical assets (particularly land), farm technology, non-farm employment opportunities, and health care and schooling, than by labor-market distortions as in the urban sector.

Since the early 1970s, the UIS has increasingly been viewed as a sub-sector with substantial growth potential in its own right, rather than as a temporary holding area for the "reserve army" – though that potential is often seen as greatly hampered by market failures (particularly credit), and excessive governmental regulations and biases in favor of the formal sector, such as in the availability of credit. An early and influential exposition of this view was ILO (1972), expanded upon in (inter alia) ILO (1985) and de Soto (1989). This has also led to some optimistic assessments of the prospects for reducing urban poverty by the deliberate promotion of the UIS, e.g. through credit subsidies and protection from competition; this has been an important element of industrial policy in India.

While there are likely gains to the poor (as both producers and consumers of the services of the UIS) from removing existing policy biases against the UIS,[62] the anti-poverty case for a pro-UIS bias in policy is more contentious. Despite the stereotype, small-scale urban manufacturing enterprises may not be significantly more labor-intensive or technically efficient than larger enterprises in LDCs [Little (1987), Little, Mazumdar and Page (1987)]. The structure of protection across industries is now thought to be a far more important determinant of aggregate labor demand [World Bank (1990, Chapter 4)].

The emphasis on housing in urban anti-poverty policy might suggest that

---

[62] Such as banning street vending, or low-cost transport from the streets, or favored treatment to large firms in access to institutional credit.

slum-dwelling provides a homogeneous environment, and hence an arena for cure, for most urban poverty risk – as agriculture does in the case of rural poverty risk. However, the ranking of fifteen Indian States by the proportion of urban people living in slums in 1981 is mildly negatively correlated with their correct ranking by incidence of urban poverty in 1983 [Minhas et al. (1991: 1676)].[63] Many of the urban poor are unaffected by slums, and many of the rural poor live in quasi-slums.

The rural-urban dichotomy has perhaps diverted some attention from even sharper regional disparities in poverty levels. In some countries, poverty incidence has been found to be lower in large cities than other urban areas [Bidani and Ravallion (1993) for Indonesia; Ravallion and van de Walle (1994) for Tunisia; Grootaert (1994) for Côte d'Ivoire]. Large disparities in rural poverty incidence have been documented for a number of countries; for example, in Indonesia in 1990 the RUPIR is estimated to be 2.2, while the ratio of the highest poverty incidence in rural areas of any province to the lowest is 4.3 [Bidani and Ravallion (1993)]. The regional variations in the incidence of rural poverty are often strongly associated with rainfall and dependence on rainfed agriculture [Bardhan (1984), Webb et al. (1991), Lipton (1992)]. Regional factor mobility has plainly not equalized poverty risk.

## 5. Growth, inequality and poverty

### 5.1. Growth and poverty reduction

The relationship between growth and poverty can be complex. Let us first make the simplifying assumption that all incomes grow at the same rate. How will poverty respond? Consider the properties of the class of poverty measures given by equation (1), which can also be written in the form:[64]

$$P = P(\mu/z, \pi)$$

where $P$ is the measure of poverty, $z$ is the poverty line, $\mu$ is the mean of the distribution of consumption or income, and $\pi$ is a vector of parameters fully

---

[63] Spearman's rank correlation coefficient is not significant even at 10 percent; but, of the five States (out of 15) with highest urban poverty incidence, three are among the half-dozen with the lowest proportions of urban population living in slums.

[64] In terms of equation (1) it is assumed that $p(y,x)$ is homogeneous of degree zero. Poverty measures with this property are "invariant to scale". In some of the literature, these are referred to as "relative poverty measures", as distinct from "absolute poverty measures", which are invariant to adding the same absolute amount to all incomes and the poverty line; see Blackorby and Donaldson (1980) and Foster and Shorrocks (1991). Almost all poverty measures currently used in practice are "relative poverty measures" in the above sense.

describing the Lorenz curve of that distribution. For every well-behaved poverty measure, the function $P$ is monotonic decreasing in $\mu/z$, holding $\pi$ constant. A growth path of the mean which maintains the same Lorenz curve implies an unambiguous reduction in absolute poverty.[65]

But how rapidly will poverty fall? Recent data indicate estimates of the elasticity of the poverty gap index (PG) w.r.t. the mean of $-2.7$ (Bangladesh and Nepal), $-3.0$ (India), $-4.1$ (Indonesia), $-2.0$ (Côte d'Ivoire), $-2.9$ (Morocco and Tunisia), and $-1.5$ (Brazil).[66] A 2 percent annual rate of growth in consumption per person at all consumption levels will result in a 3–8 percent rate of decline in PG. Other measures show similar elasticities, though estimates for H tend to be slightly lower in absolute value, while estimates for SPG tend to be higher – suggesting that the benefits of such growth are felt well below the poverty line.

The impact of changes in the Lorenz curve is less clear. Inequality can change without any absolute gains or losses to the poor. The ambiguity goes deeper for H (and other measures kinked at the poverty line, such as the Sen index). Inequality increases if there is an unambiguous outward shift in the Lorenz curve, i.e. the change in distribution satisfies the Pigou–Dalton criterion [Atkinson (1970, 1975)]. By the properties of the Lorenz curve, H is the value of $p$ at which the *slope* of the Lorenz curve equals $z/\mu$ [Gastwirth (1971), Kakwani (1980a)]. An outward shift in the Lorenz curve does not imply a lower slope at any given value of $p$, nor, therefore, a higher value of H for given $z/\mu$. However, for higher-order $P_\alpha$ measures ($\alpha > 1$) a clearer relationship between inequality and poverty emerges; unambiguous outward shifts in the Lorenz curve at a given mean must increase poverty.

Now relax the assumption that growth is distributionally neutral. During the 1970s and 1980s, it was widely believed that growth in low-income countries would be inequitable. A foundation for this view was provided by Kuznets (1955), and has come to be known as the "Inverted U Hypothesis". [Also see Adelman and Morris (1973), Robinson (1976), Ahluwalia (1976), Ahluwalia et al. (1979), and Adelman and Robinson (1988)]. This assumes that growth proceeds under a "Kuznets process". Specifically, the economy is conceived of as a low-mean, low-inequality rural sector and a high-mean, high-inequality urban sector, and the migration of workers from the former to the latter is

---

[65] This assumes that $z$ is constant, though this can be readily relaxed to the assumption that $z$ has an elasticity with respect to $\mu$ below unity; from the cross-sectional relationship between national poverty lines and mean income that assumption is plausible for developing countries [Ravallion et al. (1991)].

[66] The sources and dates for these estimates are as follows: Bangladesh (1991/1992): Ravallion and Sen (1994a); Nepal (1984/1985): calculations for this paper from World Bank data; India (1987/1988): Datt and Ravallion (1992) (up-dated); Indonesia (1987): Ravallion and Huppi (1991); Côte d'Ivoire (1985): Kakwani (1990); Brazil (1988): Datt and Ravallion (1992); Tunisia (1993): Ravallion and van de Walle (1994). All calculations are based on local poverty lines.

assumed to be "representative": a representative "slice" of the rural distribution is transformed into a representative slice of the urban distribution, preserving distributions within each sector.

What does such a process imply about the relationship between growth and inequality? Assume that everyone is initially in the rural sector. When the first sub-group of the rural sector moves into the urban sector under the Kuznets process inequality will appear that was not there before, namely that between a typical urban resident and a typical rural resident. Inequality will increase. Consider the last sub-group to leave the rural sector; the same inequality will now disappear. Extending this reasoning, an inverted U can be derived linking certain indices of inequality and the population share of the urban sector can be derived [Robinson (1976), Anand and Kanbur (1984, 1993), Kakwani (1988)].

What will happen to aggregate poverty? For all additive poverty measures, if poverty is initially higher in the rural sector then aggregate poverty must fall under the Kuznets process.[67] To see why, note that the aggregate cumulative distribution function is given by

$$F(z) = n_u F_u(z) + n_r F_r(z) \tag{6}$$

where $n_i$ $(i = u, r)$ and $F_i$ $(i = u, r)$ are the population shares and distribution functions for the urban and rural sectors respectively (where $n_u + n_r = 1$). Under the Kuznets process, the distribution functions $F_i$ are independent of the population shares. Thus

$$\partial F(z)/\partial n_u = F_u(z) - F_r(z) < 0 \tag{7}$$

for all $z$. Consider the sequence of CDFs resulting from successive increments in $n_u$. From (7), each CDF will lie entirely below the previous one; all poverty measures and poverty lines will show an unambiguous decline in poverty (Section 3.3.3).

However, the poverty levels of the two sectors do not converge (the vertical distance between distribution functions is also unaffected by urbanization; see equation 7); this follows from the assumption of representative migration. That assumption simplifies the analytics, but it is not appealing. Relaxing it can alter the conclusion that modern-sector enlargement is pro-poor. For example, Anand and Kanbur (1985) show that in Todaro's (1969) model (in which

---

[67] Anand and Kanbur (1985) prove this for FGT measures, though it readily generalizes to all other sub-group consistent poverty measures. Kakwani (1988) proves a similar result for generalized Lorenz curves (and, hence, all monotonic poverty measures), though it will also hold for the poverty incidence curves (Section 3.3). Anand and Kanbur (1993) contains the essential analytic results, though the implications for poverty are not drawn out.

migration is a response to the expected income differential between sectors), aggregate poverty could increase with migration to the urban sector.[68] This is because (under the Todaro model) some new migrants will fail to find formal work in the urban sector, and will end up worse off than they would have been in the rural sector (though this is still an equilibrium, since expected incomes are equalized). Depending on the parameter values, economic growth through urban sector enlargement may increase or decrease aggregate poverty.

The way one models the migration decision could matter greatly to the results. The Todaro model is quite restrictive. A broader set of motives is now seen to underlie migration behavior than expected wage differentials; individual migration is also increasingly seen as an outcome of family decision-making, particularly in response to uninsured risks [Stark (1991)]. Empirical work suggests that relatively advanced but unequal villages are more likely than others to produce two types of emigrants. The better off go to towns to seek education and known jobs; the relatively poor go first to other rural areas or small towns, and then chain-migrate towards uncertain urban work [Connell et al. (1976)]. This urbanization process may raise migrants' expected income but increase inequality. It is not clear what the impact on aggregate poverty will be of these more complex processes of migration.

Urbanization is not the only way growth can occur. Following Fields (1980) one can distinguish three sources of growth: "modern sector enlargement", "modern sector enrichment" and "rural sector enrichment". The latter is unambiguously pro-poor in these models (at least while the rural sector remains the poorer sector), while the effect on aggregate poverty of modern sector enrichment – rising mean income in the urban formal sector, without any change in rural sector incomes – is unlikely to be pro-poor; there will be no change in aggregate poverty under Fields's (1980) assumptions (in which there is no urban sector poverty), though under the weaker assumptions of the Anand-Kanbur model (in which there is a poor urban informal sector) there will be an unambiguous increase in aggregate poverty.

The outcome will also depend on (inter alia) consumer preferences and openness to trade. Eswaran and Kotwal (1993) offer a simple general equilibrium model in which hierarchical preferences (whereby the non-poor are sated with agricultural goods while the poor have zero propensity to consume industrial goods) in a closed economy entail that modern sector growth has no impact on poverty – the preferences and trade assumptions imply that real wages will not rise since labor is not attracted out of agriculture, and the poor do not benefit from the cheaper industrial goods. The poor will, however, gain from agricultural growth under these conditions. If instead the economy were

---

[68] Fields's (1980) opposite conclusion, that migration into the urban sector reduces aggregate poverty, is due to his assumption that no urbanite is poor.

opened to trade then export of the extra industrial output would allow the poor to benefit from enlargement of the modern sector.

Empirical investigations have explored these issues. Compilations of country-level data on inequality and growth did suggest an inverted U relationship [Paukert (1973), Ahluwalia (1976), Tsakloglou (1986)], though the robustness of these results has been questioned [Saith (1983); Anand and Kanbur (1993)]. A careful study that provided some statistical support for the inverted U [Lecaillon et al. (1983)] suggests that the impact on poverty is small, since the changes in distribution amongst the "poorest" 95 percent of persons were negligible. Other studies have not supported the view that inequality will increase in the early stages of development; from the (limited) time-series evidence, it appears to be just as likely to decrease [Saith (1983), Fields (1989), World Bank (1990, Chapter 3), Squire (1993), Ravallion (1993b)]. The current consensus is that several factors influence the effects of growth on inequality: the initial distribution of physical and human assets, preferences, the degree of openness to trade, and the effectiveness of governmental redistributive policies.

However, even when growth has been associated with rising inequality, it appears that poverty has typically fallen [Fields (1989), World Bank (1990, Chapter 3), Squire (1993)]. One recent study has looked at the experience of 16 countries for which distributional data were available for two points in time during the 1980s from nationally representative household surveys [Ravallion (1993b)]. Poverty measures were estimated using the same real poverty line at each date, with constant purchasing power exchange rates to assure that the poverty lines have similar real value across countries, and the estimation methods adjusted for some of the comparability problems, and allowed for measurement errors in the underlying household surveys.[69] About half of the variance in the rate of reduction in H was attributed to differences in the rate of growth in mean household consumption per capita, and the elasticity of H to the mean was −3.5 to −2.4, depending on the estimator used. However, there is likely to be considerable variation between countries, depending on initial conditions (both the mean, and inequality). For India – the only country where a reasonably long time series of poverty measures is available – the historical elasticity of H to mean consumption is about −1.5 [Ravallion and Datt (1994b)]. Also for India, Bell and Rich (1994) estimate that the rural H responds to real agricultural output per head with an elasticity of −1.5 to −0.8, depending model specification. A common finding of those studies which have

---

[69] An important concern is the possibility that measurement errors in the poverty measure will be correlated with those in the survey mean; if, for example, survey measurement error leads one to overestimate the rate of growth in the real mean then it will lead to an overestimation of the rate of reduction in poverty incidence. Ravallion (1993b) uses an instrumental variables estimator, with instruments derived from independent data sources, such as the National Accounts.

also looked at higher-order measures such as PG and SPG [Ravallion (1993b), Ravallion and Datt (1994b), Bell and Rich (1994)] is that these measures tend to have a higher (absolute) elasticities to growth, so the benefits of growth are typically felt well below the poverty line.

While one strand of the literature has concerned how growth affects inequality (as one of the links from growth to poverty), the reverse causation – from initial inequalities to growth – has also received attention. This link has arisen in a number of models, though a unified theory is not yet available. A classic argument assumes that the marginal propensity to save rises with income, and deduces that aggregate savings and growth will depend on the distribution of income, though this link appears to be weak [Gersovitz (1988)]. As a general proposition, however, with incomplete markets there will be efficiency implications of changes in distribution [Geanakoplos and Polemarchakis (1986), Hoff (1993)]. Various examples exist of how equalizing redistributions of wealth can increase aggregate output in a competitive economy, such as under the efficiency wage hypothesis [Dasgupta and Ray (1987), Dasgupta (1993)], or when inequality impedes prospects for efficient (cooperative) management of common property resources [Kanbur (1992)]. Capital-market imperfections influencing occupational choice can also entail that differences in initial inequalities alter growth paths [Banerjee and Newman (1993)]. Under certain restrictions on preferences, even the initial composition of demand (itself influenced by the initial distribution of assets) will also influence the type of growth observed [Murphy et al. (1989), Falkinger (1992)], again with the prediction that high initial inequality can impede the prospects for a pro-poor growth process. The cross-country evidence in Persson and Tabellini (1994) and Clarke (1993) suggests that high initial inequality lowers the future rate of growth, controlling for other factors.

## 5.2. The pattern of growth

Some observers have read the recent evidence that economic growth is rarely associated with sufficiently adverse changes in relative inequalities to prevent a decline in absolute poverty as suggesting that the role of government in reducing poverty can safely be confined to promoting growth. That does not follow. Even though past growth has often helped reduce poverty, some growth processes may do so more effectively than others. One role of government may be to foster a "pattern of growth" conducive to poverty alleviation.

The sectoral and regional pattern of investment – and hence of the resulting income gains – has often been identified as an important policy instrument. It is now widely believed that many LDCs could grow faster, as well as more equitably, by shifting investments towards rural, labor-intensive or "backward" activities. But such a shift need not indefinitely increase mean income *and* reduce poverty, because rates of return (as conventionally calculated) to investments across sectors or regions need not remain positively correlated with the relevant poverty indicators.

How much impact on aggregate poverty is possible by altering the sectoral pattern of economic growth? The answer depends in part on the performance of existing allocations of investment. If past policies have been biased against poor regions or sectors with high rates of return then suitable policy reforms may allow *both* higher impacts on current poverty, and higher rates of growth and, hence, poverty alleviation in the future. There is strong evidence that this is so in a number of developing countries, notably those which have followed excessively capital-intensive, pro-urban development strategies through a variety of pricing, external trade, and public expenditure policies [Lipton (1977), Krueger et al. (1988), World Bank (1990, 1991c)].

The key sector identified for pro-poor growth in most LDCs is the rural farming sector. Agricultural growth, especially growth and stabilization of food staples production, is likely to benefit poor people. First, many of the poor – including the rural poor – are net food buyers. Smooth and ample local food supplies, even in open economies, carry special advantages for them, especially if international or national transport costs of food staples are high. Second, while poor people's entitlements to food (rather than local availability per se) determine their nutritional levels [Sen (1981a)], their exchange entitlements depend – directly or indirectly – on earnings from growing food. For these and other reasons, some policy discussions have been optimistic about the potential for pro-poor growth through well designed pro-agricultural interventions, often citing the East Asian experience [Timmer (1992), World Bank (1993)].

The empirical debate on the effect of agricultural growth on rural poverty continues.[70] Counter-examples to the proposition that agricultural growth is necessarily pro-poor do exist.[71] These indicate that there are some important contingent factors that mediate between some forms of growth and poverty reduction [Prahladachar (1983) emphasizes appropriate rural institutions]. It is also unclear to what extent agro-technical progress and the nature of rural institutions can be viewed as exogenous in this relationship.[72] This has implications for the type of policies that are needed to promote agricultural

---

[70] On India alone see: Ahluwalia (1985), Saith (1981), van de Walle (1985), Mellor and Desai (1985), Dev et al. (1991), Gaiha (1989), Bell and Rich (1994), and Ravallion and Datt (1994b).

[71] A classic instance of immizerizing growth was the fate of smallholders in Chilalo, Ethiopia, following intensification in the early 1970s [Cohen (1975)].

[72] The new institutional economics emphasizes the choices made by farmers in adopting innovations, those choices being seen as dependent on (inter alia) evolving relative factor scarcities. On agro-technical progress from this perspective see Hayami and Ruttan (1985), Richards (1985), Ruttan and Binswanger (1978), and Binswanger and Rosenzweig (1986).

growth, though it need not dull the motivation for a pro-rural emphasis in anti-poverty strategies.

However, the balance of evidence is that, globally [Binswanger and von Braun (1993)] and in important specific cases such as India [Mellor and Desai (1985), van de Walle (1985), Bell and Rich (1994), Ravallion and Datt (1994b)], times and places of relatively high (growing) farm output have also featured relatively low (falling) rural poverty. High-yielding cereal varieties have benefited the poor, by restraining food prices, providing rural work, and raising incomes of small farms; but doubts remain about impacts on regions and countries unable to adopt HYVs, and on the stability of incomes and output [Lipton with Longhurst (1989)]. Tractorization and other labor-displacing sources of agricultural cost reduction, especially if subsidized, are likely to harm the poor, on balance. The impact of irrigation on poverty depends on the technical features of the type of system used [Narain and Roy (1980)].

In many LDCs the policy environment has been biased against the rural farm sector. Three sources of bias can be identified: i) the direct effect of sector-specific pricing policies, appearing as a wedge between domestic producer prices and border prices for agricultural outputs; ii) the direct effect of non-price, sector-specific, policies, such as public spending on roads, schools, services, and research; and iii) the indirect effect on the farm sector of economy-wide distortions operating through exchange rate and external trade policies. (Overvalued exchange rates hurt producers of tradeables – typically including many agricultural outputs – and policies to protect the manufacturing sector tend also to depress the relative price of farm outputs.) Krueger et al. (1988) look at price biases [(i) and (iii), though not (ii)] for 18 developing countries in the period 1975–1984 and find that the indirect effect is stronger than the direct price effect. It would be interesting to expand such an inquiry to include the direct non-price biases, particularly through public spending on physical and social infrastructure (Section 6.4.3).

Once the possibilities for eliminating these biases have been exploited, attempts to alter the pattern of growth in favor of the poor may come at a cost. Positive and even quite high elasticities of substitution between labor and capital have been found in LDC industries [Pack (1974); Behrman (1982)], so the growth cost of a labor-intensive bias in technology choice need not be large. It is less clear what costs would be incurred in attempting to shift resources across industries, sectors or regions. In the interests of the poor it is at least clear that the immediate aim is neutrality.

Cross-sectoral spill-over effects may strengthen the case for a pro-rural bias, with or without other distortions. Such spill-over effects can arise in a number of ways, including migration across regions and trade. In distorted economies, cross-sectoral linkages through migration and trade can readily create multiplier effects which enhance sector-specific policy impacts on the poor [Ravallion (1990b]. There is evidence that rural growth has helped reduce both rural *and* urban poverty in India [Ravallion and Datt (1994b)]. It has also been argued that agricultural growth can generate sizable positive spill-over effects on productivity in other sectors [Timmer (1992)].

## 5.3. Macroeconomic adjustment and poverty

For most LDCs, the 1980s saw macroeconomic instability, with rapidly rising servicing costs on foreign debt, external terms-of-trade shocks, and rising fiscal and external imbalances entailing an unsustainable excess of aggregate demand over supply.[73] An "adjustment program" is a set of policies to restore macroeconomic balance. The typical program combines fiscal contraction – cutting government spending and/or raising taxes – with supply-side measures aimed at reducing inefficiency (cutting, for example, trade distortions or wasteful parastatal organizations).

Unless there is a rapid supply-side response, somebody's consumption must fall. Lack of adjustment may thus be an attractive short-term option, though there must eventually be a (potentially hard) landing. The case for an adjustment program depends on showing that the present social value of the future sequence of consumptions is higher with adjustment than without. How will adjustment (relative to not adjusting) affect the poor? To what extent are those impacts contingent on the initial conditions of an economy and the details of policy reform?

### 5.3.1. Models

The main model underlying discussions of the effects of adjustment on real incomes identifies two categories of goods: *traded* and *non-traded*. Only for the latter do domestic demand and supply conditions affect price.[74] Adjustment will reduce domestic demand for both traded and non-traded goods. Producers of traded goods can sell to foreigners instead, but producers of non-traded goods will initially suffer unemployment and reduced incomes. To restore full

---

[73] Many developing countries are heavily dependent on a few primary commodities for both foreign exchange and as a source of revenue for public spending. The prices of these commodities proved to be highly volatile in the 1970s and 1980s. Increases in their prices often led to public spending sprees, which led to large budget deficits when primary commodity prices fell.

[74] For an exposition relevant to the present discussion see Edwards and van Wijnbergen (1989). For analyses of the distributional impacts of adjustment within this framework see Knight (1976), Addison and Demery (1985), and Kanbur (1987b). This type of model also underlies the analysis on this issue using computable GE models, such as in the recent OECD project [Bourguignon et al. (1991a)].

employment, the price of the non-traded goods must fall, relative to the traded goods – a real devaluation.

How will this affect the poor? Assume that the poor are net suppliers of labor, and fairly mobile across sectors. From what we know about the characteristics of the poor in most developing countries, these assumptions are believable though we comment on exceptions below. Then, from the Stolper–Samuelson theorem, the real wage in terms of non-traded goods will rise during the adjustment if (and only if) the traded goods sector is more labor-intensive than the non-traded goods sector. Policy discussions often assume this (on the grounds that LDCs' comparative advantage lies in labor-intensive products), and therefore predict that the poor will gain as employees from the relative price shifts associated with adjustment.

There are a number of caveats to that prediction:

- The employment effects of real devaluation are often more ambiguous, given that some non-tradeables in LDCs are relatively labor intensive, such as parts of the construction sector and informal sub-sectors of many other industries [Streeten (1987)].
- The speed of adjustment is also of concern. If domestic prices (both outputs and inputs) are flexible, and labor is mobile, then the process will be rapid. However, in reality, some prices adjust sluggishly and there are impediments to labor mobility; structural adjustment is very unlikely to remove all distortions. Some sectors of the economy, with flexible prices, will fare differently during adjustment to other sectors, where significant unemployment may persist. Then we must ask: are the poor concentrated in the sectors with relatively flexible prices? A common and plausible characterization of developing countries is that the rural sector tends to have flexible prices, while the modern sector has more rigid prices. Given that poverty tends to be concentrated more in the rural sector, this suggests that the positive impacts of adjustment via wages and employment may be felt quite quickly in the rural sector, as in a simulation for Morocco [Bourguignon et al. (1991b)].
- The welfare outcomes for the poor will depend on how adjustment affects consumer prices. If the poor do not consume traded goods, then the welfare outcome is clear: command over non-traded goods must rise. More generally, the direction of the change in welfare for a worker will depend on the magnitude of the real-wage response relative to the share of income devoted to traded goods. A key category of goods for the poor is food staples. The common presumption is that (except for most roots and tubers) these goods are tradeable. Then staple food prices rise during adjustment. Policy discussions often assume that the rural poor tend to be net producers of these goods. While this may be a reasonable assumption in

some settings [Dorosh and Shan (1993) for Africa], there is also survey evidence that the poor are quite heterogeneous with respect to their trading position in food markets. For example, while persons at the poverty line in Java, Indonesia, tend to be net suppliers of rice, the poorest tend to be net consumers, and there is also a great deal of variability in net trading position at any income level [Ravallion and van de Walle (1990)]. Some of the poor will gain and some will lose, and the assessment may then depend crucially on interpersonal comparisons of welfare amongst the poor (Section 3.3). Poor net-consumers of food staples in rural areas also rely heavily on agricultural labor markets, and can be expected to benefit from employment effects; provided that the wage response is large enough they will gain on balance. However, this process can be painfully slow; for Bangladesh, Ravallion (1990a) finds that the dynamics response of wages to rice price increases consistent with time series evidence is not fast enough to avoid sizable short-term welfare losses. Another complicating factor is that food staples sometimes behave more like non-traded goods in the short term, because government storage buffers domestic food prices from fluctuations in world prices, or because internal market integration is impeded by inadequate rural infrastructure [World Bank (1990, Chapter 7)]. Again, short- and long-term impacts may be in the opposite direction.

- The welfare impacts of adjustment will also depend on *how* public expenditures are cut. If the poor initially benefit little from public spending, then they can lose little from cuts. However, although often poorly targeted, public expenditures in many developing countries do benefit the poor. Unless adjustment is to be associated with a short-term increase in poverty, public expenditure cuts will have to spare such programs (Section 5.3.2 gives examples).

For all these reasons, we should be wary of simple theoretical arguments about the welfare impacts of adjustment. They can offer a useful guide to thinking, but evidence will typically be needed to resolve the issues. Fortunately, great strides have been made since the early 1980s in collecting relevant household level data. Also, adjustment lending to LDCs now commonly includes resources for collecting such data, and monitoring welfare impacts. Few of the issues can be resolved *solely* by such data; both theory and casual empiricism will remain essential. However, empirical work can help resolve some key ambiguities about impacts of policy reform on the poor.

Our understanding of welfare impacts of adjustment has been illuminated by combining direct observations, based largely on household level surveys, with models of alternative policy packages, typically in a general equilibrium model [e.g. Demery and Demery (1991), Thorbecke (1991), Bourguignon et al. (1991 a,b)]. Each mode of analysis has its strengths and weaknesses: household-level analysis tells us about actual impacts, and about key parameters; the aggregate models can allow richer simulations of alternative policies. However, to be tractable aggregate models invariably sacrifice realism; the assumptions need not be innocuous.[75] A class of "meso" level analyses has also emerged. These are less ambitious than the GE models, but can still isolate key links of policy to welfare [e.g. Kanbur (1987b), Azam et al. (1989), Demery et al. (1993)]. For example, one might ask what the distributional effects are of an increase in food staples prices allowing wage rates to adjust, but assuming that other prices are unchanged [Ravallion (1990a)]. Compared to a full-blown GE model, such an analysis loses detail in the channels transmitting policy changes to households, but it can often be tailored more closely to time series evidence on the way prices move with each other and on detailed household level parameters estimated from cross-sectional surveys.

### 5.3.2. Evidence

It is often difficult to isolate the role played by adjustment or lack of it. Poverty may have risen during an adjustment period; but it may have risen even further without adjustment. Some household-level evidence on the evolution of poverty indicators during adjustment is now available.[76] One of the few clear patterns is that the poverty measures tend to move with the mean consumption or income of households, increasing in recession and falling in recovery [World Bank (1990), Demery and Demery (1991), Morley (1992a,b), Ravallion and Datt (1994), Ravallion (1993b), Grootaert (1994)]. Given that a large share of the impact of adjustment on the poor appears to be mediated through its impact on economic growth, a key question is: did adjustment raise or lower the rate of growth? The answer depends on the speed of supply-side response. That depends on initial conditions in the economy, notably the flexibility of price and wage adjustment and the state of physical and social infrastructure. The usual expectation is that adjustment will be associated with initially slower growth — and more poverty — in the short term than non-adjustment, but that the poor will gain in the longer-term once growth is restored. However, this dynamic trade-off may be overstated; two studies of countries which avoided or

---

[75] For example, it is commonly assumed that distributional effects are neutral *within* sectors; the evolution of sector mean incomes drives the aggregate distribution. However, in one test of this assumption using household data (for Indonesia), there was a great deal of distributional change within sectors during adjustment [Huppi and Ravallion (1991)]. Intra-sectoral neutrality is an analytically convenient assumption, but it can be misleading.

[76] We shall continue to focus on consumption poverty. As for social indicators, van der Gaag et al. (1991) and Maasland and van der Gaag (1992) find little evidence that their evolution differed between adjusting and non-adjusting countries.

abandoned stabilization found rapid worsening in living standards of the poor [Glewwe and Hall (1994) for Peru; Grootaert (1994) for Côte d'Ivoire].[77]

Distributional shifts can matter to the outcome, but experience is diverse. In Brazil, distributional shifts during the 1980s significantly worsened the effects of falling growth on poverty [Datt and Ravallion (1992)]. In the Philippines, adverse distributional effects resulted in higher poverty despite (modest) growth in the late 1980s [Balisacan (1993)]. A slight improvement in distribution helped the poor in Indonesia [Ravallion and Huppi (1991)]. Dorosh and Sahn (1993) find that the distributional effects of real devaluations will tend to be pro-poor in a number of African countries, since the rural poor tend to be net producers of tradeable goods.

The distributional impacts of adjustment depend heavily on the economy's initial conditions, particularly its openness, and the extent of flexibility in its output and factor markets. For example, Costa Rica's large, open, and labor-intensive traded goods sector allowed the poor to benefit from real devaluation; opposite conditions in Argentina and Venezuela induced distributional shifts, associated with adjustment, far less advantageous to the poor [Morley and Alvarez (1992)]. The importance of price flexibility is also clear from the results of Bourguignon et al. (1991b) for Morocco, who contrast the effects of adjustment under a "fix-price" closure – fixed prices in the modern sector and flexible prices in the rural sector – with a standard Walrasian closure. Impacts on the poor differ greatly. With the fix-price closure, quantity adjustments naturally determine the distributional implications.

The policy response, particularly in the *composition* of public expenditure cuts, can greatly affect the poverty outcomes of adjustment. Several countries have combined aggregate budget contraction with rising shares (and occasionally rising absolute levels) of public spending in the social sectors, including targeted transfers [Ribe et al. (1990); World Bank (1990, Chapter 7); Selowsky (1991)]. For example, the careful mix of public spending cuts during adjustment in Indonesia, and the rapid currency devaluations, helped mitigate the short-term consequences for the poor of declining growth [Thorbecke (1991)]. Elsewhere, "golden handshakes" to retrenched workers figure prominently in actual or proposed compensatory packages, even though such workers are neither poor nor evidently threatened by poverty [Ravallion and Subbarao (1992)].

The role of policy goes well beyond compensating the poor for direct losses from adjustment. Complementarities often exist between the composition of public spending and the benefits to the poor of structural adjustment. The supply response of farmers to higher prices of traded goods will typically

---

[77] Though (here too) we do not know how different the outcome would have been under a stabilization program.

depend on the quality of supportive infrastructure (both physical infrastructure, such as roads, and information) [Binswanger et al. (1993); de Janvry et al. (1991)]. There are compelling arguments for believing that such infrastructure would generally be under-provided without public provisioning. Yet the fiscal "crunch" of adjustment often tempts governments to cut exactly these infrastructural sectors.

## 6. Interventions

The desire to reduce poverty has been used to justify various direct policy interventions by LDC governments. How well have the specific forms of intervention worked? This section cannot survey the full range of interventions. It seeks only to illustrate the arguments for and against them, and to give detail on a few examples. We focus more on the rural sector, recognizing that – judged by a typical LDC's poverty profile – rural poverty should have higher priority (Section 4.6).[78]

### 6.1. Evaluating targeted interventions

Many of the problems in evaluating targeted schemes are common to other policies; for example, it is often difficult to quantify the counterfactual of what would have happened without intervention.[79] Here we comment solely on some often neglected issues concerning anti-poverty policies in LDCs.

Most recent policy discussions agree that anti-poverty schemes should aim for "cost-effectiveness", either by maximizing the gains to the poor for a given revenue cost, or by minimizing the cost of a given impact on poverty [Reutlinger and Selowsky (1976), World Bank (1986, 1990, Chapter 6)]. An advantage of this criterion is that one does not have to spell out any trade-offs between one policy objective – say poverty reduction – and others. One is concerned solely with efficiency in attaining a given objective; could one achieve greater impact at the same cost? But there is a potential hazard, particularly when efficiency rankings of policies alter with changes in the revenue cost; the most efficient policy for one outlay need not be the most

---

[78] See Section 4.6 on the urban informal sector. Discussions of the main instruments of direct intervention to reduce urban poverty include Mayo et al. (1986) and Mayo and Gross (1988) on "sites-and-services" and slum up-grading projects; World Bank (1992c) on the potential costs and benefits to the urban poor of urban infrastructure and some other urban policy interventions; and Ravallion (1989) on the cost to the poor of urban housing regulations.

[79] For a recent review of the issues in evaluating targeted interventions in the U.S. see Manski (1990). General discussions of project evaluation are Drèze and Stern (1987) and Squire (1989).

efficient for all, and then one must specify the trade-off between poverty and revenue to rank policies.

In formulating objectives, value-judgements concerning interpersonal comparisons amongst the poor can also affect the policy choice. Should a public employment scheme aim for the widest possible coverage amongst the poor, recognizing that this may entail very low wage rates, or should it aim to allow a smaller number of participants to escape poverty, by setting a higher wage rate? The answer can be shown to depend on the available budget, administrative cost, the initial wage distribution, *and* the policy maker's ethical aversion to poverty-severity [Ravallion (1991b)]. If the needs of one group increase relative to others, should an optimally allocated transfer to that group also increase, at the expense of others? Not necessarily; the answer will depend critically on (quite subtle) properties of the poverty measure used [Keen (1992)].

A popular recommendation for more cost-effective interventions has been "better targeting", meaning that more of the poor and/or fewer of the non-poor gain. Household survey data have shown that benefits of undifferentiated transfers (such as general food subsidies) often go disproportionately to the non-poor [Grosh (1991, 1993)]. This alone does not mean that targeting will have a greater impact on poverty. Participation in a targeted scheme may be more costly. If costs of participation and administrative costs are high enough, then better targeting will diminish cost-effectiveness in reducing poverty. Empirically, the size of those costs will depend on the responses of participants and others; for example, intra-household time allocation responds to new "workfare" employment opportunities in rural India in ways which *diminish* the forgone income [Datt and Ravallion (1994)].

Targeting can also undermine political support for anti-poverty policies. For example, the switch from universal food subsidies to targeted food stamps in Sri Lanka in the late 1970s was associated with a substantial contraction in real funding over subsequent years; many of the poor ended up with a larger share of a smaller cake, and absolutely worse off [Besley and Kanbur (1993)]. However, one should be wary of oversimplifying the political economy of targeting, as the set of people who will support an efficient anti-poverty scheme is often far larger than the set of direct beneficiaries; for example, rural landlords and the urban rich have supported rural relief work schemes in India [Echeverri-Gent (1988)].

Policy discussions have also distinguished a scheme's ability to avoid "type 1 errors" (incorrectly classifying a person as poor) versus "type 2 errors" (incorrectly classifying a person as not poor) [Cornia and Stewart (1994)]. The values one attaches to these two errors in targeting are implicit in the poverty measure one uses (like the role of the "loss function" in balancing type 1 and type 2 errors in statistics); the concern with these errors arises because an appropriate measure of poverty did not fall as much as it could have. While we should be concerned with avoiding leakage to the non-poor, we should also aim for a desirable coverage amongst the poor. Poverty measurement should reflect both concerns.

The most cost-effective policy need not have the lowest "errors of targeting". Given the costs of targeting, the deliberate introduction of leakage or imperfect coverage (allowing a reduction in those costs) may allow a greater impact on poverty for a given budget outlay (Ravallion and Datt, 1994a).

### 6.2. Methods of targeting

Administrative costs and related constraints on policy instruments are now widely appreciated in analytical discussions of targeted policies. These constraints are particularly relevant in underdeveloped rural economies. In rural sectors and the urban informal sector, negative income taxes are seldom feasible. Sometimes a means test is imposed, but without the administrative capability to implement it convincingly. And even with that capability, this type of scheme will entail high marginal tax rates on the poor.[80] Both the problems of observing incomes and the incentive effects of means testing have led to a variety of schemes for "indicator targeting" whereby transfers are made contingent on correlates of poverty, such as landholding, caste, or place of residence.

Geographic targeting has attractions. Substantial regional disparities in living standards are common in developing countries, and backward areas can often be readily identified. Place of residence may thus be a useful indicator of poverty. Local governments provide an administrative apparatus. This has already been exploited in many LDCs. For example, the allocation of central government disbursements across states in India has been determined, in part, by regional disparities in poverty; China's current anti-poverty strategy also relies heavily on regional targeting; Indonesia is also putting emphasis on regional targeting as a means of reducing poverty.

How much impact on poverty can be expected from such policies? While regional poverty profiles for LDCs typically show large geographic disparities (Section 4.6), regional targeting still entails a leakage of benefits to the non-poor in poor regions, and a cost to the poor in rich regions. And even with marked regional disparities these effects can wipe out a large share of the aggregate gains to the poor. For India, Datt and Ravallion (1993) consider the effects on poverty of pure (non-distortionary) transfers among states, and

---

[80] See Kanbur et al. (1994) for an analysis of the optimal benefit withdrawal rates for targeted poverty reduction schemes which affect labor supply.

between rural and urban areas. They find that the *qualitative* effect of reducing regional/sectoral disparities in average living standards generally favors the poor. However, the *quantitative* gains are small. For example, the elimination of regional disparities in the means across 20 states of India – with each state divided into urban and rural areas – while holding *intra*-regional inequalities constant, would yield only a small reduction in the proportion of persons below the poverty line, from an initial 33 percent to 32 percent.[81] Such calculations are at best suggestive, and there are clearly other factors to consider. The benefits to the poor will be greater if administrative capabilities allow finer geographical targeting. To the extent that market failures or other distortions have biased the regional/sectoral pattern of growth, there will also be positive impacts on pre-transfer incomes (Section 5.2). Yet other factors will diminish the benefits further, such as the political power of rich regions. It is not clear what effect mobility would have. Nonetheless, the evidence on regional poverty profiles does make one rather sanguine about the prospects for a really significant reduction in aggregate poverty by this means alone, beyond the likely gains from removing policy biases against the rural sector. While broad regional targeting of transfers can help reduce poverty in developing countries if the growth cost is not too large, it may be a relatively blunt policy instrument on its own.

In much of Asia, and increasingly in sub-Saharan Africa, the most promising single additional indicator is probably the land-holding class. Where land and water are reasonably adequate and reliable, one observes a negative correlation between land-holding and poverty, especially in much of rural South Asia. This has motivated interest in a variety of forms of "land-contingent targeting", such as certain land reforms, and transfer payments to the landless (Section 6.4.1). There are inherent limitations to such targeting; landholding is an imperfect correlate of poverty. Simulations confirm the advantages of targeting transfers in Bangladesh toward households owning little or no land, but also highlight the limitations. Even with complete control over the distribution of income across (but not within) six landholding classes in Bangladesh, the maximum reduction in the aggregate severity of poverty which is attainable is no more than one could obtain by an untargeted lump-sum gain to all households of about 3–5 percent of mean income [Ravallion and Sen (1994b)]. Various factors will detract from even that modest impact. For

---

[81] Similar experiments for Indonesia, where the regional disparities in the incidence and severity of poverty across islands are larger, have suggested greater gains from this type of targeting – and also that those gains are far from being realized by existing inter-regional transfer policies [Ravallion (1993c)]. But even then regional targeting is no panacea; the impact on national poverty of unrestricted income redistributions across Indonesia's provinces would be equivalent to a four percent increase in national mean consumption. We should look for other indicators to enable finer targeting *within* regions or sectors.

example, plausible restrictions on the government's redistributive powers would further diminish the gains to the poor from such policies. There may be potential for combining land-contingent targeting with other types of targeting. For example, there are poor even amongst households with relatively large landholdings in Bangladesh. If these households can be identified with reasonable precision by other indicators, such as region of residence, then greater poverty alleviation would be informationally feasible in practice.

The prospects for reaching the poor also depend on the institutional environment, including local administrative capabilities, the incentives facing local administrators, their social relations with the poor, and the extent of empowerment of the poor, through both governmental and non-governmental representation. Options for effective local-administrative targeting do arise in some settings. For example, since 1980, the Indian state of Kerala has provided a pension to agricultural workers over 60 who have low self-reported incomes (including that of unmarried adult children). An official local committee including representatives of minority groups is in charge of verification [Gulati (1990)]. Future comparative research could reveal how much the institutional environment constricts poverty alleviation possibilities; when compared to autocratic structures of power, what are the gains from broad-based participatory forms of local political organization in which representatives and administrators face incentives consistent with poverty alleviation, and can an open political environment provide suitable checks on their efforts? For example, comparing the experiences of India and China, it appears that democracy and freedom of the press can facilitate public action to prevent or relieve famines [Drèze and Sen (1989)].

Disappointment with the prospects for poverty reduction using administratively and politically feasible forms of indicator targeting has rekindled interest in *self-targeting*. This works by creating incentives which encourage participation only by the poor. This is illustrated by one of the oldest anti-poverty schemes: relief work. The argument here is not that such work alleviates poverty by creating assets (though all the better if it does), but that work requirements can provide seemingly excellent incentives for self-targeting; the reservation wage rate for unskilled manual work is negatively correlated with poverty. Some of the largest schemes in South Asia have done well in screening poor from non-poor,[82] at modest administrative cost. There may be lessons for achieving better targeting of other public services. For example, public health services can be better targeted to the poor if waiting rooms provide only minimal comforts. Fair-price outlets, free clinics, etc., can be

---

[82] For example, 70 percent of the employment provided by Bangladesh's Food-for-Work Program in the early 1980s went to the 25 percent of rural households with lowest annual income per person [Ravallion (1991a)].

located in the poorest areas (thus combining indicator targeting with self-targeting). Under certain conditions, the rationing of food or health subsidies by queuing can also be self-targeting [Alderman (1987)], as can subsidizing inferior food staples. However, none of these mechanisms is perfect: the poor may be unable to afford the work loss in queuing; the rich may jump the queue, or send their servants to queue.

There are two main caveats about self-targeted schemes. First, they screen participants by imposing a cost on them; good schemes ensure that the cost is higher for the non-poor than the poor (so that it is the poor who tend to participate), but it may not be inconsequential to the poor. An important cost is forgone income. We know little about its magnitude for rural public works schemes, though it is unlikely to be zero; the poor can rarely afford to be idle. A recent estimate using survey data for two Maharashtran villages found that the forgone income from employment on public works schemes was quite low – around one quarter of gross wage earnings; most of the time displaced was in domestic labor, leisure and unemployment [Datt and Ravallion (1994)].

Second, some sub-groups of the poor are not willing to participate in workfare schemes, often because they are physically unable to do such work. The non-poor are screened out, but so are some of the poor. Fortunately there are some obvious, relatively non-manipulatable and easily monitored, characteristics for identifying such households, such as physical disability and old age. A combination of self-selection through relief work and indicator targeting based on such characteristics could provide a comprehensive safety net for the poor [Drèze and Sen (1989)].

## 6.3. Transient poverty

A distinction is often made between attempts to reduce transient poverty (experienced for only a short period) versus chronic poverty (experienced over a long period). Both are usually substantial in LDCs,[83] though their relative importance depends on how well existing consumption smoothing and insurance arrangements work. Individuals – especially the risk-prone rural poor – act, and set up demand for local institutions, to defend themselves from fluctuations in well-being (Section 4.5). Hence the need to crowd in, not crowd out, private and community adjustments to fluctuations is an important theme of anti-poverty policy [Morris (1974)]. However, even if optimal individually,

---

[83] A panel study in six semi-arid Indian villages over 1975–1983 showed that "... only about 12 percent of households were [poor in none of] the nine years [while] 44 percent were poor for six or more years, and 19 percent were poor in every year [and] 50 percent were poor in a typical year. The transient component is large [yet] there is a substantial persistent core of chronic poverty" [World Bank (1990: 35)].

risk-avoiding responses in (typical) settings of incomplete risk markets are costly [Rosenzweig and Wolpin (1993), Morduch (1990, 1994)]. For example, low-risk crops normally produce low expected incomes. Costly forms of adjustment to borrowing constraints may thus inhibit prospects for escaping poverty in the longer term though human and physical capital formation; for example, Chaudhuri (1993) finds that the illiquidity of poor farmers in three Indian villages inhibits adoption of new technologies.

Social insurance can exist without markets or governments, but how well does it work? Community-based risk-sharing arrangements may well be less prone to moral hazard and adverse selection (in traditional village settings in which participants are well known to each other), but they must still be implementable without binding, legally enforceable contracts. This fact constrains performance for the poor, particularly in spells of transient poverty, or when the threat of destitution reduces the probability of continued participation in social insurance [Coate and Ravallion (1993), Fafchamps (1992), Besley's chapter]. All this may justify public actions to partly insure or subsidize poor people's production and price risks, or to reduce or insure their "background" risks to health or food security.

What form should such actions take? There are ample examples of ineffective interventions. Governments often try to stabilize foodgrain prices during a famine by banning "hoarding" and "profiteering"; even when current storage is excessive (relative to a rational expectation of future price) this policy can fail dismally, even making matters worse [Ravallion (1987)]. A far better approach is to work directly on current and future food availability, to undermine any destabilizing speculation. Understanding how markets and other indigenous institutions actually work – and how public action can enable them to work better – is often the key to success in the relief of transient poverty.

Compensating the victims is one approach, though with mixed results. Crop insurance often succumbs to problems of moral hazard [Hazell et al. (1986), Walker et al. (1986)]. Also, it is not obvious why this form of fluctuation should be favored; some of its poor victims might have had good fortune in other respects, while farmworkers – usually poorer, and (via unemployment) worst affected by yield decline – are unprotected by crop insurance. There are options, such as social security [Ahmad et al. (1991)], including rural public works and employment guarantee schemes readily "switched in" during bad times [Ravallion (1991a)]. All such approaches face issues of (i) cost containment; (ii) avoidance of perverse incentives (including moral hazard); (iii) ensuring coverage of the needy, while not discouraging the emergence of insurance markets for the better-off; and (iv) distributing scarce public resources fairly and efficiently among types of events for which the poor need compensation.

Policy may also shift resources toward low-risk areas, or risk-reducing inputs. Agricultural research, irrigation, or roads may be diverted to rural areas with relatively low variability in poor people's incomes: Punjab in India, Central Luzon in the Philippines, Sonora in Mexico. This approach aims, in part, to encourage migration away from riskier environments, but mainly to place a larger proportion of output and income in "safer" districts. Yet such "betting on the safe" may paradoxically increase the variability of *total* farm output and income, due to the covariance among the districts – often climatically similar – into which the policy has concentrated a larger proportion of farm output and income [Hazell (1982)]. Moreover, unless the poor respond with substantial migration towards the areas of low fluctuations, there may be a perverse poverty impact from concentrating resources upon such areas, where initial poverty is often lower [Rao et al. (1988)]. A more promising approach is often to shift public research, extension, or subsidies towards locally risk-reducing inputs (e.g. irrigation and pest management), crop-mixes (e.g. from maize, towards more drought-resistant millets), or forms of work provision. For example, the income stabilization benefits of relief work schemes have probably been as important as the transfer benefits; there is no more important example than the role these schemes have played in famine relief in South Asia [Drèze (1990a), Drèze and Sen (1989), Ravallion (1991a)].

## 6.4. Chronic poverty

Many actions affect both transient and chronic poverty. Direct interventions, such as relief work schemes, can help the poor, or near-poor, to avoid forms of adjustment to transient distress, such as asset depletion, which would otherwise be costly in the longer-term. An effective safety net may thus also help reduce chronic poverty. Conversely, one of the best defenses against the threat of transient distress is a long period of relative prosperity. For example, household vulnerability to aggregate shocks may depend greatly on the prior history of poverty [Ravallion (1994b)].

Typically, policies aimed at reducing chronic poverty try to make the poor more productive. Altered choices about land, human capital, and credit can raise incomes among the poor.[84] In each case, the poor can gain from seven sorts of event, including policy interventions, that affect inputs. The first three

---

[84] Credit, though not an input itself, facilitates production. The poverty impact of raw material input choices (on gross output) is not explicitly reviewed. Subsidies to fertilizers, irrigation, etc. normally accrue mainly to better-off farmers, though the poor may gain indirectly. Technology choices, changing input uses in ways that may reduce poverty, appear in Table 1 under col. (a), rows (4–6); and institutional choices, mainly in col. (e) (credit).

rows of Table 41.1 relate to the impact of events that improve input volumes; the next two, input productivity; and the last two, appropriate prices.

The first way in which poor people may gain from extra input volumes is by benefiting from a rise in resource availability, e.g. through a settlement scheme that provides each person (poor or not) with the same probability of extra land whatever their initial income levels. Second, at the other extreme, poor people's resources may be increased by pure redistribution from the non-poor, e.g. by land reform. Third, input volume and distribution can together shift in favor of the poor, e.g. by targeting land in a settlement scheme, or jobs in a public works program.

Fourth and fifth come events, including policies, that raise factor productivity,[85] without necessarily varying the quantities of other inputs. These are typically concentrated on one factor. Poor producers will probably share in the benefits, sometimes even more than proportionately to initial income. The latter happened in Islampur, Bangladesh, where a rise in land productivity was achieved by a subsidy on handpumps; these become attractive for irrigation only to poor people [Howes (1985)].[86]

Sixth and seventh, the poor may gain as producers (without direct changes in volume, distribution or productivity of any factor input) from changing prices. Such changes can either reduce (or stabilize) the prices of inputs bought mainly by the poor, or raise (or stabilize) the price of marketed outputs that are intensive in their use of poor people's preferred inputs, notably labor.

Table 1 uses this framework for classifying events, including policy interventions, that can alter inputs into rural production and thereby reduce poverty. Each box exemplifies one such type of event/input interaction (including some non-farm cases). Only a few boxes are reviewed below.

### 6.4.1. Land

"More land" is often what the rural poor say they need most. Also, when asked to farm in land-preserving ways, e.g. to reduce cattle stocking ratio, they often reply (demonstrably correctly) that they need more land before they can afford to do so [Drinkwater (1991, p. 145)]. Indeed, from the Neolithic Settlement to about 1750, the usual response in rural areas suffering from an

---

[85] Local knowledge about the structure of both poverty and technology, is essential before policy-makers intervene to induce, or to accelerate, gains in the productivity of labor. Do laborers own most of the capital and land that "employs" them? If not, is the price-elasticity of total farm supply low, and the elasticity of substitution between labor and other factors high? If so, "gains" in labor-productivity (e.g. better weedicides) can mean large net losses for the rural poor.

[86] Of course, output gains achieved with all inputs held constant cannot in general be attributed to "factor-specific productivity increases". However, in practice, such rises can generally be traced mainly to changes in the type, or mode of utilization, of one or another factor.

Table 41.1
Possible interventions against rural poverty

| Production input adjustment | Inputs | | | | |
|---|---|---|---|---|---|
| | a Land | b Labor | c Human capital | d Physical capital | e Credit |
| 1. Distribution-neutral volume enhancement | Settlement schemes | "Population policy"; reducing participation costs (e.g. crèches); employment information | Proportionate rise in each type and location of health, education, etc. | Rural non-farm capital assistance; area-wide irrigation ("trickle-down"); "infrastructure" | Greater competitive public supply of, or incentives to, rural lending |
| 2. Volume-neutral distribution enhancement | Land reform | Law enforcement against discrimination vs. poor groups of women ethnics, caste members, etc. | "Reverse discrimination", in access or new services, towards: school girls; poorer tribes or areas; places of high disease incidence | Landless to obtain capital (e.g. tubewells) and sell its product (e.g. water) to farmers (Proshika) | "Quotas" for poor, via instructions/ incentives to lending institutions directed credit |
| 3. Joint volume and distribution enhancement | Trans-migration of landless | "Directed" version of 1b; workfare programs | Health and education spending increases slanted towards rural primary education and health | Poor-selective rural infrastructure; support for competitive hand- and animal-tool supply and maintenance | Credit expansion or incentives in "backward" regions |

| | | | | | |
|---|---|---|---|---|---|
| 4. Distribution-neutral productivity enhancement | Yield-related "technology policy", e.g. on high-yielding varieties | Better health services for peak-season illnesses and agricultural injuries; buses to work | Extension to raise efficiency of use of skills, e.g. appropriate nonfarm stock control | Improved irrigation delivery or maintenance | Training and supervision for bankers or for borrowers |
| 5. Poor-orientated productivity enhancement | As 4a for "poor people's crops", e.g. cassava, millets | Research and extension for standard agricultural labor tasks, esp. for women | Artisan up-grading and "recycling" courses steered to poorer people's trades | As above, concentrated on tail-ends; "barefoot management consul-tants" | Small NGO-based credit user groups; management support |
| 6. Improving or stabilizing prices of inputs brought mainly by the poor | Micro-pack-aged appropriate fertilizers | Labor-demanding technical or institutional change; competitive recruitment and transport to and from jobs | Primary health/schools cheaper, nearer, or timed for lower opportunity-cost | Subsidies for small asset purchases | Poor-selective capital or interest subsidies |
| 7. Improving or stabilizing prices of outputs produced mainly by the poor | Reduced farm-price repression | Information and infrastructure for seasonal migrants | Not applicable | Marketing co-operatives for family micro-enterprises | Credit linkage to organized/coop marketing |

increase in chronic poverty was to farm new lands, often nearby, or to shorten fallows [Boserup (1965)].

Spontaneous land expansion has until quite recently been a significant response to poverty. For example, millions of farmers resettled voluntarily in Ethiopia in 1934–1977, in response to environmental problems, evictions and other pressures [Chole and Mulat (1988, p. 165)]. However, such processes have much abated under pressure of land scarcity. They remain significant in parts of West Africa and Brazil, but even there the areas of new settlement are experiencing shorter fallows, increasingly inadequate land regeneration, and hence long-run threats of diminishing returns. In such circumstances, spontaneous settlement can seldom do much to cure poverty.

The direct actions inducing land expansion for the poor are settlement schemes and land redistribution. How much can these reduce rural poverty? The rural poverty profile has bearing on the answer. The rural poor usually do overlap substantially with those who own and/or operate little or no farmland. But there are exceptions. Rural teachers, shopkeepers, and artisans are often well-off though landless; in parts of West Africa rural non-farm employment, not occupancy of farmland, appears to predict lower risk of poverty [P. Hill (1972), Reardon et al. (1992)]. Conversely, households that own and operate as much as 3 or 4 hectares of bad land can be very poor: in Western India, they are no likelier to escape poverty than are the landless [Visaria (1977), Lipton (1985)]. In better farming areas, lack of land is a clear *correlate* of poverty, but it is an imperfect one: this constrains the prospects for reducing aggregate rural poverty by land-based redistributions [Ravallion and Sen (1994b)].

Another limitation on land redistribution or settlement – even among households deriving their livelihoods entirely from farmland – is that land inequality is less than it seems. First, household size almost everywhere increases with operated land area [Singh (1990)]. In a study of the Indian Punjab, the Gini index of operated land per household was double that of land per person [Julka and Sharma (1989)]. Second, in Asia [Bhalla and Roy (1988)], smaller holdings tend to be on higher-quality land, and to embody more land improvement (wells, bunds) per hectare, than do larger holdings. Third, tenancy usually enables some non-landowners to farm; operated land is almost always distributed less unequally than owned land [Singh (1985)].

For settlement schemes (Table 41.1:1a) to be effective against poverty, there are several prerequisites. Two are normally met. There must be differences among agricultural regions in (potential) marginal productivity of labor (MPL). And the scheme must be needed, and able, to overcome barriers, or deterrents, to poor people's spontaneous migration towards the regions with a higher potential MPL. More problematic are other prerequisites: fiscal sustainablity; low "crowding out" of spontaneous settlement; motivation to identify potential settlers, genuinely willing to move and mostly poor, yet able to benefit from resettlement; and absence of severe conflicts, or environmental degradation, in the area of settlement, such that decreases in poverty among the settlers are unsustainable or are outweighed by increases among indigenous people. Oberai (1988) reviews alternative schemes.

Redistributive land reform [see the chapter by Binswanger et al. and Lipton (1993)] remains an important route to "more land for the poor". Its aims of advancing the rural poor by increasing their land rights and by defanging multi-market "rural tyrants" [Bell (1990)] have often been achieved, though seldom sufficiently to meet initial expectations. And there have been failures too. Several have involved incentives to shift control of land away from the poor. Restrictions on tenancy, without effective ownership ceilings, have harmed some of the landless poor, because landlords have responded by reducing the supply of land to rent, especially by resuming land for personal cultivation. This has prevented the poor from selling services as farm managers and entrepreneurs via tenancy.[87] State and collective farming usually excludes poor non-members (ex-employees), relies on economies of scale that seldom exist, and creates incentives to individual shirking and to farm-level capital-intensity.

These erroneous measures have often been redeemed by, or converted into, classic land redistribution. In Taiwan and Korea, tenancy restrictions were redeemed by effective ceilings on holdings, so that incentives to ex-landlords were not (as is usually the case) to evict ex-tenants, but to sell, or accept compensation for, excess lands. Across Latin America, collective and State farmers have "voted with their feet" to convert the lands into private smallholdings [Thiesenhusen (1989)], leaving State and collective farming as a "detour" on the road from unequal to equal private farming [Bell (1990)].

Public policy for land settlement, and (much more) for land redistribution, has comprised a major, and partly successful, response to the pressures created by rural poverty and population growth.

As the composition of the rural poor shifts increasingly from farmers to employees, however, the employment effects of reforms will become more critical. Fortunately, above all in the extremely unequal circumstances of (say) Brazil, it is clear that smaller family holdings are not only more labor-intensive, but more employee-intensive, than large commercial farms. Moreover, this fact (itself due mainly to costs involved in search, screening and supervision of large hired farm workforces) probably creates an "inverse relationship" between farm size and annual output per hectare, as shown in the chapter by

---

[87] Sitting tenants who escape eviction, of course, gain from rent controls. But potential tenants lose, as land-to-rent is resumed for commercial farming on own account. Tenancy almost always renders the distribution of operated farmland more equal more pro-poor, than that of owned farmland; and it is seldom a barrier to innovation [Bardhan and Rudra (1981), Lipton with Longhurst (1989), Singh (1990)].

Binswanger et al. [also see Berry and Cline (1979), Thiesenhusen (1988), Lipton (1993)]. Thus land redistribution, unlike collectivization, or in most cases tenancy reform, normally creates extra GNP, out of which the losers can in part be compensated.

However, "more land for the poor", whether through settlement or distribution, has limits as an anti-poverty policy. First, in India [Dev et al. (1991)], Zimbabwe, and elsewhere, it is often second-rate land, needing supportive expenditure or infrastructure, that reaches the poor (seldom the poorest) in such reforms. Second, there are diminishing returns to increasingly "difficult" reforms, both economic (as the poor acquire marginal land) and political. Third, even if the poor do gain some land, old farmland is being lost, not perhaps to net decertification [Bie (1989)], but certainly to salinity and urbanization [Eckholm (1976)]. Fourth, poor rural populations in many countries continue to increase. A major part of rural poverty policy, therefore, depends on higher productivity of land already owned, rented or worked by the rural poor. Fortunately, a growing body of evidence confirms that biochemical and hydraulic innovations tend to help the poor (though not generally to reduce inequality) by reducing food prices, raising demand for labor, and often stabilizing farm-specific output. The effects on poor farmers in non-adopting regions, however, may be less advantageous [Lipton with Longhurst (1989)].

### 6.4.2. Credit

In much of Asia, Latin America, and parts of Africa, rural credit has been widely regarded as the key to poverty reduction. In urban production, inputs and outputs usually flow fairly smoothly over the year. In agriculture, especially field-crop production, (i) input requirements are concentrated into a few critical, climate-related periods, especially breaking the soil and harvesting the crop; (ii) output flows are also concentrated, in rainfed annual crops typically into a month or two; and (iii) input costs are incurred months before outputs arrive. Poor rural people, with few own resources, appear to need credit to smooth consumption. Farmers, especially poor farmers, also need credit, to obtain current and capital inputs well before farm incomes become available.

Seasons and their risks are obvious; hence farm families do adapt through non-crop labor inputs, savings and storage. Yet such adaptation is costly, and itself risky; credit might reduce those costs. Also, while rural people may adapt labor supply to the rural nonfarm economy so as to be contravariant with farm requirements, the time-distribution of farm-nonfarm linkages means that some nonfarm labor demand, especially for processing and transport, is covariant with farm labor demand. Hence consumption smoothing, input finance, and investment demand generate demands for rural credit.

Is it normally supplied to the poor? It is often alleged that this or that society lacks rural credit. However, almost invariably there exist non-cash substitutes, and/or "hidden" informal cash-credit mechanisms such as "rotating credit and savings associations" [Besley et al. (1993)]. Moreover, many rural transactions, usually analyzed in the context of land and labor, also operate as forms of credit. For example, sharecropping, as a "loan" of land for a rent that varies with output, helps to address an otherwise largely unprovided farmer demand for equity loans; so does the lending of cattle by owners to managers in Botswana's mafisa system. Many of the forms of social insurance discussed in Section 6.3 are imperfect substitutes for credit markets.

To attack "wicked moneylenders" as a cause of rural poverty has long been the mode of demagogy, but seldom of economics. Yet even those who recognize the need for rural credit supply, and hence for incentives to provide it, fear local moneylender monopoly and power, sometimes operating in "interlocking markets" [Bell (1988)], e.g. lenders who insist that needy borrowers rent their land, or work for them, if they wish to borrow at all. As general concerns, these fears are exaggerated.

Informal-sector interest rates usually reflect costs of administering small loans, together with risks of default, rather than substantial monopoly profit [Bottomley (1964), Adams et al. (1984)].

Nevertheless, there has been much concern that informal credit fails to reach the poor, and is inadequate for expanded farm output. Partly due to market responses to that concern, partly to government actions and subsidies, formal credit has displaced much informal (family, trade, curb, moneylender) credit in much of Asia and Latin America.

Yet formal credit too (it is often claimed) does not address the needs of the poor. It is usually restricted to lending for productive inputs, to creditworthy persons; the rural poor are increasingly often landless, lacking in non-land assets and hence collateral, and in need of loans mainly for consumption smoothing. Further, small borrowers offer formal lenders two serious disadvantages: high fixed costs per unit of lending [Bottomley (1963)], and problems of adverse selection, moral hazard, and above all enforcement (or, in cases of genuine hardship, rescheduling) of repayment that are much more readily met face-to-face by local informal lenders than impersonally by banks or other remote organizations. Even when a means test is applied, aimed at directing subsidized credit to the poor, the outcome often falls far short of perfect targeting; for example, a comparison of the incidence by consumption group of participation in the (credit-based and income means-tested) Integrated Rural Development Programme in Maharashtra, India, reveals that the scheme is a good deal less well targeted than that state's Employment

Guarantee Scheme (which involves neither credit nor a means test) [Ravallion and Datt (1994a)]. And even poor households can save out of labor income to finance self-employment activities.

Some of these problems can be overcome. Group-based lending schemes (such as the Grameen Bank in Bangladesh) have often achieved excellent repayment rates, though some assessments of the rates of return have been less encouraging [Hossain (1984, 1988)]. The default/loan ratio of small farmers in formal credit systems is usually lower than that of large ones [Lele (1974); Lipton (1981)]. The speculation that this is largely due to more intensive screening of small farmers, and hence not replicable if formal lending to such farmers grows substantially, may be mistaken. In India, marginal farmers (below 1 hectare) operated only 12.2 percent of farmland in June 1985, yet received 33.0 percent of agricultural credit from commercial banks, the main source [Reserve Bank of India (1989, p. 85)].

However, it is hard to maintain hope that chronic poverty can be reduced appreciably by credit-based interventions. Chronic poverty is not typically due to "market failure" in credit or other markets, but to low factor productivity, and/or low endowments-per-person of non-labor factors. If these conditions prevail, even perfect responses of all factor, product and credit markets may leave substantial chronic poverty.

### 6.4.3. Public services

To what extent can chronic poverty be reduced by policies concerning the provision and pricing of public services? Infrastructure is dealt with more fully in the chapter by Jimenez in this volume; here we only flag some key issues meriting further research in the context of poverty.

There is evidence on the productivity effects of physical infrastructure development, suggesting that investments in rural infrastructure can generate sizable income gains (both farm and non-farm) in underdeveloped rural economies [Antle (1983), Binswanger et al. (1993), Jimenez chapter]. The benefits to the poor are rarely dealt with explicitly in this literature (except in the context of the use of infrastructure development in relief work schemes; see Sections 6.2 and 6.3). However, given the evidence that agricultural growth tends to reduce rural poverty (Section 5.2), there is a compelling case that rural infrastructure development is generally poverty reducing. The causal links that have been identified in the literature and policy discussions include both direct effects of improved water control on agricultural output, and more indirect effects (particularly of roads) in reducing impediments to the flow of information and commodities. There is also evidence of positive productivity effects from human infrastructure development, particularly basic health and education; for reviews see Schultz (1988), Behrman and Deolalikar (1988), and the chapters by Jimenez and Lau in this volume. Nor are those benefits confined to the urban sector [Jamison and Lau (1982)].

In all such assessments, a recurrent issue is that infrastructure is typically a locally provided good. Public decisions are made about the location of investments, which may be influenced by income level or growth rate differences between regions. Empirical assessments of income gains from infrastructure development may then be plagued by a simultaneity bias. The (few) studies which have dealt with this problem do confirm the existence of sizable productivity effects; see Binswanger et al. (1993) on physical infrastructure in India, and Pitt et al. (1993) on human infrastructure in Indonesia.

None of this implies that the expansion of public investments in local infrastructure at the expense of other public programs, including infrastructure elsewhere, is necessarily pro-poor. That depends crucially on how well markets can provide those goods (almost certainly markets will under-provide some components of infrastructure, but not all; see the Jimenez chapter), and at what prices. "Infrastructure" is also a heterogeneous category; some components are more pro-poor than others.

Consider human infrastructure. Undifferentiated subsidization of human capital formation is unlikely to be inherently pro-poor. Income elasticities of demand for education and health care of unity or higher are plausible for LDCs [Theil and Finke (1985), Schieber and Poullier (1989), Gertler and van der Gaag (1990)]. However, a consensus is emerging in favor of differentiated expansion in primary education and basic health care, as an instrument for poverty reduction [World Bank (1990)]. This is seen as desirable in its own right, and as an important complement to achieving the right conditions (incentives and infrastructure) for promoting a labor-intensive growth path.

A "social services trickle-down" argument is often made in favor of this type of intervention. The argument rests on the assumption that the non-poor are now satiated in their consumption of these social services in most LDCs, so that extra public spending on them will go disproportionately to the poor. However, these services can differ greatly in *quality* (lower staff-student ratios in schools, better facilities in health care clinics), and the non-poor (even when they have themselves reached universal enrollments) are very unlikely to be satiated for improved quality. The extra benefits of greater budgetary allocations to these social services may then go to the non-poor in the form of higher quality.

The same factors in a country's political economy which resulted in the bias against the poor will presumably continue to operate toward that end.

Another argument is based on the existing utilization of categories of public spending on social services, as revealed by household surveys (an increasingly important use of such surveys).[88] There have been a number of empirical studies of the incidence of subsidies.[89] These typically find that existing allocations to primary education and basic health care tend to be at least mildly pro-poor, in that subsidies per head received by the poor account for a relatively higher proportion of their income or expenditure, and (in some cases) are also absolutely higher than for the non-poor. The explanation appears to lie in a tendency for the rich to shift into the private market for health and education, and also for family size to be higher for the poor (so that primary education and health care subsidies act like a family allowance scheme). Allocations to education and health care above primary level tend, however, to favor the non-poor.

Such studies are informative, but they tell us little about how the benefits of public expenditure reforms – extra spending on some categories – will be distributed. What they do suggest is that targeting of primary education and health care will be pro-poor, provided that average pre-intervention incidence reliably indicates the incidence of the benefits from selective expansion. However, that need not hold; *marginal* gains to the poor may be high for categories of spending which do not currently have a pro-poor *average* incidence. This can be assessed by directly examining how the incidence of benefits of public spending on social services evolves when budgetary outlays alter. Two such studies are Hammer et al. (1994) for Malaysia (comparing 1973 with 1984) and van de Walle (1994a) for Indonesia (comparing 1978 and 1987). Both countries experienced a sizable expansion in aggregate budgetary outlays on health and education; in both cases, aggregate school enrollments and public health care utilization expanded considerably. The distribution of the benefits of subsidies to these services, already quite pro-poor, did not worsen; in the case of Malaysia, it improved somewhat. Thus the poor gained from the expansion in social sector outlays.[90] More evidence of this sort is needed, given the weight attached to this type of intervention in current policy discussions.

Similar comments can be made about physical infrastructure; some components (rural roads) are almost certainly more pro-poor than others (urban highways). However, the evidence is even more contentious than for human

---

[88] These are often termed "benefit incidence" studies. This is somewhat misleading, since one is not really quantifying *benefits* (in the sense of welfare gains), but rather *utilization*. Utilization of multiple services is then being aggregated according to the service-specific rates of subsidy (public spending less cost-recovery). So these are better thought of as "subsidy-incidence" studies.

[89] Examples include Meerman (1979) for Malaysia, and Selowsky (1979) for Colombia, Foxley (1979) for Chile, Meesook (1984) and van de Walle (1994a) both for Indonesia, World Bank (1989) for Bangladesh, Hammer et al. (1992) for Malaysia, and Selden and Wasylenko (1993) for Peru. Also see the Jimenez chapter and van de Walle (1994b).

[90] There is some evidence from cross-country data consistent with this conclusion; not only do poor people tend to have worse health status, differences in public health spending appear to matter more to them than to the non-poor [Bidani and Ravallion (1994)].

capital investments, not least because the measurement of "who benefits" is more problematic; few surveys of household living standards surveys, for example, assess road utilization, and (in any case) the pervasive second-round benefits would make such assessments unduly narrow. Compelling evidence is likely to come via the more indirect route of first establishing that a particular growth process reduces poverty, and secondly establishing that a particular infrastructure initiative will promote such growth. This is a feasible route, but needs further research.

One public service that many people perceive as the key to reducing poverty is a subsidized family planning program. This is also contentious. One issue is whether high fertility should even be considered a "cause" of poverty (Section 4.2.1). Cross-country comparisons suggest little relationship between population growth rates and the growth of real income per person [National Academy of Sciences (1985), Simon (1986)]. It has been argued that high rates of population growth have adverse distributional effects. If poor people, by producing many children because this is *individually* optimal, raise labor supply and food demand, the real wage rate for the poor is reduced [Malthus (1798)]. Thus there is a pecuniary external diseconomy [Scitovsky (1954)] to the poor *jointly* from their high fertility.[91] But there has been little empirical work on such distributional effects.[92] A second contentious issue is whether in fact family planning programs have much impact on fertility; the bulk of the cross-country variation in the total fertility rate is explicable by differences in desired fertility – access to contraceptives matters little [Pritchett (1994)].[93] None of this denies the role of family planning programs in promoting the good health of mothers and children.

## 7. Conclusions

The idea that economic development is possible, and that it can reduce poverty, dates from the eighteenth century; there was little sign of it before Adam Smith. The idea came hand-in-hand with a shift in moral and political philosophy. The emerging capitalist civil society was seen to require public

---

[91] See Dasgupta (1993) for a theoretical treatment of how externalities of this sort can entail that the aggregate outcome of these individually rational fertility decisions is excessive population growth.

[92] Using time series data by states of India, van de Walle (1985) finds that population growth had a significantly positive effect on rural poverty incidence controlling for *both* agricultural output per capita and the real agricultural wage rate. She suggests that higher population growth rates may result in higher rates of underemployment.

[93] On the determinants of fertility also see Easterlin and Crimmins (1985), Cleland and Wilson (1987), Bongaarts (1992) and Dasgupta (1993).

institutions which accepted responsibility for mass education and basic health care, and also for protecting the vulnerable in the market economy.

The early translations of this idea into the development policies of many post-colonial LDCs were (with few exceptions) failures. For the most part, the failure was in the translation, not the idea. Smith's vision of the "progressive economy" was mistranslated into overly optimistic plans for a capital-intensive industrialization path; that was how, it was believed, poverty would eventually be eradicated. (There was wide agreement that eradicating poverty was the goal). And the role of the state in providing social services was seen more in terms of universities and hospitals than primary schools and clinics.

The attempts at forced-draft planned industrialization offered little for the poor. Growth was often retarded; even when not, it brought few gains to the poor. Indeed, they were often the hardest hit by anti-trade biases since (much more than the non-poor) they earned their living by turning non-tradeables into tradeables. And, to make matters worse, the forced-draft industrialization was financed in large part by extracting a surplus from the main source of income to the poor: agriculture. The welfare of today's poor was sacrificed, but not for tomorrow's poor.

The revolt against this failed approach to poverty reduction emerged in the mid-1970s. Disillusionment with the potential of trickle-down industrialization to reach the poor, *and* with the prospects for radical redistribution of income or land, spurred a move away from the policies and projects of the previous two decades. "Urban bias" started to be seen as damaging to both growth and poverty reduction. Instead, efforts turned to rural development, supported by agro-research and investment in physical and human infrastructure in rural areas. This accompanied a smaller-scale revolution in thinking about urban sector development priorities. Like their predecessors, some of the new plans proved too optimistic, given the real constraints on finance and organization. However, from the mid-1970s, this new direction offered greater hope for the poor, and brought real benefits to them in many countries.

In this context, it remains surprising that the early responses to the macroeconomic crises of the 1980s paid so little explicit regard to the interests of the poor. There were some reasons for believing that adjustment might well benefit the poor. The traded goods sector in LDCs tends to be labor intensive, because that is usually their comparative advantage. Then the poor will probably gain from the relative price shifts associated with adjustment. However, that prediction must be qualified. The circumstances in most developing countries – the extent of price and wage flexibility, the mobility of the poor, the extent to which food behaves as a traded good in the short-term, the extent to which the poor consume traded goods, the extent to which they lose from cuts in public spending – are far more diverse than is allowed for in many of the models which guide policy-making. With the benefit of hindsight, many of the arguments that adjustment, relative to non-adjustment, had unambiguously hurt the poor were implausible. But so were some of the high expectations of supply-side response to adjustment, and hence of a rapid transition to a more favorable growth path.

A more balanced, and realistic, consensus on how poverty can be most effectively reduced started to emerge from the late 1980s, though one with deep roots in the history of thought on poverty, going back to Adam Smith. In this view, the main role of the state is to facilitate provision of privately under-supplied goods (infrastructure, but also social equity itself) in an otherwise market driven economy. With neutral incentives, growth in such an economy is seen as being in the best interests of the poor, who are intensive suppliers of the main factor of production likely to benefit, labor. Growth in private-sector economic activity is a key part of this story, both as an instrument for income poverty reduction, and as one of the means of financing public support where it is needed. But it is only a part. As much emphasis is given to successful public action, in the areas where it is called for.

What issues endure? A comprehensive list of overlapping topics should include (in no particular order): the political economy of poverty reduction; country-incentive issues in pro-poor aid policies; the costs and benefits to the poor of asset redistribution; the ways initial distribution affects the type of growth, and hence final distribution; the extent to which poverty considerations should influence macroeconomic and trade policies; measurement and causes of "persistent" versus "transient" poverty; complementarities between fighting chronic poverty and fighting vulnerability to poverty; the status of the so-called "special poverty groups" (women, children, remote areas); environmental effects (positive and negative) of poverty and its reduction; the impacts of developed country policies on distribution within developing countries.

However, one generic issue stands out: the need to better understand how to make a success of public action in fighting poverty. The history of development efforts – including some of the best intentioned – has clearly dulled expectations of what governments can do effectively. Yet how confident can we be in those expectations while we remain as ignorant as we are about the benefits and costs of much of what governments and donors do? Development agencies still devote few resources to proper evaluation. Granted, it is difficult to properly evaluate any project or policy after it is introduced, given that one is aiming to compare living standards "with" and "without" the project (which is quite distinct from "before" and "after"). The best hope is to build in the evaluation methodology – including the survey instrument – right from the start, prior to intervention. This is rarely done.

Effective public action needs good data and measurement. There are signs of an emerging consensus on poverty measurement, which might fruitfully guide future efforts at evaluation. Recent theory and practice has moved away from the earlier obsession with a single number – the count of how many people do not reach some arbitrary poverty line – or even a single measure of poverty, no matter how many axioms it satisfies. Instead, the aim is to form consistent comparisons of poverty, such as between different places or dates, or under alternative policies. Recent literature has identified a number of principles to guide such comparisons. The more challenging questions in poverty measurement now lie right at the heart of the problem of normative economics in general: how do we measure the "standard of living"? The welfarist approach – by which only information on individual utilities should be considered – infers preferences from behavior and makes ethically acceptable inter-personal comparisons of utility functions which reproduce those preferences. But the chances of convincingly retrieving individual preferences from observed behavior remain slim, recognizing that there are many non-market determinants of welfare even in the most market-oriented economy. The need for value judgements about individual utilities, and the search for convincing and applicable non-welfarist approaches, will continue.

Recognizing these pervasive uncertainties, what do we know about the world's poor, to help guide policy? The proportion of people deemed poor, by local poverty lines, decreased in most LDCs (for which we have data) between the mid-1960s and the mid-1980s. However, there has been negligible progress in the aggregate since then, and by any reasonable standard, *numbers* of poor have been increasing since the mid-1980s. Around 1990, over one billion people were living on less than one dollar per day. More striking than this observation is the marked regional imbalance in the current rate of progress in poverty reduction. Poverty is probably worsening in Africa (though data inadequacies warn against confidence), and Latin America. But in Asia the poor appear to be seeing some real gains, and can reasonably expect them to continue, albeit with ups and downs in some countries.

At micro level, much has been learnt from household-survey data. Households with low income per person tend to be larger, due mainly to more children. The children are less likely to reach average life expectancy, but it is the high replacement fertility of the poor – which is perfectly rational – that makes up the difference. The working members of poor households thus have more mouths to feed, but they also face higher risks of unemployment, and of illness preventing work. Women are worse off, though this need not be evident in the incidence of current consumption poverty, but rather in terms of the demands on their time, and their opportunities to escape poverty.

The poorest depend mainly on their labor; there is typically little else that they can derive income from. They typically face varied, and uncertain, employment prospects from one time of the year to another. Other risks pervade their lives, such as the threat of illness. They do many things to help insure themselves (including having many children), and to help insure each other, though often at a cost to longer-term prospects for escaping poverty.

In many respects relevant to policy, the poor are heterogeneous. The depth of current poverty varies, as do the endowments which might help in escaping poverty. Net trading positions (consumption minus production) in key markets – notably for food – also vary among the poor, so some gain while others lose from a given change in relative prices. In much of South and South-East Asia, for example, higher prices of the domestically produced food staple will generally benefit those near the poverty line, but many of the poorest will lose at least in the short term.

Typically, the highest incidence and severity of poverty are found in rural areas, especially if ill-watered. Concerns about the "urbanization of poverty" in LDCs are sometimes overstated. While the proportion of the poor living in urban areas is undoubtedly increasing, it remains true that virtually all aspects of poverty are generally worse in rural areas of LDCs. For many of the rural poor, their only immediate route out of poverty is by migration to towns, to face a higher expected income, though often a more uncertain one. This may or may not reduce aggregate poverty. We can be more confident that growth in agricultural output, fuelled by investment in human and physical infrastructure, is pro-poor, though not because the poor own much land.

The policies pursued by most LDCs up to the mid-1980s – and by many still – have been biased against the rural sector in various ways. The same is true – though different policies are involved – of the other major sectoral concentration of poor, namely the urban informal sector. There are clear prospects for reducing poverty by removing these biases. Looking ahead (far ahead in some cases), it is less clear how much further gain to the poor can be expected from introducing a bias in the opposite direction. That is a researchable question, but in the time being neutrality is the immediate aim.

However, provided that the sectoral composition of growth is not biased against the poor – though political-economy considerations suggest that this proviso should not be taken lightly – the overall rate of economic growth matters enormously to their well-being, more so than some past discussions of anti-poverty policy have recognized. Earlier concerns that growth in a dualistic developing country must increase inequality have largely vanished, both as a result of a deeper understanding of the contingent nature of such effects, and due to the belief that, for the poor, absolute levels of living matter more than relative positions. Elasticities of poverty measures with respect to distributionally-neutral growth in aggregate consumption of two or more are now common in LDCs, though there is considerable variation according to initial conditions, including wealth inequalities. While the potential for reducing consumption poverty through a growth process which is not biased against the poor is now undeniable, adverse initial conditions may mean that this potential is only realized painfully slowly.

Two important roles for public action can be identified. One involves fostering the conditions for pro-poor growth, particularly in providing wide access to the necessary physical and human assets, including infrastructure. The other entails helping those who cannot participate fully in the benefits of such growth, or who do so with continued exposure to unacceptable risks. Here there is an important role for interventions aiming by various means to improve the distribution of the benefits of public expenditures on social services and safety nets in LDCs. Those means range from the selection of key categories of public spending, such as primary education and basic health care, to more finely targeted transfers (including nutrition and health interventions) based on poverty indicators, or on some self-targeting mechanism such as work requirements. Though disappointing outcomes abound, many countries have demonstrated what is possible with timely and well-conceived interventions.

## References

Adams, D.W., Graham, D. and von Pischke, J., eds., (1984) *Undermining rural development with cheap credit*. Boulder, CO: Westview.

Addison, T. and Demery, L. (1985) 'Macroeconomic stabilization, income distribution and poverty: a preliminary survey', Overseas Development Institute Working Paper 15, London ODI.

Adelman, I. and Morris, C.T. (1973) *Economic growth and social equity in developing countries*. Stanford: Stanford University Press.

Adelman, I. and Robinson, S. (1988) 'Income distribution and development', in: Chenery and Srinivasan (1988).

Agarwala R. (1983) 'Price distortions and growth in developing countries', World Bank Staff Working Paper 575, The World Bank, Washington, DC.

Aghazadeh I. and Evans, D. (1985) 'Price distortions, efficiency and growth', Institute of Development Studies, Sussex, mimeo.

Ahluwalia, M.S. (1976) 'Inequality, poverty and development', *Journal of Development Economics*, 3:307–342.

Ahluwalia, M.S. (1985) 'Rural poverty, agricultural production and prices: A re-examination', in: Mellor and Desai (1985).

Ahluwalia, M.S., Carter, N.G. and Chenery, H.B. (1979) 'Growth and poverty in developing countries', *Journal of Development Economics*, 6:299–341.

Ahmad, E., Drèze, J., Hills, J. and Sen, A.K. (1991) *Social security in developing countries*. Oxford: Clarendon.

Alderman, H. (1987) 'Allocation of goods through non-price mechanisms: Evidence on distribution by willingness to wait', *Journal of Development Economics*, 25:105–124.

Alderman, H. (1993) 'New research on poverty and malnutrition; what are the implications for poverty?', in: Lipton and van der Gaag (1993).

Alderman, H. and Paxson, C. (1992) 'Do the poor insure? A synthesis of the literature on risk and consumption in developing countries', The World Bank and Woodrow Wilson School, Princeton University, mimeo.

Anand, S. (1983) *Inequality and poverty in Malaysia*. Oxford: Oxford University Press.

Anand, S. (1991) 'Poverty and human development in Asia and the Pacific', in: *Poverty alleviation in Asia and the Pacific*. United Nations Development Programme, New York.

Anand, S. and Harris, C. (1991) 'Food and standard of living: An analysis on Sri Lankan data', in: Jean Drèze and Amartya Sen, eds., *The political economy of hunger, vol. 1, Entitlement and well-being*. Oxford: Oxford University Press.

Anand, S. and Harris, C. (1992) 'Issues in the measurement of undernutrition', in: S. Osmani, ed., *Nutrition and poverty*. Oxford: Oxford University Press.

Anand, S. and Kanbur, R. (1984) 'Inequality and development: A reconsideration', in: H.P. Nissen, ed., *Toward income distribution policies*. Tilbury: EADI Book Series 3.

Anand, S. and Kanbur, R. (1985) 'Poverty under the Kuznets process'. *The Economic Journal (Supplement)* 95:42–50.

Anand, S. and Kanbur, R. (1993) 'The Kuznets process and the inequality-development relationship', *Journal of Development Economics*, 40:25–52.

Anand, S. and Ravallion, M. (1993) 'Human development in poor countries: On the role of private incomes and public services', *Journal of Economic Perspectives*, 7(Winter):133–150.

Anderson, J. and Hazell, P., eds., (1989) *Variability in grain yields*. Baltimore: Johns Hopkins University Press.

Anker, R. and Hein, C. (1985) 'Employment of women outside agriculture in third world countries: An overview of occupational statistics', International Labor Office, World Employment Programme, Population and Labor Policies Programme, Geneva.

Antle, J.M. (1983) 'Infrastructure and aggregate agricultural productivity: International evidence'. *Economic Development and Cultural Change*, 31:609–619.

Ashenfelter, O. and Oaxaca, R.L. (1991) 'Labor market discrimination and economic development', in: Birdsall and Sabot (1991).

Asian Development Bank (ADB) (1992) 'Rural poverty in Asia', Pt. III of *Asian Development Outlook*. Manila: Oxford University Press.

Atkinson, A.B. (1970) 'On the measurement of inequality', *Journal of Economic Theory*, 2:244–263.

Atkinson, A.B. (1975) *The Economics of Inequality*. Oxford: Oxford University Press.

Atkinson, A.B. (1987) 'On the measurement of poverty', *Econometrica*, 55:749–764.

Atkinson, A.B. (1989) *Poverty and social security*. New York: Harvester Wheatsheaf.

Atkinson, A.B. and Bourguignon, F. (1982) 'The comparison of multi-dimensional distributions of economic status', *Review of Economic Studies*, 49:183–201.

Atkinson, A.B. and Bourguignon, F. (1987) 'Income distribution and differences in needs', in: George R. Feiwel, ed., *Arrow and the foundations of the theory of economic policy*. London: Macmillan Press.

Azam, J.-P., Chambas, G., Guillaumont, P. and Guillaumont, S. (1989) *The impact of macroeconomic policies on the rural poor*. UNDP policy discussion paper, UNDP, New York.

Balisacan, A.M. (1993) 'Anatomy of poverty during adjustment: The case of the Philippines', mimeo, University of the Philippines, Quezon City, Philippines.

Banerjee, A.V. and Newman, A.F. (1993) 'Occupational choice and the process of development', *Journal of Political Economy*, 101:274–299.

Barbier, E. (1988) 'Sustainable agriculture and the resource-poor: Policy issues and options', Paper 88-02, London: Environmental Economics Centre.

Bardhan, K. (1985) 'Women's work, welfare and status', *Economic and Political Weekly*, 20:51–52.

Bardhan, P.K. (1970) 'On the minimum level of living and the rural poor', *Indian Economic Review*, 5:129–136.

Bardhan, P.K. (1982) 'Little girls and death in India', *Economic and Political Weekly*, 17(36):1448–1450.

Bardhan, P.K. (1984) *Land, labor and rural poverty*. Berkeley: University of California.

Bardhan, P.K. (1990) 'Symposium on the state and economic development', *The Journal of Economic Perspectives*, 4:3–8.

Bardhan, P.K. and Rudra, A. (1981) 'Terms and conditions of labor contracts in agriculture', *Oxford Bulletin of Economics and Statistics*, 43.

Bates, R. (1981) *Markets and states in tropical Africa*. Berkeley: University of California.

Bauer, P. (1965) 'The vicious circle of poverty: Reality or myth?', *Weltwirtschaftliches Archiv*, Sep.

Becker, G. and Lewis, H.G. (1974) 'On the interaction between the quantity and quality of children', *Journal of Political Economy*, 81(2, pt 2).

Behrman, J. (1982) 'Country and sectoral variations in manufacturing elasticities of substitution between capital and labor', in: A.O. Krueger et al., *Trade and employment in developing countries*. Chicago, IL: University of Chicago Press.

Behrman, J. (1990) 'The action of human resources and poverty on one another. What we have yet

Behrman, J. (1982) 'Country and sectoral variations in manufacturing elasticities of substitution between capital and labor', in: A.O. Krueger et al., *Trade and employment in developing countries*. Chicago, IL: University of Chicago Press.

Behrman, J. (1990) 'The action of human resources and poverty on one another. What we have yet to learn', Working Paper 74, Living Standards Measurement Study, Washington, DC: The World Bank.

Behrman, J. (1991) 'Nutrient intake demand relations: Incomes, prices, schooling', mimeo, Department of Economics, University of Pennsylvania.

Behrman, J. (1993) 'The economic rationale for investing in nutrition in developing countries', *World Development*, 21:1749–1771.

Behrman, J. and Deolalikar, A. (1987) 'Will developing country nutrition improve with income? A case study for rural south India', *Journal of Political Economy*, 95:108–138.

Behrman, J. and Deolalikar, A. (1988) 'Health and nutrition', in: T.N. Srinivasan and P.K. Bardhan, eds., *Rural poverty in South Asia*. New York: Columbia University Press.

Behrman, J. and Wolfe, B.L. (1984) 'More evidence on nutrient demand: Income seems overrated and women's schooling underemphasized', *Journal of Development Economics*, 14:105–128.

Bell, C. (1974) 'The political framework', in: H. Chenery, M. Ahluwalia, C. Bell, J. Duloy and R. Jolly, eds., *Redistribution with growth*. Oxford: Oxford University Press.

Bell, C. (1988) 'Credit markets and interlinked transactions', in: H. Chenery and T.N. Srinivasan, eds., *Handbook of Development Economics, Vol. I*. Amsterdam: North-Holland.

Bell, C. (1990) 'Reforming property rights in land and tenancy', *World Bank Research Observer*, 5(2, July).

Bell, C. (1993) 'Interactions between institutions and informal credit agencies in rural India', in: K. Hoff, A. Braverman and J.E. Stiglitz, eds., *The economics of rural organization*. Oxford: Oxford University Press.

Bell, C. and Duloy, J.H. (1974) 'Statistical priorities', in: H. Chenery, M. Ahluwalia, C. Bell, J. Duloy and R. Jolly, eds., *Redistribution with growth*. Oxford: Oxford University Press.

Bell, C. and Rich, R. (1994) 'Rural poverty and agricultural performance in post-independence India', *Oxford Bulletin of Economics and Statistics*, 56(2):111–133.

Bennett, L. (1991) *Gender and poverty in India*. Country Study, Washington, DC: The World Bank.

Berg, A. (1973) *The nutrition factor*. Washington, DC: Brookings Institution.

Berry, A. and Cline, W. (1979) *Agrarian structure and productivity in developing countries*. Baltimore: Johns Hopkins University Press.

Besley, T. (1994) 'How do market failures justify intervention in rural credit markets?', *World Bank Research Observer*, 9(1, January):27–48.

Besley, T. and Coate, S. (1992) 'Workfare vs. welfare: Incentive arguments for work requirements in poverty alleviation programs'. *American Economic Review*, 82:249–261.

Besley, T., Coate, S. and Loury, G. (1993) 'The economics of rotating savings and credit associations', *American Economic Review*, 83(4):792–810.

Besley, T. and Kanbur, R. (1988) 'Food subsidies and poverty reduction', *Economic Journal*, 98:701–719.

Besley, T. and Kanbur, R. (1993) 'Principles of targeting', in: M. Lipton and J. van der Gaag, eds., *Including the poor*. Washington, DC: The World Bank.

Bhalla, S. and Roy, P. (1988) 'Mis-specification in farm productivity analysis: The role of land quality', *Oxford Economic Papers*, 40(1):55–73.

Bhanoji R. (1981) 'Measurement of deprivation and poverty based on the proportion spent on food', *World Development*, 9(4).

Bhargava, A. (1991) 'Estimating short and long run income elasticities of food and nutrients for rural south India', *Journal of the Royal Statistical Society A*, 154:157–174.

Bhargava, A. (1994) 'Nutritional status and the allocation of time in Rwandese households', *Journal of Econometrics*, forthcoming.

Bhargava, A. and Ravallion, M. (1993) 'Is household consumption a martingale? Tests for rural south India', *Review of Economics and Statistics*, forthcoming.

Bidani, B. and Ravallion, M. (1993) 'A new regional poverty profile for Indonesia', *Bulletin of Indonesian Economic Studies*, 29(3):37–68.

institutions affect agricultural output and investment in India', *Journal of Development Economics*, 41:337–366.

Binswanger, H. and McIntire, J. (1987) 'Behavioral and material determinants of production relations in land-abundant tropical agriculture', *Economic Development and Cultural Change*, 36(1):73–99.

Binswanger, H. and Rosenzweig M. (1986) 'Behavioral and material determinants of production in agriculture', *Journal of Development Studies*, 22(3):503–539.

Birdsall, N. (1979) *Siblings and schooling in urban Colombia*. Doctoral dissertation (unpub.), New Haven: Yale University.

Birdsall, N. (1980) *Population and poverty in the developing world*. Staff Working Paper No. 404, Washington, DC: The World Bank.

Birdsall, N. (1988) 'Economic approaches to population growth', in: Chenery and Srinivasan (1988).

Birdsall, N. and Behrman, J. (1991) 'Why do males earn more than females in urban Brazil: Earnings discrimination or job discrimination?', in: Birdsall and Sabot (1991).

Birdsall, N. and Sabot, R., eds., (1991) *Unfair advantage. Labor market discrimination in developing countries*. The World Bank, Washington, DC.

Birgegaard, L.E. (1987) 'A review of experiences with integrated rural development', Issues Paper No. 6, Uppsala: Swedish University of Agricultural Science, Rural Development Centre.

Blackorby, C. and Donaldson, D. (1980) 'Ethical indices for the measurement of poverty', *Econometrica*, 48:1053–1060.

Bliss, C.J. and Stern, N.H. (1982) *Palanpur: The economy of an Indian village*. Oxford: Oxford University Press.

Boateng, E.O., Ewusi, K., Kanbur, R. and McKay, A. (1990) 'A poverty profile for Ghana, 1987–1988', Social dimensions of adjustment in sub-Saharan Africa, Working Paper 5, The World Bank, Washington, DC. [*Journal of African Economies*, 1 (1992)]

Bongaarts, J. (1992) 'The supply-demand framework for the determinants of fertility: An alternative interpretation', Working Paper 44, Research Division, The Population Council, New York.

Boserup, E. (1965) *The conditions of agricultural progress*. Bombay: Asia Publishers.

Bottomley, A. (1963) 'The costs of administering private loans in underdeveloped rural areas', *Oxford Economic Papers*, 15(2):154–163.

Bottomley, A. (1964) 'Monopoly profit as a determinant of interest rates in underdeveloped rural areas', *Oxford Economic Papers*, 16(3):431–437.

Bouis, H.E. (1991) 'The determinants of household-level demand for micronutrients: An analysis for Philippine farm households', mimeo, International Food Policy Research Institute, Washington, DC.

Bouis, H.E. and Haddad, L.J. (1992) 'Are estimates of calorie-income elasticities too high? A recalibration of the plausible range', *Journal of Development Economics*, 39:333–364.

Bouis, H.E. and Haddad, L. (1991) 'Effects of agricultural commercialization on land tenure, household resource allocation and nutrition in the Philippines', Research Report 79, International Food Policy Research Institute, Washington, DC.

Bourguignon, F. and Fields, G. (1990) 'Poverty measures and anti-poverty policy', *Recherches Economiques de Louvain*, 56:409–428.

Bourguignon, F., de Melo, J. and Suwa, A. (1991) 'Modeling the effects of adjustment programs on income distribution', *World Development*, 19(11):1527–1544.

Bourguignon, F., Morrisson, C. and Suwa, A. (1991) 'Adjustment and the rural sector: A counterfactual analysis of Morocco', OECD Development Centre, Paris, mimeo.

Browning, M. (1992) 'Children and household economic behavior', *Journal of Economic Literature*, 29:1434–1475.

Cain, M. (1984) 'On the relationship between landholding and fertility', Working Paper No. 106, New York: Population Council.

Cain, M. and Mozumder, A. (1981) 'Labor market structure and reproductive behavior in rural South Asia', in: G. Rodgers and G. Standing, eds., *Child Work, Poverty and Underdevelopment*. Geneva: ILO.

Caldwell, J.C. (1979) 'Education as a factor in mortality decline: An examination of Nigerian data', *Population Studies*, 33(3):395–413.

Caldwell, J.C. (1986) 'Routes to low mortality in poor countries', *Population and Development Review*, 12:171–220.

Cassen, R. (1978) *India: Population, economy, society*. London: Macmillan.

Chambers, R., Longhurst, R. and Pacey, A., eds., (1981) *Seasonal dimensions to rural poverty*. Pinter: London.

Chander, R., Grootaert, C. and Pyatt, G. (1980) 'Living standards in developing countries', Living Standards Measurement Study Working Paper No. 1, The World Bank, Washington, DC.

Chaudhri, D.P. (1979) *Education, innovations and agricultural development: A study of India*. London: Croom Helm.

Chaudhuri, S. (1993) 'Crop choice, fertilizer use and credit constraints: An empirical analysis', mimeo, Department of Economics, Princeton University.

Chaudhuri, S. and Ravallion, M. (1994) 'How well do static welfare indicators identify the chronically poor?', *Journal of Public Economics*, 53(3):367–394.

Chayanov, A.V. (1966) *Theory of Peasant Economy*. Homewood: Irwin.

Chen, L., Huq, E. and D'Souza, S. (1981) 'Sex bias in the family allocation of food and health care in rural Bangladesh', *Population and Development Review*, 17(1):55–70.

Chen L. and Drèze, J. (1992) 'Widows and well-being in rural North India', Discussion Paper 40, Development Economics Research Programme, London School of Economics, London.

Chen, S., Datt, G. and Ravallion, M. (1994) 'Is poverty increasing in the developing world?', *Review of Income and Wealth*, forthcoming.

Chenery, H., Ahluwalia, M., Bell, C., Duloy, J. and Jolly, R. (1974) *Redistribution with growth*. Oxford: Oxford University Press.

Chenery, H. and Srinivasan, T.N., eds., (1988) *Handbook of development economics: Vol. 1*. Rotterdam: North Holland.

Chole, E. and Mulat, T. (1988) 'Land settlements in Ethiopia: A review of developments', in: Oberai (1988).

Chuta, E. and Liedholm, C. (1981) *Rural non-farm employment: A review of the state of the art*. East Lansing: Michigan State University.

Clarke, G.R.G. (1993) 'More evidence on income distribution and growth', mimeo, Department of Economics, University of Rochester.

Clark, S., Hemming, R. and Ulph, D. (1981) 'On indices for the measurement of poverty', *Economic Journal*, 91:515–526.

Cleland, J. and Wilson, C. (1987) 'Demand theories of the fertility transition: An iconoclastic view', *Population Studies*, 41(1).

Coate, S. and Ravallion, M. (1993) 'Reciprocity without commitment: Characterization and performance of informal insurance arrangements', *Journal of Development Economics*, 40:1–24.

Coats, A.W. (1972) 'The classical economists, industrialization and poverty', in: IEA (1972).

Cohen, J.M. (1975) 'Effects of green revolution strategies on tenants and small-scale landowners in the Chilalo region of Ethiopia', *Journal of Developing Areas*, 9:335–358.

Colclough, C. and Manor, J., eds., (1991) *States or markets?* Oxford: Oxford University Press.

Collier, P. and Lal, D. (1986) *Labor and poverty in Kenya 1990–1980* Oxford: Oxford University Press.

Connell, J., Dasgupta, B., Laishley, R. and Lipton, M. (1976) *Migration from rural areas: The evidence from village studies*. Delhi: Oxford University Press.

Cornia, G.A., Jolly, R. and Stewart, F., eds., (1987) *Adjustment with a human face* (2 vols.). Oxford: Oxford University Press.

Cornia, G.A. and Stewart, F. (1994) 'Two errors of targeting', in: van de Walle and Nead (1994).

Cox, D. and Jimenez, E. (1994) 'Private transfers and the effectiveness of public income redistribution in the Philippines', in: van de Walle and Nead (1994).

Dandekar, V.M. and Rath, N, (1971) *Poverty in India*. Bombay: Economic and Political Weekly, for Indian School of Political Economy.

Dasgupta, B. (1977) *Village society and labor use*. Delhi: Oxford University Press.

Dasgupta, M. (1987) 'Selective discrimination against female children in rural Punjab, India', *Population and Development Review*, 13(1):77–100.

Dasgupta, P. (1992) 'The economics of destitution', in: A. de Zeeuw, ed., *Advanced lectures in quantitative economics, Vol. 2*. New York: Academic Press, forthcoming.

Dasgupta, P. (1993) *An inquiry into well-being and destitution*. Oxford: Oxford University Press.

Dasgupta, P. and Maler, I. (1990) 'The environment and emerging development issues', Helsinki: World Institute for Development Economics Research.

Dasgupta, P. and Ray, D. (1986) 'Inequality as a determinant of malnutrition and unemployment: Theory', *The Economic Journal*, 96:1011–1034.

Dasgupta, P. and Ray, D. (1987) 'Inequality as a determinant of malnutrition and unemployment: Policy', *The Economic Journal*, 97:177–188.

Dasgupta, P. and Ray, D. (1990) 'Adapting to undernourishment: The biological evidence and its implications', in: Drèze and Sen (1990).

Datt, G. (1994) 'Poverty in India, 1951–91', Poverty and Human Resources Division, The World Bank.

Datt, G. and Ravallion, M. (1992) 'Growth and redistribution components of changes in poverty measures: A decomposition with applications to Brazil and India in the 1980s', *Journal of Development Economics*, 38:275–295.

Datt, G. and Ravallion, M. (1993) 'Regional disparities, targeting and poverty in India', in: Lipton and van der Gaag (1993).

Datt, G. and Ravallion, M. (1994) 'Transfer benefits to the poor from public works employment', *The Economic Journal*, forthcoming.

Deaton, A. (1980) 'The measurement of welfare. Theory and practical guidelines', Living Standards Measurement Study Working Paper No. 7, The World Bank.

Deaton, A. (1992) *Understanding consumption*. Oxford: Oxford University Press.

Deaton, A. (1994) *The analysis of household surveys. Microeconometric analysis for development policy*. Poverty and Human Resources Division, The World Bank, Washington, DC, mimeo.

Deaton, A. and Muellbauer, J. (1980) *Economics and consumer behavior*. Cambridge: Cambridge University Press.

Deaton, A. and Muellbauer, J. (1986) 'On measuring child costs: With applications to poor countries', *Journal of Political Economy*, 94:720–744.

Deaton, A. and Paxson, C.H. (1991) 'Patterns of aging in Thailand and Côte d'Ivoire', Working Paper No. 81, Living Standards Measurement Study, Washington, DC: The World Bank.

de Janvry, A. and Sadoulet, E. (1989) 'Investment strategies to combat rural poverty: A proposal for Latin America', *World Development*, 17(8):1203–1223.

de Janvry, A. and Sadoulet, E. (1993) 'Rural development in Latin America: Relinking poverty reduction to growth', in: Lipton and van der Gaag (1993).

de Janvry, A., Fafchamps, M., Raki, M. and Sadoulet, E. (1991) 'Structural adjustment and the peasantry in Morocco: A computable household model approach', Department of Agricultural and Resource Economics, University of California, Berkeley, mimeo.

Demery, L. and Demery, D. (1991) 'Poverty and macroeconomic policy in Malaysia 1979–87', *World Development*, 19:1615–1632.

Demery, L., Ferroni, M. and Grootaert, C. (1993) *Understanding the social impact of policy reform*. Washington, DC: The World Bank.

Deolalikar, A. (1988) 'Nutrition and labor productivity in agriculture: Estimates for rural south India', *The Review of Economics and Statistics*, 70:406–413.

Dervis, K., de Melo, J. and Robinson, S. (1982) *General equilibrium models for development policy*. Cambridge: Cambridge University Press.

de Soto, H. (1989) *The other path: The invisible revolution in the third world*. New York: Harper and Row.

Dev, S.M., Parikh, K.S. and Suryanarayan, M.H. (1991) 'Rural poverty in India: Incidence, issues and policies', Discussion Paper No. 55, Ahmedabad: Indira Gandhi Institute of Development Research.

Domar, E. (1957) *Essays in the theory of economic growth*. Oxford: Oxford University Press.

Dorosh, P.A. and Sahn, D.E. (1993) 'A general equilibrium analysis of the effect of macro-economic adjustment on poverty in Africa', Cornell University Food and Nutrition Policy Program, mimeo.

Drèze, J. (1990a) 'Famine prevention in India', in: Drèze and Sen (1990), Vol. 2.

Drèze, J. (1990b) 'Widows in rural India', DEP No. 26, London: London School of Economics, Development Economics Research Programme.

Drèze, J. and Mukherjee, A. (1989) 'Labor contracts in rural India: Theories and evidence', in: S. Chakravarty, ed., *The balance between industry and agriculture in economic development 3: Manpower and transfers*. London: Macmillan.

Drèze, J. and Sen, A. (1989) *Hunger and public action*. Oxford: Oxford University Press.

Drèze, J. and Sen, A. (1990) *The political economy of hunger* (3 volumes). Oxford: Oxford University Press.

Drèze, J. and Stern, N. (1987) 'The theory of cost-benefit analysis', in: A.J. Auerbach and M. Feldstein, eds., *The handbook of public economics*. Amsterdam: North-Holland.

Drinkwater, M. (1991) *The state and Agrarian change in Zimbabwe's communal areas*. Basingstoke: Macmillan.

Easterlin, R. and Crimmins, E. (1985) *The fertility revolution: A supply-demand analysis*. Chicago: Chicago University Press.

Echeverri-Gent, J. (1988) 'Guaranteed employment in an India state: The Maharashtran experience', *Asian Survey*, 28:1294–1310.

Eckholm, E.P. (1976) *Losing ground: Environmental stress and world food prospects*. New York: W.W. Norton.

Edmundson, W. and Sukhatme, P. (1990) 'Food and work: Poverty and hunger?', *Economic Development and Cultural Change*, 38(2):263–280.

Edwards, S. and van Wijnbergen, S. (1989) 'Disequilibrium and structural adjustment', in: Chenery and Srinivasan (1989).

Eswaran, M. and Kotwal, A. (1993) 'A theory of real wage growth in LDCs', *Journal of Development Economics*, 42(2):243–270.

Fafchamps, M. (1992) 'Solidarity networks in preindustrial societies: Rational peasants with a moral economy', *Economic Development and Cultural Change*, 41:147–174.

Falkinger, J. (1992) 'An Engelian model of growth and innovation with hierarchic consumer demand and unequal incomes', Institute of Public Economics, University of Graz, Austria, mimeo.

Farah, A. and Preston, S.H. (1982) 'Child mortality differentials in Sudan', *Population and Development Review*, 8(2):365–383.

Fei, J.C.H. et al. (1979) *Growth with equity: The Taiwan case*. New York: Oxford University Press for World Bank.

Fields, G. (1980) *Poverty, inequality and development*. New York: Cambridge University Press.

Fields, G. (1989) 'Changes in poverty and inequality in developing countries', *World Bank Research Observer*, 4:167–186.

Flegg, A. (1982) 'Inequality of income, illiteracy and medical care as determinants of infant mortality in UDCs', *Population Studies*, 36(3):441–458.

Foster, J. (1984) 'On economic poverty: A survey of aggregate measures', *Advances in Econometrics*, 3:215–251.

Foster, J., Greer, J. and Thorbecke, E. (1984) 'A class of decomposable poverty measures', *Econometrica*, 52:761–765.

Foster, J. and Shorrocks, A.F. (1988) 'Poverty orderings', *Econometrica*, 56:173–177.

Foster, J. and Shorrocks, A.F. (1991) 'Subgroup consistent poverty indices', *Econometrica*, 59:687–709.

Foxley, A. (1979) *Redistributive effects of government programmes: The Chilean case*. Oxford: Oxford University Press.

Frank, Jr., C.R. and Webb, R.C., eds., (1977) *Income distribution and growth in the less-developed countries*. Washington, DC: The Brookings Institution.

Frisch, R. (1978) 'Population, food intake and fertility', *Science*, 199(6 January):22–30.

Frisch, R. (1980) 'Pubertal adipose tissue: Is it necessary for normal maturation?', *Federation Proceedings*, 39(7):2395–2400.

Frisch, R. (1982) 'Malnutrition and fertility', *Science*, 215(5 March):1272–1273.

Gaiha, R. (1989) 'Poverty, agricultural production and price fluctuations in rural India: A reformulation', *Cambridge Journal of Economics*, 13(2):333–352.

Gaiha, R. (1992a) 'On the chronically poor in rural India', *Journal of International Development*, 4(3):273–280.

Gaiha, R. (1992b) 'Design of poverty alleviation strategy in rural areas', mimeo, Rome: FAO.

Gaiha, R. and Deolalikar, A.B. (1993) 'Permanent, expected and innate poverty: Estimates for semi-arid rural south India, 1975–1984'. *Cambridge Journal of Economics*, 17(4):409–422.

Gaiha, R. and Kazmi (1982) 'Aspects of poverty in rural India', Delhi: Faculty of Management Studies, Delhi University.

Garcia, M. (1991) 'Impact of female sources of income on food demand among rural households in the Philippines', *Quarterly Journal of International Agriculture*, 30(2):109–124.

Gastwirth, J.L. (1971) 'A general definition of the Lorenz curve', *Econometrica*, 39:1037–1039.

Geanakoplos, J. and Poleemarchakis, H. (1986) 'Existence, regularity and constrained suboptimality of competitive allocations when the asset market is incomplete', in: W. Heller, R. Starr and D. Starett, eds., *Uncertainty, informations and communication: Essays in honor of Kenneth J. Arrow*. Cambridge: Cambridge University Press.

Gertler, P. and van der Gaag, J. (1990) *The willingness to pay for medical care*. Baltimore: Johns Hopkins University Press for the World Bank.

Gersowitz, M. (1988) 'Saving and development', in: Chenery and Srinivasan (1988).

Gilby, T. (1975) *Theological texts volume 38: St. Thomas Aquinas's Summa Theologica*. Oxford: Oxford University Press.

Glewwe, P. (1990) 'Improving data on poverty in the Third World. The World Bank's Living Standards Measurement Study', Policy Research and External Affairs Working Paper WPS 416, The World Bank, Washington, DC.

Glewwe, P. and Hall, G. (1994) 'Poverty and inequality during unorthodox adjustment: The case of Peru, 1985–1990', *Economic Development and Cultural Change*, 42(4):689–718.

Glewwe, P. and van der Gaag, J. (1990) 'Identifying the poor in developing countries: Do different definitions matter?', *World Development*, 18:803–814.

Greenhalgh, S. (1985) 'Sexual stratification: The other side of "growth with equity" in East Asia', *Population and Development Review*, 11(2):265–314.

Greer, J. and Thorbecke, E. (1986) 'A methodology for measuring food poverty applied to Kenya', *Journal of Development Economics*, 24:59–74.

Grootaert, C. (1994) 'Structural change and poverty in Africa: A decomposition analysis for Côte d'Ivoire', *Journal of Development Economics*, forthcoming.

Grootaert, C. and Kanbur, R. (1990) 'Policy-oriented analysis of poverty and the social dimensions of structural adjustment', Washington, DC: Social Dimensions of Adjustment Project, The World Bank.

Grosh, M.E. (1991) 'The household survey as a tool for policy change. Lessons from the Jamaican survey of living conditions', LSMS Working Paper 80, The World Bank, Washington, DC.

Grosh, M.E. (1994) 'Towards quantifying the tradeoff: Administrative costs and targeting accuracy', in: van de Walle and Nead (1994).

Gulati, L. (1977) 'Rationing in a peri-urban community: Case-study of a squatter habitat', *Economic and Political Weekly*, 12(12):501–506.

Gulati, L. (1990) 'Agricultural workers' pensions in Kerala. An experiment in social assistance', *Economic and Political Weekly*, February 10:339–343.

Haddad, L. (1991) 'Gender and poverty in Ghana', *IDS Bulletin*, 22(1):5–16.

Haddad, L. and Kanbur, R. (1990) 'How serious is the neglect of intra-household inequality?', *The Economic Journal*, 100:866–881.

Haddad, L. and Kanbur, R. (1993) 'Is there an intrahousehold Kuznets curve? Some evidence for the Philippines', *Public Finance*, 47 (supplement):77–93.

Hagenaars, A.J.M. and de Vos, K. (1988) 'The definition and measurement of poverty', *The Journal of Human Resources*, 23:211–221.

Hagenaars, A.J.M. and van Praag, B.M.S. (1985) 'A synthesis of poverty line definitions', *Review of Income and Wealth*, 31(2):139–154.

Haggblade, S., Hazell, P. and Brown, J. (1989) 'Farm-nonfarm linkages in rural sub-Saharan Africa', *World Development*, 17(8):1173–1202.

Hammer, J.S., Nabi, I. and Cercone, J.A. (1994) 'Distributional impact of social sector expenditures in Malaysia', in: van de Walle and Nead (1994).

Hansen, B. (1969) 'Employment and wages in rural Egypt', *American Economic Review*, 59:298–313.

Hanson, C. (1972) 'Welfare before the welfare state', in IEA (1972).

Harriss, B. (1990) 'The intrafamily distribution of hunger', in: Drèze and Sen (1990).

Hart, G. (1980) 'Household labor allocation in a rural Javanese village', in: H. Binswanger et al., eds., *Rural Household Studies in Asia*. Singapore: University Press.

Hartwell, M. (1972) 'Consequences of the industrial revolution in England for the poor', in: IEA (1972).

Hayami, Y. and Ruttan, V. (1985) *Agricultural development: An international perspective*. Baltimore: Johns Hopkins University Press.

Hazell, P. (1982) *Instability in Indian Foodgrain Production*. Research Paper No. 30, Washington, DC: IFPRI.

Hazell, P. and Ramasamy, C. (1991) *The green revolution reconsidered*. Baltimore: Johns Hopkins University Press.

Hazell, P. and Haggblade, S. (1993) 'Farm/non-farm growth linkages and welfare of the poor', in: Lipton and van der Gaag (1993).

Hazell, P., Pomareda, C. and Valdés, A., eds., (1986) *Crop insurance for agricultural development*. Baltimore: Johns Hopkins University Press.

Hegel, G.W.F. (1821/1991) *Elements of the philosophy of right*. ed. A. Wood, Cambridge: Cambridge University Press.

Heston, A. (1992) 'A brief review of some problems in using national accounts data in level comparisons and growth studies', Department of Economics, University of Pennsylvania, presented at 'Conference on Data Base of Development Analysis', Yale University, May 1992, mimeo.

Hill, A. (1981) *The demographic situation in sub-Saharan Africa*. Discussion Paper No. 81–22, Population and Human Resource Division, Washington, DC: The World Bank.

Hill, C. (1972) *The world turned upside down: Radical ideas during the English revolution*. London: Temple Smith.

Hill, P. (1972) *Rural Hausa: A village and a Sesting*. Cambridge: Cambridge University Press.

Hill, P. (1982) *Dry grain farming families*. Cambridge: University Press.

Himmelfarb, G. (1984) *The idea of poverty*. London: Faber.

Hoff, K. (1993) 'The second theorem of the second best', STICERD Working Paper, London School of Economics (*Journal of Public Economics*, forthcoming).

Hoff, K., Braverman, A. and Stglitz, J.E., eds., (1993) *The economics of rural organization*. Oxford: Oxford University Press.

Holleman, C.F. (1991) *The effects of the green revolution on household food acquisition behavior in Eastern province, Zambia*. Cornell University M.Sc. thesis (unpublished).

Home, T.A. (1978) *The social thought of Bernard Mandeville*. London: Macmillan.

Hont, I. and Ignatieff, M. (1983) *Wealth and virtue*. Cambridge: Cambridge University Press.

Hopper, W.D. (1955) 'Seasonal labor cycles in Eastern Uttar Pradesh', *The Eastern Anthropologist*, 8,(3–4).

Hossain, M. (1984) 'Credit for the rural poor: The experience of the Grameen Bank', Bangladesh Institute of Development Studies Research Monograph No. 4, Dhaka.

House, W.J. (1989) 'Demography, employment and poverty at the household level in urban Juba, Southern Sudan', (Population and Labor Policies Programme), WEP Working Paper No. 168, Geneva: ILO.

Howes, M. (1985) *Whose water?* Dhaka: Bangladesh Institute of Development Studies.

Howes, S. (1993) 'Mixed dominance: A new criterion for poverty analysis', Distributional Analysis Research Programme Working Paper 3, London School of Economics.

Huffman, S.L. et al. (1987) 'Nutrition and fertility in Bangladesh', *Population Studies*, 41(3):447–462.

Hull, T. and Hull, V. (1977) 'The relationship of economic class and fertility', *Population Studies*, 31(1):43–57.

Huppi, M. and Ravallion, M. (1991) 'The sectoral structure of poverty during an adjustment period. Evidence for Indonesia in the mid-1980s', *World Development*, 19:1653–1678.

IEA (Institute of Economic Affairs) (1972) *The Long Debate on Poverty*. London: Unwin.

IFAD (International Fund for Agricultural Development) (1992) *The state of world rural poverty: An enquiry into causes and consequences.* New York: New York University Press.

Iliffe, J. (1987) *The African poor.* Cambridge: Cambridge University Press.

International Labor Office (ILO) (1972) *Employment, income and equality: A strategy for increasing productive employment in Kenya.* Geneva: ILO.

Iliffe, J. (1985) *Informal Sector in Africa.* Addis Ababa: Jobs and Skills Programme for Africa.

Irfan, M. (1989) 'Poverty, class structure and household demographic behavior in rural Pakistan', in: Rodgers (1989).

Isenman, P. (1980) 'Basic needs: The case of Sri Lanka', *World Development,* 8(3):237–258.

Jain, L.R. and Tendulkar, S.D. (1990) 'Role of growth and distribution in the observed headcount ratio measure of poverty: A decomposition exercise for India', Technical Report No. 9004 (Indian Statistical Institute, Delhi).

Jamison, D. and Lau, L. (1982) *Farmer education and farm efficiency.* Baltimore: Johns Hopkins University Press.

Jodha, N.S. (1986) 'Common property resources and rural poor in dry regions of India', *Economic and Political Weekly,* 21:1169–1181.

Jodha, N.S. (1988) 'Poverty debate in India: A minority view', *Economic and Political Weekly,* 23:45–47.

Jorgenson, D.W. and Slesnick, D.T. (1984) 'Aggregate consumer behavior and the measurement of inequality', *Review of Economic Studies,* 60:369–392.

Julka, A.C. and Sharma, P.K. (1989) 'Measurement of land inequality in India: A revision of the Lorenz-Gini ratio', *Indian Journal of Agricultural Economics,* 44(4):423–429.

Kadekodi, G.K. and Murty, G.V.S.N., eds., (1992) *Poverty in India. Data base issues.* Vikas, New Delhi.

Kakwani, N. (1980a) *Income inequality and poverty. Methods of estimation and policy applications.* Oxford: Oxford University Press.

Kakwani, N. (1980b) 'On a class of poverty measures', *Econometrica,* 48:437–446.

Kakwani, N. (1988) 'Income inequality, welfare and poverty in a developing economy with applications to Sri Lanka', in: W. Gaertner and P.K. Pattanaik, eds., *Distributive justice and inequality* Berlin: Springer-Verlag.

Kakwani, N. (1994) 'Poverty and economic growth, with application to Côte d'Ivoire', *Review of Income and Wealth,* 39:121–139.

Kakwani, N. (1993) 'Testing for the significance of poverty differences with application to Côte d'Ivoire', in: Lipton and van der Gaag (1993).

Kakwani, N. and Subbarao, K. (1990) 'Rural poverty and its alleviation in India', *Economic and Political Weekly,* 25:A2–A16.

Kakwani, N., Makonnen, E. and van der Gaag, J. (1993) 'Living conditions in developing countries', in: Lipton and van der Gaag (1993).

Kanbur, R. (1987a) 'Measurement and alleviation of poverty', *IMF Staff Papers,* 36:60–85.

Kanbur, R. (1987b) 'Structural adjustment, macroeconomic adjustment and poverty: A methodology for analysis', *World Development,* 15:1515–1526.

Kanbur, R. (1990a) 'Poverty and the social dimensions of structural adjustment in Côte d'Ivoire', Social Dimensions of Adjustment in sub-Saharan Africa, Policy Analysis, The World Bank, Washington, DC.

Kanbur, R. (1990b) 'Poverty and development: The Human Development Report and the World Development Report', WPS 618, Washington, DC: The World Bank.

Kanbur, R. (1992) 'Heterogeneity, distribution and cooperation in common property resource management', Policy Research Working Paper 844, The World Bank, Washington, DC.

Kanbur, R., Keen, M. and Tuomala, M. (1994) 'Labor supply and targeting in poverty alleviation programs', in: van de Walle and Nead (1994).

Keen, M. (1992) 'Needs and targeting', *Economic Journal,* 102: 67–79.

Keys, A. et al. (1950) *The biology of human starvation.* Minneapolis: Univ. of Minnesota.

Keynes, J.M. (1923) 'Preface', in: H. Wright, *Population.* Cambridge: Cambridge University Press.

Kennedy, E. and P. Peters (1992) 'Household food security and child nutrition: The interaction of income and gender of household head', *World Development,* 20(8):1077–1085.

Kennedy, E. and von Braun, J. (1989) 'Commercialization of agriculture: Income and nutritional effects in developing countries', Washington, DC: International Food Policy Research Institute.

Killick, A. (1991) *A reaction too far*. London: Overseas Development Institute.

King, M.A. (1983) 'Welfare analysis of tax reforms using household level data', *Journal of Public Economics*, 21:183–214.

Knight, J. (1976) 'Devaluation and income distribution in less-developed countries', *Oxford Economic Papers*, 38:161–178.

Kravis, I.B., Heston, A. and Summers, L. (1982) *World product and income: International comparisons of real gross product*. Baltimore: Johns Hopkins University Press.

Krueger, Anne O., Maurice Schiff and Alberto Valdés (1988) 'Agricultural incentives in developing countries: Measuring the effect of sectoral and economywide policies', *World Bank Economic Review*, 2:255–271.

Kuo, S.W.Y. (1983) *The Taiwan economy in transition*. Boulder, CO: Westview Press.

Kuznets, S. (1955) 'Economic growth and income inequality', *American Economic Review*, 45:1–28.

Lanjouw, P. and Ravallion, M. (1994) 'Poverty and household size', Policy Research Working Paper 1332, The World Bank, Washington, DC.

Lanjouw, P. and Stern, N. (1993) 'Markets, opportunities and changes in Palanpur 1957–1984', in: Hoff et al. (1993).

Lanjouw, P. and Stern, N. (1991) 'Poverty in Palanpur', *World Bank Economic Review*, 23–56.

Lazear, E. and Michael, R. (1980) 'Family size and the distribution of per capita income', *American Economic Review*, 70:91–107.

Leach, M. and Mearns, R. (1991) 'Environmental change, development challenge', *IDS Bulletin*, 22(4):1–5.

Lecaillon, J., Paukert, F., Morrisson, C. and Germidis, D. (1984) *Income distribution and economic development: An analytic survey*. Geneva: ILO.

Leibenstein, H. (1957) *Economic Backwardness and Economic Growth*. London: Wiley.

Lele, U. (1974) 'The role of credit and marketing in economic development', in: N. Islam, ed., *Agricultural policy in developing countries*. London: Macmillan.

Lenaghan, T. (1992) 'Adjustment and the poor in Africa', *Development Alternatives*, 3(1):8–17.

Leonard, J. (1989) *Environment and the poor*. New Brunswick: Transaction Books.

Levinson, F.J. (1974) *Morinda: An economic analysis of malnutrition among young children in rural India*. Cornell/MIT International Nutrition Policy Series.

Lewis, W.A. (1954) 'Economic development with unlimited supplies of labor', *Manchester School*, 139–191.

Lewis, W.A. (1955) *Theory of economic growth*. London: Allen and Unwin.

Limcaoco, J.A.A. and Hulme, D. (1990) 'On not throwing the baby out with the bathwater: Integrated rural development in the Philippines', Discussion Paper No. 19, Manchester: Institute of Development Policy and Management, Manchester University.

Lipsey, R.G. and Lancaster, K. (1956) 'The general theory of second best', *Review of Economic Studies*, 26:11–32.

Lipton, M. (1968) 'Urban bias and rural planning: Strategy for agriculture', in: P. Streeten and M. Lipton, eds., *The crisis in Indian planning*. Oxford: Oxford University Press.

Lipton, M. (1977) *Why poor people stay poor: Urban bias and world development*. London: Temple Smith.

Lipton, M. (1981) 'Agricultural finance and rural credit in poor countries', in: P. Streeten and R. Jolly, eds., *Recent issues in world development*. Oxford: Pergamon.

Lipton, M. (1983a) *Labor and poverty*. World Bank Staff Working Paper No. 616, Washington, DC: The World Bank.

Lipton, M. (1983b) *Demography and poverty*. World Bank Staff Working Paper No. 623, Washington, DC: The World Bank.

Lipton, M. (1983c) *Poverty, undernutrition and hunger*. World Bank Staff Working Paper No. 597, Washington, DC: The World Bank.

Lipton, M. (1985) *Land asets and rural poverty*. World Bank Staff Working Paper No. 744, Washington, DC: The World Bank.

Lipton, M. (1987a) *Improving the impact of aid for rural development*. Discussion Paper No. 233, Brighton: Institute of Development Studies.

Lipton, M. (1987b) 'Limits of price policy for agriculture: Which way for the World Bank?', *Development Policy Review*, 5:197–215.

Lipton, M. (1989) 'Attacking undernutrition and poverty: Some issues of adaptation and sustainability', Pew/Cornell Lecture Series, Ithaca: Food and Nutrition Programme.

Lipton, M. (1990) 'Responses to rural population growth: Malthus and the moderns', in: G. McNicoll and M. Cain, eds., *Rural development and population: Institutions and policy*. New York: Oxford University Press.

Lipton, M.(1992a) 'Accelerated resource degradation by Third World agriculture: Created in the commons, in the West, or in bed?', in: Vosti, Reardon and von Urff (1992).

Lipton, M. (1992b) 'Forces for change in dryland areas: options for poverty policy', Rome: International Fund for Agricultural Development.

Lipton, M. (1993) 'Land reform as commenced business: The evidence against stopping', *World Development*, 21(4).

Lipton, M. (1994) 'Review of Partha Dasgupta, *An enquiry into well-being and destitution*', *European Journal of Nutrition*. forthcoming.

Lipton, Michael with R. Longhurst (1989) *New seeds and poor people*. London: Unwin Hyman.

Lipton, M. and Maxwell, S. (1992) 'The new poverty agenda: An overview', Brighton: Institute of Development Studies, mimeo.

Lipton, M. and van der Gaag, J. (1993) 'Poverty: A research and policy framework', in: Lipton and van der Gaag (1993).

Lipton, M. and van der Gaag, J., eds., (1993) *Including the poor*. Washington, DC: The World Bank.

Little, I.M.D. (1987) 'Small manufacturing enterprises in developing countries', *World Bank Economic Review*, 1:203–235.

Little, I.M.D., Mazumdar, D. and Page, J.M. (1987) *Small manufacturing enterprises: A comparative study of India and other countries*. New York: Oxford University Press.

Lloyd, C.B. and Brandon A.J. (1991) 'Women's role in maintaining households: Poverty and gender inequality in Ghana', Washington, DC: International Centre for Research on Women.

Lluch, C. and Mazumdar, D. (1981) 'Wages and employment in Indonesia', Washington, DC: The World Bank, mimeo.

Louat, F., Grosh, M. and van der Gagg, J. (1993) 'Welfare implications of female headship in Jamaican households', LSMS Working Paper 96, The World Bank, Washington, DC.

Maasland, A. and van der Gaag, J. (1992) 'World Bank-supported adjustment programs and living conditions', in: V. Corbo, S. Fischer and S.B. Webb, eds., *Adjustment lending revisited. Policies to restore growth*. Washington, DC: The World Bank.

Mahalanobis, P.C. (1963) *The approach of operational research to planning in India*. Bombay: Asia.

Mahmud, S. and McIntosh, J.P. (1980) 'Returns to scale from family size: Who gains from high fertility?', *Population Studies*, 4(3):500–506.

Malthus, T.R. (1798/1960) *Essay on the principle of population* (ed. G. Himmelfarb), New York: Modern Library.

Mamalakis, M. (1970) *The theory of sectoral clashes*. Paper No. 152, New Haven: Yale University, Economic Growth Center.

Mann, H.H. (1968) *The social framework of agriculture*. London: Cass.

Manski, C. (1990) 'Where we are in the evaluation of federal social welfare programs', *Focus, a publication of the Institute for Research on Poverty*, 12(4):1–15.

Marx, K. (1853/1951) 'The British rule in India' (10 June) and 'Further results of British rule in India', *New York Daily Tribune*, 25 June and 8 August, in: K. Marx and F. Engels, *Selected Works* (Vol. 1), London: Lawrence and Wishart.

Mayo, S.K, and Gross, D.J. (1987) 'Sites and services – and subsidies: The economics of low-cost housing in developing countries', *World Bank Economic Review*, 1:301–336.

Mayo, S., Malpezzi, S. and Gross, D.J. (1986) 'Shelter strategies for the urban poor in developing countries', *World Bank Research Observer*, 1:183–204.

Mazumdar, D. (1976) 'The rural-urban wage gap, migration and the shadow wage', *Oxford Economic Papers*, 28(3):406–425.

McGillivray, M. and White, H. (1993) 'Measuring development? The UNDP's Human Development Index', *Journal of International Development*, 5(2):183–192.

McNamara, R.S. (1973) *Address to the Board of Governors at the Nairobi Meeting.* Washington, DC: The World Bank.

Meesook, O. (1979) *Income, consumption and poverty in Thailand.* Working Paper No. 364, Washington, DC: The World Bank.

Meesook, O. (1984) 'Financing and equity in the social sectors in Indonesia: Some policy questions', World Bank Staff Working Paper 703, The World Bank, Washington, DC.

Mellor, J.W. and Desai, G.M., eds., (1985) *Agricultural change and rural poverty.* Baltimore: Johns Hopkins University Press.

Meerman, J. (1979) *Public expenditure in Malaysia: Who benefits and why?* New York: Oxford University Press.

Mill, J.S. (1848–1871/1965) *Principles of political economy, Books I–II,* (Variorum ed. J.M. Robson). Toronto: Toronto University Press.

Minhas, B.S. (1972) 'Objectives and policy frame of the fourth Indian plan', in: M. Faber and D. Seers, eds., *The crisis in planning* (Vol. 2). London: Chatto and Windus.

Minhas, B.S., Jain, L.R. and Tendulkar, S.D. (1991) 'Declining incidence of poverty in the 1980s: Evidence versus artifacts', *Economic and Political Weekly*, July 6–13:1673–1682.

Mitra, A. (1978) *India's population: Aspects of quality and control* (Vol. 1), Abhinav, New Delhi: Family Planning Association/ICSSR.

Morduch, J. (1990) 'Risk, production and saving: Theory and evidence from Indian households', Department of Economics, Harvard University.

Morduch, J. (1991) 'Consumption smoothing across space: Tests for village-level responses to risk', Department of Economics, Harvard University, mimeo.

Morduch, J. (1994) 'Poverty and vulnerability', *American Economic Review*, 84(2):221–225.

Morley, S.A. (1992) 'Macroconditions and poverty in Latin America', Department of Economic and Social Development, Inter-American Development Bank, Washington, DC

Morley, S.A. and Alvarez, C. (1992) 'Policy and adjustment in Venezuela', Department of Economic and Social Development, Inter-American Development Bank, Washington, DC

Morris, M.D. (1974) 'What is a famine?', *Economic and Political Weekly*, 9(November 2):1855–1864.

Morris, M.D. (1979) *Measuring the condition of the world's poor: The PQLI index.* Oxford: Pergamon.

Morris, M.D. and McAlpin, M. (1982) *Measuring the condition of India's poor.* New Delhi: Promilla.

Mueller, E. and Short, K. (1983) 'Income and wealth as they affect the demand for children in developing countries', in: R.A. Bulatao et al., eds., *Determinants of fertility in developing countries.*

Muhavi, D.K. and Preston, S.H. (1991), 'Effects of family composition on mortality differentials by sex among children in Matlab Thana, Bangladesh', *Population and Development Review*, 17(3).

Mukhopadhyay, S. (1989) 'Differentials of infant mortality in rural West Bengal: A case study', *Demography India*, 18(1–2):155–169.

Murphy, K., Shleifer, A. and Vishny, R. (1989) 'Income distribution, market size and industrialization', *Quarterly Journal of Economics*, 104:537–564.

Musgrove, P. (1980) 'Household size and composition, employment and poverty in urban Latin America', *Economic Development and Cultural Change*, 28(2).

Myrdal, G. (1968) *Asian drama* (3 volumes). New York: Pantheon.

Naoroji, D. (1901) *Poverty and un-British rule in India.* New York: Swan Sonnenschein.

Narain, D. and Roy, S. (1980) *Impact of irrigation and labor availability on multiple cropping: A case study of India.* Research Report No. 20, Washington, DC: IFPRI.

National Academy of Sciences, Committee on Population (1985) *Population growth and economic development: Policy questions.* Washington, DC: National Academy Press.

National Institute of Urban Affairs (1989) *Profile of the urban poor*. Delhi: Ministry of Urban Development.

National Sample Survey Organization (NSSO) (1990) *Sarvekshana: Results of the fourth quinquennial survey of employment and unemployment*. Delhi: NSSO.

Natrajan, K. (n.d.) 'Child mortality: Analysis of 1972 fertility survey', Bombay: Indian Institute of Technology (for Registrar-General's Office, Delhi), mimeo.

Nehru, J. (1946) *The discovery of India*. New York: J. Day.

Nelson, J.A. (1988) 'Household economies of scale in consumption: Theory and evidence', *Econometrica*, 56:1301–1314.

Nelson, J.A. (1993) 'Household equivalence scales: Theory versus policy?', *Journal of Labor Economics*, 11:471–493.

Nestlé Foundation (1987, 1988, 1989, 1990) *Annual Reports*: Lausanne.

Nurkse, R., (1963) *Problems of capital formation in less developed countries*. Oxford: Oxford University Press.

O'Brien, D. (1975) *The classical economists*. Oxford: Clarendon.

Oberai, A.S., ed., (1988) *Settlement policies and population redistribution in developing countries*. New York: Praeger.

Osmani, S.R. (1982) *Economic inequality and group welfare*. Oxford: Oxford University Press.

Osmani, S.R. (1987) 'Controversies in nutrition and their implications for the economics of food'. WIDER Working Paper 16, World Institute for Development Economics Research, Helsinki.

Osmani, S.R. (1991) 'Wage determination in rural labor markets. The theory of implicit co-operation'. *Journal of Development Economics*, 34:3–23.

Otsuka, K., Cordova, V. and David, C.C. (1992) 'Green revolution, land reform and household income distribution', *Economic Development and Cultural Change*, 40:719–742.

Parikh, K. and Srinivasan, T.N. (1993) 'Poverty alleviation policies in India: Food consumption subsidy, food production subsidy and employment generation', in: Lipton and van der Gaag (1993).

Pack, H. (1974) 'The employment-output tradeoff in LDCs – a microeconomic approach', *Oxford Economic Papers*, 26:388–404.

Paukert, F. (1973) 'Income distribution at different levels of development', *International Labor Review*, 108(2–3):97–125.

Paul, S. (1991) 'On the measurement of unemployment', *Journal of Development Economics*, 36:395–404.

Payne, P.R. and Lipton, M. (1993) 'How Third World rural households adapt to dietary energy stress', Washington, DC: International Food Policy Research Institute.

Pebley, A.H.D. and Brinemann, E. (1979) 'Fertility desires and child mortality in Guatemala', *Studies in Family Planning*, 10:129–136.

Pelletier, D. (1991) 'Relationships between anthropometry and mortality in developing countries', Monograph No. 12, Ithaca: Cornell Food and Nutrition Policy Programme.

Persson, T., and Tabellini, G. (1994) 'Is inequality harmful for growth?', *American Economic Review*, 84:600–621.

Pinstrup-Andersen, P. (1989) 'The impact of macroeconomic adjustment: Food security and nutrition', in: S. Commander, ed., *Structural adjustment and agriculture*. London: ODI.

Pitt, M. (1983) 'Food preferences and nutrition in rural Bangladesh', *The Review of Economics and Statistics*, 65:105–114.

Pitt, M., Rosenzweig, M. and Gibbons, D. (1993) 'The determinants and consequences of the placement of government programs in Indonesia', in: van de Walle and Nead (1993).

Platteau, J.-P. (1988) 'Traditional systems of social security and hunger insurance: Some lessons pertaining to Third World village societies', DEP No. 15: Development Economics Research Programme, London School of Economics, mimeo.

Polak B. and Williamson, J. (1993) 'Poverty, policy and industrialization in the past', in: Lipton and van der Gaag (1993).

Pollak R.A. (1991) 'Welfare comparisons and situation comparisons', *Journal of Econometrics*, 50:31–48.

Pollak, R.A. and Wales, T.J. (1979) 'Welfare comparisons and equivalence scales', *American Economic Review*, 69:216–221.

Prahladachar, M. (1983) 'Income distribution effects of the green revolution in India: A review of empirical evidence', *World Development*, 11(11):927–944.

Preobrazhensky, E. (1924/1965) *The new economics*. Clarendon: Oxford.

Preston, S.H. (1975) 'The changing relationship between mortality and level of economic development', *Population Studies*, 29(July):231–248.

Pritchett, L. (1994) 'Desired fertility and the impact of population policies', *Population and Development Review*, 20(1):1–55.

Pryer, J. (1990) *Socioeconomic and environmental aspects of undernutrition and ill-health in an urban slum in Bangladesh*. London: University Ph.D. thesis.

Psacharopoulos, G. (1981) 'Returns to education: An updated international comparison', Reprint Series, No. 210, Washington, DC: The World Bank.

Pyatt, G. and Round, J. (1980) 'The distribution of income by factor components', Reprint No. 162, Washington, DC: The World Bank.

Quibria, M.G. and Srinivasan, T.N. (1991) 'Rural poverty in Asia: Priority issues and policy options', Manila: Asian Development Bank, mimeo.

Rao, C.H.H., Ray, S.K. and Subbarao, K. (1988) *Unstable agriculture and droughts*. Delhi: Vikas.

Ravallion, M. (1987) *Markets and famines*. Oxford: Oxford University Press.

Ravallion, M. (1988) 'Expected poverty under risk-induced welfare variability', *The Economic Journal*, 98:1171–1182.

Ravallion, M. (1989) 'The welfare cost of housing standards: Theory with application to Jakarta'. *Journal of Urban Economics*, 26:197–211.

Ravallion, M. (1990a) 'Rural welfare effects of food price changes under induced wage responses: Theory and evidence for Bangladesh', *Oxford Economic Papers*, 42:574–585.

Ravallion, M. (1990b) 'Market responses to anti-hunger policies: Wages, prices and employment', in: J. Drèze and A. Sen, eds., *The Political Economy of Hunger: Vol. 2*. Oxford: Oxford University Press.

Ravallion, M. (1990c) 'Income effects on undernutrition', *Economic Development and Cultural Change*, 38:489–516.

Ravallion, M. (1991a) 'Reaching the rural poor through public employment: Arguments, experience and lessons from south Asia', *World Bank Research Observer*, 6:153–175.

Ravallion, M. (1991b) 'On the coverage of public employment schemes for poverty alleviation', *Journal of Development Economics*, 34:57–79.

Ravallion, M. (1992) 'Does undernutrition respond to incomes and prices? Dominance tests for Indonesia', *World Bank Economic Review*, 6:109–124.

Ravallion, M. (1993a) *Poverty comparisons*. Fundamentals of Pure and Applied Economics Volume 56, Harwood Academic Press, Chur, Switzerland.

Ravallion, M. (1993b) 'Growth and poverty: Evidence for developing countries in the 1980s', *Economics Letters*, forthcoming.

Ravallion, M. (1993c) 'Poverty alleviation through regional targeting: A case study for Indonesia', in: Hoff et al. (1993).

Ravallion, M. (1994a) 'Measuring social welfare with and without poverty lines', *American Economic Review*, 84(2):359–364.

Ravallion, M. (1994b) 'Household vulnerability to aggregate shocks: Differing fortunes of the poor in Bangladesh and Indonesia, in: K. Basu, P. Pattanaik and K. Suzamura, eds., *Development, welfare and ethics: A Festschrift for Amartya Sen*. Oxford, Oxford University Press, forthcoming.

Ravallion, M. (1994c) 'Poverty rankings using noisy data on living standards', *Economics Letters*, 45:481–485.

Ravallion, M. and Bidani, B. (1994) 'How robust is a poverty profile?', *World Bank Economic Review*, 8(1):75–102.

Ravallion, M. and Chao, K. (1989) 'Targeted policies for poverty alleviation under imperfect information: Algorithms and applications', *Journal of Policy Modeling*, 11:213–224.

Ravallion, M. and Chaudhuri, S. (1993) 'Testing risk-sharing in three Indian villages', Policy Research Department, The World Bank.

Ravallion, M. and Datt, G. (1994a) 'Is targeting through a work requirement efficient?', in: van de Walle and Nead (1994).

Ravallion, M. and Chaudhuri, S. (1994) 'How important to India's poor is the urban-rural composition of growth?', Policy Research Department, The World Bank, Washington, DC.

Ravallion, M. and Datt, G. (1994b) 'Growth and poverty in India', Poverty and Human Resources Division, World Bank, mimeo.

Ravallion, M., Datt, G. and Chaudhuri, S. (1993) 'Does Maharashtra's employment guarantee scheme guarantee employment? Effects of the 1988 wage increase', *Economic Development and Cultural Change*, 41:251–276.

Ravallion, M., Datt, G. and van de Walle, D. (1991) 'Quantifying absolute poverty in the developing world', *Review of Income and Wealth*, 37:345–361.

Ravallion, M. and Dearden, L. (1988) 'Social security in a "moral economy": An empirical analysis for Java', *Review of Economics and Statistics*, 70:36–44.

Ravallion, M. and Huppi, M. (1991) 'Measuring changes in poverty: A methodological case study of Indonesia during an adjustment period', *World Bank Economic Review*, 5:57–84.

Ravallion, M. and Sen, B. (1994a) 'When method matters. Towards a resolution of the debate over Bangladesh's poverty measures', Policy Research Working Paper 1359, The World Bank.

Ravallion, M. and Sen, B. (1994b) 'Impacts on rural poverty of land-based targeting', *World Development*, forthcoming.

Ravallion, M. and Subbarao, K. (1992) 'Adjustment and human development in India', *Journal of the Indian School of Political Economy*, 4:55–79.

Ravallion, M. and van de Walle, D. (1991) 'The impact on poverty of food pricing reforms: A welfare analysis for Indonesia', *Journal of Policy Modeling*, 13:281–299.

Ravallion, M. and van de Walle, D. (1994) 'A profile of poverty in Tunisia', Poverty and Human Resources Division, The World Bank.

Reardon, T., Delgado, C. and Matlon, P. (1992) 'Determinants and effects of income diversification among farmer households in Bukina Faso', *Journal of Development Studies*, 28(2):264–296.

Reserve Bank of India (1989) *A review of the agricultural credit system in India*. Bombay: Reserve Bank of India.

Reutlinger, S. and Selowsky, M. (1976) *Malnutrition and poverty. Magnitude and policy options*. Baltimore: Johns Hopkins University Press for the World Bank.

Ribe, H., Carvalho, S., Liebenthal, R., Nicholas, P. and Zuckerman, E. (1990) 'How adjustment programs can help the poor', World Bank Discussion Paper 71, The World Bank, Washington, DC.

Ricardo, D. (1817/1972) *Principles of political economy and taxation*. London: Everyman.

Richards, P. (1985) *Indigenous agricultural revolution*. London: Hutchinson.

Richards, P. and Leonor, M., eds., (1982) *Target setting for basic needs*. Geneva: International Labor Office.

Robinson, S. (1976) 'A note on the U-hypothesis relating income inequality and economic development', *American Economic Review*, 66:437–440.

Rodgers, G. (1989) 'Demographic patterns and poverty among households in rural Bihar', (cited in Rodgers (1989)).

Rodgers, G., ed., (1989) *Population Growth and Poverty in Rural South Asia*. Geneva: ILO.

Rosenhouse, S. (1989) 'Identifying the poor: Is headship a useful concept?', Living Standards Measurement Survey, Working Paper No. 58, Washington, DC: The World Bank.

Rosenstein-Rodan, P. (1943) 'Problems of industrialization in Southern and Eastern Europe', *Economic Journal*, 53:202–211.

Rosenzweig, M. (1988) 'Labor markets in low-income countries', in: Chenery and Srinivasan (1988).

Rosenzweig, M. and Schultz, T.P. (1982) 'Market opportunities, genetic endowments and intrafamily resource distribution: Child survival in rural India', *American Economic Review*, 72:803–815.

Rosenzweig, M. and Stark, O. (1989) 'Consumption smoothing, migration and marriage: Evidence from rural India', *Journal of Political Economy*, 97(4):905–926.

Rosenzweig, M. and Wolpin, K.I. (1993) 'Credit market constraints, consumption smoothing and the accumulation of durable production assets in low-income countries: Investments in bullocks in India', *Journal of Political Economy*, 101(2):223–245.

Roth, E. and Kurup, B. (1989) 'Child mortality levels and survival patterns from Southern Sudan', *Demography India*, 18(1–2):139–146.

Rowntree, B.S. (1901) *Poverty: A study of town life*. London: Macmillan.

Ruttan, V. and Binswanger, H., eds., (1978) *Induced innovation: Technology, institutions and development*. Baltimore: Johns Hopkins University Press.

Ruzicka, L. (1984) 'Mortality in India: Past trends and future prospects', in: T. Dyson and N. Cook, eds., *India's demography*. New Delhi: South Asia.

Safilios-Rothchild, C. (1991) 'Gender and rural poverty in Asia: Implications for agricultural projects', *Asia Pacific Journal of Rural Development*, 1, 1.

Saha, A. (1993) 'A two-season agricultural household model of output and price uncertainty', mimeo, Department of Agricultural Economics, Texas A&M University.

Sahn, D. (1989) 'Seasonal fluctuations in factor and product markets: Is there a nutritional risk?', Pew/Cornell Lecture Series on Food and Nutrition Policy, Ithaca: Cornell Food and Nutrition Policy Programme.

Sahn, D., ed., (1989) *Seasonal variability in Third World agriculture*. Baltimore: Johns Hopkins University Press.

Sahn, D. and Alderman, H. (1993) 'The effect of food subsidies on labor supply', in: van de Walle and Nead (1993).

Sahn, D. and Sarris, A. (1991) 'Structural adjustment and rural smallholder welfare: A comparative analysis', *World Bank Economic Review*, 5:259–290.

Saith, A. (1981) 'Production, prices and poverty in rural India', *Journal of Development Studies*, 19, 196–214.

Saith, A. (1983) 'Development and distribution: A critique of the cross-country U hypothesis', *Journal of Development Economics*, 13:367–368.

Schieber, G. and Poullier, J.P. (1989) 'Overview of international comparisons of health care expenditures', *Health Care Finance Review* Summer Supplement.

Schiff, M. and Valdès, A. (1990) 'Poverty, food intake and malnutrition', *American Journal of Agricultural Economics*, 72(5):1318–1322.

Schofield, S. (1974) 'Seasonal factors affecting nutrition in different age groups', *Journal of Development Studies*, 11(1):22–40.

Schofield, S. (1979) *Development and the problems of village nutrition*. London: Croom Helm.

Schultz, T.P. (1988) 'Education investments and returns', in: Chenery and Srinivasan (1988).

Schultz, T.W. (1975) 'The value of the ability to deal with disequilibria', *Journal of Economic Literature*, 13(3):827–846.

Schultz, T.W. (1981a) *Investing in people*, Berkeley: University of California Press.

Schultz, T.W. (1981b) *Economics of population*. New Haven: Addison Wesley.

Schutjer, W. and Stokes, C. (1982) 'The human fertility implications of food and agricultural policies in LDCs', Bulletin 35, Agricultural Experiment Stn, Pennsylvania State University.

Scitovsky, T. (1954) 'Two concepts of external economies', *Journal of Political Economy*, 62:70–82.

Seers, D. (1972) 'What are we trying to measure?', IDS Communication Series No. 106, Brighton: Institute of Development Studies.

Selden, T.M. and Wasylenko, M.J. (1994) 'Measuring the distributional effects of public education in Peru', in: van de Walle and Nead (1994).

Selowsky, M. (1979) *Who benefits from government expenditure?* New York: Oxford University Press.

Selowsky, M. (1991) 'Protecting nutrition status in adjustment programmes: Recent World Bank activities and projects in Latin America', *Food and Nutrition Bulletin*, 13:293–302.

Sen, A. (1976) 'Poverty: An ordinal approach to measurement', *Econometrica*, 46:437–446.

Selowsky, M. (1979) 'Personal utilities and public judgements: or what's wrong with welfare economics?', *The Economic Journal*, 89:537–558.

Selowsky, M. (1981a) *Poverty and famines: An essay on entitlement and deprivation*. Oxford: Oxford University Press.

Selowsky, M. (1981b) 'Public action and the quality of life in developing countries', *Oxford Bulletin of Economics and Statistics*, 43(4):287–319.

Selowsky, M. (1985) *Commodities and capabilities*. Amsterdam: North-Holland.

Selowsky, M. (1987) *The standard of living*. Cambridge: Cambridge University Press.

Shetty, P. (1984) 'Adaptive changes in BMR and body mass in chronic undernutrition', *Human Nutrition Clinical Bulletin*, 38C.

Simon, J.L. (1986) *Theory of population and economic growth*. Oxford: Blackwell.

Singer, H. (1965) 'External aid: For plans or projects?', *Economic Journal*, 75:539–45.

Singh, B. (1985) *Agrarian structure, technical change and poverty: Microlevel evidence*. New Delhi: Agricole Publishing.

Singh, I.J. (1990) *The great ascent: The rural poor in South Asia*. Baltimore: Johns Hopkins University Press.

Smith, A. (1776/1884) *The wealth of nations* (ed. J.S. Nicholson). London: Nelson.

Squire, L. (1989) 'Project evaluation in theory and practice', in: Chenery and Srinivasan (1989).

Squire, L. (1993) 'Fighting poverty', *American Economic Review*, 83(2):377–382.

Squire, L. and Van der Tak, H. (1975) *Economic analysis of projects*. Baltimore: Johns Hopkins for World Bank.

Srinivasan, T.N. and Bardhan, P.K., eds. (1988) *Rural poverty in South Asia*. New York: Columbia University Press.

Standing, G. (1985) *Labor force participation and development*. Geneva: ILO

Standing, H. (1985) 'Women's employment and the household: Some findings from Calcutta', *Economic and Political Weekly*, 20(17):WS23–38.

Stark, O. (1991) *The migration of labor*. Oxford: Basil Blackwell.

Stiglitz, J.E. (1988) 'Economic organization, information and development', in: Chenery and Srinivasan (1988).

Stoeckel, J. and Chowdhury, A. (1980) 'Fertility and socio-economic status in rural Bangladesh', *Population Studies*, 34(3):519–524.

Strauss, J. (1986) 'Does better nutrition raise farm productivity?', *Journal of Political Economy*, 94:297–320.

Streeten, P., Burki, S.J., ul Haq, M., Hicks, N. and Stewart, F. (1981) *First things first: Meeting basic needs in developing countries*. New York: Oxford University Press.

Streeten, P. (1987) 'Structural adjustment: A survey of issues and options', *World Development*, 15:1469–1482.

Streeten, P. (1993) 'Markets and states: Against minimalism', *World Development*, 21:1281–1298.

Sukhatme, P. (1981) *Relationship between malnutrition and poverty*. Delhi: Indian Assn. of Social Science Institutions.

Summers, R. and Heston, A. (1988) 'A new set of international comparisons of real product and price levels estimates for 130 countries, 1950–1980', *Review of Income and Wealth*, 34:1–26.

Summers, R. and Heston, A. (1991) 'The Penn World Table (Mark 5): An extended set of international comparisons, 1950–1988', *Quarterly Journal of Economics*, 106:327–368.

Sundaram, K. and Tendulkar, S.D. (1988) 'Towards an explanation of interregional variations in poverty and unemployment in rural India', in: Srinivasan and Bardhan (1988).

Svedberg, P. (1990) 'Undernutrition in sub-Saharan Africa: Is there a gender bias?', *Journal of Development Studies*, 26(3):469–486.

Taylor, C. et al. (1978) 'The Narangwal experiment on interactions of nutrition and infections: 1. Project design and effects upon growth', *Indian Journal of Medical Research*, 68 (Supplement).

Taylor, L. (1993) 'Review of World Development Report, 1991', *Economic Development and Cultural Change*, 41:430–441.

Taylor, L. and Arida, P. (1988) 'Long-run income distribution and growth', in: Chenery and Srinivasan (1988).

Telles, E.E. (1993) 'Urban labor market segmentation and income in Brazil', *Economic Development and Cultural Change*, 41:231–250.

Theil, H. and Finke, R. (1985) 'Income and price elasticities of demand at low levels of real income', *Economics Letters*, 18:1–5.

Thiesenhusen, W.C., ed. (1989) *Searching for agrarian reform in Latin America*. Boston: Unwin Hyman.

Thomas, D., Lavy, V. and Strauss, J. (1992) 'Public policy and anthropometric outcomes in Côte d'Ivoire', LSMS Working Paper No. 89, Washington, DC: The World Bank.

Thomas, D. (1990) 'Intrahousehold resource allocation: An inferential approach', *Journal of Human Resources*, 25(4):635–664.

Thon, D. (1979) 'On measuring poverty', *Review of Income and Wealth*, 25:429–440.

Thorbecke, E. (1991) 'Adjustment, growth and income distribution in Indonesia', *World Development*, 19:1595–1614.

Thorbecke, E. and Berrian, D. (1992) 'Budgetary rules to minimize societal policy in a general equilibrium context', *Journal of Development Economics*, 39:189–206.

Thorbecke, E. and Jung, H.-S. (1994) 'A multiplier decomposition method to analyze poverty alleviation', *Journal of Development Economics*, forthcoming.

Thorner, D. (1968) 'Preface', in: Mann (1968).

Timmer, P. (1992) 'Agriculture and economic development revisited', *Agricultural Systems*, 40:21–58.

Todaro, M.P. (1969) 'A model of labor migration and urban unemployment in less developed countries', *American Economic Review*, 59:138–148.

Townsend, R. (1994) 'Risk and insurance in village India', *Econometrica*, 62:539–591.

Tsakloglou, P. (1988) 'Development and inequality revisited', *Applied Economics*, 20:509–531.

Tuma, E.H. (1965) *Twenty-six centuries of agrarian reform*. Berkeley: University of California.

Udall, A. and Sinclair, S. (1982) 'The luxury unemployment hypothesis: A review of evidence', *World Development*, 10(2):49–62.

Udry, C. (1989) 'Rural credit in Northern Nigeria', in: Hoff et al. (1992).

United Nations Development Programme (UNDP) (1990, 1991, 1992) *Human Development Report*. New York: United Nations.

Udry, C. (1983, 1988) *Demographic Yearbook* 1983, 1988. New York: United Nations.

Usher, D. (1963) 'The transport bias in national income comparisons', *Economica*, May:140–158.

Vakil, C.N. and Brahmanand P.R. (1956) *Planning for an expanding economy*. Bombay: Vora and Co.

van de Walle, D. (1985) 'Population growth and poverty: Another look at the Indian time series data', *Journal of Development Studies*, 21:429–439.

van de Walle, D. (1994a) 'The distribution of subsidies through public health services in Indonesia, 1978–87', *World Bank Economic Review*, 8:279–309.

van de Walle, D. (1994b) 'Incidence and targeting; An overview of implications for research and policy', in: van de Walle and Nead (1994).

van de Walle, D. and Nead, K., eds. (1994) *Public spending and the poor: Theory and evidence*. Baltimore: Johns Hopkins University Press, forthcoming.

van der Gaag, J., Makonnen, E. and Englebert, P. (1991) 'Trends in social indicators and social sector spending', PRE Working Paper 662, Washington, DC: The World Bank.

Vartia, Y.O. (1983) 'Efficient methods of measuring welfare changes and compensated income in terms of ordinary demand functions', *Econometrica*, 51:79–98.

Visaria, P. (1977) *Living standards, employment and education in Western India*. Working Paper 1, ESCAP/IBRD project on Asian income distribution data, Washington, DC: The World Bank.

Visaria, P. (1980) 'Poverty and living standards in Asia: An overview of the main results and lessons of selected household surveys', Working Paper 2, Living Standards Measurement Study, Washington, DC: The World Bank.

Visaria, P. (1981) 'Poverty and unemployment in India: An analysis of recent evidence', *World Development*, 9(3):277–300.

von Braun, J., Puetz, D. and Webb, P. (1989) *Irrigation technology and commercialization of rice in the Gambia: Effects on income and nutrition*. Research Report 75, International Food Policy Research Institute, Washington, DC.

Vosti, S.A., Reardon, T. and von Urff, W., eds. (1992) *Agricultural sustainability, growth and poverty alleviation: Issues and policies*. Proceedings of the conference held 23–27 September 1991, Feldafing, IFPRI/DSE/ZEL, Feldafing.

Waaler, H.Th. (1984) 'Height, weight and mortality: The Norwegian experience', *Acta Medica Scandinavica* (supplementum 679), Stockholm, Sweden.

Wade, R. (1991) *Governing the market*. Princeton: Princeton University Press.

Walker, T.S. and Ryan, J.G. (1990) *Village and household economies in India's semi-arid tropics*. Baltimore: Johns Hopkins University Press.

Walker, T.S., Singh, R.P. and Asokan, M. (1986) 'Risk benefits, crop insurance and dryland agriculture', *Economic and Political Weekly*, 21:A81–A88.

Watts, H.W. (1968) 'An economic definition of poverty', in: D.P. Moynihan, ed., *On understanding poverty*. New York: Basic Books.

Webb, P., Bisrat, G. and Coppock, D.L. (1991) 'Food sustainability and sustainable growth for pastoral systems in semi-arid Africa', in: Vosti et al. (1992).

Welch, F. (1970) 'Education in production', *Journal of Political Economy*, 78(1):35–59.

Williamson, J. (1991) *Inequality, poverty and history*. Cambridge (Mass.): Blackwell.

Winch, D. (1987) *Malthus*. Oxford: Oxford University Press.

Wood, A.W. (1991) 'Editor's introduction', in: Hegel (1991).

World Bank (1975) *Land Reform*. Washington, DC

World Bank (1980a, 1984, 1990, 1991c, 1991b) *World Development Report*. New York: Oxford University Press.

World Bank (1980b) *Poverty and basic needs*. Washington, DC

World Bank (1986) *Poverty and hunger. Issues and options for food security in developing countries*. Washington, DC

World Bank (1988) *First report on adjustment lending*, R88–199. Washington, DC

World Bank (1989) *India. Poverty, employment and social services*. A World Bank Country Study, Washington, DC

World Bank (1991a) *Assistance strategies to reduce poverty*. A policy paper, Washington, DC

World Bank (1991b) *Indonesia. Strategy for a sustained reduction in poverty*. Washington, DC

World Bank (1991d) *Nepal: Poverty and incomes*. A World Bank Country Study, Washington, DC

World Bank (1992a) *Poverty reduction handbook*. Washington, DC

World Bank (1992c) *Access to basic infrastructure by the urban poor*. EDI Policy Seminar Report No. 28, Washington, DC

World Bank (1992d) *China: Strategies for reducing poverty in the 1990s*. Washington, DC

World Bank (1993) *The East Asian miracle*. New York: Oxford University Press.

World Health Organization (1985) *Energy and protein requirements*. Technical Report 724, Geneva.

Zeitlin, M.F., Mansour, M. and Bajrai, J. (1987) 'Positive deviance in nutrition: An approach to health whose time has come', in: Jelliffe (1987).

*Chapter 42*

# POWER, DISTORTIONS, REVOLT AND REFORM IN AGRICULTURAL LAND RELATIONS

HANS P. BINSWANGER, KLAUS DEININGER and GERSHON FEDER

*The World Bank\**

## Contents

\* This paper has benefitted from discussions at the Asian Development Bank, the International Food Policy Research Institute, the Land Tenure Center at the University of Wisconsin, the University of Minnesota, The World Bank. Comments and suggestions by A.S.P. Brandao, D. Bromley, J. Bruce, M. Carter, R. Christiansen, Y. Hayami, K. Hoff, M. Lipton, S. Migot–Adholla, K. Otsuka, M. Roth, V. Ruttan, and T.N. Srinivasan were particularly helpful.

*Handbook of Development Economics, Volume III, Edited by J. Behrman and T.N. Srinivasan*
© *Elsevier Science B.V., 1995*

**Contents** (continued)

### Glossary

Irrespective of their historical and cultural or ideological origins, the following terms are used in this paper with the definition given below:

*Collective farm*: A farm jointly owned and operated under a single management for the benefit of and with work input from the owners of the collective.

*Communal ownership system*: A system of land ownership in which specific plots of land are assigned temporarily or permanently to members for family cultivation, while other areas are held in common for pasture, forestry, and collection of wild plants and game. Individual plots may or may not be inheritable or tradeable in internal rental or sales markets. But sales to nonmembers are always forbidden or subject to community approval.

*Contract farming*: A contract between a farmer and a purchaser in advance of the growing season for a specific quantity, quality and date of delivery of an agricultural output at a price or price formula fixed in advance. The contract provides the farmer an assured sale of the crop and sometimes provides for technical assistance, credit, services, or inputs from the purchaser.

*Corvée*: Unpaid labor and sometimes the service of draft animal provided by serfs, tenants, or usufruct right holder to the owner of the manorial estate.

*Debt peonage, Bonded labor services*: A tribute payment or labor service originating in a defaulted loan.

*Family farm*: A farm operated primarily with family labor, with some hiring in or out of labor. Family farming systems may be socially stratified, with wide dispersion in farm sizes and technology levels.

*Hacienda*: A manorial estate in which part of the land is cultivated as the home farm of the owner and part as the family farms of serfs, usufructuary right holders, or tenants.

*Home farm*: That part of the manorial estate or large ownership holding cultivated by the lord, landlord or owner under his own management using corvée and sometimes partly remunerated labor.

*Landlord estate*: A manorial estate in which all of the land is cultivated by tenants or usufructuary right holders.

*Junker estate*: A large ownership holding producing a diversified set of commodities operated under a single management with hired labor. Laborers do not receive a plot of land to use for their own cultivation as part of their remuneration, except perhaps for a house and a garden plot.

*Large commercial farm*: A large ownership holding producing several different commodities operating under a single management with a high degree of mechanization using a few long term hired workers who may reside on the farm and seasonally hired workers who do not reside permanently on the farm.

*Manorial estate*: An area of land allocated temporarily or as a permanent ownership holding to a manorial lord who has the right to tribute, taxes, or rent in cash, in kind or in corvée labor of the peasants residing on the estate. This paper uses the same term whether the peasants are there by choice or are bound by restrictions on their mobility. Manorial estates can be organized as haciendas or as landlord estates.

*Rent* is used in several ways:

   • *Residual rent*: The residual payment to a productive factor in inelastic supply after all factors have been renumerated at their respective market rates, whether the other markets are competitive or not.

   • *Rent-seeking rent*: The additional reward received as a result of regulations and restrictions that raise the level of rewards above its undistorted level. Where markets are thin or uncompetitive, measuring rent-seeking rent may be very difficult.

   • *Land rent*: A tenant's payment to a landowner in a voluntary contractual relationship. Rent may be paid as a fixed or share payment in cash, kind, or labor services. It may or may not be equal to residual rent. If the reservation utility of tenants has been reduced by distortions associated with rent seeking, the land rent includes a component of rent seeking.

*Reservation utility or reservation wage*: The level of utility (including the risk attributes) or the wage which is available outside the manorial estate to a potential tenant or worker on a manorial estate.

*Share contract*: A rental contract in which the tenant is paying a portion or all of his rent by delivering a certain proportion of the output, the crop share, to the landowner.

*State farm*: A farm belonging to the state and operated like a Junker estate or a large commercial farm under a single management with a largely resident labor force paid in wages, and sometimes, profit shares in cash or in kind. Laborers may be allocated a small garden plot.

*Surplus*: Output or labor available over and above that required to reconstitute and maintain the energy and life of peasants, serfs or slaves.

*Tribute*: A payment in cash, kind or labor services to a landlord based on restrictions on mobility and/or other forms of state-sanctioned coercion. Tribute may also be called rent or corvée.

*Usufructuary rights*: Rights to use the land. May be temporary, long-term, lifetime, or inheritable, but always exclude the right to unrestricted sale of the land.

*Wage plantation*: A large ownership holding specializing in a single crop under a single management using wage labor, a large share of which resides on the plantation but does not receive more than a garden plot for self cultivation as part of the remuneration.

## Introduction

This paper began as an inquiry into the efficiency and equity consequences of rental and sales markets for agricultural land in the developing world. Most of the work on the relationship between farm size and productivity strongly suggests that farms that rely mostly on family labor have higher productivity levels than large farms operated primarily with hired labor. If that is so, why have markets for the rental and sale of agricultural land frequently not reallocated land to family farmers? Why do extraordinarily unequal distributions of ownership and operational holdings persist in many parts of the world? Why has land reform seemed to be necessary to change these land ownership distributions?

What began to emerge from this study was the clear sense that the great variations in land relations found across the world and over time cannot be understood in a simple property rights and markets paradigm. Section 2 explains the idealized sequence of the emergence and definition of property rights which occurred in only few areas of the developing world. As that paradigm would have it, increasing land scarcity leads to better definition of rights, which are then traded in sales and rental markets that are equally accessible to all players. The outcome should be the allocation of land to the most efficient uses and users. Yet this often did not happen, as great observed deviations from efficiency demonstrate.

An examination of the historical evolution of land rights shows the reason for the deviations: rights over land and the concentration of ownership observed in most developing countries at the end of World War II are outgrowths of power relationships. Landowning groups used coercion and distortions in land, labor, credit, and commodity markets to extract economic rents from the land, from peasants and workers, and more recently from urban consumer groups or taxpayers. Such rent-seeking activities reduced the efficiency of resource use, retarded growth, and increased the poverty of the rural population. We describe the variety of land relations and their consequences for the efficiency of agricultural production,[1] using a consistent set of terminology which is summarized in the glossary of definitions. Furthermore we examine how these power relations emerged and what legal means enabled relatively few landowners to accumulate and hold on to large landholdings.

Because land ownership distribution has often been determined by power relationships and distortions, and because land sales markets do not distribute

---

[1] A large literature elaborates the implications of spatial models of land use following the tradition of von Thuenen for the optimal use of land and the associated problems of localized monopolies [Fujita and Thisse (1986)], regional and urban planning, and the determinants of land values [Randall and Castle (1985)]. The references cited provide a good overview of this literature.

land to the poor (the key point of Section 5), land reform has often been necessary to get land into the hands of efficient small family owners (Section 4 shows that they are indeed efficient). The successes and failures of reform in market and socialist economies and the perversions of reforms in both these systems, manifested in large commercial farms or collectives, are discussed in Section 3. The social cost of failing to undertake reform, including losses in productivity as well as peasant revolt and civil war, are also considered.

But land reform would not be necessary if there were economies of scale in agriculture beyond those that a family could take advantage of with a given level of technology. In that case it would not have been necessary to use power to aggregate large holdings or coercion and distortions to recruit workers. And in modern times it would not have been necessary to subsidize large commercial farms so heavily through credit subsidies and other distortions. Voluntary transactions in undistorted markets would have achieved these ends, and small peasants might have found it attractive to join collectives. Section 4 examines the work that has been done on the presence-or not- of economies of scale in agriculture, finding in measurements of the relative efficiency of small versus large farms only exceptional cases which are consistent with the myth of the efficient large farm.

Similarly, if land sales markets could allocate land from inefficient large owners to small family farmers, land reform would not be necessary. Abolishing the special subsidies to large farms and the conditions that permit coercion would be all that would be required to lead to the breakup of large farms through sales to small farmers. Showing why sales markets are often not capable of facilitating these efficiency-enhancing transfers – covariance of risks, imperfections in credit markets, distortions in commodity market and subsidies to large farms are among the reasons – is the topic of Section 5.

Section 6 then shows that tenancy and sharecropping are not as inefficient as often assumed. They are second best adaptations to incomplete or distorted markets for labor, credit, and risk diffusion. Such rental agreements are also necessary to allow large ownership holdings to be operated by tenants as small family farm units. Regulating tenancy or outlawing it has perverse efficiency and equity effects for the poor.

The sections of the paper are grouped in three parts. Part I covers the history of land relations and the legacies it leaves today. Part II covers the three analytical controversies surrounding economies of scale, and the efficiency of the land rental and the land sales market. Part III discusses the major land policy issues left behind by the various distortions and successful and unsuccessful reforms in the developing world. These include land registration and titling, land taxation, regulations limiting land sales and land rentals, fragmentation of land, redistributive land reform and decollectivization. Policy implications are discussed using the insights gained in the previous sections. Finally, the methodological epilogue examines how various strands of economic theory have contributed, or failed to contribute, to the explanation of variations in policies, distortions and land relations over space and time.

## PART I: THE HISTORICAL LEGACY

### 1. The emergence of property rights in land

The critical issue in land-abundant settings is access to labor, not land. At low population densities, there is no incentive to invest in soil fertility, and because fertility is restored by long tree fallow, ownership security is not required to induce investment. When population densities rise, fallow periods are gradually shortened until the land is continually cultivated. Then plows, manure, artificial fertilizers, and other investments and labor-intensive methods are required to maintain soil fertility [Boserup (1965), Ruthenberg (1980), Pingali et al. (1986)]. Marginal lands are also brought under cultivation requiring higher investments still to make them productive. Only now, ownership security becomes an important incentive for making the required investments. As the demand for credit to finance inputs and investments in land improvements rises, the issue of land as collateral becomes important.

Thus as population density increases private rights to land emerge in a slow and gradual process that exhibits great regularity (Figure 42.1, arrows 1 to 4). Boserup's (1965) discussion of this process is unsurpassed and so is quoted here at length:

Virtually all the systems of land tenure found to exist before the emergency of private property in land seem to have this one feature in common: certain families are recognized as having cultivation rights within a given area of land while other families are excluded.... "Free" land disappears already before the agricultural stage is reached. Tribes of food collectors and hunters consider that they have exclusive rights to collect food and to hunt in a particular area....

Under the system of forest fallow, all the members of a tribe .... have a general right to cultivate plots of land.... This general right to take part in the cultivation of the land which the group dominates – or imagines to dominate – can never be lost for any member of the cultivator families. They may voluntarily leave the territory for a time, but they can then reclaim their right when they return....

.... A distinction must be made between the general cultivation right – as described above – and the more specific right a family may have to cultivate a particular plot of land. Under all systems of fallow a family will retain the

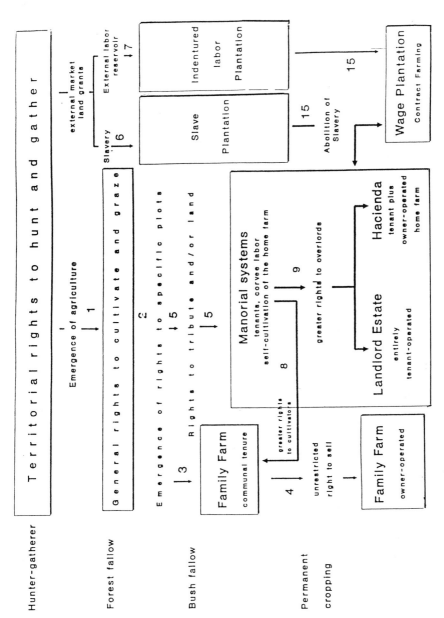

Figure 42.1. Evolution of production relations & property rights.

exclusive right to the plot it has cleared and cultivated until the harvest has been reaped. . . . But if, after the lapse of the normal period of fallow, the family does not re-cultivate a given plot, it may lose its right to this particular plot. . . . Thus, the general cultivation right is an inseparable element of the status as member of the tribe and, therefore, in principle inalienable, while the specific right to cultivate an individual plot is lost by desuetude. . . . As long as a tribe of forest-fallow cultivators has abundant land at its disposal, a family would have no particular interest in returning to precisely that plot which it cultivated on an earlier occasion. Under these conditions a family which needed to shift to a new plot would find a suitable plot, or have it allocated by the chief of the tribe. . . .

But the situation is apt to change with increasing population, as good plots become somewhat scarce. Under such conditions, a family is likely to become more attached to the plots they have been cultivating on earlier occasions. . . .

At this stage, when the attachment of individual families to individual plots becomes more permanent, the custom of pledging land is also likely to emerge. If a family does not need to use a given plot for a certain period it may pledge it to another family. . . . subject to the condition that the land must be returned, upon request. . . . This custom of pledging. . . . must be distinguished sharply from the sale of land where the former occupier of the land loses all rights in it.

Thus, the attachment of individual families to particular plots becomes more and more important. . . . As more and more land is subject to specific cultivation rights, little land will be available for redistribution by the chief. . . .

As long as the general right of cultivation has not lost all its importance a sharp social distinction exists in rural communities between cultivator families on one hand and families without cultivation rights on the other, the latter group consisting of strangers, whether they be slaves or free. . . even those strangers, who are not slaves in a legal sense, are nevertheless left with no other choice than to do menial work for chiefs or for ordinary members of the dominating tribe. . . .

Under both long- and short-fallow systems the land lying fallow at any given time is at the free disposal for grazing by domestic animals belonging to families with cultivation rights. . . . . The cultivators' communal rights to use fallow land for grazing will usually survive long after the general right to clear new forest land has disappeared. . . . [Boserup (1965), pp. 79–86]

Boserup's discussion makes clear that property rights in land are not simple and are rarely unrestricted. As land becomes more scarce, general and inheritable cultivation and grazing rights are complemented by rights to resume cultivating specific plots after fallow (arrow 2), to inherit specific plots rather than just general cultivation rights, to pledge or rent out the plots, to use them as collateral in informal credit transactions, and to sell them within the community (arrow 3). When the right to sell includes sales to members outside the community (arrow 4), the last vestiges of general cultivation rights are lost and private property rights are complete. General rights survive only as grazing and collection rights on communal grazing areas and forests, whose soils are usually unsuitable for crop or intensive pasture production.

Even where communal land rights and management systems prevail, as in indigenous communities of the Americas, or tribal communities in Asia and Africa, families have strong specific land rights. These rights provide substantial "ownership" security as long as the plots are farmed by individual family units [Noronha (1985), Downs and Reyna (1988)]. Land rental and sales usually occur within the community, especially among close kin.

While the internal rules and structures of these systems exhibit a bewildering variety, all communal systems have one thing in common: Sales to outsiders are either forbidden or subject to approval by the whole community.

The right to sell is often proscribed by laws that assign ultimate ownership to the state or that regulate the land tenure of tribal or indigenous communities. Colonial powers often legislated a uniform system of communal tenure to be applied to all land held by indigenous populations (although tribal societies have often circumvented formal prohibition of land sales; Noronha 1985). Under communal tenure family-owned plots can be used only for pledging in informal credit markets and not as collateral in formal credit markets.

## 2. Extracting tribute and rent from peasants

History has few examples of the uninterrupted transformation of general cultivation rights to land into owner-operated family farms (along arrows 1 to 4 in Figure 42.1). Nearly always, there has been an intervening period under a class of rulers who extracted tribute, taxes or rent from cultivator families (arrow 5). The landholdings of these overlords (referred to here, for expositional simplicity, as *manorial estates*, whatever the cultural or historic setting) were allocated temporarily or as permanent patrimony or ownership holding, along with the right to tribute, taxes, or rent (in cash, kind, or corvée labor) from the peasants residing on the estate. Frequently, peasants' freedom to move was restricted by bondage or by prior claims to land by members of the ruling group. The rights of the ruling group were acquired and enforced by violence or the threat of violence and institutionalized in tradition, custom, and the law and order forces of the state.[2] The rights took numerous forms and left

---

[2] For Western Europe, North and Thomas (1971) interpret the right to tribute as the emergence of a contract between peasants and manorial lords, with the lords providing protection and other public goods in exchange for tribute. This view ignores the asymmetry in the possession of the means for violence and judicial power.

historical legacies in the distribution of land once land rights became fully private. Again, Boserup (1965) says it best:

Above the group of families with cultivation rights is usually found an upper class of tribal chiefs or feudal landlords who receive tribute from the cultivators. . . . The emergence of a kind of nobility or aristocracy often seems to follow the introduction of short-fallow cultivation with animal draft power. . . . Usually the position of a cultivator with regard to his rights in land does not change because a feudal government imposes itself and levies taxes and labor services. The cultivator families continue to have their hereditary cultivation rights, both general and specific, and redistribution of land by village chiefs may continue without interference from the feudal landlords. Nor does land become alienable by sale; grants of land by overlords to members of the nobility and others are simply grants of the right to levy taxes, and do not interfere with the hereditary cultivation rights of the peasants. In other words, the beneficiaries of such grants do not become owners of the land in a modern sense. . . . (pp. 82–84)

## An analytical structure for the evolution of agrarian relations

For an analysis of the evolution of agrarian relations and the associated land ownership distribution, several points are key. The first is that favorable agricultural conditions generate the potential for *rent-seeking rent* or *surplus* and provide an incentive for groups with political and military power to try to capture the rents or surpluses. The second is that under simple technology there are no economies of scale in farming and that independent family farms are economically the most efficient mode of production except for a very limited set of plantation crops (see section 4). Compared to large farms based on hired or tenant labor, owner-operated family farms save on supervision costs of labor or eliminate the inefficiencies and supervision cost constraints associated with tenancy.

Therefore, where population density is very low, peasants will establish their own farms in the bush and thereby escape paying tribute, taxes or rent to the overlord. Extracting tribute under these conditions requires *coercion*. This implies that the utility of free peasants must be sufficiently reduced so that they will offer themselves voluntarily as workers or tenants to holders of large tracts of land at wages, rents or crop shares that provide the same level of utility as would independent self-cultivation.[3] Coercion is no longer necessary. Utility can be reduced by changing the free peasants' access to high quality land.

---

[3] Taking into account any risk reduction the landowner may be able to provide as part of the bargain.

Large landowners can also try to increase the supply of labor or tenants to their holdings by influencing governments to intervene through differential taxation of owners and workers in large and small holdings, or by limitations on market access that drive down profitability for independent peasants and thus reduce the reservation price of labor. Such economic distortions increase the rent that goes to large-scale farmers at a cost to the economy of lower productive efficiency.

When peasants can freely establish their own farms, it becomes very difficult to operate large farms with hired labor under a single management. With simple technology, there are usually no technical economies of scale (Section 4). Lumpy inputs such as draft animals provide for declining economies of scale at very small farm sizes. For larger farms the same draft-animal and driver combination has to be repeated several times over, leading to constant technical returns. Disincentives associated with hired labor give the family-operated farm a cost advantage over large farms: for family members, there are no hiring costs, they have greater incentives to work than do hired wage labor because they receive a share of profits, and third, site-specific learning costs are lower.

Renting out entire small farms to sharecropper families (share tenancy) or granting usufructuary rights to peasants in exchange for tribute allows large landowners to circumvent many of the disincentive effects inherent in large wage-based farming and take advantage of the tenant family's labor. Share tenancy has some incentive costs of its own, however, (Section 6) and even under fixed-rent tenancy there are problems of supervision and moral hazard.

Once a labor supply becomes available, large landowners can organize their operations either as *landlord estates*, with the entire estate cultivated by *tenanted* peasants, or as *haciendas*, with workers cultivating portions of the hacienda for their own subsistence as tenants or holders of usufructuary rights and providing unpaid *corvée* or labor services to cultivate the *home-farm* of the owner. Since share tenants do not receive their full marginal product, landlord estates based on a lump-sum rent payment would, without risk, be the most efficient form of operation, followed by landlord estates based on share rents. The hacienda would be less efficient since labor tenants have few incentives to invest, and landowners' cultivation of the home farm entails labor supervision cost. These points are more fully elaborated now.

*Coercion:* As Boserup (1965) points out, "Bonded labor is a characteristic feature of communities with hierarchic structure, but surrounded by so much uncontrolled land suitable for cultivation by long fallow methods that it is impossible to prevent the members of the lower class from finding alternative means of subsistence unless they are made personally unfree" (p. 73). Four ways have traditionally been used to tie labor to large farms: slavery, serfdom, indentured labor contracts, and debt peonage.

Meillassoux (1991), shows that for *merchant slavery* in which the slaveholders purchase, rather than capture slaves, they must produce for the market to finance the slaves.[4] In areas with sparse populations of hunters and gatherers and with ties to external markets, such as in the United States' southeast, the east coast of Brazil, and the South African Cape, large farms had to import slaves as workers (arrow 6).[5] The native hunter-gatherers were too few to provide a steady labor supply, or simply moved away. Large farms in areas with access to abundant labor reservoirs such as the sugar islands of the Caribbean and Mauritius, Ceylonese (Sri Lankan) and Assamese tea plantations, Malaysia, Sumatra, and South Africa were able to rely on indentured labor instead of slaves (arrow 7). The workers had to be indentured to prevent them for the period of indenture at least from establishing plots of their own or going into mining. Laws and police forces were used to enforce indentured labor contracts and to ensure the recapture and return of escaped slaves. The capital cost of slaves, the cash requirements for recruiting indentured labor from distant lands, and the absence of cash markets for food in fact implied that these systems could be used only for crops that had an export market.[6]

Serfdom or bondage could be used in somewhat more densely populated regions with a settled peasant population and production primarily for local consumption (arrow 5). Peasants would have had to move to more marginal lands to escape bondage. Slaves could not be imported because there were no export earnings with which to purchase them. Overlords obtained the right to tie subsistence-oriented populations to the land and to extract tribute or labor services. This pattern arose during feudal periods in Western Europe, China, and Japan, and pre- and post-Columbian America, and survived in Eastern Europe until the late nineteenth century [Blum (1977)].

---

[4] Mesailloux also shows that these systems of *merchant slavery* were dependent on systems of *aristocratic slavery* which engaged in the reproduction of the slave population through raids and warfare on widely dispersed subsistence-oriented peasant populations. Domar (1970) relates ownership rights in people – slavery and serfdom – to land abundance, which makes extracting residual land rents impossible. What he did not distinguish is that slavery, the purchase of the labor force, requires high levels of capital, which can be financed only if there is a market, while serfdom involves extracting tribute without a purchase transaction, and so no market is needed.

[5] Meillassoux (1991) distinguishes *merchant slavery*, were purchased slaves are used for market production, from systems of *aristocratic slavery* which regularly replenished a pool of domestic slaves through warfare and raids of subsistence-oriented peasant populations.

[6] The temperate zones of the Americas (Canada, North Eastern US, Southern Brazil, and Argentina) escaped slavery because their products could not be exported competitively to temperate zone Europe until the advent of the steamship and the railroad at a time when slavery had gone out of style. The tropical and subtropical crops, sugar, cotton, and tobacco faced no competition in European markets.

Debt peonage or bonded labor, another form of coercion, survived in many areas even under high population densities. Where manorial estates had to compete with mines for labor and therefore faced acute labor shortage, as in Guatemala and Mexico in the nineteenth century or in South Africa in the twentieth century, vagrancy laws kept a pool of potential workers in prison for a variety of petty offenses (see Table 42.1). In South Africa farmers could invest in prisons in exchange for rights to prison labor; these rights could even be traded.

## Economic distortions

Where coercion was no longer possible, or sufficient, influential groups were able to get governments to intervene to create economic distortions that would generate a labor supply for their farms. Once population density was high enough for long fallow agriculture to replace hunting and gathering, peasants would establish independent farming operations in areas without slavery and bondage. With identical technology and a competitive output market, cultivation of the home farm with wage labor would not be competitive with the free family farm because of incentive disadvantages and labor supervision costs.

To get free peasants to move to the manorial estate required lowering expected utility or profits in the free peasant sector in order to reduce peasants' reservation utility – expected utility from family farming, including the risk attributes of the corresponding income stream – or shift their labor supply curve to the right. This was achieved through four mechanisms:

- *Reducing the land available for peasant cultivation* by allocating rights to "unoccupied" lands so that they went to members of the ruling class only and thus confining free peasant cultivation to infertile or remote areas with poor infrastructure and market access. (Table 42.1 lists a variety of cases from all continents in which access to high quality land was restricted). Farm profits or utility on free peasant lands were thus reduced by the higher labor requirements for producing a unit of output on poor land, by increased transport and marketing costs, and by increased prices for consumer goods imported to the region.
- *Imposing differential taxation* by requiring free peasants to pay tribute, hut, head or poll taxes (in cash, kind, or labor services) while often exempting workers or tenants in manorial estates or taxing them at much lower rates. Such systems were used widely in Western Europe during the feudal period, in ancient Japan, China, India and the Ottoman Empire, and by all colonial powers (Table 42.1). Tribute systems in Eastern Europe and Japan survived

Table 42.1
Intervention to establish and support large farms

| Country | Land market interventions | Taxes and interventions in Labor and output markets |
|---|---|---|
| **ASIA:** | | |
| India (North) | Land grants from 1st century | Hacienda system; 4th century BC<br>Corvee labor; from 2nd century |
| China (South) | | Limitations on peasant mobility; ca 500<br>Tax exemption for slaves; ca 500<br>Gentry exemption from taxes & labor services; ca 1400 |
| Japan | Exclusive land rights to developed wasteland; 723 | Tribute exemption for cleared and temple land; 700 |
| Java and Sumatra | Land grants to companies; 1870 | Indentured labor; 19th century<br>Cultivation System; 19th century |
| Philippines | Land grants to monastic orders; 16th century | Encomienda<br>Repartimiento<br>Tax exemption for hacienda workers; 16th century |
| Sri Lanka | Land appropriation; 1840 | Plantations tax exempt; 1818<br>Indentured labor; 19th century |
| **EUROPE:** | | |
| Prussia | Land grants; from 13th century | Monopolies on milling and alcohol<br>Restrictions on labor mobility; 1530<br>Land reform legislations; 1750–1850 |
| Russia | Land grants; from 14th century<br>Service tenure; 1565 | Restrictions on peasant mobility:<br>–Exit fees; 1400/50<br>–Forbidden years; 1588<br>–Enserfment; 1597<br>–Tradeability of serfs; 1661<br>Home farm exempt from taxation; 1580<br>Debt peonage; 1597<br>Monopoly on commerce; until 1830 |
| **S. AMERICA:** | | |
| Chile | Land grants (*mercedes de tierra*); 16th century | Encomienda; 16th century<br>Labor services (*mita*); 17th century<br>Import duties on beef; 1890<br>Subsidies to mechanization; 1950–1960 |
| El Salvador | Grants of public land; 1857<br>Titling of communal land; 1882 | Vagrancy laws; 1825<br>Exemption from public and military services for large landowners and their workers; 1847 |

Table 42.1 (Continued)

| Country | Land market interventions | Taxes and interventions in Labor and output markets |
|---|---|---|
| Guatemala | Resettlement of Indians; 16th century Debt peonage; 1877 | Cash tribute; 1540 Manamiento; ca 1600 |
| Mexico | Resettlement of Indians; 1540 Expropriation of communal lands; 1850 | Encomienda; 1490 Tribute exemption for hacienda workers; 17th century Debt peonage; 1790 Return of debtors to haciendas; 1843 Vagrancy laws 1877 |
| Viceroyality of Peru | Land grants; 1540 Resettlement of Indians (congregaciones); 1570 Titling and expropriation of Indian land; 17th century | Encomienda; 1530 Mita: Exemption for hacienda workers; 1550 Slavery of Africans; 1580 |
| **AFRICA:** Algeria | Titling; ca 1840 Land grants under settlement programs; 1871 "Settlers' law" 1873 | Tax exemption for workers on European farms; 1849 Credit provision for European settlers |
| Angola | Land concessions to Europeans; 1838, 1865 | Slavery; until 1880 Vagrancy laws; 1875 |
| Egypt (Ottomans) | Land grants; 1840 | Corvée labor; from 16th century Corvée exemption for farm-workers; 1840s Land tax exemption for large landlords; 1856 Credit and marketing subsidies, 1920 and 1930s |
| Kenya | Land concessions to Europeans; ca 1900 No African land purchases outside reserves; 1926 | Hut and poll taxes; from 1905 Labor Passes; 1908 Squatter laws; 1918, 1926 and 1939 Restrictions on Africans' market access; from 1930: −Dual price system for maize −Quarantine and force of destocking for livestock −Monopoly marketing associations −Prohibition of African export crop cultivation Subsidies to mechanization; 1940s |
| Sokotho Caliphate | Land grants to settlers; 1804 | Slavery; 19th century |
| Malawi | Land allotments to Europeans; 1894 | Tax reductions for farm-workers; ca 1910 |

Table 42.1 (Continued)

| Country | Land market interventions | Taxes and interventions in Labor and output markets |
|---|---|---|
| Mozambique | Comprehensive rights to leases under prazo; 19th century | Labor tribute: 1880<br>Vagrancy law: 1899<br>Abolition of African trade: 1892<br>Forced cultivation: 1930 |
| South Africa | Native reserves; 19th century<br>Pseudo-communal tenure in reserves: 1894<br>Native Lands Act; 1912<br>–Demarcation of reserves<br>–Elimination of tenancy<br>–Prohibition of African land purchases outside reserves | Slavery and indentured labor; 19th century<br>Restrictions on Africans' mobility; 1911, 1951<br>Monopoly marketing; from 1930<br>Prison labor; ca 1950<br>Direct and indirect subsidies; 20th century |
| Tanganyika | Land grants to settlers; 1890 | Hut tax and corvée requirements; 1896<br>Compulsory cotton production; 1902<br>Vagrancy laws (work cards); 20th century<br>Exclusion of Africans from credit; 1931<br>Marketing coops to depress African prices; 1940 |
| Zimbabwe | Reserves; 1896 and 1931 | Poll and hut taxes; 1896<br>Discrimination against tenancy; 1909<br>Monopoly marketing boards; from 1924<br>–Dual price system in maize;<br>Forced destocking in livestock; 1939 |

into the second half of the nineteenth century. As long as free peasants could pay tribute or taxes in kind or cash and have equal access to output markets, taxation alone was insufficient to bring forth a supply of workers or tenants. It was therefore often complemented by output market interventions.

- *Restricting market access*, by commonly setting up cooperative or monopoly marketing schemes that buy only from the farms of the rulers. The *prazo* system in Mozambique combined rights to labor and tribute from peasants with monopolies on inputs and outputs. In Kenya the production of coffee by Africans was prohibited outright until the 1950s. European monopolies on sales of tobacco in Zimbabwe and Malawi were directly transferred to large farms after the countries gained independence.
- *Confining agricultural public goods and services* (roads, extension, credit) *to*

*the farms of the rulers* or subsidizing these farms directly was another means of increasing their profitability relative to peasant farms.[7]

Sometimes the four types of distortions were supplemented by coercive interventions in the labor market – vagrancy laws, debt peonage, and agrestic slavery are examples – to make it easier to retain workers or tenants on manorial estates.

Since these four mechanisms involved legal or customary rules backed by the state, they required a coalition between the overlords and the state. The combinations of distortions used to establish manorial estates under conditions of low population density have been remarkably similar across continents and over time (Table 42.1). The earliest recorded incidence we found was in the Arthasastra in the fourth century B.C. Once members of the ruling group began to establish viable agricultural production getting enough workers for their estates required interventions in more than one market. The most common pattern was to combine restrictions on land use with differential taxation. Groups with widely different cultures, religions, and ethnic backgrounds – Ottomans, the Hausa and Fulani in Africa, the Fujiwara in Japan, and all European colonial powers – imposed such systems on people of the same or different ethnic backgrounds when faced with similar material conditions. Material conditions of production and rent seeking rather than culture seem to have led to the emergence of such distortions.

*Production relations on the manorial estate*

On both landlord estates and haciendas, all or part of the land is cultivated by peasants under tenancy contracts or usufructuary rights. In the classical type of hacienda, the unpaid labor services of peasants (corvée) who hold usufruct rights to some plots on the estate is used to cultivate the home farm of the owner. There is, however, considerable variation in the detailed specification of production relations on manorial estates. Corvée may include the services of their draft animals and plows. The labor services of tenants may constitute all or a part of their rental payments for the use of the land. Peasants may be free

---

[7] In Zimbabwe, Africans had been encouraged to cultivate maize through the "Master Farmer Program" in the late 1920s when European farmers found it more profitable to grown tobacco and cotton. When those markets collapsed, monopoly marketing and dual price systems were introduced and the Master Farmer Program was abandoned, with responsible officials publicly declaring that they had never intended to "teach the natives to grow maize in competition with European producers" (Phimister 1988: 235).

to leave the manorial estate or may be bound to it. The resident labor force may be complemented by seasonally hired wage workers. Sometimes peasants may, in addition to usufructuary rights to a plot of land, receive a wage payment as part of the remuneration for their labor.

The extreme variation in the names and details of these arrangements and in their local evolution over time has long stood in the way of comparative analysis in a single theoretical framework. Yet common elements seem clear.

Landlord estates were prevalent in China, Korea, Japan, Eastern India, Pakistan, Iran, Egypt and Ethiopia. In many colonial environments, it was easy for landlords to restrict peasants' alternatives and maintain control over land and labor and sometimes over output markets. Haciendas emerged as the predominant form of manorial estates in Algeria, Egypt, Kenya, South Africa, Zimbabwe, Bolivia, Chile, Honduras, Mexico, Nicaragua, Peru, and other countries in Latin America, in the Philippines, in Prussia and other parts of Eastern Europe.

The home farm of the landlord often vastly exceeded the area actually cultivated. A major purpose of the huge landholdings was to restrict the indigenous population's possibilities for independent cultivation, and much of the land remained under forest or fallow or was devoted to extensive livestock grazing. At the height of the feudal period in Western Europe, between one-quarter and one-half of the total area on manorial estates was cultivated by the owner in the home farm. On Latin American and African haciendas, that share was initially a much lower, in some cases only about one-tenth [Palmer (1979), Chevalier (1963)].

Many historical accounts have noted the lack of competitiveness and limited profitability of large-scale cultivation of home farms relative to landlord estates in which all land is rented out. That relative disadvantage is also confirmed by a range of quantitative studies. Records for the eighteenth and early nineteenth centuries show that in all of the cases investigated, hacienda owners in Mexico would have been better off by renting out all of their land at rents actually paid by tenants rather than cultivating their home farms [Brading (1978)]. Many overlords survived economically against competition from independent producers only because of their access to capital markets and large-scale storage of maize, which could be sold at high prices in poor years [Florescano (1969)]. The same applies to many Chilean and Peruvian haciendas in the sixteenth and seventeenth centuries which yielded a return on capital of about 4.5 percent, considerably below the market rate at which the overlords borrowed funds to keep up their living standards. They were able to repay mortgages only because of a rapidly devaluing currency and the appreciation of their land [Moerner (1973: 204)]. Labor productivity and total production on the patrons' plots were about half that on tenants' plots in Peru and one quarter in Ecuador [Pearse (1975: 91)].

What explains the total amount of tribute, surplus, or rent that could be extracted from the peasants on the manorial estate? The predominant explanation for European estates was a demographic–economic model based on Malthus and Ricardo [see, for example, Postan (1973), Le Roy Ladurie (1966, and (1985), North and Thomas (1971), Brenner (1985), Hilton (1977)] that relates tribute burdens to relative scarcities of land and labor. Before ruling groups controlled most of the land or were able to coerce labor, attracting or retaining peasants to manorial estates in areas of low population density required that peasants' utility on the manorial estate exceeded their reservation utility for subsistence farming in the bush or in areas from which they had to be induced to emigrate. In Europe east of the river Elbe such terms usually included a grant of hereditary usufruct rights. Similarly, most corvée labor was initially devoted to the provision of public goods such as infrastructure.

As long as population densities were low, corvée requirements had to be regulated and enforced by the state. But as rising population densities and increased land scarcity reduced peasant mobility, it became possible to increase the amount of tribute extracted and to increasingly transform that tribute into obligations to work on the landlord's home farm. Labor requirements, of two to three days a week in feudal Europe, nineteenth century Russia, Kenya in 1918, and Central and South America, began to rise with growing land scarcity. In Kenya, corvée requirements for squatters and their families had risen to five days a week by the end of the colonial period (Resident Labor Ordinance of Kenya, 1939).

This simple demographic–economic model fails to explain, however, why European regions reacted so differently to the plague-induced declines in population in the fourteenth century. The associated drop in tribute contributed to the erosion of serfdom in Western Europe, but led to the reimposition of serfdom in Eastern Europe. In the debate over the demise of feudalism in Europe, Brenner (1976, 1982) clearly established that economic factors such as population density and market access alone are insufficient to determine the income distribution between peasants and lords in the manorial estate. At best, they determine a range of possible solutions to the game between landlords and peasants. The lords' success in extracting tribute depended on their political power to claim the land, monopolize markets, and control the movement of peasants relative to the power of peasants to resist these efforts.

*Bargaining between peasants and lords and the distribution of income*

The amount of rent extracted thus depended on the outcome of a bargaining game, the political conflict, or the class struggle, over the definition of "property rights" in the widest sense. That means that the cohesiveness of the landlords relative to that of the peasants and the success of the alliances they could forge – with the King, the bureaucracy, other production sectors, the financial sector, and external interests – are central to an analysis of change in the instruments of surplus extraction by landed classes.

In the bargaining over the terms of income distribution between peasants and landlords on the manorial estate, two sets of issues must be dealt with. One is to define the admissible set of property rights and of coercive or voluntary exchange relationships, including the instruments used to enforce such relationships. This problem includes the ability of overlords to impose restrictions on peasant mobility and output markets, the broad terms of legitimate leases (inheritable usufruct, long-term leases, short-term rental), the forms of rental payment available (cash, kind, labor, fixed rent, crop share) and the sanctions (eviction, physical punishment, fines) or instruments that can be used to enforce such changes. The other is to determine optimal mix and level of use of each instrument for maximizing surplus extraction, taking the available options as given. Although this question is more amenable to economic analysis than is the problem of the admissible set of instruments, there has been little formal modeling of this bargaining problem, even for environments without coercion (see, for example, Carter and Kalfayan 1990; Carter and Zimmerman 1992; and Sadoulet 1992).[8]

This second problem could be set up as a bargaining process between landlord and potential tenants. The landlord who maximizes his income or utility subject to the tenant's reservation utility constraint, determines the terms of the tenancy, the size of the tenant's plot, and the size of his own home farm according to the following considerations: he can set the overall rent burden of the tenant. He can partition the rent into corvée, fixed rent payments in cash or kind, and crop shares, each having its own incentive problems. He can choose the amount of land allocated to home farm cultivation, knowing that incentives are required to bring forth effort and that supervision is costly. He can choose the size of the plot allocated to the tenants, knowing that family farms provide high incentives to produce but may

---

[8] Carter and Kalfayan (1990) show that the combination of a labor supervision constraint and a working capital constraint can result in the emergence of tied labor contracts. Carter and Zimmerman (1992) provide a dynamic extension of this model and demonstrate the emergence of a number of the salient characteristics of dual agrarian societies as a consequence of credit and labor supervision problems. Sadoulet (1992) explains the emergence of labor service tenancy as a device adopted by the landlord in order to enforce an optimal level of insurance against default by the tenant in the case of crop failure. Covariance of yields between the landlord's home farm and tenants' plots is ignored however. But in years of crop failure the tenants' labor has no value on the home farm either, and forcing him to provide it only leads to extra supervision costs. Sadoulet's explanation therefore fails.

lead tenants to concentrate on their own plot and not supply sufficient effort for home farm cultivation.

With peasants free to leave, the major constraint faced by the landlord is that he cannot drive the utility received by his tenants below their reservation utility – the utility they could receive working in the free peasant sector outside the manorial estate or in an urban labor market. The tenant, for his part, can vary the labor effort on his own farm or leave for frontier areas, indigenous reserves, or urban labor markets. So even without coercion or the ability to affect the reservation utility, the landlord seems to have an abundance of instruments for driving the tenant down to his reservation utility. Without further restrictions on the bargaining problem, its solution may be indeterminate.

Constraints on the bargaining problem imposed by the state – restrictions on peasant mobility, on the size of parcel to be allocated to peasants in inheritable usufruct, or on the tribute, rent and corvée requirements, for example – can simplify the structure of the bargaining problem for specific historical settings. But these outside regulations did change, albeit slowly, in response to such forces as population densities and political conflict, so they can not truly be regarded as exogenous. Thus the complexity of the problem remains.

*Rent seeking, coalitions and conflict*

The analytical problem becomes even more complex if it incorporates rent seeking or surplus extraction through efforts to change the set of instruments available to landlords. A coalition or class of landlords can try to induce the state to manipulate the reservation utility of peasants and may succeed if peasants or workers are poorly organized to resist the change. We have not found any models addressing these choices or game theory problems formally, but the literature is rich in discussions of changes in the degree of coerciveness of the systems and of changes in other instruments. North and Thomas (1971), for example, in an informally stated bargaining model, analyze the choice between tribute in cash or kind and corvée labor, suggesting that corvée was preferred over tribute in kind where output markets were limited, and the relative prices of goods were highly variable. There are many other examples, however, of frontier societies without external markets in which tribute was collected in kind.

While the bargaining problem has received little formal analysis, manorial systems have sometimes been interpreted as the outcome of an efficiency-enhancing contract between peasants and landlords: the landlords provide protection and other public goods (which are produced with economies of scale and require some specialization) in exchange for tribute or rent [North and Thomas (1971), for example]. This is a plausible interpretation for land-abundant settings, where tribute rates or labor rents have to be set low enough to attract immigrants. However, there are two major problems with this view.

First, it ignores the asymmetry between contracting parties in access to weapons, laws, and public investment budgets. The systematic use of these instruments throughout history has depressed the utility of peasants and workers to far below the reservation utility that would obtain in a system without such symmetric access. Moreover, there is little doubt that substantial deadweight losses and dynamic inefficiencies have been associated with taxes and tribute, with inequalities in factor ratios between farming sectors, and with restrictions on access to credit and output markets.

Second, the contract view ignores the likely competition in rent seeking between landlords, which would add to the deadweight loss associated with restrictions. Competitive rent seeking, the literature shows, is likely to result in the dissipation of the rent into such rent-seeking costs as competitive armies, arsenals, and fortifications, which provide no consumption value. Brenner (1985) argues that at the height of the feudal period, rents were completely dissipated into the costs of competing in the system. Periodic conflicts over the right to extract rent have caused destruction and decline in many flourishing kingdoms and empires, so the efficiency characteristics of the contractual system are only third or fourth best.

*Conclusion*

The major issue in land relations, then, is the evolution of the relationship between peasants and landlords over time. The best developed literature in this area relates to the demise of the manorial estate, corvée, and bondage and the emergence of capitalism in Europe. Dobb (1976) interprets the emergence of capitalist farming and the loss of rights to tribute as the consequence of increased population density alone, while Sweezy et al. (1976) emphasizes the role of increased access to markets. Brenner (1985) shows that these explanations alone are inadequate, arguing the need to introduce the cohesiveness of the two groups and the strength of the coalitions they can form with kings or urban groups. Hilton (1977) also discusses these issues, as well as broader non-economic theories. In particular, Brenner stresses the importance of the cohesiveness of the peasant community in resisting attempts by the lords to increase the instruments available to them or the intensity of their use.

## 3. Success and failure in land reform

How does the manorial estate disappear? Again Boserup (1965) explains succinctly: "The process by which the feudal landlord tenure [the manorial estate] is abandoned may take different forms: sometimes the position of the feudal landlords in relation to the cultivators is weakened; they lose their power over all or most of the peasants and they end up as private owners of their home farms only [Figures 42.1 and 42.2, arrows 8, 10, and 11]. In other cases, the feudal landlords succeed in their efforts to completely eliminate the customary rights of the cultivators, and they end up as private owners of all the land over which they had feudal rights, whilst the cultivators have sunk to the status of tenants-at-will. England, of course, is the classical example of this last kind of development" pp. 79–87. In transitions of the first kind the peasants end up with the land rent, while in those of the second kind, the landlords retain the rent.

Since land reform involves the transfer of rents from a ruling class to tenant workers, it is not surprising that most large-scale land reforms were associated with revolts (Bolivia), revolution (Mexico, Chile, China, Cuba, El Salvador, Nicaragua, Russia), conquest (Japan and Taiwan), or the demise of colonial rule (Eastern India, Kenya, Mozambique, Vietnam, Zimbabwe). Attempts at land reform without massive political upheaval have rarely succeeded in transferring much of a country's land[9] (Brazil, Costa Rica, Honduras) or have done so very slowly because of a lack of political commitment to provide the funding to compensate owners (see Section 5).

The outcome of land reforms has been conditioned by three factors: whether

[9] Horowitz (1993) models land reform as the outcome of a Nash bargaining between two agents representing landed elites and the poor. Each party can either agree to a reform proposal or initiate "revolt", defined as a lottery over the three outcomes "victory for the rich", "victory for the poor", and "maintenance of the status quo". The power-structure which, in the case of revolt, determines the probabilities for each of these events is taken to be exogenous and time-invariant. This leads to the definition of a *safe reform plan* as the evolution of landholdings over time which constitutes a Nash equilibrium in the bargaining game between landlords and peasants which, at any point in time, provides each party with a level of utility at least equal to their expected utility in the case of revolt. Horwitz shows that in the case of risk neutrality (i) there exists a unique safe reform plan for every initial distribution of landholdings which can entail either redistribution from the rich to the poor or accumulation of land by the rich; (ii) for any given power structure, the extent of land transfer is the greater of the higher of the initial imbalances in landholdings; (iii) except in special cases, the safe land reform plan is a prolonged process consisting of a sequence of individual reform events rather than a one-time redistribution. This approach is the first formal model in which the dependence of the equilibrium landholding pattern on the power structure is clearly elaborated. The determinants of power, such as coalitions with third groups and internal cohesiveness are not modeled, however, but from the model it is clear that changes in the power structure (such as the changes taking place in many parts of the world after 1945) and the instruments available to landlords to reduce peasants' reservation utility will have major implications for the possible evolution of land ownership distributions.

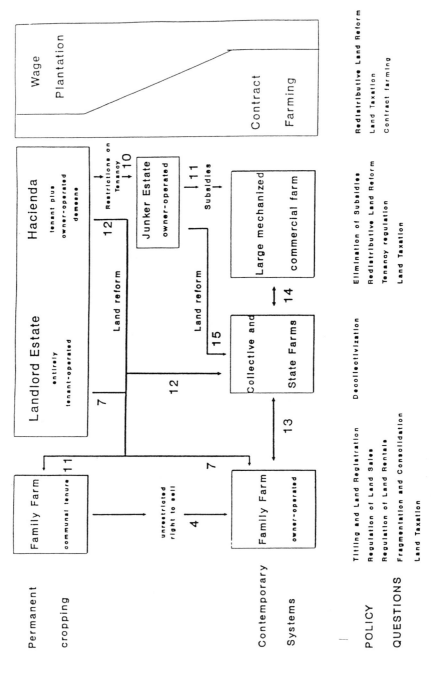

Figure 42.2. Production relations, property rights and land policy issues. . .

the system was a landlord estate or a hacienda system, whether reform was gradualist with compensation or took place all at once, and whether the reform was undertaken in a market or a socialist economy. We consider the first two factors in the context of the third, the type of economy.

*Reform in market-based economies*

Rapid transition from *landlord estates* to *family farms* in a market economy (Figure 42.2, arrow 7) has led to stable systems of production relations. The organization of production remains the same family farm system. The only change is that ownership is transferred from large landlords to tenants who already farm the land and have the skills and implements necessary to cultivate their fields.

Government involvement in the transition has often been substantial, ranging from a ceiling on the size of landholdings and the amounts to be paid for the land, to the establishment of financial obligations of beneficiaries. Many reforms, that followed this pattern provided stronger incentives for tenant-owners to work and invest in their farms and led to increases in output and productivity. The resulting systems have had great stability. Since the end of World War II, landlord estates in Bolivia, large areas of China, Eastern India, Ethiopia, Iran, Japan, Korea, and Taiwan have been transferred to tenants in the course of successful land reforms.

Theoretically, the productivity gains associated with such reforms come about because of improved work and investment incentives associated with increased security of tenure. These gains may be modest if tenants had to compensate landowners at near-market prices, if security of tenure had already been high, if cash-rent contracts had prevailed, or if the disincentive effects associated with share-tenancy had been low as suggested by Otsuka and Hayami (1988). Empirical evidence shows that the reform of landlord estates led to considerable investment, adoption of new technology and increases in productivity [Callison (1983), Koo (1968), King (1977), Dorner and Thiesenhusen (1990)] and that costs to the government of complementary investments supporting the transition in ownership structure, such as infra-structure, housing, training in management skills, were low because the structure of the smallholder production system was already in place.

By contrast with the relatively smooth transition from landlord estates to family farms, reform of *hacienda* systems has been very slow and difficult. The outcome has frequently been the emergence of large owner-operated *Junker estates*[10] with greatly increased home farm cultivation (arrow 10). Junker estates produce a wide variety of crops and livestock products using a hierarchy of supervisors, permanent workers who sometimes are given a house and garden plot, and external workers hired on a seasonal or daily basis. Junker estates are less specialized than plantations, which produce and process a narrow range of crops (discussed in section 4 on economies of scale), and less capital-intensive than large-scale commercial farms.

Expansion of the landlord's home farm at the cost of land cultivated by tenants for their own use would be associated with losses in efficiency. Therefore, rational landowners would not establish Junker estates unless induced to do so by such external constraints as the threat of land reform or restrictions on tenancy designed to protect tenants' rights. Anticipating such reforms, landowners often tried to reduce their exposure to expropriation by evicting tenants who usually are the beneficiaries of land reform. The lack of competitiveness of Junker estates with the more efficient smallholder sector made Junker estates an unstable form of production relations and led to intensive lobbying for protection and for subsidies to introduce and expand mechanization.

By substituting subsidized capital for labor, the Junker estate was transformed into a *large-scale mechanized commercial farm* (arrow 11) that no longer depended on large amounts of labor. Intensive mechanization of large commercial farms reduces the potential for land reform since there are not enough families with farming skills and implements available on these capital intensive farms to result in the establishment of efficient small farms able to rely on low-cost family labor. A similar result can be achieved by converting haciendas or junker farms to livestock ranches, which require very little labor.

The early rounds of land reform in Prussia gave freehold property rights to hereditary tenants, requiring them to give between one-half to one-third of their hereditary land to the Junkers as compensation for the loss of their corvée services. Fearing that further land reform would include tenants at will or holders of nonhereditary usufruct rights, the Junkers evicted many of the remaining tenants and reverted to cultivation with hired labor.

In Latin America, ever since the Mexican Revolution in 1910, land reform movements have legally enshrined the principle that land belongs to the tiller and that indirect exploitation of the land through tenants constitutes a cause for expropriation. The Brazilian Land Law of 1964 puts a low ceiling on rental rates and crop shares and conveys permanent usufruct rights to tenants after a few years of tenancy by protecting them from eviction. Similar provisions exist

---

[10] This "Junker path" has been described by Lenin (1974) who considered it to be part of a necessary differentiation of the peasantry. It has been extensively analyzed by de Janvry (1981) who was the first to show the compelling impact of "reformist" land legislation in Latin America on the elimination of traditional forms of labor relations and the expulsion of internal peasants.

in some land laws in Asia (Chuma et al. 1990). Restrictions on tenant cultivation in South Africa had different roots – they were imposed to make tenancy less attractive to Africans who were needed as workers in the mines. Whatever the motivation, these legal restrictions on tenancy induced owners of haciendas to evict their tenants and to expand home farm cultivation with hired labor, or shift to ranching, or to adopt mechanization.[11]

That Junker estates emerged only in response to pending land reform and tenancy restrictions supports the view that there are no technical economies of scale in unmechanized agriculture and that the incentive problems associated with supervising hired or corvée labor far exceed the efficiency losses associated with long-term whole-farm tenancy contracts. To compete successfully with family farms, Junker estates had to find ways to reduce their labor costs or to increase their revenues. Having lost their rights to rent or labor services from tenants or workers, landowners often sought to secure rents from the expanding urban and industrial sectors through trade barriers and subsidies for mechanizing production [de Janvry (1981)]. Trade barriers, by banning or reducing foreign agricultural competition, forced consumers to subsidize Junker estates. Examples include the German Zollverein at the end of the nineteenth century [Gerschenkron (1965)], tariffs on beef imports in Chile in 1887 [Kay and Silva (1992)], and selective price support to products from large-scale units in Kenya, Zimbabwe, and South Africa [Deininger and Binswanger (1993)]. Subsidies for mechanization led to the transformation of nearly all *Junker estates into mechanized commercial farms* (arrow 11). Huge sums were provided either through direct mechanization subsidies, as in Kenya, or through cheap credit, as in South Africa, Zimbabwe, and virtually all of South America, where real interest rates were even negative [Abercrombie (1972)]. Mechanization eliminated the need to rely on hired labor and resulted in widespread tenant evictions even in countries with cheap labor – hardly an optimal transformation from a social point of view.

In some market economies haciendas were converted to *communal family farm systems* (arrow 11). Communal tenure was adopted first in Mexico's ejido system and later, under land reforms in Bolivia, Zimbabwe, and elsewhere. Beneficiaries were granted inheritable usufructuary rights, but constraints on land sales and rentals often prevented using the land as collateral for credit.

---

[11] de Janvry and Sadoulet (1989) argue that the threat of land reform and their ability to lobby in coalition with the urban sector for subsidies and provision of public goods led large landowners to mechanize and make the transition from haciendas to large mechanized commercial farms in Colombia (1961–1968), Ecuador (1936–1957), Peru (1964–1969), Venezuela (1959–1970), and in Chile (after 1972). In Ecuador, two separate stages can be distinguished. Widespread eviction of tenants and the formation of Junker estates, until 1957 was followed by a period of increased emphasis on the family-farm sector together with widespread mechanization (1958–1973).

Attempts to provide alternative sources of credit through special banks or credit programs proved ineffective [Heath (1992), World Bank (1991)]. In Mexico, recent constitutional amendment legalizes land rental and sales within all ejidos and allows each ejido to remove restriction on sales to outsiders, by a majority vote, effectively converting the ejidatarios to owner-operated family farms.

### *Reforms in socialist economies*

Reform in socialist economies (Figure 42.2, arrows 10, 11, and 12) has followed different paths. *Landlord estates* in the former Soviet Union, Vietnam, and China were initially converted into *family farms* (arrow 10), in much the same way as in market economies. The redistributed farmlands were later consolidated into single management units or collectives (arrow 13), in which land is owned and operated jointly, under a single management. Families do not operate their own plots as they do in systems of communal ownership.

In Algeria, Chile, East Germany, Mozambique, Nicaragua, and Peru, *Junker estates or large commercial farms* were converted directly into *state farms* (arrows 14 and 15). In most cases, workers continued as employees under a single management, with no change in internal production relations. Over time, the organizational differences between collectives and state farms tended to disappear.

A desire to maintain presumed economies of scale in production and related activities (input supply, marketing) or to educate the beneficiaries of reform during a limited transitional period (Chile), motivated the establishment of collective and state farms. But to achieve efficient production, *collectives* have to deal with two incentive problems. One is to provide incentives to workers, a problem addressed by the adoption of piece-rate remuneration systems designed to reward labor at least partially on the basis of effort. Even where members of collectives were not able to divert effort to private plots, lack of incentives and of disciplinary measures by central management led to serious labor shortages following the transformation of private into collectively owned farms in Cuba [MacEwan (1981)] and Nicaragua [Enriquez (1992)].

The other incentive problem concerns investment and savings decisions, which are made jointly by the collective. Bonin (1985) shows that as long as equity financing is precluded and members cannot market their share in the cooperative, the representative worker will not make efficient investment decisions. Mitchell (1990) also examines problems associated with the inter-temporal allocation of consumption and shows that the distribution of decision-making power between old (who would rather consume) and young (who prefer to invest) determines the rate of growth for a cooperative enterprise. Successful collectives tend to degenerate into capitalist enterprises (or wage-labor-operated state farms) by successively substituting cheaper wage laborers for more expensive members [Ben Ner (1984)]. McGregor (1977) provides a theoretical justification and empirical examples of the tendency of cooperative enterprises to disinvest and to reduce membership in order to increase current consumption by members. Barham and Childress (1992) showed that Honduran collectives decreased their membership over time by about one fifth. Thus, the problems associated with provision of workers' effort and intertemporal consumption proved at least as serious in collectives as in haciendas [Bonin and Putterman (1986), Putterman (1989)]. The poor performance of agriculture under a collective mode of production is well documented and it is not surprising that the expected increases in production from economies of scale were not usually realized [see, for example, Colburn (1990) for Nicaragua; Ghai, Kay, and Peek (1988) for Cuba; Ghose (1985), Wuyts (1982), and Griffin and Hay (1985) for Ethiopia and Mozambique, Lin (1990) for China]. Once given the chance to do so, members of collective farms often voted to redistribute plots to family-sized farms,[12] a decision that rational farmers would not have taken if there existed true economies of scale in production [Putterman and Giorgio, (1985)]. In the absence of other possibilities of insurance, collective forms of production would be chosen, due to the implicit insurance they provide against noncovariate risks, even in the absence of economies of scale [Carter (1987)]. However, cooperative production does not insure against covariate risks. Empirical evidence indicates that social ties may be a less costly way to insure against risks that are not covariate [Walker and Ryan (1990)].

In China, agricultural output in the first six years after decollectivization in 1978 grew by 42 percent, with most of the growth attributable to the change in production organization [Lin (1992), Fan (1991), McMillan et al. (1989), Nolan (1988)]. Vietnam experienced similar productivity gains from breaking up large unmechanized collective farms into tiny family units [Pingali and Xuan (1992)]. The small family farms in these densely populated countries expanded

---

[12] Ortega (1990) offers quantitative evidence for the decline of the collective sector throughout Latin America. In Peru, the absence of economies of scale led reform beneficiaries to effectively subdivide reform collectives by concentrating effort on their private plots and to press for legal subdivisions and individual land titles [Kay (1983), Horton (1972), McClintock (1981)]. Collectives failed in Zimbabwe and were soon abandoned in favor of a smallholder-oriented strategy [Weiner (1985)]. Similarly, collectives failed in the Dominican Republic and were replaced by cooperatives, with individually owned plots [Meyer (1991)]. Land reform cooperatives in Panama are highly indebted and use labor far below profit-maximizing levels [Thiesenhusen (1987)]. Algerian production cooperatives experienced low productivity, membership desertion, high use of mechanization, and considerable underemployment of the workforce [Pfeiffer (1985), Trautman (1985)]. The same pattern of declining output and transformation into a "collective Junker estate" has been observed in Mozambique [Wuyts (1985)].

the labor input and were able to reduce machinery and fertilizer use. Clearly, the incentive advantages of individual farming outweighed any efficiency losses due to the extremely small size and fragmentation of farms [Wenfang and Makeham (1992)].

Under different conditions, as in Algeria and Peru [Melmed-Sanjak and Carter (1991)], the privatization and breakup of mechanized state farms or collectives has been less successful. Mechanization of these large farms had occurred and had reduced the number of workers or tenants before their collectivization. When these collectives were turned over to their relatively few remaining workers, the resulting family farms were relatively large and unlike in China and Vietnam could not be operated efficiently without additional hired workers or high levels of mechanization. But hiring additional workers dilutes the incentives advantage of the family farm, and the farms had neither the access to subsidized credit nor the large amounts of equity needed to finance hired labor or the mechanization. To make reform work under these capital-constrained conditions and reap the efficiency benefits of family farming may require including more beneficiary families in the reform program than those employed on the highly mechanized farms, by resettling landless or near landless workers from outside the farms (Part III).

*The social cost of delayed reform: revolts and civil wars*

Maintaining an agricultural structure based on relatively inefficient hacienda systems is costly. In addition to the static efficiency losses[13] there are dynamic efficiency losses associated with the reduced profitability of free peasant cultivation and the accompanying lack of incentives to invest in physical and human capital in the sector. Then there are the resource costs used in rent-seeking to create and maintain the distortions that support the large farms and contribute to rural poverty and inequality. In a competitive rent-seeking equilibrium these costs are equal to the rents. The distortions reduce employment in the sector, imposing an equity cost. Finally, the social costs of failing to reform have often included peasant uprisings and civil war.

Consider Brazil, where the emergence of an agricultural structure dominated by large farms owes much to a policy which – through subsidization of immigration to relieve large farms' labor constraint in the late 19th century, various interventions to maintain high prices especially for coffee and sugar, and subsidized credit since the 1950s – was continuously biased in favor of large

---

[13] Quantitative estimates of this efficiency loss are scarce, but Loveman (1976) estimates that Chile could have saved roughly $100 million a year in agricultural imports during 1949–1964 had the 40 percent of land left uncultivated by large landlords been cultivated.

farms [Graham, Gauthier and de Barros (1987)]. The social costs of distortions in favor of large farms appear to have been substantial. Between 1950 and 1980, agricultural value added in real terms grew at a remarkable 4.5 percent a year, land area expanded at 3.2 percent a year, but agricultural employment grew at only 0.7 percent a year [Maddison et al. (1993)]. Large-scale farms, assisted by large amounts of subsidized rural credit, mechanized and evicted most of their internal tenants and workers, many of whom migrated to urban slums or ended up as highly insecure seasonal workers (*boias frias*) lacking specific farming skills [Goodman and Redclift (1982)]. An alternative growth path based on smaller family farms could have provided rural employment and self-employment opportunities for many of these people and gainfully absorbed a substantial share of the rapidly growing population.

In many countries, protracted and violent struggles have significantly reduced the performance of the agricultural sector and the economy as a whole. While peasants have rarely been the initial protagonists in radical class struggles or revolutionary movements, many revolutionary movements took refuge in remote areas of limited agricultural potential – sometimes designated "communal areas", "reserves", or "homelands" – where peasants have provided both active and passive support for guerrilla fighters. Many analysts have emphasized the important role of peasant discontent in incidents of regional and national violence [Moore (1966), Wolff (1968), Huizer (1972), Migdal (1974), Scott (1976), Skocpol (1979), Christodoulou (1990), Goldstone (1991), Kriger (1991), Wickham-Crowley (1991), Rueschemeyer et al. (1992)]. The losses from such conflicts are, of course, difficult to measure, but some notion of their magnitude can be gauged from the duration and intensity of such struggles, as these cases show:

- In Mozambique, peasants escaped from forced cultivation, vagrancy laws, and forced labor to inaccessible rural areas. Some of these areas were also centers of support for the Frelimo guerrillas from 1961 until independence in 1975 [Isaacman & Isaacman (1983)]. Land reforms which were initiated after independence, however, resulted in highly mechanized collective farms. The Felimo government did little to address the problems of the free peasant sector. The counter-revolutionary Renamo movement in turn took advantage of the resulting peasant discontent. Violence continues to this day.

- In Zimbabwe, large scale eviction of some 85,000 families from European-owned farmlands during 1945–1951, led to a general strike among Africans in 1948 and provided the basis for peasants' support of ZANU (Zimbabwean African National Union) guerrillas in 1964 [Mosley (1983), Ranger (1985), Scaritt (1991) and Kriger (1991)]. Guerrilla fighters took up the peasants' grievances over unequal distribution of land and state interference with production and used the Tribal Trust Areas as bases to attack European farms. While a substantial settlement program after independence provided land to Africans, a number of shortcomings limited the success of this program [see Deininger and Binswanger (1994)]. Policy distortions remained in place despite evidence that large farms are not more efficient than small holder farmers [Masters (1991)] and land reform continues to be a major political issue.

- In Guatemala, communal lands were in effect expropriated in 1879 by a law giving proprietors three months to register land titles after which the land would be declared abandoned. Most of the "abandoned" land was then allocated to large coffee growers. Redistribution attempts in 1951–1954 were reversed following a military coup in 1954, when virtually all the land which had been subject to land reform was returned to the old owners and farms expropriated from foreigners were allocated in parcels averaging more than 3,000 hectares [Brockett (1984)]. Since then, there has been a repeated pattern of suppression and radicalization of resistance. Suppression of the cooperative movements of the 1960s led to formation of the guerrilla army of the poor (EGP) in 1972, with its main base in Indian highlands. Peasants responded to a wave of government-supported assassinations in 1976 with the formation of the committee for peasant union (CUC) in 1978. Government massacres of protesting peasants followed [Davis (1983)]. Almost 40 years after the first attempt at reform, continuing peasant demonstrations signal the cost of failure.

- Smallholder land in El Salvador was similarly appropriated. A decree of 1856 stated that all communal land not at least two-thirds planted with coffee would be considered underutilized or idle, and would revert to the state. Communal land tenure was abolished in 1888. Sporadic revolts led to such countermeasures as the 1888 "security tax" on exports to finance rural police forces, a 1907 ban on rural unions, and the creation of a National Guard in 1912 [McClintock (1985)]. Areas where land pressures were particularly severe emerged as centers of the revolt of 1932, during which some 10,000 to 20,000 peasants were killed [Mason (1986)]. Guerrillas promising land and other agricultural reform gained considerable support in rural areas, in particular, following the tenant evictions in the cotton growing lowlands during 1961–1970. These evictions led to a 77 percent decline in the houseplots available to tenants, as the number of tenants dropped from 55,000 to 17,000. Violence continued to escalate until 1979, when reform-minded officers engineered a coup and introduced land reform in an attempt to preempt a shift in popular support to the FMLN-FDR guerrilla forces. Narrow eligibility rules sharply limited the number of beneficiaries of land reforms and more than a decade of civil war ensued. The peace accord of 1992 mandates additional land reform.

- Colombia also demonstrates the perils of incomplete land reform. Conflicts over land between tenants and large-scale farmers at the frontier escalated from isolated local attacks in the early 1920s to more coordinated tenant actions by the late 1920s. While various kinds of reform legislation were considered during the 1930s, the law finally passed in 1936 vested rights in previously public lands with large landlords rather than the tenants cultivating the land [Le Grand (1982)]. A series of tenant evictions followed, leading to a quarter century of violence (1940–1965) during which guerrillas recruited support from peasant groups. Land reform legislation in 1961 and 1968 regularized previous land invasions but did nothing to improve the operational distribution of land holdings and far fewer peasants benefitted from the reforms than had previously been evicted [Zamosc (1989), de Janvry and Sadoulet (1993)]. Peasant land invasions intensified during the early 1970s, leading to the declaration of a state of emergency after 1974. Regional mobilizations, strikes, and blockades flared up again in 1984, indicated that the conflict is not yet resolved.
- Much of the rural support for the Shining Path guerillas in Peru can be traced to the exclusion of most of the highland Indians from agricultural benefits and the benefits of agrarian reform of 1973, which benefitted primarily the relatively few workers in the coastal area. As a result of the guerilla activity, more than half the departments in the country have become virtually inaccessible to government forces [McClintock (1984)], and public investment in these regions has halted, inducing further economic decline and large-scale migrations to the cities, thus exacerbating social tensions and conflicts. Poor economic management during the 1980s and continued activity by Shining Path have led to capital flight and economy wide decline.

Other countries that have experienced prolonged conflicts over land include Angola, Chile, and Nicaragua. While the policies that created and maintain dual land ownership distributions do not necessarily lead to violent struggle – other intervening factors are likely to be important – they clearly played a significant role in many cases.

## PART II: ANALYTIC CONTROVERSIES

The first question which is central to the analysis of past and future reforms in agricultural land relations is: Are Junker estates and large mechanized farms economically more efficient than smaller, family-operated holdings? The answer is important because if they are not, equalizing the ownership distribution or breaking up collective or state farms into family farms would enhance both efficiency and equity. In examining the relationship between farm size and productivity, we look first at the sources of economies of scale: economies of scale in processing plants that are transmitted to the farm and generate wage plantations, lumpy inputs that cannot be used below a certain minimum level such as farm machinery and management skills, and advantages in the credit market and in risk diffusion arising from larger ownership holding (Section 4). We then summarize the empirical findings on scale economies and diseconomies.

This leads to the second central question for land reform: if, as we find, large operational holdings are usually inefficient, why do large landowners in market economies not rent to family farmers (Section 6)? The rental market has historically been the most important mechanism to circumvent the diseconomies of scale associated with large ownership holdings despite the incentive issues associated with tenancy and sharecropping, which are reviewed in Section 6. Yet the history of land reform shows that long-term rental of entire farms often implies a high risk of loss of land to tenants, and long term tenancy is no longer an option. Short-term rental of parcels of land cannot create small family-operated holdings. But if tenancy is no longer an option, what prevents the land sales markets from bringing ownership holdings in line with the optimal distribution of operational holdings? Our analysis in Section 5 shows that it is the result of imperfections in other markets, brought about by land-credit linkages and policy distortions.

## 4. Farm size and productivity

*Economies of scale in processing*

Plantations have historically been established to produce specialized export crops in areas of extreme land-abundance and therefore have had to import slaves or indentured labor. But even after the abolition of slavery or indentured labor, *wage plantations* survived in selected crops as highly specialized large ownership holdings using hired labor to produce a single cash crop. Most workers lived in labor camps on these *wage plantation*s and had no subsistence plots of their own to cultivate.

Labor is the largest component of total costs. Grigg (1974) and Courtenay (1980) discuss how the ability to use labor nearly year-round favored the organization of production of these crops under plantations, rather than with tenants or outgrowers. Tree crops such as oil palm, rubber, and tea have the most even demand for labor. Labor demand is more seasonal for sugar and coffee, although irrigation (for sugar) or specific processing (for coffee) can help even out demand.

Wage-based plantations continue to exist for the typical plantation crops –

sugarcane, bananas, oil palm and tea – because of another technical characteristic. Economies of scale arise from the processing or marketing stage rather than in the farming operations and are transmitted to the farm because of the need to process the crops within hours of harvesting [Binswanger and Rosenzweig (1986)]. Only for these crops can wage plantations compete with smallholders without relying on coercion to acquire labor.

Economies of scale in processing alone are not a sufficient condition for plantations. The sensitivity of the timing between harvesting and processing is crucial. Easily stored products such as wheat or rice can be bought at harvest time in the open market and stored for milling throughout the year. Therefore, the economies of scale in milling are irrelevant for the organization of the farm. In the case of sugarcane, by contrast, harvesting and processing must be carefully coordinated. If cut cane is left unprocessed for more than a day, much of the sugar is lost to fermentation. And to keep the expensive capital stock operating throughout most of the year processing cane into sugar, cane must be planted at different times of the year, even at times when the sugar yield is not at its maximum. Independent farmers would be unwilling to plant cane during those times without compensation. One way to circumvent this problem is for sugar factories to run their own plantations, with a single manager who decides on the tradeoffs between harvesting cane at suboptimal times and leaving the capital stock idle. Another way is *contract farming* [Hayami (1992), Glover (1990)]. Contracting with small farmers is widespread throughout India, Thailand, and elsewhere where sugarcane was introduced into an existing smallholder system.

Production of bananas is another example of the coordination problem. Mature bananas must be put into a cold boat within 24 hours of harvest, an immense challenge for the plantation and shipping company. Coordination is required to ensure that the boat will arrive when the bananas are ready to be shipped and that a boat can be filled when it arrives. For that reason, some of the world's largest owner-operations are banana companies whose holdings include dozens of plantations operated by hired managers and workers. In Central America, when legislation made it more difficult for multinationals to own plantations, the major banana companies increased their supplies by buying from contract farms. These farms typically have hundreds of hectares and their contracts are so tight that they virtually remain managed by the multinationals [Ellis (1985)].

Similarly, rapid deterioration of the harvested product together with economies of scale in processing are the main factors leading to the continued cultivation of tea and oil palm on plantations. Thus the superiority of the plantation depends on a *combination of economies of scale in processing and a coordination problem*. Plantations do not arise – or do not survive once labor coercion is abolished – unless both these conditions exist. Bananas for local and national markets, which are supplied by individual trucks requiring little coordination, are supplied by family farms all over the world. Similarly, traditional unrefined forms of sugar such as muscovado in Central America, where processing did not involve economies of scale, were produced by family farms even in economies dominated by sugar plantations. In many countries coffee and rubber are also cultivated under smallholder systems. They have lower capital requirements for processing than do sugarcane, tea, or oil palm, and therefore, have a smaller optimal cultivated area associated with a single processing unit. Despite their even labor demand over the year, the plantation mode of production has therefore declined sharply at the expense of small-holder production.

The different outcomes for plantations following the abolition of slavery also support the combination hypothesis. United States cotton and tobacco planta-tions, which had no coordination problem, abandoned large-scale cultivation and rented the land out to their former slaves, creating landlord estates (arrow 17). The same thing happened in Latin America, except that some farms became landlord estates and some haciendas (arrows 16 and 17). Slave-operated sugar plantations in the Caribbean and South America, however, converted to wage plantations (arrow 15). There are, of course, other factors at work as well determining what precise pattern of production relations results after slavery is abolished. Klein and Engerman (1985) distinguish three patterns according to relative land abundance and the presence of government intervention.

Today, wage plantations survive in areas where they were first established under conditions of low population density and with a large land grant. Where the same crops were introduced into existing smallholder systems, contract farming prevails. Processors seem not to have found it profitable to form plantations by buying out smallholders and offering them wage contracts. This suggests either that the coordination problem associated with plantation crops can be solved at a relatively low cost by contract farming or that imperfections in land sales markets are so severe that it is prohibitively expensive to create large ownership holdings by consolidating small farms (Section 5).

*Lumpy inputs*

Draft animals for plowing were the first lumpy input in agriculture. Because of the difficulty of farming using rented draft animals [Binswanger and Rosen-zweig (1984)], small farmers who lose their draft animals frequently rent out their land until they can acquire new animals [Jodha (1984)]. *Farm machinery* – threshers, tractors, combine harvester – are much lumpier than draft animals. Tractors and harvesters reach their lowest cost of operation per unit area at a much larger scale than do draft animals, so the optimum operational farm size rises with their introduction. Karl Marx and his followers believed that the economies of scale associated with agricultural mechanization were so large as to make the family farm obsolete. Yet small owners can rent out their land to larger operators (consolidators) rather than sell it, as the ejidatarios in irrigated areas of Mexico have often done. So the initial economy of scale associated with machines does not imply that reverse land reform is needed in areas with many small ownership holdings.

The employment of lumpy capital inputs that leads to an initial portion of declining average costs is more profitable, the higher the wage rate relative to the cost of capital. Therefore, changes in relative prices or distortions in favor of capital (see Section 5) rather than genuine economies of scale may explain part of the growth of average farm sizes in industrialized countries. If opportunity wages increase and if the input of management is not fully variable, farm operators will need to obtain a remuneration for their management input comparable to incomes in other sectors of the economy. This would lead them to substitute capital for labor and increase their farm size over time [Kislev and Peterson (1982)].

Studies in high-wage economies find that, due to the presence of lumpy capital inputs, average costs of production decline up to a size of about 110–150 ac in British mixed farms [Britton and Hill (1975)], or 500 to 700 tillable acres in cash-grain farms in Illinois [Batte and Sonka (1985)]. Similarly, in Australia, average costs decreased substantially up to a gross revenue of about $20,000 (in 1966/1967) for sheep and $30,000 for wheat [Anderson and Powell (1973)]. It is important to note that, given the capital stocks, these farm sizes are still managed largely by family labor. In the following we will investigate determinants and empirical evidence concerning farm size from developing countries where cost of labor is considerably lower and does not constitute a major source of farm size growth.

Machine rental can permit small farms to circumvent the economies of scale advantage associated with machines in all but the most time-bound of operations, such as seeding in dry climates or harvesting where climatic risks are high, where farmers compete for first service and therefore prefer to own their own machines.[14] But threshing can be done at any time of the year and as in European agriculture in the late nineteenth century, the expansion of stationary threshers in developing countries today reflects a well developed, efficient rental market. Harvest combines are often rented in the developed and developing world. Most Midwestern U.S. farmers rent them from operators who follow the progress of the harvest season from Oklahoma to

---

[14] Binswanger and Rosenzweig (1986) discuss the limits to rental markets imposed by moral hazard and seasonality.

Canada. Tractors too are widely rented out for plowing to small farmers in Asia, Africa, and Latin America, but the markets are not as problem-free as those for threshers [World Bank (1984)]. Rao's (1975) analysis of India shows that small farms' productivity advantage over large farms initially disappeared following the introduction of tractors in Northwest India, but once the size of operational holdings was adjusted upwards, the smaller farms re-emerged with higher productivity rates.

Thus, the economies of scale associated with machines increase the minimum efficient farm size, but by less than expected because of rental markets. The use of draft animals and machines – lumpy inputs – leads to an initial segment of the production function that exhibits increasing returns with operational scale, but these technical economies would vanish when farm size is increased by replicating the optimal scale with lumpy inputs or when rental markets make the lumpiness of machines irrelevant. Under constant technical returns to scale and with perfect markets for land, capital, and labor, the ownership – distribution of land would be irrelevant for production and would only affect the distribution of income. Landowners would either rent the necessary factors of production (labor and capital) and make zero profits operating their own holding or, if there were transaction costs in the labor market, rent in or rent out land to equalize the size of operational holdings.

*Management skills* like machines, are an indivisible and lumpy input, so the better the manager, the larger the optimal farm size. Technical change strengthens this tendency: fertilizers and pesticides – and arranging the financing to pay for them – require modern management skills. So does the marketing of high-quality produce. In an environment of rapid technical change, acquiring and processing information becomes more and more important, giving managers with more formal schooling and technical education a competitive edge in capturing the innovator's rents.

Therefore, optimal farm sizes tend to increase with more rapid technical change. Some management and technical skills, like machinery, can be contracted from specialized consultants and advisory services or provided by publicly financed extension services. Contract farming often involves the provision of technical advice. But key farming decisions and labor supervision cannot be bought in a market. So limits on management skills will lead to an upward sloping segment in the unit cost curve as operational holding size increases.

*Access to credit and risk diffusion*

Land, because of its immobility and robustness, has excellent potential as collateral, making access to credit easier for the owner of unencumbered land (the issue is discussed in detail in Section 5). Rural credit markets are difficult to develop and sustain. There is therefore severe rationing, which can be partly relieved by the ability to provide land as collateral. The high transaction costs of providing formal credit in rural markets implies that the unit costs of borrowing and lending decline with loan size. Many commercial banks do not lend to small farmers because they cannot make a profit. Raising interest rates on small loans does not overcome this problem, since it also leads to adverse selection [Stiglitz and Weiss (1981)]. For a given credit value, therefore, the cost of borrowing in the formal credit market is a declining function of the amount of *owned land*. Land ownership may serve as a sign of creditworthiness in informal credit markets as well.

Access to credit is particularly important in developing countries because they usually lack other intertemporal markets to insure against crop or price risks. Insurance is sometimes available for very narrowly defined specific risks such as hail or frost, but only for very large farms. Forward markets are often banned or discouraged by policy intervention. An interested local insurer would have enough information to overcome the moral hazard problem, but the covariance of crop yields makes the risk uninsurable at the local level. A national insurer could overcome the covariance problem, but lacks the local information to overcome the moral hazard problem. The absence of a market for multi-risk crop insurance is the result of the combination of moral hazard and the local covariance of production risk. The absence of crop insurance and forward markets confers special importance on access to credit as an insurance substitute, but the combination of covariance and moral hazard also sharply reduces the potential of financial intermediation in rural areas [Binswanger and Rosenzweig (1986)].

Providing funds to overcome emergencies is a common function of informal rural credit markets. But the amounts small farmers can borrow for consumption are usually tiny – and often at high interest costs [Binswanger (1985), Christensen (1989), Morooka and Hayami (1990), Udry (1990), Deaton (1991)]. Investigations into how farmers and workers cope with disaster show that credit finances only a small fraction of their consumption in disaster years [Jodha (1978)]. Access to formal commercial bank credit therefore gives large modern commercial farms a considerable advantage in risk diffusion over small farmers without such access.

Farmers and workers with little or no access to credit can attempt to diffuse their risk by relying on accumulated reserves and wealth, social relationships, and risk-sharing arrangements in land, labor, output and input markets [Jodha (1978), Bidinger and others (1990), Rosenzweig (1988), Deaton (1990)]. Wealthy individuals can self-insure much more easily than the poor both directly, as a consequence of their wealth, and indirectly, because of geographically dispersed social networks on which they can rely in years of (locally covariate) poor harvests. Wealthy farmers should therefore be better able to accumulate profit-maximizing portfolios than poorer farmers, giving them an allocative efficiency advantage.[15] In land-scarce environments, the bulk of a farmer's wealth is in the form of land, so large ownership holdings are correlated with a better ability to diffuse risks through the wealth effect and land's robustness as collateral for credit. Florescano (1969) suggests that in high risk environments, the superior ability of land-rich individuals to diffuse risk through storage and better access to credit markets might have been an important reason that allowed otherwise unprofitable large farms to survive in the face of competition from family farms.

*Evidence on farm size – productivity relationship*

The literature demonstrates that imperfections in a single market would not be sufficient to introduce a systematic relationship between farm size and productivity per unit of land. For example, if credit is rationed according to farm size, but all other markets are perfect, land and labor market transactions will produce a farm structure that equalizes yields across farms of different operational size. But if there are imperfections in two markets, land rental and insurance, or credit and labor, a systematic relationship can arise between farm size and productivity.

Srinivasan (1972) has shown that under conditions of fixed farm size (no land rental) and no insurance, uncertainty and risk aversion can lead to an inverse relationship between farm size and productivity, provided that absolute risk aversion does not increase and that relative risk aversion does not decrease with wealth. With credit and labor market imperfections, the relationship is not necessarily inverse. For example, Feder (1985) and Carter and Kalfayan (1989) demonstrate that with certain model parameters, the combination of credit and labor market imperfections can lead to a U-shaped relationship. Eswaran and Kotwal (1985) obtain an inverse relationship by adding a fixed cost of production to labor and credit market imperfections. Generally, the presence of multiple market failure can explain a variety of farm size distribution and productivity structures.

The implications of imperfections in labor, credit, and land markets are illustrated by Feder (1985) whose model is replicated in Appendix 2. By assumption, the efficiency of hired labor depends on the intensity of supervision by family labor, implying that family labor and hired labor are comple-

---

[15] As explained in Binswanger and Rosenzweig (1986), they are not able to provide insurance to small farmers because covariance of income would require large reserves in order to be able to offer credible contracts.

ments and that the amount of labor effort or "efficiency" units supplied increases with supervision.

If credit and land rental markets are perfect, the supervision constraint alone would lead each household to lease in or lease out the amount of land required to maintain a uniform ratio of family labor endowment to operated area. The ratio of effective labor input to operated area would be constant for all cultivators, whatever the distribution of land ownership. No farm size-productivity relationship would exist.

But if there is a binding constraint in the credit market whereby the supply of working capital depends on the amount of land owned, the optimal size of the operational holding would vary systematically with size of the owned holding even if land rental markets were perfect. The magnitude (and direction) of this variation would depend on the relative elasticities of output with respect to effective labor and of labor effort with respect to supervision.

Now, if, in addition to a supervision constraint and a credit constraint, there are no rental markets for land – whether by law or because of the threat of land reform – a negative relation between farm size and land productivity is likely to emerge. Of course, the capital cost advantage of large farms does not necessarily lead to higher investments on the farm if the capital can be invested elsewhere in the economy at higher returns than in agriculture.

*The evidence for diseconomies of scale*

The discussion thus far suggests several approaches to the measurement of the farm size-productivity relationship:

- Since the supervision costs vary with the *operational holding* size while the capital constraint is related to the *ownership holding size*, the separate effects of operational and ownership holdings should be distinguished in any test of the farm size-productivity relationship. To eliminate errors resulting from the raw correlation of farm size and household size, regressions of an efficiency indicator on operational and ownership holding size should also include the number of adult family members who can act as supervisors. None of the existing studies has taken full account of these distinctions.
- *Proper measures of relative efficiency are the difference in total factor productivity between small and large farms and the difference in profits, net of the cost of family labor, per unit of capital invested.* Using market prices to measure productivity assesses differences in private efficiency. Using social opportunity costs as a measure eliminates the impact of distortion and measures differences in social efficiency. Few studies have made this distinction.

- Most of the literature has analyzed *physical yields* of specific crops or the *value of agricultural output* per unit of operated area. These are not relevant measures of overall private or social efficiency since they are but partial productivity indices that do not take into account differences in input and labor use. Because part of the adjustment to incentive problems and other market imperfections is to vary the output mix so as to save on the factors with the highest scarcity value in the specific farm, focusing on a single crop is inappropriate except in monocrop farming systems. Individual crop studies are therefore not relevant to the farm size-productivity relationship problem.
- Normalizing any productivity measure by *total land area* or regressing it on land area raises severe measurement problems because agroclimatic potential and land quality differ across regions. The same problem afflicts any comparisons that involve pooled data or use the means from several regions [e.g. Thiesenhusen (1990), Deolalikar (1981)]. Land quality differences within regions are often so large that adjustments must be made for those differences if productivity is measured per unit area rather than per capital invested [Bhalla and Roy (1988)]. Only if there is no correlation between land quality and farm size is such an adjustment unnecessary[16] – or if the differences arise from farmer investments in tubewells, land levelling, drainage, or the like.

The following test of the farm size-productivity relationship is one way to take these considerations into account describing not a causal relationship but a multiple correlation:

$$P/K = g(OP, OW, H, Z) \text{ with expected signs } g_1 < 0, \ g_2 > 0, \ g_3 > 0, \quad (1)$$

where $K$ is assets, $L$ is labor, $P$ is private or social profits net of private or social cost of family labor, $OP$ is operated area or value of operated land, $OW$ is owned area or value of owned land, $H$ is the number of household workers, and $Z$ is a vector of exogenous land quality, distance from infrastructure, and exogenous land improvement variables. $g_1$ should be negative because of rising supervision costs. $g_2$ should be positive because ownership provides better access to credit. And $g_3$ should be positive because family members have incentive to work and can supervise.

None of the studies of the farm size-productivity relationships have applied this full specification and few studies have even looked at total factor

[16] Both distress sales [Bhagwati and Chakravarty (1969)] and differential patterns of investment [Sen (1964)] could explain theoretically why small farmers could systematically end up with higher quality land within a given village. Few empirical studies exist at a sufficiently disaggregated village level to confirm this association. For six villages in semi-arid India, Walker and Ryan (1990) reject the existence of a systematic association between farm size and land quality.

productivity or farm profits net of the cost of family labor. So we must be content to summarize the findings of farm-level studies within small regions that look at value of output per operated area. Typical findings are presented in Table 42.2, which is extracted from Berry and Cline (1979), and similar results are found in a range of other studies.[17]

These studies support the following generalizations:

- The productivity differential favoring small farms over large one increases with the differences in size. That means it is largest where inequalities in land holdings are greatest, in the relatively land-abundant countries of Latin America and Africa, and smallest in land-scarce Asian countries where farm size distributions are less unequal.
- The highest output per unit areas is often achieved not by the smallest subfamily or part-time farmers but by the second-smallest farm size class,

Table 42.2
Farm-size productivity differences, selected countries

| Farm size[a] | Northeast Brazil[b] | Punjab, Pakistan[c] | Muda, Malaysia[d] |
|---|---|---|---|
| Small farm (hectares) | 563 (10.0–49.9) | 274 (5.1–10.1) | 148 (0.7–1.0) |
| Largest farm (hectares) | 100 (500 +) | 100 (20 +) | 100 (5.7–11.3) |

*Notes:* [a]100 = largest farm size compared with second smallest farm size. Second smallest farm size used in calculations to avoid abnormal productivity results often recorded for the smallest plots.
[b]Table 4-1. Northeastern Brazil, 1973; Production per Unit of Available Land Resource, by Farm Size Group, p. 46. Index taken using average gross receipts/areas for size group 2 (small) and 6 (large), averaged for all zones excluding zone F, where sugarcane and cocoa plantations skew productivity average for large farms.
[c]Table 4-29. Relative Land Productivity by Farm Size: Agricultural Census and FABS Survey-based Estimates Compared, (1968–1969) p. 84. Index taken using value added per cultivated acre for second smallest size group and largest.
[d]Table 4-48. Factor Productivity of Muda River Farms by Size, Double Croppers, 1972–1973 p. 117. Index taken from value added in agriculture/relong (0.283 ha = 1 relong).
*Source:* Berry and Cline (1978)

[17] For six Latin American countries Lau and Yotopoulos 1971, and 1979, Barraclough and Collarte 1973; for northeastern Brazil Kutcher and Scandizzo 1981; for fifteen countries in Africa, Asia, and Latin America Cornia 1985; for the Indian Punjab Sen 1981; for India and West Bengal Carter 1984; and for India disaggregated into seventy-eight agroclimatic zones Bhalla and Roy 1988. Dyer 1991 describes the array of instruments used by large producers in Egypt to increase their competitiveness with small farmers, demonstrating that large producers can successfully lobby for measures to counteract the inverse farm-size productivity relationship. The need for such rent-seeking implies the continued validity of this relationship although Dyer interprets it to mean the opposite.

which includes the smallest full-time farmers. This suggests that the smallest farms may be the most severely credit constrained.

- Plantation crops as represented by sugarcane production in Brazil, do not exhibit a negative farm size-productivity relationship [Cline (1971), Kutcher and Scandizzo (1981)].
- When land is adjusted for differences in quality using land value or exogenous land quality measures, the negative productivity relationship weakens but does not disappear, especially where it is very large.
- Introduction of the green revolution technology in India led to a weakening but not the disappearance of the raw productivity differentials [Bhalla and Roy (1988)].

Three studies came closer to the specification in equation 1. For the Muda River region of Malaysia, Berry and Cline (1979) found that value added per unit of invested capital for the second smallest farm size group exceeded that of the largest farm size group by 65 percent, more than the difference in value of output reported in Table 42.2. The use of value added adjusts for costs of purchased inputs, but this measure is still likely to bias the test in favor of small farms to the degree that small farms use labor more intensively than do large farms. But since the result holds for raw output, the negative relationship would probably hold as well if the test were based on net farm profits. The results suggest that well-developed rental markets, as in the Muda area for tractors and threshers, enable small farmers to circumvent the economies of scale associated with tractors, leaving labor supervision costs to dominate.[18]

In the second study, Berry and Cline (1979) first split the data for Northeast Brazil (see Table 42.2) into agroclimatic zones, which sharply reduced the observed negative relationship. "Social" profits were then calculated by imputing a real opportunity cost of 15 percent to capital and valuing family labor at 0, 50 and 100 percent of the minimum wage, a wage rarely paid in

---

[18] Only a few studies explicitly test for the separability of family and hired labor. Pitt and Rosenzweig (1986) show for a sample of Indonesian farmers that profits are independent of the short-term health status of the household head, but since short-term illness does not interfere with supervision the result says little about whether wage labor can complement family labor on a permanent basis. Deolalikar and Vijverberg (1987) reject the hypothesis of perfect substitutability between family and hired labor based on samples from India and Malaysia, but because they estimate a production function using cross-section data, statistical problems vitiate their findings. Benjamin (1992) estimates a demand function for aggregate labor services. He rejects the hypothesis of nonseparability for Indonesian rice farmers on the basis of the joint lack of significance of demographic variables. Since his model includes area harvested as a dependent variable, it does not allow for adjustments of area operated (via rental) in response to family size. In effect, then, the model measures only the conditional impact of demographic variables, given operated area, on the demand for hired labor. The fact that area operated (which, has significant influence on labor demand) is correlated with family composition suggests that a strong supervision constraint might be found if the unconditional effect were considered.

agriculture. Even when family labor is valued at the full opportunity wage, social profits are clearly higher by 23 to 150 percent for the second smallest farm size group (10 to 50 hectares) than for the second largest and the largest farm size groups (200 to 500 hectares) in four of six non-sugar growing zones. For the two zones where the relationship does not hold as clearly (Bahia and Sertao), the weakness of the results appears to be due to paucity of observations [Kutcher and Scandizzo (1981)]. The negative productivity relationship still holds in the technologically advanced Agreste region, where mechanization was most pronounced if social profits are considered.

In the third study, Rosenzweig and Binswanger (1993) estimate a profit function similar to equation (1) which includes total assets, the composition of the asset portfolio, family labor, education, age, and the onset date of the monsoon. They use the complete ICRISAT panel data from ten villages in high-risk semi-arid India to estimate a model that allows for separate testing of technical economies of scale on the one hand and the impact of supervision cost advantages of poorer farmers relative to the capital cost and risk diffusion advantages of wealthier farmers on the other hand. Fixed-effects estimation techniques were used to eliminate problems of land quality differences. The results reject the hypothesis that the composition of investments reflects technical scale economies. They support the hypothesis that the asset portfolios of farmers are significantly affected by farmers' risk aversion, wealth, and the degree of monsoon onset variability (a measure of weather risk). In an environment of slowly changing technology, the profitability of the portfolio is not affected by formal schooling, but it does rise with age, a proxy for experience. Profits (net of their wage costs) also increase with the number of adult family members, suggesting that their contribution arises from their management and supervision function.

Rosenzweig and Binswanger also estimate the impact of weather risk and wealth on the riskiness and profitability of farmers' asset portfolios. Figure 42.3 plots the profit per unit of asset for four wealth classes as a function of rainfall variability (onset of the monsoon). The profit rate of farmers at the eightieth percentile of wealth is insensitive to increases in weather risk, suggesting that they are confident enough in their ability to diffuse risk through credit, savings, or social relationships that they do not need to choose portfolios that reduce risk up front at some cost in profits. Farmers in the 20th percentile, however, sharply reduce the profitability of their portfolios as rainfall risk rises.

Despite these portfolio adjustments, in this high risk environment with relatively little mechanization and slow technical change, the smaller farm size groups have higher profits per unit of wealth at all levels of rainfall risk observed in the data. The supervision and labor cost advantages of family labor are apparently greater than the advantages that the lumpiness of management skills and machines and the better access to credit and other risk-diffusion

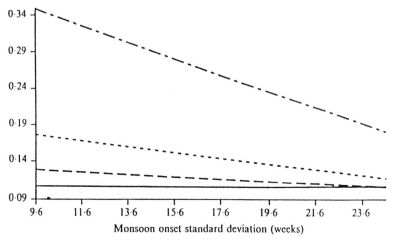

Figure 42.3. Profit-wealth ratios and weather variability, by wealth class. Percentiles: ——, 20th; – – –, 40th; ---, 60th; – - – -, 80th. *Note*: The onset date of the Monsoon was the single most powerful of eight different rainfall characteristics to explain gross value of farm output.

measures confer on large farms. Only in the most risky environments does the advantage of the poorer farmers nearly disappear.

Using a nonparametric approach to estimate a production function for Wisconsin farmers, Chavas and Aliber (1993) study farms in a very modern and dynamic environment. They find virtually no scale economies in dairy production and only very limited initial scale economies due to lumpiness of inputs.

*Conclusion*

Most of the empirical work on the farm size-productivity relationship in the developing world has been flawed by methodological shortcomings, and has failed to deal adequately with the complexity of the issues involved. Studies that come to grips with some of the shortcomings and use a more refined measure of land quality and a productivity variable instead of simple yields find that even in fairly technologically advanced and mechanized areas, such as the Muda scheme in Malaysia or the Agreste region of Northeast Brazil, small farms retain a productivity advantage over large farms. This finding suggests that rental markets can substitute to a certain degree for the indivisibility of machines and some management skills. The methodologically sounder study based on the ICRISAT data confirms both the mechanisms leading to differential performance by scale and the superiority of smaller farms in an environment with little mechanization and slow technical change. While there is evidence on the negative relationship between farm size and production, more work is needed on this subject. Such work should follow the lines sketched out in equation 1, using recent farm level data for developing country regions with high quality agroclimatic and soil conditions, substantial mechanization, and dynamic technical change.

## 5. The effects of land-credit links and policy distortions on land sales markets

The farm-size productivity studies indicate that for given technology, factor prices, land quality, and farming skills there is an optimal *operational holding* size at which the disincentive costs of adding more workers fully offsets the economies of scale from lumpy inputs, access to credit and management skills. Taking into account differences in farming skills and land quality, this finding translates into an optimal distribution of operational sizes. For any given distribution of ownership holdings, one would expect tenancy and land rental markets to bring the distribution of operational holdings close to that optimal distribution. If incentive problems associated with tenancy are minor and can be ignored, the distribution of ownership holdings would be independent of the distribution of operational holdings, since large landholders would simply rent out their land with no loss in efficiency.

But if legal restrictions on tenancy make this option infeasible or unprofitable we need to ask whether the sales market will bring about a more nearly optimal distribution of ownership-operational holdings – that is, whether it will be profitable for the owners of large and relatively unprofitable farms to split them up and sell them to small family farmers. Covariate risk, imperfect intertemporal markets, and policy distortions affecting the functioning of the land sales market will prevent this market from achieving a first-best solution. But increases in efficiency are still likely to result from sales transactions that transfer land from bad to better managers.

### Covariate risks and imperfect credit markets

Land is often a preferred store of wealth, so with imperfect inter-temporal markets the utility derived from landownership will exceed the utility derived from farm profits. Its immobility makes land a preferred form of collateral in credit markets which confers additional utility from landownership, especially in an environment where production risk cannot be insured.

The collateral value of land and the high positive correlation of incomes in a given area imply that there would be few land sales in periods of normal weather.[19] Landowners would be made better off by selling land only if they could earn a higher return from the sales proceeds than from cultivating or renting out the land. So, where non-agricultural investment opportunities for rural residents are limited and national credit markets are underdeveloped, little land will be supplied for sale in normal years. The number of bidders for land is constrained by the level of household savings since mortgaging the land would be unprofitable. Because land has collateral value, its equilibrium price at given credit costs will always exceed the present discounted value of the income stream produced from the land. Mortgaged land, however, cannot be used as collateral for working capital, so the owner does not reap the production credit advantage and thus will be unable to repay the loan out of increased income from the land. With imperfect insurance markets, only unmortgaged land yields a flow of income or utility, the present value of which equals the land price. As discussed, if land ownership provides access to credit and helps in risk diffusion, the buyer has to compensate the seller for the utility derived from these services of land [Feder et al. (1988)]. Since only un-mortgaged land provides these services, a buyer relying on credit cannot pay for the land out of agricultural profits alone. Thus land sales are likely to be financed out of household savings, so that the purchased land can be used as collateral for working capital. This need to purchase land out of savings tends to make the distribution of landholdings more unequal, despite the greater utility value of land to smaller owners arising from its insurance value and their lower labor costs.

Spatial covariation in yields suggests that in particularly good crop years, when savings are high, there would be few sellers and many potential buyers of land. Good years are thus not good times for land purchases. In bad crop years, farmers would have little savings with which to finance land purchases. And in particularly bad periods – say after consecutive harvest failures – moneylenders would be the only ones in the local rural economy with assets (their debt claims). Moneylenders would prefer to take over rather than sell the landholdings offered as collateral by defaulters since the price of land would be lower than average in bad years. So, in bad crop years land would be sold mainly to moneylenders as distress sales, or to individuals with incomes or assets from outside the local rural economy. We should expect, then, that in areas with poorly developed insurance and capital markets, land sales would be

---

[19] Such paucity of land sales is also observed in developed countries where land sales markets are usually very thin. The percentage of farmland transferred on average each year is 3 percent of the total in the US, 1–1.5 percent in Britain, 1.5 percent within the white sector in South Africa, 0.5 percent in Ireland and Kenya [Moll (1988: 354)].

few and limited mainly to distress sales. Results from India and Bangladesh confirm this hypothesis. Farmers in India experiencing two consecutive drought years have been found to be 150 percent more likely than other farmers to sell their land [Rosenzweig and Wolpin (1985)].

The implications of different insurance mechanisms on distress sales and the land ownership distribution are demonstrated by a comparison of the evolution of ownership holdings from about 1960 to 1980 for predominantly agricultural villages in India and Bangladesh [Cain (1981)]. These villages faced very high environmental risks but were characterized by distinct differences in mechanisms of risk-insurance: In Maharashtra, India, an employment guarantee scheme operated throughout the period and attained participation rates of up to 97 percent of all households during disasters. Such schemes were absent after the major flood episodes in Bangladesh. With other insurance-mechanisms either absent or exhausted, 60 percent of land sales in Bangladesh were undertaken to obtain food and medicine. Downward mobility affected large and small farmers equally, suggesting that even large farmers had insufficient possibilities to diffuse risks. 60 percent of the currently landless had lost their land since 1960 and the Gini coefficient of landownership distribution increased from 0.6 to almost 0.7. This contrasts sharply with the Indian villages, where land sales for consumption purposes accounted only for 14 percent and were incurred mainly by the rich to meet social obligations. 64 percent of land sales were undertaken in order to generate capital for productive investment (digging of wells, purchase of pumpsets, children's education and marriages), leading to an equalization of the land-ownership distribution in India, and suggesting that the poor were not only able to avoid distress sales, but actually could acquire some land as rich households liquidated agricultural assets to be able to pursue non-agricultural investment.

Historically, distress sales have played a major role in the accumulation of land for large manorial estates in China [Shih (1992)] and in early Japan [Takekoshi (1967)] and for large landlord estates in Punjab [Hamid (1983)]. The abolition of communal tenure and the associated loss of mechanisms for diversifying risk are among the factors underlying the emergence of large estates in Central America [Brockett (1984)].

Moral hazard, covariance of income, and collateral value of land imply absent insurance and imperfect credit markets. In such environments, land sales markets are likely to become a means for large landowners to accumulate more land. Even where markets for labor, current inputs, and land sales and rentals are perfectly competitive, weak intertemporal markets for risk diffusion may therefore prevent land sales markets from bringing about pareto improving trades and an efficient farm size distribution – an illustration of the theorem of the second best.

*The impact of policy distortions*

The existence of common policy distortions intensifies the failure of the land sales market to distribute land optimally. Consider an idealized case of competitive and undistorted land, labor, risk and credit markets. The value of land for agricultural use would equal the present value of agricultural profits capitalized at the opportunity costs of capital. If the poor have to borrow to buy land at its present value, the only income stream available for consumption is the imputed value of family labor. The remaining profits go to pay for the loan. If the poor can get the same wage in the labor market, they are no better off as landowners than they would be as wage-laborers. And this example assumes ideal conditions, with the poor paying the same interest rate as most creditworthy borrowers.

While higher productivity of family labor as compared to wage labor would provide an advantage to small family farmers in buying land, this advantage is normally more than offset by a number of factors and distortions that increase the price of land above the capitalised value of the agricultural income stream. This would make it impossible for the poor to buy land without reducing their consumption below the level of their potential earning in the labor market.

The most important factors and distortions are the following:

- With populations growing and urban demand for land increasing, the price of land is expected to appreciate, and some of this real appreciation is capitalized into the current land price. Robinson et al. (1985) find much higher implicit rates of return (cash rents to land values) to farming in predominantly agricultural states in the United States than in states where nonagricultural land demand is high. The impact of closeness to urban areas on agricultural land prices is well known. Since these returns are realized only when the property is sold, the only way a poor person could tap into that income stream is by regularly selling off a small parcel of land to pay the interest costs – hardly a feasible option for small landowners.
- In periods of macroeconomic instability, nonagricultural investors may use land as an asset to hedge against inflation, so that an inflation premium is incorporated into the real land price. If expected inflation is fully reflected in interest rates, inflation alone will not affect agricultural land prices [Feldstein (1980)]. But if expected inflation is not fully reflected in current or expected future interest rates, and if land is perceived to be no riskier than alternative assets, excess demand for land will increase the price of land as a speculative asset. Inflation and changes in real returns on alternative uses of capital are the main factors explaining changes in land prices for the United States (Just and Miranowski 1989). For Iowa, in addition to fundamentals (the present value of the discounted future income stream), an additive fad

term closely associated with expected inflation has a significant impact on land prices (Falk 1991).[20] In a simulation using results of econometric estimation for Brazil (1966–1989), Brandao and Rezende (1992) find that six percent of the increase in land prices is attributable to credit subsidies, 28 percent to macroeconomic instability (inflation).

- Credit subsidies are capitalized into land values, as shown in the Brandao and Rezende (1992) study and by Feder and Associates (1988). For the U.S., Shalit and Schmitz (1982) show that most of the increasing debt on farm real estate during 1950–1978 was translated into higher land prices, whereas farm income increases had a much smaller impact.[21] Even where there are no credit subsidies, large landowners have a transactions cost advantage in securing credit, which is capitalized into land values and may even block access to mortgage credit altogether for small borrowers.
- Many countries exempt agricultural income from income tax, and even where there is no general exemption, agricultural income is de facto subject to lower tax rates. These preferences will be partly or fully capitalized into land values. Since the poor pay no taxes and so cannot benefit from the tax break, they do not receive the corresponding income stream. Any other subsidies or tax preferences for large farms similarly increase the difficulty the poor have in buying land.

Where any of these factors pushes the price of land above the price justified by the fundamentals of expected agricultural profits in the absence of distortions associated with farm size, the poor have difficulty buying land. Even if they are provided with credit on market terms, that difficulty persists unless their productivity advantage from lower supervision cost is very large. Of these factors, nonagricultural demand, inflation, credit constraints, and credit subsidies have been investigated empirically; income tax preferences for agriculture have not. Most of the empirical studies concentrate on the United States since the paucity of land transactions in developing countries makes research difficult. More work needs to be done.

---

[20] Although overvaluation due to misperception – bubbles – would lead to observationally equivalent predictions, myopic behavior on the part of land purchasers seems a more satisfactory explanation. On the possibilities for rational bubbles see Asako (1991) and Diba and Grossman (1988). Empirical and experimental evidence on bubbles is provided buy DeLong and Shleifer (1991), Smith et al. (1988), and Evans (1986).

[21] While this demonstrates the significance of the policy and institutional environment in aggregate models, microeconomic evidence on the importance of credit rationing on land prices is limited. Carter (1989), Carter and Kalfayan (1989), and Carter and Wiebe (1990) use a roughly calibrated model to determine the reservation price of land as a function of farm-size and obtain a U-shaped curve. Because of the roughness of their data, the results indicate orders of magnitude rather than exact figures, but they are certainly in the appropriate direction.

## 6. Incentives, land-credit links and land rental markets

As long as there are imperfections and/or distortions in other markets, land sales markets are unlikely to bring a skewed distribution of land ownership holdings closer to an optimal distribution of operational holdings. The question, then, is whether land rental markets can increase efficiency by improving the access of the poor to land under conditions in which they can not buy land.

Land tenancy markets might not increase efficiency if tenants lack incentives to invest in land improvements, to work hard, or to apply sufficient inputs. These problems will be particularly severe under sharecropping arrangements, with the tenant receiving only a share of the marginal product of the inputs (the Marshallian inefficiency). Quantitative measurement of the inefficiency associated with share contracts in different environments is necessary to determine the importance of such disincentives. The empirical discussion shows that the inefficiencies of share-cropping, measured at the farm level, are not large.

Despite the disincentives associated with tenancy and sharecropping their widespread use all over the world suggests that, in an environment where capital constraints and risk considerations make fixed rent tenancy contracts infeasible or undesirable, share rental contracts may in fact emerge as efficiency enhancing, especially if the incentive problems associated with them are low. Since both the theoretical literature [Otsuka and Hayami (1988) Otsuka, Chuma, and Hayami (1992)] and the empirical literature [Bell (1988)] have been reviewed recently, the discussion here is brief.

*Choice of contract and the incentive problems*

In the basic model of land-leasing, renting out land under a fixed-rent or share contract or employing wage labor are substitutes along a continuum on contractual choices. The landlord maximizes income by choosing the number of tenants, the fixed payment and the output-share parameter subject to the constraint that tenants achieve their (exogenously given) reservation utility. The tenant determines the level of effort that will maximize utility, yielding an effort-reaction function.

The basic model consists of a constant returns to scale production function $Q = \theta F(e, h)$ where $Q$ is output, $e$ is effort, $h$ is number of tenants, and $\theta$ is a stochastic element. The landlord's income is $y = h[(1 - \alpha)Q - \beta]$, and the representative tenant's income is $Y = \alpha Q + \beta$. The fixed rent contract is obtained for $\{\alpha = 1, \beta < 0\}$, the pure wage contract for $\{\alpha = 0, \beta > 0\}$; and the share contract for $\{0 < \alpha < 1\}$, with the sign and magnitude of $\beta$ a function of the landlord's choice of $\alpha$ and the tenant's reservation utility level.

Under conditions of certainty and the rather unrealistic assumption of perfect enforceability of effort, all contracts lead to equivalent outcomes and the choice of contract type does not matter [Cheung (1969)]. If the assumption of perfect effort enforceability is dropped, the tenant receives only a fraction $\alpha$ of his marginal product for all but the pure cash rental contract. Therefore, with effort unobservable and under conditions of certainty (or equivalently, risk neutrality), the fixed-rent contract clearly dominates the fixed-wage and the share contracts and will always be chosen in equilibrium. Given supervision costs for workers or sharecroppers, any type of contract other than fixed rent would result in an undersupply of effort by the tenant or worker, which would lower total production.

With risk aversion and uncertainty, a share contract provides the possibility of partly insuring the tenant against fluctuations in output. Where intertemporal markets are weak or unavailable, the Pareto optimal contract always involves a trade-off between the risk-sharing properties of the fixed-wage contract, under which the tenant's residual risk is zero, and the incentive effects of the fixed-rent contract, which would result in optimal effort-supply by the tenant. (Note that with effort as the only variable input, effort supply completely determines total production.) With risk averse agents and incomplete intertemporal markets, the one-period contract can achieve only a second-best solution. Increases in the output share parameter above the second-best equilibrium value would increase expected production, but expose the utility to greater uncertainty and thus lower his expected utility.

Recasting the problem in a multiperiod context and allowing for reputation effects, however, provides options for bringing this second-best optimum closer to the first-best outcome. Otsuka, Chuma, and Hayami (1992) discuss the conditions under which, in a multiperiod context, the threat of loss of reputation will prevent the tenant from shirking – or equivalently the landlord from cheating if he provides essential inputs to production (as in Eswaran and Kotwal 1985) – and so the fixed-rent contract will tend to dominate the fixed-wage contract as it does in the certainty case just described. They argue that in relatively closed villages, such implicit enforcement by the community may be strong enough to bring the inefficient outcome under the unenforceable contract closer to the first-best outcome even if risk is present. This conclusion is consistent with the empirical observation that fixed-wage contracts are found only where the institutional environment discriminates against tenancy contracts (see Section 3 and below) but is inconsistent with the overwhelming prevalence of share-cropping relative to fixed-rent tenancies.

*Choice of contracts and factor market constraints*

There is considerable theoretical justification and evidence [Bliss and Stern (1982), Pant (1983), Nabi (1985), Binswanger and Rosenzweig (1986), Skoufias (1991), Shaban (1991)] that where markets for lumpy inputs such as management skills and draft animals are imperfect, households seek to achieve the optimal operational holding size through land tenancy contracts. Given the nontradeable factor endowment, land rental would be expected to increase efficiency if a fixed-rent contract is chosen. The relevant question is whether share contracts would increase efficiency as well.

A limit on the working capital available to the tenant (or to landlord and tenant) because of imperfection in the credit market, can lead to the adoption of a share contract as the optimal solution to the bargaining problem. Laffont and Matoussi (1981) show that a working capital constraint imposes limits on the share parameter $\alpha$ that may make the first-best fixed-rent contract infeasible. Their model implies positive correlation between the tenants' working capital and his output share $\alpha$. A positive correlation between working capital and output in the share contract but the absence of such an effect in the fixed rent contract would indicate presence of an incentive problem. Consideration of the joint working capital available to tenant and landlord does imply a negative relationship between the landlord's working capital and the tenant's share. All of these predictions are confirmed empirically for a set of data from Tunisia. This direct dependence of the optimal choice of contract on the working capital available to both landlord and tenant may account for the coexistence of a variety of contracts in the same environment among parties with roughly similar risk aversion but different endowments of working capital.

Thus the main reason that *interlinked contracts* and cost-sharing arrangements are so common may be that they implicitly provide the credit or insurance a tenant needs in an environment where credit and insurance markets are imperfect [Otsuka, Chuma and Hayami (1992)]. The traditional interpretation that these interlinkages are devices used by landlords to bring the second-best equilibrium closer to the first-best outcome by increasing the tenant's supply of effort [Braverman and Stiglitz (1982), Mitra (1983), Braverman and Srinivasan (1981)] requires strong assumptions that are generally not satisfied in developing countries [Otsuka, Chuma, and Hayami (1992)].

A tenant may be able to meet only part of his (working) capital requirements in the credit market because of the limited suitability of unharvested crops as collateral – and at higher interest rates than the landlord would get by offering land as collateral. The landlord is often in a better position than other financial intermediaries to provide a tenant with credit and actuarially fair insurance because of economies of scope in supervision and informational advantages concerning the value of the tenant's unharvested crop. Since the amount of credit provided will be related to the tenant's expected future income, the landlord can set the contractual fixed payment to zero and still be free to adjust the interest rate, or accept the customary interest rate and adjust the fixed payment and share parameter, to realize an optimal outcome [Otsuka, Chuma, and Hayami (1992)].

A popular form of implicit credit is the landlord's provision of inputs to the tenant under a *cost-sharing arrangement*. Providing inputs this way is formally identical to an implicit production loan which, like interlinked contracts, would be adopted where credit markets are imperfect. Static analysis of cost-sharing arrangements may thus be inappropriate if credit constraints are to be taken fully into account. Calculating the implicit interest rate charged for such production loans would help determine the equity and efficiency consequences of share-cropping arrangements. The few empirical studies that have been done suggest that the interest rates may not be significantly different from those charged by moneylenders, rates reaching as high as 50 percent [Fujimoto (1986)] or even more [Morooka and Hayami (1986)]. Where there are imperfections in credit markets, it is possible to derive the precise conditions for share contracts under which the benefits from overcoming the credit market imperfections would be greater than the loss resulting from the Marshallian inefficiency [Shaban (1991)].

If tenants are assumed to be willing to bear greater risk as their wealth rises (decreasing absolute risk aversion), then both working capital constraints with imperfect credit markets and risk aversion by tenants would generate observationally equivalent outcomes. For a sample of Tunisian farmers, Laffont and Matoussi (1988) found that a credit constraint rather than risk aversion led farmers to prefer share over fixed-rent contracts. Since credit and insurance are at least partly substitutable, it is likely that improvements in financial markets and in the insurability of risk will lead to a decrease in share contracts in favor of fixed rent contracts, and to a gain in overall efficiency.

None of the land rental models discussed here, or even Marxian-inspired models of semifeudalism [Bhaduri (1986)] considers the tenant's reservation utility – usually the market wage – to be endogenously determined. Instead they explain inefficiency and inequities as consequences of the contracts themselves, despite the fact that such contracts are entered into voluntarily by both parties (see epilogue). But in light of the discussion in Section 2, it would be surprising indeed if landlords with some political power did not try to find ways to reduce the reservation utility of potential tenants and workers.

Governments the world over have been concerned about the efficiency and distributional implications of such tenancy arrangements, which in essence depend on the relative bargaining power of each of the contracting partners. Tenancy and sharecropping have therefore been heavily regulated. The empirical evidence suggests that government interventions into these have had little success in achieving their stated objective of protecting tenants, which is hardly surprising given the market imperfections leading to the emergence of share tenancy, and the difficulty in designing welfare-improving interventions. Historically, land reform that resulted in establishing owner-operated farms appears to have been a far more successful way of addressing the equity question.

*Evidence on efficiency of tenancy arrangements*

Several principles should guide the empirical evaluation of the efficiency properties of share contracts:

- Using cross-sectional data to determine the effect of share tenancy on productivity is likely to involve simultaneity problems, since the decision to rent in or rent out land is endogenous, and it fails to control for unobservable attributes of plots and tenants. The appropriate approach is to use panel data and fixed-effects techniques to compare rented and sharecropped (or owned and sharecropped) plots of the same farmer and to adjust for differences in land quality.
- The loss associated with a share contract may be greater than the measured reduction in production if landlords use resources to enforce tenant effort. Community-based enforcement mechanisms may, however, reduce the inefficiency associated with sharecropping at relatively moderate cost. [22]
- Share contracts are likely to arise in response to imperfect information, supervision costs, imperfections in credit and insurance markets, and constraints imposed by government. Share contracts should not be blamed for the inefficiencies that result from such exogenous constraints.
- Share contracts may have positive effects in a dynamic environment by providing a way for tenants to acquire experience or capital.

Bell (1976) was the first to compare output on owned and share-cropped plots for the same farmers, thereby controlling for unobservable farmer

---

[22] Community enforcement and insurance mechanisms have been discussed mainly in the Asian context [Scott (1984), Hayami and Kikuchi (1984)]. In the literature on Europe, Brenner (1985) suggests that better developed community ties in Western Europe enabled peasant farmers to resist tribute requirements. A complete framework of production relations would have to explain differences in the strength of community ties endogenously. For example, one would expect such community relations to be better developed in densely populated areas as compared to more recently frontier regions. This is consistent with variations observed by Hayami and Kikuchi in the Philippines.

attributes. Applying the same methodology, Shaban (1987) found that a 32 percent loss in output associated with tenant plots declined to 16 percent if adjustments were made for differences in land quality. Inputs of family labor and draft animals were significantly lower on sharecropped plots than on owned parcels. No statistically significant differences in efficiency were found between owned plots and plots rented on a fixed-rent basis, supporting the hypothesis of the productive efficiency of fixed-rent contracts. Other results point in the same direction [Sen (1981)], and Otsuka and Hayami's (1988) review of the literature finds, at most, small efficiency losses associated with tenancy.

Government interventions have given rise to efficiency-reducing share contracts in a number of countries. Otsuka, Chuma, and Hayami (1992) argue that in India, where the Bell and Shaban studies were conducted, there were a number of government constraints on long-term fixed rent contracts. That implies that the 16 percent in production losses adjusted for land quality derived by Shaban are likely to constitute an upper bound.

Land transactions to circumvent imperfections in credit markets have been important in West Africa in the past [Robertson (1985)], and continue to be observed in a number of developing countries where credit markets are absent or credit is highly rationed. Usufruct mortgage is still reported to be common in Bangladesh [Cain (1981), Java [Morooka and Hayami (1986)], and Thailand [Fujimoto (1988)]. In the Philippines, tenancy transactions emerged as a credit substitute in response to limitations on the transferability of land [Nagarajan et al. (1991)].

Where there is imperfect information on tenants' unobservable characteristics, landlords may interpret the tenants' acceptance of certain types of contracts as a signal that can be used as a self-selecting screening device [Newbery and Stiglitz (1979)]. The preference for tenants who already possess some land and draft animals, which is well documented in the literature [Quibria and Rashid (1986), Shaban (1991)] points in the same direction.

Tenancy has often been described as a rung on the "agricultural ladder" that rises from worker to share tenant, to fixed rate tenant, to owner and permits farmers to acquire capital and agricultural knowledge. In a static framework this has been modeled by making production a function of tenants' effort and the landlord's provision of management skills [Eswaran and Kotwal (1985)]. Although quantitative evidence is limited, Reid (1973) argues that this function of tenancy played an important role in the U.S. South after the abolition of slavery. Lehman (1986) noted the importance of tenancy in facilitating capital accumulation in the intergenerational transfer of farm holdings in Ecuador. Tenancy would be expected to facilitate capital accumulation where land is abundant relative to labor and where rents or owners' shares are low. Longitudinal studies of changes in tenancy patterns and capital accumulation over the life cycle of tenants would help shed more light on the relative importance of this phenomenon in different environments.

*Conclusion*

Because of the productivity advantage of small over large farms, it is more profitable for large landowners to rent out land under fixed-rent contracts than to work it using hired labor, if there are no other market imperfections. If effort is unobservable and credit is rationed or insurance markets are imperfect and tenants risk averse, the fixed-rate tenancy contract may no longer be attainable or desirable and a second-best share contract would be adopted instead.

Empirical investigations show that share tenancy arrangements under a wide variety of conditions are a highly flexible tool for adjusting to such constraints with relatively modest losses. Since effort is not fully enforceable and even limited enforcement is likely to be associated with some cost, the adoption of share tenancy (or wage labor) contracts would still be associated with some loss of efficiency. Removing the conditions that prompt the emergence of share tenancy are likely to lead to modest efficiency gains and will be more effective than legal prohibition of such contracts (see Part III). Greater efficiency gains may be associated with the removal of the distortions that lead to the adoption and perpetuation of wage labor contracts, and large commercial farms rather than fixed-rent or share contracts.

## PART III: LAND POLICY

Many institutional arrangements in land markets emerge as a result of attempts by the contracting parties to overcome problems of asymmetric information, moral hazard, and covariance of risk. Other types of institutional arrangements represent interventions by the government or community intended to produce outcomes that are more congruent with the society's objectives than those that would be generated by market forces alone. Here, we will evaluate interventions in land markets from the point of view of efficiency and equity, two objectives that are sometimes, but not always compatible. As shown in appendix 1, governments often intervened in land markets pursuing goals other than efficiency or equity.

Four broad types of land distribution and production relations remain today (Figure 42.1), each with its own characteristic policy problems. Family farm systems under freehold or communal tenure face problems of access to credit, land registration and titling, tenancy regulation, fragmentation, and taxation.

Communities in which communal tenure prevails face decisions about allowing sales to outsiders. Where large scale mechanized commercial farms coexist with low wages and unemployment, governments have to consider ways, such as the elimination of tenancy regulation, the elimination of agricultural subsidies and/or land reform, to make farm size distributions more compatible with equity and efficiency objectives. In wage plantation systems, contract farming and taxation are the important issues. For collective and state farms systems, the key concern is whether decollectivization or privatization should aim to establish large commercial farms or small family farms.

## 7. Land registration and titling

*The issues*

Land titles and registration reduce the problems of asymmetric information and thus provide the institutional framework to facilitate land sales. Such transfers can enhance efficiency by transferring land from bad managers to better farmers and by facilitating the use of land as collateral in the credit market. Transfers of land, which are facilitated by land titles, may reduce equity as well as efficiency if economic and institutional distortions encourage accumulation of land by influential or wealthy individuals. As establishment and maintenance of land titles is not costless, whether to introduce titling has to be based on a comparison of the benefits of land titles over and above existing arrangements to regulate land transactions and the likely cost of such arrangements.

In the early stages of agricultural development, transactions in land take place mainly among individuals who are members of the same community and who generally share information about the rights enjoyed by a renter or a seller, and about rights to specific tracts of land. With more advanced agriculture and increased mobility, communal constraints on sales to outsiders are abandoned and transactions are increasingly with individuals who are not members of the same community. The scope for asymmetric information increases, generating inefficiencies in the land market since the price of land may no longer reflect its true social value and the extent of land transactions becomes less than optimal. To reduce these informational inefficiencies and the associated welfare losses, societies develop institutional arrangements to reduce risk, such as the requirement in the Arthsastra (4th century B.C. in India) that land transactions be conducted in public with witnesses or the establishment of a centralized public register that tracks land plots and those who have rights over these plots. As early as 600 B.C., the Bible describes a land transaction between the prophet Jeremiah and a relative in which a written record of the transaction was kept in two copies with a certain priest in Jerusalem.

Public registers provide potential buyers or renters of land with a way to verify that the rights they are about to purchase belong to the seller. A functioning legal system and effective enforcement mechanisms are other institutional arrangements designed to reduce the uncertainty related to land transactions. Without such arrangements to reduce the risk of challenges to land rights, the incentives to invest and to work hard are weakened. Theoretical analysis [de Meza and Gould (1992)] indicates that private profit-maximizing decisions to enforce property rights may not be socially optimal. It is often more efficient to reduce the risk through the provision of public goods (land records, police, judiciary), than through the private individual allocation of resources (guards, elaborate fences).[23]

Asymmetric information and risk are at their extremes in frontier areas, where specific plots have no previous owners, though the government usually claims formal ownership. While often the land is subject to a general claim by tribal groups who have been using it for hunting, gathering, or livestock grazing, some of it is also claimed by individuals who have migrated from other areas. Since there is no culturally unified community from which to obtain knowledge, the administrative infrastructure (land record, offices, courts, police) typically becomes overloaded by claims and counter claims. It is not uncommon then to find private (and necessarily segmented) institutions protecting property rights over land (gunmen, fortified property). And if the institutions for recording property are not well developed, the method to establish land claims itself can be associated with environmental hazard [Southgate, Sierra and Brown (1991)].

Institutional arrangements for land records and title documents also have beneficial implications for credit markets. In lending, asymmetric information provides ample scope for moral hazard. Collateral has long served as a means of minimizing the efficiency losses associated with asymmetric information and moral hazard, and land has traditionally been viewed as an ideal collateral asset in areas where land is scarce [Binswanger and Rosenzweig (1986)]. For land to be useful as collateral, however, the lender needs to be assured that the borrower-operator has the right to dispose of the land by sale or the transfer of use rights. Thus the documentation of land rights makes land a form of credible collateral, affects the willingness of lenders to make loans and may make credit markets more efficient [Feder, Onchan, and Raparla (1988)]. Where the inability to use untitled land as collateral for credit is the relevant

---

[23] In Uganda and Côte d'Ivoire, land privatization significantly decreased risks and transaction costs associated with transferring land resulting in increased land transfers, a factor commonly associated with higher productivity in agriculture [Barrows and Roth (1990), Atwood (1990)].

constraint, the issuance of titles can provide a solution in the long term. But where other constraints such as small farm size prevent the operation of credit markets, land titles may fail to be useful until these obstacles are removed [Atwood (1990)].

Under ideal conditions government intervention in land registration is theoretically neutral in its effect on equity. In practice, however, titling can lead to greater concentration of land and to the dispossession of groups that have enjoyed land rights under a customary system that predated the formal system. When titling is introduced, wealthier and better connected individuals may use their information advantages to claim land over which other, less informed, individuals have customary rights. Even when there are no information advantages, titling based on the on-demand principle involves fixed and relatively high transaction costs for surveys and bureaucratic processing that put smallholders at a disadvantage. The equity-reducing impacts of titling on this basis are well-known. The introduction of selective titling on demand greatly facilitated the emergence of haciendas in Central Luzon [Hayami and Kikuchi (1984), Guatemala [Cambranes (1985), El Salvador Lindo-Fuentes (1990), and Nicaragua [Newson (1987)]. In Bolivia during the 1980s, the titling agency granted titles to very large farms in the Eastern Lowlands within one to two years, while applications from smallholders without the benefit of helpful lawyers have an average processing time of 12 years. Bruce (1988) notes that land grabbing by influential individuals during titling programs who are able to use the rules in their favor did more to facilitate land concentration than transactions in the land market following the issuance of titles. The profitability of consolidating several small untitled holdings and getting a single title provides incentives for wealthy individuals to buy out smallholders and to concentrate their own holdings. Titled land also provides advantages in the credit market [Feder, Onchan and Raparla (1988)] that are likely to increase income disparity.

### The policy implications

To avoid these undesirable effects, titling programs should be accompanied by publicity campaigns to ensure widespread knowledge of the rules and procedures. Both equity and efficiency considerations argue that titling programs be systematic rather than on demand. Efficiency is increased through economies of scale and equity by the fact that *all* claims in an area are registered at the same time. The *ryotwari* system introduced by the British in Southern India around 1820 and similar systematic titling programs elsewhere show that conflicting claims can be dealt with through a relatively quick administrative procedure rather than through lengthy and costly legal channels.

Because titling programs can be expensive, the issue of optimal expenditure is relevant [see Malik and Schwab (1991)]. Feder and Feeny (1991) have demonstrated that when individual willingness to pay for titling determines the aggregate public expenditure, there may be a tendency for over-investment from a social welfare perspective. Frequently, some less costly arrangement than formal titling may significantly lessen the problem of asymmetry of information. In Rwanda, the local municipality issues affidavits that attest to the ownership rights of specific individuals over specific tracts of land but are not based on precise surveys [Blarel et al. (1992)]. A lower cost system was also used in Thailand prior to the introduction of formal titling (Siamwalla et al. (1990), Feeny (1988)].

Communal systems constitute a special case. Communal land is not considered adequate collateral in formal credit systems because of constraints on sales to outsiders. Issuing individual titles in communities that maintain such constraints may improve neither the security of tenure nor access to credit, although individual titles would be helpful to avoid barriers to the emergence of rental markets within the community. Until the restrictions on transfers to outsiders are eliminated, a community title could be issued to ensure the community's security of ownership against well-connected outsiders. Platteau (1992) advocates registering land as "corporate property" as a way of decreasing the costs associated with titling while reaping many related benefits such as insurance, flexibility of land allocation, and the utilization of genuine scale economies in subsidiary activities. Experience with group ranches in Kenya suggests that imposing group titles from above is unlikely to be successful, while issuing individual titles does not prevent farmers from taking advantage of scale where they exist [Grandin (1989)].

Another case for community titles concerns common property resources, such as communal pastures, forests, or other marginal lands. Such areas constitute an important safety net for the poor that may be particularly important in high-risk environments where alternative means of insurance are unavailable. Community mechanisms for managing common property resources have tended to weaken with economic development [Lawry (1991), Jodha (1986) and (1990)], and privatization of such resources in India has led to significant increases in yields. But the preservation of common property resources could be desirable from an equity perspective since privatizing these lands takes away a part of the social safety net for the rural poor. Providing a community title for these lands can protect communal rights from outside encroachment and prevent the poor from being excluded from communal property. We need to learn more about the management and the relative importance of such areas to specific social groups.

Assessments of the impact of individual titling on efficiency vary. Atwood emphasizes that in a distorted environment, introduction of land titles may decrease equity and efficiency. Feder et al. (1988) find that in Thailand, where possession of a title can be considered exogenous[24], output is 14 to 25 percent higher on titled land than on untitled land of equal quality. The market value is also much higher for titled land than for untitled land of similar quality. For Indian reservations in the US, characterized by the coexistence of different (exogenous) tenure arrangements, Anderson and Lueck (1992) find that output on tribal and individual trust land was lower by 85–90 and 30–40 percent, respectively, than on fee simple land. Less rigorous evidence is provided for Costa Rica by Salas et al. (1970), who estimate a positive correlation of .53 between farm income and title security. Studies in Brazil and Ecuador also suggest a positive association between farm income and titles (IDB 1986). But several studies have demonstrated that the credit market advantages of titles account for the lion's share of their effects [Feder (1993)] and that ownership security is not significantly correlated with titling [Migot-Adholla et al. (1991)]. Titling may have no significant effect at all when legal or customary rules limit land transactions and credit markets are weak. In Latin America where credit markets are more developed, recent land titling programs appear generally to have led to increases in the value of land, without encouraging increased concentration – at least in the short term [Stanfield (1990)].

## 8. Land tax

*The issues*

In most developing countries, land taxes have evolved from tribute payments to feudal lords or to a colonizing power. Because the taxes went to central government budgets, local compliance depended on strong enforcement by tax collectors, who shared in the revenues. Inflation and the difficulty of central-ized collection eventually led to the erosion or complete disappearance of such taxes. Today, the policy question is whether to reinstate land taxes and, perhaps to use them to finance investments and services in local jurisdictions, as is done successfully in the United States. In theory, a tax on land has three main advantages over a tax on agricultural output or exports: (1) if a land tax is based on the potential monetary yield of a certain plot under normal conditions, a land tax has minimal disincentive effects; (2) it facilitates taxation of the domestic agricultural sector while being much less regressive than poll taxes; and (3) if the tax basis is changed infrequently, a land tax does not discourage investment in land improvements.

---

[24] If the decision to acquire title is endogenous, estimation of the effects of titling using cross-sectional data is subject to simultaneity bias [Boldt (1989), Stanfield (1990)].

If risk is high and insurance markets are unavailable or imperfect, introducing a significant land tax (based on average incomes) can lead to increasing land concentration, as Hamid (1983) has shown for India. When insurance markets are imperfect, a mix of output tax and land tax Pareto-dominates either tax in isolation, for the same reason that a sharecropping contract is preferable to a fixed rental agreement [Hoff (1991)].

Administering a tax on land effectively and equitably requires having an official record, or cadastre, of the size, value, and ownership status of each tract of land, its productive capacity and information on the costs of outputs and inputs. If land quality can not be observed costlessly, a land tax may impose higher effective tax rates on landowners with low quality land than on those with high quality land. With plausible parameter values this effect may be large enough to make a land tax less desirable than an output tax [Skinner (1991)]. Land tax administration also requires a property tax law that assigns property rights and tax obligations and an administrative organization that keeps the register up to date and assesses, collects, and enforces the tax [Bird (1974)]. Even in the few developing countries able to meet these conditions, land taxes are relatively unimportant, suggesting that the administrative or political costs may be higher than the incentive advantages associated with a land tax.

Progressive land taxes are often advocated as a means of making land speculation less attractive and inducing large landowners to sell out or use their land more intensively [see Hayami, Quisumbing, and Adriano (1991) on the Philippines]. Landowners often find ways around such taxes, however, from establishing dummy divisions of their holdings to lobbying for exemptions from progressive rates associated with effective use of the land (as in Brazil), which sharply diminish the effectiveness of progressive land taxes in breaking up large commercial farms. Such an approach was applied and failed in Argentina, Bangladesh, Brazil, Colombia, and Jamaica [Strasma, Alsm, and Woldstein (1987), Bird (1974)]. Carter (1992) in a simulation model calibrated to Nicaragua finds that a progressive land tax is unlikely to significantly alter the distribution of land. And even if such taxes did work, it is not obvious why such an indirect approach would be politically more acceptable than direct redistribution of land. Progressive land taxes are also likely to be associated with higher administrative costs and protracted litigation.

*Policy implications*

Where the administrative infrastructure – an up-to-date cadastre plus administrative organization – is only rudimentary, flat or mildly progressive land taxes based on rough classification of holdings may still be useful for raising revenue and providing some modest incentives for owners to sell off poorly utilized land. The United States has found success by assigning the administration of land taxes to local authorities and earmarking tax revenues for local infrastructure and local government services. By increasing the local visibility of the benefits financed with the tax revenue, this approach may increase willingness to pay a land tax. It may also reduce administrative costs since local governments should be better able to assess land values and land ownership.

## 9. Regulations limiting land sales

Governments and local authorities have often placed restrictions on land transactions. Restrictions are typically placed on land sales and rentals when major changes are introduced to alter the land ownership pattern (redistributive land reform or settling programs). The restrictions are designed to prevent an increase in the number of landless and in the social tensions that accompany landlessness. Since these restrictions also prevent some transfers of land from worse to better farmers or managers, there is likely to be some efficiency loss. Such restrictions are frequently evaded, however, through disguised sales and rentals, which are likely to involve transaction costs that constitute a loss to society.

Restrictions on the rights of land reform beneficiaries or settlers on state-owned land to sell the land also reduce their access to credit. Often new owners are forbidden to mortgage their land during an initial probation period. Since that period coincides with the establishment phase, when their need for credit is most urgent, the efficiency losses may be considerable. Land rental contracts (usufruct-mortgaging) that have arisen as credit substitutes in some places, such as the Philippines [Nagarajan, Quisumbing and Otsuka (1991)], have caused transfer of land rights from the poor to the rich and resulted in increased use of inefficient labor contracts (*kasugpong*) [Hayami and Otskuka (1993)].

Sometimes restrictions on sales are not total, as in communal systems that permit sales only among members of the community. The welfare losses from the sales restrictions are less than in the case of a total ban, but they are not completely eliminated.

In the early years after a redistributive land reform in areas where land markets are thin and accurate information may not be available on the expected stream of incomes from the land, it may be reasonable to impose a temporary restriction on sales of say, three to four years. That would allow sufficient time to acquire knowledge about a farm's potential and to avoid sales at prices below the real value of the land, which would run counter to efficiency and equity objectives. Such restrictions would not be needed, however, in areas where former tenants receive land they have been tilling since they can be assumed to have adequate knowledge of the land. In the case of partial restrictions under communal systems, the ban on sales to outsiders may serve a protective role in environments where outsiders with strong political connections may attempt to take over land in the community. Where appropriate institutions for intragroup decision-making are available [Libecap (1986)], permitting the community to limit sales and giving it the right to decide whether to eventually allow sales to outsiders may be an acceptable compromise between equity and efficiency concerns (see Barrows and Roth 1990). As traditional social ties loosen or the efficiency loss from the sales restriction becomes too high, groups are likely to allow sales to outsiders. The recent constitutional reform of the land rights system in Mexico allows for free sales and rental within all *ejidos* and for decision-making by majority vote on whether to eliminate the restriction on sales to outsiders.

The most common means of restricting land sales are upper and lower bound size restrictions and zoning regulations. *Land ownership ceilings* have often been imposed in an attempt to break up large estates or to prevent their reconcentration. Among countries that have imposed ceiling are Bangladesh [Abdullah (1974)], India [King (1977)], Indonesia, Japan, Korea, Pakistan, South Vietnam, Taiwan, Egypt, Ethiopia, Iran, Iraq, Zimbabwe, Bolivia, Cuba, El Salvador, Guatemala, Mexico, and Peru. While such ceilings can theoretically increase efficiency where a negative relationship exists between size and productivity, in practice the ceilings have been evaded through fictitious subdivisions or have become superfluous over time through inheritance. Ceilings were often commodity specific providing much larger limits for sugarcane, bananas or livestock ranching. Therefore, they encouraged inefficient conversion to products with the highest ceilings. Rarely did ceilings alone enable the poor landless or extremely small farmers to purchase land; rather, they enabled farmers with medium-sized holdings, who had already acquired some equity, to enlarge their holdings (Chile).

Despite these flaws and loopholes in practice, several studies do credit land ownership ceilings with a major role in preventing new large consolidations after land reform [Cain (1981), Mahmood (1990)]. In Japan and Korea, success in preventing the reaggregation of land may be attributed as much to the availability of attractive investment opportunities outside agriculture and to noneconomic factors such as attachment to land as to the ceilings on land holdings. Ceilings imposed following a land reform that results in fairly homogeneous holdings might be effective and less distortionary in preventing massive reconcentration of land.

At the opposite end, *restrictions on minimum holding size* are intended to prevent excessive fragmentation of farms. While it is not clear that fragmentation is always a negative phenomenon (see below), a floor on farm size might provide a useful countervailing effect in a society where inheritance customs lead to extremely small farms. Whether the intervention improves efficiency depends on the specific circumstances. Also to be considered is that many restrictions on subdivision of land or minimum holding size have historically been used to prevent ex-slaves, tenants, and other powerless groups from acquiring ownership rights to land and thus eventually competing with farms established by the ruling group. Restrictions on the subdivisions of large farms in Kenya and Zimbabwe have limited the prospects for land resettlement schemes [Leys (1974)] and in these circumstances clearly reduced efficiency.

Governments often adopt *zoning regulations*, i.e. assign specific uses to certain lands to overcome environmental externalities rather than allowing market forces to determine land usage. In urban areas, the objective of zoning is to prevent commercial or industrial activities from locating in residential areas and creating noise and pollution. In rural areas, zoning of land for agricultural use provides benefits such as tax credits, exemption from assessments for urban type services, eligibility for soil conservation programs, and protection from nuisance suits, but forecloses the option of selling the land as a residential property.[25] In general, zoning is justified if negative externalities need to be reduced by more than the cost of zoning enforcement.

Zoning laws established for social or environmental reasons may run counter to economic incentives. Zoning may then need to be supported by some type of incentive mechanism, and political support for implementation of the regulations becomes essential to their enforcement [Barrows and Neuman (1990)]. If there are sharp conflicts between private profitability of land uses and zoning regulations in a country with weak institutional infrastructure, and little popular support for the zoning measures, zoning may lead to excessive rent-seeking and corruption. If zoning results in the emergence of extensive rent-seeking the benefits may greatly decrease or even become negative [Mills (1989)]. Zoning laws affect supply and demand for land and may lead to consumer mobility in response to zoning (Tiebout effects). The attempt to counteract production or agglomeration externalities through zoning laws also generates the potential for rent seeking behavior by landowners who either try to evade existing zoning regulations or lobby for the imposition of a set of laws which would provide them with a differential advantage. All of these issues have been analyzed largely in isolation of each other and a comprehensive analytical treatment is not yet available [Pogodzinski and Sass (1990)].

---

[25] Henneberry and Barrows (1990) find that parcel characteristics in general determine whether agricultural zoning has positive or negative price effects, in particular parcel size and distance from urban areas. [For a review of the effects of urbanization on agriculture, see Bhadra and Brandao (1992)].

## 10. Fragmentation and consolidation

*The issues*

While governments often intervene to prevent fragmentation of farm land, such intervention is not always economically justified. To justify such intervention it is necessary that inheritance customs or other exogenous forces be responsible for most of the fragmentation, that losses from fragmentation be substantial, and that existing markets be unable to counter fragmentation.

While inheritance customs probably explain much of the fragmentation of farm land, it may also reflect conscious decisions by farmers seeking to reduce their risk by diversifying their farm land and thus their crops [McCloskey (1975)]. This factor is likely to be important where other risk-diffusion mechanisms such as insurance, storage, or credit are unavailable or are associated with higher costs than fragmentation. Fragmentation may also help to smooth out labor requirements over time where labor requirements are highly seasonal [Fenoaltea (1976)].

Among the disadvantages associated with fragmentation are physical problems (increased labor time, land loss, need for fencing, transportation costs, and limitations to access); operational difficulties (unsuitability of certain equipment, greater difficulty with pest control and management and supervision, foregone improvements such as irrigation, drainage, and soil conservation); and social externalities [need for extensive road and irrigation networks; Simons (1987)]. The few studies which quantify losses from fragmentation in developing countries suggest that the losses involved are modest, although further studies of the efficiency of farms or losses from fragmentation are clearly needed. Indeed, Heston and Kumar claim that in Asia "it is hard to find instances where fragmentation had involved high losses in output" (1983: 211), and in Ghana and Rwanda, Blarel et al. (1992) find fragmentation does not seem to hurt productivity and does improve risk diversification and the allocation of family labor over time.

*Policy implications*

Relying on the market to eliminate fragmentation is likely to involve high transaction costs to coordinate transfers among large numbers of landowners. Transaction costs are much lower under government programs, which are normally coercive and include a range of other development initiatives, and returns can be high – Simons (1987) finds returns of 40 percent for France.

However, if the forces that led to fragmentation remain unchanged, land consolidation programs are unlikely to have any long-term effect [Simons (1987), Elder (1962)].

When should something be done about fragmentation? Experience in industrialized countries shows that fragmentation becomes a serious constraint requiring intervention once it impedes the ability to use machinery on a large scale in areas with a rapidly decreasing agricultural population [Bentley (1987)]. This is rarely the case in developing countries, with their high population densities. In addition, consolidation programs are likely to take a long time to complete, and they require considerable human capital and well-developed cadastres and land titles. Immediate government action to consolidate holdings does not appear to be a high priority in most developing countries, considering the high costs and the potential reduction of land fragmentation through voluntary transactions as rural credit and insurance markets improve.

## 11. Restrictions on land rentals

*The issues*

Governments have often introduced *tenure security and rent control legislation* to protect tenants from arbitrary eviction or to limit the amount of rent landlords can change. The unintended result has often been the eviction of tenants at the first hint of such legislation and the landlords' resumption of self-cultivation on the home farm, resulting eventually in the formation of Junker estates. In India, attempts to provide greater land security for tenants could be enforced only in states that imposed land ownership ceilings [King (1977)], and even there, landlords found ways to evade the legislation by signing tenants to short-term contracts which were exempt from protection, or by rotating tenants from plot to plot.

Where rent controls have been effectively implemented and combined with protection from eviction as in the Philippines or Taiwan, they do increase tenants' income, but since there is no transfer of ownership, they are still likely to result in dynamic efficiency losses. In the longer term, unless landowners find ways to circumvent the restriction on rents, such policies are likely to reduce incentives for renting out land, resulting in efficiency losses from constraints on adjustments in operational farm sizes. Investment is also likely to fall on farms on which tenants have a protected status since landlords are unlikely to invest heavily in land from which they are prevented from evicting tenants, while tenants' incentives to invest are weakened by uncertainty about the inheritability of the protected status.

Bans on share tenancy or low ceilings on the landlord's share are widespread even where other forms of land rental are allowed, such as the Philippines [Hayami and Otsuka (1993)], Brazil [Estatuta da Tierra (1964)], Zimbabwe [Palmer (1979)], South Africa [Bundy (1985)], Honduras, and Nicaragua [Dorner (1992)]. These restrictions are motivated in part by the common belief that share tenancy is exploitative (because, under conditions of land scarcity, tenants are likely to receive incomes close to their reservation wage) and in part by efforts to eliminate the Marshallian inefficiency associated with share contracts. But if the choice of contract is endogenous and if share contracts provide efficiency gains under circumstances of credit constraints and high risk and supervision costs, simply prohibiting share contracts without changing the underlying framework of market imperfections is likely to result in efficiency losses [Otsuka and Hayami (1988)]. More likely, the bans will give rise to disguised transactions or less efficient wage labor contracts that improve neither equity nor efficiency. Tenancy has long been an important transitional stage allowing peasants to accumulate capital and gain agricultural experience, so elimination of sharecropping as a rung on the agrarian ladder will certainly not contribute to equity in the long run. And considerable inefficiency in production may be associated with the absence of sharecropping as an option, especially where restrictions on private ownership of land impede the functioning of fixed-rent markets [Noronha (1985)]. Collier (1989) estimates static efficiency losses of more than ten percent associated with unavailability of share contracts in Kenya. From all perspectives then, bans on sharecropping and a low ceiling on landlord's share have no merit.

## 12. Redistributive land reform

*The issues*

Most redistributive land reform is motivated by public concern about the rising tensions brought about by an unequal land distribution. The common pattern is concentration of landownership among relatively few large owners in an economy where labor is abundant and land is scarce. Thus the masses of landless laborers and tenants who derive their livelihoods from agriculture receive relatively less income because their only asset is labor. Redistributive land reform can also increase efficiency, by transferring land from less productive large units to more productive small, family-based units (Section

4).[26] Yet, because of other market imperfections, land markets will not typically affect such transformations of ownership patterns. The value of the land to large owners may exceed the discounted sum of agricultural income smallholders can expect to receive despite their productivity advantages from lower supervision costs if there are policy distortions favoring large owners or if the access of small farmers to long-term credit has already been exhausted by mortgage-based land acquisition.

Market values of land are determined in a way that prevents small farmers who lack equity from building up viable farms and improving their standard of living while repaying their land mortgage. Land reform schemes that require payment of the full market value of the land are likely to fail unless special arrangements are made. In the simplest case, beneficiaries soon default and the program ends. Many ambitious land reform programs simply run out of steam because full compensation of old owners at market prices imposes fiscal requirements that the political forces are unwilling to meet – that was the fate of programs in Brazil, the Philippines and Venezuela. Some programs attempt to avoid this problem by compensating landowners (with bonds) whose real value erodes over time. Not surprisingly, landowners oppose this thinly disguised confiscation, and such programs are politically feasible only in circumstances of political upheaval (Cuba, Japan, Korea, Taiwan or Vietnam). Another approach is to finance land purchases through foreign grants or from internal tax revenues or inflationary monetary expansion – or some combination.

*Policy implications*

Before any land redistribution program is introduced, the implicit and explicit distortions which drive land prices above the capitalized value of agricultural profits need to be eliminated. Otherwise, small farmers will continue to have an incentive to sell out to larger farmers since the environment would still favor large ownership holdings. The poor must be provided with either the land or a grant to help them buy it to compensate for their lack of equity. Credit to beneficiaries for land purchases can only play a subsidiary role[27] but removing distortions also lowers the amount of grant assistance needed by small farmers

[26] Under circumstances of extreme poverty and landlessness redistribution of land can also enhance efficiency by improving the nutritional wellbeing and thus the productive capacity of the population [Dasgupta and Ray (1986) and (1987), Moene (1992)].

[27] Organizations such as the Penny Foundation in Guatemala have been able to buy land from owners and distribute it to small farmers with little apparent government subsidies [Forster (1992)]. These cases usually involve some grant element or subsidy in the credit provided to the smallholders, or the purchase of the land below market prices on account of liabilities of the former owner to government institutions or the workers which are forgiven as part of the deal.

to support their acquisition of land. The macro-economic and political environment also strongly affect the outcome of land reform policies.[28]

The type of manorial estate has a substantial bearing on the gains to be expected from land reform. On landlord estates, would-be beneficiaries are already managing operational units so land reform addresses primarily the equity concerns of society, transferring the entitlement to land rents while leaving operational farm structure largely unchanged. Potential efficiency gains are associated with improved investment incentives and increased security of tenure (Section 3). With haciendas, the threat of land reform legislation often leads to the eviction of tenants and reductions in the resident work force. The large commercial farms that result are more difficult to subdivide than landlord estates or haciendas [de Janvry (1981), Castillo and Lehman (1983), de Janvry and Sadoulet (1989)]. Land reforms of Junker estates and large mechanized farms involve major changes in the organization of production. The resident labor force and external workers have little or no independent farming experience, and in many cases, neither the infrastructure nor the investments in physical capital provide an appropriate basis for smallholder cultivation.[29]

The availability of technology and of competitive input and output markets thus becomes a crucial determinant for the potential of land reform to increase efficiency. Appropriate institutional arrangements are needed to ensure access to extension services, credit, and markets. Such institutions are especially important where land reform involves resettling beneficiaries on former Junker estates or large mechanized commercial farms. To reap the efficiency gains of family farming under these conditions seems to require increasing the density of family labor, and that may require resettling landless workers from outside.[30] Reform of these systems is likely to be difficult, but where the alternative to reform is the perpetuation of large economic and social costs, including the possibility of revolt and civil war, the cost of failing to reform may be enormous.

Opinions are divided on redistributive reform of wage plantations in the

---

[28] In Chile, substantial increases in output followed the expropriation and redistribution of almost 20 percent of the total agricultural land in 1964–1970, much of it due to the increase in investment induced by the favorable macroeconomic and political conditions [Jarvis (1985, 1989)]. In contrast, output failed to increase significantly during the decollectivization and breakup into family farms in 1975–1983, a period of extremely unfavorable government policies. Not until some of the debts incurred to pay for the land had been forgiven and structural impediments affecting small farmers had been eliminated did the program become fully effective.

[29] The differential outcomes of reform of Junker-estates in Kenya and Zimbabwe can be used to highlight the importance of appropriate institutional and policy-arrangements [Binswanger and Deininger (1993)].

[30] To some extent, credit and other public support can substitute for the advantage of more family labor per hectare. Leys (1978) found for Kenya that there was very little difference in economic performance between high density schemes, with small plots and low public investment, and low density schemes with larger plots and substantial public support.

classic plantation crops: banana, sugar, tea and oil palm. The fact that contract farming in these plantation crops is practiced successfully in many parts of the developing world indicates that converting plantations to contract farming is feasible. Indeed, Hayami, Quisumbing, and Adriano (1990) describe the successful conversion of even a banana plantation into a contract farming system in the Philippines, and strongly argue for bringing about more such conversions through a progressive land tax. The efficiency gains from lower supervision costs associated with such a step are likely to be offset, however, because of the genuine economies of scale in plantation crops.

Trying to replace plantations with collectives rather than contract farming has been unsuccessful. In Peru, the failure of collectivized sugar plantations to invest and their increased exploitation of external workers who were denied membership rights led to strikes by collective members that were put down by military intervention. Continuing losses – in part due to falling world sugar prices – provoked increased government intervention and the effective trans-formation of the collectives into state farms (Kay 1982). In Malaysia, rubber plantations which had been established on a collective basis were split up and allocated to individual farmers at maturity to ensure proper tapping [Pickett (1988)].

## 13. Decollectivization

The poor performance of collectives and state farms the world over is so obvious that the question facing the liberalizing economies of Eastern Europe and the Commonwealth of Independent States is not whether to privatize but rather how quickly and in what form – as large commercial farms or as family farms.

*Policy implications*

The discussions in this paper imply that four issues appear to be of overriding importance in determining this policy choice:

- The small farm option is viable only if there are competitive input and output markets. Otherwise the land rent and the entrepreneurial rents from agriculture will be captured by the monopolistic output marketers and input suppliers rather than by the new farm owners. Risk diffusion mechanisms also need to be functioning adequately, or else covariate weather or price shocks can force distress sales by new landowners, who do not have other assets or income streams. Work on creating competitive input and output marketing systems and a viable financial system therefore has to start before large farms are split up into individual landholdings.

- Experience from China, Vietnam, and East Germany shows that inputs and machinery services, which have previously been supplied by the cooperative, are more efficiently provided by private contractors who lease or buy the machinery stock from the cooperative in a competitive process (Nolan 1988, Pingali and Xuan 1992, Pryor 1992). The Chinese experience also suggests that farmers and machinery suppliers respond to the changes in operational holding size by adopting a different and generally more efficient pattern of mechanization (Lin 1991). This suggests that the excessive lumpiness of the existing machine stock is not a serious constraint to smaller scale farming.
- Agricultural research, extension, and other production support services take on special importance since many farm workers are likely to lack the skills needed to manage their own farms. Some of the structures that served quasi-governmental functions on collective and state farms, particularly by providing education and health services, could be retained as well. They might also eventually develop into independent cooperatives for supplying machinery, custom plowing, machine rentals, inputs, and possibly credit – all in competition with the private sector [Nolan (1988), Pryor (1992)].
- Where capital, skills, technology, infrastructure, or competitive markets for inputs and outputs are lacking, enthusiasm for independent farming may be lacking as well. If only a few entrepreneurs are willing to farm, the resulting farms are then likely to be too large for the cost advantage associated with the use of family labor, and large commercial farms, heavily mechanized or dependent on large numbers of hired workers, will emerge in their stead. Most likely such large farms would continue to press for subsidies, emerge as rent-seekers from the rest of society and, if successful, generate insufficient employment. Therefore, countries may need to find temporary arrangements, including long-term land leases, that will provide a greater number of households with opportunities to acquire the necessary skills needed to allow the emergence of a structure of smaller family farms more consistent with the income and wage levels and rural labor forces that can be expected for these economies in the next few decades.

## EPILOGUE ON METHODOLOGY

Scholars of various ideological persuasions and methodological commitments have attempted to explain the great variations in land relations over space and time which have been the topic of this paper. Much of the discordance among these scholars is closely associated with their choice of modeling strategies and assumptions. This epilogue relates the analytical results and the observed variations in land relations discussed in this paper to the minimum set of assumptions needed to derive the results or explain the variations. We distinguish several levels of assumptions.

*Level A* assumes self-interested behavior, such as expected utility maximization or other forms of purposive behavior, of all actors, who compete on a level playing field in an environment with risk using voluntary transactions, with symmetrically distributed information and exogenously given endowments of land, capital and skills. Technology is characterized by constant or diminishing returns to scale. Virtually none of the variations in land relations discussed in this paper can be explained with these assumptions alone.

*Level B* adds constraints in the credit market or assumes that this market is entirely absent. Formal models of surplus value from Marx to the generalized version of Roemer (1982) use this approach to explain capitalist exploitation and the endogenous differentiation of maximizing individual economic agents – who operate in a competitive environment with voluntary transactions – into economic classes as the consequence of differences in their exogenous endowments of physical capital and absent credit markets. Eswaran and Kotwal (1985) apply Roemer's approach to agriculture, imposing in addition constant costs (Section 4).

*Level C* adds asymmetric information, moral hazard, and incentive problems, arriving at the analytical apparatus of agency theory. As Stiglitz (1986) summarizes, these assumptions are sufficient to explain credit rationing, thereby giving an analytical underpinning to level B models. They also explain various combinations of reasons for sharecropping and interlinked credit (Section 6). These assumptions are also sufficient to establish the superiority of family farms, as discussed in the mathematical model of Feder (Section 4 and Appendix 2) and the historically widespread use of tenancy by large owners of land at moderate to high population density to circumvent the diseconomy of scale (Section 2). Incentives issues of collectives are also analyzed with this analytical apparatus (Section 4).

Level C models provide little insight into the process by which large landownership holdings could accumulate or be perpetuated in systems characterized by voluntary transactions and competition, and with constant or diminishing returns.

*Level D* adds several material conditions relating specifically to agricultural production, generating the analytical apparatus used by Meillassoux (1981) or Binswanger, Rosenzweig, and McIntire (1986, 1987). The material conditions most frequently used in this paper are covariance of risk and returns among farmers and workers in a given agricultural region, the immobility of land, which – when it is scarce – makes it a preferred store of wealth (relative to stocks and livestock, for example) and of collateral, and exogenously given population density and processing characteristics of specific agricultural commodities.

Covariance creates enormous difficulties for intertemporal markets for crop insurance and credit. Because of land's preferred role as store of wealth and as collateral, an insurance and collateral benefit is associated with landownership. Together with the failure of intertemporal markets this preferred role explains the prevalence of distress sales and the accumulation of large landownership holdings even in a competitive environment with strictly voluntary contracts and diseconomies of scale (Section 5). The potential failure of land sales markets to improve efficiency in an environment with missing or imperfect intertemporal markets is a powerful and historically relevant illustration of the theorem of second best [Lipsey and Lancaster (1957)] of neoclassical economics.

The explanation of variations over time and space of property rights to specific plots of land (Sections 1 and 2) requires the introduction of population density and its association with the farming systems and the farm technologies, as explained by Boserup (1965). The seasonality of production, the timeliness requirements of specific crops, and the economies of scale of the processing plants or transport facilities required for them are necessary material conditions to explain the survival, in only a few specific plantation crops, of wage plantations in the absence of slavery or indentured labor (Section 4). Note that anthropologists, like Marvin Harris, who use behavioral-materialist approaches also carefully specify their detailed material assumptions, although their themes extend well beyond those discussed in this paper.

*Level E* partly abandons the assumption of voluntary contracts (for the case of slavery and bondage) and extends the analysis beyond individualistic approaches and transactions by introducing rent seeking, coalition building, and the coercive power of the state to enforce laws. These additions facilitate the explanation of the use of bondage and slavery, tribute systems, state allocations of preferential land rights and enforcement powers to ruling groups, distortions in commodity and factor markets, and distortions in public expenditures specifically intended to extract rent and make large ownership or operational holdings competitive with independent family farms (Sections 2 and 3). The historical literature has sharply differentiated between coercive and noncoercive methods of rent extraction and has often equated the elimination of coercive means with the leveling of the playing field. While there are certainly important qualitative differences between coercive and noncoercive means, the differentiation seems to have obscured the continuity of rent seeking or surplus extraction along alternative paths such as taxation of the free peasant sector, land allocation, monopoly marketing, and the allocation of public spending.

Level E explains the emergence and persistence over time of highly dualistic farm size structures as the result primarily of a rarely broken chain of rent seeking (Sections 2 and 3). It explains the poor economic performance of many such systems as the result of a dissipation of rents into the cost of competition for them among rent-seeking groups.[31] Within the chain of rent-seeking, the officially sanctioned set of legitimate instruments of rent seeking may be progressively reduced by gradually eliminating slavery and serfdom, tribute and corvée, and land rental, until only output and factor market distortions and differential allocation of public expenditure remain. With exogenous variation in the set of instruments available for rent seeking, this framework of analysis can explain a substantial proportion of the variation over space and time in the level of use of each of the available instruments. For given instruments, modeling at level D can also, in principle, investigate the income distributions and efficiency costs associated with the resulting distortions, while the theory of rent seeking behavior [Tollison (1982)] can be used to investigate the extent to which rents are dissipated in the process of competing for them.

Finally, *level F* asks questions that are touched on only lightly in this paper about what determines endogenously the changes in the set of instruments available for rent seeking or surplus extraction in a given country at a given time. Population density and its distribution over space becomes an endogenous variable. The questions include the extensively debated issues of the demise of feudalism and bondage [Marx, Dobb (1977), Brenner (1985); the abolition of slavery [Fogel and Engerman (1977), Meillassoux (1991); the elimination of corvée, tribute, and debt peonage; the power to monopolize output and input markets [Anderson and Hayami (1986); elimination of the land rental option; and land reform [de Janvry (1981)]. The questions analyzed also include why revolt and revolution are necessary in some cases, while in others a change in the set of instruments available is successfully accomplished by reform, and why some reforms lead to stable and efficient production relations, while others result in institutions that are unsuccessful to promote either equity or efficiency.

These are the grand themes of historians, classical economists, and Marxist historical materialist analysis. These issues usually involve coalitions (or their

---

[31] Brenner (1976, 1985) argues that under feudalism the rents extracted from peasants by landed elites were almost completely dissipated and that the resulting failure by peasants and landlords to reinvest in land improvements and draft animals was responsible for the extension of arable farming to marginal lands and the declining productivity associated with population growth in feudal European agriculture. Thus it was the rent seeking itself that led to the Neo-Malthusian or Ricardian subsistence crises of the twelfth and thirteenth centuries, rather than to population-induced positive Boserup-sequences of investment, change in technique, increased division of labor, and agricultural productivity growth. This explanation of stagnant or declining productivity is similar to that documented by Bates (1983) and Krueger, Schiff, and Valdes (1992) to explain the recent stagnation of agriculture and limited technical change in much of Africa as a consequence of the extraordinarily high taxation of (mostly smallholder) agriculture in many African countries by urban-dominated states.

breakdown) that, except in purely agrarian societies, extend beyond opposing rural groups to include manufacturing, trading, financial, bureaucratic, or foreign interests. Therefore additional exogenous elements (including material ones) from outside agriculture must be factored into the exploratory framework. Much of the work on these themes that we have come across neither explicitly specifies assumptions about the distribution of information (level C) nor formally includes into the analysis specific material conditions of agriculture (introduced in level D) or other sectors of the economy. And while rent seeking at level E is implicit in the questions asked, and coalitions or their breakdown are discussed, the coalition building associated with rent seeking is rarely modeled explicitly. There may be some gains to be had from more formal considerations of these omitted elements and their incorporation into the structure of the analysis of these grand themes.

## Appendix 1

### Interventions to establish and support large farms

The literature on emergence and evolution of manorial estates and the production relations prevailing within such estates has focussed largely on examples from Europe (mainly Britain, France, Germany, and Eastern Europe). This appendix, which explains table 1 in the text, provides evidence on the establishment and evolution of large farm systems from a wider range of settings and covers a longer time period.

The examples discussed here all suggest that neither the establishment nor the continued existence of large farms was due to their superior economic efficiency and/or the presence of economies of scale in agricultural production. The establishment of large farms was due to government intervention in favor of large landholders via land grants and differential taxation. Withdrawal of these privileges led either to their disintegration into landlord estates or to a shift towards rent seeking and more subtle forms of support for large farms.

### Asia

*India (North)*

*Land market interventions.* The hacienda system is already described in the Arthshastra from the 4th century BC. In the first century, land grants comprising some ten or more villages each were made to priests and to a few members of the ruling family and high officers of the state [Sharma (1965)].

This process of land grants "culminated in the 11th and 12th centuries, when Northern India was parcelled into numerous political units largely held by secular and religious donees who enjoyed the gift villages as little better than manors" [Sharma (1965: 273)].

*Differential taxation and labor levies.* Corvée labor emerged in the second century and remained prevalent until the tenth century. Between the fifth and tenth centuries, where population density was high enough, as in Gujarat, Rajasthan, and Maharastra, permanent tenants were reduced to tenants at will. Where population density was low, tenants and artisans were tied to the soil in the same manner as serfs in medieval Europe (Sharma 1965).

## China (South)

*Differential taxation and labor levies.* The equitable land allotment system introduced around 600 under conditions of land abundance allocated land equally among all members of the community in return for tax payments. Slaves received the standard size of plot but had to pay only half the taxes demanded from free men [Chao (1986)]. Peasants, however, could not escape the tax burden since farmers who fled to uncultivated lands were returned to their village by the authorities. DeFrancis (1956) quotes reports of 600,000 "refugees" having been collected in a single year (544). To escape the tax, many cultivators presented themselves as serfs or "bondservants" to large landholders or monasteries, leading to the emergence of large estates. In a major land reform in 1369 under the Ming dynasty, the estates were broken up into small freehold farms [Eastman (1988)]. Following the land reform, tax captains were installed to administer tax collection from units of 110 households each and to deliver grain taxes to government warehouses. Using corvée labor and bondservants, they were also active in land clearing to expand their revenue base [Shih (1992)]. They accumulated modest estates of their own thanks to their ability to provide credit. Increasingly heavy tax demands (to finance wars) left many tax captains in a desperate situation.

The new gentry class that began to emerge in the fourteenth century was exempt from both taxes and labor services. Since gentry landlords did not pay taxes, they were able to reap higher returns from land and accumulate wealth. They were able to further increase their holdings after periods of disaster by foreclosing on lands they had accepted as collateral for credit [Shih (1992)]. These advantages made it easy for members of the gentry to accumulate land, decrease the tax captains' revenue base, and finally buy out bankrupt tax captains, who by the end of the century had lost most of their land to gentry landlords. As gentry landlords increased their moneylending activities, small owners in financial difficulties had to resort to selling their land or selling themselves to gentry landlords as serfs or bondservants, thereby obtaining partial exemptions from their tax obligations. Gentry estates grew to several thousands of hectares in size, with a labor force of over 10,000. The estates were often split up into smaller farms of about 500 hectares, managed by specially educated bondservants [Shih (1992)].

Following the change from the Ming to the Qing dynasty in 1644, gentry landlords lost their tax privileges. Declining population and greater opportunities for off-farm employment during 1630–1950 increased the amount of land available and, as in Western Europe, improved the position of peasants [Shih (1992)]. In the second half of the seventeenth century, the heritability of serf status was repealed, and serfs were fully emancipated in 1728. Operation of a large home farm using wage labor was no longer profitable, and landlord estates emerged [Wiens (1980)], considerably improving the position of tenants. Tenancy allowed operational holdings to adjust to household size and led to very labor-intensive cultivation and high yields [Feuerwerker (1980)].

## Japan

*Land market interventions.* To provide incentives to make the investments required to transform wasteland into paddy land, the land reclamation bill of 723 made such land the heritable personal property of the developer. This provision led to the emergence of a separate category of private land that was tax exempt and excluded from the communal tenure system in which land was redistributed every six years among all members of the community (Takekoshi 1967).

*Differential taxes and labor levies.* In return for such land allotments, farmers had to pay tribute in kind as well as special labor services of up to 140 days a year [Takekoshi (1967)]. Cleared and temple lands, as well as land belonging to the nobility, were exempt from all tribute requirements. In order to obtain immunity from tributes, many landowners transferred their lands to temples or members of the nobility. While they had to give up the heritable right to the land, original landholders did in most cases continue to manage the land and home farm cultivation remained minimal. Higher officials could accumulate manors of enormous size, but in turn had to commend their properties to higher-ranking individuals to protect the immunity of their manor from tribute requirements, leading to a complex tenure-hierarchy in which shares of manors and associated rights to income were traded [Sato (1977)]. Around the end of the fourteenth century increasing land scarcity, as evidenced by physical fragmentation of fields due to intergenerational transfers, led to a gradual conversion to landlord estates [Keirstead (1985)], which remained in place until the nineteenth and twentieth centuries.

## Java and Sumatra

*Land market interventions.* The Agrarian Land Law of 1870 declared all uncultivated land inalienable state property and leased it to European companies which established large scale plantations.

*Differential taxes and labor levies.* These plantations were operated almost exclusively using indentured labor [Breman (1989)]. Laws such as the "coolie ordinance" from 1880 imposed severe penalties on indentured workers who absconded and prison terms on anybody employing such runaway workers, thus indicating the scarcity of labor [Stoler (1985)]. Large scale cultivation was limited to these plantations.

Where individual peasant holdings prevailed at the beginning of colonial rule, authorities used the "cultivation system" (1820) to appropriate surplus without expending resources for capital investment, and relying on traditional land tenure and labor exchange arrangements. This system required farmers to grow cash crops (predominantly coffee or sugar) for the government on one-fifth of village lands in lieu of a land tax [Hart (1985)]. Both of these crops were integrated into the local systems of rice or upland cultivation [Geertz (1963)].

## Philippines

*Land market interventions.* Land grants were given to private individuals and religious orders after 1571 [Roth (1977)] and by 1700 all of the best land was under the control of large estates [Cushner (1976)].

*Differential taxation and labor levies.* The Philippines, like countries in Latin America, had both *encomienda* – the right to tribute in labor, cash, or kind from a particular region – and *repartimiento* – which distributed workers for public works and private Spanish businesses. The systems differed from those in Latin America, however, in that the right to labor services was hereditary and often included whole villages. Workers on European haciendas were exempted from heavy public works and from taxes, making hacienda employment highly attractive. Despite this advantage, the lack of economies of scale led to almost immediate disintegration of rice-cultivating haciendas into landlord estates. Moreover, by the nineteenth century, sugar production as well as processing were controlled by tenants [Roth (1977)].

## Sri Lanka

*Land market interventions.* Upland areas where slash and burn cultivation was practiced were declared crown land in 1840 [Bandarage (1983)] and sold to private cultivators, mainly British, who established coffee plantations.

*Differential taxation and labor levies.* Corvée labor was abolished on public lands in 1818 and replaced by a grain tax amounting to 10 percent of gross produce. Export agriculture – all land under coffee, cotton, sugar, indigo, opium poppies, and silk – was exempted from the tribute [Bandarage (1983)].

While landed interests had successfully opposed the imposition of a general land tax, the opportunity to earn income from coffee cultivation, together with the absence of a totally landless labor caste, severely limited the willingness of local people to supply labor to estates. Thus almost the entire agricultural work force on coffee estates had to be imported: Census figures indicate that in 1871 and 1881, 97 percent of some 200,000 plantation workers were indentured Tamils, mainly from India. The 3 percent of Singhalese plantation workers were mostly low-country artisans who were paid competitive wages and used their position to accumulate capital for own land purchases [Bandarage (1983)].

## Europe

### Prussia

*Land market interventions.* Land grants in Prussia date from the thirteenth century and were made to knights and nobles who were to colonize the largely unpopulated territory and provide military services to the king. Initially, population density was so low that very favorable terms were required to attract peasants: peasants received hereditary usufruct leases to about 32 hectares of land each. Noble knights operated modestly sized demesnes of about two to three times the size which was provided to settlers (Hagen 1985) to supplement the rents they received from peasants. They were "not the master but the neighbor" of the farmer, and in economic terms they often fared worse than full peasants (Lütge 1979). Depopulation caused by the Black Death increased the amount of land available to the nobility who became "land rich but labor poor". Productive use of this land could be maintained only by attracting and settling new farmers, often on terms which were quite favorable to the settlers.

*Differential taxation and labor levies.* While settler farmers had a legal right to leave without the lords' consent as late as 1484 [Hagen (1985)], the *Landesverordnung* of 1526 no longer mentioned the right of the farmer to take legal action against a landlord who would not allow him to leave [Abel (1978)], indicating landlords' increased bargaining power (due to higher population density). Such restrictions on peasants' mobility facilitated more widespread adoption of labor rents and an increase in labor requirements from two days of service a week for full peasants in 1560 to three days around 1600 [Hagen (1985)]. Still, landlords had to rely on hired workers in addition to compulsory labor services, estates were relatively small: In 1624, Junkers' demesne took up only 18 percent of the cultivated land [Hagen (1985)]. The main benefit of labor services for landlords was the obligation of full peasants to supply a pair of oxen or horses and a driver rather than the contributions made by non-full peasants (*nicht spannfähige Bauern*) to demesne cultivation.

Although landowners increased the size of their demesne by adding the land of families who died during the plague years of the fourteenth century and the Thirty Years War of 1618–1648, large farms began to dominate in Prussia only after the land reform in 1807–1850 [Lütge (1979)]. Three aspects of the reform contributed to the emergence of large farms: the terms of separation requiring farmers with hereditary or nonhereditary lifetime leases to cede one-third or one half their land to the Junkers in return for freedom; the initial limitation of reform benefits to "full peasants" and its extension to other peasants without long-term lease rights only in 1850 when, most people agree, it was "already too late" [Dickler (1975)]; and repeal of tenancy protection laws, which had been in place since 1750. These factors allowed Junkers to vastly increase their demesnes and to draw on an increased pool of wage labor. The typical Junker style of cultivation with permanent laborers residing on house plots emerged as the predominant form of production organization [Lütge (1979)]. After farm workers became free to migrate in 1868 and began moving westward [Wunderlich (1961)], they were gradually replaced by salaried and migratory seasonal workers, especially from Poland, where population density was high and landlessness was widespread [Dickler (1975)].

*Input and output market interventions.* From the earliest settlement days, knights had certain rights of jurisdiction and monopolies on milling and on the manufacture and sale of alcohol. However, the fact that they were willing to cede a good deal of their trade-related privileges to entrepreneurs who engaged in land-clearing and attracting settlers from the west illustrates just how pressing the labor scarcity was.

*Russia*

*Land market interventions.* In the fourteenth century, princes, considering all land in their princedom as their patrimony (votchina), granted land to nobles who could provide the labor force necessary to cultivate the land and pay taxes. These landlords in turn had to attract peasants with very favorable terms. In-kind payments (obrok) remained the predominant type of peasant obligation, and, due to the limited ability to impose labor rents (barshchina), home farm cultivation was almost nonexistent [Blum (1961)].

In 1565, Ivan IV confiscated the property (votchina) of almost all the old princedoms, converting it into state land (oprichnina) and then using it for land grants to reward servitors. Servitors did not receive freehold title, acquiring only usufruct rights under service tenure (pomestye) which became the dominant form of lay seignorial tenure. As a result, "the personal possession of landed property became a monopoly of a single class of Russian society – the servitors of the tsar" [Blum (1961: 169)]. As land rights could be terminated at will by the tsar, continued possession of the land was conditional on the performance of service to the state. Indeed, landlords who could not provide payment in service or money were evicted, and the class of servitors was subject to high fluctuations, competition for labor was fierce, and home farm cultivation remained very limited. The economic situation of the servitor was often precarious until tenures gradually became heritable in the seventeenth century [Blum (1961)].

*Restrictions on labor mobility and differential taxation.* The extent of labor scarcity is illustrated by continuously more severe restrictions on peasant cultivators' mobility. Between 1400 and 1450, the right of peasants to terminate leases and move on to another landlord was restricted to two weeks each year. Even then peasants were required to pay formidable "exit fees" (equivalent to 300 bushels of oats or 120 bushels of wheat; Blum 1961) before leaving. Landlords competed fiercely for labor and resorted to "labor pirating", i.e. attracting workers from other estates by promises. In fact, such labor pirating became "the principal lawful way by which renters transferred from one lord to the other", though illegal means were often resorted to as well [Blum (1961)]. The introduction in 1588 of "forbidden years" during which the peasants' right to move was temporarily suspended did not prevent labor pirating because the law could not be enforced. Decrees in 1597 and again in 1607 bound all peasants to the place they were residing at the time of the census of 1592, which facilitated enforcement of the law. The Assembly Code of 1649, which remained valid until about 1850, abolished statutes of limitation on the return of fugitive peasants to their original landlord. It also made serfdom heritable by prohibiting the peasant's wife and progeny from moving as well. After 1661, fines for peasant raiding had to be paid "in serfs": for every illegal peasant found on a landlord's holding, the landlord had to give up one of his own serf families. Serfs could be freely sold; restrictions prohibiting the sale of serfs without land were unsuccessful. Serfs were also used as collateral, to be auctioned off if their landlord went bankrupt. In 1859, two-thirds of all serfs were mortgaged. After 1719, the privileges of peasants – mainly at the frontiers – who had escaped serfdom were successively eliminated. They became serf-like state peasants, subject to taxes, quitrent, and conscription. By 1850 more than 90 percent of the male population were serfs [Blum (1961)].

In 1580, landlords' home farms (demesnes) were exempted from taxation. With revenue requirements also rising, the tax burden on peasants increased substantially, significantly lowering the potential return from cultivation [Blum (1961)]. Peasants responded by running off to the frontiers where landlords were keen to attract labor and, because of temporary exemptions from taxes, were able to offer better conditions.

Landlords attempted to tie peasants to their holdings through debt peonage. Under laws passed between 1586 and 1597, a debtor automatically fell into debt servitude if he was unable to repay the loan on time. He then had to work continuously for the creditor just to pay the recurrent interest. Without any possibility of repaying the principal, debt servitors' only advantage over slaves was that they were to be freed following the creditor's death [Blum (1961)].

*Input and output market interventions.* Since neither serfs nor state peasants were allowed to engage in independent business until the 1820s or 1830s, landlords enjoyed a de facto monopoly over commerce in their area, in addition to their formal monopoly on alcohol manufacture and sale.

## Latin America

### Chile

*Land market interventions.* In the mid-sixteenth century, town councils, free of the central supervision by a viceroy or governor that was common in Mexico and Peru, handed out land to settlers "with utmost generosity and . . . in the face of royal legislation to the contrary" [Bauer (1980: 4)]. In contrast to other Latin American countries, where the right to tribute was legally distinguished from land grants, and the de jure protection of Indian communal land was enforced by central authorities, *encomenderos* in Chile received land grants in the middle of "their" Indians' communal lands early on. The *encomenderos* were thus provided with cheap and abundant labor services such that "by the

1650s landownership and *encomienda* were fully integrated ... [and] the *encomienda* was absorbed by the land" [Bauer (1980: 8)].

*Differential taxation and labor levies.* The main means to provide labor to the mines was the *mita* which required all Indian settlements to supply a certain proportion of their labor force for agriculture or public works, but in most cases the mines. Hacienda workers were exempt from the *mita* and many Indians sought refuge from the cruel forced labor requirements by joining the ranks of the *yanaconas*, a group which had given up all ties, including land rights, to their original communities and, living in total dependence on individual Spaniards, formed the nuclear labor force of the Spanish estates.

A rise in demand for wheat from Lima in 1687 led to a considerable increase in such labor requirements with landowners relying on either reconstituted *encomienda* or on *yanaconas* who were virtually enslaved and only given 3 days off a year to tend their house-plots [Pearse (1975)]. As on the Eastern European Junker estates, able tenants were used as "labor brokers" and obliged to supply the hacienda with workers (*peones obligados* or *reemplazantes*) nearly year-round [Kay (1977)].

*Input and output market interventions.* Large wheat growing farms in the Central region could not compete against wheat produced on the more dynamic (and smaller sized) farms in the South and were converted into livestock ranches. In order to protect them from competition from Argentina they lobbied successfully for the imposition of import taxes on beef at the end of the 19th century. Such taxes were maintained despite consumer riots caused by high food prices in 1905 [Kay (1992)].

In this century, large landowners received special treatment to reduce the cost of mechanization. They received exemptions from import tariffs and low interest rate loans; real interest rates on mechanization loans in most of Latin America during the 1950s and early 1960s were actually negative. Farmers in Chile, Argentina, Brazil, and Venezuela paid back only 50 to 80 percent of their equipment loans [Abercombie (1972)].

*El Salvador*

*Land market interventions.* Public land was granted to anybody who was planting it at least two third with coffee beginning in 1857 [Lindo-Fuentes (1990)]. A large land titling program, initiated in 1882, which was intended to speed up the growth of coffee production, is thought to have directly affected up to 40 percent of the territory of the country [Lindo-Fuentes (1990)] and led to extraordinary concentration of land ownership. The 1882 law required all occupants of ejido lands to register their claims (i.e. prove that they were cultivating the land and pay the titling fee) within a period of six month. All lands not claimed in this way was to be sold at public auctions. Illiterate Indians, were often not aware of these requirements and well-connected individuals could take considerable advantage of the legislation. The goal of establishing a successful export agriculture could have been achieved by modernizing the credit system and providing education to Indians as well, in particular as Indians had proven to be responsive to market incentives before. Choice of the land market as the instrument to achieve the transformation illustrates the administrative difficulties as well as the power of the elites who would benefit from such legislation [Lindo-Fuentes (1990)].

*Differential taxation and labor levies.* In 1825 vagrancy laws were passed requiring Indians to carry work cards certifying their employment (Lindo-Fuentes 1990). The penalty for vagrancy was imprisonment. In 1847, land-owners planting more than 15 000 coffee trees obtained exemption from public and military services for themselves and all their workers.

### Guatemala

*Land market interventions.* While the Spanish made some land grants in Guatemala in the early sixteenth century, their main land market intervention was resettlement of the Indian population in centralized villages to facilitate tax administration and conversion of Indians to Christianity. They limited their activities to ranching for which no land title was required [MacLeod (1973)]. Titles, which were issued to Spaniards through land grants, became important only in 1590–1630, following a shift to cultivation of indigo.

*Differential taxation and labor levies.* Initially, Spaniards had little interest in establishing intensive agriculture and collected tribute instead [such Indian tribute contributed more than 80 percent of royal government revenue; Brockett (1990)]. From 1540, tribute assessments were made in cash, and the need for cash income was an important force inducing Indians from the highlands to migrate to plantation areas [MacLeod (1973)]. By the 1560s and 1570s, Indians who had migrated from the highlands in this way constituted the majority of the coastal Indian population.

Beginning around 1600, Indian headmen were required to provide labor contingents (*mandamiento*) – which could be as high as a quarter of the work force – for tasks of public interest (MacLeod 295). *Mandamiento* labor was ideally suited to the seasonal demands of indigo processing. Employment of Indians in indigo factories was widespread, despite its legal prohibition to prevent further decline of the decimated Indian population [Lindo-Fuentes (1990)]. The *mandamiento* system survived well into the 1880s, when it was used to provide cheap labor for European coffee plantations [Cambranes (1985)].

Debt peonage was legalized in 1877, and by forcing debtors to work off their debts, provided landowners with official means of enforcing the continuation of a flow of cheap labor. Following the abolition of debt peonage, vagrancy laws were adopted in 1933 in response to the severe labor shortage. All Indians who could not prove owner-operatorship of a minimum of 1.1 to 2.8 hectares of land were forced to work – mainly on plantations – for 100 to 150 days a year to discharge their "debt to society". The requirement to carry work cards facilitated enforcement [Pearse (1975)].

*Mexico*

*Land market interventions.* Resettlement of Indians beginning in 1540 deprived them of their traditional lands and placed them on smaller, less productive holdings. While the intention of the resettlement program was primarily to raise money for the crown by selling the Indians' land to Europeans, the expropriations seriously reduced the productive basis of the Indian agricultural economy [Gibson (1965), Taylor (1988)].

Communal lands were expropriated in the 1850s, and as land became increasingly scarce, fewer alternative opportunities were open to potential tenants. "The expropriation of communal villages brought about two contradictory tendencies. On the one hand, cheap temporary labor became more readily available than before. This made it economically less and less necessary for the hacienda in central Mexico to rely on forced labor. On the other hand, as the haciendas acquired more and more land, much of it of mediocre quality, they preferred not to work it themselves but to shift the risk to sharecroppers and tenants. The condition of these occupants was so precarious that many of them . . . inevitably incurred debts with the hacienda which they could not repay" [Katz (1974: 41)].

*Differential taxation and labor levies.* Spanish settlers received, after 1490, *encomiendas*, i.e. rights to Indian villages from which they could extract tribute in kind and labor services. Restrictions limiting the use of tribute labor in agriculture were imposed in some regions, in order to secure labor supply for public works.

In 1542, the original *encomiendas* were restricted to the right to collect tribute and the system of *repartimiento* was used to distribute Indian labor, supposedly in a more equitable way. While this restricted the power of the original beneficiaries of the *encomienda*, it worsened the lot of Indians who still had to pay tribute to *encomenderos* and to render labor services under *repartimientio*.

Tribute requirements remained in place but could be avoided by working on haciendas (the hacienda paid the tribute). Tribute was often required to be paid in cash, forcing many highland Indians to migrate to lowland areas to obtain the necessary cash income [Moerner (1978)].

Debt peonage was not significant in the early period of colonization, but it later acquired importance as a means of tying laborers to the hacienda and lowering their wages. In 1790, 80 percent of peons in one area had a total debt higher than the legal limit; their average debt was equivalent to eleven months' wages [Taylor (1972)]. As landlords let debt accumulate up to the point of the expected future value of work performed, the system came very close to slavery (debt peons were even being traded by redeeming the debt to their current employer). A law enacted in 1843 secured not only state enforcement to "collect" debts incurred to haciendas but also made it illegal to hire laborers who had left their hacienda without paying their debts and required that they be returned [Katz (1974)]. Vagrancy laws passed in 1877 and strictly enforced led to a considerable increase in the employment of deportees and "criminals" [Katz (1974)].

*Viceroyality of Peru (present day Peru, Bolivia, and Ecuador)*

*Land market interventions.* Beginning in 1540, land grants became common in this region, with grants of 120–800 hectares being relatively easy to obtain. The main beneficiaries were the *encomenderos*, i.e. Spaniards who had received rights to labor services from whole villages (see below), since without Indian tribute labor to work the land, the latter was virtually worthless. Once all the land set aside for this purpose had been exhausted, around 1557, "private" Indian land was expropriated and distributed among Spaniards [Gonzales (1985), Davies (1984)].

In the coastal areas, resettlement under Viceroy Toledo in 1570 moved Indians into newly established towns where they were assigned farmlands of often inferior quality. Programs to review existing Spanish land titles under which "Spaniards could legally acquire land that they had previously stolen from Indians by paying a fee to the Crown" [Gonzales (1985: 15)] were introduced in 1589. In 1641 the same pattern was applied even more rigorously to improve the financial position of the Spanish crown: there were large-scale expropriations of Indian land, and all surplus land was sold to Europeans. Indians "suffered a considerable reduction in their holdings; they now possessed some of the worst farmland in the valley" [Davies (1984: 130)]. In the

Arequipa Valley, adult married men were allotted an area of only about half a hectare.

*Differential taxation and labor levies.* Beginning around 1530, the *encomienda* conferred rights to tribute (in labor, cash, or kind) from a particular region to Europeans, who replaced local overlords. Holders of this privilege (*encomenderos*) were, at least at the beginning, completely unregulated as to how much or what form of tribute to assess [Ramirez (1986)]. While many used labor tributes to cultivate large farms, assessment of tributes in cash did reportedly force Indians to borrow funds and sell off abandoned lands to repay their debt [Davies (1984)]. The right of individual *encomenderos* to the exclusive use of Indian tribute labor for personal services was abolished about 1550, mainly to free labor for public works and the mines. The other benefits of *encomienda* remained, however.

With the abolition of *encomienda*, the Spaniards transformed the *mita*, an Incan institution for recruiting labor for public works projects, into a permanent labor-recruitment arrangement for the mines. In addition to paying tribute to the *encomendero*, each village had to supply a percentage of its work force for "public works", which mostly meant work in the mines. As work for Spanish haciendas exempted from the *mita* and tribute requirements, many workers in the *altiplano* are reported to have accepted work on haciendas. The class of *yanaconas*, who were resident on haciendas and had completely abandoned their tribal identities, emerged [Pearse (1975)].

Slavery was extensive after 1580 in the coastal valleys for the production of sugar, cotton, and wine [Davies (1984)]. When slavery was abolished, sugar plantations resorted to indentured labor from China and Japan, which comprised more than 90 percent of the work force on some estates [Gonzales (1985)]. Other crops, predominantly cotton were, however produced under tenancy contracts [Gonzales (1991)] after slavery was no longer available, suggesting that this form of labor was more profitable than farming the area under large farms.

**Africa**

*Algeria*

*Land market interventions.* With the French occupation, all state, religious, and tribal land became state property; uncultivated and waste land was subject to titling which allowed settlers to acquire land at no price and "amounted to little short than robbery" [Ageron (1991)]. In some cases, such titling left the Muslims with slightly more than 5 percent of the land area and much of the land declared waste included land grazed by nomads in the course of their migrations. Since the number of settlers remained limited, various forms of settlement (including establishment of native villages) were tried to make the colony economically viable.

The desire to impose French rule in Algeria after the 1870/71 rebellion led to initiation of a large colonization and settlement program between 1871 and 1882. At a huge cost to government, settlers were provided free land and infrastructure but either sold out or farmed their land with native sharecroppers [Ageron (1991)]. The so-called "settlers" law' from 1873 allowed Europeans to acquire rights to vast amounts of community land by purchasing a small share thereof and led to the accumulation of vast estates at little cost [Ageron (1991)].

*Differential taxes and labor levies.* Beginning in 1849, all Arabs had to pay head taxes from which those working as sharecroppers or wage laborers on European farms were exempt [Bennoune (1988)]. Still, while "they had always been willing to cultivate for the French as khammes or sharecroppers", at the beginning of the 20th century only about 12 percent of Arabs were working as farm laborers. French viticulturalists relied on foreign, immigrant labor from mediterranean countries. Differential provision of credit to Europeans, led to rapid growth of vine-cultivation. Market fluctuations, together with additional land grants to the newly rich settlers, led to the consolidation of large estates of between 4000 and 5000 ha.

## Angola

*Land market interventions.* In 1838 and again in 1865, all "unoccupied" land could be given as concessions to Europeans. "The settlers were given lands, seeds, tools, and slaves by the government, and measures were taken to ensure that their products could be sold" [Clarence-Smith (1979, 15)]. From 1907 to 1932, 98 square miles were set aside for native reserves, 4 square miles were given to Africans along with land titles, and about 1,800 square miles of the best land was given to Portuguese settlers and other foreigners [Bender (1978)].

*Differential taxation and labor levies.* After the abolition of domestic slavery in 1875, slavery continued in a variety of forms but due to tremendous demand for labor from the cocoa plantations of Sao Tome, prices for slaves increased steadily, making it more profitable to export workers than to use them on inefficient settler farms [Clarence-Smith (1979)]. Vagrancy laws passed in 1875 subjected all "nonproductive" Africans to nonremunerated labor contracts

[Bender (1978)]. The laws were replaced in 1926 by native laws, which provided for payments of wages but retained the provision that all Africans had to work for European landlords or could be contracted by the state [Henderson (1980)].

## Egypt

*Land market interventions.* Land grants of the 1840s gave some 40 percent of the land to Turko-Egyptian landlords and facilitated the formation of large estates [Richards (1982)]. Expropriation of communal lands which took place in 1850–1870, exacerbated this trend. Land taxes in 1856 (per acre) were four to six times higher for smallholders than for the large land holdings [Richards (1982)] and in many cases large landowners did not pay taxes at all [Owen (1986)].

*Differential taxation and labor levies.* In contrast to their usual practice, the Ottomans in the sixteenth century did not distribute Egyptian lands to military leaders but assessed collective tribute. They wished to avoid disrupting agricultural production in Egypt, "the granary of the Ottoman Empire" [Richards (1983: 7)]. Corvée laborers were recruited initially for public works to set up an extensive irrigation system and later for cotton production on the ruler's home farm. Following the large land grants made in the 1840s, "large landowners arranged to have corvée laborers work on their estates and to get their peasants exempted from the corvée" [Richards (1982: 23)], thus closely paralleling events on the Latin American *hacienda*.

Large landowners obtained considerable direct government subsidies for cotton-price stabilization programs in the early 1920s and 1930s, supplemented by an official limitation of the amount to be planted to cotton and financial support to lower interest rates for large landowners which, by the 1930s, were heavily indebted. Similarly, imposition of tariffs on imported flour in 1932 and 1934 and protection of the market for domestically produced sugar, directly supported large landowners [Owen (1986)].

## Kenya[32]

*Land market interventions.* With the arrival of Europeans, all vacant land was declared to be Crown land and sold to European settlers at extremely

---

[32] For more detail on Kenya, South Africa, and Zimbabwe, see Deininger and Binswanger (1994).

favorable conditions. Much of the land continued to be farmed by African tenants, which were called squatters [Mosley (1983)]. Africans' land rights were limited to reserves and a formal prohibition of African land purchases outside the reserves was codified in 1926.

*Differential taxation and labor levies.* The British introduced a number of regressive hut and poll taxes in order to "increase the native's cost of living" [Berman (1990: 509)]. To pay these taxes, Africans initially did not seek wage labor but increased production, mainly on tenanted land. Despite repeated requests from settlers to grant tax-exempt status to Africans working on European farms, such taxes had to be paid by workers as well, thus large estates based on wage labor remained relatively unprofitable as compared to tenancy.

The squatter law from 1918 required tenants to provide at least 180 days a year in labor services to their landlord at a wage not to exceed two-thirds of the wage for unskilled labor. This ordinance was amended twice (in 1926 and 1939), both times increasing the minimum amount of labor services (to 270 days per year in 1939), limiting the area allowed to be cultivated as well as the amount of stock owned per tenant, and making eviction of tenants easier. Labor passes, which had been introduced in 1908, limited the mobility of Africans; leaving without the employer's consent was a criminal offense [Berman (1990)].

*Input and output market interventions.* A dual price system for maize, adopted in the 1930s, reduced the returns African farmers could obtain for the same produce as supplied by their European counterparts and, in addition, unloaded most of the price risk on Africans [Mosley (1983)].

Grower associations that excluded Africans were formed for most of the important cash crops. High licensing fees kept Africans out of pyrethrum production, and they were prohibited outright from cultivating coffee [Berman (1990)].

During World War II, European farmers received direct subsidies to mechanize their farms [Cone and Lipscomb (1972)].

*Sokotho-Caliphate (present day Burkina Faso, Cameroon, Niger, and northern Nigeria)*

*Land market interventions.* After 1804, land was granted to settlers by the caliphate government in the areas around defensive centers, the amount of land depending on the number of slaves owned. Thus "anyone with slaves could obtain enough land to start a plantation" [Lovejoy (1980)]. There were about 100–200 slaves per plantation, although there are reports of officials who managed to obtain holdings of more than 1,000 slaves [Lovejoy (1978)].

*Differential taxation and labor levies.* The pattern of "slavery" in the area, which was populated by Hausa and Fulani, was characteristic of many parts of Africa in the nineteenth century [Lovejoy (1980)].[33] Slaves which made up some 50 to 75 percent of the local population were acquired by warfare, direct seizure, or as tribute from subjected tribes. Limited export markets and the relatively low price of slaves [landowners could replenish their bonded work force through independent raids; Lovejoy (1980)] allowed relatively lenient treatment of slaves who enjoyed more rights, e.g. the possession of heritable house-plots [Hogendorn (1977)] and the right to self-redemption often using funds acquired by cultivating surplus land [Hill (1978)] than the slaves acquired for cash by market-oriented plantations in the Americas. Land and the absence of economies of scale meant, however, that slave owners had to take measures to prevent slaves from escaping and establishing their own operations [Hogendorn (1977)]. Eventually, these factors led to the demise of the large holdings [Hopkins (1973)].

### Malawi

*Land market interventions.* In 1894, Europeans were allotted more than 1.5 million hectares, or about 15 percent of total arable land.

*Differential taxation and labor levies.* Attempts to introduce labor tenancy on European-owned cotton lands were unsuccessful as farmers abandoned the land and fled to uncultivated crown land. The situation improved only as a law was introduced in 1908 which allowed Africans to gain a significant reduction in the head tax they had to pay by working for European cotton growers for at least one month a year. Africans' possibility to gain a similar reduction of the head tax by producing cotton on tenanted land, was, due to landowners' pressure, eliminated [Mandala (1990)].

### Mozambique

*Land market interventions.* Exclusive property rights in land and quasi-governmental authority, the institution of *prazo*, existed since the 17th century

---

[33] There is some discussion in the literature on the appropriate nomenclature for this system, which combines elements of slavery and serfdom.

and were granted for a period of three generations. In the 19th century such property rights were often granted to companies. The prazo-holder had to provide minimal public services, cultivate part of the property, pay quitrent and tithe, but could levy annual tributes (in cash, kind, or labor) on the local population and (see below) was endowed with a complete monopoly on all trade within and outside the area [Vail and White (1980)].

*Differential taxation and labor levies.* Hut taxes were established in 1854. After 1880, at least half of the tax had to be paid to the local *prazo-holder* in the form of labor services [Vail and White (1980)].

Under the vagrancy law of 1899, all male Africans between fourteen and sixty years old were legally obliged to work. The area of crops to be grown or the wage-employment required to satisfy this obligation could be varied by local *prazo*-holders, providing them with ample instruments to increase the supply of labor. Contingents of migratory labor were often "sold" to other areas (such as South Africa) where labor was relatively scarce [Vail and White (1980)]. Vagrancy laws were repealed in 1926 – at about the time many *prazos* were expiring – and the use of forced labor for "private purposes" (i.e. non-quota production) was banned. The labor code of 1942 instituted an obligatory labor requirement of six months for all African men.

*Input and output market interventions.* In 1892 all itinerant African trade within *prazos* was abolished, conferring a monopoly on *prazo*-holders of all commerce in their prazo [Vail and White (1980: 132)]. *Prazos* turned into a kind of mini-state, each with its own closed economy and unlimited freedom for the prazo-holder to determine the terms of trade. As a consequence, African producers almost completely withdrew from cash-crop productions and the *prazos* became "private labor pools from which the companies, by direct force or by indirect manipulation of the economy, could compel the labor they required" [Vail and White (1980: 132)]. Following their expiration about 1930, *prazos* were replaced by a "concession system". Concession holders received monopoly rights to purchase cotton and rice at state-administered low prices from African growers in return for enforcing Africans' work obligations and providing inputs and supervision [Isaacman (1992)]. Although exactions from Africans were still high, (forced) cultivation of all but sugar reverted to smaller scale units rather than large scale farms.

## South Africa

*Land market interventions.* Native reserves were firmly established at the end of the 19th century, although they were legally defined only in 1912. For example in Transvaal in 1870, the area allocated to African reserves was less than a hundredth of the area available to whites [Bundy (1985)].

The Glen Grey Act (1894) restricted African land ownership in the reserves to a parcel of no more than about 3 hectares and instituted a perverted form of "communal tenure" which banned the sale, rental, and subdivision of land in order to prevent the emergence of a class of independent African smallholders [Hendricks (1990)]. The inability to sell land in the reserves, which persists up to this day, is recognized to be the major reason for the low productivity of agriculture in the homelands [Lyne and Nieuwodt (1991)].

Various legal measures to discourage tenancy on European farms, such as a limit on the amount of tenants per farm in 1895 and assessment of license fees for tenants in 1896, did not lead to the desired results. The Native Lands Act (1912) circumscribed the extent of African reserves and declared real tenancy on European farms illegal, forcing all African tenants to either become wage laborers or labor tenants on European farms or to move to the reserves.

*Differential taxes and labor levies.* Prior to state intervention on their behalf, very limited market production by European farmers was based on slaves or, after the prohibition of slavery in 1834, indentured labor.

Masters and Servants Laws and the Mines and Workers Act (1911) restricted Africans' occupational mobility and excluded them from skilled occupations in all sectors except agriculture [Lipton (1985)]. Restrictions on mobility were reinforced and tightened by pass laws (influx controls) from 1922 and the establishment of labor bureaus to enforce the legislation from 1951 [Lipton (1985)].

In addition to restricting Africans' ability to obtain jobs outside agriculture, more rigid pass laws and rigorous enforcement of such laws also provided a flow of cheap labor for white agriculturalists. It is estimated that, in 1949, about 40,000 pass-law offenders were supplied to farms as prison laborers [Wilson (1971)].

*Input and output market interventions.* European farmers were assisted by a large array of monopolistic commodity marketing boards and direct credit subsidies. In 1967, the amount spent on subsidizing about 100,000 white farms was almost double the amount spent on education for more than 10 million Africans [Wilson (1971)].

*Tanganyika (part of present day Tanzania)*

*Land market interventions.* From the late 1890s until 1904 it was common practice to allocate several villages apiece to incoming German settlers.

*Differential taxation and labor levies.* A hut tax, to be paid in cash or labor services, was imposed in 1896 "not so much for the revenue which resulted but as a means of propelling them into the labor market" [Rodney (1979, 131)] although half of the hut-tax income went directly to settlers' District Councils. Village headmen were required to provide a fixed number of workers each day to provide labor for the settlers to cultivate their rubber and sisal plantations. Every African was issued a work card that obligated him to render services to an employer for 120 days a year at a fixed wage or else to work on public projects [Illife (1979)]. In 1902, the Germans introduced compulsory cotton production in certain coastal areas; it is widely accepted that this scheme was one of the main causes leading to the outbreak of the Maji Maji revolt in 1905 [Coulson (1982)].

Africans were excluded from credit by the Credit to Natives Ordinance of 1931 which required that an African have specific government permission before he could even request a bank to lend him money [Coulson (1982)]. Attempts by Africans to set up a marketing cooperative for coffee led to the attempt to outlaw traditional practices of coffee growing in 1937, which led to riots. Settler-dominated marketing monopolies for African-grown crops were set up in the 1940s and creamed off most of the profits from those crops [Coulson (1982)].

## Zimbabwe

*Land market interventions.* Reserves for Africans in remote areas of often low fertility were established in 1896 although their boundaries underwent some changes until 1931 [Palmer (1977)], when African land purchases outside the reserves and specifically designated "African Purchase Areas" were declared illegal.

*Differential taxation and labor levies.* While all Africans were subject to poll and hut taxes, specific taxes discriminated against cash rental and share tenancy contracts from 1909 [Palmer (1979)]. The prospect of (temporarily) easing the tax load led to large-scale migration of Africans into the reserves when commodity prices were extremely low in the early 1920s [Arrighi (1970)].

*Input and output market interventions.* Volatility and downturns in output markets were smoothed by government interventions such as increased land bank loans, debt moratoria (especially during the depression in 1930) and, after protracted lobbying by European producers, the establishment of monopoly marketing boards (for tobacco, dairy, pigs, and cotton) in selected crops and the establishment of export subsidies.

African maize and livestock producers were discriminated against by dual price systems. Pressure by European miners who were interested in cheap supplies of maize limited the extent of price discrimination against African producers in maize. Quarantine-based restrictions on African livestock sales initially led to the buildup of large herds and the associated soil degradation in the reserves. To ease this problem, in 1939, compulsory destocking was mandated; prices paid for African cattle were between one third and one sixth of the prices fetched for comparable European stock [Mosley (1983)].

## Appendix 2

### How market imperfections affect the farm size – productivity relation[34]

Consider a region where each farm household consists of $F$ family members capable of conducting farm operations as well as supervising the work of hired laborers. The household owns $V$ acres of land, but the size of farm it actually operates, denoted by $A$, is determined through renting in or renting out land at the going rental rate $R$. Output depends on effective labor $(L)$ and land $(A)$. Effective labor is defined as the product of the number of individuals employed and the effort $(e)$ they exert. While family members can be expected to perform farm tasks with maximum effort, say $\bar{e}$, hired laborers' work effort depends on the intensity of supervision. The intensity of supervision is represented by the ratio of household members to operational farm size $(F/A)$. It is assumed that the marginal returns to supervision intensity are diminishing,

$$e = e(F/A), \ e' > 0, \ e'' < 0, \ \lim_{F/A \to \infty} e = \bar{e} \tag{1}$$

With $N$ hired laborers per operated acre and a total of $F$ household members, the effective labor input is given by

$$L = F \cdot \bar{e} + A \cdot N \cdot e(F/A) . \tag{2}$$

Output is determined by a neoclassical production function that depends on effective labor and land,

$$Q = Q(L, A) . \tag{3}$$

Assuming constant returns to scale, and substituting equation 2 in equation 3, output per operated acre is given by

[34] This appendix is based on Feder (1985).

$$q = Q[\bar{e} \cdot (F/A) + N \cdot e(F/A);1] = q[\bar{e} \cdot (F/A) + N \cdot e(F/A)] , \tag{4}$$

where $q = Q/A$ and $q' > 0$, $q'' < 0$.

A simple but realistic way to introduce a credit market imperfection to the present model is to assume that the supply of credit depends on the amount of land owned by the household, denoted $S$:

$$S = S(V), \; S' > 0 . \tag{5}$$

With the wage rate denoted by $w$, intermediate input costs per acre by $c$, and cash consumption expenditures per family member during the season by $\theta$, the cash requirements of a family with an operational holding of size $A$ are $w \cdot N \cdot A + c \cdot A + R \cdot (A - V) + \theta \cdot F$, and the working capital constraint faced by the farm is:

$$w \cdot N \cdot A + c \cdot A + R \cdot (A - V) + \theta \cdot F \leq S(V). \tag{6}$$

The farmer's objective is to maximize end-of-season profits (accounting for interest charges $i$ per dollar borrowed), subject to the working capital constraint. Formally,

$$\max_{A,N} \prod = A \cdot q[\bar{e} \cdot (F/A) + N \cdot e(F/A)]$$
$$-[w \cdot N \cdot A + c \cdot A + R \cdot (A - V)] \cdot (1 + i) ,$$

subject to inequality (6) and $A \geq 0$, $N \geq 0$.

Defining the Lagrangean function $\Psi \equiv \prod + \lambda \cdot [S(V) - w \cdot N \cdot A - c \cdot A - R \cdot (A - V) - \theta \cdot F]$, where $\lambda$ is the shadow price of the credit constraint, the Kuhn-Tucker conditions for optimization imply:

$$\frac{\partial \psi}{\partial A} = q - q' \cdot [e \cdot [F/A] + N \cdot (F/A) \cdot e'] - (w \cdot N + c + R) \cdot (1 + i + \lambda)$$
$$\leq 0 , \tag{7a}$$

$$\frac{\partial \psi}{\partial A} \cdot A = 0 , \tag{7b}$$

$$\frac{1}{A} \cdot \frac{\partial \psi}{\partial N} = e \cdot q' - w \cdot (1 + i + \lambda) \leq 0 , \tag{8a}$$

$$\frac{\partial \psi}{\partial N} \cdot N = 0 \,, \tag{8b}$$

$$\frac{\partial \psi}{\partial \lambda} = S(v) - w \cdot N \cdot A - c \cdot A - R \cdot (A - V) - \theta \cdot F \geq 0 \,, \tag{9a}$$

$$\frac{\partial \psi}{\partial \lambda} \cdot \lambda = 0 \tag{9b}$$

$$A \geq 0, \ N \geq 0, \ \lambda \geq 0 \,, \tag{10}$$

We start with the case in which the credit constraint is not binding ($\lambda = 0$); solving first-order conditions (7a) and (8a) for the optimal values of $A$ and $N$ and differentiating yields:

$$\frac{\mathrm{d}A}{\mathrm{d}F} = \frac{A}{F} \tag{11}$$

and

$$\frac{\mathrm{d}N}{\mathrm{d}F} = 0 \,. \tag{12}$$

Equation (11) implies that in the absence of binding credit constraints, the elasticity of the optimal operational size with respect to household size is unity, i.e. there is a fixed operational holding to household size ratio. The amount of owned land does not affect the optimal ratio. This outcome is intuitively expected in a situation of constant returns to scale with perfect rental and capital markets.

Equation (12) implies that the optimal number of hired laborers per acre is not affected by household size (neither is it affected by the size of the owned holding). Since the earlier results imply that the operational holding is proportional to household size, it follows that the number of hired laborers per acre is identical on all farms, whatever the size of the operational holding (and that the ratio of family to hired labor declines with operational holding size). A trivial extension of these results is the observation that the level of effective labor per acre is identical on all farms (since the ratio $F/A$ is fixed and $N$ is the same on all farms), assuming all other farm and farmer attributes are identical. It therefore follows that output per unit of land operated is not affected by the size of the operational farm or by the amount of land owned.

The analysis and the presentation in the case where the credit constraint is binding ($\lambda > 0$) are greatly simplified by assuming that the functions $q(\cdot)$ and $e(\cdot)$ are of fixed elasticity with respect to their arguments, that is, that $(q'/q) \cdot (L/A) \equiv \eta$, the elasticity of output with respect to effective labor, and $(e'/e) \cdot (F/A) \equiv \mu$, the elasticity of effort with respect to supervision, and where

$\mu$ and $\eta$ are parameters within the interval $(0, 1)$. The standard treatment of labor in the literature – the assumption that hired labor is not affected by family supervision – is then the special case $\mu = 0$ in the present model.

Differentiation of equations (7a), (8a), (9a), under the assumption of an internal solution, yields after some manipulation

$$\frac{dA}{dV} = \frac{(1 - \eta - \eta \cdot \mu) \cdot \dfrac{(S' + R)}{w}}{\dfrac{(1 - \eta \cdot \mu) \cdot (c + R)}{w} - \dfrac{\mu \cdot (1 - \eta) \cdot \bar{e} \cdot F}{e \cdot A}} \tag{13}$$

The denominator can be shown to be positive if second-order conditions hold. It follows that the sign of equation (13) is determined by the sign of $(1 - \eta - \eta \cdot \mu)$, which is the limit value of total output elasticity with respect to land as the share of family labor tends to zero.

To demonstrate that the relation between per-hectare yields and operational holding size can follow different patterns within the framework of the present model, we use the definition of effective labor and the first-order conditions to calculate the optimal per-hectare input of labor:

$$(L/A)^* = \eta\{[c + R] \cdot e/w] - [\mu \cdot \bar{e} \cdot F/A]\}/(1 - \eta - \eta \cdot \mu) . \tag{14}$$

Differentiation of equation 14 with respect to owned holding size $V$ yields

$$\frac{d(L/A)^*}{dV} = \mu \cdot \eta \cdot \left[\frac{\bar{e}}{e} \cdot \frac{F}{A} - \frac{c + R}{w}\right] \cdot \frac{e}{A} \cdot \frac{dA}{dV}\bigg|(1 - \eta - \eta \cdot \mu) . \tag{15}$$

Clearly, if the labor market is perfect ($\mu = 0$), labor per hectare of land does not vary with farm size. Inspection of equation 13 verifies that **dV** and the sign of equation 15 thus depends on the term in square brackets.

In the case where $1 - \eta - \eta \cdot \mu > 0$, the relation between the effective labor input per hectare and owned holding size can be negative or positive. Consider, for instance, the case where the output elasticity $\eta$ equals $\frac{1}{2}$. First-order conditions imply $[(1 - \eta)(\bar{e}/e)] \cdot (F/A) - \eta \cdot [(c + R)/w] < 0$, hence, in the case where $\eta = \frac{1}{2}$, it follows that $d(L/A)/dV < 0$, i.e. the effective labor input (and yields) declines with owned holding size. The same result can be obtained for all $\eta < \frac{1}{2}$. By an argument of continuity, since in the case $(1 - \eta - \eta \cdot \mu) = 0$ it holds that $d(L/A)/dV > 0$ (in that case there is a finite operational farm size regardless of wealth), there must exist some low (but positive) values of the term $(1 - \eta - \eta \cdot \mu)$ for which $d(L/A)/dV > 0$ holds. The conclusion is, therefore, that one may observe a positive or a negative relation between operational holding size and per-hectare yields, depending on the relative magnitudes of $\eta$ and $\mu$. In the case $(1 - \eta - \eta \cdot \mu) = 0$ there will be no correlation between operational holding size and per-hectare yields.

# References

Abdullah, A. (1974) 'Land reform and agrarian change in Bangladesh', *Bangladesh Development Studies*, 2:67–99.

Abercombie, K.C. (1972) 'Agricultural mechanization and employment in Latin America', *International Labour Review*, 106:11–45.

Anderson, J.R. and Powell, R.A. (1973) 'Economics of size in Australian farming', *Australian Journal of Agricultural Economics*, 17:1–8.

Anderson, T.L. and Lueck, D. (1992) 'Land tenure and agricultural productivity on Indian reservations', *Journal of Law and Economics*, 35:427–454.

Alston, L.J., Datta S.K. and Nugent, J.B. (1984) 'Tenancy choice in a competitive framework with transaction costs', *Journal of Political Economy*, 92:1121–1133.

Asako, K. (1991) 'The land price bubble in Japan', *Ricerche Economiche*, 45:167–184.

Aston, T.H. and Philpin, C.H.E. eds. (1985), *The Brenner debate: Agrarian class structure and economic development in pre-industrial Europe*. New York: Cambridge University Press.

Atwood, D.A. (1990) 'Land registration in Africa: the impact on agricultural production', *World Development*, 18:659–671.

Barham, B.L. and Childress, M. (1992) 'Membership desertion as an adjustment process on Honduran agrarian reform enterprises', *Economic Development and Cultural Change*, 40:587–613.

Barraclough, S. and Collarte, J.C. (1973) *Agrarian structure in Latin America: A resume of the CIDA land tenure studies of Argentina, Brazil, Chile, Colombia, Ecuador, Guatemala and Peru*. Lexington, MA: Lexington Books.

Barrows, R. and Neuman, M. (1990) A review of experience with land zoning. Land Tenure Center, mimeo.

Barrows, R. and Roth, M. (1990), 'Land tenure and investment in African agriculture: Theory and evidence', *Journal of Modern African Studies*, 28:265–297.

Bates, R.H. 1989, *Beyond the miracle of the market. The political economy of agrarian development in Kenya*, Cambridge: Cambridge University Press.

Batte, M.T. and Sonka, S.T. (1985), 'Before- and after-tax size economies: An example for cash grain production in Illinois', *American Journal of Agricultural Economics*, 67:600–608.

Bell, C. (1977) 'Alternative theories of sharecropping: Some tests using evidence from northeast India', *Journal of Development Studies*, 13:317–346.

Bell, C. (1988) 'Credit markets and interlinked transactions', in: H. Chenery and T.N. Srinivasan, eds., *Handbook of development economics*. Vol. I. Amsterdam, North-Holland.

Ben-Ner, A. (1984) 'On the stability of the cooperative type of organization', *Journal of Comparative Economics*, 8:247–260.

Benjamin, D. (1992) 'Household composition, labor markets and labor demand: Testing for separability in agricultural household models', *Econometrica*, 60:287–322.

Bentley, J. (1987) Economic and ecological approaches to land fragmentation: In defense of a much-maligned phenomenon', *Ann. Rev. Anthropol*, 16:31–67.

Berry, R.A. and Cline, W.R. (1979) *Agrarian structure and productivity in developing countries*. Geneva: ILO.

Bhaduri, A. (1976) 'The evolution of land relations in eastern India under British rule', *Indian Economic and Social History Review*, 13:45-58.

Bhaduri, A. (1986) 'Forced commerce and agrarian growth', *World Development*, 14:267–272 .

Bhalla, S.S. and Roy, P. (1988) 'Mis-specification in farm productivity analysis: The role of land quality', *Oxford Economic Papers*, 40:55–73.

Bidinger, P.D., Walker, T.S., Sarkar, B., Murty, A.R. and Babu, P. (1991) 'Consequences of mid-1980s drought: Longitudinal evidence from Mahbubnagar', *Economic and Political Weekly*, 26:A105–A114.

Binswanger, H.P. (1989) 'Brazilian policies that encourage deforestation in the Amazon', *World Development*, 19:821–829.

Binswanger, H.P. and Deininger, K. (1993) 'South African land policy: The legacy of history and current options', *World Development*, 21(9):1451–1475.

Binswanger, H.P. and Elgin M. (1988) 'What are the prospects for land reform', in: A. Maunder and A. Valdes, eds., *Agriculture and governments in an interdependent world*. Proceedings of the Twentieth International Conference of Agricultural Economists, 1988.

Binswanger, H.P. and McIntire, J. (1987) 'Behavioral and material determinants of production relations in land abundant tropical agriculture', *Economic Development and Cultural Change*, 36:75–99.

Binswanger, H.P. and Rosenzweig, M.R. (1986), 'Behavioral and material determinants of production relations in agriculture', *Journal of Development Studies*, 22:503–539.

Bird, R. (1974) *Taxing agricultural land in developing countries*. Cambridge, MA: Harvard University Press.

Blarel, B., Hazell, P., Place, F. and Quiggin, J. (1992) 'The economics of farm fragmentation: Evidence from Ghana and Rwanda', *World Bank Economic Review*, 6:233–254.

Bliss, C.J. and Stern, N.H. (1982) *Palanpur: The economy of an Indian village*. Oxford: Clarendon Press.

Blum, J. (1977) *The end of the old order in rural Europe*. Princeton, NJ: Princeton University Press.

Boldt, R.A. (1989) 'The effects of land title on small farm production in the highlands of Ecuador', Land Tenure Center Research Paper. 30.

Bonin, J.P. (1985) 'Labor management and capital maintenance: Investment decisions in the socialist labor-managed firm', in: D.C. Jones and J. Svejnar, eds., *Advances in the economic analysis of participatory and labor managed firms*. Vol. I, Greenwich, CT: JAI Press.

Bonin, J.P. and Putterman, L. (1986) *Economics of cooperation and the labor-managed economy*, Fundamentals of Pure and Applied Economics 14. Harwood Academic Publishers.

Boserup, E. (1965) *Conditions of agricultural growth*, Chicago: Aldine Publishing Company.

Britton, D.K. and Hill, B. (1975), *Size and efficiency in farming*, Farnborough, Hants: Saxon House.

Brading, D.A. (1977) 'The transition from traditional hacienda to capitalist estate', in: K. Duncan and I. Rutledge, *Land and labour in Latin America*, Cambridge: Cambridge University Press.

Brandao, A.S.P. and de Rezende, G.C. (1992) Credit subsidies, inflation and the land market in Brazil: A theoretical and empirical analysis, Washington: World Bank, mimeo.

Braverman, A. and Stiglitz J.E. (1982) 'Sharecropping and the interlinking of agrarian markets', *American Economic Review*, 72:695–715.

Braverman, A. and Srinivasan, T.N. (1981) 'Credit and sharecropping in agrarian societies', *Journal of Development Economics*, 9:289–312.

Brenner, R. (1976) 'The origins of capitalist development: A critique of neo-Smithsian Marxism', *New Left Review*, 104:25–92.

Brockett, C.D. (1984) 'Malnutrition, public policy and agrarian change in Guatemala', *Journal of Interamerican Studies and World Affairs*, 26:477–497.

Brown, M.R. (1989) 'Radical reformism in Chile:1964–1973', in: W. Thiesenhusen, ed., *Searching for agrarian reform in Latin America*, Boston: Unwyn Hyman.

Bruce, J.W. (1988) 'A perspective on indigenous land tenure systems and land concentration', in: R.W. Downs and S.P. Reyna, eds., *Land and society in contemporary Africa*.

Burt, O. (1986) 'Econometric modeling of the capitalization formula for farmland prices', *American Journal of Agricultural Economics*, 68:10–26.

Caballero, J.M. (1983) 'Casual labor in Peruvian agrarian cooperatives', in: F. Steward, ed., *Work, income and inequality*.

Cain, M. (1981) 'Risk and insurance: Perspectives on fertility and agrarian change in India and Bangladesh', *Population and Development Review*, 7:435–474.

Callison, C.S. (1983) 'Land to the tiller in the Mekong delta: Economic, social and political consequences of land reform in four villages of South Vietnam', Bloomington, IN: University Press of America.

Cambranes, J.C. (1985) *Coffee and peasants in Guatemala*. Stockholm.

Carter, M.R. (1984) 'Identification of the inverse relationship between farm size and productivity: An empirical analysis of peasant agricultural production', *Oxford Economic Papers*, 36:131–145.

Carter, M.R. (1987) 'Risk sharing and incentives in the decollectivization of agriculture', *Oxford Economic Papers*, 39:577–595.

Carter, M.R. (1989) 'The impact of credit on peasant productivity and differentiation in Nicaragua', *Journal of Development Economics*, 31:13–36.

Carter, M.R. and Kalfayan, J. (1989) 'A general equilibrium exploration of the agrarian question', Madison, Wisconsin, mimeo.

Carter, M.R. and Wiebe, K.D. (1990) 'Access to capital and its impact on agrarian structure and productivity in Kenya', *American Journal of Agricultural Economics*, 72:1146–1150.

Castillo, L. and Lehman, D. (1983) 'Agrarian reform and structural change in Chile, 1965–1979', in: A.K. Ghose, ed., *Agrarian reform in contemporary developing countries*. New York: St. Martins Press.

Chavas, J.P. and Aliber, M. (1992) 'An analysis of economic efficiency in agriculture: A nonparametric approach'. mimeo.

Chayanov, A.V. (1991) *The theory of peasant cooperatives*. Ohio State University Press.

Cheung, N.S. (1969) *The theory of share tenancy*. Chicago: University of Chicago Press.

Chevalier, F. (1963) *Land and society in colonial Mexico: The great hacienda*. University of California Press.

Christensen, G.N. (1989) *Determinants of private investment in rural Burkina Faso*. Dissertation, Cornell University, Ithaca, New York.

Christodoulou, C. (1990) *The unpromised land: Agrarian reform and conflict worldwide*. London: Zed Books.

Chuma, H., Otsuka, K. and Hayami, Y. (1990) 'On the dominance of land tenancy over permanent labor contract in agrarian economies', *Journal of the Japanese and International Economies*, 4:101–120.

Cline, W.R. (1970) *Economic consequences of a land reform in Brazil*. Amsterdam: North-Holland.

Colburn, F.D. (1990) *Managing the commanding heights: Nicaragua's state enterprises*. Berkeley, University of California Press.

Collier, P. (1989) 'Contractual constraints on labour exchange in rural Kenya', *International Labour Review*, 128: 745–768.

Cornia, G.A. (1985) 'Farm size, land yields and the agricultural production function: An analysis of fifteen developing countries', *World Development*, 13:513–534.

Courtenay, P.P. (1980) *Plantation agriculture*, Boulder, CO: Westview Press.

Dasgupta, P. and Ray, D. (1986) 'Inequality as a determinant of malnutrition and unemployment: Theory', *Economic Journal*, 96:1011–1034.

Dasgupta, P. and Ray, D. (1987) 'Inequality as a determinant of malnutrition and unemployment: Policy', *Economic Journal*, 97:177–188.

Davis, S.H. (1983) 'State violence and agrarian crisis in Guatemala', in: M. Diskin, ed., *Trouble in our backyard: Central America and the United States in the eighties*. New York: Pantheon Books.

De Janvry, A. (1981) *The agrarian question and reformism in Latin America*. Baltimore, MD: Johns Hopkins University Press.

De Janvry, A. and Sadoulet, E. 1993, 'Path dependent policy reforms: From land reform to rural development in Colombia', in: K. Hoff, A. Braverman, J. Stiglitz, eds., *The economics of rural organization*. Oxford University Press.

De Janvry, A. and Sadoulet, E. (1989) 'A study in resistance to institutional change: The lost game of Latin American land reform', *World Development*, 17:1397–1407.

De Janvry, A., Sadoulet, E. and Wilcox Young, L. (1989) 'Land and labour in Latin American agriculture from the 1950s to the 1980s', *Journal of Peasant Studies*, 16:396–424.

De Meza, D. and Gould, J.R. (1992), 'The social efficiency of private decisions to enforce property rights', *Journal of Political Economy*, 100:561–580.

Deaton, A. (1989) 'Savings in developing countries: Theory and review', Woodrow Wilson School, Princeton University Discussion Paper 144.

Deaton, A. (1991) 'Household savings in LDC's: Credit markets, insurance and welfare', Woodrow Wilson School, Princeton University, Discussion Paper 153.

Deininger, K. (1993) *Cooperatives and the breakup of large mechanized farms: Theoretical perspectives and empirical evidence*. World Bank Discussion Paper 218, Washington, DC.

Deininger, K. and Binswanger, H.P. (1993) Rent seeking and the development of agriculture in Kenya, South Africa and Zimbabwe, *Economic development and cultural change*. forthcoming.

Deolalikar, A.B. (1981) 'The inverse relationship between productivity and farm size: A test using regional data from India', *American Journal of Agricultural Economics*, 71:275–279.

Diba, B.T. and Grossman, H.I. (1988) 'The theory of rational bubbles in stock prices', *Economic Journal*, 98:746–54.

Dobb, M. (1963) *Studies in the development of capitalism*. London: Routledge and Keegan Paul.

Domar, E.D. (1970) 'The causes of slavery or serfdom: A hypothesis', *Journal of Economic History*, 30:18–32.

Don, Y. (1985) 'The economics of transformation from agricultural to agro-industrial production cooperatives: The case of the Israeli kibbutz', in: E. Duelfer and W. Hamm, eds., *Cooperatives in the clash between member participation*. Organizational Development.

Dorner, P. and Thiesenhusen, W.C. (1990) 'Selected land reforms in East and Southeast Asia: Their origins and impacts', *Asian Pacific Economic Literature*, 4:69–95.

Downs, R.W. and Reyna, S.P., eds., *Land and society in contemporary Africa*. Hanover and London: Published for University of New Hampshire by University Press of New England.

Elder, J.W. (1962) 'Land consolidation in an Indian village: A case study of the consolidation of holdings act in Uttar Pradesh', *Economic Development and Cultural Change*, 11:16–40.

Ellis, F. (1983) 'Las transnacionales del banano en centroamerica', Editorial Universitaria Centroamericana, San Jose, Costa Rica.

Eswaran, M, Kotwal, A. 'Access to capital and agrarian production organisation', *Economic Journal*, 96:482–498.

Evans, R.J. and Lee, W.R., eds. (1985), *The German peasantry: Conflict and community in rural society from the eighteenth century to the present*. London.

Falk, B. (1991) 'Formally testing the present value model of farmland prices', *American Journal of Agricultural Economics*, 73:1–10.

Fan, S. (1991) 'Effects of technological change and institutional reform on production and growth in Chinese agriculture', *American Journal of Agricultural Economics*, 73:266–275 .

Feder, G. 1993, 'The economics of land and titling in Thailand', in: K. Hoff, A. Braverman and J. Stiglitz, eds., *The economics of rural organization*. Oxford University Press.

Feder, G., Onchan, T., Chalamwong, Y. and Hongladarom C. (1986) *Land policies and farm productivity in Thailand*. Baltimore, MD: John Hopkins University Press.

Feder, G. (1985) 'The relation between farm size and farm productivity: The role of family labor, supervision and credit constraints', *Journal of Development Economics*, 18:297–313.

Feder, G. and Feeny, D. (1991) 'Land tenure and property rights: Theory and implications for development policy', *World Bank Economic Review*, 5:135–155.

Feder, G., Onchan, T. and Raparla, T. (1988) 'Collateral, guarantees and rural credit in developing countries: Evidence from Asia', *Agricultural Economics*, 2:231–245.

Feeny, D. (1988) 'The development of property rights in land: A comparative study', in: R.H. Bates, ed., *Toward a political economy of development: A rational choice perspective*. Berkeley: University of California Press.

Feldstein, M. (1980) 'Inflation, portfolio choice and the prices of land and corporate stock', *American Journal of Agricultural Economics*, 62:910–916.

Fenoaltea, S. (1976) 'Risk, transaction costs and the organization of medieval agriculture', *Explorations in Economic History*, 13:129–175.

Finkler, K. (1978) 'From sharecroppers to entrepreneurs: Peasant household production strategies under the edged system of Mexico', *Economic Development and Cultural Change*.

Florescano, E. (1969) 'Precios del maiz y crisis agricolas en Mexico (1708–1810): Ensayo sobre el movimiento de los precios y sus consecuencias economicas y sociales', Mexico.

Fogel, R.E. (1971) *The reinterpretation of American economic history*. New York: Harper and Row.

Forster, N.R. (1992) 'Protecting fragile lands: New reasons to tackle old problems', *World Development*, 20:571–585.

Fujimoto, A. (1988) 'The economics of land tenure and rice production in a double-cropping village in southern Thailand', *Developing Economies*, 26:189–211.

Gerschenkron, A. (1965) 'Agrarian politics and industrialization in Russia, 1861–1917', *Cambridge Economic History of Europe*. Vol. 6.

Ghai, D., Kay, C. and Peek, P. (1988) 'Labour and development in rural Cuba', Geneva: ILO and Macmillan Press.

Graham, D.H., Gauthier, H. and de Barros, J.R.M. (1987) 'Thirty years of agricultural growth in Brazil: Crop performance, regional profile and recent policy review', *Economic Development and Cultural Change*, , 1–34.

Griffin, K. and Hay, R. (1985) 'Problems of agricultural development in socialist Ethiopia: An overview and suggested strategy', *Journal of Peasant Studies*, 13:37–66.

Glover, D. (1990) 'Contract farming and outgrower schemes in East and Southern Africa', *Journal of Agricultural Economics*, 41:303–315.

Goldstone, J.A. (1992), *Revolution and rebellion in the early modern world*, Berkeley: University of California Press.

Goodman, D. and Redclift, M. 1982, *From peasant to proletarian: Capitalist development and agrarian transition*. New York: St. Martin's Press.

Grandin, B. (1989) 'Land tenure, subdivision and residential change on a Maasai group ranch', *Institute for Development Anthropology Newsletter*, 9–13.

Grigg, D.B. (1974) *The agricultural systems of the world*. Cambridge University Press.

Grindle, M.S. (1990) 'Agrarian reform in Mexico: A cautionary tale', in: R.L. Prosterman, et al., *Agrarian reform and grassroots development: Ten case studies*. Boulder, CO: Lyenne Rienner Publishers.

Hagen, W.W. (1985a) 'How mighty the Junkers? Peasant rents and seigneurial profits in sixteenth-century Brandenburg', *Past and Present*, 108:80–116.

Hagen, W.W. (1985b) 'The Junkers' faithless servants: Peasant insubordination and the breakdown of serfdom in Brandenburg–Prussia, 1763–1811', in: R.J. Evans and W.R. Lee, eds., *The German peasantry*.

Hamid, N. (1982) 'Dispossession and differentiation of the peasantry in the Punjab during colonial rule', *Journal of Peasant Studies*, 10:52–72.

Hayami, Y. and Kikuchi, M. (1984) *Asian village economy at the crossroads: An economic approach to institutional change*. University of Tokyo Press.

Hayami, Y., Quisumbing, M.A.R. and Adriano, L.S. (1990) *Toward an alternative land reform paradigm: A Philippine perspective:* Manila: Ateneo de Manila University Press.

Hazell, P., Pomareda, C. and Valdes, A. (1986) *Crop insurance for agricultural development: Issues and experience*. Baltimore, MD: John Hopkins University Press.

Heath, J.R. (1992) 'Evaluating the impact of Mexico's land reform on agricultural productivity', *World Development*, 20:695–711.

Hendricks, F.T. (1990) *The pillars of apartheid land tenure, rural planning, and the chieftaincy*, Uppsala, Sweden: Almquist & Wiksell.

Henneberry, D.M. and Barrows, R.L. (1990), 'Capitalization of exclusive agricultural zoning into farmland prices', *Land Economics*, 66:249–258.

Heston, A. and Kumar, D. (1983) 'The persistence of land fragmentation in peasant agriculture: South Asia', *Explorations in Economic History*, 20:199–220.

Hilton, R. ed. (1978) *The transition from feudalism to capitalism*, London: New Left Books.

Hoff, K. (1991) 'Land taxes, output taxes and sharecropping: Was Henry George right? *World Bank Economic Review*, 5:93–111.

Horton, D.E. (1976) 'Haciendas and cooperatives: A study of estate organization, land reform and new reform enterprises in Peru', Ithaca, NY: Ph.D. dissertation, Cornell University.

Huizer, G. (1972) *The revolutionary potential of peasants in Latin America*. Lexington, MA: Lexington Books.

Iliffe, J. (1979) *A modern history of Tanganyika*, Cambridge University Press.

Inter-American Development Bank (IDB), (1986) 'Jamaica land titling project: Feasibility report', Washington, DC.

Isaacman, A. and Isaacman, B. (1983) *Mozambique: From colonialism to revolution, 1900–1982*. Boulder, CO: Westview Press.

Jarvis, L.S. (1985) *Chilean agriculture under military rule: From reform to reaction, 1973–1980*. Institute of International Studies, University of California, Berkeley.

Jarvis, L.S. (1989) 'The unraveling of Chile's agrarian reform, 1973–1986', in: W. Thiesenhusen, ed., *Searching for agrarian reform in Latin America*.

Jodha, N.S. (1975) 'Famine and famine policies: Some empirical evidence', *Economic and Political Weekly*, 5:1609–1623.

Jodha, N.S. (1986) 'Common property resources and rural poor in dry regions of India', *Economic and Political Weekly*, 21:1169–1181.

Jodha, N.S. (1990) 'Rural common property resources: Contributions and crisis', *Economic and Political Weekly*, 25:A65–A78.

Just, R.E. and Miranowski, J.A. (1989) 'U.S. land prices: Trends and determinants', in: A. Maunder and A. Valdes, eds., *Agriculture and governments in an interdependent world*. Proceedings of the Twentieth International. Conference of Agricultural Economists, 1988.

Kay, C. (1983) 'The agrarian reform in Peru: An assessment', in: A.K. Ghose, ed., *Agrarian reform in contemporary developing countries*. London: St. Martin's Press.

Kay, C. and Silva, P. eds. (1992) *Development and social change in the Chilean countryside: From the pre-land reform period to the democratic transition*. Amsterdam: CEDLA.

King, R. (1977) *Land reform: A world survey*. London: G. Bell and Sons.

Kislev, Y. and W. Peterson (1982), 'Prices, technology and farm size', *Journal of Political Economy* 90:578–595.

Klein, H.S. and Engerman, S.L. (1985) 'The transition from slave to free labor: Notes on a comparative economic model', in: M.M. Fraginals, F.M. Ponse and S.L. Engerman, *Between slavery and free labor: The Spanish-speaking Caribbean in the nineteenth century*, Baltimore MD: Johns Hopkins University Press.

Koo, A.Y.C. (1968) *Land reform and economic development: A case study of Taiwan*. New York: Praeger.

Kriger, N.J. (1992) *Zimbabwe's guerrilla war: Peasant voices*. Cambridge: Cambridge University Press.

Krueger, A.O., Schiff, M. and Valdes, A. (1991) *The political economy of agricultural pricing policy*, Vol. 5, Summary and conclusions, Baltimore, MD: Johns Hopkins University Press.

Kutcher, G.P. and Scandizzo, P.L. (1981) *The agricultural economy of Northeast Brazil*. Washington, DC: The World Bank.

Laffont, J.J. and Matoussi, M.S. (1988) 'Moral hazard, financial constraints and sharecropping in El Oulja', Californian Institute of Technology and Social Science Working Paper 667.

Larson, B.A. and Bromley, D.W. (1990) 'Property rights, externalities and resource degradation: Locating the tragedy', *Journal of Development Economics*, 33:235–262.

Lau, L.J. and Yotopoulos, P.A. (1971), 'A test for relative efficiency and application to Indian agriculture', *American Economic Review*, 61:94–109.

Lau, L.J. and Yotopoulos, P.A. (1979) eds., 'Resource use in agriculture: Applications of the profit function to selected countries', *Food Research Institute Studies*, 17:1–115.

Lawry, S.W. (1990), 'Tenure policy towards common property natural resources in sub-Saharan Africa', *Natural Resources Journal*, 30:403–422.

Le Roy Ladurie, E. (1974) *The peasants of Languedoc*. Urbana: University of Illinois Press.

Lehmann, D. (1986) 'Sharecropping and the capitalist transition in agriculture: Some evidence from the highlands of Ecuador', *Journal of Development Studies*, 23:333–354.

Lenin, V.I., *The development of capitalism in Russia*. Moscow: Progress Publishers 1974.

Leo, C. (1978) 'The failure of the "progressive farmer" in Kenya's million-acre settlement scheme', *Journal of Modern African Studies*, 16:619–678.

Leys, C. (1974) *Underdevelopment in Kenya: The political economy of neo-colonialism, 1964–1971*. Berkeley: University of California Press.

Libecap, G.D. (1986) 'Property rights in economic history: Implications for research', *Explorations in Economic History*, 23:227–252.

Lin, J.Y. (1990) 'Collectivization and China's agricultural crisis in 1959–1961', *Journal of Political Economy*, 98:1228–1249.

Lin, J.Y. (1991) 'The household responsibility system reform and the adoption of hybrid rice in China', *Journal of Development Economics*, 36:353–372.

Lin, J.Y. (1992) 'Rural reforms and agricultural growth in China', *American Economic Review*, 82:34–51.

Lindo-Fuentes, H. (1990) *Weak foundations, the economy of El Salvador in the nineteenth century*. University of California Press.

Lipsey, R.G. and Lancaster, K. (1956/57) 'The general theory of the second best', *Review of Economic Studies*, 24:11–32.

Loveman, B. (1976) *Struggle in the countryside: Politics and rural labor in Chile, 1919–1973*. Bloomington, IN: Indiana University Press.

Ludden, D. (1985) *Peasant history in south India*. Princeton, NJ: Princeton University Press.

Luetge, F. (1979) *Deutsche Sozial und Wirtschaftsgeschichte: Ein Ueberblick*, Berlin: Springer.

Lyne, M.C. and Nieuwoudt, W.L. (1991) 'Inefficient land use in KwaZulu: Causes and remedies', *Development Southern Africa*, 8:193–201.

Maddison, A. et al. *The political economy of poverty, equity and growth: Brazil and Mexico*, A World Bank comparative study, Oxford University Press.

Mahmood, M. (1990) 'The change in land distribution in the Punjab: Empirical application of an exogenous-endogenous model for agrarian sector analysis', *Pakistan Development Review*, 29:149–289.

Malik, A. and Schwab, R.M. (1991) 'Optimal investments to establish property rights in land', *Journal of Urban Economics*, 29:295–309.

Mason T.D. (1986) 'Land reform and the breakdown of clientelist politics in El Salvador', *Comparative Political Studies*, 18:487–516.

Masters, W.A. (1991) 'Comparative advantage and government policy in Zimbabwean agriculture', Ph.D. dissertation, Stanford University, Palo Alto, CA.

McClintock, M. (1985) '*The American connection*. Vol. 1, *State terror and popular resistance in El Salvador*. London: Zed Books.

McClintock C. (1981), *Peasant cooperatives and political change in Peru*. Princeton, NJ: Princeton University Press.

McClintock, C. (1984) 'Why peasants rebel: The case of Peru's sender luminoso', *World Politics*, 37:48–84.

McCloskey, D.N. (1975) 'The persistence of English common fields', in: W. Parker and E. Jones, eds., *European peasants and their markets*. Princeton, NJ: Princeton University Press.

McGregor A. (1977) 'Rent extraction and the survival of the agricultural production cooperative', *American Journal of Agricultural Economics*, 59:478–488.

McMillan, J., Whalley, J. and Zhu, L. (1989) 'The impact of China's economic reforms on agricultural productivity growth', *Journal of Political Economy*, 97:781–807.

Meillassoux, C. (1981) *Maidens, meal and money: Capitalism and the domestic community*. Cambridge University Press.

Meillasoux, C. 1991, *The anthropology of slavery: The womb of iron and gold*, Chicago: University of Chicago Press.

Melmed-Sanjak, J. and Carter, M.R. (1991) 'The economic viability and stability of capitalized family farming: An analysis of agricultural decollectivization in Peru', *Journal of Development Studies*, 190–210.

Meyer, C.A. (1989) *Land reform in Latin America: The Dominican case*. New York: Praeger.

Migdal, J.S. (1974) '*Peasants, politics and revolution: Pressure toward political and social change in the third world*. Princeton, NJ: Princeton University Press.

Migot-Adholla, S., Hazell, P., Blarel, B. and Place, F. (1991) 'Indigenous land rights systems in sub-Saharan Africa: A constraint on productivity?', *World Bank Economic Review*, 5:155–175.

Mills, D.E. (1989) 'Is zoning a negative sum game?', *Land Economics*, 65:1–12.

Mitchell, J. (1990) 'Perfect equilibrium and intergenerational conflict in a model of cooperative enterprise growth', *Journal of Economic Theory*, 51:48–76.

Mitra, P.K. (1983) 'A theory of interlinked rural transactions', *Journal of Public Economics*, 20:167–191.

Moene, K.O. 1992, 'Poverty and landownership', *American Economic Review*, 82:52–64.

Moerner, M. (1973) 'The Spanish American hacienda: A survey of recent research and debate', *Hispanic American History Review*, 53:183–216.

Moll, P.G. (1988) 'Transition to freehold in the South African reserves', *World Development*, 16:349–360 .

Moore, B. (1966) *Social origins of dictatorship and democracy: Lord and peasant in the making of the modern world*. Boston: Beacon Press.

Morooka, Y. and Hayami, Y. (1990) 'Contract choice and enforcement in an agrarian community: Agricultural tenancy in upland Java', *Journal of Development Studies*, 28–42.

Mosley, P. (1983) *The settler economies: Studies in the economic history of Kenya and Southern Rhodesia, 1900–1963*. Cambridge University Press.

Murrell, P. (1983) 'The economics of sharing: A transactions cost analysis of contractual choice in farming', *Bell Journal of Economics*, 14:283–293.

Nabi, I. (1986) 'Contracts, resource use and productivity in sharecropping', *Journal of Development Studies*, 22:429–441.

Nagarajan, G., Quisumbing, M.A. and Otsuka, K. (1991) 'Land pawning in the Philippines: An exploration into the consequences of land reform regulations', *Developing Economies*, 29:125–144.

Newbery, D.M.G. and Stiglitz, J.E. (1979) 'Sharecropping, risk sharing and the importance of imperfect information', in: J.A. Roumasset et al. eds., *Risk, uncertainty and agricultural development*. Agricultural Development Council.

Nolan, P. (1988) *The political economy of collective farms: An analysis of China's post-Mao rural reforms*. Boulder, CO: Westview Press.

Noronha, R. (1985) 'A review of the literature on land tenure systems in sub-Saharan Africa', World Bank Discussion Paper, Washington, DC.

North, D.C. and Thomas, R.P. (1971), 'The rise and fall of the manorial system: A theoretical model', *Journal of Economic History*, 31:777–803.

Oldenburg, P. (1990) 'Land consolidation as land reform in India, *World Development*, 18:183–195.

Ortega, E. (1990) 'De la reforma agraria a las empresas asociativas', *Revista de la CEPAL*, 40:105–122.

Otsuka, K. (1991) 'Determinants and consequences of land reform implementation in the Philippines', *Journal of Development Economics*, 35:339–355.

Otsuka, K., Chuma, H. and Hayami Y. (1992) 'Land and labor contracts in agrarian economies: Theories and facts', *Journal of Economic Literature*, 30:1965–2018.

Otsuka, K. and Hayami, Y. (1988) 'Theories of share tenancy: A critical survey', *Economic Development and Cultural Change*, 37:31–68.

Palmer, R. (1977) *Land and racial domination in Rhodesia*, Berkeley: University of California Press.

Pant, C. (1983) 'Tenancy and family resources: A model and some empirical analysis', *Journal of Development Economics*, 12:27–39.

Pearse, A.C. (1975) *The Latin American peasant*. London: Cass.

Pfeiffer, K. (1985) *Agrarian reform under state capitalism in Algeria*. Boulder, CO: Westview Press.

Phimister, I. (1988) *An economic and social history of Zimbabwe 1890–1948: Capital accumulation and class struggle*. London: Longman.

Pickett, L.E. (1988) *Organizing development through participation. Co-operative organization and services for land settlement*. A study prepared for the ILO. London: Croom Helm.

Pingali, P., Bigot, Y. and Binswanger H.P. (1987) *Agricultural mechanization and the evolution of farming systems in sub-Saharan Africa*. Baltimore, MD: Johns Hopkins University Press.

Pingali, P.L. and Xuan, V.T. (1992) 'Vietnam: Decollectivization and rice productivity growth', *Economic Development and Cultural Change*, 40:697–717.

Pitt, M.M. and Rosenzweig, M.R. (1986) 'Agricultural prices, food consumption and the health and productivity of Indonesian farmers', in: I. Singh, L. Squire and J. Strauss, eds., *Agricultural household models. Extension, applications and policy*. Baltimore MD: Johns Hopkins University Press.

Platteau, J.P. (1992) 'Formalization and privatization of land rights in sub-Saharan Africa: A critique of current orthodoxies and structural adjustment programmes', London School of Development Economics Paper 34.

Pogodzinski, J.M. and Sass, T.R. (1990) 'The economic theory of zoning: A critical review', *Land Economics*, 66:294–314.

Prosterman, R.L. and Hanstad, T.M. (1990) 'China: A fieldwork-based appraisal of the household responsibility system', in: R.L. Prosterman, M.N. Temple and T.M. Monstad, *Agrarian Reform and Grassroots Development*. Boulder, CO: Lyenne Rienner Publishers.

Prosterman, R.L., Temple, M.N. and Hanstad, T.M. (1990) Agrarian reform and grassroots development: Ten case studies. Boulder, CO: Lyenne Rienner Publishers.

Pryor, F.L. (1993) 'Problems of decollectivization with special attention to East Germany', in: L. Somogyi, eds., *Problems on transition to a market economy*. forthcoming.

Putterman, L. (1989) 'Agricultural producer cooperatives', in: P.K. Bardhan, ed., *The economic theory of agrarian institutions*, Berkeley: University of California Press.

Putterman, L. and DiGiorgio, M. (1985) 'Choice and efficiency in a model of democratic semi-collective agriculture', *Oxford Economic Papers*, 37:1–21.

Quibria, M.G. and Rashid, S. (1984) 'The puzzle of sharecropping: A survey of theories', *World Development*, 12:103–114.

Randall, A. and Castle, E.N. (1985) 'Land resources and land markets', *HNRE*, Vol. II, 571–620.

Ranger, T. (1985) *Peasant consciousness and guerrilla war in Zimbabwe: A comparative study*. London: James Currey.

Rao, C.H.H. (1975) *Technological change and distribution of gains in Indian agriculture*. Delhi: Macmillan.

Ravallion, M. (1991) 'Reaching the rural poor through public employment: Arguments, evidence and lessons from South Asia', *World Bank Research Observer*, 6:153–176.

Ray, R. (1975) 'The Bengal Zamindars: Local magnates and the state before the permanent settlement', *Indian. Economic and Social History Review*, 12:263–2292.

Reid, J.D. (1976) 'Sharecropping and agricultural uncertainty', *Economic Development and Cultural Change*, 24:549–576.

Robertson, A.F. (1982) 'Abusa: The structural history of an economic contract', *Journal of Development Studies*, 18:447–478.

Robison, L.J., Lins, D.A. and VenKatraman, R. (1985) 'Cash rents and land values in U.S. agriculture', *American Journal of Agricultural Economics*, 67:795–805.

Roemer, J.E. (1982) *A general theory of exploitation and class*. Cambridge: Harvard University Press.

Rosenzweig, M.R. (1978) 'Rural wages, labor supply and land reform: A theoretical and empirical analysis', *American Economic Review*, 67:847–861.

Rosenzweig, M.R. (1988) 'Risk, implicit contracts and the family in rural areas of low-income countries', *Economic Journal*, 98:1148–1170.

Rosenzweig, M.R. and Binswanger, H.P. (1993) 'Wealth, weather risk and the composition and profitability of agricultural investments', *Economic Journal*, 103:56–58.

Rosenzweig, M.R. and Stark, O., (1989) 'Consumption smoothing, migration and marriage: Evidence from rural India', *Journal of Political Economy*, 97: 905–926.

Rosenzweig, M.R. and Wolpin, K.I. (1985) 'Specific experience, household structure and intergenerational transfers: Farm family land and labor arrangements in developing countries', *Quarterly Journal of Economics*, 100:961–987.

Rosenzweig, M.R. and Wolpin, K.I. (1993) 'Credit market constraints, consumption smoothing and the accumulation of durable production assets in low-income countries: Investments in bullocks in India', *Journal of Political Economy*, 101:223–244.

Rueschemeyer, D., Huber Stephens, E., Stephens J.D. 1992, *Capitalist development and democracy*, Chicago: University of Chicago Press.

Ruthenberg, H. (1980) *Farming systems in the tropics*. Oxford University Press.

Sato, E. 1974, 'The early development of the shoen', in: J.W. Hall and J.P. Mass, eds., *Medieval Japan. Essays in institutional history*. New Haven: Yale University Press.

Sadoulet, E. (1992) 'Labor-service tenancy contracts in a Latin American context', *American Economic Review*, 82:1031–1042.

Scaritt, J.R. (1991) 'Zimbabwe: Revolutionary violence resulting in reform', in: J.A. Goldstone, T.R. Gurr and F. Moshiri, eds., *Revolutions of the late twentieth century*. Boulder, CO: Westview Press.

Schwartz, S.B. (1984) 'Colonial Brazil, c.1580–c.1750: Plantations and peripheries', in: *Cambridge history of Latin America*, Vol. II.

Scott, J.C. (1976) *The moral economy of the peasant: Rebellion and subsistence in Southeast Asia.* New Haven, CT: Yale University Press.

Sen, A.K. (1981) 'Market failure and control of labour power: Towards an explanation of "structure" and change in Indian agriculture', Parts 1 and 2, *Cambridge Journal of Economics,* 5:201–228 and 327–350.

Shaban, R.A. (1987) 'Testing between competing models of sharecropping', *Journal of Political Economy,* 95:893–920.

Shaban, R.A. (1991) 'Does the land tenancy market equalize holdings?', Working Paper, University of Pennsylvania, mimeo.

Shalit, H. and Schmitz, A. (1982) 'Farmland accumulation and prices', *American Journal of Agricultural Economics,* 64:710–719.

Shih, H. (1992) *Chinese rural society in transition: A case study of the Lake Tai area, 1368–1800.* Berkeley: University of California Press.

Siamwalla, A. et al. (1990) 'The Thai rural credit system: Public subsidies, private information and segmented markets', *World Bank Economic Review,* 4:271–295.

Simons, S. (1987) 'Land fragmentation and consolidation: A theoretical model of land configuration with an empirical analysis of fragmentation in Thailand', Ph.D. thesis, University of Maryland, College Park.

Singh, B., Bal, H.S. and Kumar, N. (1991) 'A spatio-temporal analysis of land-lease markets in Punjab', *Indian Journal of Agricultural Economics,* 46:355–360.

Skinner, J. (1991) 'If agricultural land taxation is so efficient, why is it so rarely used?', *World Bank Economic Review,* 5:113–133.

Skinner, J. (1991) 'Prospects for agricultural land taxation in developing countries', *World Bank Economic Review,* 5:493–512.

Skocpol, T. (1979) *States and social revolutions: A comparative analysis of France, Russia and China,* Cambridge: Cambridge University Press.

Skoufias, E. (1991) 'Land tenancy and rural factor market imperfections revisited', *Journal of Economic Development,* 16:37–55.

Southgate, D. (1990) 'The causes of land degradation along "spontaneously" expanding agricultural frontiers in the third world', *Land Economics,* 66:93–101.

Southgate, E., Sierra, R. and Brown, L. (1991) 'The causes of tropical deforestation in Ecuador: A statistical analysis', *World Development,* 19:1145–1151.

Srinivasan, T.N. (1972) 'Farm size and productivity. Implications of choice under uncertainty, *Sankhya, The Indian Journal of Statistics,* Series B, 34:409–420.

Srinivasan, T.N. (1979) 'Agricultural backwardness under semi-feudalism: Comment', *Economic Journal,* 89:416–419.

Stanfield, D. (1990) *Rural land titling and registration in Latin America and the Caribbean: Implications for rural development Programs.* Land Tenure Center, mimeo.

Stiglitz, J.E. (1986), 'The new development economics', *World Development,* 14:257–265.

Stiglitz, J.E. and Weiss, A. (1981) 'Credit rationing in markets with imperfect information', *American Economic Review,* 71:393–409.

Strasma, J., Alsm, J., Shearer, E. and Waldstein, A. (1987) 'Impact of agricultural land revenue systems on agricultural land usage', Madison WI: Land Tenure Center, mimeo.

Sweezy, P.M. et al. (1976) *The transition from feudalism to capitalism,* London: NLB, Atlantic Highlands, NJ: Humanities Press.

Sweezy, P. (1978) 'A critique', in R. Hilton, ed., *The transition from feudalism to capitalism.*

Takekoshi, Y. (1967) *The economic aspects of the history of the civilization of Japan.* London: Dawsons of Pall Mall.

Taslim, M.A. (1988) 'Tenancy and interlocking markets: Issues and some evidence', *World Development,* 16:655–666.

Taylor, W.B. (1972) *Landlord and peasant in colonial Oaxaca,* Stanford, CA: Stanford University Press.

Thiesenhusen, W.C. (1987) 'Incomes on some agrarian reform asentamientos in Panama', *Economic Development and Cultural Change,* 809–831.

Thiesenhusen, W.C. and Melmed-Sanjak, J. (1990) 'Brazil's agrarian structure: Changes from 1970 through 1980', *World Development,* 18:393–415.

Trautman, W. (1985) 'Rural development in Algeria: The system of state-directed cooperatives', *Quarterly Journal of International Agriculture*, 24:258–267.

Udry, C. (1990) 'Credit markets in northern Nigeria: Credit as insurance in a rural economy', *World Bank Economic Review*, 4:251–270.

Vail, L. and White, L. (1980) *Capitalism and colonialism in Mozambique. A study of Quelimane district*. St. Paul: University of Minnesota Press.

Vaillancourt, F. and Monty, L. (1985) 'The effect of agricultural zoning on land prices', Quebec, 1975–1981, *Land Economics*, 61:36–42.

Walker, T.S. and Ryan, J.G. (1990) *Village and household economies in India's semi-arid tropics*. Baltimore, MD: Johns Hopkins University Press.

Weiner, D. (1988) 'Land and agricultural development', in: C. Stoneman, ed., *Zimbabwe's prospects: Issues of race, class, state and capital in southern Africa*. London: Macmillan.

Wenfang, Z. and Makeham, J. (1992) 'Recent developments in the market for rural land use in China', *Land Economics*, 68:139–162.

Wickham-Crowley, T.P. 1991, *Guerrillas and revolution in Latin America*, Princeton: Princeton University Press.

Wilson, F. (1971) 'Farming 1866–1966', in: *Oxford history of South Africa*, Vol. II, Oxford University Press.

Wolf, E. (1968) *Peasant wars of the twentieth century*. New York: Harper and Row.

World Bank (1984) 'Agricultural mechanization: A comparative historical perspective', 673. Washington, DC.

Wuyts, M. (1985) 'Money, planning and rural transformation in Mozambique', *Journal of Development Studies*, 22:180–207.

Zamosc, L. (1989) 'Peasant struggles and agrarian reform'. Washington: The Smithsonian Institute.

Zimmerman, F. and Carter, M. (1992) 'A dynamic simulation of endogenous structural evolution in an imperfect-market, agrarian, two asset market economy', Madison WI: Land Tenure Center, mimeo.

*Chapter 43*

# HUMAN AND PHYSICAL INFRASTRUCTURE: PUBLIC INVESTMENT AND PRICING POLICIES IN DEVELOPING COUNTRIES

EMMANUEL JIMENEZ*

*The World Bank*

## Contents

The views expressed herein are the author's own and do not reflect the official position of The World Bank or any of its affiliated institutions. I would like to acknowledge the comments of T. N. Srinivasan, Jere Behrman, Justin Lin, Haidy Pasay, and other participants at the ADB conference, numerous colleagues at The World Bank, but particularly Paul Glewwe, Kyu Sik Lee and Lant Pritchett, as well as the help of Ruben Suarez Berenguela and Masako Ii in assembling some of the material.

*Handbook of Development Economics, Volume III, Edited by J. Behrman and T.N. Srinivasan*
© *Elsevier Science B.V., 1995*

## 1. Introduction and overview

Almost by definition, infrastructure is the basis for development.[1] For an economy, it is the foundation on which the factors of production interact in order to produce output. This has been long recognized by development analysts, and infrastructure, often termed "social overhead capital," is considered to include:

> ... those services without which primary, secondary and tertiary production activities cannot function. In its wider sense it includes all public services from law and order through education and public health to transportation, communications, power and water supply, as well as such agricultural overhead capital as irrigation and drainage systems [Hirschman (1958) p. 83].

These seemingly diverse services share some common traits that are important in economic analysis. They are generally not tradeable. Although they may affect final consumption directly, their role in enhancing output and household welfare can also be indirect – in facilitating market transactions or in making other economic inputs more productive. Finally, and perhaps most importantly, the many infrastructure services share characteristics, such as scale economies in production, consumption externalities and non-exclusivity, that have been used to justify a large role for public policy in their provision and financing.

This chapter will focus not only on what has traditionally been considered the "core" infrastructure sectors, which enhance the productivity of physical capital and land (mainly transportation and power). It will also include human infrastructure – or those services that raise the productivity of labor (health, education, nutrition). This is a broadening of the definition that was given great prominence by Schultz (1963) and Becker (1964) and that has since been widely accepted by both scholars and practitioners.

Public investment will be defined broadly to include all government spending in these sectors, rather than just capital expenditures as traditionally defined in official statistics. This is to ensure that the economic issues regarding recurrent as well as capital spending are covered, since both have been the focus of the recent literature. Moreover, the chapter will emphasize recent policy debates, but will not present in detail the basic theoretical concepts underlying them.

---

[1] The dictionary's definition of "infrastructure" is "the underlying foundation or basic framework". See *Webster's Ninth Collegiate Dictionary*, 1985, p. 621.

These can be obtained from standard public finance textbooks, and appropriate references will be made when necessary. There have been some recent shifts in emphasis on the analytic approach to infrastructure – such as a greater focus on the efficiency of use, rather than on construction, and an increased role for private sector participation in providing infrastructure services. But the most dramatic advances that have been made have been in the way the concepts are applied to the particular circumstances of developing countries.[2]

Because of its wide coverage, this chapter will stress the following common cross-sectoral themes regarding the pricing of, and investment in infrastructure services in developing countries, rather than detailed issues within sectors:

- Recent studies at both the macro and micro level have reinforced the point that investments in human and physical infrastructure are critical elements for economic growth and for reducing poverty, although there has been less consensus on the magnitude of that effect (Section 2).
- While the literature continues to accept the key role of government in investment policy, there has been more of a debate about the nature of that role in order to improve efficiency and equity. There are two key questions: (1) how much and what type of service should be provided? and (2) what is the appropriate public-private balance in providing it? (Section 3).
- Given that the government has decided where to invest, how should these investments be financed? Section 4 shows that the recent literature has been reconsidering pricing policy so that it can play a greater role in financing.

The paper will sum up briefly and then discuss areas where future research will be necessary, both in terms of substance and of the data needed to undertake that research (Section 5).

## 2. The role of infrastructure in the development process

There are two types of evidence regarding the contribution that infrastructure makes to development. Aggregate evidence at the country, regional or sectoral level has most often been used to show how infrastructure can affect economic indicators, such as levels and growth of output. There has also been some work on the impact that infrastructure has had on aggregate social indicators. Micro evidence is used to depict how infrastructure influences household or individual welfare (human infrastructure) and the profitability of firms (physical infrastructure).

---

[2] For example, two of the World Bank's influential *World Development Reports* have been on Health (1993) and Infrastructure (1994).

This section reviews this evidence, but the discussion will be succinct and selective. The literature is large and cross-references will be used to direct the reader to more detailed reviews (some of which are published in this *Handbook* or in its earlier editions). Also, the discussion will not focus on the differential impacts of publicly or privately provided infrastructure, since this will be the subject of the later sections regarding policy.

## 2.1. National and cross-country evidence

A key question is whether variations in national economic growth and aggregate indices of welfare can be explained by (and attributed to) changes or differences in infrastructure variables. Before reviewing the empirical evidence, a brief overview of the underlying concepts might be useful.

Infrastructure can contribute to output directly as a measurable final product. Medical staff and hospitals combine to provide curative services that are valued for consumption and that improve a nation's social indicators. Buses and drivers combine with highways to provide passenger transport services.[3]

But its more important contribution may be indirect. As an intermediate input, it enhances the productivity of all inputs in producing output.[4] The quality of labor is enhanced by human capital improvements such as schooling. Physical capital and land are made more productive by investments that facilitate the transport of goods or the provision of power.

Moreover, as has recently been argued in the "new growth" economic literature, these indirect effects can give rise to externalities, which, if taken into account in investment decisions, can cause long-run growth to accelerate.[5] The more celebrated theoretical contributions have focused on human capital, although similar types of externalities are posited for physical capital. Romer (1986, 1990) argues that technological innovation, which is produced by human

---

[3] For example, gas, water and electricity are included as industrial sectors in national accounts calculations, while transport and communications are included as service sectors – together their combined share in GDP varies between 5–11 percent in most countries [Kessides (1993)].

[4] Formally, infrastructure's direct and indirect effects can be represented [Hulten and Schwab (1991)] as:

$$(1) \quad Y_t = A(I_t, t) * f(K_t, L_t, T_t, I_t),$$

where output ($Y$) is determined by physical capital ($K$), labor ($L$), land ($T$), infrastructure ($I$) and technical progress ($A$) through a twice-differentiable function $f(.)$ and $t$ is a time variable that allows for other differences in productive efficiency. Equation (1) varies from standard neoclassical formulations because of the effect of infrastructure investment in affecting $A(.)$. Even if $f(.)$ exhibits constant returns to scale inclusive of $I$, the presence of $I$ in the technical progress term gives rise to externalities, as suggested by recent proponents of the "new growth" literature.

[5] Chapter 41 by Lau in this volume contains a thorough review of the theoretical and empirical literature.

capital, is a public good so that private capital investment increases the level available to all entrepreneurs. Lucas (1988) emphasizes the externality associated with private investment in human capital – because one worker increases the productivity of others (as well as his or her own) in the process of interaction.[6] Becker et al. (1990) discusses increasing returns to human capital because investing in the quality of children has higher returns when human capital is abundant relative to investments in quantity.[7] These models assume that, because of externalities, factor returns do not necessarily diminish. Thus, increasing investment can accelerate economic growth – hence the term, "endogenous growth".

In contrast, the neoclassical formulations associated with Solow (1956) invoked the simplifying assumptions of constant returns to scale, diminishing factor returns and the exogenous nature of the factors themselves to obtain closed form solutions.[8] These assumptions assured that all countries will converge to the same exogenously determined steady state growth path – a characteristic that is difficult to support empirically.

Ultimately, the validity of the competing theories rests on empirical work. What is the aggregate evidence regarding growth, investment and social outcomes?

*Growth and human capital.* The early aggregate studies using growth accounting methods [Denison (1967), Kendrick (1976)] measured the contribution of variables that enhance the productivity of the measured inputs (like education) to the average annual rate of growth by inferring it from the residual of a growth equation, after the growth of labor and capital are taken into account. In education, for example, a review [Psacharopoulos (1984)] concluded that, although the quantitative results were widely disparate across countries, qualitatively education had a positive effect on growth. But these studies were rooted in the neoclassical formulations of the Solow-type growth models and failed to isolate the effects of the possible externalities mentioned above.

Another approach that allows for possible externalities comes from econo-

---

[6] None of these arguments are particularly new, as is admitted by most of the recent authors, many of whom formalize ideas posited earlier. Selowsky (1992) makes this point forcefully. Romer's (1986) ideas are close to those of Arrow (1962) and Phelps (1966) on learning by doing, while Lucas (1988) builds on Uzawa's (1962) work on increasing the returns that arise from external effects associated with human capital. What is innovative is that they are being used in formal models of economic growth with closed form solutions.

[7] Summers (1992) and Gill and Bhalla (1992) extend this argument to the importance of female human capital by stressing the positive association between the education of women and better health and greater enrollment of children in school.

[8] These assumptions lead to the "convergence" hypothesis. Diminishing returns and the diffusion of technology guarantee that all countries will have the same steady-state rate of economic growth.

metric analysis of the relationship between output levels or growth and human infrastructure variables from historical and cross-section data. This link has been reviewed in several chapters of this *Handbook* – Birdsall on population (Chapter 12), Schultz on education (Chapter 13), Behrman and Deolalikar on health and nutrition (Chapter 14) and Lau on general issues (Chapter 41) – as well as other recent papers [for example, Behrman (1990b), Weale (1992) and Easterly et al. (1992)]. These reviews have generally found that, while there is some evidence that human resources contribute to growth, there is less consensus on the importance of that contribution – both with respect to its magnitude and its nature (whether the externalities are pecuniary or technical). For example, two studies of about 100 countries find that a 10 percent increase in secondary school enrollment rates is associated with an increase in the growth rate of GDP per capita of 0.2 percent [Barro (1991)] and 0.7 percent [Baumol et al. (1989); see Weale (1992) for further comparisons].

The apparent lack of empirical consensus concerns important measurement and methodological problems that are only slowly being resolved. One set of issues has to do with obtaining an appropriate measure of human capital as an explanatory variable. This complexity can be illustrated for the case of education, where data are arguably more readily available than in other infrastructure sectors. Popular measures used in numerous early studies are school enrollment ratios and adult literacy rates [for example, Romer (1990)]. These variables may not capture the contribution of changes in the directly measured stocks of human capital. School enrollment ratios refer to flows of schooling, which may be inappropriate since there are usually long time lags before the results of the educational process emerge; and adult literacy rates capture only a very early stage of human capital formation that does not include numeracy, reasoning and other aspects that may have a major impact on productivity. Both measures, which are typically obtained by U.N. specialized agencies from surveys of developing country institutions, also produce data of doubtful quality because of non-comparability across nations as well as a lack of monitoring on the production of the numbers.

More recently, census survey data have been used to construct measures of educational attainment. For example, Psacharopoulos and Arriagada (1986) use census-based data to compile the total educational stock of the labor force for 99 countries (although only 34 have more than one observation). Lau et al. (1991) and Nehru et al. (1993) take a slightly different approach in using annual enrollment figures in perpetual inventory models to estimate stocks of educational attainment for the working-age population. Barro and Lee (1993) uses census-based data (for 129 countries, 77 of which have three or more observations) as a benchmark and then combines them with enrollment ratios to estimate the educational attainment of the overall population aged 25 and above. While these studies are able to resolve the stock-flow issue, the data they use are still subject to criticism on quality grounds because: the enrollment ratios contain substantial measurement error; they are not sensitive to completion and retention rate differences across countries; and the interpolation techniques to fill in missing data points may not be duly sensitive to individual country conditions. This may be one reason why the results tend to be sensitive to what is included in the regression equations, which remain surprisingly ad hoc, in relation to the elegant theoretical models on which they are based.

The measurement issue also affects studies that attempt to use health, nutrition and population outcomes.[9] Available aggregate demographic and health data are notoriously incomplete and are difficult to compare because of varying definitions. The UN's *Demographic Yearbook* distinguishes between "reliable" and "other" statistics by using italics. The World Bank's *1993 World Development Report* explicitly highlights estimates based on old data, models and other approximations. The quality of the data is improving due to better collection methods and the availability of new data, such as from the Demographic and Health Surveys (DHS) sponsored by USAID, although census coverage still leaves much to be desired. Data regarding child mortality and, to a lesser degree, total fertility are considered to be of better quality than data regarding adult mortality, which are very incomplete.

Another set of issues has to do with technical concerns about the estimation. Most important is the concern about simultaneity. Aggregate output and its growth can obviously affect many of the human capital variables that are used as explanatory variables.[10] Early attempts by Wheeler (1980) to correct for simultaneity suffered from a lack of instruments [see Behrman (1990b)]. Recent studies with access to more and better quality data have been able to argue that some of the variables used are indeed exogenous because of the way the lagged relationships are modeled [Barro and Lee (1993)]. Still, even these studies are criticized because of concerns that some variables may have been omitted, such as the effect of environmental variables on health outcomes and continued measurement error in the variables for which data do exist.

*Growth and physical capital.* The evidence on the link between physical infrastructure and growth is more diffuse and is only beginning to be reviewed [see, for example, Kessides (1993) and Chapter 1 of the *World Development Report 1994* on "Infrastructure for Development" (World Bank (1994))]. The nature of infrastructure services is much more variable, and it is difficult to develop aggregate measures of physical capital analogous to indicators of the

---

[9] I am grateful to Ken Hill for his help in this assessment.

[10] Indeed, as is evident below, there is a whole literature about how national income determines socio-economic indicators such as educational and health outcomes, which are often the same variables used as proxies for human capital.

human condition. Aggregate infrastructure (which is usually a combination of diverse sectors like transport and communications and some components of the "economic services" category of the national accounts) has shown that there can be a substantial positive effect. Aschauer's (1989) study of the U.S. evidence, using a production function approach, indicates that the contribution of basic infrastructure services is very large.

But such single-country studies over time are difficult to replicate in developing countries because of data constraints. Lakshaman and Elhance (1984) show that transport and power have a positive effect on industrial production in India. Among the few other studies in developing countries, one for Mexico (using a restricted cost-function approach) finds that there is some evidence that public physical infrastructure makes both labor and capital inputs more productive [Shah (1992)], although the rate of return is lower than that for private capital.

Cross-country evidence does exist that links a variety of specific infrastructure outcomes with growth or other measures of overall economic performance. Table 43.1 cites some aggregate evidence of the results mentioned above for agriculture, the sector in which the coverage of data is probably best. Roads and road density have a strong positive effect on agricultural output. Irrigation also has a significant effect on aggregate output.

Other variables that have been used in cross-country analysis include: telephone coverage per capita [Hardy and Hudson (1981)] and the extent of paved road networks [Querioz (1992)]. These have been shown to be significant in explaining differences in GDP per capita across countries. One study finds that an indicator of spending on transport and communications services has a significant effect on some categories of sectoral output, such as agricultural productivity [Antle (1983)]. Manufacturing investment is also found to depend on infrastructure quality [Wheeler and Mody (1991)]. These studies found strong correlations between lagged values of these variables and GDP per capita, but econometric problems may persist as the lag structures may not fully account for simultaneity.

Table 43.1
Effects of infrastructure on agriculture: Cross-country evidence[a]

| Due to 1% increase in | Increase of aggregate crop output (%) |
|---|---|
| Irrigation | 1.62* |
| Paved roads | .26* |
| Rural road density | .12* |
| Adult literacy rate | .54 |

* Statistically significant at 10%.
[a] Cross-country study – 58 countries.
*Source*: Binswanger, H. (1990).

Studies that use physical measures of capital, such as those cited above, are few. A more popular approach is to use data on the shares that each sector (typically transportation and communication, but also gas, water and electricity) contributes to total output [World Bank (1987b)] or to public spending as explanatory variables of per capita GDP levels or growth. A recent review of multicountry studies [World Bank (1994)], as well as country-level studies of Korea, Israel and Mexico, reveals a wide range of estimates – with elasticities (output with respect to changes in levels of aggregate measures of transport, power, water and communication spending) of .01 − .44, suggesting rates of return on the order of 5 to over 60 percent. Most of these studies suffer from many of the same econometric and measurement problems described above for human infrastructure. For example, they cannot control adequately for simultaneity, so that the causality between economic growth and the provision of infrastructure is not clear. Moreover, many of the studies cannot be used directly for policy analysis because the sector definitions are too broad or because they do not consider variations in quality or utilization.

Interpretation of the results is also a concern. First, using overall sectoral shares confounds the differential effects of public and private spending, making it nearly impossible to derive clear policy implications. Correcting for this may be difficult since data on private spending are scarce and many private infrastructure utilities receive large amounts of public subsidies. Moreover, it is critical not to lump together wasteful infrastructure "white elephants" with productive investments. Second, studies that rely on public spending patterns may not capture the true effect of infrastructure if there is widespread waste in spending [see Devarajan et al. (1992)].

Another way to measure the impact of public infrastructure investment on development is to consider its effect on private investment. Studies using data from developing countries [see reviews in Chhibber and Dailami (1990), Serven and Solimano (1992)] indicate that public infrastructure investment "crowds in" private investment, while the opposite is true for non-infrastructure investment. These points are discussed in the next section on investment policy.

*Social indicators and infrastructure.* Levels and growth of aggregate output measure only one aspect of overall economic development. Another important set of indicators is the direct measure of health and social variables. For an in-depth discussion on the reasons for distinguishing between these two aspects, see the chapter by Lipton and Ravallion (Chapter 42).

Aggregate data have been used to illustrate that social indicators have been improving over time [World Bank (1990), Kakwani (1992)]. Infant mortality rates have been dropping, although Kakwani (1992) finds that the progress made by the low-income countries, which was superior to that made by middle-income countries until the mid-1970s, seems to have lost momentum in subsequent periods. Literacy rates have shown a strong upward trend, consistent with the parallel gains in primary school enrollment rates. Moreover, policy documents have loosely used broad correlations to show that access to infrastructure, particularly social services and water, has had much to do with these gains. One such example is the World Bank's 1990 *World Development Report*:

> In 1985, spending on primary education as a percentage of GNP was more than four times higher in Botswana, where the enrollment rate was 99 percent, than in Haiti, where it was only 55 percent. Similarly, in countries that have achieved broad provision of health care, such as Chile and Mauritius, spending as a percentage of GNP is several times greater than in countries such as India and Pakistan, where under 5 mortality remains exceptionally high and the percentage of children immunized is low (p. 46).

While intuitively appealing, these contentions cannot be considered to be rigorous evidence of the impact of infrastructure on social indicators. The quality of the data on aggregate educational and health outcomes has already been discussed above. Moreover, there is the taxing question of simultaneity – it is likely that educational outcomes, for example, proxy for overall levels of economic development and can equally explain the amount of investment countries can afford to make. Finally, questions about the efficacy of public investment can be raised because there are typically no controls in these studies for differences in quality.

*Conclusions*. The positive link between measures of infrastructure and development is fairly robust across studies and methodologies. However, it is more difficult to pin down the quantitative evidence regarding this impact, particularly that of aggregate measures of physical infrastructure [see Polenske and Rockler (1993)]. This is because of the difficulty in measuring and deriving a precise methodology that clearly defines causality between infrastructure outcomes and development measures. Consequently, while such studies are useful for raising overall consciousness about the importance of infrastructure, they are less useful for guiding policy. Moreover, even if the measurement and methodology questions were addressed, policy instruments at the aggregate level are often difficult to interpret. This is because of the need to differentiate between publicly versus privately provided capital. The studies that do differentiate in this way rely on spending data, but such spending may not lead to great improvements in the physical capital stock if they are not done efficiently; also they measure flows and not stocks of capital.

## 2.2. Microeconomic links

The uneven nature of the aggregate evidence has meant that much more of the burden of documenting the effects of infrastructure on productivity has rested on microeconomic data at the individual or enterprise level. This evidence also has a direct bearing on the question of what effect infrastructure has on poverty reduction since increasing productivity is one of the principal ways for the poor to escape poverty and since many of the studies also focus on poorer households and smaller firms.

*Direct effects of human capital.* The link between human resources and productivity has been the subject of a large number of studies, particularly in education, health and nutrition, which is only briefly summarized in what follows.[11]

Much of the microeconomic evidence comes from studying the impact of education on wages. Studies (mainly using earnings functions) consistently find that there is a large labor market premium on attaining additional years or levels of schooling. Table 43.2 shows the magnitude of this impact for a number of countries. When compared to the costs of obtaining that education, many conventional estimates put these rates of return at levels that are typically above those of physical rates of return [Psacharopoulos (1985)]. These estimates, summarized in Table 43.3 as averages of individual studies, also reveal that returns to education tend to be highest for basic levels. Many of these studies have been criticized for a number of valid reasons, such as the possibility that these returns to education are due to credentialism, the inability to control for quality [Behrman and Birdsall (1983)], the possibility that the returns may have been dropping over time, and their failure to control for inter-regional differences. While some of these corrections could cause a decline in some of the estimates (particularly in the returns to expanding primary education versus improving its quality), in general, the general qualitative results and supporting evidence have been taken very seriously in policy advice.

There is also evidence from the non-wage sector. Educated farmers are more likely to adopt new technologies, and virtually all studies on agricultural productivity show that better-educated farmers get a higher return on their land. Studies of Africa, for example, have found that farmers who have completed four years of education (the minimum many analysts conclude is

---

[11] See Behrman (1990a) for a more thorough review of these issues. Some of these ideas also arise in the context of the discussions in previous chapters of this *Handbook* by Strauss and Thomas in this volume, Behrman and Deolalikar (Chapter 14) and Schultz (Chapter 13).

Table 43.2
The effect of an additional year of schooling on wages and farm output, selected countries and years

| | Percentage increase in wages | | | Percentage increase in farm output |
|---|---|---|---|---|
| | Male | Males and Females | Female | |
| Côte d'Ivoire, 1987 | | 12 P | | |
| | | 21 S | | |
| Ghana, 1988/89 | | 5 | | |
| Korea, Rep. of, 1976, 1974 | | 6 | | 2 |
| Indonesia, 1986 | 8 | | 12 S | |
| France, 1987 | | | 11 | |
| Peru, 1986 | 13 P | | 12 P | 3 |
| | 8 S | | 8 S | |
| Malaysia, 1987 | 16 | | 18 | 5 |
| Nicaragua (urban), 1985 | 10 | | 13 | |
| Philippines, 1980 | | | 18 | |
| Spain, 1979 | | | 10 | |
| Thailand, 1986; 1973 | 17 P | | 13 P | 3 |
| | 7 S | | 25 S | |
| United States, 1967 | | | | |
| Whites | 6 | | 7 | |
| Blacks | 5 | | 11 | |

P = primary school level.
S = primary school level.
*Note*: These results were all estimated controlling for other factors such as work experience and other individual characteristics. In most cases, the estimated effects have also been corrected for any statistical bias resulting from selecting a sample of wage earners only. The estimates for Côte d'Ivoire, Ghana and Korea pertain to combined samples of men and women.
*Source*: World Bank, 1991 (which has the references to the original studies).

necessary for literacy) produce, on average about 8 percent more than farmers who have not gone to school [Jamison and Lau (1982)]. Similar positive effects have been found in studies in Korea, Malaysia and Thailand [see references in Behrman (1990a)]. Although there is not as much evidence that schooling improves informal sector employment and earnings in the rural non-agricultural sector, some studies – including one of family businesses in Peru – show that the more education a person has had, the wider the range of possibilities that is open for enhancing income [Moock et al. (1989)]. These findings, since they use physical measures of productivity or are concerned with the self-employed, can conceptually be used to counter the criticism that the returns to education are due to credentialism reflected in money wages in the labor market. However, to the extent that they do not adequately control for unobserved characteristics such as individual motivation and ability, the findings could suffer from the same econometric biases that affect studies of money wages.

Similarly, there is a burgeoning literature on the effects of better health and

Table 43.3
Returns to investment in education, by country type and level

| Region | Social | | | Private | | | Number countries reporting |
|---|---|---|---|---|---|---|---|
| | Primary | Secondary | Higher | Primary | Secondary | Higher | |
| Africa | 28 | 17 | 13 | 45 | 26 | 32 | 16 |
| Asia | 27 | 15 | 13 | 31 | 15 | 18 | 10 |
| Latin America | 26 | 18 | 16 | 32 | 23 | 23 | 10 |
| Europe, Middle East and North Africa | 13 | 10 | 8 | 17 | 13 | 13 | 9 |
| Developing countries | 24 | 15 | 13 | 31 | 19 | 22 | 45 |

*Note*: Private returns take into account only the cost of education to the individual. In contrast, social returns are based on the full cost of education to society, but as they do not attempt to measure social benefits, they are necessarily lower.
*Source*: Psacharopoulos (1985).

nutrition on productivity, especially in those activities in which the poor are engaged. While these studies are not used to estimate rates of return as in education (the outcomes are often not valued so as to be comparable to costs), they show the impact on productivity of physical measures of nutrition and health. Several such measures have been used including anthropometric measures (such as height, weight or body mass), mortality or morbidity histories, loss of capacity for normal activities and nutrient intake (in terms of calories). For example, studies of agricultural productivity indicate that an increase in caloric intake results in a substantial increase in the efficiency of an hour of labor among agricultural workers in Sri Lanka, India and Guatemala, as well as among Kenyan road crews [see Behrman (1990a) for citations and a critique]. Since a full review of this literature is beyond the scope of this paper, it is informative simply to quote from Behrman's review:

> ... though the studies that attempt to control for simultaneity are limited and not without their problems, there is growing evidence of positive effects of health and nutrition on labor productivity of at least poorer individuals in developing countries (p. 62).

*Externalities and human capital.* Aside from these direct effects on one's own labor productivity, investments in human capital for one individual can affect the well-being of others also. Some of these external effects can accrue to society as a whole. For example, primary education may foster "good citizenship" in a number of ways – increasing patriotism, lessening crime or, through literacy, easing the administrative burdens of tax collection. While it is almost impossible to obtain quantitative measures of these general impacts, it is also difficult to argue that they are not important.[12] There is evidence that, beyond a certain level (fourth grade), schooling leads to a decline in fertility [Cochrane (1979)], although a debate still rages on the effects of lower population growth on economic growth (Birdsall, Chapter 12).

There is more evidence that investments that make one individual more productive can have a positive effect on other individuals. But to what extent should such evidence be used to justify public intervention in the name of externalities? One issue hinges on the answer to the question: "external to whom?" Parental education will influence children's schooling positively. Studies in Malaysia and the Philippines found, for example, mothers' schooling affects daughters' schooling significantly [Behrman (1990a)]. A similar argument can be made for health. But systematic evidence outside the family situation has yet to be gathered, so that the issue depends partly on whether benefits that are external to the individual but are internal to the household are important for public policy. This implies addressing some fundamental questions regarding the short-sightedness and altruism of a household with respect to resource allocation among its members.

Another issue is whether all indirect effects should be treated as externalities. There is now more evidence regarding important indirect and non-pecuniary effects of human resource investments. The effects of social sector investments tend to complement each other. Schooling achievement can affect nutrient intake; nutrition depends on the type of food used, which, in turn, depends on the characteristics of the preparer. In Nicaragua, for example, a study shows that the more schooling women have, the better nourished are households [Behrman and Wolfe (1989)]. Several studies indicate that schooling has a strong positive effect on health indicators. Mothers' schooling is associated with lower infant mortality, more appropriate weight-for-age of children, greater use of medical facilities such as vaccinations and better household water quality [see Behrman (1990a) for a comprehensive review of these studies]. But important though they are, there is less evidence to what extent such non-monetary effects are truly external to the one directly consuming the service.

A final issue concerns methods of analysis. Just as education can enhance child nutrition, better nutrition improves the child's capacity to learn. Recent studies [for Nepal by Moock and Leslie (1986) and for China by Jamison (1986)] show, for example, strong correlations between anthropometric indicators of child health and various measures of child schooling achievement. However, these associations need not necessarily imply causality, since it is

---

[12] The magnitude of these non-wage effects can be substantial. Although no aggregate numbers are available in developing countries, in the United States, it has been estimated that these effects amount to up to two fifths of the full economic value of education [Haveman and Wolfe (1984)].

likely that household decisions about child health and schooling are determined simultaneously. A recent paper [Behrman and Lavy (1992)] examines the nature of the possible biases, which may work in opposite directions. If unobserved characteristics (such as differences in parents' preferences as to their children's attainment at school) lead to greater schooling achievement as well as better child health, there will be an upward bias. But some unobserved characteristics (such as parental concern or local labor market conditions) may lead parents to direct their resources towards enhancing intellectual as opposed to physical outcomes, leading to a downward bias. Behrman and Lavy's conclusion, using data from Ghana, is that these effects tend to offset each other so that, for the range of observed health and achievement measures in their sample, the true effect of health on school success is negligible. It will be important in future studies to examine the robustness of this result given other initial conditions.

*Physical infrastructure.* Physical infrastructure affects the profitability of private enterprises. Improving it can lower the cost of producing a given level of output or, alternatively, can increase the amount of output produced by all other inputs for a given cost. The benefits of the typical "infrastructural" or "public utilities" project in developing countries embody estimates of these effects [Squire (1989)]. Infrastructure also enables markets to work better. Transactions are made less costly and this increases the benefits of trade, both international and domestic. For example, major advances in transport and communications technologies have considerably lowered storage costs by permitting producers to respond rapidly to changing consumer demands in international trade [Peters (1992) and Kessides (1993) refer to this as "modern logistics management"].

However, despite this widespread application, there are relatively few econometrically-based studies of such effects at the level of firms. The main reason for this is the availability of data. While there is now a reasonably large set of household and individual data from surveys that allow the direct measurement of human capital on earnings, firm-based information in developing countries is only beginning to be made available and utilized by researchers. Where data do exist, researchers have had trouble obtaining access to them because of overzealous attempts to protect confidentiality. Also, most firm-based surveys do not contain adequate infrastructure measures with which to relate to costs and output.

The situation is beginning to change as several researchers are collecting their own data [Lee and Anas (1992)] or are managing to augment firm-level data available from official sources with infrastructure variables. The preliminary evidence from this type of analysis indicates that unit costs tend to rise due to unreliable or inaccessible public infrastructure. Firms, both large and small, spend a significant portion of their expenditure on buying infrastructure services and suffer when these are not available. In Nigeria, for example, unreliable public utilities have led private firms to produce their own infrastructure services at high unit costs as they are unable to take advantage of scale economies [Lee and Anas (1992)]. A recent study of small firms in Ghana named electricity outages as among the top four constraints to expansion [Steel and Webster (1991)]. In agriculture, infrastructure provision has made a considerable impact in marketing. Transport, for example, can account for about half the costs of marketing agricultural commodities – an activity that itself accounts for 25–60 percent of the final prices of goods [Beenhakker (1987)]. This is reflected in improved prices, the diffusion of technology and the use of appropriate inputs, as was found in a study in Bangladesh [Ahmed and Hossain (1990)], which compared villages that had more developed infrastructure services with those that did not. Rural roads are shown to reduce transaction costs in India [Binswanger et al. (1989)], Colombia [cited in Kessides (1993), p. 27), where they were associated not only with increased production but also greater use of credit and in Thailand [Binswanger (1983)].

These studies are still far from conclusive because they rely on very small sample sizes and do not control for difficult econometric issues, such as simultaneity bias. For example, if improvements in infrastructure are systematically located where firms are most likely to succeed for other reasons, then the estimated effects would be biased upwards.

The impact of infrastructure on poor households can be manifested in the greater income-earning opportunities they can afford. Improvements in firm profitability are likely to induce entry opportunities and enhance employment opportunities in general, although the net effect would depend on the substitutability between labor and physical capital inputs. Improved infrastructure can make it easier for poor households who own their own businesses or who are agricultural producers to make market transactions and to take advantage of profit-making opportunities. However, there is little econometric evidence that has been systematically brought to bear on either of these issues.

There is more micro-level evidence that infrastructure improves social indicators of welfare, particularly among the poor. The direct effect of physical infrastructure on welfare is most obvious in the case of water. The poor can spend large amounts of resources on obtaining water, either through private vendors or, in rural areas, by traveling to water sources [see Kessides (1993) for citations]. As will be seen later, there is often a great deal of willingness to pay for improved services [Briscoe et al. (1993)]. The use of clean water may have as much to do with social indicators such as infant mortality as access to health clinics [see, for example, World Bank (1993)]. It is intuitively appealing to suppose that a positive association exists between educational outcomes and the provision of infrastructure, such as electricity in the home, (for example, students in homes with such infrastructure may find it easier to study);

however, it has been difficult to obtain strong empirical support for this contention because infrastructure tends to be highly correlated with physical inputs to education such as building quality and the availability of teaching materials [Glewwe and Jacoby (1993)].

*Conclusions.* Micro-economic studies of the impact of infrastructure on the profitability of firms and household welfare are difficult to undertake in developing countries. One critical issue is the availability of data, particularly for studies of physical infrastructure and outcomes regarding enterprises. Another issue that affects all studies is one that also afflicts macro-level studies – simultaneity.

Despite these drawbacks, micro-level studies are better able to demonstrate the link between infrastructure and productivity than those at the country level. More data exist, except possibly in the case of physical infrastructure. There are also more recent attempts to account for difficult econometric questions by explicitly modeling the source of the possible errors. Applying these techniques tends to confirm the macro-level associations and predictions from theory about the links between infrastructure, productivity and household welfare.

## 3. Public investment: The role and challenges

In most countries (both developing and developed), governments provide and finance most human and physical infrastructure. Over 90 percent of primary school children and three-quarters of secondary school children attend public schools, all of which are heavily subsidized and most of which are free. Almost half of all health spending is attributable to the public sector. It is thus not surprising that central government spending in all of these sectors accounts for an average of about 5 percent of GDP in developing countries [World Bank (1992a)].

The comparable figures for physical infrastructure are more difficult to summarize since the institutional arrangements under which providers operate may not be so clearly delineated as a spending item of the central government. Many services are provided by state-owned enterprises, such as public utilities. However, these enterprises are heavily subsidized, and the evidence that exists shows that the bulk of infrastructure in most countries is financed by governments [see, for example, World Bank (1988c), Chapter 8].[13]

---

[13] Aside from direct budgetary burdens from non-performing public enterprises, there are also indirect contributions in the form of unpaid taxes and debt service guaranteed by the government. For example, the state power company of The Gambia owed its treasury the equivalent of 16 percent of current government revenue in 1984; its own unpaid claims on the government amounted to one quarter of these arrears [World Bank (1988c)].

Public spending does not give a full picture of the extent of government involvement. Even those infrastructure services that are provided by the private sector are subject to varying degrees of regulatory control, including constraints on the rate of return (particularly for natural monopolies) and on the type of service being delivered [such as curricula in schools – see, for example, James (1991)].

This section reviews the principles guiding such involvement, the challenges to those principles given the experience of applying them and recent suggestions that have been made to improve the situation.

### 3.1. The principles

Economic theory justifies an important role for government intervention in efficient and equitable infrastructure use and provision. The arguments rest on several "traditional" notions of market failure, such as: externalities in consumption and production; scale economies; failures in related markets, like credit (education and physical infrastructure), insurance (health) and labor markets (all sectors); non-excludability; information problems about benefits and costs; and the need to achieve objectives such as equity or poverty alleviation. These standard arguments are well known in the traditional public finance literature and need not be discussed in detail here.[14] But infrastructure services are diverse and each exhibits these characteristics to varying degrees. Indeed, as will be discussed below, policies often fail when they do not make such distinctions within infrastructure. For example, while street sweeping and traffic signalling are non-rival and non-excludable services with high externalities, and urban bus transport is more nearly a private good, one public urban transport entity may be in charge of, and heavily subsidize, them all. As discussed in the previous section, the challenge is that empirical research quantifying the importance of these externalities is far from definitive. Thus, the general principles can only be a rough guide to the appropriateness of government intervention.

*Externalities.* When one individual's consumption affects the well-being of others, the individual should be induced by public action to consider the social rather than just the private costs and benefit of his or her behavior. In the case of human infrastructure, most of these effects are assumed to be positive, thus requiring intervention by government. These might include general effects on

---

[14] For a thorough review of basic principles, see Atkinson and Stiglitz (1980). There are also many treatments of market failures within sectors, such as the classic article by Arrow (1963) for the health field.

society "at large", such as in eradicating certain types of diseases through mass immunization programs. While there is little solid empirical work on this issue, more evidence is beginning to be marshalled on externalities that affect smaller groups of identifiable individuals. These include the positive impact of schooling and parents' health investments on children's access to these services (which may constitute an externality if parents are myopic or are not altruistic towards their children – which are important and controversial assumptions, as was already discussed in the previous section).

With physical infrastructure services, negative externalities have been used more in justifying government investment. Congestion and pollution are the most important reasons cited in the literature as to why private markets may not lead to optimal results. In the case of roads, another externality is that associated with damage to users caused by other users [vehicles cause potholes which cause damage to other vehicles – see Small et al. (1989)].

*Scale economies.* Some infrastructure investments, especially in physical infrastructure, entail large fixed costs, and this argument is often used to justify natural monopolies which can deliver the service at lower than average costs due to scale effects. Another aspect is the need to integrate service delivery into networks that cover a wide geographic area. An example would be the distribution of hydroelectricity; dams require a large long-term investment and the electricity they generate needs to be distributed over a large area via efficient trunk-feeder lines in order to lower unit costs [Munasinghe and Warford (1982)].

*Non-excludability and monitoring use.* This is particularly important for physical infrastructure and some health-related programs (such as vector-control activities through spraying). Roads and other transport modes have traditionally been thought to be too non-exclusionary for a private market to work well, although the setting up of private toll roads in a number of locations has led some to reconsider this proposition [Hau (1990)]. In the water sector, many argue that it is impossible to monitor all those who benefit from a very large irrigation scheme [see, for example, Repetto (1986)] although beneficiaries of residential water supply can be reached more easily.

*Information about benefits.* While information needs to be disseminated regarding all infrastructure services, it is widely accepted to be most essential in the case of health. Much of the focus on why health costs are so high has to do with the simple fact that an asymmetry of knowledge exists between consumers and doctors; in other words, consumers cannot be expected to be able to gather enough information to make informed decisions about the kind of health care they need (even this is controversial as the patient may have the most information about how he or she truly feels). Thus, even in the United States, where consumers are perhaps some of the best informed in the world, lack of information is considered to be the most important reason why a primarily private system fails to provide health care cost-effectively.[15]

*Meeting equity and non-economic objectives.* Particularly in the case of human infrastructure, governments may have objectives other than narrowly defined effectiveness and cost-efficiency criteria. One is poverty reduction. Indeed, the provision of infrastructure has been center stage in many of the recent policy pronouncements from international agencies as a way for the poor to enhance their capacity to take advantage of income-earning opportunities.[16] Other possible objectives include investments to promote national security or solidarity.

## 3.2. The record regarding technical efficiency

Lately, however, concern about the effectiveness, cost and equity of public intervention has sparked an often spirited debate about the need to temper these market failure arguments with analyses of possible government failure. The rest of this section discusses these concerns. For convenience, it first deals with more narrowly-defined efficiency issues – in other words, resource allocation under the assumption of distribution neutrality. It then goes on to assess the evidence regarding equity.

*Investing in the right type of service.* An issue that has received much attention in the policy debate is that the most productive types of infrastructure services are under-provided. Many recent policy studies have argued that investment has not been sufficiently directed towards those infrastructure services that have the highest social rates of return. This is a reflection of both an under-emphasis on relatively inexpensive investments and a lack of government attention to those services that exhibit the most important public good characteristics.

The evidence supporting this point has been more indicative and anecdotal, rather than analytically rigorous. For example, Table 43.4 shows that, for 24 developing countries, when governments faced tough expenditure choices due to macroeconomic crises, economic infrastructure spending bore a larger burden of fiscal adjustments. These are sectors that have a high ratio of capital to recurrent spending. When countries have had to make difficult spending

---

[15] For work on developing countries on the nature of externalities see World Bank (1993).
[16] World Bank (1990); UNDP (1991).

Table 43.4
Expenditure trends by sector for 24 countries that experienced real declines in total expenditure (1979–1989)

|  | Percentage change | Elasticity[a] |
|---|---|---|
| Total expenditure | −17.2 | 1.00 |
| General public | −9.2 | 0.53 |
| Defence | −6.25 | 0.38 |
| Social sectors | −11.4 | 0.66 |
| Productive | −18.7 | 1.08 |
| Infrastructure | −25.4 | 1.47 |
| Others[b] | −1.4 | 0.08 |

[a] Percentage change in the *i*th sectoral over the percentage change in total expenditures.
[b] Includes interest, transfers to local governments and other non-sector specific expenditures
*Source*: Hicks (1991).

decisions, they have tended to start by cutting longer-term capital investment. While some of these declines in expenditure on physical infrastructure may be long overdue because of overcapacity or may simply reflect constraints in the capital market, a persistent trend in this direction may begin to compromise long-term growth.

In human resources, Table 43.4 indicates that, during times of adjustment, governments do try to preserve spending on social services and welfare, at least in relative terms. But many argue that such a trend is hardly an advance – more resources are needed as demands are increasing. And most important, investment in human resources, particularly in basic education and health, continues to be a high-return but relatively neglected spending category. The World Bank's review of adjustment lending is typical of such criticism, citing, in the case of Brazil:

> . . . resource concentration at tertiary levels and of declining allocations for basic social services, despite poor social indicators. . . [The neglect is reflected in a lack of] critical complementary inputs, such as basic drugs, textbooks, and supplies, at the expense of continued overstaffing. . . Similar problems can be found in many other . . . countries [World Bank (1992c)].

These anecdotal examples, while dramatic, do not use careful studies comparing the economic costs of misallocations across sectors. As will be discussed below, the methodology for making such comparisons has yet to become practical – particularly when one is dealing with investments for which benefit calculations are difficult to obtain due to externalities and public good characteristics.

*Effectiveness of public spending.* A growing literature points out that publicly-provided infrastructure services can be made much more effective in terms of measurable outcomes. The concern is not so much with an inability to produce quantity, as it is with poor quality. The descriptive evidence refers to low achievement scores and high repetition rates in education [Lockheed et al. (1991)] and the lack of drugs in clinics [World Bank (1987a)]. In the power sector, it is a lack of system reliability [World Bank (1992)]. A recent review indicates that in 85 developing countries, a quarter of the paved roads outside urban areas need reconstruction – as do a third of the unpaved roads [World Bank (1988b)].

The economic costs of such ineffectiveness can be enormous. The repair bill for the roads in developing countries that need to be reconstructed would amount to $40–45 billion – considerably more than the $12 billion it might have taken in timely preventive measures to keep these roads operational [World Bank (1988b)]. In Nigeria, because of persistent breakdowns in publicly provided infrastructure, 92 percent of surveyed firms owned their own electricity generators [Lee and Anas (1992)]. These costs were excessively high because the firms had to invest relatively large fixed costs for small volumes of output (they were also prevented from selling their excess output). Thus, when governments fail to provide reliable services, enterprises can improvise by trying to compensate, but at a larger cost to society.

More rigorous evidence to support the anecdotal evidence on the effectiveness of government intervention is only beginning to be found. One such strand of research indicates that, while the empirical link between infrastructure-related outcome measures (for example, percentage enrollment rates or the availability of road networks) and economic growth is strong, the quantitative evidence on the link between public spending on these infrastructure categories and growth is weak [see, for example, Devarajan et al. (1992)]. This result could partly be attributed to the difficulty in getting good cross-country data on government spending, or to differences across countries in the cost of infrastructure. More research is warranted to test the robustness of this aggregate result.

*High unit costs.* Another issue that is symptomatic of inefficiency is that the unit costs of providing the services are too high for a given level of output quantity or quality. One indicator of this comes from comparisons of costs for public and private providers. These comparisons must be carefully done in order to ensure that unit costs are computed at the same levels of quantity (in other words, net of scale effects) and quality.

In human resources, several studies on education estimate the determinants of student achievement and use these calculations to conclude that, with secondary level student characteristics held constant, a randomly chosen student would perform better in a private school compared to a public school in five developing countries [Jimenez et al. (1992)].[17] For the average student, the gains in academic achievement to attending private school rather than public school are shown in column 1 of Table 43.5. At the same time, unit costs for the private schools are on average lower than those in public schools, due primarily to lower wage bills – teachers are as effective in private schools, although they are paid less and have lower official teaching qualifications (column 2 of Table 43.5).

Studies of the relative effectiveness of publicly and privately provided physical infrastructure tend not to control as carefully for quality and scale effects, making it more difficult to evaluate the unit cost comparisons. Still, the descriptive studies are indicative of the magnitude of the possible discrepancy. In transport, for example, studies indicate that bus transport for intra-city travel is much less costly when in the hands of the private sector [World Bank (1988c)]. Private bus companies also tend to have a higher fleet utilization rate, a lower staffing ratio and a lower incidence of fare evasion than their subsidized public counterparts [Armstrong and Thierez (1987)]. In the power sector, losses during transmission and distribution (partly through theft) are notoriously high; as a percentage of generation, the losses are 31 percent in

Table 43.5
Relative average cost and efficiency of public and private schools

| Country | (1) Ratio of private to public effectiveness | (2) Ratio of private cost to public cost | (3) Ratio of relative cost to effectiveness[a] |
|---|---|---|---|
| Colombia | 1.13 | 0.69 | 0.61 |
| Dominican Republic | | | |
| Non-elite private | 1.31 | 0.65 | 0.50 |
| Elite private | 1.47 | 1.46 | 0.99 |
| Philippines[b] | | | |
| Math | 1.00 | 0.83 | 0.83 |
| English | 1.18 | 0.83 | 0.70 |
| Philippino | 1.02 | 0.83 | 0.82 |
| Tanzania | 1.16 | 0.69 | 0.59 |
| Thailand | 2.63 | 0.39 | 0.15 |

[a] Col(2)/Col(1).
[b] Public cost estimates and weighted average of national and local costs. Costs are assumed to be the same for all three subjects and are based on World Bank estimates.
*Source*: Jimenez et al. (1991).

[17] Since it is likely that high-performing students come from affluent homes, which provide a more conducive atmosphere for education and self-select themselves into private school, these studies also control for possible sample selection bias via Heckman's two-step technique. The identifying restriction for the equations varies. In the Philippines case study, for example, the relative distance of alternative public and private schools from the household is used to explain the choice of school type but is not used in the achievement equations.

Bangladesh, 28 percent in Pakistan and 22 percent in Thailand and the Philippines compared to only 8 percent in the U.S. and 7 percent in Japan [World Bank (1992a, p. 137)]. These lead to very high costs.

### 3.3. The record regarding equity

Poverty reduction is often cited as another major justification for government intervention. Equal access to some infrastructure services are particularly crucial as they either alleviate some of the main consequences of being poor (for example, access to health services or clean water has a direct bearing on individual well-being) or they enhance the opportunities for the poor to escape their plight (for example, education enhances future labor productivity).

The record for access to publicly provided infrastructure services is, at best, a mixed one.[18] In order to review the available evidence adequately, it is first useful to review some of the data and methodologies that analysts have used.

*Data needs.* The data requirements for incidence analysis can be heavy. The basic need is for a representative sample survey that includes information not only on the level of well-being of the relevant population but also on their use of the infrastructure service under discussion. This means that consumption or household budget surveys that included no data on the use of public facilities would be insufficient. If the analysis were to take into account behavioral concerns as well, then the data requirements would increase accordingly.

Can anything be done without specialized household surveys? One way would be to conduct incidence analysis by sector of economic activity or by geographic region, if it can reasonably be ascertained that certain income groups are concentrated in such sectors or regions.

*Methods of estimating benefit incidence.* Human and physical infrastructure spending typically accounts for about 5–10 percent of all public spending. The general question addressed in studies of benefit incidence analysis of such expenditures in developing countries is: who benefits from various components of public spending? In particular, how does the receipt of the benefits of public spending vary across groups with different levels of well-being?[19]

The most popular method – and one employed in the seminal analyses by

---

[18] This chapter focuses only on infrastructure services, most of which are targeted broadly, that is, have no explicit mechanism for distinguishing among recipients. The Lipton and Ravallion chapter will deal explicitly with subsidies that are narrowly targeted with explicit selection mechanisms; I will only make brief cross-references here.

[19] There have been several reviews: de Wulf (1975), Jimenez (1986) and Selden and Wasylenko (1991).

Meerman (1979) and Selowsky (1979) – consists of the following steps. First, everyone is ranked by level of well-being – usually a measure of income or consumption. Second, the average use of the relevant infrastructure service for each income or consumption group is then estimated. Third, the cost to the government of providing that service is used as a proxy for the benefit of consuming that service. Fourth, the level of well-being is compared before and after the intervention by adding the assumed benefit level to the pre-intervention welfare measure.

There are several key assumptions in using this methodology. One set of assumptions has to do with how to measure the level of well-being. This issue is well-covered in Lipton and Ravallion's chapter of this volume. Income is probably the most popular measure, despite its obvious drawbacks for developing countries – some forms of income are hard to value, particularly those of the self-employed and farmers (who are important in less developed countries) and, on top of this, income tends to vary, and not just seasonally. Consumption is probably easier to measure (although it is similarly difficult to make an accurate assessment of spending on items such as housing). Overall, consumption does not vary as much as income and, as such, it is consistent with the utility maximizing model, since consumption is simply the amount of money required to reach a certain level of welfare. A related consideration is which unit of observation to choose, whether household or individual [again, see Lipton and Ravallion]. If intra-household distribution is important, then the individual is a more appropriate basis of analysis.

The most complicated set of assumptions revolves around the argument that the public cost of the service is an appropriate proxy for the benefits accruing to the individual who gets initial access to the subsidy. This may not be so for a number of reasons. First, if the beneficiary can resell the access to the subsidy, then the benefits will be shared, depending on the resale price.[20] This is unlikely to be an issue in the case of the services with which we are dealing since it is rather difficult to resell access to infrastructure services.

Second, the benefit to an individual of an in-kind subsidy may not be equivalent to the cash value of purchasing that service. The equivalence holds if the in-kind subsidy can be resold in the open market; it would still hold even if resale were not possible, provided that the consumption of that service after the subsidy is infra-marginal. However, if consumption is not infra-marginal, then the value to the individual of the in-kind subsidy may well be less than that of its cash value to the government. For example, a review of "social housing programs" in the U.S. and Germany demonstrates that the value to beneficiaries ranged from 58–62 percent of the cost of provision [Mayo (1986)].

Third, the benefit of an in-kind infrastructure subsidy may be more or less

---

[20] The analysis will be similar to that in tax incidence work [see Atkinson and Stiglitz (1980)].

than the cost of government provision if it precipitates behavioral adjustments by households that would affect the welfare of the recipients. For example, public transfers may substitute, at least in part, for the provision of private transfers. A series of research studies for developing countries shows that private transfers are targeted towards recipients of public subsidies in education and health [Cox and Jimenez (1990)]. In fact, a case study for Peru indicates that private transfers would have been about one fifth more had there not been a publicly-funded social security system for old-age support [Cox and Jimenez (1991)].

Finally, there may be a difference between marginal and average benefits. Most incidence analysis is concerned with measuring average benefits. However, what is important for policy prescriptions are marginal benefits – the benefits of another unit of access. This may be very different for certain income groups. For example, studies indicate that the marginal gain for an additional unit of access to health services, as measured by willingness-to-pay, may decrease for lower income groups [Gertler et al. (1989), Gertler and van der Gaag (1991)].

*Results.* These considerations are rarely addressed for the majority of incidence studies that have been implemented for developing countries. Nevertheless, with appropriate caveats, these studies using standard assumptions have been found to be useful [see reasons outlined in Selden and Wasylenko (1991)].

Given that the standard methodology is benefit incidence analysis, three important factors will generally determine which services benefit poorer income groups the most. One factor is the relative costs of different types of services. For example, in education, the unit costs of higher education are very much higher than those of other levels. In all developing countries, the opportunity cost of one higher education student is 26 primary school students; in Africa, the ratio is 53:1. In health, present subsidies are also unevenly distributed, partly because urban-based hospital care is much more expensive than other types of intervention [World Bank (1988c)].

A second factor is whether access to these various services is distributed evenly across the population. In most cases, they are not. In education, for example, because only a few people benefit from the large subsidies in higher education, 71 percent of the population gets only 22 percent of the subsidies [World Bank (1988c)].

A third factor is the characteristics of those who do get access. Despite zero prices, there is often a high private cost to access. Materials (drugs), opportunity cost and transport can be a large proportion of private cost even though fees are minimal. When there is supply-side quantity rationing, it often favors the rich. One important reason for this is location – richer urban households often have better access than poorer rural households to both physical and human infrastructure. Also, there are ways to buy into access. For example, in education, examples abound of private tutoring in order for households to get access to free, high-quality public schools whose quantity is controlled. In health, coverage in those systems covered by formal social security is often better – but this means that it is open primarily to better-off workers in the formal sector.

Given these considerations, it is thus not surprising that, while the distribution of the benefits of overall public social spending (human and some physical infrastructure) tends to be pro-poor, there is considerable variation depending on the type of service one considers. For example, Table 43.6a shows that, for five Latin American countries, the impact of the sum of government subsidies on education, health, social security, housing and water on the distribution of income is equalizing (in terms of a lower gini coefficient). However, the results vary by type of service. Basic services, such as primary education and most public health interventions (particularly if they are concentrated in rural areas) tend to be strongly pro-poor. However, the poor are systematically under-represented in terms of their access to those services that tend to be the most subsidized per unit of service, such as higher education and urban-based hospital care. Table 43.6b shows the percentages of subsidies received by various income groups in various countries [see also Selden and Wasylenko (1991) for other citations].

There are fewer studies that measure benefit incidence for public enterprises dispensing physical infrastructure [Selden and Wasylenko (1991)]. Studies in

Table 43.6a
Benefit incidence of various expenditure categories

|  | Argentina | Costa Rica | Chile | Dominican Republic | Uruguay |
|---|---|---|---|---|---|
| Sum of education, health, social security, housing and water | + | + | + | + | + |
| All education | + | + | + | − | + |
| Basic education | + | + | + | − | + |
| Secondary education | + | + | + | − | + |
| Higher education | − | − | − | − | − |
| Health | + | + | + | + | + |
| Social security | − | − | − | − | − |
| Housing | + | − | + | − | − |
| Water | − | − | − | − | − |

*Source*: Petrei, 1987.
*Note*: + = contribute to equality (lower gini); − = contribute to inequality.

Table 43.6b
Who gets social sector subsidies?

| Country and sector | Year of survey | Percentage of government subsidy received by income group | | |
|---|---|---|---|---|
| | | Lower 40 percent | Middle 40 percent | Upper 20 percent |
| *All education* | | | | |
| Argentina | 1983 | 48 | 35 | 17 |
| Chile | 1983 | 48 | 34 | 17 |
| Colombia | 1974 | 40 | 39 | 21 |
| Costa Rica | 1983 | 42 | 38 | 20 |
| Dominican Republic | 1976–77 | 24 | 43 | 14 |
| Uruguay | 1983 | 52 | 34 | 14 |
| Indonesia | 1978 | 46 | 25[a] | 29[a] |
| Malaysia | 1974 | 41 | 41 | 18 |
| *Higher education* | | | | |
| Argentina | 1983 | 17 | 45 | 38 |
| Chile | 1983 | 12 | 34 | 54 |
| Colombia | 1974 | 6 | 35 | 60 |
| Costa Rica | 1983 | 17 | 41 | 42 |
| Dominican Republic | 1976–77 | 2 | 22 | 76 |
| Uruguay | 1980 | 14 | 52 | 34 |
| Indonesia | 1978 | 7 | 10[a] | 83[a] |
| Malaysia | 1974 | 10 | 38 | 52 |
| *Public health* | | | | |
| Argentina | 1980 | 69 | 27 | 4 |
| Colombia | 1974 | 42 | 40 | 20 |
| Costa Rica | 1983 | 49 | 38 | 13 |
| Chile | 1983 | 51 | 47 | 11 |
| Dominican Republic | 1984 | 57 | 44 | 9 |
| Uruguay | 1983 | 64 | 25 | 12 |
| Indonesia | 1978 | 19 | | 45[b] |
| Iran | 1977 | 51 | 37 | 13 |
| Malaysia | 1974 | 47 | 37 | 17 |
| Philippines | 1975 | 27 | 33 | 40 |
| Sri Lanka | 1978 | 46 | 39 | 14 |
| *Hospitals* | | | | |
| Colombia | 1974 | 23 | 53 | 23 |
| Malaysia | 1974 | 36 | 34 | 20 |

[a] These figures are for the middle 30 percent.
[b] These figures are for the upper 30 percent.
*Sources*: Jimenez (1987), Petrei (1977), World Bank (1986).

Malaysia and Colombia have found that the distribution of subsidies for electricity, residential piped water and sewerage services are generally not pro-poor [Meerman (1979), Selowsky (1979)]. These studies emphasize the fact that these services tend to be located in urban areas, where average income is higher than in rural areas. Table 43.7a summarizes shows for more recent incidence analyses the relative access of the richest and pooorest to infrastructure services. Moreover, within urban areas, there is some clear case study evidence that higher income families have better access than poorer ones

Table 43.7a
Who gets access to infrastructure services
Percentage of poorest and richest quintiles with access

| Country/yr | Public Water Supply | | Sewers | | Electricity | |
|---|---|---|---|---|---|---|
| | Bot 20% | Top 20% | Bot 20% | Top 20% | Bot 20% | Top 20% |
| Côte d'Iv./85 | 2.4 | 62.1 | 3.4 | 57.0 | 13.2 | 74.8 |
| Ghana/87 | 10.5 | 30.6 | 0.5 | 14.6 | 5.6 | 46.0 |
| Guatem./89 | 46.9 | 86.8 | – | – | 16.1 | 86.1 |
| Mexico/89 | 50.2 | 95.0 | 14.2 | 83.2 | 66.2 | 99.0 |
| Peru/86 | 31.0 | 82.0 | 12.3 | 70.0 | 22.8 | 82.5 |
| *Urban only*: | | | | | | |
| Bolivia/89 | 84.8 | 89.9 | 52.6 | 87.4 | – | – |
| Paraguay/90 | 53.7 | 88.8 | 10.4 | 62.2 | 94.5 | 99.2 |

–: not available.
*Source*: World Bank 1994.

Table 43.7b
Ratio of the price charged by private water vendors to the price charged by the public utility in selected cities, mid-1970s to early 1980s

| City, country | Price ratio |
|---|---|
| Kampala, Uganda | 4:1 to 9:1 |
| Lagos, Nigeria | 4:1 to 10:1 |
| Abidjan, Côte d'Ivoire | 5:1 |
| Lome, Togo | 7:1 to 10:1 |
| Nairobi, Kenya | 7:1 to 11:1 |
| Istanbul, Turkey | 10:1 |
| Dhaka, Bangladesh | 12:1 to 25:1 |
| Tegucigalpa, Honduras | 16:1 to 34:1 |
| Lima, Peru | 17:1 |
| Port-au-Prince, Haiti | 17:1 to 100:1 |
| Surabaya, Indonesia | 20:1 to 60:1 |
| Karachi, Pakistan | 28:1 to 83:1 |

*Source*: World Bank (1988c).

in terms of individual physical connections to main lines [see bottom two rows of Table 43.7a and Whittington 1990)]. Poorer families must thus rely on private water vendors for their water supply and must pay higher unit prices than richer households, as shown in Table 43.7b.[21]

## 3.4. Towards improving public investment policies

The preceding analysis has identified the following needs:

- across sectors, to set priorities more appropriately by focusing on subsidized public investments in those activities that have the highest marginal returns to public funds and that are used primarily by the poor;
- within sectors, to distinguish among subsectors and apply the same criteria as those governing the choice among sectors;
- to mobilize more resources in a non-distortionary way;
- to improve management and internal efficiency; and
- to improve targeting to the poor.

If followed, these actions will lead to socially efficient policies, as they are roughly equivalent to taking into account appropriate shadow prices. But meaningful and sustainable policy reform must investigate more deeply into the root causes of policy failure – what led to the present unsatisfactory outcomes and what reforms can be instituted to correct for them?

An extensive inquiry is beyond the scope of this paper, but it is useful to focus on several general reasons that have preoccupied analysts trying to improve investment policy in infrastructure. There appears to be a general consensus that investing more money in much the same way as before will not solve the problems and that, therefore, appropriate policy reform is the key. If so, one must understand the policymakers – their abilities, the information and techniques available to them and their incentives. The rest of this section reviews some recent work addressing some of these parameters, including developing better tools of analysis, fostering institutional reform that increases efficiency, such as decentralization and greater private sector involvement, and taking political economy into account in analyzing infrastructure investment.

*Better tools of analysis.* One important area is to develop more practical tools of analysis or guidelines for allocating resources across spending categories – that is, choosing among spending alternatives by weighing benefits and costs

---

[21] Private water vendors are those who sell water in the street, mainly in low-income communities. This term does not apply to those who sell bottled water in specialty stores.

through an analysis of their social rates of return. This is often a problem because the tools for doing so for both human and physical infrastructure are far from perfect.

Formal cost-benefit exercises are often not used to evaluate investments in human infrastructure.[22] One reason may be that it is often difficult to evaluate benefits for many human resource investments. In education, although there are a growing number of studies that estimate the rate of return to different levels of education (see Table 43.3), they are not available for many countries, are of variable quality and generally ignore some high cost-services, such as alternative disciplines in higher education. Moreover, as discussed earlier, most of the benefit estimates (which are typically inferred from wage differentials) are unable to take into account such difficulties as externalities or quality effects. On the health side, rates of return are only very rarely computed because evaluating benefits requires explicit calculations of the value of life (or healthy life-years). The methodological difficulty of doing this has forced analysts to conduct instead cost-effective analyses that allow only limited inter-sectoral comparisons of spending options.

Because of these factors, combined with the misleading but lingering view that "social" services cannot inherently be compared with "productive" services, rate-of-return comparisons are not used to guide specific investment decisions in the social sectors. This view has recently been challenged by those who claim that rates of return can indeed be computed for education and health services [Psacharopoulos (1985)] and that, in any case, the pitfalls in deriving benefit estimates for these services are no worse than those that plague physical infrastructure.

Another possible reason why cost-benefit methodology is not so widely used as a planning tool is that the most important spending decisions in human resources are not about discrete capital investments but about more continuous flows of recurrent spending. In theory, the techniques can be adapted to evaluate recurrent spending, a larger component in social expenditures than in infrastructure expenditures, which are heavily weighted by new investments [see Besley (1989b) for suggestions on how to make such concerns operational]. In practice, implementation is more difficult because data on recurrent spending categories are often not neatly subdivided in a way that is relevant for policy – for example, the joint costs of producing various levels of education and health expenditures are difficult to sort out. Thus, the need to develop practical economically oriented guidance on inter-sectoral spending choices remains a priority item on the conceptual agenda. Even in the absence

---

[22] For example, the World Bank's operational guidelines for the economic analysis of projects acknowledge that, "while it may be possible to use quantitative criteria in such [social] sectors more often than is customary, both conceptual and statistical difficulties limit their application". (The World Bank, 1980, OMS 2.21 "Economic Analysis of Projects").

of hard data, however, the discipline of going through steps of benefit-cost calculation in making broad sectoral allocations can help to make the logic of spending decisions more transparent and explicit.

In the case of physical infrastructure, rate of return analysis has a well-established methodology and a long accepted tradition in development [see Dreze and Stern (1991) and Squire (1989) for recent comprehensive treatments of the concepts]. But a recent review by Little and Mirrlees (1990) indicates that the analytical principles are not being applied systematically:

> We have claimed that much in the rules [about cost-benefit analysis] we collected and prescribed in 1969 and 1974 has survived analytical scrutiny, that these procedures are capable of being used effectively, and that many important aspects of them have been neglected by project evaluators. We have found that the extent to which they are used and have real influence is not great... (p. 376).

The authors then suggest that this is one reason why investment in developing countries has had very low returns in the aggregate, leading to low growth during the 1980s.[23]

The question is, how can this process be improved? At issue is the complexity of the methods, as well as the incentives of the institutions to take them seriously. Squire (1991) suggests the following practical principles: (1) basing project costs on historical experience (rather than on overly optimistic projections), (2) using shadow pricing, but only when it is critical (that is, for those projects whose profitability is highly sensitive to the choice of the standard conversion factor) and (3) explicitly building in analyses for cost recovery to those projects that result in a net cost to the public sector but a net benefit overall.

Another methodological issue is that conventionally estimated rates of return may be an inadequate guide to investment choice in the absence of an analysis of the general economic environment in which the project is operating. Table 43.8 depicts how rates of return to public projects – particularly those in infrastructure – vary with various indices of market distortions resulting from trade restrictions, exchange rate interventions, the real rate of interest and the public deficit. Fewer distortions are highly correlated with greater rates of return.[24] While these calculations are based only on World Bank projects, they

---

[23] However, they do note that World Bank projects tended to have relatively high rates of return. But the rest of the investment portfolio for these countries did not fare as well, which raises the important issue of fungibility.

[24] It is not possible to infer causality strictly because of a possible source of bias in the comparisons if the observed policy distortions are caused by the same factors (say, political economy) that affect the rates of return.

Table 43.8
Economic policies and average economic rates of return for projects
Financed by The World Bank Group, 1968–1989 (1%)

| Policy distortion index | All public projects | Public projects in non-tradeable sectors |
|---|---|---|
| *Trade restrictiveness* | | |
| High | 13.6 | 14.6 |
| Moderate | 15.4 | 16.0 |
| Low | 19.3 | 24.3 |
| *Foreign exchange premium* | | |
| High (200 or more) | 7.2 | 11.5 |
| Moderate (20–200) | 14.9 | 17.2 |
| Low (less than 20) | 18.0 | 19.3 |
| *Real interest rate* | | |
| Negative | 15.4 | 17.9 |
| Positive | 17.5 | 17.9 |
| *Fiscal deficit*[a] | | |
| High (8 or more) | 13.7 | 16.6 |
| Moderate (4–8) | 15.1 | 16.8 |
| Low (less than 4) | 18.1 | 18.2 |

[a] Percentage of GDP.
*Source*: Kaufmann (1991).

are from an extensive database of 1,200 projects over a 20-year period [Kaufmann (1991)]. A similar study on the success of human resource projects (measured by ex-post evaluation rankings rather than by rates of return, which are not calculated) finds similar results [Kaufmann and Wang (1992)].

The problem of inter-sectoral resource allocation can be approached using the modern theory of optimal taxation [Besley (1989a) is an example of this].[25] The problem would be to derive a set of optimal subsidies, which can be interpreted simply as negative taxes. Given costs, these would imply a set of optimal prices for all public services. These would presumably depend upon the relative elasticities of demand for the range of goods and services. If, for example, demand for transport services were more inelastic than that for some health service, then cross-subsidies from transport to health might be in order. Contingent on the continued growth of a literature on the price elasticities of different public services, this could be a promising avenue for future research, although implementation could be constrained by heavy data requirements.

[25] See also the discussion in Atkinson and Stiglitz (1980) or Stern (1987) for a full discussion of optimal public pricing and how the principles are similar to those of the optimal taxation literature.

*Providing better incentives through less centralized institutions.* Public sector management is partly a question of applying a range of techniques from budgeting to personnel administration. These techniques are obviously important factors in improving investment performance, and it is important for staff to receive adequate training and technical assistance. However, these are issues that are not germane to infrastructure and are not treated any further here. Public management is also a question of building incentives within institutions where objectives may not be clear and competitive pressures may not exist, leading to a lack of accountability and undermotivated workers. Many have argued that, in order to address such incentive issues within government, more than a piecemeal reform of public administration will be necessary. In this regard, two initiatives have received much attention lately in the field of infrastructure – decentralization and privatization.

The debate about decentralization ranges over a wide set of issues regarding the appropriate balance of financial and administrative responsibility among central governments, sub-national (state and local) governments and the institutions and communities themselves.[26] It is an issue that is particularly important for human infrastructure where the provision and financing of infrastructure services has traditionally been very heavily centralized [Winkler (1991), World Bank (1993)]. The issue is whether more decentralization would be desirable on efficiency grounds. There are two principal arguments. One is largely technical. The scale economies in providing infrastructure services may be overestimated, once administrative and information costs are taken into account. For example, when even small questions have to be referred to central authorities (such as individual curricula in schools), unit costs tend to be very high. Also, central authorities may have less information than those who run the facilities leading to misallocation regarding input mixes. The other argument is incentive-based centralized institutions, compared to local institutions, are not as accountable to those they serve, precisely because the client group is not the funding source.

While there are not yet many empirical studies, the initial evidence tends to support these propositions. A study by Jimenez and Paqueo (1993) indicates that, in the Philippines, unit costs in schools where parents contribute more to financing tend to be lower than in other schools when quality is held constant. A similar finding is reported by James et al. (1993) for Indonesia.

Implementing decentralization reform is also an important issue. Reforms to

---

[26] In a world of many communities, each with a different tax and package of public infrastructure (as well as other services), if people are perfectly mobile, an optimal allocation of public goods will result. In this Tiebout-world, consumers reveal their preferences by moving, yielding an efficient market-like solution. But inter-jurisdictional spillovers and moving costs imply that higher tiers of government may have to intervene in such a world, taking into account these externalities and scale economies in service provision.

decentralize health care provision and education in Chile have been generally successful in delivering more services to where they are needed, but the implementation process has been more difficult and slower than anticipated. Getting local authorities prepared for taking on a different role takes time and effort [Castaneda (1992)].

By contrast to human infrastructure, physical infrastructure services tend to be provided by semi-autonomous, state-owned enterprises or by line units of municipalities and other sub-national agencies. The recent *World Development Report 1994* discusses how commercial principles could be introduced within public entities to make them more responsive and accountable for their actions. But autonomy can lead to principal-agent type issues about the ability of the central government (the principal) to affect the behavior of the provider of the service (the agent) when the two actors may have different objectives and information bases. One example would be if the central government is interested in a provider being an employer of large scale while the agent is trying to minimize costs [see Galenson (1989) for the case of roads]. However, there have been few studies that have posed the problem in this way in infrastructure and none that have addressed it empirically.

A more extensive discussion has emerged regarding privatization and how it can improve incentives in physical infrastructure. The argument is that, in many cases, the public sector has taken on more than it should – after all, the market failures described above probably do not apply to the same degree for every infrastructure service. Indeed, in the early years of many industrial countries, basic infrastructure – such as roads, railways, power and even education – was financed and built mainly by private entrepreneurs and organizations [Roth (1988)]. Disengaging the public sector in situations where its role as a provider is not justified would allow (1) a private sector that is more subject to competitive pressures to provide the services more efficiently; and (2) the public sector to focus its limited financial and administrative capacity on those services where market failures are indeed important and public provision in some form is required. There are issues associated with each point.

For what types of infrastructure services would a greater private sector involvement be viable and efficient? It is important to distinguish among various types of services, and within services, types of activities, because they have different characteristics. Some infrastructure services, for example, are not subject to scale economies and are more easily characterized by perfect competition, such as trucking and bus services. Private provision is likely to lead to efficiency gains in this case, unless there are barriers to entry due to regulatory restraints. The evidence on this point has so far only been illustrative and relies on simply comparing the unit costs of public and private providers of a given service to infer what the efficiency gains might be from privatization, without rigorous controls to ensure strict comparability. For example, data for urban transport show that, in cities where bus services are provided by both public and private operators, the cost per passenger is lower for private operators than for public operators, despite the fact that the public services are invariably highly subsidized. For these same cities, the public operators have a lower fleet utilization rate, a higher staffing ratio and a greater incidence of fare evasion than unsubsidized private operators.

Ratio of per passenger private cost to public
cost of comparable bus services, 1985

| Ankara | .48 | Jakarta | .50 |
|---|---|---|---|
| Bangkok | .63 | Karachi | .36 |
| Calcutta | .37 | Khartoum | .40 |
| Istanbul | .85 | | |

*Source*: World Bank (1988c), calculated from Table 6.3.

Recent case studies on roads have found that the unit cost of road maintenance done directly by government agencies is about 60 percent higher than that of work done by private contractors in Brazil [World Bank (1988b)]. Such cost comparisons need to be done more carefully, however, to ensure that all the components of cost are taken into account even for the private sector.

But for many infrastructure services, there are barriers to entry (either regulatory or technological) as well as scale economies that inhibit a large number of private firms from operating profitably. Thus, it is important to consider the market structure that results from a privatization effort, since a regulated private monopoly is not necessarily more efficient than a well-run, publicly owned utility.[27]

A useful framework for discussing this question is contestability analysis, under which competitive pressures can result from potential as well as actual current rivals. Thus, unlike perfect competition, it is compatible with the presence of scale economies and, consequently, a small number of large firms

---

[27] For example, prior to its break-up in 1983, the Bell telephone system in the U.S. provided excellent service (and returns to its investors) but it was needlessly expensive. The company was able to justify high local rates by adding to its cost base. (When broken up, Bell quickly shed many of its prestigious but not directly profitable operations, including its theoretically inclined economic research staff and academic economics journal). Such a monopoly puts a heavy burden on the regulatory authorities to monitor the firm closely and to develop innovative incentive schemes – a difficult task, particularly in developing countries.

subject to the threat of entry.[28] Even monopolists in a perfectly contestable market cannot earn excessive profits since these would be a profit opportunity for a potential entrant. The key is free entry and exit into the market.

This analysis has been applied to the case of infrastructural deficiencies in Nigeria, where a public sector utility such as the electric power authority is often characterized by severe shortcomings in operation and maintenance, as well as in administrative and financial management. Baumol and Lee (1991) conclude that the most promising way to correct these inefficiencies is to institute regulatory changes that would allow greater participation of the private sector – such as allowing private firms to sell any excess power to the public agency or to other firms to make the electric utility market more nearly contestable. Scale economies would allow these private firms, which already have generating capacity because of unreliable public supplies, to lower their costs. Another regulatory change would be to let industrial areas manage "utility pools," not only for power but also for other public services, such as water supply, garbage collection and telecommunications.

In such analyses, unbundling activities within sectors is an important concern, since the market for some activities may be more contestable than others. For example, in power, even though natural monopolies exist in the transmission and distribution of electricity, generation can be done by small producers, who can sell it to consumers through public utilities. In addition, services that used to be done by public agencies are now being contracted out, such as stevedoring in Chile or the sale of railway tickets in Korea. In Côte d'Ivoire, the public authority in charge of water supply is responsible for owning and financing the fixed assets while a private company is responsible for operations and maintenance. Contracting out is also being tried in education, as in Chile and also in the Philippines where there was an exploratory scheme to allow the public school enrollment surplus to be educated in private schools for a fee [World Bank (1989)]. Rigorous evaluation summarizing the lessons learned from these schemes have yet to be conducted.

Important innovations in technology and regulatory management increase the scope for introducing efficient competitive behavior. Examples are in telecommunications where cellular systems are merging as an alternative to local distribution networks and in power generation, where multi-cycle turbine generators operate more efficiently at lower output levels [World Bank (1994)].

Even when services are provided privately, the government still has a role,

---

[28] Baumol and Lee (1991) provide a very useful primer, with an application for infrastructure services in developing countries.

for example, in ensuring that acceptable safety and environmental standards are met and that the poor have access to certain key services. It would be important to consider efficiency criteria in meeting such objectives [see, for example, Eskeland and Jimenez (1993), on the choice of policy instruments in pollution control and Lipton and Ravallion's chapter in this volume and Grosh (1993) on targeting public expenditures towards the poor]. Also, the emphasis away from almost universal direct provision towards selective intervention in (and effective regulation of) certain activities entails a fundamental way in which many governments do business. For example, regulatory interventions must ensure that they do not themselves become barriers to entry for private sector involvement. One major impediment to direct private sector investment is the risk that future price controls or government interventions will reduce the returns to that investment. Another barrier is most governments' under-developed capacity to design, award and supervise contracts that assure equitable risk sharing and good performance. A promising initiative in public-private partnership in infrastructure is to operate on a "build-operate-and-transfer" (BOT) or "build-own-and-operate" (BOO) basis, under which a private firm finances some or all of the initial investment and is remunerated directly from revenues earned by the project by selling the facility or output to a public utility. BOT schemes provide for the eventual transfer of ownership to the state, when private firms do not want to assume the risks and liability of operating the facility. A recent survey indicates that since the early 1980s, 150 infrastructure projects in developing countries using such financing techniques have amounted to a total cost of over $60 billion [World Bank (1994)].

Whether the private sector or local communities respond to this challenge will depend upon local organizational abilities, as well as on the risks they face if they do not respond. A case study of 31 villages in upland South India suggests that, where the risks of crop loss and conflict caused by water shortage are high, villages tended to organize local infrastructure at little cost, ignoring the officially established local government in the process [Wade (1988)].

*Political economy.* There are several issues of political economy that can affect infrastructure investment. One is that some infrastructure investment is undertaken for non-economic reasons, such as national security (transport) or national unity (education). These must be taken into account in the process of planning infrastructure investment.

Another issue is that infrastructure, like most other public spending, is subject to "capture" by special interest groups. In human resources, this phenomenon has been blamed for the fact that public investment places such a heavy emphasis on tertiary levels (universities and urban-based hospital care) as opposed to primary levels (basic education and health care), even when the latter have higher rates of return and are more equitably distributed [Birdsall and James (1993)]. This has been attributed to the power of urban dwellers to exercise more influence over resource allocation.

Political economy can also be at the root of the problem of quality, which is linked to underinvestment in operations and maintenance (O&M), particularly in spending on non-wage categories. As pointed out by Heller (1976, 1992), governments tend:

> ... to concentrate their efforts on new investments and fail to provide adequately for the recurrent costs of operating and maintaining previous projects. Sectors in which there have been the largest shortfalls in O&M are, typically, road networks, public and government buildings, agricultural equipment, and communications equipment [Heller (1992), p. 52].

One problem is that the incentives of various decision-makers are often biased. Large economic rents in new construction lead to a coincidence of interests among beneficiary groups, the politicians they lobby and, finally, bureaucrats from infrastructure agencies, all of whom may benefit more from starting new projects rather than maintaining old ones. The resulting decision-making process leads to large suboptimal investments, even in developed countries. In the United States, for example, the value of irrigated water to some 146,000 farms served by the Bureau of Reclamation amounted to nearly $15 billion or 56 percent of the average market value of irrigated land. The 6 percent of all farmers who receive the subsidy are among the richest in the nation [Repetto (1986)].

In some infrastructure services, particularly in the area of human capital, the problem is not so much excessive new investment as underinvestment in the non-wage component of O&M. Strong labor market actions by education and health care workers often lead to protection of wage payments when budgets become tighter. In Côte d'Ivoire, for example, the proportion of the budget devoted to the wage bill went up, while the proportion going to materials fell between 1975 and 1986. Over that period, the results were a lack of teaching materials and drugs, dilapidated and unsanitary conditions and an overall decline in quality that seriously undermined productivity [World Bank (1992c)].

## 4. Pricing infrastructure services

Recently, international institutions have been advocating pricing reform in public infrastructure as another way to address many of the issues outlined in the previous section.[29] From given low levels, raising prices can mobilize revenue that can be used to increase the accessibility and improve the quality of services. At the same time, demand management will reduce waste. If done selectively so that prices for services consumed by the rich are raised, there could even be a salutary effect on equity.

This section first reviews some basic principles of public pricing, before discussing the recent issues in human and physical infrastructure.

## 4.1. Some basic principles

The basic principles for public pricing are well established in public finance [see Atkinson and Stiglitz (1980)]. Efficiency requires prices to be set according to social marginal cost. When there are no externalities, market imperfections or other distortions, and when goods and services are traded freely in the private market, the appropriate reference point would be the prevailing price. For goods that are not traded privately, such as most infrastructure services, the incremental opportunity cost of resources used in production must be considered. In these cases, the public authority must also take into account: (1) externalities (whether positive, such as decreasing the incidence of communicable diseases through a health project, or negative, such as the increased pollution caused by the increase in traffic induced by a new road); (2) scale economies, caused by large fixed costs which, in turn, imply that marginal cost pricing cannot recover costs; (3) incomplete markets (such as underdeveloped financial credit markets for education or insurance markets for health); and (4) the administrative costs of collecting certain kinds of charges (such as monitoring volumes of water used by a large number of users or being able to exclude nonpayers). In addition, prices may take into account distributional and financial objectives. The main issues in practice arise in how those principles are applied in specific sectors.[30]

Another consideration that has more recently been considered in the pricing literature is the fiscal context. While the fiscal crises of the 1980s which confronted many developing country governments drew attention to this issue, the principles behind the approach were more general and rigorously rooted in

---

[29] Publications by the World Bank on the following sectors all contain these points: health [World Bank (1987)] water [World Bank (1992), forthcoming], energy and power [World Bank (1992b)], roads [Heggie (1991)], education [World Bank (1986)].

[30] A recent review of infrastructure pricing at the World Bank [Julius and Alicbusan (1988)] indicated that while it is standard policy to compute marginal cost and explicitly adjust it to take those considerations into account, many of the adjustments are not done in practice.

ideas developed in modern public finance.[31] Public pricing decisions need to take into account the overall budget constraint since alternative forms of raising revenues through taxes on commodities, trade or labor would inevitably introduce distortions elsewhere in the economy. Distortion-free lump-sum taxes are infeasible and there are economic limits to which governments can rely on the inflation tax (which may introduce its own distortions) and increasing the deficit. Prices charged by public enterprises can thus be an efficient alternative in raising revenues. The result is that governments may provide a lower subsidy for services for which there are large externalities, once the fiscal objective is considered. Indeed, prices may generally exceed the marginal costs as conventionally calculated.

If one were to assume that the profits and losses of the public agency or state-owned enterprise delivering the infrastructure service were simply passed on to the central government, then, the problem of deriving optimal prices would be analytically the same as that of setting optimal taxes. It is beyond the scope of this paper to derive these formulas, which are discussed more fully elsewhere (see the references in footnote 30). This approach is very data intensive. Even under the strong assumption that prices elsewhere in the economy are constant (if they were not, addressing this fully would require a computable general equilibrium model), the estimates of fiscal gains would require a calculation of the change in demand of the service in question as well as the cross-price elasticities of other services that serve as substitutes and complements. Estimating the distortionary cost or "excess burden" would require similar data (although one would want the compensated demands of the relevant goods).

These ideas have been applied in a much more simplified way to the more limited, and arguably short-term, problem of setting prices within a sector or service (as opposed to setting prices optimally over the full range of government services), when the subsidy required is less than what is optimal. The partial equilibrium diagram of Figure 43.1 illustrates some of the basic arguments. Let $D_p$ and $D_s$ denote private and social demand curves. $D_s$ is to the right of $D_p$ because of externalities. (Ignore for the moment the curves marked $S$, which are iso-subsidy curves to be described below.) The optimal quantity of the service, $q^*$, will only be consumed with an optimal unit subsidy equivalent to $s^* = c - p^*$, where $c$ depicts marginal cost (assumed to be constant without loss of generality) and $p^*$ indicates the private cost to the

---

[31] The classic reference is Diamond and Mirrlees (1971). For treatments in the tradition of the recent public finance literature, see Atkinson and Stiglitz (1980). For applications in some of the sectors of concern in this paper, see Katz (1987), Besley (1989b), Hammer (1993) and Heady (1988).

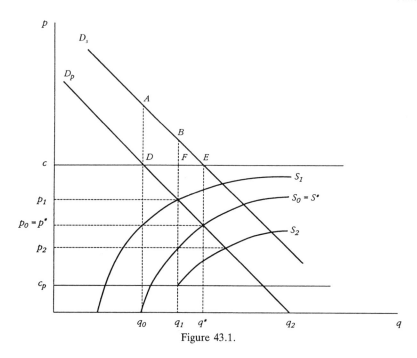

Figure 43.1.

individual, who must then pay a fee equivalent to $p^* - c_p$, the private cost of going to school. This means that total subsidy is $S_0 = S^* = cq^*$. When do these arguments justify a zero price, the most popular option for many social services? The optimal fee is zero only if the marginal private benefit curve crosses $c_p$ at $q^*$, or if the administrative costs of collecting the fee (not drawn) outweigh the benefits.

What happens when there are budgetary restraints?[32] Second-best principles apply. The government is restricted to financing the cost of providing a public service, $cq$, out of a given subsidy budget, $S_1 < S_0$ and the proceeds from a user charge, $pq$. Then, the iso-subsidy locus, which shows the combinations of $q$ and $p$ that would be consistent with a given unit cost of provision $c$ and a budget $S_1$, is in effect the supply curve. The total optimal subsidy in Figure 43.1 is $S_0$, but the optimum is not available in this case. The distance between the locus and the constant marginal cost of providing the service is the amount that needs to be "recovered" from the users. Given the binding budget constraint,[33] at a price $p_0$, there would be excess demand equivalent to $q_0 q^*$. A

---

[32] See Thobani (1983), Jimenez (1987), Besley (1989b) and Katz (1987) for more thorough discussions of these models.

[33] The budget constraint would not be binding if $S_o$ were to cross the private demand curve beyond $q^*$.

unit price increase of $p_1 - p^*$ would be welfare improving by the amount of the area ADFB. Essentially, the intuitive rule in this case would be to raise fees until the excess demand disappears.

The rest of this section discusses the extent to which these ideas have been applied to human and physical infrastructure in theory and in practice.

## 4.2. Human infrastructure[34]

Over the past 10 years, the concept of pricing education and health has once more come to the fore as a means to address some of the efficiency and equity issues outlined in Section 3. It is here that the proposed changes have been most different from past practice and advice.

*Past practice and suggested reforms.* The majority of education and health services in developing countries are provided by central governments. These services are very heavily subsidized, to the extent that they are usually provided free, or almost free.[35] In addition, there are often restrictions on the level of fees that private providers can charge users.

While it is difficult to get an accurate measure of the share of recurrent costs recovered through user charges (because definitions and categories of budgetary flows are not systematically monitored internationally), Table 43.9 provides

Table 43.9
Cost-recovery ratios in education in developing countries, early 1980s

|  | Percentage of countries with no fees | Uses fees as percentage of unit cost | Number of countries |
|---|---|---|---|
| Education |  |  |  |
| Primary | 39 | 8 | 36 |
| Secondary | 25 | 15 | 36 |
| Higher | 30 | 8 | 30 |
| Health[a] | n.a. | 7 | 17 |

[a] Percentage of recurrent public health expenditure covered by user fees.
n.a. Not available.
*Source*: Jimenez, 1987.

[34]Many of the ideas in this chapter are taken from Jimenez (1987, 1990). However, this chapter provides a conceptual and empirical update.

[35] While systematic evidence on the amount of public expenditures that is recovered is not available, there is much country-specific evidence that the most popular pricing scheme is zero-pricing, at least officially [see, for example, World Bank (1986, 1987a)]. This does not include "unofficial" prices charged by providers for access to rationed services.

rough estimates for a sample of countries. The cost figures do not account for the possibility of distorted prices, but the data are indicative and show that there is some variation across countries but that overall the shares are generally very low.

Recent studies, many sponsored by multilateral financial institutions like the World Bank [for summaries of this debate, see World Bank (1986, 1987a), Jimenez (1990) and Creese (1992)] have argued that present pricing rules ought to be changed to improve efficiency and equity. In particular, the literature focuses on three points. First, despite evidence that more investment in education and health is still profitable, there are severe constraints to tapping further central government sources. Second, uniformly low prices mean that expensive services are subsidized more than cheaper ones, which leads to the poorest having little access to subsidies. Third, the limited resources devoted to social services are often badly used. While the exact recommendations vary, the common link among them is the idea that policies that differentiate prices by type of service and by type of consumer are generally more efficient and equitable than low and uniform price policies. The rest of this section reviews the conceptual arguments and the empirical evidence regarding this proposition.

The principal recommendations have been debated in the past eight to ten years, in both the research and policy literature.[36] They include the following:

- Increase prices for some social services that have large private benefits and are consumed by the relatively well-off. For many countries, these services include higher education or curative care in urban hospitals. The extent of the increases will have to be tailored to the availability of credit (for education) and insurance (for health) markets.
- Invest revenues in socially-profitable services, focusing on expanding quantity (such as primary education, primary health care) or on quality (such as non-wage recurrent expenditure categories).
- Protect the poor's consumption of the services, with increased prices through categorical targeting or, where feasible, means testing.
- Make institutional changes to develop credit and insurance markets, particularly in education and health respectively, as well as to liberalize overly-centralized provision, thus giving institutions, local communities and private providers more responsibility.

*Efficiency: some conceptual issues.* What are the efficiency justifications for

---

[36] See, for example, World Bank (1986, 1987a), de Ferranti (1985), Jimenez (1986b, 1987), Griffin (1987) and Briscoe (1993). For examples of dissenting voices, see Abel-Smith (1987), Bray (1986) and Gilson (1988).

these proposals? One argument is that the reasons for heavily subsidized (and, in some cases, free) provision are not warranted for all types of social services. Externalities, for example, may hold more for primary education and less for higher education [World Bank (1986)]. Similarly, the benefits of curative health care and a clean water supply are particularly considered to be private, whereas those of preventive care could have external benefits. The empirical evidence offered in the literature on these issues, reviewed earlier, is still relatively limited, which is surprising given the central role that the argument currently plays in shaping policy.

Information about benefits is particularly important for health. The asymmetry of information between provider and user has long been recognized as one of the most important roadblocks to relying only on private insurance as a cost-efficient system. Profit-maximizing providers could have a moral hazard problem in prescribing high-cost treatments. In this case, subsidizing provision could be important for users. However, subsidies alone will not solve the problem and could exacerbate it if providers know users have access to the "deep pockets" of government. There is more of an argument for increasing regulation or for eliminating the moral hazard problem through pre-payment arrangements in which both the provider and consumer have a stake in keeping the latter healthy. Health maintenance organizations are motivated by this principle.

Another argument for reconsidering pricing options in the social sectors is fiscal – for a variety of reasons, budgets are severely restrained, even though the returns to some investments are high. There are several reasons for this outcome that have been discussed earlier. For example, the costs of mobilizing revenues through general taxes are particularly high in developing countries because of their heavy reliance on distortionary indirect domestic and trade taxes [World Bank (1991b), Newbery and Stern (1987)]. Also, central governments fail to allocate sufficient amounts from the main treasury because of technical constraints, such as the failure to measure benefits and costs of social programs accurately in order to make the appropriate investment choices, or because of political roadblocks [see Birdsall and James (1993)].

But the welfare improvement from a fee increase is dependent not only on demand-side parameters, but also on the supply responsiveness of providers. The foregoing analysis assumes that increased prices will finance service expansion. Thus, in evaluating the welfare implications, it is also important to capture supply responses. This is true not only for quantity but also for quality, which is often sacrificed in a budget-restrained environment. Some analysts have argued that fee revenues can be earmarked for certain non-wage operations and maintenance spending since this is where government tends to underspend [Heller (1976)].

What evidence is there that these effects are important? The ultimate objective of policy reform is to maximize social welfare. However, this is too general to be useful as an operational criterion for making an empirical evaluation of policy change. The literature has instead focused on various arguments for pricing reform – namely that increasing prices will: (1) increase government revenues, which can be used to expand the supply and quality of priority services; (2) stimulate the use and consumption of those services; and (3) improve key indicators, such as gains in consumer surplus or by direct measure of health and educational outcomes, such as health status or literacy (although attribution may be difficult due to lags between policy changes and expected impacts).

The growing literature on price effects in the use of education and health are of roughly two types: (1) studies that primarily simulate the revenue, supply, use and welfare effects and (2) those that attempt to monitor the impact of actual attempts to raise prices. Both types of evaluations are reviewed here.

*Efficiency: evidence from simulation studies.* Some policy studies have simply used some rough order of magnitude to get a sense of what kinds of financing can be generated if demand were completely inelastic and a price increase were used to finance service expansion. The results can be dramatic. For example, it has been estimated that the impact of raising user costs in higher education, by eliminating university student allowances and introducing tuition payments to cover operating costs, would be sufficient to finance substantial increases in enrollment ratios in some countries in sub-Saharan Africa (Table 43.10).

Table 43.10
Potential impact on primary education in Africa of increasing fees in higher education

| Country | Current enrollment ratio | Potential primary enrollment ratio with full cost recovery in higher education[a] |
|---|---|---|
| Benin | 65 | 81 |
| Burkina Faso | 20 | 25 |
| Central African Republic | 68 | 79 |
| Congo | n.a. | n.a. |
| Côte d'Ivoire | 76 | 100 |
| Malawi | 59 | 91 |
| Mali | 27 | 35 |
| Niger | 23 | 26 |
| Senegal | 48 | 81 |
| Sudan | 51 | 73 |
| Tanzania | n.a. | n.a. |
| Togo | n.a. | n.a. |
| Average | 49 | 66 |

[a] Full cost recovery refers to the elimination of university student allowances and introduction of tuition payments to cover operating costs.
n.a. Not available.
*Source*: World Bank (1986, pp. 22, 23).

Such estimates are only illustrative of what is feasible. More recent studies incorporate behavioral concerns. The general empirical approach is to use micro-econometric techniques to estimate the effects price changes have on behavior and then to use the results as parameters to simulate the eventual effects on the use and availability of the service.

Most of the studies focus on the demand side to estimate the effects of price changes on utilization and revenue. A series of studies on the impacts of price changes on health demand has been done on Malaysia [Heller (1982)], the Philippines [Akin et al. (1986)], Côte d'Ivoire [Dor and van der Gaag (1987) and Gertler and van der Gaag (1991)], Ghana [Gertler and van der Gaag (1991) and Lavy and Quigley (1991)], Kenya [Ellis and Mwabu (1991), Mwabu (1986) and Mwabu et al. (1992)], Nigeria [Akin et al. (1991)], Peru [Gertler et al. (1987)] and Pakistan [Alderman and Gertler (1989)]. While a detailed review of these studies is beyond the scope of this paper, a general outline of the procedures used would be useful.

Discrete choice models are typically used to obtain estimates of demand price elasticities. The left-hand side dependent variable is often measured as the incidence of use of various kinds of health facilities (for example, private doctor, public facility, traditional healer), though the Lavy and Quigley study is different in that it also measures intensity of use. These price elasticities are then used to show how revenues will be affected by increasing prices, as measured by independently collected unit prices in a locality or as proxied by the time costs of access. Table 43.11 shows some basic results. A common finding is that the utilization of health services tends to be relatively price inelastic, so that a unit increase in prices will lead to an increase in revenues. Moreover, these are estimates at a single point along the demand curve – many of the studies show that demand may be relatively more price elastic at lower levels of utilization and income.

The models of education demand are similar to those of health [Peru, Gertler and Glewwe (1990), Malawi, Tan et al. (1984)]. More measures are used for demand. At the household level, it could be the number of children in school; at the individual level, the use of various types of discrete categories of education facilities and completed years of schooling (relative to the number of years possible) are also used. The qualitative results, also shown in Table 43.11, do not differ much from those found in health.

These price elasticities can be used to compute the welfare gain associated with a price increase, given the budget-constrained analytical framework outlined above.[37] The estimated revenue generated from the user charges can finance either an expansion of supply or an improvement in quality. Some of

---

[37] If the public sector rationed efficiently across sectors, the shadow value of a dollar of public revenue would be sufficient to infer welfare improvements. However, the pricing literature for education and health assumes that insufficient funds are being devoted to education and health services.

Table 43.11
Price elasticities of demand for health and education services

| Year of data | Country and service | Price range (U.S. dollars) | Overall | Price elasticity by income group | |
| --- | --- | --- | --- | --- | --- |
| | | | | Lowest quartile | Highest quartile |
| | *Health* | | | | |
| 1985 | Côte d'Ivoire[a] | | | | |
| | Clinic | Free to $.11 | n.a. | − 0.61 | − 0.38 |
| | | $.11 to $.22 | n.a. | − 1.16 | − 0.05 |
| | Hospital | Free to $.11 | n.a. | − 0.47 | − 0.29 |
| | | $.11 to $.22 | n.a. | − 0.86 | − 0.51 |
| 1985 | Peru[a] | | | | |
| | Private doctor | Free to $1.56 | − 0.14 | − 0.20 | − 0.06 |
| | | $1.56 to 3.12 | − 0.29 | − 0.44 | − 0.12 |
| | Hospital | Free to $1.56 | − 0.41 | − 0.67 | − 0.33 |
| | | $1.56 to $3.12 | − 0.64 | − 1.18 | − 0.05 |
| | Clinic | Free to $1.56 | − 0.46 | − 0.76 | − 0.03 |
| | | $1.56 to $3.12 | − 0.68 | − 1.28 | − 0.06 |
| 1975 | Malaysia | | | | |
| | Outpatient visits | n.a. | − 0.01 | n.a. | n.a. |
| 1981 | Philippines | | | | |
| | Prenatal child care | n.a. | − 0.01 | n.a. | n.a. |
| 1980–81 | Kenya | $5.80 | inelastic[b] | n.a. | n.a. |
| 1985 | Ethiopia | | | | |
| | Outpatient care | n.a. | − 0.05 to − 0.50 | n.a. | n.a. |
| 1986 | Sudan | n.a. | | | |
| | Outpatient services | n.a. | − 0.37 | n.a. | n.a. |
| | *Education* | | | | |
| 1985 | Peru[a] | | | | |
| | Secondary education | Free to $1.56 | − 0.14 | − 0.18 | − 0.20 |
| 1982 | Mali[c] | n.a. | − 0.98 | n.a. | n.a. |
| 1983 | Malawi[d] | n.a. | − 0.52 | n.a. | n.a. |

[a] These are price elasticities, which is why price ranges are relevant.
[b] Uses household enrollment ratio as dependent variable.
[c] Uses distance as price variable.
[d] Magnitude could not be computed from available data.
n.a. Not available.
*Sources*: Gertler and van der Gaag (1988) for health in Côte d'Ivoire and Peru; Gertler and Glewwe (1988) for education in Peru; Akin et. al. (1986) for the Philippines; Mwabu (1988) for Kenya; Dunlop (1987) for Ethiopia; Birdsall et al. (1983) for Mali; Tan et. al. (1984) for Malawi; Schwabe (n.d.) for Sudan.

the studies outlined above take this additional step in the analysis. For example, analysts use the quality variables being held constant in the demand equation to try to infer willingness to pay for marginal changes in some of these characteristics, and they conclude that significant quality improvements can be

Table 43.12
Individual willingness to pay for access to social services and the cost of provision
(1985 U.S. dollars)

| Country and service | Willingness to pay for obtaining access to a nearby facility when the alternative is: | | |
| --- | --- | --- | --- |
| | One hour away | Two hours away | Marginal cost |
| *Côte d'Ivoire* | | | |
| West Forest Health Clinic[a] | 0.10 | 0.17 | 1.30 |
| Savannah Health Clinic[a] | 0.03 | 0.06 | 1.30 |
| *Peru* | | | |
| Coastal Health Clinic[a] | 0.09 | 0.17 | 2.73 |
| Sierra Health Clinic[a] | 0.00 | 0.02 | 2.73 |
| Secondary School[b] | 14.29 | 104.64 | 35.71 |

[a] Dollars per visit.
[b] Dollars per academic year.
*Sources*: Health: Gertler and van der Gaag (1988, Tables 5 and 6). Education: Gertler and Glewwe (1989).

financed by user charges (Table 43.12). Mwabu et al. (1992) finds that, in Kenya, the availability of drugs and trained personnel affects demand and should be taken into account in the analysis.

While these recent studies have gone a long way towards addressing a gap in policy analysis, the literature still needs to evolve. First, future policy work must have more studies on which to rely. The methods and results of the studies that are currently available are varied enough to caution against deriving many conclusions that can be widely applied. Future studies will continue to confront the problem that little information is available that combines users' socioeconomic characteristics with data on utilization and on the characteristics of facilities like schools and hospitals. For example, the prices of using a service like education and health are very difficult to obtain. In education, many public schools charge no prices at all; in health, provider-reported average prices of visits to clinics, such as those used by Akin et al. (1985), do not take into account ad hoc price discrimination by providers or the possible existence of health insurance, both of which complicate pricing measurement. Many studies have thus tended to use proxy variables or indirect measures for prices, such as those from hedonic price equations [for example, Gertler et al. (1987)], travel time [for example, Dor et al. (1987) and Gertler and van der Gaag (1990)] or the charge at the nearest alternative facility of each type [for example, Mwabu et al. (1993)]. It is thus difficult to compare the parameters estimated from the studies.

Data concerns are being alleviated by recent initiatives to collect multi-purpose surveys in developing countries. One such initiative, the Living

Standards Measurement Study (LSMS) of the World Bank, has been applied in almost a dozen countries, and the data have been used in many of the studies cited earlier [see Grosh and Glewwe (1993) for a description].

There are also empirical challenges that go beyond data. The studies discussed above tend to underestimate the true benefits of a policy reform if there are externalities and no studies take such effects into account. Another issue is that many of the empirical models impose a great deal of structure on household models (such as logarithmical additive utility functions). While such models allow the analyst to map out the preference function and use it for behavioral models, most of the studies have not tested for the robustness of their conclusions in case other structures might imply different results.

Finally, most of these empirical studies are flawed by simplistic assumptions about supply-side responses. Most assume constant cost. One study that directly estimates the cost functions of the facilities to infer what the supply response might be is that of Akin et al. (1991). They use this to do simulations on the effects of different types of investment policy. Unfortunately, they use a very limited Nigerian sample that consists only of those households that report an incidence of illness. More studies about the cost structure of education and health services are needed.

Another assumption is that resources will actually be used to finance expansion or improvements in quality. This is partly dependent on the specific actions of government and can only be evaluated on the basis of actual experience. Where this experience exists, this evidence will also be useful to use against those who argue that such policy changes cannot be made because of reasons of political or administrative costs.

*Efficiency: evidence from actual experiments.* There have been relatively few attempts to raise fees in education, health and water services, and even fewer instances where such attempts have been rigorously documented and evaluated. In health, detailed case studies of four African, two Asian and four Latin American countries have been documented; these include studies in Ghana [Waddington and Emyimayew (1989)], Zaire [Creese, (1991)], Swaziland (Yoder), Lesotho [Creese (1991)], Bangladesh [Santon and Clemens (1989)], Cameroon [Litvack and Bodart (1992)], Dominican Republic, Honduras, Jamaica and Brazil [Lewis (1991a,b)] and Indonesia [RAND (1994)].[38] These actual case studies share the following conclusions. First, they show that raising charges is feasible and that political and administrative costs can be overcome. This is particularly true in health – the evaluation of education reform has yet

---

[38] There are other cases in which fee increases have been attempted. However, either they have only just begun as experiments (such as in Indonesia) or they have not been fully documented in scholarly work.

to be done. In this regard, incentives matter; hospitals and clinics that retained control of their funds were able to generate more funds.

Second, the impact on revenue mobilization has also been positive – user fees can raise substantial amounts, although it remains to be seen what the government has actually done with the money. In the Latin American examples, the fees actually went to buy more supplies and drugs.

Third, the impact on the utilization of services is mixed. In almost all countries, utilization in the facility went down – partly because the fees were raised dramatically (so that this finding is not necessarily inconsistent with the demand findings above). In several of the case study countries, they recovered after only two years. It is also important to note that many of the studies are unable to characterize the full utilization consequences since some individuals switch to other providers, both public and private. In addition, if there is a substantial enough effect on private demand of public fee increases, the private sector prices could also rise, and this feedback could dampen the tradeoff between revenue and utilization – a finding of the Indonesia case study [RAND (1994)].

The number of actual cases is still relatively small and is practically non-existent in the case of education. Perhaps most important, the experiments in the case studies are not rigorously designed. These types of studies are still being designed and until they are finished, the debate is likely to continue to rage.

*Equity: some conceptual issues.* The earlier section has already shown that free provision does not necessarily mean that the poorest income groups have access to certain services. There are several reasons for this. One is that, even at zero or a very low price, social services are costly to use. The private cost includes payments for transport, materials (medicine in the case of health, or school books in the case of education) and opportunity cost (particularly high for education, but might be high in terms of waiting time for other services). For education, the opportunity cost alone can amount to 25 to 50 percent of the total social (private plus public) cost of education [Jimenez (1987), p. 19]. Even though poor adults may have a lower opportunity cost of time than richer adults, this relationship may be reversed for children – poor children may tend to work at home and may find it more difficult to attend school.

Another reason is that, when demand is rationed, the rationing system often favors those who are relatively well off, unless the services are carefully and deliberately targeted. For example, rationing of school places, nominally by ability, may in fact favor richer households that can afford to pay for tutoring or to let their children repeat a grade. The same may be true of rationing by concentrating the service in certain areas, like urban centers.

Rationing by means of requiring beneficiaries to spend time waiting for a service such as health care or to travel long distances for water can favor the relatively poor if the price of a wait is higher to those with a higher opportunity cost of time [Briscoe et al. (1993)]. But the benefits from redistributing income in this way should be compared to the benefits of improved benefits financed by higher taxes. Moreover, the costs can be high if the government can redistribute income effectively by direct transfers [Bucovetsky (1984)] or other allocation mechanisms [Sah (1987)], or if the benefits are unevenly distributed among those who wait.

When such considerations are important, differential prices for different services can significantly improve efficiency and equity. It has been shown empirically, for example, that higher income groups tend to benefit disproportionately from higher education, so that shifting government spending from that level to more basic levels will have a bigger impact on reducing poverty [World Bank (1986, 1987a), Mingat and Tan (1985, 1986), Griffin (1992)].

Moreover, the inequalities of government spending have also been used as an argument for using targeting to redistribute wealth. The benefits and costs of targeting are discussed more fully in the chapter by Lipton and Ravallion. Recent evidence for targeted health or educated programs indicate that such techniques could be administratively feasible [Grosh (1993)], particularly if they do not involve explicit means testing but instead target by category (such as age, gender or location) using characteristics that are highly correlated with indicators of poverty.

*Equity: evidence.* The previous section has shown that the popular method for ensuring access has been to provide all social services at a heavy per unit subsidy through uniformly low or zero prices, accompanied by quantity rationing or low quality when budgets are tight. This has not been successful as the highest subsidies often go to services used mainly by the rich such as higher education and urban-based health care. In principle, differential pricing – increasing prices (or lowering subsidies) for those services that are consumed primarily by the rich and increasing subsidies for those services that are consumed primarily by the poor – is bound to have beneficial effects, particularly when the initial differences in cost are great and the distribution of access to various service levels is very unequal.

For example, according to figures in Table 43.13, Asian countries fall roughly into three groups: (1) those where education subsidies are roughly equitably distributed according to levels of education (Korea and the Philippines); (2) those with moderately equitable distributions (China, Indonesia, Malaysia, Sri Lanka and Thailand); and (3) those with fundamentally inequitable distributions (Bangladesh, India, Nepal and Papua New Guinea). Since students from richer families will tend to be overrepresented at higher levels of

Table 43.13
Distribution of public spending on education, selected Asian countries, mid-1980s

| Country | Index of Gini coefficient[a] | Cumulative spending received by 10 percent best-educated (percentage of total cumulative spending) |
|---|---|---|
| Bangladesh | 81.9 | 71.7 |
| China | 44.4 | 31.1 |
| India | 65.8 | 60.8 |
| Indonesia | 27.3 | 21.4 |
| Korea | 15.9 | 13.4 |
| Malaysia | 37.9 | 32.0 |
| Nepal | 57.9 | 53.5 |
| Papua New Guinea | 62.1 | 53.5 |
| Philippines | 18.6 | 14.1 |
| Sri Lanka | 32.6 | 28.1 |
| Thailand | 32.9 | 23.3 |
| Regional average | 43.4 | 36.3 |

[a] This statistic has a range of 0 to 100. The closer it is to 100, the more unequal is the distribution of public spending on education in a school-age population.
*Source*: Tan and Mingat (1992).

education, it can reasonably be concluded that differential pricing would be more progressive in the last group of countries.

One consideration is that there are relatively few human services that are not consumed by rich and poor alike. Some urban-based specialty hospitals cater solely to diseases that afflict the relatively wealthy, and, in Africa, education is so selective that, by the tertiary level, the elite form a vast majority of all applicants [World Bank (1986, 1987a)]. However, in other countries and services, the poor represent a minor but still significant portion of students at primary or middle levels or of patients in urban hospitals. In these cases, it is important to measure the initial distribution of subsidies very carefully and to make appropriate judgments as to how they might change as a result of the change in policy.

Another consideration is that there may be externalities or other reasons why ensuring that the poor have access to higher-level services is important to a society. There may also be political reasons for wanting to guarantee, for example, that poor students who have managed to work their way through secondary school have a chance to enter university or that poor children with an operable heart condition have a chance to have life-saving operations. More importantly, there may be economic efficiency reasons for this because credit markets for education and insurance markets for health are only just starting up in many developing countries. Such concerns are validated some recent empirical work [Gertler et al. (1987), Gertler and van der Gaag (1988) and Gertler and Glewwe (1989)] that shows that the price elasticity of demand for social services may be higher among the poor than among the rich. Thus, for a given price increase, the consumption of the poor would fall proportionately more than that of the rich. This is corroborated by some recent case work in Ghana. When fees for attendance at health stations were raised, there was an initial drop in attendance at urban-based stations, but the numbers soon went up again, whereas attendance at small, rural-based health stations remained at a lower level, even after two and a half years [Waddington and Enyimayew (1989)].

As a result, many argue that, where possible, user charges, even if differentiated by type of service, should also be accompanied by more narrowly targeted subsidies to ensure that the poor continue to have access to the service in question. As reviewed in the chapter by Lipton and Ravallion, however, the relative costs of various targeting mechanisms have to be weighed carefully. Means testing of individuals, while generally administratively costly to implement, may be quite appropriate for relatively small programs that draw from a limited population where monitoring is easier [see Grosh (1993) for a comprehensive review]. One such example may be university scholarships where a student's background is arguably relatively easy to determine and where parents are likely to be reasonably well educated [see Klitgaard (1986) for an interesting discussion of some cases].

There are various alternatives to individual means testing. Studies of food subsidies have found that targeting using physical criteria, such as nutrition level, is generally more effective in reaching target populations and in keeping others out than using income criteria, although individual testing may be costly [for example, see Edirisinghe (1987)]. Similar criteria that have been applied in developing countries are health status (incidence of certain diseases) or adult literacy [Griffin (1989)]. A more realistic category to use for targeting is geographic location. The rule of exempting institutions from fees in urban slums or obviously poor rural areas also makes it easier to implement. The one drawback is that, if two neighboring locations have vastly different rates, people may migrate in order to qualify for the cheapest alternative [Rosenzweig and Wolpin (1986)].

Self-selecting mechanisms are often suggested as a way to target in a way that minimizes the administrative burden. Most of these are based on the concept of quality. For example, long waiting lines can be used to take advantage of the fact that the opportunity cost of time is greater for rich than for poor people. Another example is that lower quality facilities tend to attract only the poor [Besley and Coate (1992)].

*Feasibility*. One aspect of feasibility is administrative cost. While it is true that public administration in many developing countries is generally weak, a few case studies indicate that the administrative problems associated with collecting fees can generally be overcome if the appropriate incentives are put in place. For example, the salaries of the administrative staff could be related to the amount of fee income they recover. Even more importantly, institutions could be allowed to retain a percentage of the fee income that they raise. In many countries, these fees must be remitted to the central finance ministry. According to Vogel (1988, 1991), in Côte d'Ivoire and Senegal, almost 100 percent of fees has to be handed over to the finance ministry, while in Mali, it is all remitted to the central health ministry. However, in Ghana, the institution was able to keep 25 percent.

The financial costs of recovering fees are not overwhelming. Generally, the cost of collecting fees, including incentive payments to collectors, amounts to about 10 percent of total fees collected – some outliers indicate 25 percent [Vogel (1988)]. Hecht et al. (1992) documents a plan for a relatively comprehensive proposal for price reform in Zimbabwe, and concludes that fee collection is indeed administratively feasible [see also Wouters (1991) and Yoder (1989)].

Another aspect of feasibility is political. Governments may be acting in their own rather than in the public interest. Another possibility is that some governments may be unable to withstand pressure from powerful minority interests [Birdsall and James (1993)]. Such pressures may explain the persistence of the unequal distributions found in certain countries in terms of access to higher education and health care.

Political constraints can be a real barrier to reform. However, it is possible to take measures to counteract them. One is to compensate those who will lose out as a result of the reform and, at the same time, to mobilize those who will gain from it. This can only be done by a massive public information campaign, as occurred in Ghana, to alert the population to the inequities of the existing distribution of subsidies [World Bank (1988c)]. Another is to rely on rules rather than discretion – for instance, by greater earmarking. This may not work if the discretionary portion of the funds is used to counteract the non-discretionary portion. Moreover, there may be heavy efficiency losses associated with this [McCleary (1988)].

*Conclusions.* In short, although there is much merit in the conceptual arguments for increasing prices in the social sectors, empirical support is only now beginning to build. There is strong evidence that there is much room for improvement, in that present subsidies could be directed more towards the poor. Moderate increases in user fees would raise revenues because demand is relatively price inelastic, but dramatic increases designed to recover costs in full would not be feasible because of the lack of adequate credit or insurance markets and because demand elasticities may rise. Finally, practical methods exist for protecting the poor.

The remaining problems are the need to:

- assess the feasibility of measures to protect the poor;
- reach agreement on which services should have fees raised and by how much, in other words, a need for operational "rules of thumb";
- gather information about the cost structure of service provision; and
- make systematic evaluations of actual attempts to raise prices.

### 4.3. Physical infrastructure

For most physical infrastructure services, the pricing discussion has primarily been motivated by a different set of externalities than those emphasized in human infrastructure, where most of the consumption externalities are positive. In physical infrastructure, many of the externalities are decidedly negative – congestion in the use of electricity, road and water services, damage caused to other users from a road that deteriorates with each use, and, increasingly, pollution from road and water traffic and some forms of power generation.

The discussion on pricing physical infrastructure has also been influenced heavily by the fact that most investments have large fixed costs. This means that, in many instances, marginal costs are below average costs, so that some subsidy is required. Also, while pricing at short-run marginal cost would give the firm information about the appropriate time to invest (prices would rise as the plant operated closer to capacity), the price rise at capacity may be unacceptably high before further investment finally alleviates the constraint. Many argue [Anderson (1989)] that long-run marginal costs would thus be a better guide, although this is not universally accepted.

There has been a widespread and longstanding recognition that prices should play a role in resource allocation in physical infrastructure (unlike human infrastructure). The prices should be positive and should approximate marginal costs, at least in the long run if not in the short run.[39] The principles of sound demand management and the important role that prices play in signaling the provider how much to invest are generally accepted. But, for many of the physical infrastructure sectors, present practice far from reflects these principles.

*Efficiency issues: raising more revenue to cover supply costs.* Recent policy

---

[39] See, for example, a series of studies for the World Bank by Churchill (1974), Walters (1968), Bennathan and Walters (1979), Saunders and Warford (1976), Saunders et al. (1983), Turvey and Anderson (1977), Bahl and Linn (1992) and Munasinghe and Warford (1982), which cover most of the physical infrastructure sectors with which institutions work.

studies have found that, in practice, infrastructure prices in developing countries have two disturbing general characteristics relative to what is efficient – they are too low, and they are structured in a way that does not reflect the nuances of the various market failures mentioned in the preceding paragraphs.

There is considerable evidence that present prices in most sectors are very low and are below not only financial requirements but also marginal costs. Electric power is judged to be underpriced in most developing countries. Prices amount, on average, to just above a third of supply costs and are half as much as those in industrial countries [World Bank (1992b)]. While consumers in most industrial countries pay all of the recurrent costs of both water and sewerage services plus a large proportion of capital costs, in developing countries, consumers pay much less. For example, a recent review of projects financed by the World Bank showed that the effective price paid for water is only about 35 percent of the average cost of supplying it [World Bank (1992d), see also Katko (1990), Sampath (1992)].

Some subsectors like ports, railways and telecommunications tend to be run more autonomously as state-owned enterprises and have a better record than other sectors in implementing a cost-based tariff structure. While the calculations regarding costs are admittedly crude, a selected review of some countries where systematic data exist found that the ratio of revenues to operating costs tended to exceed well over 100 percent for ports and to be close to 100 percent for railways. Cost recovery is also usually high in telecommunications [Julius and Alicbusan (1989)]. Some recent analysts have defined road taxes and charges broadly – including the purchase tax on vehicles, taxes on diesel fuel and gasoline and license fees, as well as tolls and other direct prices – and have ignored any pure tax elements in concluding that many developing countries collect considerably more user charges than is spent on roads [Heggie (1991)]. While it is difficult to accept the assumption that all such taxes and charges can be interpreted as user charges, even for these sectors, the efficiency issues are similar to those posed for the sectors that experience chronic deficits. The expenditures fall far short of what is required for maintenance [Anderson (1989) and Heggie (1991)]. Moreover, some raise the question of whether prices should be increased even more, given that other methods of revenue raising are costly.

Given these initial conditions, the magnitude of the revenues that can be generated by increasing prices can be substantial. Table 43.14 summarizes some calculations made in the case of Africa [Anderson (1989)]. For electricity and water, the gain was computed by assuming that an increase in the real financial rate of return of around 5 to 10 percent was feasible. For telecommunications, actual tariffs were compared to long-run marginal costs. For roads, a substantial increase in user charges of 50 to 75 percent above current

Table 43.14
Incremental effects of raising prices and user charges in sub-Saharan Africa (1980s)

| Sector | Current contribution to public revenue | Potential contribution as percentage of public revenue |
|---|---|---|
| Electricity | Small or negative | 5–10 |
| Water | Small or negative | 2–5 |
| Telecommunications | Marginal | 5–10 |
| Roads | 10–15% | 5–10 |

*Source*: Anderson, D. 'The Public Revenue and Economic Policy in African Countries', World Bank Discussion Paper No. 19, 1987.

levels appeared justified to take into account the costs of maintenance. The calculations imply an increase in revenue of about 23 percent, which is sufficient to cover recurrent costs and earn adequate financial rates of return. Moreover, as most of this is in the form of user charges, deadweight losses would be low; even for road taxes, elasticities are shown to be relatively small. Anderson also points out that raising revenues in this way would ensure the financial autonomy of institutions, which could then attract private capital for investment.

Are these gains feasible? Anderson states that:

The financial surpluses from marginal costs pricing (and also from any infrastructure taxes) would be relatively easy and inexpensive to administer. They would be a near costless part of the billing services for electricity, telecommunications and water supply, and of the user charges for roads (license fees, parking fees, gasoline taxes, etc.) (p. 530).

Unfortunately, he does not present any evidence on this point, and the issues of calculating, monitoring and administering efficient user charges remains an important debating area in the literature, and will be discussed further below in the context of addressing externalities.

Does this mean that infrastructure prices can be a good instrument for general revenue raising, given the high deadweight losses associated with commodity taxes?[40] If these charges are to be considered as an indirect tax, they should be evaluated like one. The case of roads has been examined in this way [Newbery (1988)]. The road price can be considered to have two elements: a road user charge to ensure sectoral efficiency (in other words, to take into account congestion and road damage, as discussed below) and a pure tax element, which is the amount by which road taxes exceed road use cost. If the

---

[40] Heggie (1991) and Heggie and Fon (1991) advocate such a policy for developing countries. See also Laferriere and Nalo (1992), Mwase (1988, 1989).

economy were competitive and externalities could be corrected,[41] then policies should be designed to achieve production efficiency and all distortionary taxes should fall on final consumers (to avoid cascading effects of distortions). Newbery (1988) points out that, under these conditions, "freight transport should pay the efficient road user charge; passenger transport may be subject to additional pure taxation" (p. 121). The latter is particularly attractive in light of Deaton's finding (1987) that household spending on gasoline car purchase and maintenance is relatively income-elastic in developing countries [see also Oum et al. (1990)].

Should the funds be earmarked for operations and maintenance, given that so many recent studies pinpoint this as the most important priority area for further investment, as discussed in Section 3? This is an argument made by many who work within the sectors [see, for example, Johanson (1989)], while analysts and policymakers dealing with general economics feel that earmarking is a controversial policy subject. The pros and cons of earmarking are beyond the purview of this paper.[42] However, some general principles are reasonably clear. The user charge portion of the price should be spent on expanding or maintaining the infrastructure, depending on which has the higher return. Revenues from the tax portion of the price should be treated like taxes – and, if the government has reasonable expenditure allocation mechanisms, operations and maintenance should be considered along with other worthwhile investments. If not, then one should investigate the possibility of removing discretion from central authorities as the best way to achieve better resource allocation.

*Efficiency issues: correcting for negative externalities.* Prices in physical infrastructure can be used to correct for the principal negative externalities imposed by a user on others: congestion (as in the decreasing reliability of power supply as more users are connected to the grid), damage to the infrastructure (as in road damage causing higher costs of maintenance to the public authority and of repair to other vehicle owners) and, in some cases, pollution. The principles are reasonably clear for each of the subsectors.

In road transport, the ideal is to charge vehicles the cost of using the road each time. This cost will include damage and congestion. Road damage is relatively straightforward – a combination of vehicle-specific and distance-related charges (such as on axles, fuels, vehicle parts or purchase have been suggested).[43] Congestion is more problematic because of the large differences

---

[41] These meet a more general set of conditions discussed formally by Diamond and Mirrlees (1971) – that production efficiency is feasible and that any resulting private profits are negligible or can be taxed away.

[42] For a good summary of the principal issues, see McCleary (1991).

[43] Small et al. (1989) and Newbery (1988).

between peak and off-peak road usage. Metering can be especially difficult, unless some new electronic technology is developed as has been tried on a pilot case in Hong Kong [see Hau (1990)]. Otherwise, proxies are used as second-best instruments. One of the most successful has been access charges that are area-specific, as has been tried and is still in practice in Singapore [see Watson and Holland (1976) for a thorough evaluation]. Fuel taxes are a particularly blunt instrument in this regard since they are related to distance rather than congestion. One simulation of how these various types of charges can be combined are summarized for commercial vehicles in Tunisia in Table 43.15. The table shows that different types of prices will have differential impacts on various types of vehicles.

Road prices have implications for pollution and, depending on the form they take, on other sectors in the economy. It has been shown that the pollution externality would add another term to the optimal price formula.[44] However, there have been no studies that explicitly measure how a charge can be made for pollution in road pricing in developing countries. Eskeland (1992), in the context of Mexico, estimates that the range of instruments to do so would vary and could very well include regulatory as well as tax-related interventions. Another consideration is that blunt instruments like fuel taxes may have substantial repercussions elsewhere in the economy and, if so, their effects should be taken into account. Studies by Hughes (1986) in Indonesia, Thailand

Table 43.15
Illustrative road user charges for commercial transport in Tunisia, 1983

| Vehicle class | Road use costs (U.S. cents per kilometer) | | | | Diesel tax rate (U.S. cents per liter)[a] | Purchase tax rate (percent)[b] |
|---|---|---|---|---|---|---|
| | Road damage (1) | Non-urban congestion (2) | Urban congestion (3) | Total (4) | | |
| Utility (pickup) | 0.03 | 0.15 | 1.46 | 1.64 | 18.22 | 26 |
| *Truck class* | | | | | | |
| Light | 0.12 | 0.21 | 1.94 | 2.27 | 15.13 | 20 |
| Medium | 0.51 | 0.33 | 0.44 | 1.28 | 6.40 | −4 |
| Heavy single | 2.18 | 0.39 | 0.52 | 3.09 | 7.92 | 2 |
| Heavy tandem | 4.46 | 0.39 | 0.52 | 5.37 | 12.07 | 17 |
| Articulated | 5.64 | 0.41 | 0.44 | 0.44 | 13.33 | 11 |

[a] The diesel tax rate is that needed to cover road use costs fully through a tax on diesel.
[b] The purchase tax stipulates a diesel tax of six cents per liter, a tire tax of 10 percent, and a tax on parts of 10 percent. The purchase tax rate is the rate needed to equate charge to cost.
*Source*: Newbery (1988).

[44] See Eskeland and Jimenez (1992) for an intuitive explanation and for applications to developing countries.

and Tunisia used an input-output table, a model of price-shifting behavior and an estimated system of demand equations to analyze these effects. The data requirements were obviously very heavy, for the study had to be replicated in many other countries.

For water, the issues are rather different. Here, the literature has stressed the metering issue, particularly for irrigation where it is virtually impossible to control who has access to the service. One option is for the government to deal with water users' associations (WUAs), which are charged with dealing and negotiating prices with the national irrigation authority. The WUA then negotiates with individual farmers and monitors use locally. Such schemes have worked well in the Philippines and elsewhere [World Bank (1988c)].

*Equity issues.* There have been relatively few studies of the impact of various infrastructure pricing schemes on equity. Since the majority of infrastructure services are in urban areas and the distribution of income favors those living in these areas, raising prices there will not affect the poor as much as raising them elsewhere would do. Even within urban areas, coverage is often such that the rich are the ones who obtain access.

For example, Table 43.7 has already shown that prices charged by private water vendors in selected cities around the world are much higher than those charged by public utilities, and it is often the poor who must buy water from the former and the rich who have connections to the latter. This is partly the reason that, in the few case studies in Latin American comparing the incidence of various types of infrastructure intervention, urban-based water subsidies are relatively regressive (Table 43.6b). Thus, charging more for such utilities may not be that regressive.

Moreover, recent research has found a high level of willingness to pay even in rural areas [Briscoe et al. (1993)], although it is important to distinguish among different types of communities. In studies of rural water demand in Brazil, Haiti, India, Nigeria, Pakistan, Tanzania and Zimbabwe, researchers used both contingent valuation and revealed preference methods of inference to conclude that most rural people want and are willing to pay for a relatively high level of service (yard taps) and are willing to pay substantially more if that service is reliable. In other types of communities, only a minority of households are willing to pay for private connections, but most are willing to pay for some if not all of the costs of public connections. In some of the poorer communities where supply costs are high, public taps could be subsidized.[45]

There are also ways to protect the poor by block pricing in which higher unit

---

[45] The study also identified communities where the willingness to pay for any kind of improved service is low because traditional water supplies are relatively easy to get or the provision of this service is seen as the financial responsibility of government.

prices are charged at higher levels of consumption, as has been tried in Brazil, Colombia and Indonesia [World Bank (1988c)]. An extreme example of this would be a lifeline rate in which, up to a certain threshold, consumption is free and is charged at marginal cost thereafter. However, such charges should take into account patterns of use. The poor could end up paying higher unit prices than the rich if the former relied on communal taps (which have high volumes) and the latter relied on private taps (which have low volumes). In such a case [documented in the case study by Whittington (1990)], volume-based pricing would not serve the poor as well.

For road taxes, evidence indicates that, in transport, some combinations of instruments are neutral; for example, gasoline taxes are progressive while diesel plus kerosene taxes are regressive and so they balance each other out [Newbery (1988)].

*Conclusions*. For physical infrastructure, unlike in education and health, there has been a longstanding acceptance that prices should be set high enough to cover marginal costs. The main issues have to do with implementing these principles – particularly in practical ways to account for congestion and pollution externalities; metering problems; accounting for fiscal realities in pricing; and in adjusting prices to account for distributional objectives.

## 5. Summary and future directions

The recent literature has reinforced the point that human and physical infrastructure are critical elements for economic growth and for the reduction of poverty. Despite data limitations and methodological difficulties, studies espousing these ideas, briefly reviewed in Section 2, have permeated the formulation and application of policies, as practiced by governments and as supported by international funding agencies.

There is also a continuing recognition that, because of externalities, scale economies, other public goods characteristics, and because of distributional objectives, the government has a key role to play in financing and supplying infrastructure. But recent studies summarized in Section 3 have raised fundamental concerns with how such intervention has been practiced. The efficiency objective is often not met – the highest return investments are not being given priority; and the services that are being provided are not being provided at least cost. Even more alarming is the fact that, despite spirited rhetoric and clearly stated national goals to ensure access to all, but especially the poor, the equity objective is often not met either. At the root of those failures are constraints that are often neglected in planning models: administrative capacity of government is weak; rents are often sought and obtained by private interest groups, leading to distorted outcomes; operational tools to implement conceptual sound advice are often lacking.

But what then can be done to ensure that infrastructure services are more adequately financed and that what is spent is better directed towards priority investments? The recent literature on these issues is vast and diverse, even within each of the sectors that can be classified as "infrastructure."[46] Section 3 presented selected examples of how received textbook analysis is being revisited in the policy debate, only some of which is backed by rigorous and empirically-based analysis. Recent initiatives have attempted to relieve the two main constraints to sound public decision-making – a lack of information and a lack of incentives. These initiatives have included refining economic tools of analysis, particularly those for making inter-sectoral allocation decisions in spending and those that take into account general policies in setting sectoral policies, building better incentives into investment choices, particularly through decentralization, and allowing for greater private sector provision in certain subsectors, while ensuring that the government maintains an important regulatory role.

Pricing reform is another of the policy initiatives that has recently been given much attention. Once a government has decided where to invest, it must then decide how much to charge for the use of that service. Section 4 focused on the recent literature on pricing reform, which fundamentally revisits the public-private balance in the financing of infrastructure. There has been an often emotional debate about pricing those services that produce human capital, since education and health have traditionally been provided for free by the public sector. In physical infrastructure, the issues are somewhat different. In transport, energy and, to a lesser extent, water, pricing to achieve economic efficiency has always been accepted in principle. However, the principles have traditionally not been applied so the recent literature on these sectors has also focused on the need for reform.

This review has also identified key areas for future research. First is the need to improve data quality and availability. At the aggregate level, the empirical link between infrastructure and productivity can be strengthened with improved measures of outcomes (particularly in human resources). At the household level that combines information about socioeconomic characteristics of consumers as well as their access and use of infrastructure.

Second, while there have been major recent advances, there is a need to apply more widely and selectively econometric corrections to problems regarding selectivity and simultaneity bias. This includes research in topics such as the

---

[46] Moreover, many of the papers are interesting and policy-relevant but cannot be classified as scholarly research – they tend to be position papers, although many are indeed based on rigorous background studies. See, for example, the recent *World Development Reports* of the World Bank.

microeconomic link between productivity and infrastructure, as well as in behavioral studies of household demand for infrastructure services. For example, there are relatively few studies using such corrections showing how roads, power and other forms of physical infrastructure affect productivity of firms and household welfare. Also, more research would be useful on how household utilization of physical and human infrastructure services are affected by changes in price and quality, the most important variables affected by government policy.

Third, some key areas remain relatively unexplored empirically. For example, estimates of the benefit incidence of infrastructure services generally do not adjust for household behavior. This may be important if private transfers are affected by public transfers thus influencing the net impact of receivers of publicly subsidized infrastructure. Another example of a relatively unexplored area is how decentralized provision of infrastructure – whether by local public institutions or by private firms – can affect efficiency and equity. These become especially important in light of the recent calls for the introduction of commercial principles in the operation of publicly provided services and of more direct private sector provision.

Fourth, some conceptual issues remain to be solved. These include political economy questions and how policy recommendations may change when endogenous government behavior is taken into account. Another issue is to develop analytical tools to address the issue of intersectoral allocation. Finally, given that much of infrastructure will continue to be provided or regulated by public institutions, there is a need to look into the incentive framework influencing such sectors.

## References

Abel-Smith, B. (1987) 'Book review of *Financing health services in developing countries: An agenda for reform* [World Bank 1987]'. *Health Policy and Planning* 2, No. 4:355–358.

Ahmed, R. and Hossain, M. (1990) *Development impact of rural infrastructure in Bangladesh.* Research Report 83, International Food Policy Research Institute, Washington, DC.

Ainsworth, M. (1984) 'User charges for cost recovery in the social sectors: Current practices', Discussion Paper No. 1984–1986. Country Policy Department, World Bank, Washington, DC.

Akin, J.C., Griffin, C., Guilkey, D.K. and Popkin, B.M. (1986) 'The demand for primary health care services in the Bicol region of the Philippines'. *Economic Development and Cultural Change*, 34:755–782.

Akin, J.S., Denton, H., Guilkey, D.K., Vogel, R.J. and Wouters, A. (1991) 'Health care costs, demand and cost recovery in Ogun State, Nigeria', December. Washington, DC: The World Bank.

Alderman, H. and Gertler, P. (1988) 'The substitutability of public and private medical care providers for the treatment of children's illnesses in urban Pakistan', Washington, DC: International Food Policy Research Institute, processed.

Anderson, D. (1989) 'Public revenue and economic policy in developing countries', *World Development.*

Antle, J. (1983) 'Infrastructure and aggregate agricultural productivity: International evidence', *Economic Development and Cultural Change*, 31(3).

Armstrong-Wright, A. and Thiriez, S. (1987) *Bus services: reducing cost, raising standards*. World Bank Technical Paper No. 68, Washington, DC.

Arrow, K. (1962) 'The implications of learning by doing', *Review of Economic Studies*, 29: 661–669.

Arrow, K. (1963) 'Uncertainty and the welfare economics of medical care', *American Economic Review*, 53:941–973.

Aschauer, D. (1989) 'Is public expenditure productive?', *Journal of Monetary Economics*, 23:171–200.

Atkinson, A.B. and Stiglitz, J.E. (1980) *Lectures on public economics*. McGraw-Hill, London.

Bahl, R. and Linn, J.F. (1992) *Urban public finance in developing countries*. New York: Oxford University Press.

Barro, R.J. (1991) 'Economic growth in a cross section of countries', *Quarterly Journal of Economics*, May 1991, Vol. 106(2):407–444.

Barro, R.J. and Lee, J.-w. (1993) 'International comparisons of educational attainment', Presented in conference on 'How do national policies affect long-run growth', February, Washington, DC. The World Bank.

Baumol, W., Blackmann, S.A.B. and Wolff, E.N. (1989) *Productivity, growth and American leadership: The Long View*. MIT Press.

Baumol, W. and Lee, K.S. (1991) 'Contestable markets, trade and development', *World Bank Research Observer*, 6(1): 1–17.

Becker, G.S., Murphy, K. and Tamura, R. (1990) 'Human capital, fertility, and economic growth', *Journal of Political Economy*, 98(5).

Beenhakker, H. (1987) *Issues in agricultural marketing and transport due to government intervention*. Report No. TRP7, Transportation Department, The World Bank, Washington, DC.

Behrman, J. (1990a) 'The action of human resources and poverty on one another', LSMS Paper No. 74, The World Bank.

Behrman, J. (1990b.) *Human resource led development?: Review of issues and evidence*. New Delhi: International Labour Office – Asian Regional Team for Employment Promotion, ILO-ARTEP.

Behrman, J. and Lavy, V. (1993) 'Child health and schooling achievement: Causality or correlation?', Policy Research Department, The World Bank, processed.

Behrman, J. and Wolfe, B. (1987) 'How does mother's schooling affect family health, nutrition, medical care usage and household sanitation', *Journal of Econometrics*, 36:185–204.

Behrman, J. and Birdsall, N. (1983) 'The quality of schooling: quantity alone is misleading', *American Economic Review*, 73:928–946.

Bennathan, E. and Walters, A. (1979) *Ports pricing and investment policy for developing countries*. New York: Oxford.

Besley, T. (1989a) 'Reforming public expenditures: Some methodological issues', World Bank Country Economics Department. Washington, DC, processed.

Besley, T. (1989b) 'Welfare-improving user charges for publicly provided private goods', Woodrow Wilson School of Public and International Affairs, Princeton University, processed.

Besley, T. and Coate, S. (1991) 'Public provision of private goods and the redistribution of income', *American Economic Review*, 81(4):979–984.

Binswanger, H. (1983) 'Growth and employment in rural Thailand', Washington, DC: The World Bank, processed.

Binswanger, H. et al. (1989) 'Output and investment in Indian agriculture: Effects of agroclimate, infrastructure, banks and prices', Washington, DC: The World Bank, processed.

Binswanger, H. (1990) 'The policy response of agriculture', *Proceedings of the World Bank Annual Conference on Development Economics 1989*. Washington, DC.

Birdsall, N. and James, E. (1993) forthcoming. 'Government and the poor: The case for the private sector', in: M. Lipton and J. van der Gaag, eds., *Including the Poor*, Regional and Sectoral Studies Series, Washington WC: The World Bank.

Birdsall, N., Orivel, F., Ainsworth, M. and Chuhan, P. (1983) 'Three studies on cost recovery in social projects', Country Policy Department Paper No. 1983–1988, Washington, DC: The World Bank.

Bitran, R. (1991) 'Health care demand in developing countries: A model of household demand and a market simulation model of health care financing', Ph.D. thesis. Boston University.

Bray, M. (1986) 'Book review' of World Bank 1986. *International Journal of Educational Development*, 7(2).

Briscoe, J. and the Water Demand Research Team. (1993) 'The demand for water in rural areas: Determinants and policy implications', *The World Bank Research Observer*, 9(1):47–70.

Bucovetsky, S. (1984) 'On the use of distributional waits', *Canadian Journal of Economics*, 11(4):699–717.

Castaneda, T. (1992) *Combating poverty: Innovative social reforms in Chile during the 1980s*. San Francisco: International Center for Economic Growth Press.

Chhibber, A. and Dailami, M. (1990) 'Fiscal policy and private investment in developing countries: Recent evidence on key selected issues', Policy and Research Working Paper WPS 559, Washington, DC: The World Bank.

Churchill, A. (1972) *Road user charges in Central America*. Baltimore: Johns Hopkins University Press.

Cochrane, S. (1979) *Fertility and education: What do we really know?* Baltimore: Johns Hopkins University Press.

Cox, D. and Jimenez, E. (1992) 'Social security and private transfers the case of Peru', *World Bank Economic Review*, 6:155–169.

Creese, A. (1991) 'User charges for health care: A review of recent experience', *Health Policy and Planning*, 5:260–270. Switzerland: World Health Organization.

Deaton, A. (1987) 'The demand for personal travel in developing countries', Infrastructure and Urban Development Department, INU Discussion Paper 1, Washington, DC: The World Bank.

de Ferranti, D. (1985) *Paying for health services in developing countries: An overview*. World Bank Staff Working Paper 721. Washington, DC.

Denison, E. (1967) *Why growth rates differ: Post-war experience in nine Western countries*. Washington, DC: Brookings Institution.

Devarajan, S., Swaroop, V. and Zou, H.-f. (1992) 'What do governments buy? The composition of public expenditures and economic performance', Country Economics Dept., The World Bank, processed.

Diamond, P.A. and Mirrlees, J.A. (1971) 'Optimal taxation and public production, Part I: Production efficiency', and 'Part II: Tax rules', *American Economic Review*, 61(1): 8–27; (3): 261–278.

Dor, A., Gertler, P. and van der Gaag, J. (1987) 'Non-price rationing and medical care provides choice in rural Côte d'Ivoire', *Journal of Health Economics*, 6:291–304.

Dreze, J. and Stern, N. (1987) 'The theory of cost benefit analysis', in: Alan J. Auerbach and Martin Feldstein, eds., Chapter 14 *Handbook of Public Economics*. Amsterdam: North-Holland.

Dunlop, D. (1987) 'A study of health financing: Issues and options, Ethiopia', Washington, DC: The World Bank, processed.

Easterly, W., King, R., Levine, R. and Rebelo, S. (1992) *Do national policies affect long-run growth? A research agenda*. Washington, DC: World Bank Discussion Paper No. 164.

Easterly, W. and Rebelo, S. (1993) 'Fiscal policy and economic growth: An empirical investigation', presented in conference on 'How do national policies affect long-run growth', February. Washington, DC: The World Bank.

Edirisinghe, N. (1987) 'The food stamp program in Sri Lanka: Costs, benefits, and policy options', International Food Policy Research Institute, Washington, DC.

Ellis, R.P. and Mwabu, G.M. (1991) 'The demand for outpatient medical care in rural Kenya', September. Boston University and Kenyatta University.

Eskeland, G. (1991) 'Demand management in environmental protection: Fuel taxes and air pollution in Mexico City', Public Economics Division, The World Bank.

Eskeland, G. and Jimenez, E.. (1992) 'Policy instruments for pollution control in developing countries', *World Bank Research Observer*.

Galenson, A. (1989) 'Labor redundancy in the transport sector', Working Paper No. WPS 158. Washington, DC: The World Bank.

Gertler, P., Locay, L. and Sanderson, W. (1987) 'Are user fees regressive?: The welfare implications of health care financing proposals in Peru', *Journal of Econometrics*, 33:67–88.

Gertler, P. and Glewwe, P. (1990) 'The willingness to pay for education in developing countries: Evidence from rural Peru', *Journal of Public Economics*, 42:251–275.

Gertler, P. and van der Gaag, J. (1990) *The willingness to pay for medical care: Evidence from two developing countries*, Baltimore: Johns Hopkins University Press.

Gilson, L. (1988) 'Government health care charges: Is equity being abandoned?: A discussion paper', EPC Publication No. 15, London: School of Hygiene and Tropical Medicine.

Gill, I.S. and Bhalla, S.S. (1992) 'Externalities in new growth theory: The importance of female human capital', presented at Western Economic Association Meetings.

Glewwe, P. and Jacoby, H. (1992) 'Estimating the determinants of cognitive achievement in low-income countries', LSMS Working Paper No. 91. Washington, DC: The World Bank.

Griffin, C.C. (1987) *User charges for health care in principle and practice*. Economic Development Institute Seminar Paper 37. Washington, DC: The World Bank.

Griffin, C. (1992) 'Health care in Asia: A comparative study of cost and financing', Washington, DC: The World Bank.

Gronau, R. (1991) 'Are Ghana's roads paying their way? Assessing road use cost and user charge in Ghana', Policy, research and external affairs, Working Paper WPS 773. Washington, DC: The World Bank.

Grosh, M. (1993) *From platitudes to practice: Targeting social programs in Latin America*. Regional and Sectoral Studies Series, Washington, DC: The World Bank.

Grosh, M. and Glewwe, P. (1993) 'An introduction to the World Bank's living standards measurement study household surveys', Poverty and Human Resources Division, The World Bank, mimeo.

Hardy, A. and Hudson, H.. (1981) 'The role of the telephone in economic development: An empirical analysis', ITU-OECD, May.

Hau, T.D. (1990) 'Electronic road pricing: Developments in Hong Kong 1983–1989': Developments in transport policy', *Journal of Transport Economics and Policy*, May:203–214.

Hammer, J. (1993) 'Prices and protocols in public health care', Policy Research Working Paper WPS 1131, Washington, DC: The World Bank.

Haveman, R. and Wolfe, B. (1984) 'Nonmarket returns to schooling', *Journal of Human Resources*.

Heady, C. (1988) 'Public sector pricing in a fiscal context', World Bank Policy, Planning and Research Working Paper 179. Washington, DC: The World Bank, processed.

Hecht, R., Overholt, C. and Holmberg, H. (1992) 'Improving implementation of cost recovery for health: Lessons from Zimbabwe', World Bank, Africa Technical Dept. Working Paper No. 2, June.

Heggie, I. (1991) 'Improving management and charging policies for roads: An agenda for reform', Infrastructure and Urban Development Department, INU Report 92. Washington, DC: The World Bank.

Heggie, I. and Fon, V. (1991) 'Optimal user charges and cost recovery for roads in developing countries', Policy Research Working Paper WPS 780. Washington, DC: The World Bank.

Heller, P. (1979) 'The underfinancing of recurrent development costs', *Finance and Development*.

Heller, P. (1982) 'A model of the demand for medical and health services in peninsular Malaysia', *Social Science and Medicine*, 16:267–284.

Heller, P. (1992) 'Operations and maintenance', IMF, processed.

Hicks, N. (1991). 'Expenditure reduction in developing countries revisited', *Journal of International Development*, 3(1):29–37.

Hughes, G. (1986) 'A new method for estimating the effects of fuel taxes: An application to Thailand', *The World Bank Economic Review*, 1(1):65–102.

Hulten, C. and Schwab, R. (1991) 'Is there too little public capital? Infrastructure and economic growth', University of Maryland (January).

James, E. (1991) 'Public policies toward private education: An international comparison', *International Journal of Educational Research*, 15(5):359–76.

James, E., King, E. and Suryadi, A. (1993) 'Education outcomes and the state and resources of schools in Indonesia', Presented at the International symposium on the economics of education, The British Council, 19–21 May.

Jamison, D. and Lau, L. (1982) *Farmer education and farm efficiency*. Baltimore: Johns Hopkins University Press.

Jansson, J.O. and Cardebring, P. (1989) 'A comparative study of road user taxation in different countries', *International Journal of Transport Economics*, XVI(1), February.

Jimenez, E. (1986a) 'The public subsidization of education and health in developing countries: The impact of equity and efficiency', *World Bank Research Observer* 1, No. 1:111–129.

Jimenez, E. (1987) *Pricing policy in the social sectors: Cost recovery for education and health in developing countries*. Baltimore: Johns Hopkins University Press.

Jimenez, E. (1990) 'Social sector pricing policy revisited: A survey of some recent controversies', *World Bank Economic Review/Research Observer*, Proceedings of The World Bank Annual Conference on Development Economics 1989.

Jimenez, E., Lockheed, M. and Paqueo, V. (1988) 'The relative efficiency of public and private schools in developing countries', *World Bank Research Observer*.

Jimenez, E., Paqueo, V. and de Vera, Ma. L. (1988) 'Does local financing make primary schools more efficient?: The Philippine case', Policy, Planning and Research Working Paper, WPS 69. Washington, DC: The World Bank.

Johansen, F., ed., (1989) 'Earmarking, road funds and toll roads: A World Bank symposium', Infrastructure and Urban Development Department, Policy Planning and Research Staff, Report INU 45. Washington, DC: The World Bank.

Julius, DeA. and Alicbusan, A.P. (1988) 'Public sector pricing policies: A review of bank policy and practice', Policy Planning and Research Working Paper, WPS 49, Washington, DC: The World Bank.

Kakwani, N. (1992) 'Structural adjustment and performance in living standards in developing countries', World Bank, Population and Human Resources Department, Washington, DC, processed.

Katko, T.S. (1990) 'Cost recovery in water supply in developing countries', *Water Resources Development*, Vol. 6(2), June.

Katz, M. (1987) 'Pricing publicly supplied goods and services', in: D. Newbery and N. Stern, eds., *The theory of taxation for developing countries*. New York: Oxford University Press.

Kaufmann, D. (1991) 'The forgotten rationale for policy reform: The productivity of investment projects', The World Bank, processed.

Kaufmann, D. and Wang, Y. (1992) 'How macroeconomic policies affect project performance in the social sectors', Policy Research Working Paper WPS 939, The World Bank.

Kessides, C. (1993) *The contribution of infrastructure to economic development: A review of experience and policy implications*. Washington, DC: World Bank Discussion Paper (September).

Klitgaard, R. (1986) *Elitism and meritocracy in developing countries: Selection policies for higher education*. Baltimore: Johns Hopkins University Press.

Laferrière, R. and Nalo, D.S.O. (1992) 'Optimal road user charges and income distribution in Kenya', *International Journal of Transport Economics*, XIX(1), February, pp. 61–83.

Lakshaman, T.R. and Elhance, A. (1984) 'Impacts of infrastructure on economic development', Presented at the Annual Workshop of the Building Sector, Boston, MA.

Lau, L., Jamison, D. and Louat, F. (1991) 'Education and productivity in developing countries: An aggregate production function approach', Policy, Planning and Research Working Paper, WPS 612. Washington, DC: The World Bank.

Lavy, V. and Quigley, J.M. (1991) 'Willingness to pay for the quality of intensity of medical care: Evidence from low income households in Ghana', Living Standards Measurement Study Working Paper No. 94. Washington, DC: The World Bank.

Lee, K.-S. and Anas, A. (1992) 'Impacts of infrastructure deficiencies on Nigerian manufacturing', Infrastructure Department Discussion Paper No. INU 98. Washington, DC: The World Bank.

Lewis, M. (1991) 'User fees in public hospitals: Comparison of three country case studies', *Economic Development and Cultural Change*.

Lewis, M. and Parker, C. (1991) 'Policy and implementation of user fees in Jamaican public hospitals', *Health Policy*.

Little, I. and Mirrlees, J. (1990) 'Project appraisal and planning 20 years on', *World Bank Proceedings of the Annual Conference on Development Economics*, pp. 351–382.

Litvack, J. and Bodart, C. (1993) 'User fees plus quality equals improved access to health care: Results of a field experiment in Cameroon', *Social Science and Medicine*, 37(3): 369–383.

Lockheed et al. (1991) *Improving primary education in developing countries*. New York: Oxford University Press.

Lucas, R. (1988) 'On the mechanics of economic development', *Journal of Monetary Economics*, 22 (July):3–42.

Mayo, S. (1986) 'Sources of inefficiency in subsidized housing programs', *Journal of Urban Economics*.

Mayo, S.K. and Gross, D.J. (1987) 'Sites and services – and subsidies: The economics of low-cost housing in developing countries', *The World Bank Economic Review*, 1(2).

McCleary, W.A. (1991) 'The earmarking of government revenue: A review of some World Bank experience', *World Bank Research Observer*, 6(1):81–104.

Meerman, J. (1979) *Public expenditure in Malaysia: Who benefits and why*. New York: Oxford University Press.

Mingat, A. and Tan, J.-P. (1985) 'On equity in education again: An international comparison', *Journal of Human Resources*, 20(2):298–308.

Mingat, A. and Tan, J.P. (1986) 'Who profits from the public funding of education? A comparison by world regions', *Comparative Education Review*, 30:260–270.

Moock, P., Musgrove, P. and Stelcner, M. (1989) 'Education and earnings in Peru's informal family enterprises', Policy Planning and Research Working Paper, WPS 236. Washington, DC: The World Bank.

Moock, P. and Leslie, J. (1986) 'Childhood malnutrition and schooling in the Terai region of Nepal', *Journal of Development Economics*, 20(1):33–52.

Munasinghe, M. and Warford, J. (1982) *Electricity pricing: Theory and case studies*. Baltimore: Johns Hopkins University Press.

Mwabu, G. (1986) 'Health care financing in Kenya: A simulation of welfare effects of user fees', *Social Science and Medicine*, 22(7):763–767.

Mwabu, G. (1989) 'Nonmonetary factors in the household choice of medical facilities', *Economic Development and Cultural Change*, 37:383–392.

Mwabu, G. (1991) 'Financing health services in Africa: An assessment of alternative approaches', Washington, DC: The World Bank, mimeo.

Mwabu, G., Ainsworth, M. and Nyamete, A. (1992) 'Quality of medical care and choice of medical treatment in Kenya: An empirical analysis', May. Kenyatta University and The World Bank, mimeo.

Mwase, N.R.L. (1988) 'Road transport pricing in developing countries: The Tanzania case, *International Journal of Transport Economics*, 15:327–343, October. Italy.

Mwase, N.R.L. (1989) 'Railways tariffs in Southern Africa: A case study of the Tanzania–Zambia railway tariff', *International Journal of Transport Economics*, XVI(2), June.

Nehru, V., Swanson, E. and Dubey, A. (1993) 'A new database on human capital stock: Sources, methodology and results', Policy Research Working Paper, WPS 1124, Washington, DC: The World Bank.

Newbery, D.M. (1988) 'Charging for roads', *World Bank Research Observer*, 3(2):119–138.

Oum, T. et al. (1990) 'A survey of recent estimates of price elasticities of demand for transport', Policy, Planning and Research Working Paper WPS 359. Washington, DC: The World Bank.

Pan American Health Organization (PAHO). (1988) 'Financing health services in developing countries: An agenda for reform', *Bulletin*, 22(4).

Peters, H. (1992) 'Service: The new focus in international manufacturing and trade', Policy Research Working Paper WPS 950, Washington, DC: The World Bank.

Petrei, A.H. (1987) *El gasto publico social y sus efectos distributivos*. Rio de Janiero: Estudios Conjuntos de Integracao Economia da America Latina.

Polenske, K. and Rockler, N. (1993) 'Infrastructure and productivity', DUSP, MIT, Cambridge, MA.

Psacharopoulos, G. (1985) 'Returns to education: A further international update and implications', *Journal of Human Resources*, Fall:583–604.

Psacharopoulos, G. and Arriagada, A.M. (1986) 'The educational attainment of the labor force: An international comparison', *International Labor Review*, 125:561–574.

Querioz, C. and Gautam, S. (1992) 'Road infrastructure and economic development: Some diagnostic indicators', Policy Research Working Paper WPS 921, Washington, DC: The World Bank.

RAND Corporation. (1994) 'Financing health care: Lessons from the Indonesian resource mobilization study', June, Santa Monica, CA, mimeo.

Raut, L. and Srinivasan, T.N. (1992) 'Theories of long-run growth: Old and new', September, mimeo.

Repetto, R. (1986) *Skimming the water: Rent-seeking and the performance of public irrigation systems*. Research Report 4. Washington, DC: World Resources Institute.

Romer, P. (1986) 'Increasing returns and long-run growth', *Journal of Political Economy*, 94:1002–1037.

Romer, P.M. (1990) 'Human capital and growth: Theory and evidence', Carnegie–Rochester Conference Series on Public Policy.

Rosenzweig, M. and Wolpin, K. (1986) 'Evaluating the effects of optimally distributed public programs: Child health and family planning interventions', *American Economic Review*, 76:470–482.

Roth, G. (1987) *The private provision of public services in developing countries*. New York: Oxford University Press, EDI Series in Economic Development.

Sah, R.K. (1987) 'Queues, rations and markets', *American Economic Review*, 77(1):69–77.

Sampath, R.K. (1992) 'Issues in irrigation pricing in developing countries', *World Development*, 20:967–977.

Santon, B. and Clemens, J. (1989) 'User fees for health care in developing countries: A case study of Bangladesh', *Social Science and Medicine*, 29:1199–1205.

Saunders, R. and Warford, J. (1976) *Village water supply*. Baltimore: Johns Hopkins University Press.

Saunders, R., Warford, J. and Wellenius, B. (1983) *Telecommunications and economic development*. Baltimore: Johns Hopkins University Press.

Schwabe, C., (no date) 'The demand for curative health services in Juba, Sudan: An empirical investigation into the potential for introducing user fees', Graduate Research Paper, Syracuse University, Syracuse, NY.

Selden, T. and Wasylenko, M. (1992) 'Benefit incidence analysis in developing countries', Policy Research Working Paper, WPS 1015, Washington, DC: The World Bank.

Selowsky, M. (1979) *Who benefits from government expenditure? A case study of Colombia*. New York: Oxford University Press.

Selowsky, M. (1992) forthcoming, 'Comment on Romer', *Proceedings of The World Bank annual conference on development economics*.

Serven L. and Solimano, A. (1992) 'Dynamics of public infrastructure, industrial productivity and profitability', *The Review of Economics and Statistics*, 74:28–36.

Shepard, D.S. and Benjamin, E.R. (1986) 'Mobilizing resource for health: The role of user fees in developing countries', Development Discussion Paper No. 23. Cambridge, MA: Harvard Institute for International Development.

Small, K., Whinston, C. and Evans, C. (1989) *Road work: A new highway pricing and investment policy*. April. Washington, DC: The Brookings Institution, processed.

Solow, R. (1956) 'A contribution to the theory of economic growth', *Quarterly Journal of Economics*, 70:65–94.

Squire, L. (1989) 'Project evaluation in theory and practice', in: H. Chenery and T.N. Srinivasan, eds., *Handbook of Development Economics, Vol. 2*, Amsterdam: North-Holland.

Squire, L. (1991) 'Comment on Little and Mirrlees', *Proceedings of The World Bank annual conference on development economics*.

Steel, W. and Webster, L. (1992) 'How small enterprises in Ghana have responded to adjustment', *World Bank Economic Review*, 6(3):423–438.

Tan, J.-P., Lee, K.H. and Mingat, A. (1984) 'User charges for education: The ability and willingness to pay in Malawi', World Bank Staff Working Paper 661, Washington, DC.

Tan, J.-P. and Mingat, A. (1992) *Education in Asia: A comparative study of cost and financing.* Washington, DC: World Bank Regional and Sectoral Studies.

Thobani, M. (1983) 'Charging user fees for social services: The Malawi education case', World Bank Staff Working Paper 572, Washington, DC.

Turvey, R. and Anderson, D. (1977) *Electricity economics: Theory and case studies.* Baltimore: Johns Hopkins University Press.

Uzawa, H. (1962) 'Optimal technical change in an aggregative model of economic growth', *International Economic Review*, 6:18–31.

Vogel, R.J. (1988) *Cost recovery in the health care sector: Selected country studies in West Africa.* Technical Paper No. 82. Washington, DC: The World Bank.

Vogel, R. (1991) 'Cost recovery in the health-care sector in sub-Saharan Africa', *International Journal of Health Planning and Management*, 6:167–191.

Waddington, C.J. and Enyimayew, K.A. (1989) 'A price of pay: The impact of user charges in Ashanti-Akim district, Ghana', *International Journal of Health Planning and Management*, 4:17–47.

Wade, R. (1988) *Village republics: Economic conditions for collective action in South India.* London: Cambridge University Press.

Walters, A. (1968) *The economics of road user charges.* World Bank Occasional Paper No. 5. Baltimore: Johns Hopkins University Press.

Watson, P.L. and Holland, E.P. (1976) 'Relieving traffic congestion: The Singapore area license scheme', World Bank Staff Working Paper No. 281, June.

Weale, M. (1992) 'Education, externalities, fertility, and economic growth', Policy Research Working Papers, WPS 1039, Washington, DC: The World Bank.

Wheeler, D. (1980) 'Human resource development and economic growth in developing countries: A simultaneous model', World Bank Staff Working Paper No. 407, July.

Wheeler, D. and Mody, A. (1993) 'International investment location decisions: The case of US firms', *Journal of International Economics.*

Whittington, D. (1990) 'Problems with the use of increasing block water tariff structures in developing countries', Infrastructure and Urban Development Department, The World Bank.

Winkler, D. (1989) 'Decentralization in education: An economic perspective', Policy Planning and Research Working Paper WPS 143, Washington, DC: The World Bank.

World Bank (1986) *Financing education in developing countries: An exploration of policy options.* Washington, DC: The World Bank.

World Bank (1987a), *Financing health services in developing countries: An agenda for reform.* A World Bank Policy Study, Washington, DC: The World Bank.

World Bank (1988b), *Road deterioration in developing countries: Causes and remedies.* Prepared by H. Clell and A. Faiz, with contributions by E. Bennathan, G. Smith and A. Bhandari. A World Bank Policy Study. Washington, DC.

World Bank (1987b, 1988c, 1990, 1991, 1992a, 1993, 1994) *World development report.* Oxford University Press.

World Bank (1989) *Developing the private sector.* Washington, DC.

World Bank (1991b) *Lessons of tax reform.* Washington, DC.

World Bank (1992b) *Energy efficiency and conservation in the developing world.* Washington, DC.

World Bank (1992c) *Adjustment lending and mobilization of private and public resources for growth,* Policy and Research Series 22, Washington, DC.

World Bank (1992) *Water resources management.* Washington, DC.

Wouters, A. (1991) 'Essential national health research in developing countries: Health-care financing and the quality of care', *Journal of Health Planning and Management*, 6:253–271.

Yoder, R.A. (1989) 'Are people willing and able to pay for health services?', *Social Science and Medicine*, 29:35–42.

*Chapter 44*

# STRUCTURAL ADJUSTMENT, STABILIZATION AND POLICY REFORM: DOMESTIC AND INTERNATIONAL FINANCE

VITTORIO CORBO and STANLEY FISCHER*

## Contents

* Corbo is Professor of Economics at Universidad Catolica, Santiago, Chile. At the time of writing, Fischer was Professor of Economics at MIT, and a Research Associate of the NBER; he is currently at the IMF. We thank Jere Behrman and T.N. Srinivasan for comments, and Max Alier and Paul Cashin for efficient research assistance.

*Handbook of Development Economics, Volume III, Edited by J. Behrman and T.N. Srinivasan*
© *Elsevier Science B.V., 1995*

## 1. Introduction

In the 1980s many developing countries faced a combination of severe balance of payments problems, high and variable inflation, slow growth, and high unemployment. These problems emerged from the cumulative effects of weak national policies and institutions which combined with a drastic and unfavorable change in external conditions (terms of trade shocks, interest rate shocks, a worldwide recession, and a severe reduction in commercial bank lending) to lead to the debt crisis. In contrast, in that same decade, a group of countries located in East Asia escaped the debt crisis and achieved an annual rate of growth of over 6 percent.

In the wake of the Great Depression and the apparent success of the Soviet planning model from the 1930s until the 1960s, economic policy in the post-World War II period had been dominated by skepticism about market mechanisms, and a corresponding belief that government intervention could successfully be used to correct market failures. The most notable and most important examples in the developing countries are the widespread preparation of national economic plans, and the pursuit of import substituting industrialization (ISI). Until the early 1970s, such policies were generally supported by academic development economists and policy advisers, with a few notable exceptions, such as Haberler (1959) and Viner (1953). Given the high tariff levels of industrial countries, the inherent appeal of protectionist policies to the practical person, the use of protectionist policies by the United States and European countries during their periods of industrialization, and the role of industrialization in the process of economic development, ISI seemed an obvious development strategy. Rapid growth in most developing countries in the 1950s and 1960s appeared to justify the basic ISI approach.

State intervention took place on a broad scale [Krueger (1992), Larrain and Selowsky (1991)]. Public enterprises were created to achieve industrialization directly, as well as provide employment; state marketing boards helped enforce pricing policies that in many countries discriminated against agriculture to the benefit of urban dwellers. The financial system was repressed to ensure appropriate financing for both the industrial firms favored by the state, and to provide cheap financing for the government. In many countries, especially in Latin America, the growth in the size of the public sector's spending obligations surpassed its capacity to collect revenues, and budget deficits increased to levels that were unsustainable in the international environment of the 1980s. Frequently, domestic currencies were overvalued as a result of domestic inflation and the attempt to use the nominal exchange rate as an anchor in the fight against inflation.

While economists such as Little, Scitovsky and Scott (1970) were sharply critical of the prevailing approach to development policy, and although the free-market critique of state intervention gained strength in the 1970s, it is only in retrospect that the disasters of the 1980s appear inevitable. The large-scale foreign borrowing by developing countries that helped create the debt crisis was initially applauded as part of the successful recycling of the balance of payments and saving surpluses of the oil producers. Even at the end of the 1970s, the final outburst of commercial bank lending between 1979 and 1982 helped conceal the unsustainability of the macroeconomic policies then being followed in many developing countries. But when the debt crisis struck, adjustment became unavoidable.

*Structural adjustment defined*

*Structural adjustment is a process of market-oriented reform in policies and institutions, with the goals of restoring a sustainable balance of payments, reducing inflation, and creating the conditions for sustainable growth in per capita income.* Structural adjustment programs generally start with a conventional stabilization program, intended to restore the viability of the current account and the budget, but they are distinguished from pure stabilization programs by the inclusion of a set of microeconomic-institutional policy reforms. In some cases, including Mexico starting in the mid 1980s, and Argentina in the late 1980s, important structural changes have been made even before the country achieved macroeconomic stabilization.[1]

Stabilization measures aimed at restoring macroeconomic balance and reducing inflation focus on bringing the level of demand and its composition (tradeable relative to non-tradeable goods) into line with the level of output and the financeable level of the trade deficit. Typically stabilization requires a reduction in both the public sector deficit and monetary financing of the government, in order to reduce the inflation rate. The structural transformation component focuses on the removal of microeconomic obstacles to the efficient allocation of resources. Typical measures include: liberalizing the trade regime; removing price controls; deregulating domestic goods markets; reforming the public sector, including the tax system, the structure of government spending, and state-owned enterprises; removing constraints on factor employment and mobility; deregulating domestic financial markets and removing obstacles to saving and investment; and creating and strengthening institutions to support stabilization and structural transformation. In short,

---

[1] We have not pursued the etymology of structural adjustment, a term that does not appear as a separate entry in the *New Palgrave*. The literature tends to reserve the term "structural" for the more microeconomic or sectoral reforms; see for instance OECD (1988).

structural adjustment policies aim to restore macroeconomic balance, to integrate the economy into the global economy, to greatly increase the role of (relatively undistorted) markets in allocating resources, and to create the institutions needed to achieve these goals.

*Adjustment programs before 1980*

Since the early 1980s, structural adjustment has been closely identified with the role of International Financial Institutions (IFIs) in fostering policy reforms in developing countries. However, since any country implementing wide-ranging economic reforms can be described as pursuing a structural adjustment program, many have in the past undertaken structural adjustment programs without knowing they were doing so. Prominent among the many structural reform programs undertaken between the end of World War II and 1980 are the German adjustment program of the late 1940s and 1950s, the Spanish reforms initiated in 1959, the Korean and Taiwanese programs of the first half of the 1960s, and the Chilean adjustment program of the second half of the 1970s.

The German program included a currency reform to stop inflation and a structural transformation component focusing on reestablishing a market system. While the German currency reform was implemented overnight, the liberalization of trade and the introduction of currency convertibility took place gradually. Indeed, adjustment in western Europe was very gradual: for instance price controls in Britain were not removed until 1954, and current account convertibility was not achieved until the late 1950s (Kaplan and Schleiminger, 1989).

Up to the early 1960s Korea, like most of the Latin-American countries, pursued a classic import substitution strategy.[2] Import competing manufacturing was encouraged through a host of incentives in the form of import restrictions (quotas, tariffs, and multiple exchange rates), tax concessions, subsidized credit, and the creation of public enterprises in the import competing sector. Slow growth and a military coup helped Korea recognize the limitations of the import substitution strategy, and achieve a shift in the early 1960s to an export-oriented development strategy.

The new strategy combined stabilization with a reduction in the anti-export bias of the trade regime by dismantling or offsetting previous protectionist policies, and by introducing explicit export promotion incentives. One of the most important pro-export measures was the unification of the exchange rate system and the implementation of a successful large real devaluation in the

---

[2] The experience of Korea is analyzed in the World Bank's (1993a) study of the East Asian economies.

period 1963–1964. Export activities were also encouraged by cheap banks loans for exporters, an aggressive indirect tax drawback system that included the remission of indirect taxes on inputs into exports and on the exports themselves, and discounts in the prices of transportation and electricity for export oriented activities. Fiscal and monetary policies succeeded in achieving low to moderate inflation and a fairly stable real exchange rate adjusted for changes in fundamentals [Kim and Roemer (1979), Frank et al., (1975), Scitovsky (1990), Suh (1992)].

The transformation of the Korean economy was dramatic. The average annual rate of growth of per capita GNP increased from 0.7 percent between 1952 and 1962, to 6.9 percent in the period 1962–1971. In the latter 10 years, the dollar value of exports grew at the astonishing average annual rate of 39 percent [Suh (1992)]. There are significant differences of opinion about the role of the state in promoting the expansion of exports. Some researchers claim that direct state intervention in the 1960s through selective incentives for exporters had a major role in export growth [Dornbusch (1985), Sachs (1987), Amsden (1989), Wade (1990)], while others argue that the export promotion initiatives merely compensated for the anti-export bias of import restricting policies [Westphal (1978), Nam (1985), Krueger (1985)]. Of course these restrictions and incentives still created distortions at the margins between domestic production and importing, and between domestic production and exports. There is no disagreement on the role played by macroeconomic policies: researchers of the Korean experience accept that the stable macroeconomic situation with low inflation, small fiscal deficits and a manageable balance of payments situation made a substantial positive contribution to its dramatic economic performance [Dornbusch (1985), Sachs (1987), Collins (1990), Corbo and Suh (1992)].

The structural transformation of the Taiwanese economy was as impressive as that of Korea. Taiwan's transformation from a backward agricultural economy to an industrial power started in 1958 when the basic exchange rate was devalued, and exporters of non-traditional products were allowed to trade their exchange surrender certificates for the full foreign exchange value of their exports [Tsiang (1985)]. These measures were followed by a gradual liberalization of the foreign trade regime, and the unification of the multiple exchange rate system in 1959. At this time the system of foreign exchange certificates was eliminated and another large devaluation took place. These measures were followed in the 1960s by aggressive policies to create a close to free-trade, free-market regime for exports. The liberalization of controls and the changes in the trade regime made it increasingly profitable to produce for foreign markets, and unleashed unprecedented export growth.

Monetary and fiscal policy have been used in Taiwan to keep inflation under control since 1958. Taiwan relied on markets to allocate resources more than did Korea. For example, while economic policies in Taiwan encouraged saving mobilization through a positive real interest rate for deposits and loans, Korea made much more use of credit subsidies in the early stages of its reforms.

The Taiwanese economy responded impressively to these measures. The average annual rate of growth of GNP per capita reached 6.7 percent in the 1960s, while it had been only a little over 2 percent in the second half of the 1950s. In the same decade dollar exports grew at an average annual rate of 21.3 percent, compared with an annual rate of 6 percent in the 1950s [Tsiang (1985)].

The structural transformation of the Chilean economy was initiated in the middle of the 1970s, after the economic collapse and 600 percent inflation which accompanied the end of the Allende government. The adjustment program included macroeconomic stabilization, significant trade liberalization, and a consistent return to the use of markets. The key macroeconomic measure was a cut in the public sector deficit from nearly 25 percent of GDP in 1973 to a mere 0.9 percent of GDP in 1975, and a surplus starting in 1976. The government also undertook a large nominal devaluation to assist in attaining the real devaluation required to switch the pattern of demand and production.

Structural transformation measures included a reform of the trade regime, the liberalization of markets, and an aggressive privatization program. The change in the trade regime relied mostly on the dismantling of the import restriction regime, accompanied by the successful real devaluation. It relied much less on special measures for the encouragement to exports than had the Korean and even the Taiwanese programs. Competitive markets were promoted by the opening to trade, and the deregulation of factor markets. The role of the private sector was also enhanced through the privatization of public enterprises [Corbo (1985a), Edwards and Edwards (1987)].

Subsequent developments in Chile, which included a deep crisis in 1982 and the eventual recovery of growth at the end of the 1980s, are discussed in the Chilean case study in Section 6.

*Adjustment programs of the 1980s*

The term structural adjustment came into common use only in the 1980s, after the World Bank (International Bank for Reconstruction and Development, IBRD) proposed structural adjustment lending in 1979 [Stern (1983)] – before the debt crisis began, though not before some Bank member countries were experiencing severe balance of payments difficulties at the onset of the second oil price shock. While the debt crisis made the need for stabilization and external financial assistance clear, the emphasis on trade liberalization and the other structural components owed much to the increasing weight of experience – such as that of Korea and Taiwan – and research [for instance, Bhagwati (1978), Krueger (1978), and Balassa and associates (1982)].

The World Bank proposed the introduction of structural adjustment lending at its Annual Meetings in September 1979. In the words of Ernest Stern, who played a central role in the introduction of these loans by the Bank:

"This new form of lending would:

- support a program of specific policy changes and institutional reforms designed to reduce the current account deficit to sustainable levels
- assist a country in meeting the transitional costs of structural changes in industry and agriculture by augmenting the supply of freely usable foreign exchange
- act as a catalyst for the inflow of other external capital to help ease the balance of payments situation". [Stern (1983, p. 89)].

In February 1980, Robert McNamara[3] set out the goals of adjustment as being increased efficiency of resource use and "improved responsiveness of the economy to changes in economic conditions", a goal that in later years was shortened to "enhanced supply response". It was envisaged that these programs would involve the reassessment of domestic investment programs, changes in the trade regime, domestic resource mobilization, and price incentives. Read in the light of the World Bank's approach of the 1980s, McNamara's discussion of trade reform was surprisingly eclectic, including the possibility that it might be desirable to reorient investment to domestic markets to stimulate domestic demand in the face of limited export prospects. The memorandum envisaged that implementation of structural adjustment programs would take several years and that their results would only gradually become visible. It also emphasized the need for enhanced coordination between the World Bank and the IMF in the process of adjustment lending.

World Bank adjustment lending started in 1980 with three SALs (structural adjustment loans) and one SECAL (sectoral adjustment loan). Most of the early adjustment loans were SALs, but after 1982 the bulk of adjustment lending took the form of SECALs. A textbook adjustment lending program starts with one or more SALs, designed to support economy wide institutional and policy reforms aimed at reducing the trade balance deficit, while also creating the conditions for sustainable growth. Further adjustment lending will focus on reforms in particular sectors, supported by SECALs. Alternatively,

---

[3] World Bank (1980).

SECALs may be used to support important sectoral reforms before a government can implement economy-wide reforms.

Structural adjustment loans typically disburse within 18 months, but have a maturity of 17 to 50 years.[4] During the 1980s the IMF introduced facilities that provide loans for more than its customary three years, the Extended Fund Facility (EFF) and the Structural Adjustment Facility (SAF). The rationale for Fund adjustment lending was that, in the context of the reduced net capital inflows of the debt crisis, consumption and investment levels in the developing countries – and thus current and future output levels – would be cut too hard if countries had to be in a position to repay Fund loans within the otherwise standard three years.

As the 1980s progressed, the success of additional countries in Asia (Indonesia, Malaysia and Thailand), the sustained performance of the Chilean economy, the difficulties suffered by non-adjusting countries in Latin America, and the collapse of the socialist model in Eastern Europe and the former Soviet Union, made the need for reform increasingly evident in many countries. During the decade, virtually all countries in Latin America entered structural adjustment programs, and some of them, especially Mexico and Argentina, succeeded in implementing them. While many countries in Africa also entered adjustment programs, there were fewer success stories and more failures.

Adjustment programs were not confined to developing countries: New Zealand undertook a radical adjustment program starting in the 1980s; and the OECD increasingly laid stress on efficiency-oriented reforms in its member countries [OECD (1988)]. Nor was structural adjustment in the developing countries confined to those receiving financial support from the IFIs: China pursued its reform program with strong World Bank intellectual and financial support, but without the benefit of Bank adjustment lending until late in its adjustment process.

By the beginning of the 1990s, the structural adjustment model had to an extraordinary extent become the accepted approach to reform,[5] with erstwhile critics increasingly accepting the general approach while attempting to soften the rigors of its application. However, some institutional and intellectual opposition to the structural adjustment policies recommended by the IFIs remains. The ECA has been a persistent critic of World Bank adjustment programs in Africa (UN Economic Commission for Africa, 1989), but in recent years some convergence has emerged between ECA and World Bank views on the type of reforms more suited to Africa. In particular, both institutions put

---

[4] Adjustment loans may be provided either under IBRD terms (at market interest rates) or, for the poorest countries, IDA (International Development Association) terms, which are essentially interest free, except for a small fee.
[5] World Bank (1991) summarizes and develops this consensus.

strong emphasis on the need to strengthen institutions, the high payoff from investment in human capital, and the need to restructure the public sector. While intellectual criticism of the type of policy recommendations of the IFIs has diminished, as there has been a large convergence of views on development, some criticism still remains [Helleiner (1989), Taylor (1988), and Cornia et. al. (1987).] Also, many students of the East Asian experience (for example, Amsden 1989, Wade 1990) argue that its real lessons are very different from those drawn by the Bank.[6]

## 2. Basic data, and the nature of a typical adjustment program

The data we present in this section are based on World Bank adjustment lending through 1992, and are drawn from the Bank's third report on adjustment lending.[7] Our statistical observations are therefore based on the adjustment programs of developing countries that adjusted with World Bank financial support; they omit both structural adjustment programs in industrialized countries[8] and developing country programs undertaken without Bank support. The data cover a total of 258 World Bank adjustment loans, made to 75 countries, over the period 1980–1991 [World Bank (1992)]. It is striking that at least 75 developing countries have formally declared themselves to be undertaking structural adjustment programs.

Countries that institute structural adjustment programs typically are suffering from a balance of payments crisis, manifested in an inability to obtain foreign financing. Such a crisis is frequently accompanied by a run on the currency, a large current account deficit, and – if there are capital controls – a large black market premium. The presence or expectation of a balance of payments problem is a necessary condition for IMF assistance, and is almost a necessary condition for the World Bank to provide rapidly disbursing loans.[9]

There are two potential sources of the balance of payments difficulties with which adjustment lending is associated. First, many adjusting countries were hit hard by the disturbances associated with the international debt crisis – the worldwide recession and sharp rise in real interest rates in 1982, and the decline in commodity prices. Table 44.1 presents estimates of the magnitude of external shocks suffered by countries that received World Bank adjustment loans. The data show that the intensive adjustment lending countries, most of which received adjustment loans before 1986, in aggregate suffered large shocks in the early 1980s, and that these shocks persisted through the rest of

---

[6] See too the World Bank's (1993a) attempt to deal with this question.
[7] Published as World Bank (1992).
[8] We present a case study on New Zealand below.
[9] This is one reason China did not receive World Bank adjustment loans until recently.

Table 44.1
External shocks to adjusting countries (percent of GDP)

| Country group | Magnitude of shock | |
|---|---|---|
| | 1981–1985/1971–1980 | 1986–1990/1971–1980 |
| Intensive adjustment lending (IAL) | −5.0 | −4.9 |
| Other adjustment lending (OAL) | 2.9 | −4.4 |
| No adjustment lending (NAL) | −3.5 | −2.0 |

*Source*: World Bank (1992), Table A.2, p. 27.
*Note*: Intensive adjusters are the 27 countries that received at least two structural adjustment loans or three adjustment loans (i.e. including sectoral adjustment loans) by June 1990, with the first effective before June 1986; there are 30 other adjustment lending countries, and 20 countries that did not receive adjustment loans. Although 75 countries received adjustment loans, data for statistical analysis are available only for 57. The external shock is the sum of the interest rate and the terms of trade shock. Both shocks are measured with respect to the base period.

the decade. Other countries that received adjustment loans were not adversely affected by the shocks of the early 1980s, but were hit hard in the second half of the decade. Countries that received no adjustment loans were also adversely affected by the shocks of the first half of the 1980s, but these shocks had moderated by the second half of the decade.

The second type of balance of payments crisis arises as a result of a country following unsustainable policies, which would sooner or later have led to a crisis even without external shocks. The transition economies fit this category, as do some of the other adjustment lending recipients whose balance of payments difficulties appear to be chronic rather than closely related to particular shocks.

The two elements – shocks and unsustainable policies – are present in different proportions whenever IMF or Bank adjustment lending takes place (see Table 44.2). If the problem is mainly an external shock, IMF loans should be sufficient. The original rationale for adjustment lending, that it would help countries reform in a period of years, applies well to a country such as Korea, whose basic approach to development was successful, but whose policies in the late 1970s were poor. After four Fund standbys and three adjustment loans between 1980 and 1985, Korea has returned to vigorous growth, and has no need for IFI financing. But there are many countries with more profound development policy problems, which have been receiving continuing Fund and Bank support for a decade or more. For instance, between 1981 and 1991 Ghana received six Fund loans and 11 Bank adjustment loans; Côte d'Ivoire received seven Fund loans and eight Bank adjustment loans.

The first column of Table 44.3 confirms that most adjustment lending programs start with a Fund loan. If the first loan is not from the Fund, then it is more likely to be a SECAL than a SAL – a contrast with the proportions of the second and third loans. There are two possible reasons for this relationship. One is that adjustment loans are being made to countries in such good shape that they do not need a Fund program or a SAL; the other is that the country's macroeconomic situation is not yet sufficiently stable to justify a Fund loan or SAL. The second possibility is more likely. The news in the second and third columns is that there is no clear trend at that point to SECALs, and that a significant share of early adjustment lending takes place through SECALs. If the Bank continues to make adjustment loans, they tend eventually to become SECALs; most of the SALs in the last column were recorded as SAL IV.

The loan sequence data in Table 44.3 suggest that structural adjustment typically starts with macroeconomic stabilization, and then moves on to

Table 44.2
Policy indicators, adjusting countries

| Group | 71–80 | 81–82 | 83–85 | 86–90 |
|---|---|---|---|---|
| Trade deficit, percent of GDP | | | | |
| IAL | 5.7 | 8.0 | 4.0 | 3.4 |
| OAL | 6.1 | 8.7 | 4.7 | 4.3 |
| NAL | 5.5 | 10.9 | 6.1 | 4.4 |
| Fiscal deficit, percent of GDP | | | | |
| IAL | 5.9 | 8.4 | 6.4 | 6.2 |
| OAL | 4.9 | 6.4 | 7.3 | 8.0 |
| NAL | 4.4 | 7.5 | 6.5 | 6.3 |
| Inflation rate, percent p.a.* | | | | |
| IAL | 15 | 15 | 20 | 17 |
| OAL | 11 | 13 | 10 | 11 |
| NAL | 11 | 10 | 10 | 16 |

* Median.
*Source*: World Bank (1992), Tables A.2 and A.5.

Table 44.3
Sequence of loans

| First loan | | | Second loan | | Third loan | | Fifth loan* | |
|---|---|---|---|---|---|---|---|---|
| Fund | SAL | SECAL | SAL | SECAL | SAL | SECAL | SAL | SECAL |
| 60 | 7 | 8 | 40 | 33 | 31 | 23 | 5 | 14 |

* Excluding Venezuelan debt reduction loan.
*Source*: Based on World Bank (1992), Table A.1.5. See footnote 10 for details.

sectoral reforms. However, the table no doubt also to some extent reflects World Bank doctrine, which argues that the first few loans should achieve a viable macroeconomic situation.

The record of World Bank conditionality provides evidence of the nature of the policies that are the focus of adjustment programs. Table 44.4 shows the share of each type of loan-agreement conditions in all adjustment loans.[10] The distribution of loan conditions is striking: conditions relating to each of trade policy, of government finance and administration, public enterprise reform, and fiscal policy conditions are found in about half or more of all adjustment loans. Thus, *adjustment programs focus primarily on the trade regime, and on the operations of the public sector.* In sectoral terms, reforms focus on the agriculture sector and the financial sector.[11]

Table 44.4
Loan-agreement conditions*

|  | 1979–1985 | Fiscal 1980–1988 | Fiscal 1989–1991 |
|---|---|---|---|
| **I. Supply side** |  |  |  |
| Trade policies | 58 | 57 | 50 |
| Sectoral |  |  |  |
| Industry | 22 | 21 | 15 |
| Energy | 15 | 15 | 16 |
| Agriculture | 45 | 45 | 31 |
| Financial sector | 31 | 32 | 32 |
| Rationalization of govt. finance & admin. | 51 | 57 | 82 |
| Public enterprise reforms | 44 | 44 | 56 |
| Social sector | 11 | 13 | 24 |
|  |  |  |  |
| **II. Absorption reduction** |  |  |  |
| Fiscal policy | 51 | 49 | 60 |
| Monetary policy | 16 | 13 | 20 |
|  |  |  |  |
| **III. Switching policies** |  |  |  |
| Exchange rate | 16 | 14 | 13 |
| Wage policy | 13 | 13 | 18 |

*Percent of loans with conditions in these areas. The loan agreement conditions are in percentage terms. Typically each loan contains many conditions so the row column sums exceed 100 percent.
*Source*: Based on World Bank (1990), Table 4.2, and World Bank (1992), Table A2.2

[10] There are also conditions that are mentioned in the loan agreements or the report of the President to the Board that are not formal legal loan conditions. In the period to 1989 these related mostly to trade policies, the budget, monetary and exchange rate policies, and the financial sector. In the period 1988–1991, they were mostly related to financial sector and public enterprise reform.
[11] World Bank (1992), Table A2.4 reports that at least 85 percent of these conditions are substantially fulfilled in every category in Table 44.4.

Finally, in this section we examine the amount of funding provided by adjustment lending. Although the share of such lending has not risen to more than 10 percent of *total* loans disbursed to developing countries (excluding India and China), *net* adjustment lending was by 1990 a major source of whatever net official disbursements were being made to the developing countries. Examining the regional breakdown of adjustment lending, approximately 25 percent has been to Africa, and 36 percent to Latin America and the Caribbean. Adjustment loans provided over half the net flow of official resources to Latin America in 1990, the year in which debt reduction operations began. Thus adjustment lending is important not only because it may encourage adjustment, but also because it is a vehicle for providing resources to developing countries.

## 3. Analytic underpinnings of structural adjustment programs

In this section we discuss aspects of the analytics of structural adjustment, starting from the causes of the crisis and the need for adjustment. We then examine the economics of stabilization, the economics of the microeconomic aspects of structural adjustment, the sequencing of adjustment measures, and the political economy of the maintenance of support for adjustment policies.

### 3.1. The source of the crisis

Most adjustment programs in the 1980s started from an economic crisis, when the government and private sector were no longer able to continue commercial borrowing to finance current account deficits. In these circumstances, *some* adjustment is inevitable. Typically the country suffering an external crisis also has a large and unsustainable fiscal deficit, and in many cases is experiencing very rapid inflation.

The questions with which we start are: first, what does it mean for policies to be unsustainable; and second, why is adjustment so often delayed. We should note, though, that appearances on the second issue may be deceiving: crises that do not happen do not get much attention, and most countries avoid the type of adjustment crises that the severely indebted countries suffered in the 1980s.

More usually, countries change policies because there is sufficient domestic dissatisfaction over the economic situation for the government to attempt to improve it. For instance, New Zealand's radical adjustment program (discussed below) was not in any sense inevitable. Rather, a political party was able to articulate the view that the country's relative decline could be stopped, and that both macroeconomic and structural policy changes would improve economic performance. A similar description applies in the case of the Thatcher adjustment program of the 1980s in the UK. China's leaders are supposed to have decided to undertake their reform program when they realized that their neighbors (specifically, it is said, Indonesia) were growing more rapidly than they were. The adjustment initiated by Malaysia in the second half of the 1980s also fits this description. General and gradual trade liberalization in the industrialized world in the period since World War II has taken place not because of a crisis, but because of a general agreement on the long-run benefits that it would bring.

*Unsustainable policies. A policy is unsustainable when it cannot continue forever.* The unsustainability of a particular macroeconomic policy is most clearly evident in the foreign exchange markets, when a country is unable to continue borrowing to finance its current account deficit. A policy may be unsustainable and yet continue for some time, either because market participants do not recognize its unsustainability, because the government is using controls to suppress the market forces that would impose a change, or because market participants expect the policy to change. A *crisis* occurs when economic or political pressures to change economic policy immediately become essentially overwhelming.[12]

Policies may be unsustainable for two reasons: first, as an economic matter, budget constraints imply that current policies have to change; and second, as a political matter, because political opposition will make it impossible for the government to continue these policies. We deal first with economic unsustainability, which can arise either because the domestic budget or external payments cannot be financed, unless policy changes.

*Debt dynamics.* The dynamics of government debt and external debt are analytically similar; we examine the case of government debt. Let $B_t$ be the real value of government debt (internal and external), $X_t$ the real value of the primary budget surplus (i.e. the budget exclusive of interest), and $S_t$ be the value of seigniorage obtained by the government in the current period. Then the government budget constraint is:

$$B_t = (1 + r_t)B_{t-1} - X_t - S_t \tag{1}$$

where $r_t$ is the realized real interest rate on the debt outstanding at the end of

[12] The qualifier "essentially" is needed because occasionally a government may ride out a crisis without fundamentally changing policy.

the last period, and

$$S_t = (H_t - H_{t-1})/P$$

where $H_t$ is the stock of high-powered money, and $P_t$ is the price level.[13]
It is convenient to define

$$q_T \equiv \prod_{i=1}^{T} (1 + r_{t+i})^{-1} \tag{2}$$

where $q_T$ is the discount factor that applies to cash flows $T$ periods from period $t$.

Now solving equation (1) forward, we obtain:

$$B_t = q_T B_{t+T} + \sum_{i=1}^{T} q_{t+i}(X_{t+i} + S_{t+i}) \tag{3}$$

If

$$\lim_{T \to \infty} q_T B_{t+T} = 0, \tag{4}$$

then equation (3) implies that a government that has a positive stock of bonds outstanding has to expect to run future budget surpluses or print sufficient money to pay off the debt. In practice, since the future tax rates or discount rates are not known at time $t$, equation (3) is usually used by taking expected values on the right hand side.

Several authors have used (3) to examine the sustainability of United States fiscal policy.[14] One question is whether the transversality condition (4) holds. This can be tested by creating a time series or other model to forecast $q_T B_{t+T}$, and examining its limiting behavior. If the condition (4) does not hold, then the present fiscal policy is not sustainable, *in the sense that policy will have to be changed.* Wilcox (1989) finds that U.S. fiscal policy was not sustainable in the post-World War II period.[15]

Equation (3) is an accounting identity. If current policies are unsustainable, then something has to give: in particular either some $X_{t+i}$ have to change, so

---

[13] Seigniorage could be included as government revenue in $X_t$. This is in effect done in countries that include central bank profits as part of government revenue. In countries that pay interest on bank reserves – a common practice in high inflation countries – the monetary base should be adjusted to reflect the extent to which it represents non-interest bearing government debt. There are two reasons to separate out $S_t$ in the budget constraint: first, when the government finances through non-interest bearing debt, no future interest liabilities are incurred, so that the adverse debt dynamics do not come into play; and second, explicit inclusion of $S$ emphasizes the route through which budget deficits may be inflationary.

[14] For example, Hamilton and Flavin (1986) and Wilcox (1989).

[15] See also Blanchard et al. (1990).

that the primary budget surplus will have to increase, perhaps through a capital levy on the debt, or through other taxes, or seigniorage, $S_{t+i}$, will have to be increased. But because both the non-interest budget surplus and seigniorage are bounded by the size of the economy, it will at some point become clear that the debt cannot be serviced through these means, and then a capital levy – formal or informal – becomes inevitable. Well before that point is reached, the government is likely to find itself paying higher interest rates on the debt, and forced into adjusting its macroeconomic policies.

An almost identical analysis applies to the external sector. Here the counterpart of the primary deficit in the budget is the non-interest current account of the balance of payments. Except for countries which receive transfers, or whose currencies are held abroad, there is no counterpart of seigniorage. The interpretation of equation (3) is that a country with an external debt has to be expected to run future non-interest current account surpluses to pay off the debt. And when the debt is on an unsustainable path, the adjustment will have to come either from a write-down of the debt or from adjustment of the current account, through devaluation and supportive measures.

The sustainability of the paths for domestic and external debt are closely connected. For many developing country governments with underdeveloped domestic capital markets, external borrowing was the main source of deficit financing. Further, correction of excessive external deficits typically requires a fiscal adjustment that also affects the path of government debt.

An alternative representation of debt dynamics focuses on the relationship between the real interest rate and the growth rate.[16] Here we work with ratios of the variables in (1) to GNP, represented by lower case symbols:

$$b_t = [(1 + r_t)/(1 + g_t)]b_{t-1} - x_t - s_t \qquad (2)'$$

where $(1 + g_t) \equiv (Y_t/Y_{t-1})$.

For given $x_t$ and $s_t$, the key question for debt dynamics is whether the real interest rate exceeds or is less than the growth rate of real GNP.[17] If

$$r < g \qquad (5)$$

then equation (2)' describes a stable difference equation. This means that the economy is growing fast enough that the amount borrowed by the government today is a greater share of GNP than the amount that has to be repaid. Under

[16] The comparison can be made between nominal growth and nominal interest rates, or real growth and real interest rates. For a simple exposition of debt dynamics along these lines, see Fischer and Easterly (1990).

[17] Depending on the context, either GNP or GDP might be the more useful scale variable. The growth rate in (2)' should be the growth rate of whichever scale variable is used.

these high growth or low real interest rate conditions, the economics of government borrowing is relatively benign. Under such conditions, a government can run a primary *deficit* that is a constant share of GNP, and rely on growth to (more than) take care of the consequent interest burden.

For many countries, especially in the 1960s, the relationship (5) seemed to hold. However, that is not necessarily the normal situation over long periods. Indeed in simple growth models without uncertainty, the economy is operating inefficiently if condition (5) holds.[18] In any case, if (5) does not hold, then a country cannot run a primary deficit forever. Put more strongly, if (5) does not hold, then a country that runs a constant primary deficit will find its debt to GNP ratio rising. Thus the relationship between the interest rate and the growth rate, (5), provides a useful first check on the sustainability of a fiscal deficit or deficits in the non-interest current account. Using (5), the onset of the debt crisis can be attributed to the rise in $r$ and the decline in $g$ that took place in the early 1980s.

Another short-hand method for judging sustainability is to use a simple model that respects budget and external debt identities, such as the World Bank's Revised Minimum Standard Model (RMSM), to project forward the paths of domestic and external debt under alternative policy scenarios.[19] If a particular policy leads to an ever-increasing domestic or foreign debt relative to GNP, then the policy will have to be changed. The RMSM model is in fact used in this way.

*Timing of the crisis.* There remains the question of when and if a crisis will occur if a country's current policies are non-sustainable. As already noted, many countries change policies without going through a crisis. We may say that a crisis will occur when the markets – for government debt, or foreign markets for the debt of the country's private sector – conclude that the current path is non-sustainable, and that the government is unlikely to change its policies in time. At that point, the government or the country may be unable to sell its debt, and has to adjust. The need to adjust may also result from an unanticipated change in external conditions, for instance a change in the world interest rate or the terms of trade.

Krugman (1979) presents a model of a predictable run on a country's foreign exchange reserves in a fixed exchange rate system. Assuming that the government shifts to a flexible exchange rate after the reserves run out, and that agents have perfect foresight, the crisis takes place at that moment when the post-attack adjustment path would commence at the existing exchange

---

[18] See Blanchard and Fischer (1989), p. 103.
[19] The RMSM of the World Bank is a version of a Domar growth model with disaggregation on the debt side and in the balance of payments.

rate. The timing of the crisis is thus determined by the perfect foresight implication that asset prices do not take anticipated jumps. Generalizations of the Krugman analysis allow the government to react before the point at which its reserves would be totally exhausted by the anticipated run on the reserves.

Alternatively, domestic political pressures may force a policy adjustment. However, domestic political pressures may sometimes push governments away from sustainable policies rather than towards them [Dornbusch and Edwards (1992)].

*Why is stabilization delayed?* If economists know what has to be done to avoid crises, and to increase growth, why are those policies not implemented? Part of the answer must be that economists have not succeeded in convincing the relevant political decision-makers (including the voters) that their answers are correct – and indeed sometimes economists are wrong. Another part is that the medicine may be too bitter for significant parts of the society, and thus for the body politic as a whole.

A growing theoretical and empirical literature deals with the political economy of reform, including the question of why stabilizations are delayed.[20] This helps answer the question of why countries sometimes find themselves in crisis. Alesina and Drazen (1991) argue that although there could be agreement on the need for a fiscal adjustment, conflict could emerge on how to distribute the burden of higher taxes or expenditure cuts among the different socioeconomic groups. In their model, stabilizations are delayed because of a conflict over which socioeconomic group will bear the greater part of the burden of adjustment. In a model with two groups, stabilization takes place only when one group concedes, in effect agreeing to bear the greater part of the burden, even though the total burden of stabilization is increased by delay. The delay is a result of each group's uncertainty about the burden being borne by the other before stabilization, and thus uncertainty about the date at which the other group would be better off agreeing to bear the greater burden in stabilization rather than continue in the pre-stabilization situation.

The source of their results can be understood from the fact that stabilization is immediate if it is known that the burden will be equally shared. The greater the difference between the burdens borne by the winners and losers, the later is the expected date of stabilization. The model predicts that the expected date of stabilization is later the more polarized is the society. Alesina and Drazen argue that their model explains why countries often fail in their first attempts at stabilization, and why a stabilization program may succeed when an apparently similar program failed earlier. In a war of attrition, the cost of waiting forces one group to concede.

Fernandez and Rodrik (1991) present a model in which uncertainty about

---

[20] The literature is concisely reviewed by Rodrik (1993).

the beneficiaries of reform similarly delays action, even for programs which will receive majority support if adopted, and even though individuals are risk neutral. Rodrik (1993) explains this result, which of course requires that the reform not be a Pareto-improvement, in a very useful survey of the developing theory of the political economy of reform.

Political scientists have also studied why stabilization in particular, and adjustment policies in general, are delayed when it appears that current policies are unsustainable. This literature has considered several factors that could account for a delay in responding: the source of the crisis; the intensity of the crisis; and the political support for carrying out a stabilization program. Nelson (1990), summarizing a set of case studies, claims that the response was usually delayed when a crisis could be clearly identified with an external shock. Others have formulated the hypothesis that the demand for stabilization increases with the intensity of the crisis [Krueger (1993) Haggard and Webb (1993)]. Usually a change in government precipitates the introduction of a stabilization program. As Haggard and Kaufman (1992, p. 30) put it, "Incoming governments . . . have capitalized on honeymoon periods and the disorganization or discrediting of the opposition to launch ambitious new reform initiatives". However, they also claim that weak governments may fail to assemble enough support for a stabilization effort, which will then have to wait for the next government.

## 3.2. The economics of stabilization

In discussing the analytics of adjustment programs, it is useful to distinguish between countries that start with low inflation, and those which have also to deal with high inflation.

Many of the African countries that had to adjust in the 1980s, including members of the franc zone, as well as India in the 1990s, had avoided high inflation. Nonetheless, the gap between domestic demand and output exceeded the financeable level of the current account deficit, and adjustment was necessary.

We start this section by illustrating the typical adjustment problem faced by a country where inflation is not a major issue. Then we extend the analysis to high inflation countries, by dealing explicitly with inflation reduction as an added adjustment problem.

### 3.2.1. Stabilization and structural adjustment in low inflation countries

The economics of structural adjustment for a small open economy can be well understood in terms of the dependent economy model of Salter–Swan–Corden–Dornbusch [Salter (1959), Swan (1961), Corden (1960) and Dornbusch

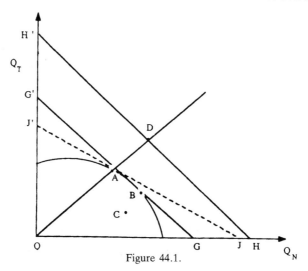

Figure 44.1.

(1980)]. Figure 44.1 shows the typical model. There are two types of good, tradeables on the vertical axis, and nontradeables on the horizontal axis. Their relative price, $(P_T/P_N)$, where $P_T$ and $P_N$ are the prices of tradeables and nontradeables respectively, is defined as the real exchange rate, the price of tradeable goods (a composite of importable and exportable goods, which has been aggregated assuming that the country is a price taker in world markets) in terms of domestic goods. When tradeable goods become more expensive, the real exchange rate rises, corresponding to a real devaluation.

The need for adjustment starts with the country consuming at $D$ and, if there are no distortions in commodity or factor markets, producing at $B$, with producers and consumers facing the same real exchange rate. The country is running a trade deficit equal to GH, measured in terms of non-tradeables. The market for non-tradeables clears, as can be seen from the fact that the output of non-tradeables at $B$ is equal to their consumption, at $D$. Assuming the trade deficit has to be restored to balance, the country has to reach a new equilibrium on the production possibility frontier.

Typically the country also has many impediments – in the form of distortions in product and factor markets, as well as institutional weaknesses – to the efficient use of resources, and is therefore operating well within the production frontier at a point like $C$ in Figure 44.1. For countries that start their adjustment programs with severe distortions, there is a potential output gain from removing the structural impediments. However, it will generally take time for such supply side measures to affect output positively, and the initial adjustment effort is likely to reduce demand and output.

Since a large fiscal deficit is the most likely cause of the excess of expenditures over output, fiscal contraction will be a key component of the expenditure reduction package. Pure expenditure reducing policies, which shift the budget line in but do not change prices, are incapable of restoring external balance without creating an imbalance between the demand for and supply of non-tradeable goods. What is needed is the combination of an expenditure reducing policy, which shifts in the budget line (for example to GG'), and a (production and expenditure) switching policy, which changes relative prices, ending at an equilibrium like point A. Note that between budget lines GG' and JJ', the relative price of tradeables has risen, i.e. there has been a real devaluation.

Figure 44.1 provides a metaphor for structural adjustment: for an economy operating close to the frontier typically macroeconomic adjustment is needed to reduce expenditures relative to income (as between points *D* and *A*); and, in the structural component, resources have to be reallocated (as between points *C* and *A*). But the figure is only a metaphor: macroeconomic adjustment typically involves dealing with inflation as well as excess spending, and there are choices about the methods (fiscal, monetary, exchange rate) by which macroeconomic adjustment is attained; the structural component involves more than getting prices right; and there are issues about the sequencing of reforms. Furthermore, in economies that have many distortions the structural component includes also their removal to increase output levels out of existing resources.

The dependent economy model can also be presented in terms of the real exchange rate and expenditure and output in terms of non-tradeables, $E/P_N$ and $Q/P_N$ respectively [Dornbusch (1980)]. Figure 44.2 shows the basic diagram, which is a transformation of Figure 44.1. The schedule YY shows the value of output in terms of non-tradeable goods, for each value of the real exchange rate. It is the intercept of the tangent to the production frontier traced out in Figure 44.1 as the real exchange rate changes: the value of output measured in non-tradeable goods rises as the real exchange rate rises. *BB* is the locus of external balance, combinations of the level of real spending and real exchange rate that maintain the demand for traded goods equal to their supply: when income increases, the real exchange rate has to rise to maintain external equilibrium.[21] Finally, *NN* is the locus of non-tradeable-goods market equilibrium, which is negatively sloped on the assumption that substitution effects dominate.

Both the markets for tradeable and non-tradeable goods are in equilibrium at point *E*. At any other point, the exchange rate and/or the level of income and output have to change to bring about equilibrium; typically both spending

---

[21] In terms of Figure 44.1, the level of income OH and the relative price shown at B and D represent a point on the BB locus.

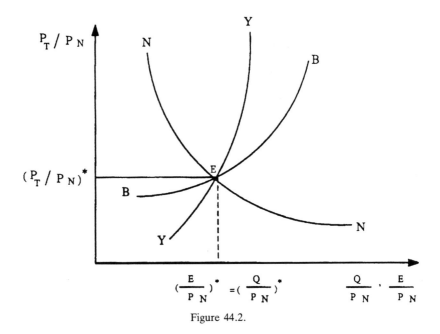

Figure 44.2.

and the real exchange rate have to change.[22] The model can conveniently be used to analyze the effects of disturbances, such as the receipt of a transfer, or fiscal policies that affect the level of spending. Dornbusch (1980) shows also how to modify the dependent economy model to allow for endogenous terms of trade changes.

This analysis illustrates the direct relationship among expenditures, the real exchange rate, and the trade deficit. We can use the model to illustrate the effects of an expansionary aggregate demand policy for an economy operating close to the frontier. Consider the case of a country that starts in equilibrium at a point like $E$ in Figure 44.2; then aggregate demand expands. The real exchange rate will depreciate along the NN locus, and the country will develop a trade deficit. Suppose now that the external financing – for example, foreign aid or loans from multilateral institutions – is reduced. Then there will be a trade balance deficit at the initial real exchange rate and level of real expenditures. In the absence of financing, the country has to adjust. The adjustment program will include expenditure reduction and supply expansion policies, along with a real devaluation. Structural reforms play a central role in facilitating the reallocation of resources and in moving the economy towards

----

[22] Dornbusch (1980) reviews both the anatomy of disequilibrium, and the policy measures needed to return to equilibrium.

the production frontier. Structural reforms are also important in creating conditions for sustainable growth by improving the economic environment for physical and human capital accumulation.

The effects of the demand reduction programs are likely to dominate in the short run. As domestic expenditures are reduced, the real exchange rate has to depreciate to avoid creating an excess supply of non-tradeable goods and unemployment. Unemployment will result if the real exchange rate is for whatever reason not allowed to increase, due for example to insufficient adjustment (or none at all) of the nominal exchange rate, or through real wage resistance. This situation is represented by point $F$ in Figure 44.3. There is a trade balance deficit at point $F$, given by $GF$, and the real exchange rate is $(P_T/P_N)_o$. The expenditure reduction brings the economy to point H: with exchange rate $(P_T/P_N)_o$, there is an excess supply of non-tradeable goods and unemployment.

This model illustrates that following a reduction in domestic expenditures, a real devaluation is required to produce the larger trade surplus which can prevent the emergence of an excess supply of non-tradeable goods.

The analytics of the two components of structural adjustment – stabilization and macroeconomic adjustment, and structural or microeconomic adjustment – are not generally dealt with simultaneously. And even on the macroeconomic side, the economics of stabilization is generally dealt with separately from the

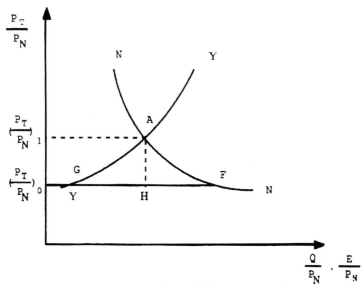

Figure 44.3.

analysis of the investment and growth that is supposed to result from stabilization and adjustment.

Any comprehensive policy model of the stabilization process thus has to include the government budget constraint and its financing, the external sector and its financing, and the dynamics of asset stocks and inflation.[23] In practice a wide variety of analytic models, many of which do not explicitly include the government budget constraint or external sector dynamics, are used in studying the dynamics of adjustment. Macroeconomic stabilization is usually analyzed in a one-good model, for example in the financial programming model of the IMF or the RMSM or extended RMSM models of the World Bank. Recently attempts have been made to broaden these models in three directions: to introduce the tradeable-non-tradeable breakdown; to deal more explicitly with the relevant budget constraints; and to introduce expectations explicitly.[24]

A stabilization program generally includes fiscal consolidation, monetary contraction, exchange rate adjustments, and sometimes incomes policies. The starting point is a target external deficit, based on the availability of external financing including assumptions about debt service. This implies the adjustment that has to be made in domestic absorption relative to domestic output. Absorption can be reduced through direct declines in government spending and declines in private spending induced by monetary and fiscal policies. It is rarely the case that domestic output can be increased much in the short run. Often it is found that the required reductions in domestic demand are too difficult to implement politically, and in such a case the government or international agencies will have to seek additional external funding, sometimes in the form of arrears.

The real exchange rate will typically have to be devalued as part of the adjustment process. The required devaluation can be calculated from a net export equation with domestic income and the real exchange rate as arguments.[25] Thus the preliminary calculations for a stabilization program provide estimates of the fiscal policy variables and the real exchange rate in the new equilibrium; there will probably also be an inflation target. It is then necessary to decide on the adjustment path by which these targets are to be attained – whether in a big bang or gradually, and what exchange rate and credit policies correspond to the planned adjustment path.

---

[23] See for instance the models in Bryant et al. (1988) and (1993).

[24] Caballero and Corbo (1986); Haque et al. (1991); Devarajan and de Melo (1987); Schmidt-Hebbel and Serven (1993); Bryant et al. (1993).

[25] See Krugman (1992) for a discussion of the question of whether exchange rate changes are a necessary part of the adjustment mechanism of the current account.

## 3.2.2. *Stabilization and structural adjustment in high inflation countries*

In high inflation countries, adjustment has a third dimension beyond the expenditure reduction-output expansion and real devaluation issues analyzed in the previous section – the need to break the dynamics of inflation.

Inflation generates seigniorage revenues for the government, but at the same time generally reduces real government revenues through the erosion of the real value of tax revenues due to collection lags in a situation of accelerating inflation, the so called Keynes–Olivera–Tanzi effect [Tanzi (1977)]. Whether a fiscal contraction is necessary to reduce inflation permanently can be decided in each case by calculating a *low inflation budget* for the country. This is a calculation of what the budget deficit would be, given planned tax rates and real government spending, if the economy were operating at a specified low inflation rate. The calculation thus takes account of the Keynes-Olivera-Tanzi effect, of any reductions in nominal interest rates that would result from lower inflation, of the potential loss in seigniorage from operating at a low inflation rate,[26] and all the distortions that inflation puts into the government accounts. At the same time, a judgment would have to be reached on a desirable path for the government debt and the overall budget deficit. If the low inflation deficit is consistent with the desired deficit, then no fiscal correction is needed to deal with inflation – though one may still be needed to deal with the external deficit.

Bruno and Fischer (1986) identify an extreme case of dual equilibria in which inflation is high even though the economy could, with the same fiscal policy, be in a low inflation equilibrium. This result derives from the seigniorage Laffer curve. Alternatively, inflation may have risen to high levels as the private sector adapts to ongoing inflation by reducing its money holdings, and the government attempts to reduce its costs to the private sector, for instance through indexing of government wages, and by paying interest on bank reserves. In such a situation, there is a low inflation equilibrium available with relatively little loss of fiscal revenue, but getting there is costly and some of the reduced demand for real balances may be irreversible. Similarly, a country may find itself inadvertently in a high inflation equilibrium as a result of accommodating monetary policy operating rules, such as attempting to hold the real exchange rate and the real interest rate constant.[27]

---

[26] Dornbusch and Fischer (1993) review the public finance aspects of inflation, which starts with Keynes' (1923) superb analysis in the *Monetary Tract*, and which were later taken up by Cagan (1956) and Bailey (1956).

[27] In the 1980s, the Chilean central bank has used these operating rules. In practice, though, it has tightened policy when inflation has risen, so that the rule is not purely accommodating.

While it is possible that fiscal correction is not needed to stabilize inflation, it has to be recognized that calculations of the desired deficit and the low-inflation deficit are imprecise and that wishful thinking – especially about the size of the Tanzi effect – often plays a large part in such calculations. Despite the theoretical possibility, it is advisable to be skeptical about claims that no fiscal correction is needed to reduce inflation: more stabilizations have failed – in Brazil alone – because of overoptimism about the size of the Tanzi effect than because the fiscal adjustment was too ambitious.[28]

Similar calculations have to be made for the external accounts, to attempt to ensure that the current account deficit is consistent with available financing. This is typically done in a model of the type discussed in the previous section.

*Dynamics of disinflation.* The dynamics of disinflation can be studied using a simple macroeconomic model such as that presented in Dornbusch and Fischer (1993).[29]

$$\Pi = \alpha w + (1 - \alpha)e + \mu \quad 0 < \alpha < 1 \tag{6}$$

$$w = \Pi_{-1} - \lambda u \tag{7}$$

$$e = \beta \Pi + (1 - \beta)\Pi_{-1} \quad 0 < \beta < 1 \tag{8}$$

$$\Pi = \Pi_{-1} + \theta \mu - \alpha \lambda \theta u \quad \theta = 1/[1 - \beta(1 - \alpha)] \tag{9}$$

$$u = u_{-1} - \gamma(m - \Pi) - \theta(e - \Pi) - \sigma f \tag{10}$$

Equation (6) represents cost-based pricing, with the inflation rate from the supply side reflecting wage changes ($w$) and the rate of depreciation of the currency ($e$), which affects the prices of imported commodities; $\mu$ is an adverse supply stock. Equation (7) is a stylized Phillips curve: the lagged inflation term reflects either adaptive expectations about inflation, or indexation of nominal wage adjustments, which is of course widespread in high inflation economies. Equation (8) is an exchange rate adjustment rule, in which the government is assumed to try to maintain the real exchange rate constant, but in which – because of lags in measuring or perceiving price changes – inflation surges result in real appreciation. Equation (9) is obtained from replacing equations

---

[28] It is quite certain once the economic calculations have been made that the political decisionmakers will shave the extent of the fiscal (or external sector) correction from the recommended level. This opens up the question of whether the economist should correspondingly shade his or her calculations in the opposite direction. We are sure this happens in practice but recommend against it, as well as against the opposite error – of shading the calculation in the direction the politician would like to hear.

[29] A similar model, with a richer lag structure, is used in Edwards (1993a).

(7) and (8) in (6). Equation (10) represents goods market equilibrium: increases in real balances, real depreciation, and fiscal expansion ($f$) reduce unemployment.

While the lag structures and the treatment of expectations in this model are excessively simple, the model summarizes well the essential problem of stabilization. By adding and subtracting $\Pi_{-1}$ on the right hand side of (6) we obtain

$$\Pi = \Pi_{-1} + \alpha(w\text{-}\Pi_{-1}) + (1 - \alpha)(e - \Pi_{-1}) + \mu \qquad (6)'$$

On the supply side, inflation today will be equal to inflation yesterday except for any combination of the following:

(a) Wage inflation falls below past price inflation. This requires a break with any implicit or explicit backward price indexation, otherwise the real wage tends to rise when inflation is reduced [Simonsen (1983), Corbo (1985b) Fischer (1988)]. The suspension of indexation, the replacement of backward looking by forward looking indexation, or introduction of an incomes policy, could achieve this.

(b) Exchange depreciation falls below the past rate of inflation. This is the major attraction of exchange-rate based stabilizations, particularly in very open economies.

(c) Favorable supply shocks lead to disinflation without the need for the exchange rate or wages to take the lead. Just as the unfavorable supply shocks of the 1970s increased inflation, the favorable oil price shock of late 1985 helped the Israeli disinflation program that started in July that year.[30]

By using equation (9), we also obtain the Phillips curve conclusion:

(d) Inflation can be cut the old-fashioned way, by increasing unemployment, through restrictive aggregate demand policies.

*Heterodoxy and orthodoxy.* The stabilization problem is to reduce inflation, the balance of payments deficit, and the fiscal deficit at minimum cost in terms of unemployment and to the poor, with minimum damage to growth, and in ways that will increase long-run growth. The attraction of supply side policies – incomes policies, wage-price freezes, changes in indexation rules – is that they appear to hold out the prospect of reducing inflation costlessly. The danger of using such policies is that they cannot permanently reduce inflation unless the underlying fiscal and monetary causes of the inflation have been dealt with. But by combining the necessary fiscal and monetary measures with supply side

---

[30] Of course, as the 1985 Argentine case shows, favorable supply shocks are not sufficient without resolute fiscal action.

measures, in so-called *heterodox* policies, the unemployment costs of stabilization can in principle be reduced.[31]

In equation (6), heterodoxy would seek to reduce $w$ below the level it would take without direct intervention, either by freezing wages, or by suspending indexation that would otherwise set $w$ at the level $\Pi_{-1}$. More generally, heterodoxy could be seen also as seeking to produce a negative $\mu$ by controlling price increases. We discuss the role of the exchange rate in disinflation below.

*Wage controls, pacts, and taxes.* Heterodox programs often seek to control wages, either through controls or through pacts with labor, as in the Mexican "Pacto" among the government, labor, and industry. Wage taxes, TIPs (tax incentive plans), have been used in some formerly socialist economies, including Poland and Russia. In these cases, firms paid taxes on wage increases above some specified rate. While the macroeconomic case for reducing the rate of wage increase is clear from the above model, wage controls that are maintained for any length of time either begin to break down, or else distort relative wages. Thus wage controls should be viewed at best as a transitory measure to help stabilize inflation.

*Seigniorage and public finance.* The public finance analysis of the inflation tax starts from Keynes' *Tract on Monetary Reform*, which emphasizes that inflation is a tax of last resort; the discussion took more analytic shape with Cagan (1956) and Bailey (1956), and is summarized and extended in Dornbusch and Fischer (1993). The inflation tax was placed in an intertemporal context by Mankiw (1987), who argued that an optimally chosen (from the viewpoint of the inflation tax) inflation rate would display a unit root, and be positively correlated with other tax rates. This latter implication appears not to hold (Edwards and Tabellini, 1991).

In classic hyperinflations, seigniorage eventually became the main source of revenue as the Keynes-Tanzi effect eroded the tax system. But typically the amount of seigniorage collected in modern high and moderate inflations is only a few percentage points of GNP. This fact immediately raises the question of why the country cannot undertake the fiscal effort that would make it possible to reduce inflation to single- or low double-digit levels.

We identify two possible explanations. First, raising taxes or cutting spending by 2–4 percent of GNP is politically more difficult than it sounds. By contrast with explicit taxation, the inflation tax and its incidence are almost invisible

---

[31] The term "heterodox" was supposed to mean "orthodox plus", but etymologically actually means "other than orthodox". This is not the meaning that those who use the word would like it to have: "polydox" is closer to the intended meaning.

and can be imposed without legislation. Second, inflation may continue because the politicians believe it too costly to stop, even though the fiscal effort to stop it would be politically possible.

The literature identifies at least two costs of disinflation: distributional costs; and output costs. The distributional costs of ending inflation play a prominent role in political economy models that seek to explain stabilization delays,[32] but little is known about their empirical importance.[33] The output cost emerges from the traditional Phillips curve approach to inflation.

Once the role of expectations in the Phillips curve is recognized, the output costs can in principle be avoided if the private sector can be persuaded to expect lower inflation by some route other than lower inflation. Thus in models where credibility is important, credible pre-announced reductions in money growth can reduce the output costs of disinflation.[34] Even in the presence of long-term contracts, credible disinflations announced sufficiently far in advance, or sophisticated paths of money growth, in principle make it possible to disinflate costlessly. However, the evidence suggests that disinflation is costly,[35] except perhaps for disinflations that are based on an exchange rate anchor (Kiguel and Liviatan, 1992).

*Nominal anchors. A nominal anchor is a nominal variable which guides monetary policy.* The term appears to be new,[36] but the concept is at least as old as the gold exchange standard, where the price of gold was the nominal anchor that determined the quantity of money. In modern discussions, the nominal anchor is typically thought of as either the quantity of money or some other nominal asset (e.g. credit), or the exchange rate. The exchange rate may be fixed, or may follow a preannounced crawling peg path, as in the *tablitas* of the late seventies in the Southern Cone of South America. The exchange rate path may be reset from time to time, as for instance in the Israeli diagonal band system introduced in 1991.

The exchange rate and the quantity of money can be regarded as anchors in the sense that the central bank can, at least for some time, control them. In principle, the price level, or the target inflation rate, could be nominal anchors, but those variables are less directly under the control of the central bank. Of course, no nominal anchor can keep inflation low for long unless the underlying real fundamentals, in particular the budget deficit, are consistent

---

[32] Such as Alesina and Drazen (1991), and Mondino, Sturzenegger, and Tommasi (1992).

[33] World Bank (1990), examines the distributional impact of adjustment policies.

[34] The role of credibility was brought home forcefully by Sargent's (1982) well-known article on the ends of four hyperinflations; later work has suggested that even the hyperinflations were not ended without output costs. See also Sargent (1983) and the comments by Summers.

[35] See Solimano (1990) for a review of experience, including that of the hyperinflations.

[36] We are not aware of when the term was first used; one of the authors recalls using it in 1984, and it must have been used much earlier.

with the specified path of the anchor. Also, the behavior of the anchor should be consistent with the mechanism of adjustment in other nominal prices; otherwise large distortions in relative prices could develop, and damage the effectiveness of the program. In particular, backward-looking wage indexation is often incompatible with the use of a fixed exchange rate anchor. Chile's stabilization program of 1978–1982 illustrates this problem [Corbo (1985b), Edwards and Edwards (1987), Corbo and de Melo (1987), Corbo (1993) and Corbo and Fischer (1994)].

The general need for a nominal anchor arises from the property, emphasized by Patinkin (1956), that the price level and other nominal variables are indeterminate unless at least one nominal variable is specified exogenously. The specific need for a nominal anchor during a stabilization arises from the likelihood that the system has been without a nominal anchor during the preceding inflation – indeed, inflation could not have risen to such levels if an effective nominal anchor had been in place. It is not uncommon for monetary policy in high-inflation countries to target real variables such as the real supply of credit, the real exchange rate and the real interest rate, and not to adjust these real targets in response to inflation.[37]

In practice, the choice between the exchange rate and the quantity of money as nominal anchor during a stabilization has almost always been settled in favor of an exchange rate peg.[38] The extent of the commitment to the exchange rate anchor varies. At one extreme is the Argentine 1991 convertibility law, which embodies the nominal anchor in legislation; at the other is an exchange rate peg that is simply announced without any longer term commitment being made.

The exchange rate has several advantages over the quantity of money as a nominal anchor: the central bank knows precisely what it has to do; the public knows at every moment whether the central bank is succeeding; and the exchange rate affects import prices and the prices of tradeables directly. An exchange rate peg can quickly garner credibility, at least for the short term; in the long term, credibility can be retained only by success in maintaining the exchange rate peg. By contrast, there is bound to be great uncertainty about the demand for real balances during a stabilization, both because it is not known to what extent the preceding inflation has permanently reduced the demand for money, and as a result of uncertainty over the success of the stabilization attempt. Consequently the central bank adhering to a money stock

---

[37] If the real targets are adjusted in response to inflation, e.g. the real interest rate is raised when inflation increases, then the system in effect is operating with a nominal anchor (cf. the discussion of Chilean monetary policy in footnote 27).

[38] The choice between these two anchors is analyzed in Fischer (1986) and Bruno (1991). Edwards (1993a) discusses the notion of a nominal anchors and, empirically, the effect of different anchors on the dynamic properties of the economy.

target may find itself with an exchange rate and interest rates that are far out of line with the needs of the situation. The recent instability of the demand for money in many of the industrialized countries, including the US and the UK, has further reduced confidence in the efficacy of a monetary anchor.

Kiguel and Liviatan (1992) argue that, contrary to the usual pattern in stabilizations, exchange-rate based stabilizations (ERBSs) in chronic inflation countries start with a boom (perhaps after a brief recession) rather than a recession. Then, if the exchange rate peg is maintained, there is a period of overvaluation which results in a recession. Thus, they argue, the ERBS does not avoid the recession that accompanies stabilization, but only delays it. During the ERBS, the trade balance and current account deteriorate, real wages generally increase, the real exchange rate appreciates, and either or both consumption and investment boom. In several cases, the consumption boom took place despite a significant cut in the budget deficit and higher taxes. Real interest rates declined in some cases, and rose sharply in the recent successful Mexican and Israeli stabilizations.

Kiguel and Liviatan identify several possible explanations for the stylized facts of the differences between ERB and money-based stabilizations, including the role of sticky prices, the possibility that lower real interest rates encourage spending, that uncertainty about the success of the stabilization combined with concern over the policies that will follow (e.g. imposition of tariffs, tax increases) can account for the spending boom, and the possibility that the increase in real wages encourages consumption.[39]

Calvo and Vegh (1991) present a model based on a cash-in-advance constraint, with staggered contracts, that attempts to account for the different dynamic responses to exchange rate- and money-based stabilizations.[40] With a credible permanent exchange rate peg, the inflation rate declines immediately to its new steady state level, and the real equilibrium is unaffected. If the exchange rate peg is not credible, in the sense that it is expected to be temporary, then the real exchange rate appreciates as a result of price stickiness, and the cash-in-advance constraint produces a consumption boom during the peg, because the lower rate of devaluation temporarily reduces the effective price of consumption. This model is thus capable of accounting for some of the basic empirical characteristics of ERBSs reported by Kiguel and Liviatan, even if the cash-in-advance constraint route to the consumption boom is not compelling. Another empirical implication, that the recession comes when the policy fails, is also questionable: in the Mexican and Israeli cases, the

---

[39] Of course, the real wage is generally endogenous, so the question arises of what is causing the real wage increase in the first place. In the Israeli stabilization of 1985–1986, the real wage increase six months after the start of the stabilization was essentially exogenous, negotiated between the government and the unions six months earlier.

[40] The results of this and related papers are well summarized in Vegh (1992).

recession appears to have come as a result of the real appreciation that took place as the stabilization policy was maintained, rather than as a result of policy failure.

The issue of the nominal anchor has received renewed attention in the context of socialist economy reform. An exchange rate peg was central to the Polish stabilization. In such a situation, where the fundamentals are not known, and where it is unlikely the pegged exchange rate can be sustained for more than a year, the authorities have to worry about when and how to switch away from the peg. A typical change is to switch to a crawling peg, maintaining exchange rate discipline, but not committing to an unsustainable rate.

*The role of external financing.* Stabilization programs in both low and high inflation developing countries have typically been undertaken with the assistance of loans from the international financial institutions (IFIs). Even in industrialized countries, stabilizations have often been supported by foreign loans, for instance the British stabilization of 1976, undertaken with IMF support. However, foreign financing is not necessary for adjustment, as the Chile and New Zealand examples discussed below show.

Most structural adjustment programs in recent years have been financially supported by the international institutions. In presenting the rationale for adjustment lending, the World Bank (1992, p. 7) explains that policy reform is a typical investment, with short run costs and longer run benefits that outweigh the costs.[41] "But transitional financing is usually needed to spread the costs over time, minimizing the reductions in consumption (especially important in poor countries) and making the reform feasible for policymakers". Critics of adjustment lending sometimes describe the loans as a bribe to undertake policy reform, but this is not a particularly useful formulation[42] of the complexities of putting together and maintaining a domestic coalition in support of reform.

Of course, the debt and adjustment crisis was partly a result of the easy and unconditional availability of external financing for developing countries. In adjustment loans, conditionality is imposed to deal with the dynamic inconsistency that arises after the loan contract has been agreed. However, even when loan conditions are imposed, borrowers who are indebted to an IFI know that it too has a stake in maintaining their relationship. The theoretical complexities of conditionality and the incentives it creates to undertake reforms are analyzed in Mosley (1992). A review of the extent to which loan conditions are met can be found in Webb and Shariff (1992).

Between 1980 and 1991, the World Bank committed $41 billion to 258

---

[41] Krueger (1984) presents this argument.

[42] See World Bank (1992), Box 2, p. 9, for a useful discussion of the argument that adjustment lending is unnecessary because countries that do not want to reform should not be bribed to reform and countries that do want to reform will do so anyway.

Table 44.5
Volume and share of adjustment lending (AL)

|  | 1980–1982 | 1983–1985 | 1986–1988 | 1989 | 1990 | 1991 |
|---|---|---|---|---|---|---|
| Commitments ($ bill)* | 0.8 | 2.2 | 4.5 | 6.1 | 6.9 | 7.0 |
| Disbursements ($ bill) |  |  |  |  |  |  |
| Gross | 0.8 | 1.5 | 3.6 | 3.9 | 6.6 | 6.2 |
| Net | 0.8 | 1.5 | 3.0 | 3.1 | 5.6 | 3.6 |
| AL/total loans disbursed (percent) | 0.9 | 2.2 | 5.4 | 5.9 | 10.0 | 8.7 |
| AL/total official disbursements (percent) | 2.9 | 5.5 | 10.1 | 10.3 | 16.3 | 12.4 |
| AL net/official net disbursements (percent) | 3.9 | 8.5 | 17.7 | 20.8 | 30.2 | – |

\* At average annual rates.
*Source*: World Bank (1992), Tables A1.1 and A1.4.

adjustment loans. Gross disbursements of adjustment loans during that period amounted to $35 billion. As seen in Table 44.5, total disbursements under adjustment loans never amounted to as much as 20 percent of total official disbursements. Nonetheless, for several countries, particularly in Africa, there can be no question that adjustment loans and associated IMF loans were crucial to covering substantial external financing gaps.

We are not aware of studies that analyze what would have happened to the reform process in a country if adjustment loans had not been available. We suspect that when these studies are made, and the relevant theory developed, they will show that countries would have gone into deeper crises before adjusting, and that the adjustment would have been more painful. Quite likely they will also show that some countries prolonged their adjustment to ensure that future policy reforms could be supported by adjustment loans. This is not necessarily a bad outcome.

## 3.3. Sectoral reforms and sequencing

The range of potential efficiency-enhancing policy changes that can be made in any economy is enormous. Table 44.4 shows the types of policy changes that have been undertaken in World Bank-supported adjustment programs. Policy measures supported in these areas are intended to increase the efficiency of the economy and improve its ability to respond appropriately to price signals – in brief, to improve the supply response of the economy. As already noted, conditions relating to trade reform, to public enterprise reform, and to the rationalization of government finance and administration appear in at least 50 percent of loans. These are the predominant areas of reform. The most common sectoral reforms are in agriculture and the financial sector.

The rationale for the central role of trade reform is discussed in Thomas et al. (1990), Dornbusch (1992), and in Chapter 45 by Dani Rodrik in this volume. The emphasis on public sector reform is a result both of the inefficiencies demonstrated in this sector in many countries, and the fact that these inefficiencies generally have an impact on the whole economy. With the bulk of output in many developing countries being produced in agriculture, and given the pronounced anti-agriculture bias of development strategies in many developing countries during the 1960s and 1970s, the sectoral emphasis on agriculture is easily understood.

"Getting prices right", trying to move prices closer to social marginal cost, is a large part of the emphasis of trade, agriculture, industrial and other supply side reforms.[43] But in several areas, it is also generally recognized that getting prices right is not sufficient, that for instance export promotion measures are needed to help producers take advantage of the right prices, and that institutional capacity within the government has to be built up. The new trade theory research that shows that interventions may sometimes be welfare-enhancing, for instance because they help develop domestic technological capacity, has not generally been reflected in structural adjustment programs. One reason is that it is difficult in practice to identify policies that will work, leading to the conclusion that free trade is a good rule of thumb.[44] Conceivably the World Bank's (1993a) study of the East Asian miracle economies will lead eventually to cautious departures from the liberalization approach.[45] However, the negative record of the great majority of developing countries in pursuing industrial policies in the last twenty five years should encourage a sense of caution before embarking on industrial policy.

The prominent role of financial sector reform is a result of both the perception that an efficient financial sector is essential to growth, the generally poor performance of development banks, and the widespread failures of financial institutions during the debt crisis.[46] This is an area where recent research finds many possibilities of market failure [Villanueva and Mirakhor (1990), McKinnon (1991), Stiglitz (1993)], and where some proponents of the East Asian model of development advocate the directed allocation of credit.

Initial conditions play a central role in the design and implementation of financial reforms. If a large proportion of the assets of financial institutions are held at below market rates, or are not performing, then financial reforms will

---

[43] We discuss interactions among distortions – second best issues – in the discussion of sequencing that follows.

[44] See for example, Helpman (1989) and Krugman (1987).

[45] It is necessary to distinguish between rhetoric and practice when discussing trade liberalization and intervention. Trade reform loans are made to countries with highly distorted trade regimes, provided they are on balance moving in the right direction.

[46] For the remarkably long list of countries in which the banking system was essentially bankrupt, see the World Bank's (1989) study of the financial system.

create difficulties for existing institutions. In particular, if deposit and lending rates are deregulated simultaneously, and free entry is permitted into the banking system, then existing banks will be forced to pay market interest rates. They will then suffer substantial losses, jeopardizing the banking system's solvency and macroeconomic stability. It may be necessary in such cases to allow for a transition phase, in which lending rates are deregulated first, with deposit rates following only gradually [World Bank (1989)]. In other cases, most banks may already be insolvent before the financial reforms are implemented. The banks have then to be closed down or recapitalized before deregulation. Otherwise, as the banks have already lost their capital, moral hazard problems will be exacerbated, and the future collapse of many financial institutions could be very costly.

Financial sector reforms are especially difficult because the running of such institutions requires a great deal of specific business knowledge and experience. They are also difficult to evaluate, in particular because undercapitalized institutions can run for some time without problems becoming evident. It is also necessary before liberalizing to have in place an appropriate regulatory and supervisory capacity in an independent Superintendency of Banks, or similar organization [Villanueva and Mirakhor (1990), Stiglitz (1993)].

Adjustment programs in the financial sector recognize the complexities of the credit markets by emphasizing the need for prudential supervision and regulation of financial institutions. In moderate and high inflation countries, controlled interest rates are typically well below the inflation rate, and adjustment programs generally seek to raise real interest rates to positive levels.

Initially, adjustment was expected to last just a few years, and there was little attention to its distributional impact. The poverty impact of adjustment measures was increasingly taken into account as it became clear that the adjustment process would be prolonged, and as critics of adjustment pointed to the apparent worsening of poverty in adjusting countries.[47] Analysis of Bolivia's emergency social fund and other anti-poverty mechanisms suggested that targeted anti-poverty programs, including employment, education, and health care, could help protect the poor during adjustment at a reasonable budgetary cost – sometimes funded entirely, and apparently additionally, by donors.[48]

*Sequencing.* Given the many reforms needed in most adjusting countries, the question naturally arises as to whether they should be carried out in any

---

[47] See for example Cornia et al. (1987); and for a later World Bank study, Maasland and van der Gaag (1992).
[48] See the World Bank (1990) report on poverty.

particular order. Obviously, everything depends on everything else, but since both the implementation of reforms and their effects take time, and since the ability of any administration is limited, perhaps certain changes should be in place before others are attempted. In a very useful article, Edwards (1989b) reviews the literature on the sequencing of reforms,[49] and sets out an analytic model to analyze the issues.

Key issues that have been discussed in the literature are: the order of liberalization of the current and capital accounts of the balance of payments; the order of macroeconomic stabilization and structural reforms; and the sectoral order of liberalization of the trade account. Edwards presents the arguments that have been made on the ordering of trade liberalization and macroeconomic stabilization. The arguments for the primacy of stabilization are: unless the fiscal deficit is corrected, liberalization will be carried out at too low (overly appreciated) a real exchange rate; that inflation distorts price signals; and that there are insufficient instruments to set the exchange rate at a level appropriate for both stabilization and structural reforms. To these should be added the fact that tariffs provide an important revenue source in many countries, and cannot be reduced unless compensating fiscal revenues have been found.

Several authors argue that trade liberalization and stabilization should be simultaneous, since there is very little connection between the state of the macroeconomy and trade orientation, and there is no point in prolonging the inefficiencies of the restrictive trade regime. Political economy arguments have also been used to recommend that macroeconomic stabilization and trade liberalization should be undertaken simultaneously. In general, stabilization and trade reforms offer mixed results. Haggard and Webb (1993) argue that in a well-designed reform program, groups that lose from one element (e.g. trade reform) can be compensated by gains from another element (e.g. stabilization).

Although the general presumption is that macroeconomic stabilization should come first [Sachs (1987), Rodrik (1990)], there has been little systematic collection of evidence on the issue. There are examples of countries whose trade liberalizations have failed, apparently because of macroeconomic instability, for example, Sri Lanka in 1978–1979, Chile in 1959–1961, and Israel in 1981–1982 [Michaely et al. (1991)]. There are also countries that successfully started liberalizing trade before stabilizing, for example Mexico and Argentina. There is also a difference between recommending macroeconomic stabilization first if there is a choice – a view we share, and arguing that trade liberalization should not be attempted if macroeconomic stabilization is for whatever reason out of reach.

In 1973 McKinnon argued that trade liberalization should precede capital

---

[49] Edwards traces the analysis of the issue to Little, Scitovsky and Scott (1970) and McKinnon (1973).

account liberalization, since liberalization of the capital account tends to produce a capital inflow and real appreciation, at a time when the real exchange rate should be depreciating to reflect the reduction in protection. Frenkel (1983) adds the observation that the speed of adjustment in asset markets is more rapid than that in flow markets, so that if both are liberalized at the same time, adjustment will be complete in the capital market well before prices are right in the flow market [see also Krueger (1985) and (1992)]. Again, while the trade reform first argument is generally accepted, trade reforms have been carried out successfully by countries whose capital accounts were already open, for instance Indonesia and Mexico.

In his analytic model, Edwards identifies four distortions: a tariff; a labor market distortion; a tax in the non-tradeables market that drives a wedge between producer and consumer prices; and a financial market distortion that causes the domestic interest rate to differ from the world rate. Edwards emphasizes the interactions of intertemporal and inter-sectoral distortions, but finds few general results on optimal sequencing. This is an area where practice has moved far ahead of theory, and where the difficulties of second-best suggest that interesting general results will be sparse.

*Big bang, gradualism, and credibility.* The issue of the optimal speed of trade reform was discussed by Little, Scitovsky and Scott (1970), in the Bhagwati–Krueger NBER project [Bhagwati (1978), and Krueger (1978)] and in the Michaely–Papageorgiou–Choksi World Bank comparative study (1991). It has become even more prominent in the reforming East European and former Soviet countries, under the heading of the big bang versus gradualism, with the successful gradualist Chinese approach often being contrasted with the Polish big bang. The discussion has also moved from just trade liberalization to economy wide liberalization.

The analysis takes place at two levels. First, assuming all policy changes are credible, that is that all market participants believe that announced policies will be implemented, what is the optimal timing and ordering of reforms? The starting point is that in the absence of other distortions, the first best solution is immediate and simultaneous removal of all policy distortions. If this is not possible, for example because administrative capacity is limited, or because some policy distortions cannot be removed immediately, the analysis is in the realm of the second best. Edwards and Van Wijnbergen (1989) present examples where gradual policy reform is optimal in this context.

It is difficult to discern a coherent set of analytic results on the speed of reform under full credibility of policy. The case for gradualism must be closely related to the presence of capital market imperfections. Suppose that the adjustment of the private sector to relative price changes takes time, and that during the adjustment period, some firms that should optimally survive would have negative cash flows if all prices were adjusted to their optimal level at the beginning of the program. With perfect capital markets, firms that should survive would be able to borrow to cover their negative cash flows. But if capital markets are imperfect, it might be better to allow prices to adjust gradually toward their optimal level, to ensure that some firms that should survive do survive.

Credibility adds another dimension to the analysis. Big bang advocates argue that a government that acts quickly strengthens the public's belief that reforms will be maintained without backtracking [Calvo (1989), Przeworski (1991)]. Since the economic response to reforms depends on expected incentives, it is important to create a firm expectation of the overall direction of reform as soon as possible. Advocates of a more gradual approach argue that a big bang runs the risk of backtracking as its short-run costs provoke resistance.

Political arguments also do not provide a clear answer. Advocates of the big bang conclude that multiple reforms can create coalitions in favor of reform that would not be put together in a more gradual process; they also frequently argue that since reforms have short-run costs, it is essential to strike on as broad a front as possible, as soon as possible, before the costs of reform begin to erode government support [Douglas (1990), Krueger (1993), Haggard and Webb (1993)]. They argue that a new administration that inherits a crisis should start quickly: "A new government that takes office in the middle of a severe crisis and acts immediately can blame the decline in living standards on actions of the previous government. The longer the government delays, the more likely that the costs of adjustment will be attributed to the current government, increasing the level of opposition". [Haggard and Webb (1993, p. 159)]. Advocates of gradualism argue that large short-run costs can defeat a reform, whereas the same aggregate costs spread over time will not at any point generate sufficient opposition to defeat the reform. The latter has been interpreted as one of the main lessons from the reforms in China [McMillan and Naughton (1992)].

Political scientists and economists have started to assemble some initial evidence on these hypotheses [Nelson (1990), Thomas and Grindle (1991), Haggard and Kaufman (1992), Krueger (1993), Williamson (1994), Haggard, Kaufman and Webb (1994)], but it is too early to have clear cut conclusions.

Both the credibility and political economy considerations bearing on the speed of reform have to be modified to take into account the institutional and technical capacity of the government to carry out the reform program.

## 4. Evaluations of structural adjustment programs

Although judgments on the effects of policies are made all the time, the scientific basis for these judgments is typically not well-established. For anyone equipped with a true model, which includes the endogenous response of economic agents to changes in policies, the problem would be easy. But there is no known true model. Another complication arises because the data used to estimate the models are usually of very low quality [Srinivasan (1994)]. Furthermore, the evaluation of programs using data for a cross-section of countries faces the additional problem of cross-country comparability [Ahmad (1994)]: the data for different countries have to be converted to common units, but the sharp differences in relative prices across countries make most of the standard adjustment methods highly questionable. Some progress has been achieved in this area in recent years with the work related to the International Comparisons Project of Summers and Heston, but many problems still remain [Heston (1994)]. Problems also exist with the population numbers that are used to obtain per capita figures [Chamie (1994)]

The difficulties in evaluating structural adjustment programs in particular are compounded because they seek to achieve both macroeconomic stabilization and a structural transformation of the economy, with the ultimate objective of achieving a sustainable and high rate of growth of GDP while reducing poverty. Some of these objectives may be reached in the medium term, while success in achieving a sustainable high growth rate can only be evaluated over a longer period.

Typically adjustment programs are implemented over periods of five or more years. Given the length of the program implementation process, examination of performance two or three years after the initiation of an adjustment program is likely to reveal little about its eventual benefits. Rather, it probably picks up mainly the short-term avoidable and unavoidable costs of stabilization [Corden (1989)]. Therefore, in evaluating the effectiveness of adjustment programs it is desirable to measure outcomes for a period much beyond the initiation of the program.

A second element to consider in evaluating adjustment performance is the selection of performance indicators. The most common measures of program performance used in the literature are: the rate of growth of GDP; the ratio of investment to GDP; the ratio of saving to GDP; the ratio of exports to GDP; the inflation rate; and the current account deficit relative to GDP. The first measure does not need justification. The saving, investment and exports measures are indicators of progress in structural transformation, and also to some extent of the restoration of macroeconomic stability. The last two indicators are, to a greater extent, indicators of the success of stabilization.

A third element is the need to isolate the marginal contribution of an adjustment program from other non-program determinants of performance. The problem is that there is no clear counterfactual that represents the performance that would have been obtained in the absence of the program. This problem is common to the evaluation of any policy or institutional change.

As a survey in *The Economist* put it: "In economics, questions about what might have been are practically unanswerable; questions about what is are hard enough" (The Economist, September 19–25, 1992).

The counterfactual should include the effects on performance of the initial conditions, the external environment in the program period, and the policies and institutions that would have been in place in the program period had there has not been a program in place [Goldstein and Montiel (1986), Khan (1990), Corbo and Rojas (1992)]. The difficulties arise because this counterfactual has to be estimated.[50] Alternative approaches used to evaluate program effectiveness differ in the methods used to estimate the counterfactual.

Three approaches have been used to estimate the counterfactual in crosssectional work: the country's performance for a period before the program was put in place; the observed performance of a comparator group of countries without a program for the same period; and a simulated performance of what would have been observed in the absence of a program if everything had been the same except the presence of a program. These methods are known as the before-and-after approach, the control-group approach, and the modified control-group approach respectively.[51] There are many versions of the modified control-group approach, differing in the method used to deal with the selectivity bias problem [Corbo and Rojas (1992)], that is, on how to deal with the problem that countries that undertake programs are *ipso facto* different from those that do not.

Although the before-and-after approach has been the most commonly used in the literature on the evaluation of program performance, Reichmann and Stillson (1978) [see, for example, Donovan (1981) and (1982)], the results are likely to provide a biased and inconsistent estimate of program effects. The obvious problem is that this approach embodies the assumption that absent the program, the performance indicators would have taken their base period values. Since countries do not undertake adjustment programs out of a clear blue sky, this assumption is implausible. Suppose for example that there had been no change in the external environment, but that a country was living well beyond its means in the base period. Then the before-and-after approach underestimates the effects of the program, because the previous situation was unsustainable.

The control-group approach implicitly attempts to control for the external environment, but it uses the restrictive assumption that the external environment should affect program and non-program countries equally. In the context

---

[50] Similar problems have been encountered in the evaluation of training programs in labor economics, and the work on the evaluation of the effectiveness of adjustment programs has been much influenced by that literature. See for instance Heckman (1978).

[51] In the evaluation of IMF programs, some evaluations have been made comparing outcomes with program targets [Edwards (1989a), Guitian (1981)].

of the oil shock, this would imply that oil importers and exporters would be affected in the same way. Obviously, this assumption fails whenever external factors have different effects on the performance of program and non-program countries.

The modified control-group approach, to be described shortly, provides an unbiased and consistent estimate of program effects if the model to estimate the counterfactual is unbiased. The basic idea behind the modified control-group approach is to accept that program countries are different than non-program countries, to identify the differences between them in the pre-program period, and then to control statistically for these differences in assessing program performance in the post reform period. This is equivalent to assuming that program countries are not randomly selected. Instead, they are adversely selected, since only countries with poor performance undertake a program. The modified control-group approach can also control for world economic conditions.

A counterfactual is also needed to evaluate the impact of an adjustment program, or any other policies, for an individual country. The most common methods here are the before-and-after approach, and model based estimates of the counterfactual for the program period. Models used have typically been either econometric [Corbo and de Melo (1989), Mosley et al. (1991)], or computable general equilibrium [Bourguignon and Morrisson (1992), Harrigan and Mosley (1990)].

We now describe in detail the methodology used in the evaluation of adjustment lending for a cross-section of countries.

*Statistical analysis of performance across countries*

The before-and-after approach estimate of program performance is simply the mean change in a selected performance indicator over some relevant period. With $y$ the *change* in the selected performance indicator between the program evaluation period and the base period, the before-and-after estimate ($\beta$) involves calculating the mean change across the reduced sample of program countries only, for each of the selected performance indicators:

$$\bar{y}_i = \beta \quad \text{(for program countries)} \tag{4.1}$$

The control-group estimate is calculated by running the following regression for the complete sample of program and non-program countries:

$$y_i = \beta_o + \beta_1 d_i \tag{4.2}$$

where $d_i$ is a dummy variable with a value of one for program countries, and zero otherwise. The estimated value of $\beta_1$ is equal to the difference in the mean change in the performance indicator $y$ between program and non-program countries. Thus, using this methodology, a statistically significant value for $\beta_1$ would indicate that the change in the performance indicator $y$ for the program countries was different from the corresponding change in non-program countries (the control-group).

The modified control-group approach specifies a reduced-form equation that links policy instruments, initial conditions, and world economic conditions to performance. The method starts from the basic reduced form equation for the performance indicator $y_i$, given by

$$y_i = x'_i \phi + W'_i a + \beta_4 d_i + e_i \tag{4.3}$$

where $x_i$ is a $K$-element vector of macroeconomic policy instruments that would have been observed, in the post-program period, in the absence of a program in country $i$; $W_i$ is an $M$-element random vector of world economic conditions that affect the $y_i$ performance indicator in country $i$; and $e_i$ is a random error with mean zero and constant variance.

To complete the methodology one needs to specify also a policy reaction function, which shows how policy instruments change in response to changes in the state of the economy. Following Goldstein and Montiel (1986), the policy vector $x_i$ is estimated from a policy reaction function of the form:

$$x_i = \tau[y_i^d - (y_i)_{-1}] + u_i \tag{4.4}$$

where $y_i^d$ is the desired value of the performance indicator $y_i$ and $u_i$ is an unobservable error term. The policy variables $x_i$ react to the difference between the desired and the actual value of the performance indicator. The model is completed by endogenising the country's decision on whether to enter an adjustment program $(d_i)$.[52]

*Program evaluations*

Much work on program evaluation has been done in recent years, based on both cross-sectional country data, and data for individual countries. Evaluations have been made of IMF stabilization programs, and of World Bank-supported structural adjustment programs, by the staff of the IFIs and by other researchers.

This recent work has evaluated the effectiveness of programs rather than of policies. The transmission mechanism from program to performance indicators is implicit in the analysis; programs are assumed to work both by changing the

---

[52] For details on two approaches to the estimation of this model, see Goldstein and Montiel (1986), and Corbo and Rojas (1992).

values of policy variables and by enhancing the impact of policy variables on performance by changing the structure of the economy. Numerous individual country studies have been done for programs that include stabilization and structural transformation components.

The work on the evaluation of IMF programs has illustrated quite clearly the limitations of the before-and-after and the control group techniques. For instance, Goldstein and Montiel (1986) evaluated the effectiveness of IMF programs for four indicators of performance: the ratio of the overall balance of payments to nominal GNP; the ratio of the current account to nominal GNP; the rate of CPI inflation; and the rate of growth of real GDP. They found that, by not controlling for other factors, the before-and-after approach produced results that were extremely sensitive to the year of the program. Even the sign of the effects changed depending on the year in which the programs were initiated.

When they pooled all the programs and used equation (4.1) to estimate the before-and-after effects for the full sample of program countries, they found that the programs had negative effects on the four indicators of performance. When they used the control-group approach to control for external conditions, the data implied that Fund programs are associated with an improvement in the current account and with slightly better growth, but with slightly worse inflation and balance of payment situations. However, these differences were not statistically significant. The latter test was done on the coefficient of $\beta_1$ in model (4.2).

When Goldstein and Montiel used the modified control-group approach, they found that countries with IMF programs did a little better on inflation but worse on the other three indicators of performance. Once again, however, the differences between the performance of program and non-program countries were not statistically significant.

Pastor (1987) used the control-group approach to analyze the effectiveness of IMF programs in 15 Latin American countries during the period 1965–1981. He found that the balance of payments improved, while inflation and the share of labor income deteriorated. He did not find an effect of IMF programs on growth. One limitation of these evaluations is that they do not correct for selectivity bias and they use a crude method to control for external conditions.

Another comprehensive study of the effectiveness of IMF programs was undertaken by Khan (1990). Khan used the Goldstein and Montiel version of the modified control-group approach. However, the model is estimated using pooled time-series, cross-section data. Khan used four performance indicators: the change in the ratio of the balance of payments to GDP; the change in the ratio of the current account to GDP; the change in the inflation rate; and the change in the rate of growth. In the comparisons he used two alternative current periods: the program year; and the average of the program year and the succeeding year. The second alternative allows for the slow response of the economy to program changes. For the first definition of the current period, Khan found that programs had a positive effect on the current account balance, and a negative effect on the rate of growth. Both effects were statistically significant. The effects on inflation and the balance of payments, although favorable, were not statistically significant. Using the second definition of the current period, Khan found that the balance of payments, the current account, and the growth effects were statistically significant. Further, the size of the balance of payments and current account effects was larger. However, the negative and significant effect on growth was maintained.

World Bank (1988) evaluates the effectiveness of its structural adjustment lending, using both cross-sectional data and country studies. The cross-sectional work concluded that the 30 countries receiving adjustment lending before 1985 performed better on average, by the end of 1987, than developing countries not receiving such loans. Two methods were used for the evaluations: before-and-after, and control-group. The evolution of eight indicators of performance was studied: GDP growth; the ratio of investment to GDP; export growth; the ratio of the current account balance to GDP; the ratio of the budget balance to GDP; the inflation rate; the ratio of external debt to exports; and the ratio of debt service to exports. The control-group results showed that the thirty countries that received adjustment lending before 1985 performed somewhat better than the sixty-three that did not, even though the adjusting countries experienced more severe external shocks. The better performance was especially marked in the twelve countries that received three or more adjustment loans before 1987 and those that are substantial exporters of manufactured goods. Improvements were smaller in the highly indebted countries and in sub-Saharan Africa. However, no statistical analysis of the significance of the differences was performed [World Bank (1988)].

The work reported in World Bank (1990) benefited from a larger sample of countries that had received adjustment loans from the World Bank. It also focused mainly on the contribution of adjustment lending to sustainable growth. For this purpose, it examined the performance of intermediate indicators of structural transformation-saving, investment, and export ratios – along with the rate of GDP growth. The statistical evaluation was based on a version of the modified control-group approach.

When comparing changes in these indicators between 1981–1984 and 1985–1988, it was found that after explicitly controlling for external shocks, initial conditions, levels of external financing, and estimated policies that would have been followed without adjustment lending, the annual average rate of growth of GDP of countries that received two or more adjustment loans was close to 2 percentage points of GDP higher than that for countries which were not heavy users of adjustment lending. It was also found that the domestic saving to GDP ratio increased over 4 percentage points when measured at current prices, and 5.8 percentage points when measured at constant prices. The investment ratio was practically unaffected, while the export to GDP ratio increased 5 percentage points at current prices and 2.3 percentage points at constant prices. However, the latter effect was not statistically significant.

When comparing performance in the 1980s with that in the 1970s, the results were somewhat different. In particular, the investment to GDP ratio at constant prices decreased 5.6 percentage points between 1970–1980 and 1985–1988. This result was strongly statistically significant (World Bank, 1990, p. 18).

World Bank (1992) continued the evaluation of adjustment programs by adding more information and by investigating differences in model structure for different country groupings. This report also made progress in understanding the behavior of the investment ratio, which declined by a statistically significant 3.5 percent between the 1970s and 1985–1990.[53] However, when different groups of countries were examined, it was found that this result is due mostly to a large drop in this ratio for the low income countries. Middle-income country performance improved by all the indicators, while the low income countries did well on growth and the export to GDP ratio, but worse on the investment to GDP ratio; there was no significant difference between periods in the saving ratio. For the low income countries the only statistically significant effects were the increase in the rate of growth of GDP and the drop in the investment rate.

Mosley, Harrigan and Toye (1991, Table 7.1) evaluate the effectiveness of adjustment *policies* rather than of adjustment lending. In their multiple regression analysis they include beside external economic variables and initial conditions, two variables related to the program: a program implementation variable, and the size of the loan. From their empirical work the authors conclude that for the period 1980–1986, compliance in the current period and in the previous two years has a positive effect on growth. However the amount of financing in the previous period has a (surprising) negative effect on growth. All in all, they conclude that Bank programs have a weak positive effect on GDP growth. This is the net of a positive effect of program compliance on growth and a significant and negative effect of the amount of program finance. The authors also find a negative effect of Bank programs on investment rates. They attribute this to the compression of government expenditures, the shift from project finance to adjustment lending, and the effect of the stabilization-induced recession on private investment through aggregate demand factors.

Conway (1990), using a panel data approach for a sample of 76 developing

---

[53] A similar drop was found in World Bank (1990).

countries, also concludes that there is a significant positive association between participation in a World Bank adjustment lending program and more rapid growth in real GNP, an improved current account as a percentage of GNP, and a lower ratio of domestic investment to GNP.[54]

The statistical cross-sectional studies provide an aggregate and reasonably consistent picture of the effectiveness of adjustment programs. However, except for the work of Mosley et al. (1991), this research has not empirically evaluated the economics behind the programs; nor has it taken the extent of compliance into account with any care. Some criticisms of IMF and World Bank-supported programs have followed these routes.

Edwards (1989a) evaluated IMF programs, examining both compliance and some of the assumptions behind their design. He finds that compliance in recent programs has been low, and that there has been a profusion of waivers. On this basis, he concludes that recent programs were not fully adequate to deal with the sharp external shocks of the early 1980s that culminated in the debt crisis. He also questioned the scant attention that IMF programs paid to income distribution. In examining the economic assumptions behind programs, Edwards examined the output-effects of devaluations. From his empirical work based on a group of 12 countries,[55] he concluded that devaluations have had a negative short-run effect on output. However, he supports the assumption used in Fund programs that exchange and trade controls have negative effects on output growth.[56]

Another common critique is that adjustment programs have not followed an appropriate sequencing of reforms and, in particular, have started trade liberalization while the macroeconomic situation was still unstable. In the latter case, it is argued that the low credibility of the reform program could be welfare deteriorating [Sachs (1987), Rodrik (1990)].

In the case of Africa, it has been argued that the policy reforms introduced in the adjustment programs do not properly take into account the institutional constraints facing these countries. Indeed, several researchers have suggested that existing institutional constraints could imply program effects far removed from those expected when the programs were put in place [Killick (1984), Helleiner (1992), Taylor (1988)]. It has also been argued that World Bank-supported adjustment programs have been used to buy reforms, whose continuity would be questionable, even if they were implemented initially [Mosley et al. (1991)].

---

[54] Conway also introduced country dummies to control for country characteristics.

[55] India, Malaysia, Philippines, Sri Lanka, Thailand, Greece, Israel, Brazil, Colombia, El Salvador, South Africa, and the former Yugoslavia.

[56] For a reply to Edwards see Goldstein (1989).

## 5. Beyond adjustment to longer-term growth

Structural reforms that contribute to the reduction of macroeconomic imbalances and the improvement of resource allocation create the foundations for a recovery of growth [Fischer (1987), Dornbusch (1990)]. There are five main economic requirements for sustained growth: stable macroeconomic conditions [Fischer (1991)]; an appropriate structure of incentives, generally provided through markets; an adequate physical and human capital base; an adequate level of saving; and efficient institutions to turn saving into productive investment.

We have already discussed some of the elements needed to meet the first two requirements. The last three are more important for sustaining growth. In the initial stages of development, growth frequently comes from the use of natural resources. In later stages, investment in human and physical capital, and the introduction of new technologies, become relatively more important.

In most developing countries in the 1980s, the upgrading of the infrastructure and the human capital base, which has a public good character, required a profound restructuring of the public sector. This essentially involved getting rid of activities that are more efficiently undertaken in the private sector, to make space in the public sector budget to finance these infrastructure and human capital expenditures. Some countries have also developed a framework in which the private sector can invest in these activities. Chile has gone far in this direction by promoting the participation of the private sector in the production of education and health services. Lately it has also developed a framework in which the private sector can invest in infrastructure, including roads and port facilities.

The participation of the private sector in the provision of health and education has been made possible by decentralizing production. For example, the provision of these services for the poorest groups, who would otherwise have gone without them, has been encouraged by providing state subsidies (per student or per patient), while the production of the service has been decentralized into the private sector. Mexico has also made progress in encouraging private sector participation in infrastructure, but has been less successful in moving the private sector into the provision of health and education services [World Bank (1990)].

In principle, the increase in investment could be financed by borrowing in international capital markets, though it is rare that as much as 5 percent of GNP can be borrowed on a sustainable basis [Krugman (1993)]. Further, heavy reliance on capital inflows in the early stages of an adjustment program could lead to a premature real exchange rate appreciation. Since aid prospects also appear to be worsening, developing countries which want to increase their investment rates will have to increase national saving.

The weight of the empirical evidence suggests that private saving rates are not very sensitive to policy variables, and in particular to interest rates [Giovannini (1985), Corbo and Schmidt-Hebbel (1991)]. However negative real interest rates probably discourage saving – certainly they reduce the amount and efficiency of financial intermediation and encourage capital flight.

Increased public saving will contribute to increasing national saving provided it is not offset by a decrease in private saving. Empirical evidence presented by Corbo and Schmidt-Hebbel (1991) shows that changes in public saving generally are not greatly offset by the response of private saving. This evidence on saving highlights the central importance of fiscal balance.

The last factor, an increase in the rate and efficiency of private investment, is much affected by the stability of the macroeconomic framework and by clear and predictable tax rules and property rights [Rodrik (1989), Serven and Solimano (1992)]. However, there will inevitably be doubts about the final success of an adjustment program in its early stages. Typically investors will wait to have a clearer assessment of the most likely evolution of the economy, both the level of activity and relative prices, before committing to investment. This slow response is a common characteristic of most adjustment programs [Dornbusch (1990), Serven and Solimano (1992)].

The belief that economic policies and the investment rate are major determinants of economic growth has long been expressed in the writings of economists. However it is only recently that the links among policy, investment, and long-term growth have been captured in simple analytic models, in the endogenous growth literature [Romer (1986, 1990), Lucas (1988), Fischer (1991), Easterly (1993)].

The ideas underlying these models – economies of scale, externalities, and public goods – and the argument that the removal of distortions promotes growth, have been familiar in the development literature for a long time. At a minimum, the new models provide a framework that may improve understanding of the operation of growth-promoting policies that have been proposed in the past; perhaps they will also improve the quality of growth-promoting policies in the future.

This literature highlights a number of channels through which public policies can affect growth. The promotion of human capital accumulation, through education and even through improvements in nutrition, can foster growth. So can investment in R&D. The models also point to the possibility of economies becoming stuck in a poverty trap: a situation in which low income and low human capital levels create incentives for high population growth and low human capital investment, thus perpetuating the state of poverty. Policies that stimulate investment in human capital can help the economy break out of the trap. The new theories also point to the many routes through which fiscal policies can affect growth.

Recent work that has used these new theories to examine the links between trade policy and growth indicates that, after adjusting for factor accumulation, countries with more open economies have had higher rates of growth [Easterly and Wetzel (1989), de Melo and Robinson (1989), Nishimizu and Page (1991), Dollar (1992), Levine and Renelt (1990), Edwards (1993b)]. Countries that are more open to trade produce with more up-to-date technology and invest more in quality improvement and research and development than countries more closed to trade [Dornbusch (1992)].

The impact of financial policies and structure on growth has also been the focus of recent scrutiny. Gelb (1989) and Easterly and Wetzel (1989) present evidence suggesting that severe financial distortions such as sharply negative real interest rates and very small formal financial systems adversely affect growth [see also King and Levine (1993)].

New growth theory insights have been used recently to study the difference in growth performance across Latin American countries. Corbo and Rojas (1993) find that variation in the investment ratio is the most important single factor affecting growth; this accounts for 37 percent of the variation in the per capita growth rate. Of course, at a deeper level investment is endogenous, and it too needs to be explained. The addition of other new growth theory variables – such as the initial level of GDP per capita, the ratio of government expenditure to GDP, measures of human capital, and the inflation rate and the ratio of the trade deficit to GDP – raises the $R^2$ to 62 percent. The inflation rate, the trade deficit ratio, and the human capital proxy were the most significant of these additional variables.

Stabilization and adjustment programs typically reduce growth in their early years. The question then arises of how long it takes until sustained growth begins [Dornbusch (1990)]. This is obviously a question that has no unique answer, for it depends on the extent of the disarray at the start of the reform program, on the speed and comprehensiveness of the adjustment program, on the financing available to cushion the reforms, and on the credibility and stability of government policies. Nonetheless, observation of even such successful programs as those of Chile and Mexico in the 1980s suggests that it takes a long time, perhaps five or more years, until growth begins to revive. The delays are due to the complexity of the necessary policy changes, and on lags in the investment response of the private sector. Such a long transition period increases the political difficulty of sustaining the adjustment program.

## 6. Case studies

In this section we present brief case studies of adjustment programs in three countries, Chile, Ghana and New Zealand, chosen to provide examples of adjustment in Latin America, Africa, and an industrialized country, respectively. We are interested in each case in: the cause of the crisis; the program and its political economy; and the results.

## 6.1. Chile

Chile initiated its adjustment program in the mid-1970s. The economy grew rapidly in the late 1970s but went into deep crisis in 1982. By 1984 the Chilean program was widely seen as a failure. Yet today Chile is viewed as one of the great success stories of adjustment and growth. Here we examine the Chilean reform program, the causes of the crisis of 1982–1983, and the nature of the economic recovery program initiated in 1984. We conclude by drawing some lessons from the reforms.

### 6.1.1. Causes of the crisis

From the 1930's, Chile pursued an active import substitution policy, along with active government participation in the production and marketing of private goods. These policies reached their peak in the early 1970s during the Allende administration. Agrarian reforms initiated in the previous decade were drastically accelerated during the Allende government, and ended with the expropriation of practically all large estates. The Allende government also took over the banking system. Multinationals were expropriated, in some cases, as with copper enterprises, without compensation payments. This caused international conflicts for the government, especially with the US.

On the macroeconomic front, the Allende government started with an aggressive expansion of aggregate demand. In 1971, current government spending grew by 12.4 percent and the fiscal deficit reached 10.7 percent of GDP. Pulled by this demand expansion, GDP grew 9 percent in real terms (Table 44.7) and the money supply grew 66 percent in real terms (see Tables 44.6 and 44.7).

Measured inflation was relatively low but price controls and commodity and factor market rationing were widespread. Price controls were intensified during the next few years. With the continuation of expansionary policies, the fiscal deficit increased from 2.7 percent of GDP in 1970 to close to 25 percent of GDP in 1973. As the budget deficit was mostly financed by borrowing from the central bank, and because the economy was fairly closed to trade, pressures on domestic prices had to be contained by tighter price controls. Not surprisingly, active black markets developed in which consumer goods were available at a multiple of the official price. At the enterprise level, excess demand was

Table 44.6
Chile: Annual financial indicators. 1969–1993

|      | Trade balance surplus (in US$*) (1) | Total net cap. inflow except reserves (in US$*) (2) | Net foreign reserves central bank (in US$*) (3) | Net foreign reserves banking system (in US$*) (4) | Rate of change in nom. M1A (5) | Short term real interest rate (peso loans) (6) |
|------|-------|--------|--------|---------|-------|------|
| 1969 | 246.5 | 222.5 | 285.2 | 10.7 | 40.5% | N.A. |
| 1970 | 155.9 | 267.5 | 393.5 | 16.0 | 51.9% | N.A. |
| 1971 | −16.3 | −26.5 | 162.7 | −42.9 | 100.0% | N.A. |
| 1972 | −253.4 | 327.4 | 75.8 | −149.8 | 99.5% | N.A. |
| 1973 | −138.3 | 397.0 | 167.4 | −235.3 | 271.6% | N.A. |
| 1974 | 135.0 | 139.0 | 94.0 | −221.3 | 291.6% | N.A. |
| 1975 | −118.3 | 373.0 | −129.2 | −162.4 | 257.2% | 15.9 |
| 1976 | 460.6 | 66.0 | 107.9 | −131.6 | 231.8% | 64.2 |
| 1977 | −231.8 | 577.0 | 273.3 | −254.1 | 161.0% | 57.1 |
| 1978 | −728.6 | 1946.0 | 1058.0 | −373.6 | 86.6% | 42.3 |
| 1979 | −873.0 | 2247.0 | 2313.8 | −386.6 | 67.1% | 16.9 |
| 1980 | −1055.0 | 3165.0 | 4073.7 | −832.7 | 60.1% | 12.2 |
| 1981 | −2869.0 | 4698.0 | 3775.3 | −1107.0 | 33.4% | 38.9 |
| 1982 | −388.2 | 1215.0 | 2577.5 | −1175.4 | −5.7% | 5.1 |
| 1983 | 659.7 | 508.0 | 2022.7 | −721.9 | 16.8% | 15.9 |
| 1984 | −3.2 | 1940.0 | 2055.9 | −54.5 | 18.8% | 11.3 |
| 1985 | 816.3 | 1384.0 | 1866.7 | −252.0 | 21.0% | 11.1 |
| 1986 | 1308.0 | 741.0 | 1778.3 | −390.1 | 39.4% | 7.6 |
| 1987 | 1308.6 | 944.0 | 1871.1 | −637.7 | 28.1% | 9.4 |
| 1988 | 1760.0 | 1009.0 | 2549.9 | −894.1 | 40.2% | 7.4 |
| 1989 | 1578.1 | 1264.0 | 2948.1 | −1268.0 | 24.4% | 11.8 |
| 1990 | 1273.1 | 3048.7 | 5357.5 | −1243.2 | 14.4% | 16.4 |
| 1991 | 1575.9 | 829.2 | 6640.5 | −996.0 | 41.1% | 8.3 |
| 1992 | 749.2 | 2882.8 | 9009.2 | −2535.7 | 36.9% | 9.9 |
| 1993 | −978.6 | 2763.6 | 9758.6 | −2538.9 | 13.0% | 0.4 |

* In millions of US$
*Column sources*:
   (1) Social and economic indicators 1960–1988 (SEI), Central Bank, FOB value since 1973. Since 1989 *Monthly Bulletin* of the central bank.
   (2) Up to 1973, SEI, Central Bank. Since 1974 until 1976, Corbo (1985b). Thereafter *Monthly Bulletin*, Central Bank.
   (3) and (4) SEI, Central bank. Since 1983 does not include assets and liabilities from liquidated banks.
   (5) SEI and *Monthly Bulletin*, Central Bank (Dec. to Dec.).
   (6) SEI and *Monthly Bulletin*. This corresponds to the cumulated ex-post monthly real interest rates charged for short term loans.

manifested in chronic shortages of basic inputs at the official prices. As a result, black markets for inputs also emerged.

By August 1973 the government had run out of net foreign reserves. Strong political opposition was developing from the groups whose assets had been expropriated. When the economic situation started to take a sharp turn for the worse, the political crisis intensified.

### 6.1.2. The adjustment program[57]

The government that took power through a military coup in September 1973 inherited an economy characterized by a dominant role of the public sector, severe macroeconomic imbalances, and an extremely distorted set of price incentives. Resources were being allocated mainly by bureaucratic rules. The labor market was dominated by a few militant unions, which were highly politically motivated. The central bank's gross international reserves were down almost to zero, and the budget was out of control. Inflation was running at close to 500 percent a year.

On the economic front, the initial 18 months of the new administration were spent implementing a costly gradual stabilization program, aimed at reducing the inflation rate; the government attempted to reestablish the price system as the main mechanism to allocate resources, and initiated a deep fiscal reform.

By 1975 a team of economists with very strong (classical) liberal ideas began emerging within the government. This new team was about to initiate an economic transformation that would result in a competitive, market-oriented, open Chilean economy. Reforms were introduced in four areas: public sector reforms, to attain macroeconomic stability and improve efficiency; trade reforms; goods and labor market reforms, to facilitate the needed drastic reallocation of resources; and financial sector reforms, to improve efficiency and to facilitate the reallocation of resources.

The initial price liberalization of the Pinochet government was undertaken before the macroeconomic situation was stabilized, and inflation rose to near 1000 percent. The economic team's first move was to initiate a stabilization program, while continuing price reforms. The main components of the stabilization program were the restructuring of the public sector and the elimination of the fiscal deficit.

### Public sector reforms

A major tax reform was initiated in 1974. Its main purpose was to reduce the fiscal deficit by increasing tax revenues. As part of the reforms a value added tax was introduced to replace a cascaded sales tax. The VAT became the main source of fiscal revenue in the years to come. Another important goal sought by the reform was to improve the incentives to work by reducing marginal tax rates. On the expenditure side, public employment and public investment were

---

[57] For more details on the reforms, see Corbo (1985b) and Ramos (1986).

sharply reduced. The 1974 fiscal adjustment was drastic: the deficit was reduced from 24.7 percent of GDP in 1973 to 3.5 percent of GDP in 1974 (see Table 44.7). In 1975 Chile suffered severe terms of trade shocks. The lack of external funding forced a drastic reduction of expenditures to face the emerging trade balance deficit. This second fiscal adjustment was as severe as the first. A further 26 percent cut in real public expenditures, imposed in the middle of a severe contraction, reduced the fiscal deficit to a mere 0.9 percent of GDP.[58]

The privatization process which started in 1975 also contributed to fiscal adjustment. The process started with the sale or restoration of enterprises that had been taken over or bought during the Allende government. When the restitution of private property was completed, the privatization of large public enterprises was initiated. This process would continue until 1989.

The recession of 1975 slowed the retrenchment of the public sector. In 1976 the fiscal deficit was maintained at almost the 1975 level, −0.6 percent of GDP, and inflation was 232 percent. Most of the fiscal adjustment had been done by this time. Current expenditures in real terms stayed at their 1975 level. From then on, the fiscal deficit was gradually reduced and in 1979–1981 there were fiscal surpluses (see Table 44.7).

Improvements in the administration of the tax system were implemented throughout the 1970s. The government instituted a radical pension system, with important fiscal effects, in 1981. In that year, the old pay-as-you-go system was substituted by one based on individual capitalization. Gradually, most of the labor force moved into the new system. As the old system had been partially funded by a payroll tax, the transfer of the labor force into the new system tended to increase the fiscal deficit. Of course, although tax collection decreased, future pension payments also decreased. Nonetheless, some adjustment needed to be made in the fiscal system to prevent an increase in the recorded deficit.

*Trade reforms*

As a consequence of the trade policies of the previous 40 years, the Chilean trade regime was very distorted by 1973. The average nominal tariff at the end of 1973 was 105 percent [Corbo (1990)]. Tariffs ranged from 0 percent for some consumer goods to 750 percent for some goods considered as luxuries. There were also many non-tariff barriers, including quotas, prior approvals and licences. As a direct result of the protection system, export activities were heavily taxed.

Imports were concentrated in intermediate goods, followed by capital goods

---

[58] Note that this happened in a year that GDP dropped by 12.9 percent.

Table 44.7
Chile: Annual macroeconomic indicators: 1969–1993

| | Total GDP real growth (%) (1) | GDP growth T sectors (2) | GDP growth NT sectors (3) | Public sector deficit (% of GDP) (4) | Price of copper (USc/ pound) (5) | Inflation (% change in CPI. annual base) (6) | Unemployment rate (% of labor force) (7) | Real exchange rate (1977 = 100) (8) |
|---|---|---|---|---|---|---|---|---|
| 1969 | 3.7 | −0.8 | 6.6 | 0.4 | 66.6 | 30.7 | 5.5 | 93.5 |
| 1970 | 2.1 | 1.4 | 2.9 | 2.7 | 64.2 | 32.5 | 5.7 | 93.4 |
| 1971 | 9.0 | 9.2 | 8.8 | 10.7 | 49.3 | 22.1 | 3.9 | 85.6 |
| 1972 | −1.2 | −0.8 | −1.1 | 13.0 | 48.6 | 117.9 | 3.3 | 64.7 |
| 1973 | −5.6 | −7.3 | −3.7 | 24.7 | 80.8 | 487.5 | 5.0 | 74.4 |
| 1974 | 1.0 | 6.6 | −0.4 | 3.5 | 93.3 | 497.8 | 9.5 | 122.7 |
| 1975 | −12.9 | −16.6 | −8.4 | 0.9 | 55.9 | 379.2 | 14.8 | 147.1 |
| 1976 | 3.5 | 5.3 | 1.6 | −0.6 | 63.6 | 234.5 | 15.0 | 124.1 |
| 1977 | 9.9 | 7.8 | 9.4 | −0.1 | 59.3 | 113.8 | 13.1 | 100.0 |
| 1978 | 8.2 | 4.5 | 9.6 | −1.5 | 61.9 | 50.0 | 13.9 | 111.4 |
| 1979 | 8.3 | 7.0 | 10.0 | −3.3 | 89.8 | 36.6 | 13.9 | 112.2 |
| 1980 | 7.8 | 5.5 | 10.0 | −4.5 | 99.2 | 35.1 | 12.2 | 97.2 |
| 1981 | 5.5 | 3.8 | 5.4 | −0.8 | 78.9 | 19.7 | 11.3 | 84.5 |
| 1982 | −14.1 | −11.2 | −15.7 | 3.5 | 67.1 | 9.9 | 18.5 | 94.2 |
| 1983 | −0.7 | 0.5 | −1.4 | 3.2 | 72.2 | 27.3 | 19.8 | 113.1 |
| 1984 | 6.3 | 8.0 | 5.3 | 4.3 | 62.4 | 19.9 | 16.3 | 118.2 |
| 1985 | 2.4 | 2.5 | 2.4 | 2.5 | 64.3 | 30.7 | 13.8 | 145.2 |
| 1986 | 5.7 | 6.7 | 5.0 | 2.1 | 62.3 | 19.5 | 10.8 | 159.7 |
| 1987 | 5.7 | 3.7 | 7.0 | 0.2 | 81.1 | 19.9 | 10.5 | 166.6 |
| 1988 | 7.4 | 7.0 | 7.6 | −0.2 | 117.9 | 14.7 | 6.3 | 177.6 |
| 1989 | 10.0 | 8.4 | 11.0 | −1.0 | 129.1 | 17.0 | 5.3 | 173.5 |
| 1990 | 2.1 | 0.7 | 3.0 | −1.1 | 120.9 | 26.0 | 5.7 | 180.1 |
| 1991 | 6.0 | 4.4 | 6.9 | −1.6 | 106.1 | 21.8 | 5.3 | 169.9 |
| 1992 | 10.3 | 7.1 | 12.0 | −2.9 | 103.6 | 15.4 | 4.4 | 156.7 |
| 1993 | 6.0 | 2.3 | 7.9 | −1.9 | 86.7 | 12.7 | 4.5 | |

*Column sources*:

(1) and (5), SEI up to 1988, *Monthly Bulletin* Central bank of Chile thereafter.

(2) SEI. This sector includes: Agriculture, fishing, mining and industry.

(3) SEI. This sector includes: Electricity, gas and water, construction, trade, transportation and communications, other services. The sum of tradeable and non-tradeable GDP growth does not add up to the total GDP growth as it excludes import taxes and bank charges.

(4) Corbo and Fischer (1994) for the period 1969–1988, thereafter Government Budget office. This measure excludes amortizations.

(6) Schmidt-Hebbel and Marshall, quoted in Corbo (1985a) and actualized with *Monthly Bulletin* Central bank.

(7) Coeymans (1992) up to 1987 and *Monthly Bulletin* of the central bank thereafter. Rate is for the last quarter of the year.

(8) Corbo and Fischer (1994).

and a few consumer goods. Non-food consumer goods imports were almost nonexistent. Exports were concentrated in copper, which made export earnings highly dependent on copper prices. International trade was almost entirely in

Table 44.8
External shocks

| Year | Total external effect TXE | Terms of trade effect TTE | Real interest rate effect RIRE | Price of exports PX | Price of imports PM | Average real interest rate on foreign debt RIR | Foreign debt to GDP ratio FD/GDP | Exports to GDP ratio X/GDP | Imports to GDP ratio M/GDP |
|---|---|---|---|---|---|---|---|---|---|
| 1977–1979 | 0.00% | 0.00% | 0.00% | 1.0000 | 1.0000 | −0.0018 | 0.4104 | 0.2149 | 0.2415 |
| 1980 | 1.20% | 1.04% | 0.16% | 1.1049 | 1.0501 | −0.0056 | 0.4020 | 0.2282 | 0.2698 |
| 1981 | −0.52% | −0.55% | 0.03% | 0.9424 | 0.9715 | −0.0026 | 0.4761 | 0.1642 | 0.2675 |
| 1982 | −3.80% | −1.87% | −1.92% | 0.7437 | 0.8495 | 0.0451 | 0.7047 | 0.1936 | 0.2125 |
| 1983 | −3.37% | −0.88% | −2.49% | 0.7175 | 0.7849 | 0.0590 | 0.8816 | 0.2404 | 0.2132 |

*Note*: The indicators TXE, TTE and RIRE are calculated as follows:

TXE = TTE + RIRE

TTE = $(PX_t/PX_o)*(X/GDP)_o − (PM_t/PM_o)*(M/GDP)_o$

RIRE = $−(RIR_t − RIR_o)*(FD/GDP)_o$

where the period o is the average 1977–1979.

government hands. By 1973 there were six exchange rates, with the ratio between the highest and the lowest being 52 to 1. Private capital inflows were almost non existent as the country risk was too high.

Trade reform started with the unification of the exchange rate system, the tariffication of non-tariff barriers, and the reduction of extreme tariffs. Initially, the fiscal consequences of the trade liberalization were minimal, as there were no imports of goods with the highest tariffs, and tariffication provided additional revenues. A large nominal devaluation at the time of the unification of the exchange rate, together with the drastic fiscal adjustment, helped bring about a large real devaluation.

In the initial years of the reforms, aggressive nominal devaluations were used to achieve the real devaluation required to accompany the drastic fiscal adjustment. Inflation was still high, and devaluations were implemented in the context of a crawling peg system; the rate of devaluation was determined by the government's goal of reducing inflation, as well as changes in fundamentals. For instance, in 1975, following the first oil shock and a 45 percent reduction in real copper prices, a sharp fiscal adjustment took place which was accompanied by a nominal devaluation that reached 490 percent for the year.

The speed and extent of trade liberalization were not known when the trade reforms began. However, the reforms accelerated as the liberal economic team improved its standing in the government. By 1979, the trade reform was completed when a uniform tariff rate of 10 percent was established with just one exception for the car industry.

The exchange rate was fixed with respect to the U.S. dollar in June 1979. The fixing of the exchange rate at a time when domestic inflation was still far above international levels, and when wages were indexed, would create much trouble later.

The liberalization of the capital account was initiated much later. Up to late 1978, the central bank authorities were afraid that an early liberalization of the capital account would result in large capital inflows and a real exchange rate appreciation, given high real domestic interest rates.

*Labor market reforms*

By 1973 the labor code was very restrictive, for instance making it essentially impossible to dismiss workers. In its early years, the Pinochet regime severely curtailed the power of the labor unions. Later, a new labor code was introduced to modernize labor legislation. The new code increased the flexibility of labor contracts and the dismissal process, and instituted negotiation at the firm rather than sectoral level. But it also put in place a major rigidity in real wages, by requiring compulsory wage indexation for all workers subject to collective bargaining. When the nominal exchange rate was fixed in 1979, the dollar value of real wages increased enormously. This increase in wages fueled an expenditure expansion and a large loss of competitiveness of the tradeable sectors.

*Financial sector reforms*

Almost all the domestic financial system was in public hands at the end of 1973, and nominal interest rates were heavily regulated. The privatization of financial institutions began in 1974, and nominal interest rates were gradually liberalized too.

However, the lack of an appropriate regulatory and supervisory framework would later create major difficulties. In 1977, a recently privatized middle-sized bank, which belonged to an industrial conglomerate, entered into bankruptcy and was taken over by regulators. Corbo (1985b), and de la Cuadra and Valdés (1991), among others, suggest that this action signaled *de facto* deposit insurance and set the stage for the exacerbation of moral hazard problems. Financial groups could lend, almost without limit, to their own enterprises as their borrowing costs did not reflect the higher risks associated with the concentration of their portfolios.

Similarly, the existence of deposit insurance without prudential regulation and banking supervision also encouraged financial groups to take undue currency risks by borrowing abroad. The currency risks assumed by different Chilean economic groups was one of the causes of the very high rate of bank failures in 1981–1983 [de la Cuadra and Valdés (1991)].

### 6.1.3. Results of the adjustment program

Surprisingly, the Chilean economy grew, moderately, in 1974, the year after the coup. However, this growth was followed by a deep recession in 1975. The recovery and expansion from that recession lasted until 1981. There was then another extremely deep recession in 1982–1983, followed by a recovery that started in 1984 and that put the economy onto a sustainable growth path.

The recession of 1975 had three major causes. First, the terms of trade worsened as copper prices fell 45 percent in real terms, and the price of oil rose by a factor of three. Second, fiscal and monetary policies were extremely restrictive, attempting to stop inflation and to reduce an incipient current account deficit that could not be funded through borrowing. Third, with the change in trade incentives, some import competing sectors started to shrink.

By 1976 inflation remained high at 230 percent, the unemployment rate was 15.0 percent, and the international reserve position was weak (US$ 107.9 millions, less than one month of imports), but the fiscal deficit was −0.6 percent of GDP (see Tables 44.6 and 44.7). Stopping inflation was now the economic team's top priority, with fiscal contraction its main instrument. The use of an orthodox program to reduce a stubborn inflation became very costly in terms of output losses and higher unemployment [Corbo and Solimano (1991)]. The cost of stabilization would have been lower if the fiscal adjustment had been accompanied by coordinated deceleration of the rate of increase of wages and the exchange rate. Finally, inflation came down very slowly, and with a high cost in terms of unemployment. Nonetheless, the economy started to grow as the reforms progressed and their credibility was enhanced. GDP growth was 3.5 percent in 1976, 9.9 percent in 1977 and 8.2 percent in 1978 (see Table 44.7).

By early 1978 the economic authorities were becoming impatient with the slow progress in reducing inflation. They first instituted a crawling peg exchange rate system, and then in June 1979 fixed the exchange rate, despite a domestic inflation rate of 30 percent. There was a very clear conflict between the objective of achieving a stable equilibrium real exchange rate and the use of the exchange rate as an anchor for the price level. The growing overvaluation of the currency had deep macroeconomic repercussions and was one of the main causes of the boom that developed in the following years, as well as of the deep recession that followed.

With the introduction of a preannounced crawling peg, the cost of foreign borrowing decreased substantially. It fell from 22.6 percent per year in the fourth quarter of 1977 to 10.2 percent per year in the first quarter of 1978, and became negative from there on until the last quarter of 1980. The reduction in the cost of foreign borrowing unleashed large capital inflows and a drop in domestic real interest rates.[59] Inappropriate regulation and supervision of the banking system facilitated the increase in capital inflows. The drop in real peso and dollar interest rates and the large increase in real credit fueled a rapid increase in real domestic expenditures.

The widening gap between the rate of growth of expenditures and GDP was reflected in a growing trade deficit. The trade balance deficit as a percentage of GDP rose from 3.2 percent in 1978 to 5.2 percent in 1979, 6.7 percent in 1980, and 12.9 percent in 1981. The sharp increase in the demand for non-tradeable goods resulted in a market clearing appreciation of the real exchange rate, by 25 percent between 1978 and 1981.

By the end of 1981 and early in 1982, the large trade deficit and adverse external shocks (a worsening in the terms of trade, and a sharp increase in international interest rates)[60] began to generate doubts about the sustainability

---

[59] Some observers relate the increase in capital inflows mainly to the lifting of capital controls [Edwards (1986), Morandé (1988)].

[60] Relative to the average for the period 1977–1979, the size of the external shock is estimated as a positive shock of 1.2 percent of GDP in 1980, a loss of 0.5 percent of GDP in 1981, and a loss of 3.8 percent of GDP in 1982 (see Table 44.8).

of the exchange rate. As a result, capital inflows began to slow, and a period of capital flight started. With the loss of external funding, the key policy issue in early 1982 was how to engineer a sharp reduction in the trade deficit without causing an undue increase in unemployment. Chile was already in crisis before the international debt crisis broke in August 1982, but at that point capital inflows all but disappeared and the speed of reduction in the trade balance deficit had to be accelerated.

After a couple of years in which policies concentrated on the consequences of the recession, a medium term adjustment program was put in place in 1984. The program's main objectives were to reduce the fiscal deficit that emerged from the recession, rescue the financial system, and achieve a large real devaluation. As the traded goods sectors had achieved large efficiency improvements during the preceding period of real appreciation, there was a powerful supply response to the real depreciation, and the economy entered a sustained period of high growth. When the new democratic government took office in early 1990, and by its actions reaffirmed the main thrust of policy, a large direct foreign investment boom was initiated and growth stayed high.

For a highly indebted country, Chile's economic performance in the post 1985 period was remarkable. For the period 1986–1989, the average annual rate of growth of real GDP reached 7.2 percent, while the average annual rate of inflation declined to 17.8 percent. During the same period the unemployment rate was reduced from 14.8 percent in 1985 to only 5.3 percent in 1989 (see Table 44.7). When the new authorities took office in early 1990, the economy was overheating. The new government imposed a contractionary monetary policy early in 1990, thereby establishing the continuity of policy. After a brief period of lower growth, the acceleration of inflation was stopped, and in 1991 the economy was on its way to sustainable growth with a decreasing rate of inflation.

## 6.2. Ghana[61]

Economic adjustment and the recovery of growth have been exceptionally difficult in Africa [World Bank (1993b)]. Ghana, which started its adjustment program in 1983, has been the most successful of the African adjusters.[62]

---

[61] On conditions in the 1960s, see Clark Leith (1975); on the more recent period, see Kapur et al. (1991) and Leechor (1991).

[62] World Bank (1993b) classifies six of 29 adjusting African countries as successful adjusters. These countries all experienced an increase in GDP growth of at least 2 percent between 1981–1986 and 1987–1991. They are Ghana, Tanzania, the Gambia, Burkina Faso, Nigeria, and Zimbabwe.

*6.2.1. Causes of the crisis*

Ghana had an estimated GDP per capita of US$ 400 in 1990. The country is well endowed with natural resources such as arable land, forests, and large mineral deposits including gold, diamonds, bauxite and manganese.

When it began its Economic Recovery Program in April 1983, Ghana was submerged in a deep economic crisis, which had been building for the previous 15 years. At the time an autonomous government was established in 1951, (followed by full independence in 1957), in comparison with other African countries Ghana had a well-educated population and was receiving large external inflows. During the 1950s the economy grew at an average annual rate of 4 percent. Growth started to slow during the 1960s, when it averaged just 2.8 percent. Further, the growth rate declined as the decade progressed, and the average growth rate for the 1970s was negative. Food production decreased 18 percent during the decade, including cocoa (the main export product). The drop in cocoa production is most remarkable considering that there was a cocoa price boom in the middle of the 1970s.

The poor economic performance during the 1970s and early 1980s was due to inadequate domestic policies and severe internal and external shocks (droughts in 1975–1977 and a deterioration in the terms of trade in 1981–1983). On the macroeconomic front, a large fiscal deficit was behind an acceleration of inflation and a deteriorating current account deficit. On the microeconomic front, heavy government intervention through price controls, import controls, a multiple exchange rate system, distribution controls, as well as a massive expansion of the public sector in the production of private goods, all resulted in heavily distorted relative prices (including for cocoa) and an overextended public sector.

When balance of payments problems became acute in the early 1980s, exchange and import controls were intensified. Restrictions on imports of spare parts and basic inputs hampered production. At the same time the exchange and trade restrictions accumulated during the previous twenty years had resulted in an anti-export bias that crowded out most potential export activities. In particular, the marketing board for the main commodity export, cocoa, paid producers far less than the international price. At the same time, expansionary demand policies were fueling an acceleration of inflation. With the nominal exchange rate fixed, a large real exchange rate appreciation developed. Not surprisingly, the black market exchange rate premium increased and the implicit tax on exports increased too. To avoid this tax, cocoa smuggling became rampant.

Controls on interest rates at a time of high inflation led to highly negative real interest rates, discouraging saving, promoting inefficient investment decisions, and encouraging capital flight. The negative real interest rates and the heavy borrowing of the government resulted in financial repression and a very inefficient financial system, especially in rural areas. During the period 1981–1983, GDP declined at an annual average rate of 4.6 percent; the average inflation rate was 76 percent; the fiscal and current account deficits were around 5 percent and 7.6 percent of GDP, respectively. As the fiscal situation deteriorated, the funding and quality of basic government services and public investment started to suffer. The deterioration in the economic situation fueled international migration of the well-educated population. To make matters worse, in the early 1980s foreign capital inflows started to dry up as creditors questioned Ghana's economic policies.

By the end of 1982, the balance of payments deficit had used up the country's international reserves, and the economy had accumulated international arrears equivalent to 10 percent of the GDP (about 18 months of imports). The crisis that had been building up for the previous twenty years – GDP per capita declined by 30 percent in the period 1968–1983 – reached its climax.

### 6.2.2. The economic reform program

The goals of the Economic Recovery Program introduced in 1983 were to restore economic balance and to lay the foundation for sustainable growth with equity. These objectives were supposed to be achieved in the medium term after a thorough transformation of the existing economic system. The program included: a stabilization component aimed at reducing inflation and moving towards a trade balance deficit consistent with available financing; a series of microeconomic and institutional reforms aimed at correcting price incentives and increasing the integration of the Ghanaian economy in the world economy; the rehabilitation of the physical and social infrastructure; and the removal of impediments to the expansion of private investment. The shift away from controls toward the use of market based incentives was to be gradual, but prices that remained under control were intended to be managed flexibly and were to avoid large distortions.

The main initial measures included a large nominal devaluation of the cedi, the removal of the implicit taxation of exports resulting from the exchange system and the trade regime, an increase in the price received by cocoa producers to levels close to international prices, and an improvement in fiscal revenue collection. Important flows of external aid, soft loans and credit arrangements, supported the program of reforms in Ghana.

Public sector reforms were an integral part of the adjustment program. Fiscal contraction was needed to achieve and sustain a real devaluation. The fiscal deficit was reduced from 5.6 percent of GDP in 1982 to 0.7 percent in 1989. The deficit has remained at that level since.

Table 44.9
Macroeconomic indicators: Ghana 1978–1990

| Item | 1978 | 1979 | 1980 | 1981 | 1982 | 1983 | 1984 | 1985 | 1986 | 1987 | 1988 | 1989 | 1990 |
|---|---|---|---|---|---|---|---|---|---|---|---|---|---|
| **Constant prices (percent growth)** | | | | | | | | | | | | | |
| Gross domestic product | 9.8 | -1.7 | 0.6 | -2.9 | -6.5 | -4.5 | 8.7 | 4.5 | 5.0 | 4.8 | 5.6 | 5.1 | 3.3 |
| Total consumption | 14.0 | -3.4 | 3.5 | -3.1 | -10.1 | -0.6 | 8.2 | 4.3 | 3.4 | 5.1 | 3.1 | 3.6 | 13.5 |
| **Shares of GDP in current prices (percent)** | | | | | | | | | | | | | |
| Resource balance (BOP) | -2.1 | 0.1 | 0.8 | -9.9 | -2.5 | -3.9 | -2.0 | -3.7 | -2.2 | -5.7 | -8.4 | -9.8 | -10.8 |
| Net current transfer | -0.1 | 0.0 | -0.1 | -0.1 | 0.0 | 0.0 | 0.5 | 0.7 | 1.3 | 4.0 | 6.6 | 8.0 | 6.8 |
| Current account balance[a] | -3.0 | 1.0 | -1.2 | -12.0 | -4.8 | -1.1 | -2.7 | -4.1 | -3.5 | -4.6 | -5.1 | -6.0 | -8.2 |
| Exports of GNFS (NA) | 8.4 | 11.2 | 8.5 | 4.8 | 3.3 | 6.1 | 7.4 | 9.6 | 19.2 | 20.6 | 18.4 | 16.9 | 15.4 |
| Imports of GNFS (NA) | 9.7 | 11.2 | 9.2 | 5.3 | 3.0 | 9.3 | 7.7 | 11.7 | 22.5 | 23.6 | 24.3 | 24.5 | 24.0 |
| Private consumption | 84.7 | 83.1 | 83.9 | 87.2 | 89.8 | 90.8 | 86.0 | 83.1 | 82.6 | 81.6 | 81.7 | 82.9 | 83.1 |
| General government consumption | 11.3 | 10.3 | 11.1 | 8.8 | 6.5 | 8.6 | 7.4 | 9.3 | 11.2 | 10.6 | 10.0 | 9.2 | 10.9 |
| Gross domestic investment | 5.4 | 6.5 | 5.6 | 4.6 | 3.4 | 3.7 | 7.0 | 9.6 | 9.6 | 10.9 | 14.2 | 15.5 | 14.4 |
| Gross domestic savings | 4.0 | 6.6 | 4.9 | 4.0 | 3.7 | 0.6 | 6.6 | 7.6 | 6.3 | 7.9 | 9.1 | 9.5 | 7.9 |
| Gross national savings | 3.8 | 6.2 | 4.5 | 3.7 | 3.5 | -0.3 | 5.4 | 6.4 | 5.1 | 9.3 | 12.5 | 13.7 | 10.9 |
| Fiscal deficit (–) / surplus[b] | -9.0 | -6.4 | -4.2 | -6.5 | -5.6 | -2.7 | -1.8 | -2.2 | 0.1 | 0.5 | 0.4 | 0.7 | 0.2 |

| | | | | | | | | | | | | |
|---|---|---|---|---|---|---|---|---|---|---|---|---|
| **Debt burden ratios** | | | | | | | | | | | | |
| Total external debt / Exports | 127.2 | 107.2 | 108.3 | 175.6 | 195.5 | 334.4 | 307.9 | 321.4 | 323.7 | 345.5 | 341.8 | 359.8 | 367.4 |
| Total external debt / GNP | 34.7 | 31.1 | 29.6 | 34.6 | 34.6 | 39.4 | 42.9 | 48.3 | 46.3 | 61.7 | 59.3 | 63.6 | 57.0 |
| Interest / exports | 2.4 | 3.0 | 4.3 | 7.7 | 8.8 | 13.1 | 11.1 | 13.0 | 13.5 | 13.0 | 12.1 | 13.5 | 11.7 |
| Interest / GDP | 0.7 | 0.9 | 1.2 | 1.5 | 1.6 | 1.5 | 1.5 | 2.0 | 1.9 | 2.3 | 2.3 | 2.1 | 1.7 |
| *(percent change)* | | | | | | | | | | | | | |
| Consumer prices | 73.1 | 54.4 | 50.1 | 116.5 | 22.3 | 122.9 | 39.7 | 10.3 | 24.6 | 39.8 | 31.4 | 25.2 | 37.2 |
| Net domestic credit | 67.7 | 17.7 | 28.2 | 63.1 | 21.6 | 72.2 | 50.2 | 59.7 | 33.8 | 5.6 | 12.7 | −3.0 | 8.9 |
| Money plus quasi-money | 68.6 | 14.7 | 33.8 | 51.3 | 23.3 | 40.2 | 53.6 | 46.2 | 47.9 | 53.3 | 43.0 | 26.9 | 18.0 |
| **Indices (1980 = 100)** | | | | | | | | | | | | | |
| Real money | 149.6 | 108.0 | 100.0 | 69.9 | 70.5 | 44.4 | 48.8 | 64.7 | 76.8 | 84.2 | 93.8 | 110.2 | 88.0 |
| Terms of trade | – | – | 100.0 | – | – | – | – | 50.6 | 48.0 | 44.7 | 40.3 | 33.4 | 30.9 |
| Real effective exchange rate (decrease indicates depreciation) | 96.7 | – | 100.0 | 222.4 | 278.1 | 186.9 | 72.1 | 52.4 | 30.2 | 23.3 | 22.4 | 21.1 | 21.0 |

[a] Before net official transfers.
[b] Including grants.
*Sources*: World Bank and IMF publications.

The fiscal reform consisted of an initially painful reduction of expenditures and a substantial reduction in public enterprise losses. Revenues from traditional taxes were increased by broadening the tax base and improving tax administration.

The civil service was also reformed: the number of public employees was reduced, real wages for the remaining ones were raised, and the wage scale was decompressed. These reforms permitted the government to keep the good employees who would otherwise have left their jobs. The public sector reforms also included an increase in budgetary allocations for the rehabilitation, maintenance and construction of new economic and social infrastructure.

The reforms of public enterprises notably improved their performance. By early 1991, 23 public enterprises had been liquidated and 15 others privatized. The reduction in the fiscal deficit and the restoration of external flows enabled the government to reduce the absorption of resources from the banking system. In 1987 the government started making net payments to the banks.

The rationalization of the tax structure included reductions of income and dividend tax rates, and increases in indirect taxes (on consumption, petroleum and motor vehicles). The fiscal reforms were directed at improving incentives (specially for investment and savings), and also toward achieving an equitable distribution of the social costs of adjustment, by aiding the most vulnerable economic and social groups such as small farmers, urban unemployed and underemployed, and retrenched public employees.

Credit and monetary policies were designed to reduce inflation and the current account deficit, while at the same time providing financing for the desired growth of production. Credit was also increasingly made available to the private sector as the government diminished its absorption of resources from the banking system.

Controls on deposits and lending interest rates began to be eliminated in 1988. Quantitative controls on credit were also lifted. Deeper institutional reforms of the banking system were implemented in 1989–1990, including a revision of banking legislation and the improvement in the supervision of banks. These measures, together with restructuring plans for all the financially distressed commercial and development banks, enhanced the position of financial institutions. At the same time they created conditions for increasing the efficiency of financial intermediation.

In 1987 an auction system for treasury bills was implemented, and new financial instruments were introduced. The Bank of Ghana started using market-based instruments for monetary control. These measures led to an expansion of financial markets. Real interest rates became positive in 1990.

Important reforms were also introduced in the exchange rate system and trade policy. The reforms of the exchange rate system were initiated at the beginning of the reform program, when a series of large discrete devaluations was undertaken. The accompanying contractionary fiscal and monetary policies were designed to produce a large real devaluation.

In 1986 an exchange rate auction system was implemented, to obtain a market-determined value of the official exchange rate. The parallel market was legalized in 1988, with the creation of exchange rate bureaus that could freely trade in foreign exchange for transactions not allowed in the official market. Then, in 1990, both markets were unified by broadening access to the official market, and the recreation of an inter-bank market.

Reform of trade policies included the elimination of import licenses, reductions in tariffs, and the elimination of restrictions on current account international payments and transfers. The reforms related to the cocoa sector have been far-reaching. Producer prices were raised closer to the world level, price subsidies on inputs were eliminated, and the operating costs of the Ghana Cocoa Board were reduced; on balance these measures increased incentives for cocoa production. However, a sharp drop in the international price of cocoa in 1987–1989 discouraged cocoa output and exports just when implicit domestic taxes had been reduced.

### 6.2.3. The results

In spite of a large worsening of the terms of trade, the Ghanaian economy grew at an average rate of 4 percent during the period 1983–1990, a rate higher than population growth (2.6 percent). GDP per capita grew consistently for the first time in a decade.

In 1990, agriculture remains the largest sector of the economy, accounting for about 45 percent of GDP. It is followed by the services sector which accounts for 40 percent of GDP, and has been the most dynamic part of the economy for the last five years, growing at an average rate of 8.8 percent over 1985–1990. Although industry (including mining) generates a small share of GDP (a little over 14 percent), this sector is relatively diverse and well developed in comparison with other countries in the region. In spite of a major reduction in the anti-export bias of the trade regime, exports are still very concentrated – cocoa, wood, and gold account for over 75 percent of export earnings.

Important progress has been achieved in reducing inflation: the annual inflation rate was reduced from 142 percent in 1983 to close to 20 percent in 1991. However inflation fluctuations, year to year, have been wide. Real wages rose during the period.

The effects of the program on savings and investment have been less impressive. Although public investment has increased to rebuild infrastructure, the response of private investment has been weak. The higher growth rates were due more to the result of better utilization of the existing capacity, with the assistance of aid flows – as the severe exchange rate constraint was left behind – than to an increase in capacity itself. As in most adjustment programs, the response of private investment has been slower than envisaged in the program. A possible explanation is the slow buildup of credibility in the program, and its heavy dependence on external financial support. Negative real interest rates until 1990 most likely restricted the response of private saving, and even more, did not sufficiently reduce the incentives for capital flight.

Exports and imports both grew at an annual rate of about 15 percent between 1983–1990. The improved balance of payments, reinforced by official transfers and concessional loans, facilitated the elimination of external arrears and contributed to an improvement in the international reserves position.

The diminishing external debt/GDP ratio since 1987, and the renegotiation of the maturity structure of the external debt, reduced the external debt burden. By 1990 the external debt-service/exports ratio had fallen to 40 percent, from 70 percent in 1988. Rising aggregate income, the increase in rural incomes, and improvements in the provision of social services made possible progress in the alleviation of poverty during the last years. The Ghanaian PAMSCAD,[63] which coordinated the activities of anti-poverty agencies, helped ensure that the anti-poverty element of the adjustment program was kept at the forefront of policy concerns.

Economic performance worsened in 1990 as a result of a drought, an increase in oil prices, and a sharp drop in the terms of trade (about 26 percent). The government responded to the decline in the terms of trade by an increase in public sector saving, and with a further depreciation of the cedi. The initial increase in the current account deficit was financed with private capital inflows in the form of direct foreign investment, as well as external aid and external borrowing.

### 6.3. New Zealand[64]

New Zealand has a population of 3.4 million, and is a member of the OECD. In 1950, per capita income was third highest in the world; in 1990 it was 24th. From another perspective, per capita income in 1950 was 26 percent above the OECD average, while in 1990 it was 27 percent below the OECD average. A radical adjustment program was initiated by a newly elected Labor government in 1984. Labor won re-election in 1987, and was defeated in 1990, but the new Conservative government continued the reform program. The reformists lost

---

[63] Programme of action to mitigate the social costs of adjustment; see World Bank (1990b).
[64] On the New Zealand reforms, see Bollard (1992 and 1993), Caygill (1989), Dalziel and Lattimore (1991), and Douglas (1990).

Table 44.10
Economic performance, New Zealand:1983–1993

| | Real GDP growth (% p.a) | CPI in- flation (% p.a) | Unemploy- ment rate (%) | Budget def/ GDP (%) | | Curr. a/c /GDP (%) | Real eff. exchange rate | Short-term int. rate (% p.a) |
|---|---|---|---|---|---|---|---|---|
| | | | | (a) | (b) | | | |
| 1983 | 1.0 | 7.3* | 5.3 | 6.9 | 5.4 | −4.4 | 105.7 | 13.1 |
| 1984 | 8.6 | 6.2* | 4.5 | 9.0 | 7.0 | −8.7 | 98.3 | 15.0 |
| 1985 | 1.2 | 15.4 | 3.5 | 7.2 | 6.4 | −7.3 | 100.0 | 23.3 |
| 1986 | 0.6 | 13.2 | 4.0 | 4.2 | 3.2 | −6.3 | 101.1 | 19.1 |
| 1987 | −2.2 | 15.8 | 4.1 | 3.6 | 3.8 | −5.4 | 116.8 | 21.1 |
| 1988 | 3.0 | 6.4 | 5.6 | −0.8 | 2.1 | −1.4 | 124.5 | 15.4 |
| 1989 | −0.7 | 5.7 | 7.2 | −2.7 | 1.8 | −3.5 | 118.1 | 13.5 |
| 1990 | 0.5 | 6.1 | 7.9 | −3.8 | 0.4 | −2.9 | 114.7 | 13.9 |
| 1991 | −1.8 | 2.6 | 10.3 | | 3.6 | −1.3 | 109.4 | 10.0 |
| 1992 | 0.5 | 1.0 | 10.3 | | 3.5 | −1.9 | 98.8 | 6.7 |
| 1993 | 3.0 | 1.4 | 9.8 | | 2.3 | −1.7 | 99.9 | 6.3 |

\* Wage and price controls were in effect in 1983 and 1984.
*Sources*: Unless otherwise noted, *OECD Economic Outlook*, various issues. Budget deficits from Dalziel and Lattimore (1991); (a) includes asset transactions, (b) excludes them. Column (b) data for 1991–93 are from *OECD Economic Outlook*. Real effective exchange rate from IMF; increase represents appreciation.

ground in the election of 1993, and the new government promised to moderate the pace and impact of adjustment.

## 6.3.1. Causes of the crisis

The New Zealand economy grew at a satisfactory rate, 4 percent, in the decade to 1973. In that year New Zealand benefitted from the increase in food prices, but was adversely affected by the oil price shock. Britain's entry into the European Community had an even more profound impact on the New Zealand economy, by ending preferential access to its largest market for agricultural exports. New Zealand's terms of trade worsened by 30 percent in the year ending March 1975, and the current account deficit rose to 14 percent of GDP.

The government responded by trying to maintain domestic demand, with agricultural subsidies, and budget deficits. In 1978 it mounted a major public investment program, "Think Big", which led to larger budget deficits and a growing internal and external debt; subsidies were also extended to private sector investments. The budget deficit,[65] which had averaged 2.3 percent of GDP for the period 1964–1973, increased to an average of 6.5 percent for the period 1974–1983. The public debt correspondingly increased from 43 percent of GDP in 1975 to 73 percent in 1985, with the external debt in that year

[65] This is the budget deficit including asset transactions (from Dalziel and Lattimore, p. 57). In the source, data are given for fiscal years, which at that time ended in March. They have been shifted to the previous year, to make them coincide better with the calendar.

amounting to 32 percent of GDP.[66] Comprehensive wage and price controls were imposed in June 1982 to deal with the double digit inflation that had persisted for the entire previous decade. GDP growth averaged 1.8 percent in the decade to 1984. The registered unemployment rate rose from 0.1 percent in 1974 to 5.7 percent in 1984.[67]

By 1984 there was a widespread perception, compounded by a foreign exchange crisis just before the election, that the economy was in crisis. A new Labor government was elected on a reform platform, committed to change, though "most [voters] were clearer about what they were voting against than what they were voting for".[68] The refusal by the outgoing administration to permit a devaluation in the interim between the election and the time the new administration took office heightened the sense of crisis that greeted the incoming administration.

The key economic policy figure in the new government was Roger Douglas, the Minister of Finance. Douglas, who had been a junior minister in the first half of the 1970s, had been rethinking his views and his approach to policy during his time in opposition. By 1984 he had reached a set of conclusions about the needs for macroeconomic stability and low inflation, and the desirability of decontrolling the economy and allowing market forces to work, which were soon to become embodied in policy. He reconciled his radical pro-market views with his membership in a Labor government by arguing that state intervention in markets typically created favored groups and promoted inequality rather than efficiency, and that only a Labor government could do what was essential to restore long-run growth to the economy. On tactics, his views [see Douglas (1990)] were to move as fast as possible, wherever possible, to express no doubts, and to maintain momentum. Douglas initially received strong support from the Prime Minister, and from the appointment of two capable and relatively senior Associate Ministers of Finance.

Douglas and the economic program also received powerful intellectual support from the Treasury, whose views had been evolving during the failures of the previous administration. Treasury economists had developed a set of views, largely on microeconomic issues, and heavily influenced by trends within the economics profession, that contributed to the intellectual coherence of the reform program. For instance, on the issue of public ownership, the new Treasury view emphasized principal-agent problems, and argued that corporatization and privatization were preferable to public ownership. Similarly, they used the theory of contestability to argue for less direct regulation. In general, they wanted to reduce the dominant role of government in the

---

[66] The external debt jumped from 24 to 32 percent of GDP between 1984 and 1985.

[67] Dalziel and Lattimore (p. 55) report corresponding OECD definition unemployment rates that rise from 3 percent in 1974 to 10.5 percent in 1984.

[68] Bollard (1993, p. 24) quoting C. James.

economy and to harness competition wherever possible. They did not pay much attention to the dynamics and potential social costs of policy reform, tending to believe that growth would follow as microeconomic distortions were removed. Similarly, there was very little attention to distributional issues.

### 6.3.2. The adjustment program

Caygill (1989), one of the two Associate Ministers of Finance, describes the New Zealand economic reform strategy as consisting of three main elements: a medium-term approach to economic policy, with the emphasis on consistency and credibility; an orthodox medium-term macroeconomic strategy aimed at reducing the budget deficit and inflation; and the removal of sectoral distortions.

Despite the large budget deficit and the foreign exchange crisis in 1984, the initial focus of the adjustment program was on the third, the microeconomic, component. Figure 44.4, reproduced from Bollard (1993), shows how far the sequencing of reform in New Zealand departed from the conventional prescription of starting with macroeconomic stabilization and leaving financial liberalization for later.

The initial set of reforms were in the financial and foreign exchange markets, in trade liberalization, and deregulation, including in agriculture. Interest rate controls and credit growth guidelines were removed at the outset, as were controls on external investment and borrowing. Foreign exchange controls were lifted in 1984, a 20 percent devaluation was undertaken, and a free float instituted in 1985; an important trade agreement had been reached with Australia in 1983, import licensing was ended in 1984, and tariffs reduced gradually over the period 1986–1992.

Industrial and labor market deregulation began in earnest in 1984, and continued through 1990. By 1991, the deregulation of the New Zealand economy was almost complete.

Despite the high inflation and large budget and current account deficits, no serious attack on the fiscal problem was made until 1987. Monetary policy was tightened, and the real interest rate increased,[69] but in the absence of fiscal contraction, and with large capital inflows, the inflation rate responded very little. The absence of macroeconomic stabilization is visible not only in the continuing high budget deficits and inflation, but also in the low unemployment rate that persisted through 1987. The tightening of monetary policy in 1987 led to the continuation of very high real interest rates and a major appreciation of the New Zealand dollar. Harberger, in the introduction to Bollard (1992)

---

[69] Because price controls were in effect in 1983 and 1984, we should assume that the real interest rate was less than the interest rate minus the official inflation rate.

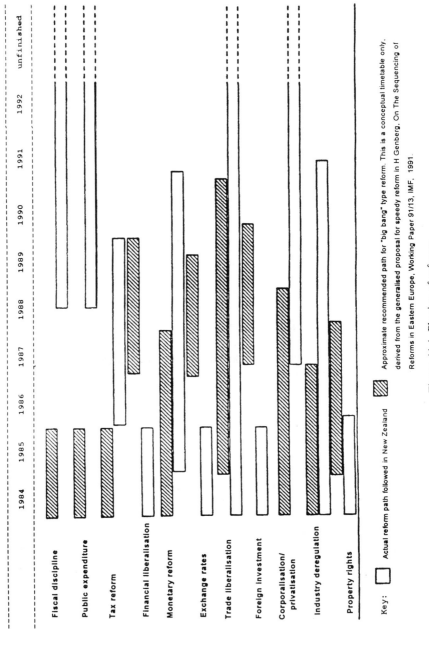

Figure 44.4. Phasing of reforms.

argues that the failure to attempt fiscal stabilization before 1987 was the major weakness of the New Zealand program.

Corporatization and privatization of government companies began on a major scale in 1987, leading to a budget surplus including privatization receipts that reached nearly 4 percent of GDP in 1991. Tax reforms to produce a neutral tax system began in 1986, with the extension of the goods and services tax to virtually all final domestic consumption, and with income tax rates being reduced and the structure simplified. More radical reforms of government services were introduced starting in 1991, with reform of the state pension and health systems on the agenda.

A major change in monetary policy was introduced in the Reserve Bank Act of 1989. Under the new law, the government reaches an agreement with the Governor of the Bank on a target path for inflation, the achievement of which is then the Governor's responsibility. If he fails, he can be dismissed. An automatic allowance is made for terms of trade changes. This innovation is important for at least four reasons: first, the policy criterion is unambiguous – the central bank has no discretion to trade off output for inflation; second, the targets can be varied by an agreement between the government and the central bank, so that some flexibility is maintained; third, this is a monetary policy rule, but it is specified in terms of the target outcome, with the means of and responsibility for achieving the target left to the central bank – this is not a monetary rule which seeks to solve the technical problem of how best to achieve a given inflation rate; and fourth, the adjustment for terms of trade changes recognizes that supply shocks should be allowed for in setting monetary policy. After achieving the initial target path, the Governor has recently been reappointed.

### 6.3.3. The results

The results of the New Zealand adjustment program have been mixed. The adjustment period was extremely long. Real GDP was essentially unchanged between 1984 and 1992. Three percent growth returned in 1993, and higher growth is predicted for the next two years as well. Thus it took eight years of adjustment before a period of sustained growth started.

A major reason for the slow adjustment is the delay in attempting fiscal stabilization. The microeconomic reforms introduced beginning in 1984 did not have a major effect on growth or unemployment, but in the presence of continuing inflation and large budget deficits did not produce much of a supply response. Monetary and fiscal tightening took place only in 1987, real interest rates increased, and the currency appreciated. The unemployment rate then began to rise, and growth stayed low as inflation was wrung out of the system.

The real appreciation three years after the start of the adjustment program meant that export growth, often the first evidence of supply response, stayed low until 1991.

The reformers argue that the early reforms, particularly the floating of the exchange rate, helped establish their credibility. It seems likely that they would have been even more credible had they attacked the budget deficit and inflation at the beginning Further, the prolonged slow growth that resulted from the New Zealand sequencing meant that the public saw very little benefit from reform for almost a decade. More resolute early adjustment would have brought a greater initial output decline, but a more rapid return to growth – albeit from a lower level of income.

Despite the program's goal of reducing the role of government in the economy, social sector spending continued to grow during the 1980s.[70] This increase in part reflects a disagreement between the Prime Minister and the Finance Minister over the social consequences of adjustment. A Royal Commission on Social Policy that reported in 1988, criticized the reform program for ignoring the equity-efficiency tradeoff, and the government's failure to compensate losers from the reforms. Bollard (1993) notes that there was a shift of income from the lower to upper quintiles during the adjustment period, but notes also that a similar change was taking place in other countries not pursuing an adjustment program. In any case, the Prime Minister rejected the Finance Minister's proposal for a flat rate income tax, and Douglas later resigned.

Inflation came down very rapidly after 1990. It is natural to give the credit for this change to the new monetary policy, though it should also be noted that Australia achieved a similar reduction in inflation without changing its monetary rule.[71] Expectations of inflation in New Zealand are however lower than those in Australia.

After nine years of persistent reform, the New Zealand economy has been transformed. The economy is deregulated, there has been extensive privatization, the budget deficit is declining, inflation is minimal. However, the 1993 election results reflected adjustment fatigue, and the pace of reform is now likely to slow and some of the reforms may even be reversed. Ironically, sustained growth appears to be returning just as the public has tired of the changes that made it possible.

---

[70] See Bollard (1992, p. 31).

[71] The New Zealand experience is compared with those of Australia and Canada in an MIT thesis by Debelle (1994).

## 7. Concluding comments

Structural adjustment touches on virtually every aspect of the economy, microeconomic and macroeconomic. Correspondingly, the analysis of adjustment has to draw on a wide range of economic analysis and the full range of any economist's skills. The topic is so all-inclusive that no single model can be used to analyze adjustment. Rather, different aspects have to be dealt with by using different models. The microeconomics of distortions and regulation, open economy macroeconomics, the macroeconomics of stabilization, static and dynamic trade theory, models of financial repression and reform, and political economy models are the main tools used in analyzing structural adjustment.

The absence of agreed-upon analytic or econometric models to analyze some of the basic problems of adjustment is striking. For instance, the analysis of sequencing problems is still underdeveloped. The important issue of the distributional impact of adjustment has received attention in computable general equilibrium models (see for instance Bourguignon and Morrisson, 1992), but it is fair to say that this work has not yet had a wide impact.

It is also striking how few empirical generalizations are yet widely accepted. In part this is because of the difficulty of constructing counterfactuals, a problem that lies at the heart of the econometric issues discussed in Section 4 of this chapter. In part it reflects the very broad and imprecise questions often asked in the analysis of adjustment, e.g. should the financial sector be deregulated before the trade sector. Almost surely the answer is "it depends", but we do not as yet have sufficient evidence or analytics to know precisely on what it depends. One thing we do know is that it depends also on political factors (see for instance Krueger, 1993). That adds both interest and complexity to the analysis of adjustment.

Of course, the inadequacies that remain in the analysis of adjustment policies are not particular to adjustment, but are the same as those that apply in almost every applied area in economics. And they have their good side: they provide the basic challenge for future research in this area.

## References

Ahmad, S. (1994) 'Improving inter-spatial and inter-temporal comparability of national accounts', *Journal of Development Economics* 44 (June):53–75.
Alesina, A. and Drazen, A. (1991) 'Why Are Stabilizations Delayed?', *American Economic Review*, 81(5) (Dec.):1170–1188.
Amsden, A. (1989) *Asia's next giant*. New York: Oxford University Press.

Bailey, M. (1956) 'The welfare cost of inflationary finance', *Journal of Political Economy*, 64(2) (April):93–110.

Balassa, B. and associates (1982) *Development strategies in semi-industrial economies*. Baltimore: Johns Hopkins University Press.

Bhagwati, J. (1978) *Foreign trade regimes and economic development: Anatomy and consequences of exchange control regimes*. Cambridge, MA: Ballinger.

Blanchard, O. and Fischer, S. (1989) *Lectures on macroeconomics*, Cambridge MA: MIT Press.

Blanchard, O., Chouraqui, J.-C., Hagemann, R.P. and Sartor, N. (1990) 'The sustainability of fiscal policy: New answers to an old question', *OECD Economic Studies*, No. 15 (Autumn):7–36.

Bollard, A. (1992) 'New Zealand, 1984–1991', International Center for Economic Growth, San Francisco.

Bollard, A. (1993) 'The political economy of liberalisation in New Zealand', NZ Institute of Economic Research (Inc.), Wellington, NZ.

Bourguignon, F. and Morrisson, C. (1992) *Adjustment and equity in developing countries: A new approach*. Paris: OECD.

Bruno, M. (1991) 'High inflation and the nominal anchors of an open economy', *Princeton essays in international finance*.

Bruno, M. and Fischer, S. (1986) 'The inflationary process: Shocks and accommodation', in Y. Ben-Porath, ed., *The Israeli economy: Maturing through crises*. Cambridge, MA: Harvard University Press.

Bryant, R., Henderson, D., Holtham, G., Hooper, P. and Symansky, S., eds., (1988) *Empirical macroeconomics for interdependent economies*. Washington, DC: Brookings Institution.

Bryant, R., Henderson, D., Holtham, G., Hooper, P., Mann, C. and Tryon, R., eds., (1993). *Evaluating policy regimes: New research in empirical macroeconomics*. Washington, DC: Brookings Institution.

Caballero, R. and Corbo, V. (1986) 'Explicando la balanza comercial: Un enfoque de equilibrio general', *Cuadernos de economia* (Dec.).

Cagan, P. (1956) 'The monetary dynamics of hyperinflation', in: M. Friedman, ed., *Studies in the quantity theory of money*. Chicago: University of Chicago Press.

Calvo, G. (1989) 'Incredible reforms' in G. Calvo et al. (ed.), *Debt, Stabilization and Development*, Cambridge, MA: Basil Blackwell.

Calvo, G. and Vegh, C. (1991) 'Exchange-rate based stabilization: The dynamics of non-credible policy', mimeo, IMF, Research Department.

Caygill, D. (1989) 'Economic restructuring in New Zealand since 1984', Per Jacobsson Lecture (IMF Press).

Chamie, J. (1994) 'Population databases in development analysis', *Journal of Development Economics*. 44 (June):131–146.

Coeymans, J.E. (1992) 'Productividad, salarios y empleo en la economía chilena: Un enfoque de oferta agregada', *Cuadernos de Economía* (Agosto).

Collins, S. (1990) 'Lessons from Korean economic growth', *American Economic Review*, 80(2) (May):104–107.

Conway, P. (1990) 'How successful is world bank lending for structural adjustment?', University of North Carolina, mimeo.

Corbo, V. (1985a) 'Reforms and macroeconomic adjustment in Chile during 1974–1984' *World Development*, 13(8):893–916.

Corbo, V. (1985b) 'International prices, wages and inflation in an open economy: A model for Chile', *Review of Economics and Statistics* 67 (Nov.):564–573.

Corbo, V. (1990) 'Public finance, trade and development: The Chilean experience', in V. Tanzi, ed., *Public Finance and Development*. Washington, DC: IMF.

Corbo, V. (1993) 'Economic reforms in Chile: An overview', documento de trabajo #160, Instituto de Economia, Universidad Catolica de Chile.

Corbo, V. and de Melo, J. (1987) 'Lessons from the southern cone policy reforms', *World Bank Research Observer*, 2(2) (July):111–142.

Corbo, V. and de Melo, J. (1989) 'External shocks and policy reforms in the southern cone: A reassessment', in: G. Calvo et al., ed., *Debt, stabilization and development*. London: Blackwell.

Corbo, V. and Fischer, S. (1992) 'World bank supported adjustment programs: Rationale and main results', in: Corbo, Fischer and Webb, loc. cit.

Corbo, V. and Fischer, S. (1994) 'Lessons from the Chilean stabilization and recovery', in: B. Bosworth et al., eds., *The Chilean economy: Policy lessons and challenges*. Washington, DC: Brookings Institution.

Corbo, V. and Rojas, P. (1992) 'World Bank supported adjustment programs: Country performance and effectiveness', in Corbo, Fischer and Webb, loc. cit.

Corbo, V. and Rojas, P. (1993) 'Investment, macroeconomic stability and growth: The Latin American experience', *Analisis Economico*, 8(1) (June):19–35.

Corbo, V. and Schmidt-Hebbel, K. (1991) 'Public policies and saving in developing countries', *Journal of Development Economics*, 36:89–115.

Corbo, V. and Solimano, A. (1991) 'Chile's experience with stabilization revisited', in: M. Bruno et al., eds. *Lessons of economic stabilization and its aftermath*. Cambridge, MA: MIT Press.

Corbo, V. and Suh, S.M. (1992) *Structural adjustment in a newly industrialized country: Lessons from Korea*. Baltimore, MD: Johns Hopkins University Press.

Corbo, V., Fischer, S. and Webb. S., eds., (1992) *Adjustment lending revisited: Policies to restore growth*. Washington, DC: The World Bank.

Corden, W.M. (1960) 'The geometric representation of policies to attain internal and external balance', *Review of Economic Studies*, 28:1–22.

Corden, W.M. (1989) 'Macroeconomic adjustment in developing countries', *World Bank Research Observer*, 4(1):51–64.

Cornia, G.A., Jolly, R. and Stewart, F. (1987) *Adjustment with a human face*, Vol. I, *Protecting the vulnerable and promoting growth*. New York: Oxford University Press.

Dalziel, P. and Lattimore, R. (1991) *A briefing on the New Zealand macroeconomy 1960–1990*. Auckland, NZ: Oxford University Press.

de la Cuadra, S. and Valdés, S. (1991) 'Bank structure in Chile', in: G. Kaufman, ed., *Banking structures in major countries*. Amsterdam: Kluwer Academic Publishers.

de Melo, J. and Robinson, S. (1989) 'Productivity and externalities: Models of export-led growth', Manuscript, The World Bank.

Debelle, G. (1994) 'Central Bank independence and inflation', unpublished Ph.D. dissertation, MIT.

Devarajan, S. and de Melo, J. (1987) 'Adjustment with a fixed exchange rate: Cameroon, Côte d'Ivoire, and Senegal', *World Bank Economic Review*, 1(3) (May):447–487.

Dollar, D. (1992) 'Outward-oriented developing economies really do grow more rapidly: Evidence from 95 LDCs:1976–1985', *Economic Development and Cultural Change*, 40(3) (April):523–544.

Donovan, D. (1981) 'Real responses associated with exchange rate action in selected upper credit tranche stabilization programs', *IMF Staff Papers*, 28:698–727.

Donovan, D. (1982) 'Macroeconomic performance and adjustment under fund-supported programs: The experience of the seventies', *IMF Staff Papers*, 29:171–203.

Dornbusch, R. (1980) 'Home goods and traded goods: The dependent economy model', Chapter 6 in *Open economy macroeconomics*. New York, NY: Basic Books.

Dornbusch, R. (1985) 'Policy and performance links between LDC debtors and industrial nations', *Brookings Papers on Economic Activity*, 2:303–368.

Dornbusch, R. (1990) 'Policies to move from stabilization to growth', *World Bank Annual Conference on Development Economics*, 19–48.

Dornbusch, R. (1992) 'The case for trade liberalization in developing countries', *Journal of Economic Perspectives*, 6(1) (Winter):69–86.

Dornbusch, R. and Edwards, S., eds., (1992) *The macroeconomics of populism in Latin America*. Chicago, IL: University of Chicago Press.

Dornbusch, R. and Fischer, S. (1993) 'Moderate inflation', *World Bank Economic Review*, 7(1) (Jan.):1–44.

Douglas, R. (1990) 'The politics of successful structural reform', *Policy*, 6(1) (Autumn):2–6.

Easterly, W. (1993) 'How much do distortions affect growth?' *Journal of Monetary Economics* 32:187–235.

Easterly, W. and Wetzel, D.L. (1989) 'Policy determinants of growth: Survey of theory and evidence', World Bank PPR Working Paper #343.

Edwards, S. (1986) 'Monetarism in Chile, 1973–1983: Analytical issues and economic puzzles', in: *Economic Development and Cultural Change*, 34 (April):535–559.

Edwards, S. (1989a) 'The International Monetary Fund and the developing countries: A critical evaluation', *Carnegie–Rochester conference series on public policy*, Vol. 31, Autumn, 7–68.

Edwards, S. (1989b) 'On the sequencing of structural reforms', NBER Working Paper No. 3138 (Oct.).

Edwards, S. (1993a) 'Exchange rates, inflation and disinflation: Latin American experiences', NBER Working Paper No. 4320 (April).

Edwards, S. (1993b) 'Openness, trade liberalization, and growth in developing countries', *Journal of Economic Literature*, 31(3) (Sept):1358–1393.

Edwards, S. and Edwards, A.C. (1987) *Monetarism and liberalization. The Chilean experience.* Cambridge, MA: Ballinger.

Edwards, S. and Tabellini, G. (1991) 'Explaining fiscal policy and inflation in developing countries', *Journal of International Money and Finance*, 10(5) (March supplement):S49–72.

Edwards, S. and van Wijnbergen, S. (1989) 'Disequilibrium and structural adjustment', in: H.B. Chenery and T.N. Srinivasan, eds., *Handbook of development economics*, Vol. II. New York: North-Holland.

Fernandez, R. and Rodrik, D. (1991) 'Resistance to reform: Status quo bias in the presence of individual-specific uncertainty', *American Economic Review*, 81(5) (Dec.):1146–1155.

Fischer, S. (1986) 'Exchange rate versus money targets in disinflation', in: S. Fischer, *Indexing, inflation and economic policy*. Cambridge, Mass: MIT Press.

Fischer, S. (1987) 'Issues in medium-term macroeconomic adjustment', *World Bank Research Observer*, 1(2) (July):163–182.

Fischer, S. (1988) 'Real balances, the exchange rate and indexation: Real variables in disinflation', *Quarterly Journal of Economics*, 103(1) (Feb.):27–50.

Fischer, S. (1991) 'Growth, macroeconomics, and development', in: O.J. Blanchard and S. Fischer, eds., *NBER Macroeconomics Annual*.

Fischer, S. and Easterly, W. (1990) 'Economics of the government budget constraint', *World Bank Research Observer*, 5:127–142.

Frank, C. et al. (1975) *Foreign trade regimes and economic development: South Korea*. New York: Columbia University Press.

Frenkel, J.A. (1983) 'Remarks on the Southern Cone', *IMF Staff Papers*, 30(1) (March):164–173.

Gelb, A. (1989) 'A cross-section analysis of financial policies, efficiency and growth', Manuscript, The World Bank.

Giovannini, A. (1985) 'Saving and the real interest rate in LDCs', *Journal of Development Economics* (Aug.) 18:197–217.

Goldstein, M. (1989) 'The International Monetary Fund and the developing countries: A critical evaluation', A comment', *Carnegie–Rochester conference series on public policy*, Vol. 31, Autumn:69–76.

Goldstein, M. and Montiel, P. (1986) 'Evaluating Fund stabilization programs with multicountry data: Some methodological pitfalls', *IMF Staff Papers*, 33(2):31–44.

Guitian, M. (1981) *Fund conditionality: Evolution of principles and practices.* IMF Pamphlet Series No. 38, Washington, DC.

Haberler, G. (1959) 'International trade and economic development', reprinted in: G. Haberler, *International trade and economic development*. San Francisco, CA: ICS Press:1988.

Haggard, S. and Kaufman, R., eds., (1992) *The politics of economic adjustment*. Princeton, NJ: Princeton University Press.

Haggard, S. and Webb, S.B. (1993) 'What do we know about the political economy of economic policy reform?', *World Bank Research Observer* 8(2) (July):143–168.

Haggard, S., Kaufman, R. and Webb, S.B. (1994) *Voting for reform: The politics of adjustment in new democracies.* New York: Oxford University Press.

Hamilton, J.D. and Flavin, M.A. (1986) 'On the limitations of government borrowing: A framework for empirical testing', *American Economic Review*, 76(4) (Sept.):808–819.

Haque, N.U., Montiel, P.J. and S. Symansky, (1991) 'A forward-looking macroeconomic simulation model for a developing country', in: M.S. Khan, P. Montiel and N. Haque, eds., *Macroeconomic models for adjustment in developing countries*. Washington, DC: IMF.

Harrigan, J. and Mosley, P. (1991) 'World Bank policy based lending: An evaluation', *Journal of Development Studies*, 27:63–94 April.

Heckman, J. (1978) 'Dummy endogenous variables in a simultaneous equation system', *Econometrica*, 46:931–60.

Helleiner, G. (1989) 'The IMF, the World Bank, and Africa's adjustment and external debt problems: An unofficial view', *World Development*, 20(6):779–792.

Helpman, E. (1989) 'The noncompetitive theory of international trade and trade policy', *Proceedings of the World Bank Annual Conference on Development Economics*: 193–216.

Heston, A. (1994) 'A brief review of some problems in using national accounts data in level comparisons and growth studies', *Journal of Development Economics*. 44 (June):29–52.

Kaplan, J.J. and Schleiminger, G. (1989) *The European Payments Union*. Oxford: Clarendon Press.

Kapur, I. et al. (1991) 'Ghana: Adjustment and growth, 1983–1991'. Occasional Paper #86, IMF, Washington, DC.

Keynes, J.M. (1923) *A tract on monetary reform*. Reprinted by the Royal Economic Society, London, 1971.

Khan, M. (1990) 'The macroeconomic effects of Fund-supported programs', *IMF Staff Papers*, 37(2).

King, R.G. and Levine, R. (1993) 'Finance, entrepreneurship, and growth: Theory and evidence', *Journal of Monetary Economics*, 32(3):513–542.

Kiguel, M. and Liviatan, N. (1992) 'The business cycle associated with exchange-rate-based stabilization', *World Bank Economic Review*, 6(2) (May):279–305.

Killick, T. (1984) 'The impact of Fund stabilization programs', in: T. Killick, ed., *The quest for economic stabilization: The IMF and the Third World*. New York: St. Martins Press.

Kim, K.S. and Roemer, M. (1979) *Growth and structural transformation*. Cambridge, MA: Harvard University Press.

Krueger, A. (1978) *Foreign trade regimes and economic development: Liberalization attempts and consequences*. Cambridge, MA: Ballinger.

Krueger, A. (1984) 'Problems of liberalization', in: A. Harberger, ed., *World economic growth*. San Francisco, CA: ICS Press.

Krueger, A. (1985) 'The experience and lessons of Asia's super exporters', in: V. Corbo, A.O. Krueger and F. Ossa, eds., *Export-oriented development strategies*. Boulder, CO: Westview Press.

Krueger, A. (1992) *Economic policy reform in developing countries*. Cambridge, MA: Blackwell.

Krueger, A. (1993) *Political economy of policy reform in developing countries*. Cambridge, MA: MIT Press.

Krugman, P. (1979) 'A model of balance-of-payments crises', *Journal of Money, Credit, and Banking*, 11(3) (Aug.):311–325.

Krugman, P. (1987) 'Is free trade passe?' *Journal of Economic Perspectives*, 1(2) (Fall):131–144.

Krugman, P. (1992) 'Adjustment in the world economy', in: P. Krugman, *Currencies and crises*. Cambridge, MA: MIT Press.

Krugman, P. (1993) 'What do we need to know about the international monetary system?' Essays in international finance #190, (July). Princeton University, International Finance Section.

Larrain, F. and Selowsky, M. (1991) *The public sector and the Latin American crisis*. San Francisco, CA: ICS Press.

Leechor, C. (1991) 'Ghana's adjustment program', in: V. Thomas et al., *Structural adjustment and the World Bank*. New York: Oxford University Press.

Leith, J.C. (1975) *Foreign trade regimes and economic development: Ghana*. New York: Columbia University Press.

Levine, R. and Renelt, D. (1990) 'A sensitivity analysis of cross-country growth regressions', Manuscript, The World Bank.

Little, I., Scitovsky, T. and Scott, M. (1970) *Industry and trade in some developing countries: A comparative analysis*. London: Oxford University Press.

Lucas, R. (1988) 'On the mechanics of economic development', *Journal of Monetary Economics*, 22(1):3–12.

Maasland, A. and van der Gaag, J. (1992) 'World-Bank supported adjustment programs and living standards', in: Corbo, Fischer and Webb, eds., op cit.

Mankiw, N.G. (1987) 'The optimal collection of seignorage', *Journal of Monetary Economics*, 20(2) (Sept.):327–341.

McKinnon, R. (1973) *Money and capital in economic development*. Washington, DC: Brookings Institution.

McKinnon, R. (1991) *The order of liberalization*. Baltimore, MD: Johns Hopkins University Press.

McMillan, J. and Naughton, B. (1992) 'How to reform a planned economy: Lessons from China', *Oxford Review of Economic Policy*, 8(1):130–143.

Michaely, M., Papageorgiou, D. and Choksi, A.M. (1991) *Liberalizing foreign trade: Lessons of experience in the developing world*. Cambridge, MA: Basil Blackwell.

Mondino, G., Sturzenegger, F. and Tommasi, M. (1992) 'Recurrent high inflation and stabilization: A dynamic game', UCLA, mimeo.

Morandé, F. (1988) 'Apreciación del peso y entrada de capitales externos, Cuál viene antes?', in: F. Morandé and K. Schmidt-Hebbel, eds., *Del auge a la crisis de 1982*, Instituto Interamericano de Mercados de Capital and ILADES, Georgetown University.

Mosley, P. (1992) 'A theory of conditionality', in: P. Mosley, ed., *Development finance and policy reform*. New York, NY: St. Martin's Press.

Mosley, P. et al. ( 1991) *Aid and power: The World Bank and policy-based lending in the 1980s*, (2 volumes). London: Routledge.

Nam, C.H. (1985) 'Trade policy and economic development in Korea', Discussion Paper 9. Seoul: Korea University.

Nelson, J., ed., (1990) *Economic crisis and policy choice: The politics of adjustment in the Third World*. Princeton, NJ: Princeton University Press.

Nishimizu, M. and Page, J. (1991) 'Trade policy, market orientation and productivity change in industry', in: J. de Melo and A. Sapir, *Trade theory and economic reform: North, South and East*. Cambridge, MA: Basil Blackwell.

Organization for Economic Cooperation and Development (1988). *Structural adjustment and economic performance*. Paris: OECD.

Pastor, R. (1987) 'The effects of IMF programs in the third world: Debate and evidence from Latin America', *World Development*, 15:249–262.

Patinkin, D. (1956) *Money, interest and prices*. Evanston, IL: Row Peterson & Co.

Przeworski, A. (1991) *Democracy and the market: Political and economic reforms in Eastern Europe and Latin America*. New York: Cambridge University Press.

Ramos, J. (1986) *Neoconservative economics in the southern cone of Latin America, 1973–1983* (Chap. 8). Baltimore, MD: Johns Hopkins University Press.

Reichmann, T. and Stillson, R. (1978) 'Experience with programs of balance of payments adjustment: Stand-by arrangements in the higher credit tranches, 1963–1972', *IMF Staff Papers*, 25:293–309.

Rodrik, D. (1989) 'Policy uncertainty and private investment in developing countries', NBER Working paper #2999, Cambridge, MA.

Rodrik, D. (1990) 'How should structural adjustment programs be designed?' *World Development*, 18(7):933–947.

Rodrik, D. (1993) 'The positive economics of policy reform', *American Economic Review, Papers and Proceedings*, 83(2) (May):356–361.

Rodrik, D. Chapter 45 in this volume.

Romer, P. (1986) 'Increasing returns and long-run growth', *Journal of Political Economy*, 94(5) (Oct.):1002–1037.

Romer, P. (1990) 'Endogenous technological change', *Journal of Political Economy*, 98(5) (Part 2) (Oct.):S71–S102

Sachs, J.D. (1987) 'Trade and exchange rate policies in growth-oriented adjustment programs', in: V. Corbo, M. Goldstein and M. Khan, eds. *Growth-oriented adjustment programs*. Washington, DC: IMF and The World Bank.

Salter, W.E.G. (1959) 'Internal and external balance: The role of price and expenditure effects', *Economic Record*, 35 (Aug.):226–238.

Sargent, T. (1982) 'The ends of four big inflations', in R.E. Hall, ed., *Inflation: Causes and Effects.* Chicago: University of Chicago Press.

Sargent, T. (1983) 'Poincare and Mrs. Thatcher', in: R. Dornbusch and M.H. Simonsen, eds., *Inflation, debt and indexation.* Cambridge, MA: MIT Press.

Scitovsky, T. (1990) 'Economic development in Taiwan and South Korea:1961–1981', in: L.J. Lau, ed., *Models of development.* San Francisco, CA: ICS Press.

Schmidt-Hebbel, K. and Serven, L. (1993) 'Dynamic response to external shocks in classical and Keynesian economics', in: D. Currie and D. Vines, eds., *North-South linkages and international macroeconomic policy.* Cambridge, UK: Cambridge University Press.

Serven, L. and Solimano, A. (1992) 'Private investment and macroeconomic adjustment: A survey', *World Bank Research Observer*, 7 (Jan.):95–114.

Simonsen, M.H. (1983) 'Indexation: Current theory and the Brazilian experience', in: R. Dornbusch and M.H. Simonsen, eds., *Inflation, debt and indexation.* Cambridge, MA: MIT Press.

Solimano, A. (1990) 'Inflation and the costs of stabilization: Historical and recent experiences and policy lessons', *World Bank Research Observer*, 5(2) (July):167–186.

Srinivasan, T.N. (1994) 'Data base for development analysis: An overview', *Journal of Development Economics.* 44 (June):3–27.

Stern, E. (1983) 'World Bank financing of structural adjustment', in: J. Williamson, ed., *IMF Conditionality.* Washington, DC: Institute for International Economics.

Stiglitz, J.E. (1993) 'The role of the state in financial markets', *World Bank Annual Conference on Development Economics.*

Suh, S.M. (1992) 'The economy in historical perspective', in: V. Corbo and S.M. Suh, ed., *Structural adjustment in a newly industrialized country: The Korean experience.* Baltimore, MD: Johns Hopkins University Press.

Swan, T. (1963) 'Economic control in a dependent economy', *Economic Record*, 36:51–66.

Tanzi, V. (1977) 'Inflation, lage in collection, and the real value of tax revenues', *IMF Staff Papers*, 24(2) (March):154–167.

Taylor, L. (1988) *Varieties of stabilization experience: Towards sensible macroeconomics in the Third World.* Oxford: Clarendon Press.

Thomas, V., Matin, K.M. and Nash, J. (1990) *Lessons in trade policy reform.* Policy research paper 2, The World Bank, Washington, DC.

Thomas, W.J. and Grindle, M.S. (1991) *Public choices and policy change: The political economy of reform in developing countries.* Baltimore, MD: Johns Hopkins University Press.

Tsiang, S.C. (1985) 'Foreign trade and investment as boosters for take-off: The experience of Taiwan', in: V. Corbo, A.O. Krueger, and F. Ossa, eds., *Export-oriented development strategies.* Boulder, CO: Westview Press.

United Nations, Economic Commission for Africa (1989) 'Statistics and policies: ECA preliminary observations on the World Bank report: 'Africa's adjustment and growth in the 1980s', Addis Ababa, United Nations.

Vegh, C.A. (1992) 'Stopping high inflation: An analytical overview', *IMF Staff Papers*, 39(3) (Sept.):626–695.

Villanueva, D. and Mirakhor, A. (1990) 'Strategies for financial reforms', *IMF Staff Papers*, 37(3) (Sept.):509–536.

Viner, J. (1953) *International trade and economic development.* Oxford: Clarendon Press.

Wade, R. (1990) *Governing the market.* Princeton: NJ: Princeton University Press.

Webb, S.B. and Shariff, K. (1992) 'Designing and implementing adjustment programs', in: Corbo, Fischer and Webb (op cit).

Westphal, L. (1978) 'Republic of Korea's experience with export-led industrial development', *World Development*:6 (3).

Wilcox, D.W. (1989) 'The sustainability of government deficits: Implications of the present-value borrowing constraint', *Journal of Money, Credit and Banking*, 21(3) (Aug.):291–306.

Williamson, J. (1994) *The political economy of policy reform.* Washington, DC: Institute for International Economics.

World Bank (1980) 'Lending for "Structural adjustment"', Memorandum to the Board, R80–17, February 5.

World Bank (1988) *Adjustment lending: An evaluation of ten years of experience*. Policy and Research Series Paper 1.

World Bank (1989) *World Development Report*.

World Bank (1990) *Adjustment lending policies for sustainable growth*. Policy and Research Series Paper 14.

World Bank (1991) *World Development Report*.

World Bank (1992) *Adjustment lending and mobilization of private and public resources for growth*. Policy and Research series Paper 22.

World Bank (1993a) *The East Asian miracle: Economic growth and public policy*. New York: Oxford University Press.

World Bank (1993b) *Adjustment in Africa: Reform, results and the road ahead*, Oxford University Press.

*Chapter 45*

# TRADE AND INDUSTRIAL POLICY REFORM

DANI RODRIK*

*Columbia University, CEPR, and NBER*

## Contents

* I am grateful to Izak Atiyas, Ann Harrison, and James Tybout for helpful conversations, and to Alice Amsden, Gene Grossman, Gerry Helleiner, Augustine Tan, Larry Westphal, and the editors for comments on an earlier draft.

*Handbook of Development Economics, Volume III, Edited by J. Behrman and T.N. Srinivasan*
© *Elsevier Science B.V., 1995*

**Contents** (continued)

## 1. Introduction

A decade or two from now, the 1980s will probably be remembered as the time when two significant, and not unrelated, set of events ocurred. First, much of the developing world, including a majority of countries in Latin America and Africa, became engulfed in a debt and macroeconomic crisis of major proportions. Per capita income scarcely grew, and, in many countries, declined over the course of the decade. It became commonplace to call this the "lost decade" for development.

But maybe not all was lost. For the second major feature of the decade was that in scores of countries, the inward-oriented, import-substituting policies of the past came under critical scrutiny from policy makers – often from the same government leaders who had enthusiastically espoused and implemented the older policies. By the end of the decade, the anti-export and anti-private enterprise bias of the prevailing policy regimes was largely discredited. Public enterprise, industrial promotion, and trade protection were out; privatization, industrial de-regulation, and free trade were in.

This paper is an attempt to review what we know about the consequences of these policy reforms. I try to cover in equal measure both theory and evidence, as it is only the interplay of the two that allows us to comprehend and interpret the world around us. Just as theory without facts is vacuous, a search for evidence in the absence of a sound conceptual framework yields unintelligible results. Research on policy reform has not been short on either theory or evidence, even though, as we shall see, there is still a need for systematic empirical studies on the consequences of the recent round of reforms. My focus is strictly on trade and industrial policies; macroeconomic stabilization issues are touched upon only to the extent that they impinge on microeconomic reforms. Further, I will emphasize the more recent literature.

Since the World Bank has been intimately involved in the policy reforms of the 1980s through its Structural Adjustment Loans, I begin the survey by considering the role of the World Bank and the concept of "structural adjustment". In the following section (Section 3), I briefly discuss the nature of the policies to be reformed. Section 4 is devoted to the rationale for trade and industrial policy reform. I identify four basic arguments: (i) improvements in static resource allocation; (ii) dynamic benefits in the form of learning and growth; (iii) improved flexibility in face of external shocks; and (iv) reduced rent-seeking. I discuss critically the theory and evidence that underlie each one of these arguments.

Sections 5 and 6 turn to two sources of "heterodoxy". First, I discuss recent revisionist accounts of the East Asian experience (Section 5). These accounts have stressed the positive role of government intervention in trade and industry, and sit uncomfortably with the orthodox emphasis on restricting the government's role. Section 6 covers recent models with imperfect competition. These models, developed in part in response to the challenge posed by East Asia to received theory, provide increased latitude for government intervention, on account of both static and dynamic effects. Section 7 is devoted to the literature on the strategy of reform, and covers recent contributions including those in the theories of piecemeal reform, timing and sequencing of reform, credibility, and political economy. Section 8 reviews the available evidence on the consequences of the reforms of the 1980s, paying particular attention to the supply response, and to static and dynamic efficiency. In Section 9, I offer some brief concluding remarks.

## 2. Policy reform, structural adjustment and the World Bank

During the 1980s, the term "structural adjustment" became virtually another name for policy reform. Almost all major episodes of policy reform during this period in the developing world were instigated and/or supported by Structural Adjustment Loans (SALs) from the World Bank. The reforms usually took place in the context of intense policy dialogues with the World Bank – as well as with the International Monetary Fund, which began to disburse medium-term assistance under its own Extended, Structural Adjustment, and Enhanced Structural Adjustment facilities. The policy dialogue with the Bretton Woods institutions, along with the conditionality that goes with the latter's lending, helps account for the remarkable uniformity that has characterized the reformists' agenda. Wherever reforms were attempted, the words "structural adjustment" became the code used to describe and legitimize them, and liberalization and outward orientation the main strategies employed. Williamson (1990) has termed this agenda the "Washington consensus".[1] Perhaps the only important exception was China, where policy developments were insulated from World Bank and IMF conditionality. But even here, the ongoing reforms since 1978 have unmistakably moved the economy in the direction of greater use of the market mechanism and private incentives, and of greater export orientation.

The role played by the World Bank in the reforms of the 1980s has been chronicled and analyzed in a number of different sources, notably by World Bank staff themselves. Thomas et al. (1991) and Corbo, Fischer, and Webb

---

[1] However, he later came to regret the implication that the choices made by reformists all over the developing world were in fact derived from a consensus reached in Washington, D.C. [Williamson (1992)].

(1992) present useful compilations of Bank studies, focusing on the effectiveness of adjustment lending. A comparable independent study including case studies is that by Mosley, Harrigan, and Toye (1991).

According to Ernest Stern, a vice president of the World Bank who was closely involved in the development of SALs, interest in such lending arose from the frustration felt in the Bank in the aftermath of the second oil shock regarding the lack of real involvement in country policies, despite substantial commitment of resources in the form of project assistance:

> Initially our thinking focused on the ways to help countries develop greater export capacity, . . . When we started, however, we were quite naive about just how profoundly distorted the development strategies of many of the developing countries were. . . . [These countries] must begin to move from highly distorted price incentives and investment frameworks to something more stable, more oriented to the market system of prices, and more open and less protected. [E. Stern (1991, 1–2)]

Hence, even though the origin of SALs lay in the external payments crisis brought on by the two rounds of oil shocks in the 1970s, the Bank's attention soon turned to correcting microeconomic distortions. Indeed, it became common to view the subsequent debt crisis of 1982 as "one of the symptoms of these distortions", as Stern himself put it (1991, 2).

The goals set forth for SALs, therefore, covered both macroeconomic stabilization and microeconomic reforms. As Thomas et al. put it:

> Two types of policy response, both labeled "adjustment", were called for [to deal with the external shocks of the later 1970s and the early 1980s]. The first was stabilization, or managed reductions in expenditures to bring about an orderly adjustment of domestic demand to the reduced level of external resources available to the country. The second was structural adjustment, or changes in relative prices and institutions designed to make the economy more efficient, more flexible, and better able to use resources and so to engineer sustainable long-term growth. It was envisioned that effective structural adjustment measures would reduce the necessary extent of stabilization. (1991, 11)

Contrast this definition of structural adjustment with the following one by Streeten:

> The essence of development is structural adjustment: from country to town, from agriculture to industry, from production for household consumption to production for markets, from largely domestic trade to a higher ratio of foreign trade. . . . In this very general sense, development is synonymous with structural adjustment and a paper on structural adjustment would be a paper on development. (1989, 3)

While one cannot help but agree with Streeten, I will use the term structural adjustment in the narrower sense used by Thomas et al.[2] In particular, I will focus on structural adjustment *policies*, i.e. policies aimed at improving an economy's efficiency and its long-term growth. Macroeconomic stabilization policies, aimed at price stability and overall balance between an economy's resources and its expenditures, are covered in the chapter by Corbo and Fischer. However, as will become clear, it is not always easy to draw clear distinctions between stabilization and structural measures.

## 3. What is to be reformed?

An exhaustive list of the policies that came under attack by the reformers would fill volumes, as does indeed any official catalogue describing the industrial incentive regime in a typical import-substituting country. In trade policy, the reforms were directed at licensing and other quantitative restrictions, high and extremely differentiated tariff rates, export taxes, and burdensome bureaucratic requirements and paperwork. In industrial policy, the targets were inefficent and loss-making public enterprises, entry and exit restrictions on private enterprise, price controls, discretionary tax and subsidy policies, and soft-budget constraints.

The best quantitative picture of the state of trade protection in developing countries is provided in Erzan et al. (1989). These authors provide a snapshot of tariff and non-tariff barriers in some 50 developing countries as of the mid-1980s. They list sectoral average tariff rates, as well as coverage ratios for non-tariff measures such as licenses, quotas and advanced import deposits. See also Kostecki and Tymowski (1985) for a review of import charges (other than customs duties) and a calculation of their ad-valorem equivalents in a smaller group of developing countries. Prevailing industrial policies are discussed, more qualitatively, in Dervis and Page (1984) Frischtak (1989), and Meier and Steel (1989). De Soto (1989) provides an influential account of the burdens imposed on private-sector activity by bureaucratic regulations and paperwork in Latin America, particularly where small business is concerned.

Policy discussions on trade policy were much influenced by the early work directed by Little, Scitovsky, and Scott (1970), Balassa (1971), and Bhagwati

---

[2] An even narrower definition is given by Edwards and van Wijnbergen (1989, p. 1482): "A structural adjustment program can be defined as a set of policy measures that attempts to permanently change relative prices of *tradeable to nontradeable goods* in the economy, in order to reallocate, or help along reallocation of, production factors in accordance with the new set of external and domestic economic conditions" (emphasis added). By focussing only on one key relative price, and the one that is most directly influenced by the exchange rate at that, this definition presents a somewhat incomplete picture of the microeconomic changes typically called for in the Bank's structural adjustment programs.

(1978) and Krueger (1978). These studies undertook quantitative descriptions and evaluations of trade regimes, notably by measuring effective rates of protection in developing countries. They demonstrated that the existing policies had resulted in haphazard and often inordinately high levels of protection, hard to reconcile with policymakers' stated objectives.

More recently, Krueger, Schiff and Valdes (1991) have completed a multi-volume study on agricultural pricing policy that promises to do for agriculture what this earlier work has done for trade policy in industry. These authors quantify the effects of policy interventions on agriculture, taking into account both direct effects (i.e. sector-specific interventions) and indirect effects (i.e. those arising from trade restrictions on manufactures and from induced changes in the equilibrium exchange rate). They document the existence of a large disincentive for agricultural production, with the explicit and implicit taxation of agriculture ranging from 25 percent in the case of Asian and Mediterranean countries to more than 50 percent in sub-Saharan African countries. Interestingly, Krueger et al. find that most of this tax originates not from direct interventions, but from the general-equilibrium implications of industrial protection and overvalued exchange rates [for a summary of their findings, see Krueger, Schiff, and Valdes (1988)]. In a sense, then, what these authors have documented is the flip side of the earlier industrial protection studies referred to above.

## 4. Why reform? The rationales for policy reform

By the late 1970s, the studies mentioned above on trade and industrialization policies had gradually erected a formidable case for policy reform in developing countries. The indisputable success of South Korea, Taiwan, Singapore and Hong Kong with what appeared to be market-oriented policies strengthened the argument (see below, however). Perhaps the clincher was that the external-payments crisis originating from the debt debacle made policy change unavoidable. However, it was by no means clear that change would take the form of liberalization: the first impulse of policy makers confronting a balance-of-payments crisis is typically to tighten quotas and impose foreign exchange rationing. That the 1980s eventually turned out differently was partly due to the fact that policy makers learned from their past mistakes. But there were other reasons as well: (i) World Bank and IMF conditionality ruled out access to external financing in the absence of at least some lip-service to reform; (ii) the depth and persistence of the macroeconomic crisis relegated to second-place distributional considerations that would have blocked microeconomic reforms in more normal times (Rodrik, 1992a).

There are four basic arguments in favor of market-oriented policy reform: (i) economic liberalization reduces static inefficiencies arising from resource misallocation and waste; (ii) economic liberalization enhances learning, technological change, and economic growth; (iii) outward-oriented economies are better able to cope with adverse external shocks; (iv) market-based economic systems are less prone to wasteful rent-seeking activities. While all four of these arguments are used widely, it is the last three that have dominated the discussion on structural adjustment policies. This is understandable since the benefits on account of the first, basically some Harberger triangles, are quantitatively minor compared to the benefits arising from the others, which usually are sizable rectangles. However, by and large, only the first of these arguments is solidly grounded in accepted economic theory.[3]

### 4.1. Static effects: Resource mis-allocation

The efficiency costs of import-substitution policies, encompassing most notably high levels of trade protection and industrial regulation, were documented extensively in the studies cited above [Little, Scitovsky, and Scott (1970), Balassa (1971), Bhagwati (1978), and Krueger (1978)]. These policies had encouraged the development of industries that were high-cost, and did little to ensure that productivity would increase over time. The resulting pattern of specialization became divorced from comparative advantage. From the perspective of resource allocation, the effects were anti-export, anti-agriculture, anti-labor, and anti-newcomers in industry.

The literature on these issues is broad, and it is impossible to provide a complete list of references. On the employment consequences of trade regimes, see in particular Krueger (1983). The dismal export performance of sub-Saharan African countries is reviewed by Svedberg (1991), who traces its roots largely to domestic economic policies. The consequences of industrial regulations are discussed in Frischtak (1989), and Meier and Steel (1989). Two recent sources on India's infamous industrial regime are Pursell (1990) and Bhagwati (1993). For additional references on the earlier literature, see the surveys by Pack (1988) and Bruton (1989).

While the theoretical and empirical arguments for the resource misallocation costs of the import-substitution syndrome are strong, it is much harder to make a compelling case regarding the *magnitude* of these costs. Reasonable estimates of the welfare cost of relative-price distortions under usual neoclassical assumptions rarely produce numbers in excess of a couple of percentage points

---

[3] My four-fold classification is not meant to be entirely exhaustive. An additional rationale for trade and industrial policy reform is improved capacity utilization in the face of bottlenecks and macroeconomic policy failures. However, as the qualifiers in the previous sentence indicate, I do not consider this to be as "basic" an argument as the others I have included.

of GNP [see, for example, Srinivasan and Whalley (1986)]. Moreover, when distortions get too large, the emergence of parallel and black markets tend to alleviate the welfare costs [see Roemer and Jones 1991)]. How, then, can such small numbers be reconciled with the large and growing performance gap between import-substituting countries and the outward-oriented countries of East Asia? To provide an answer, it is common to turn to explanations that go beyond static allocative-efficiency.

## 4.2. Dynamic effects: Technical change, learning, and growth

Import-substituting industrialization policy was supposed to enhance technological capabilities and economic growth. That it failed to do so, while outward-oriented East Asian countries continued to grow at phenomenal rates, suggested to many economists not only that the infant-industry position was untenable, but that it had it exactly backwards. The anti-export and anti-competition bias of prevailing policies, the argument now went, discouraged innovation, cost-cutting, the acquisition of technological capabilities, and therefore eventual growth. Correcting these biases would remove the technological disincentives. A representative statement is from Balassa (1988, 45):

> It has often been observed that [monopolies and oligopolies] prefer a "quiet life" to innovative activity, which entails risk and uncertainty. In turn, the carrot and stick of competition gives inducement for technological change. For one thing, in creating competition for domestic products in home markets, imports provide incentives for firms to improve their operations. For another thing, in response to competition in foreign markets, exporting firms try to keep up with modern technology in order to maintain or improve their market position.

This view became conventional wisdom as a retrospective explanation of the East Asian success, as well as a prospective argument for removal of distortions in other developing countries.

The analytical foundations of such arguments regarding the dynamic benefits of liberalization have never been too clear. Too often, the preferred method of proof is a casual appeal to common sense. In particular, no distinctions are typically made between policies for which received theory is silent as regards learning (or has ambiguous implications), and those for which a definite theoretical presumption exists.

Relative-price distortions, such as trade taxes and investment subsidies, are of the first kind. Such distortions affect *relative* profitabilities across industries and sectors. If learning in some sectors is adversely affected by intervention, others must be left in better shape. Consequently, even if changes in a sector's profitability could be presumed to have unambiguous consequences for innovative activity (which they do not), the *net* change in economy-wide innovation would still be unpredictable. Innovative activity would be reduced in some sector, but enhanced in others.

This argument applies equally well to X-efficiency: if tariffs encourage entrepreneurial slack in import-competing sectors because they increase such sectors' relative prices, by the same logic they must reduce slack in export-oriented sectors [Rodrik (1992b)]. Moreover, Balassa's statement above notwithstanding, the a priori relationship between the degree of product-market competition and innovative activity is by no means clear; for the state of the debate in the advanced-country context, see Nalebuff and Stiglitz (1983), Hart (1983), and Scharfstein (1988). Neither is it clear whether the inadequacy of incentives to upgrade quality due to informational externalities call for policy intervention [as in Bagwell and Staiger (1989)] or are aggravated by it [as in Grossman and Horn (1988)].

To rescue the conventional wisdom, one needs to resort in each case to finer arguments and special assumptions that are rarely made clear. An early exception is Corden (1974, 224–231), who dissected many of the arguments linking trade policy to cost-cutting incentives and showed their fragility. Developments in the theories of industrial organization and growth have now made learning and technical change more amenable to analysis, and some recent contributions will be reviewed in Section 6.3.

In the second group are trade and industrial policies that have unambiguously deleterious consequences for learning and technological capability. Some prominent examples are as follows. Domestic price controls on industrial commodities like steel discourage innovation and quality upgrading because they lead to excess demand; in the presence of excess demand, firms have no need to increase demand for their product by improving it [see Perez and Peniche (1987), for the case of Mexican steel[4]]. Soft-budget constraint policies similarly discourage innovation in a number of ways: when profits are taxed on the basis of ex post profitability, the benefits of any innovation are shared with the government; when the government stands ready to bail out a loss-making enterprise, it discourages the adoption of technologies that may otherwise render the firm viable [Atiyas, Dutz, and Frischtak (1992, 16–17)]. Entry and exit restrictions, through capacity licensing or prohibition of layoffs, prevent more efficient newcomers from replacing less efficient ones. More directly pernicious are restrictions on imports of technology and capital goods, and local-purchase requirements forcing firms to use inferior inputs and equipment

---

[4] The authors quote the owner of the company they studied as saying that if the sun were not visible through the steel sheets, they could be sold.

(as is common in many countries that prohibit imports when domestic substitutes exist). See Lall (1987) for relevant evidence from India.

There is a wide array of empirical evidence that has been brought to bear on these issues and to test, in particular, the hypothesized cause-and-effect relationship between protection and poor technological performance. However, since the conceptual issues are rarely sorted out as a prelude to empirical analysis, the results of these exercises are difficult to interpret. There are three types of empirical evidence that deserve mention: (i) firm-level case studies; (ii) cross-industry studies of technical efficiency and productivity change, and (iii) cross-country studies of economic growth. I will briefly discuss each in turn.

### 4.2.1. Firm-level case studies of technological change

Several in-depth case studies of technological change and learning have been carried out at the firm level, and the results are described in a number of sources, including Katz (1987), Lall (1987), and Pack (1987). See Levy (1991) for case studies of learning related to export markets among Taiwanese and Korean footwear producers. Pack (1992) provides an overview and survey of the firm-level literature on technical change. These studies show that there is a considerable amount of technological tinkering that goes on even when firms are cut off from foreign markets. They do not, however, lead to any easy generalizations regarding the extent to which trade regimes affect the pace of learning. In fact, it is easy to read the case evidence in very different ways: Katz (1987) concludes from his and his collaborators' studies that reducing costs has not been a high-priority for Latin American firms because of high levels of trade protection and little internal competition; the author of one of those studies, however, provides evidence that it was firms which could rely on steady growth in captive domestic markets that undertook the highest levels of technical effort [Pearson (1987, p. 421)].

### 4.2.2. Cross-industry studies of technical efficiency and productivity change

There exist a number of studies that correlate aspects of policy regimes with measured changes in total factor productivity (TFP) at the industry level. Among the most notable of these are Krueger and Tuncer (1982a), Nishimizu and Robinson (1984), Nishimizu and Page (1991).

Krueger and Tuncer (1982a) find that, on average, periods of slower TFP growth in Turkish industry coincided with period in which the trade regime was more restrictive. Drawing on data from Korea, Turkey, Japan, and Yugoslavia, Nishimizu and Robinson (1984) relate the increase in sectoral TFP to sources of demand growth, including export expansion and import substitution. They find a preponderance of cases where export expansion is positively associated, and import substitution negatively associated, with TFP growth. They caution specifically, however, that no causality can be attributed to these results. Nishimizu and Page (1991) analyze a panel of industries from several countries and regress TFP growth on country characteristics. They find that export growth is positively correlated with TFP growth, but only in economies that follow "market-oriented policies". However, they also find that import penetration was negatively correlated with TFP performance in the same economies in the post-1973 period. Naturally, the same comment about causality applies to this study as well.

There have not been many studies that have attempted to test the infant-industry hypothesis directly. A well-known paper by Krueger and Tuncer (1982b) compares sectoral TFP growth rates in cross-section of Turkish industries, and reports that there was no systematic tendency for more protected industries to have had higher TFP growth than less protected industries.[5] Strictly speaking, the authors' method does not constitute an appropriate test of the infant-industry argument. Such a test would require a counterfactual regarding the TFP path that the protected industries would have followed in the absence of protection; the implicit assumption that the less protected industries provide the appropriate counterfactual is not compelling.[6] Along similar lines, Dollar and Sokoloff (1990) analyze TFP growth in South Korean manufacturing industries (over the period 1963–1979), and find productivity increase to play a smaller role in the growth of heavy industries than in the growth of light and medium industries. They speculate that the reason may have to do with the prevalence of credit subsidies for heavy industries, which would have encouraged capital deepening. On the other hand, Waverman and Murphy's (1992) study of TFP growth in the automobile sectors of four countries – Argentina, Mexico, Korea, and Canada – provides a more mixed picture. Judged by the yardstick of TFP growth, the second most successful country during the 1970s was Argentina (after Korea), the most closed of the four economies. Waverman and Murphy find TFP growth to have been high in Argentina both during its trade-liberalization period (1978–1981)

---

[5] Actually, a closer look at their data leads to a conclusion more favorable to protection. Krueger and Tuncer report data on three measures of protection and two measures of productivity growth. The only correlations that are statistically significant at a 10 percent confidence level between these types of indicators are two *positive* correlations between a measure of protection and a measure of productivity growth. Moreover, one of these is statistically significant at the 1 percent level. I am grateful to Ann Harrison for this information.

[6] Krueger and Tuncer claim (1982b): "... in order for infant industry considerations to have warranted intervention in favor of industry $i$, costs per unit of output must have fallen more in $i$ than in $k$" (1145). This is not quite right. One can imagine a situation where dynamic learning externalities in industry $i$ call for intervention, but once these externalities are appropriately internalized via policy, productivity still grows slower than in other industries.

and earlier. Other, more informal evidence on infant industries are surveyed in Bell, Ross-Larson, and Westphal (1984), who suggest that the evidence is rather damaging to the case for infant-industry protection.

The above studies can be criticized for not being able to control for industry or country effects that exert an independent influence on productivity. Two firm-level studies of the Taiwanese electronics industry avoid some of these problems. Chen and Tang (1987) compare the level of technical efficiency (as measured by distance from an estimated production frontier) in two groups of firms, one that comprises firms that are constrained to export all their output, and one that includes firms that are allowed to service the protected domestic market. They find that the former group exhibits a higher level of technical efficiency than the latter. Disaggregating by four-digit product categories, Aw and Hwang (1994) find a similar result: firms that sell their output primarily in the export market tend to have higher technical efficiency than those that sell primarily in the domestic market. However, the interpretation of these results is open to question also. In both studies, causality could be running from efficiency to export orientation, rather than the other way around. For example, there is reason to suspect that the two samples of firms in Chen and Tang (1987) would be subject to selection bias: since firms know which policy regime they are going to be operating under, it would seem obvious that only firms that had reasonably high estimates of their efficiency would submit themselves to the exports-only regime.

The only paper that I am aware of which has attempted to confront this causality issue head on is Aw and Batra (1993). These authors use firm-level Taiwanese data (which include figures on R&D spending), treating both the export and technological effort decisions as endogenous. A bivariate probit estimation yields the result that export orientation has no causal effect on technical efficiency in firms that report some spending on R&D ("high-tech" firms), while it has a positive effect in those that do not ("low-tech" firms).

A paper by J.-W. Lee (1992) is significant because it focuses on the productivity consequences of Korea's industrial policy, which has been the subject of great debate (see Section 5). Lee constructs sectoral estimates of tariff and non-tariff barriers, tax incentives, and credit subsidies. His econometric analysis covers a panel of 38 Korean manufacturing sectors over four 5-year periods (during 1963–1983). He finds sectoral TFP growth rates to be negatively and statistically significantly correlated with non-tariff barriers, but positively and significantly correlated with tax incentives. These findings are interesting, as well as puzzling. It is difficult to reconcile the two sets of results theoretically, suggesting perhaps that differences in the implementation of these interventions may have had something to do with the findings.

Other empirical studies of how contacts with the outside world influence domestic technological performance include Katrak (1989), Aitken and Harrison (1992), and Prasnikar, Svejnar, and Klinedinst (1992). Katrak finds a positive relationship between the amount of imported technology and domestic in-house R&D in Indian enterprises. Aitken and Harrison look for evidence of spillovers at the plant level from foreign subsidiaries to local firms in a panel drawn from Venezuela. They find no indication that foreign presence helps domestically-owned plants' productivity. Prasnikar et al. is a plant-level econometric study of the determinants of technical efficiency in the former Yugoslavia. This study finds no evidence that export orientation or the presence of joint ventures with foreigners had beneficial effects on technical efficiency. See the chapter by Evenson and Westphal in this volume for a more complete discussion of the related literature.

Finally, a recent group of papers has been devoted specifically to the experiences of countries undergoing structural adjustment programs, and has paid close attention to econometric and conceptual issues. These papers will be discussed when we turn to the results of recent policy reforms.

### 4.2.3. Cross-country studies of economic growth

A large number of cross-crountry studies have looked at the relationship between economic growth and some measure of trade policy and/or price distortions, using various controls on the right-hand side of the regression. These studies generally conclude that openness has been conducive to higher growth.

The immediate problem in such regressions is coming up with an appropriate indicator of trade policy that would rank countries consistently among each other from least open to most open. Many candidate indicators exist, including trade shares, tariff and non-tariff measures, and residuals from factor-endowments models of trade patterns. Pritchett (1991) reviews and discusses some of the better-known measures.[7] His disturbing conclusion is that there is virtually no statistically significant positive correlation among them. Secondly, there is the usual problem of attributing causality: if governments routinely tighten restrictions when economic performance becomes worse, statistical analysis will pick up a spurious relationship between distortions and growth. This may happen even in the absence of conscious government policy. Under a fixed exchange rate, for example, the black-market premium will endogenously increase in response to a foreign-exchange crisis. If such crises are associated

---

[7] Pritchett limits his attention to "objective" measures of outward orientation. These include: the share of trade in GDP, adjusted for country characteristics and factor endowments; the average tariff and coverage ratio of non-tariff barriers; measures of deviation of actual trade patterns from the pattern predicted from a model of resource based comparative advantage; measures of real price distortions.

with lower growth, the analyst will uncover a negative relationship between the black-market premium (the trade distortion variable) and economic growth.

Hence, most of the indicators that have been used can be criticized on conceptual or empirical grounds. Balassa (1978), Feder (1983), Michaely (1977), Syrquin and Chenery (1989) and Easterly (1992) use exports (either their growth rate or their share in income) as the indicator of openness. This raises problems of endogeneity and reverse causality [Jung and Marshall (1985), Esfahani (1991)]. Alam (1987) and Easterly (1992) use the trade orientation index presented in World Bank (1987), which has been criticized as being misleading and biased [Taylor (1991), p. 107)]. Edwards (1992) uses a measure of openness computed by Leamer (1988), which attributes *all* of the residual from a cross-country factor-endowments model to government inter-vention and has serious shortcomings in the way it ranks certain countries.[8] De Long and Summers (1991) use a range of measures, among which a dummy for high levels of effective rates protection (>40%) and the World Bank (1987) trade orientation index are found to exert an independent negative effect on growth. Easterly (1993) uses a measure based on the variance of relative prices of investment goods across commodities. Barro (1991) and Dollar (1992) use the deviation of the local price level from purchasing power parity (in the case of Barro, only with respect to investment goods), derived from Heston and Summers (1988).[9]

The last method deserves separate comment, as it appears at first sight to yield an intuitive and objective measure of openness and price distortions, and has received considerable attention. What Dollar (1992) does specifically is to take a ten-year average for each country of the deviation in its price level from that of the U.S. The systematic component of cross-country differences in non-tradeables prices is purged, to the extent possible, by regressing price levels on national income.[10] Dollar claims that "a country maintaining a high price level over many years would clearly have to be a country with a relatively large amount of protection (inward orientation)" (525–526). However, it is not uncommon for countries to maintain overvalued exchange rates (as measured

---

[8] For example, one of Leamer's measures (the scaled regression-based openness measure) ranks countries like Morocco, Indonesia and Ivory Coast as more open than countries like Canada and the U.S. While Edwards (1992) limits his sample to developing countries, such anomalies reflect the inadequacy of the basic method. Leamer himself remains doubtful about his results: "As I examine these results, I am left with a feeling of skepticism regarding the usefulness of the adjusted trade intensity ratios as indicators of trade barriers. I see tastes (Japan's coffee), omitted resources (Iceland's fish), and historical accidents (Switzerland's watches). I am not sure that I see trade barriers" (1988, pp. 198–199).

[9] This is by no means a complete list of such studies. For additional references, see for example Esfahani (1991) and Helleiner (1990).

[10] In his growth regressions, this price level index is actually combined with an index of real exchange rate variability to produce what Dollar calls an outward orientation index. The inclusion of the variability index is itself problematic in this context.

by PPP) for a prolonged period of time, even in the absence of trade restrictions – think of Chile in 1979–1982 and the U.S, in 1981–1985, for example. Moreover, the converse of the statement is certainly not true: a large amount of protection need not imply a high price level for *tradeables as a group*. Trade protection raises the prices of import competing goods *relative* to exportables; it has no definite implication for the aggregate price index for tradeables. If an import tariff raises the domestic price of tradeables, by the same logic, an export tax – which has the same resource-allocation effect as an import tariff thanks to the Lerner symmetry theorem – must reduce it.

Judged from this perspective, some of the anomalies in Dollar's rankings can be better understood. For example, India and Indonesia are listed among the second least distorted group of countries (there are four groups in all), which should come as a surprise to anyone with some knowledge of these countries' trade regimes during 1976–1985. What explains this, in all likelihood, is that these two countries managed their exchange rates and macroeconomic policies rather well over the period in question, avoiding sustained overvaluations of their currencies. It is even more surprising to find Chile listed among the more closed economies, even though this economy was certainly one of the least protected ones in the world during much of this period. Since Chile also experienced a pronounced exchange rate overvaluation during part of this period, this result is however understandable in light of the methodology. In short, purchasing-power-parity-based indicators of price distortions are likely to capture the exchange-rate (and therefore macroeconomic) stance of countries, and miss out on micro price distortions when exchange rates are managed well.

An additional problem with growth regressions of the type discussed here is that they tend to be very sensitive to the precise configuration of explanatory variables included in the regression. Levine and Renelt (1992) have shown that very few explanatory variables are "robust" to the inclusion of additional variables on the right-hand side of cross-country growth regressions. The share of investment in GDP tends to be robust in this sense. Trade and price-distortion indicators are not. But they also report that the ratio of trade to GDP does appear to have a robust correlation with the *investment* share. Partly in response to this criticism, Harrison (1991) has analyzed a large set of trade and price distortions, and included them individually in a panel regression with country fixed-effects and additional controls of the type Levine and Renelt have used. Within this fixed-effect framework, she recovers a systematically negative and statistically significant correlation between trade distortions and growth.

Perhaps the most credible of the cross-country regression studies are those [like Barro (1991) and Easterly (1993)] that find a negative relationship between distortions in capital goods prices and economic growth. It should be non-controversial that physical investment is a causal factor in growth. And if so, the relative price of capital goods must matter for growth.

### 4.2.4. Summary on empirical studies on dynamic costs of price distortions

A number of problems have plagued the empirical studies surveyed here. We summarize the more important here: (i) the trade-regime indicator used is typically measured very badly, and is often an endogenous variable itself; (ii) the direction of causality is not always clear, even when a policy variable is used as the trade indicator: governments may choose to relax trade restrictions when economic performance is good; (iii) openness in the sense of lack of trade restrictions is often confused with macroeconomic aspects of the policy regime, notably the exchange-rate stance;[11] (iv) the causal mechanisms that link openness to beneficial dynamic effects are rarely laid out carefully and subjected to test themselves; this makes it very difficult for policy conclusions to be drawn.

Measurement and conceptual issues aside, it is perhaps reassuring that so many studies using so many different indicators tend to confirm that countries with fewer price distortions, particularly on the trade side, tend to grow faster. Even if we are not convinced by any single study, should we not be swayed by all of them taken together? Perhaps so. But the virtual impossibility of accurate cross-country measurement of distortions, as well as the prevalence of distortions in Taiwan and Korea in the 1960s and 1970s (see below), should make us cautious with regard to the presumption of improved technological performance in any specific country contemplating liberalization.[12]

### 4.3. Response to external shocks

The case for policy reform was much strengthened by the argument, originating most forcefully in Bela Balassa's work, that export-oriented countries are better positioned to deal with negative external shocks than inward-oriented countries. The argument was advanced by analyzing the comparative experience of countries during the second half of the 1970s. Focussing on the period following the first oil shock (1974–1978), Balassa (1981a) first calculated

[11] When foreign currency is rationed, an overvalued exchange rate is equivalent to an import tariff. However, in all other cases the consequences of exchange-rate overvaluation (or undervaluation) differ from those of trade barriers. This distinction is rarely drawn in the studies discussed above.

[12] Also, the weight of published evidence should be tempered by a selection bias at work. Such is the appeal of conventional wisdom on this issue that it is possible that many studies which find an insignificant or positive relationship between price distortions and growth do not make it beyond first-draft stage.

the foreign-exchange impact of terms-of-trade and export demand shocks for several countries. Then, he decomposed the aggregate shock into four types of what he called "policy responses": (i) additional net external financing; (ii) increase in export market share; (iii) import substitution; and (iv) import effects of lower GNP growth. He argued that export-promoting countries, unlike inward-oriented countries, were able to increase their world market shares, which in turn favorably affected their economic growth. Balassa (1981b) later confirmed these findings with a larger sample of developing countries.[13]

Focussing on the early 1980s, Sachs's (1985) comparative analysis of East Asian and Latin American experiences reinforced Balassa's conclusion. Sachs argued that the primary reason most East Asian countries were successful in avoiding protracted debt crises was the higher share of exports in their GNPs. He also went one step further in linking the Latin American outcome to the political pressure originating from powerful urban groups with a stake in inward-orientation.

At first sight it is paradoxical that more open economies should perform better in the face of negative external shocks. Here it is useful to distinguish between the impact effect of a shock and the transition out of it. With regard to the former, it is clear that a given terms of trade shock is more harmful to a country with a high export-to-GNP ratio than one with a low ratio. Similarly, a reduction in external capital flows affects a country that has actively partici- pated in international capital markets more than one that has not. Indeed, the impact effects of external negative shocks were gravest on the most open economies such as Korea in 1980 and Chile in 1982–1983, but were barely felt in a closed economy like India.

The appropriate way to think of Balassa's and Sachs's arguments, therefore, is as follows: it is not that outward oriented countries are immune to shocks, but that they have an easier time getting out of crisis. But even here there are conceptual problems. If what one understands by outward orientation is the absence of microeconomic distortions that bias incentives away from exports, it is difficult to see how such distortions could be causally related to the balance-of-payments crises that have typically followed external shocks. None of the case studies in Thomas et al. (1991), for example, makes a convincing case that microeconomic distortions were at the root of the crisis of the early 1980s. As a matter of simple economics, trade restrictions lower exports *and* imports, and have no implications for the balance between the two. The trade

---

[13] See also Balassa and McCarthy (1984). See Srinivasan (1988) for a review of these and related studies by Mitra (1986). Balassa's procedures have been criticized by Hughes and Singh (1991) for not taking into account the negative interest rate shock to Latin American countries and the positive remittance shock to certain Asian countries, thus making the comparison less favorable to the former.

balance is determined by macroeconomic policies – expenditure policies and exchange-rate policy in particular. The correct response to an adverse balance-of-payments shock is a combination of expenditure-reducing and expenditure-switching (i.e. exchange-rate) policies. The evidence is that countries that recovered relatively quickly from their respective shocks were those that applied this simple recipe (see for example Dailami, 1991, on Korea, and Moran, 1991, on Chile).[14]

These objections notwithstanding, it is still possible that outward oriented countries have greater flexibility in responding to shocks, or that their political economy more easily allows (and acommodates) a change in macro policies. The informal evidence is consistent with these views, but the studies cited above – with the exception of Sachs (1985), which explicitly links policy choices to the underlying political economy – have only scratched the surface. Consequently, we lack a good understanding of how and why certain configurations of economic policy render the economy more resilient to external shocks than others.[15]

## 4.4. Institutional effects: Reducing rent seeking

The final set of arguments in favor of policy reform has to do with governance issues. The institutional setting under which import-substitution policies have typically operated has given rise to a wide variety of incentive distortions and resource misallocations that collectively go under the name of "rent-seeking". Starting with Krueger's (1974) classic article, it has become commonplace to argue that the resource costs of the prevailing distortions are multiplied several-fold by the existence of such activities. Examples of the waste generated include: employment of lobbyists and other intermediaries in pursuit of licenses and incentives to be obtained from government officials; generation of excess capacity when import licenses are allocated in proportion to installed capacity; competition for scarcity rents in black markets when commodities and foreign exchange are rationed; smuggling, under-invoicing, and over-invoicing. See Krueger (1990) for a recent re-statement, Bhagwati (1982) for a theoretical generalization, Gallagher (1991) for an empirical application to African countries, Tarr (1992) for an application to autos and TVs in pre-transition Poland, and Murphy, Shleifer, and Vishny (1991) for an extension in the context of economic growth.

---

[14] Westphal's criticism of Dailami's account is noteworthy: "[the chapter] does not develop with sufficient clarity the point that Korea's rapid recovery from the macroeconomic crisis owed far more to stabilization policies than to concurrent structural adjustment policies" (1991, 406).

[15] See Neary (1993) for a first effort to analyze formally the relationship between responsiveness to external shocks and domestic distortions.

While the costs of rent-seeking may be genuinely immense, it does not follow that a correction of price distortions and a move to outward orientation necessarily eliminates them. As long as governments exist and they implement policy, individuals and groups will exercise political power to obtain particularistic benefits for themselves. For example, Onis (1991) shows how a new type of rent-seeking took over once Turkish policy moved towards Korean-style outward orientation: rent-seekers started to run after export subsidies instead of import licenses.

It is a plausible hypothesis, nonetheless, that certain types of policies are more conducive to rent-seeking than others. Compare tariffs and quotas. As Bhagwati and Srinivasan (1980) have noted, tariff revenue can be sought by rent-seekers just as quota premia are. Yet, it is reasonable to suppose that the anonymity of revenues that accrue to the general budget somehow shields them from the gaze of rent-seekers, something that cannot be said for quota licenses that carry hefty premia [Krueger (1990)]. Similarly, a uniform tax system may be more impervious to lobbying than one with a highly differentiated structure [see Panagariya and Rodrik (1993), for an analyis]. But the lack of overt rent-seeking in East Asia must be attributed primarily to the "hardness" of the state in that setting (see the next section), and not to outward oriented policies per se.

## 5. Heterodoxy I: Reinterpreting the East Asian experience

The East Asian success story – i.e. the stupendous growth rates achieved by Japan, South Korea, Taiwan, Singapore and Hong Kong – raises the challenge of how this experience can be emulated in other settings. Economists who prescribe openness and price liberalization to developing countries typically present a picture of the East Asian experience that differs rather sharply from that presented by East Asian specialists themselves. A usual caricature is that these countries achieved their miracles by minimizing price distortions, giving markets free rein, and emphasizing exports. In the case of Korea and Taiwan, in particular, emphasis is placed on reforms during the 1960s that greatly reduced the restrictiveness of the trade regime, eliminated financial repression, and established a free-trade regime for exporters. Analysts who have studied these countries closely describe a much more nuanced situation, and stress that government intervention has been pervasive (except for in Hong Kong). The latter credit East Asian governments for making the miracles happen, not by getting out of the way of private entrepreneurs, but by actively nurturing and protecting infant industries.

With regard to liberalizing trade restrictions, for example, it is clear that East Asian countries did not go nearly as far as some Latin American countries have done recently, and that whatever was accomplished took place a lot more gradually. Here is how Hong (1991) describes the progress of liberalization in Japan, Korea and Taiwan:

It was not until the 1960s that Japan eliminated the bulk of its formal quantitative restrictions: the nominal import liberalization ratio (by items) expanded from less than 70 percent in 1960 to about 93 percent in 1964, and to 97 percent by 1976. Similarly, Taiwan did not eliminate the bulk of its formal quantitative restrictions until the early 1970s: the nominal import-liberalization ratio increased from 61.5 percent in 1970 to 96.5 percent in 1973. . . . Korea is scheduled to eliminate the bulk of its quantitative restrictions during the period 1984–1988. (p. 245)

According to a Korean Development Institute (KDI) study (cited in Hong, 1991), the average effective rate of protection in Korea (for domestic sales only) actually rose from 30 percent in 1963 to 38 percent in 1978, after a dip to 24 percent in 1970.[16] The contrast with the rapid and no-holds-barred liberalization that has taken place in Chile in the second half of the 1970s, and in Bolivia, Mexico and Argentina in the 1980s is staggering.

With regard to industrial policy, the following evaluation of Tanzi and Shome (1992) of Taiwan's tax incentives is noteworthy:

Taiwanese policymakers believed that they could pursue an investment strategy that would second-guess the market and pick winners. As a consequence, Taiwan kept its tax rates much higher than Hong Kong but pushed the investors in the desired direction through the widespread use of tax incentives. These incentives were fine-tuned to a degree rarely seen in other countries. (p. 57)

The same objectives were pursued in Korea via selective and discretionary credit subsidies [see C.H. Lee (1992)]. On industrial activism in Singapore, see Young (1992).

The extensive involvement of the state in industrialization has long been familiar to close observers of East Asia [see for example Jones and Sakong (1980), Westphal (1982) and Pack and Westphal (1986)]. Two recent books have led the way in popularizing the reinterpretation of the East Asian experience, Amsden (1989) on Korea and Wade (1990) on Taiwan. While many of Amsden's and Wade's arguments have been made before, what is new in these books is an ambitious re-conceptualization of this experience,[17] as well

---

[16] This reflects an increase in protection of the agricultural sector, however. For manufacturing proper, the effective rate has declined from 26 percent in 1963 to 13 percent in 1978.

[17] But see Johnson (1982) for an antecedent in Japan's case, as well as Jones and Sakong (1980) on Korea.

as their extensive documentation of the government's role in allocating resources and guiding industrialization in both instances.

Amsden (1989) describes in detail the Korean government's use of trade protection, selective credit subsidies, export targets (for individual firms!), public ownership of banking sector, export subsidies, and price controls – all deployed single-mindedly in the service of acquisition of technological capabilities and of building industries that will eventually compete in world markets. She argues that government policy was successful not because it got prices right, but indeed because it got them purposefully wrong. However, a key element of the strategy, Amsden argues, was that in exchange for government subsidies and trade protection the government also set stringent performance standards. Firms were penalized when they performed poorly, as when they became subject to "rationalization" (government-mandated mergers and capacity reduction) in the wake of over-extension. They were rewarded when they fulfilled government objectives, as when they were awarded subsidized credit for fulfilling export targets. Such discipline kept the system free of the rent-seeking that has contaminated incentive regimes in other settings: "in other countries – like Turkey and India, for example – subsidies have been dispensed primarily as giveaways. In Korea the 'wrong' prices have been right because government discipline over business has enabled subsidies and protection to be less than elsewhere and more effective" [Amsden (1989, vi)].

Wade (1990) does not deny that there were elements of the free-market (i.e. Hong Kong) recipe in the Taiwanese strategy, but he qualifies the picture significantly. He calls Taiwan a governed market economy, characterized by: (i) high levels of investment; (ii) more investment in certain key industries than would have resulted in the absence of government intervention; and (iii) exposure of many industries to international competition (p. 26). He documents the pervasiveness of incentives and controls on private firms through import restrictions, entry requirements, domestic content requirements, fiscal investment incentives, and concessional credit. He argues that the Taiwanese state has consistently acted in *anticipation* of comparative advantage in such sectors as cotton textiles, plastics, basic metals, shipbuilding, automobiles, and industrial electronics: "Taiwan manages its trade differently from many other developing countries, but not less" (p. 113). Like Amsden, he stresses the "hard" nature of the East Asian state, but also argues that the emphasis on exports helped reveal policy mistakes and made reversal possible when some ventures got too costly.

These works do not make easy reading for economists, both because they so boldly contradict conventional wisdom on what constitutes good economic policy, and because their authors' analyses occasionally remain incomplete or confusing. The latter is true particularly on the question of whether the various policy interventions more or less offset each other, resulting in broad policy neutrality on balance, as liberalizers are prone to argue [e.g. Snape (1991)]. On this important issue, Amsden openly contradicts the Lerner symmetry theorem (and Walras' Law) without attempting a reconciliation.[18] Wade does the same, and also contradicts himself.[19] Nonetheless, these books cannot easily be dismissed; they present a serious challenge to those who would deny the usefulness of an activist industrial policy. Similar analyses of the East Asian experience, with varying emphases, are presented in Banuri (1991), Bardhan (1990), Biddle and Milor (1992), Biggs and Levy (1990), Gereffi and Wyman (1990), Johnson (1987), and Westphal (1990). The World Bank (1993) has recently contributed a study of its own on *The East Asian Miracle*: the study confirms that intervention was rampant, but nonetheless finds it unlikely that other developing countries can successfully replicate this experience.

It bears repeating what is perhaps the most striking aspect of the revisionist accounts of the East Asian experience: the policy instruments used to such benefit in that context are no different from those that have apparently failed so miserably in Latin America, Africa, and the rest of Asia. The policies in question are import quotas and licenses, credit subsidies, tax exemptions, public ownership, and so on. For example, export subsidies that have worked so well in Korea in the 1960s have been ineffective and a source of rent-seeking in Kenya in the 1970s, and in Bolivia, Côte d'Ivoire and Senegal during the 1980s [Rodrik (1993)].[20] A reasonable hypothesis is that the reason has to do with differences in the way that the government interacts with the private sector. One way of conceptualizing this difference is to think of the government as a Stackelberg follower vis-a-vis the private sector in much of the developing world, whereas it is the Stackelberg leader in East Asia. A model of this sort can be used to explain how identical policies can have diametrically opposite consequences in different institutional settings [see Rodrik (1992d)].

If there is a set of conclusions regarding the East Asian experience on which

---

[18] "The argument that relative prices in Korea were distorted but in the right direction, that is, toward exports, is therefore itself distorted: Prices were distorted in all directions in Korea – both for import substitutes and for exports – and often for one and the same product in the two categories" [Amsden (1989, p. 155)].

[19] "The government was trying to promote both exports and, *in different industries*, import substitution . . . ." (1990, p. 117, my emphasis). Later on, Wade writes: "[export promotion and import substitution] are mutually exclusive only if defined to refer to the overall balance of incentives between domestic and foreign sale. But at the individual industry level, import-substituting incentives and export-promoting inventives can be complementary" (p. 363). His second statement is, of course, correct, but greatly limits the force of his argument since it is a partial-equilibrium one which cannot have applied to more than a narrow segment of industry.

[20] This point was also stressed by Pack and Westphal (1986): "The differences between Japan, Korea, and Taiwan, on one side, and most less successful industrializing countries, on the other, are not to be found in the use of different policy instruments. The differences are to be found instead in different ways of using the same policy instruments – for example, in the scope of their application, in whether they are used promotionally or restrictively" (pp. 102–103).

the revisionists and the liberalizers can agree on, it probably goes as follows: (i) there has been a lot of government intervention and an active trade and industrial policy; (ii) but intervention has taken place above all in the context of stable macroeconomic policies in the form of small budget deficits and realistic exchange-rate management; (iii) equally important, the governments' emphasis on, and unmitigated commitment to exports has helped minimize the resource costs and incentive problems that would have otherwise arisen from heavy intervention; (iv) also, intervention has taken place in an institutional setting characterized by a "hard" state and strong government discipline over the private sector; (v) furthermore, such a setting is lacking in most other developing countries. What one then does with these conclusions depends on one's predilections. Some would argue that it is possible to engineer local versions of the institutions that have made Korea's or Taiwan's policies so successful [e.g. Wade (1990, Chapter 11), Fishlow (1991)]. Others would conclude that weaker governments should economize on their scarcest resource, administrative competence, and restrict their involvement in the micro-management of the economy [Krueger (1990)]. Yet others would call for an entirely hands-off approach [Lal (1990)].

## 6. Heterodoxy II: Recent models of imperfect competition

One of the common arguments against East Asian type industrial policies is that governments could not possible make informed decisions about which industries will eventually become successful and hence deserve support. Wade (1990) argues that this objection misses the point: "The governments of Taiwan, Korea and Japan have not so much *picked* winners as *made* them". (p. 334, emphasis in the original). In other words, Wade implies that under the right set of government policies, industries can be nurtured into competitiveness even if these industries are ex ante undistinguished with respect to potential comparative advantage. Now, while this statement may be true as a matter of objective description, its normative implications are not as salutary as Wade assumes. Indeed, in an economy approximating perfectly-competitive conditions, the policy just described would have to reduce the economy's real income. Making "successful" exporters out of industries that do not possess an underlying comparative advantage is a resource-subtracting policy.

This conclusion is no longer so clear in light of recent trade models with increasing returns to scale and imperfect competition. Assume for a moment that much of manufacturing operates under increasing returns to scale, at least up to a point. Assume also that industrial production exhibits demand or technological spillovers; that is, the expansion of a firm leads to an increase in demand faced by other, neighboring firms or a reduction in their costs.[21] Under these circumstances, the pattern of comparative advantage can be largely arbitrary. A policy that subsidized a sub-grouping of firms or industries exhibiting such demand complementarities or technological spillovers would permanently alter the economy's "comparative advantage" *and* raise its real income (Pack and Westphal, 1986; Murphy et al., 1989; Krugman, 1991, 1992). Moreover, the informational requirements of a policy of this sort need not be heavy: an input-output table and some knowledge of the industrial structure of more advanced countries are basically all that the policy makers would need.[22]

There are strong echoes of Rosenstein-Rodan (1943), Nurkse (1953) and Hirschman (1958) in this. Indeed, one consequence of the emergence of this new literature has been the partial rehabilitation, at least at the level of theory, of concepts such as "big push", "balanced growth" and "linkages".

This is just one example of how conventional wisdom can be upset by explicitly considering increasing returns to scale. However, the new literature is far from having yielded robust conclusions. As we shall see, more often than not it has led to a bewildering array of special cases and an embarrassingly rich set of possible outcomes from policy intervention. Consequently, it may be a mistake to think of it as having significantly enhanced the case for intervention. Some have noted that returns to scale and imperfect competition are rampant in developing countries, which makes the new ideas particularly relevant to developing countries [Krugman (1989), Rodrik (1988), Helleiner (1992a)]. Others have dismissed them as largely irrelevant to developing-country

---

[21] See Stewart and Ghani (1992) for a survey of evidence on this and other type of spillovers. Note that a demand spillover, taken on its own (i.e. in the absence of increasing returns), would not constitute grounds for policy intervention. A technological spillover normally would.

[22] This is how Wade (1990, p. 335), citing the *Economist*, describes the way MITI picked industries to support: "First, MITI officials studied income elasticities of demand for various items in the main markets of the world, especially the United States. Second, they examined trends in technological change in various industries. Third they checked industries with high income elasticities and high potential for technological change against Japan's specialization index, or the share of each industry in Japan's industrial exports over the share of that industry in world trade. . . . If world demand was growing especially fast for some particular item, the planners would get worried if Japan's specialization index for that item was not going up too. On the other hand, if Japan's specialization index was already high for an item whose world demand was not rising, they would not worry if its exports did not keep up. Fourth, they checked the trends against another index called the 'export and industrial estrangement coefficient'. This measured the relationship between an item's importance in Japan's total industrial output against its importance in exports. . . . With these measures, the government could identify sectors where measures for encouraging greater output and exports should be stepped up". None of this of course makes sense in the context of the competitive model of economy. But with increasing returns, demand spillovers, and imperfect competition, a justification can be constructed. Of course, it is also easy to credit East Asian planners with too much: even Amsden (1989) recognizes that Korean policy makers may have gone too far with their promotion of heavy and chemical industries in the late 1970s. See Yoon (1992) for a model of how a Korean producer of computer memory chips became successful *without* direct government support, and Young (1992) for an interesting critique of Singapore's industrial policy.

circumstances and concerns [Srinivasan (1989), Corden (1990)]. See Grossman (1990) for a cautious survey of recent arguments for promoting new industrial activities, and an evaluation of their policy relevance.

How important is imperfect competition in developing countries? Casual evidence would suggest that it is very important indeed. See Lee (1992) for a recent survey of studies on market structure in developing countries. However, imperfect competition is often the consequence of government policy itself: entry and exit restrictions, capacity licensing and quantitative trade barriers are among the policies that come to mind. The evidence on returns to scale is much more limited. What we have are mostly engineering studies undertaken for advanced countries [as summarized in Scherer and Ross, (1990), for example]. Serious recent econometric evidence comes in a paper by Tybout and Westbrook (1992a) who analyze a panel of plant-level data from Chile. They find no trace of significant returns to scale: none of their estimates for three-digit industries suggests departures from constant returns, and only two (out of 12) of their four-digit estimates indicate increasing returns. They caution, however, that their method is unable to pick up any set-up costs that might be present. Broadly supportive evidence comes from Little (1987), who reports that small enterprises do not face a substantial comparative dis-advantage vis-a-vis larger firms.

Perhaps the recent literature's main contribution resides in providing new tools for analysis of some age-old questions. The new tools relate to the modeling of three sets of issues in particular: strategic interactions among firms; market-size externalities; and equilibrium when returns to scale and learning-by-doing are *internal* to firms. These in turn have raised three types of policy questions: (i) strategic trade policy (i.e. profit-shifting policy); (ii) policies to promote industries with scale economies; and (iii) policies to promote learning and growth. I take up each in turn.

### 6.1. Strategic trade policy

Much of the recent interest in modeling policy in imperfectly-competitive set-tings arose from the work of Brander and Spencer (1985) on strategic trade poli-cy. The basic Brander-Spencer model consists of two oligopolists based in differ-ent countries, competing in third markets and operating under constant costs. Their competition is modeled in a static, Nash-Cournot fashion; that is, each firm selects its output taking the other firm's output as given, and the equilibrium is defined as the pair of outputs from which neither firm wishes to deviate. In this setting, Brander and Spencer showed that if one of the governments moved first and offered an export subsidy to the domestic firm, the policy would unambigu-ously increase home welfare (producer profits net of subsidy costs). What brings this result about is the first-mover advantage arising from the assumed ability of the government to credibly commit itself to a subsidy *before* firms select their output levels. In effect, this transforms the domestic firm into a Stackelberg leader vis-a-vis the foreign firm, increases the market share of the domestic firm, and enhances home welfare by shifting profits towards the latter.

What makes support of home firms a potentially worthwhile objective in imperfectly-competitive markets is the existence of excess profits, at least when there is limited entry. This makes a peso of additional activity inherently more valuable in these industries than in other, perfectly competitive sectors.

However, the practical relevance of the profit-shifting argument is quite limited. As Krugman (1992) has put it, "while an admirable piece of modeling craftsmanship, [the Brander-Spencer model] has generated intellectual and political heat out of all proportion to its long-run importance". The laundry list of objections against the result is indeed formidable. The export-subsidy prescription is reversed (into an export tax) when firms compete in prices (in Bertrand fashion) rather than in quantities [Eaton and Grossman (1986)].[23] With free entry into the industry, the rents from policy intervention are competed away and the home economy left worse off.[24] If the home government lacks perfect information about costs and demand, the intervention may be set at the wrong level. When the foreign government plays the same game, a prisoners' dilemma situation results. Last but not least, the available empirical studies (which are mostly of the calibration-simulation type) yield only small gains from strategic policy even when policies are set optimally and with perfect information. See the essays in Krugman (1986) for a good discussion of the policy issues raised by the Brander-Spencer model, and the real-world limitations to its usefulness.

Because they are rarely significant players in oligopolistic global markets, the direct implications of the Brander-Spencer model to developing-country exporters are even more limited. Baldwin (1992) conducts a calibration-style empirical analysis of one of the few exceptions: Brazilian exports of commuter aircraft (the EMB-120) to U.S. and European markets. He finds that, on

---

[23] The logic, somewhat crudely, goes as follows. When firms play Bertrand, they each assume that the other firm's price remains unchanged "in response" to an increase in own price. In actual fact, the optimal response is to *raise* prices when the competitor does the same. This means that under Bertrand conjectures the home firm is too restrained in setting its price, relative to the true (out-of-equilibrium) response by its competitor. An export tax raises the home firm's price, thereby correcting the "distortion" due to the difference between the conjectured response and the actual response.

[24] It is possible to confuse the presence of excess profits with the lack of free entry. Suppose entering an industry is risky, with a positive probability that an incumbent will make losses (and have to exit). In order for there to be any entry at all, there must also be a positive probability of excess profits. Excess profits, under free entry, will be zero ex ante, but positive ex post. Subsidizing incumbents will simply lead to additional entry, and the dissipation of additional rents created.

profit-shifting grounds alone, even an optimally-selected Brazilian subsidy would have reduced home welfare. (But he also shows that this result would be reversed once labor rents in the Brazilian aircraft industry are allowed for).

Perhaps a more promising area for profit-shifting policy is *domestic markets* in which home firms compete with local subsidiaries of multinational corporations or with direct sales from oligopolists abroad. In such markets, there is a parallel case for discriminating against the foreign firms. Such discrimination can be accomplished by import tariffs when foreign firms do not produce locally [Levy and Nolan (1992)], or by discriminatory performance requirements when they do [Rodrik (1987a)]. But in either case, many of the limitations of the original profit-shifting argument carry over to this setting as well.

Levy and Nolan (1992) systematically analyze policies in the area of trade and direct foreign investment in the presence of excess profits, and present a useful summary of the implications for developing countries. The "lessons" they list are as follows: (1) Competition from foreign firms need not always be beneficial. (2) Imports can be excessive under laissez-faire. (3) Foreign investment can be harmful, even under free trade. (4) Policies that discriminate in favor of domestically-owned firms can be beneficial. (5) Given the available empirical evidence, imperfect competition in the industrial sector of developing countries does not justify nominal tariff rates in excess of 15 percent. (6) Imperfect competition in the industrial sectors of developing countries is not an argument against trade liberalization measures of the type typically under consideration.

### 6.2. Policies to promote industries with scale economies

The "new" trade theory has investigated a second area of potential policy intervention when domestic firms operate at sub-optimal levels of capacity. In the presence of increasing returns to scale, average costs of production exceed marginal costs; and since prices cannot fall below average costs for firms to remain financially viable, there must exist a gap between price and marginal cost (even when excess profits are zero). In principle, this gap could be closed via policies of subsidization and trade protection which encourage increased scale of production.

When economies of scale are large enough, and there exist demand spillovers from one sector to another, it is even possible that otherwise profitable industries will never get established in the first place. This is the basis for Murphy, Shleifer and Vishny's (1989a, 1989b) justification for coordinated industrialization policies:

When domestic markets are small and world trade is not free and costless, firms may not be able to generate enough sales to make adoption of increasing returns technologies profitable, and hence industrialization is stalled. . . . [W]e focus [in this paper] on the contribution to industrialization of one sector to enlarging the size of the market in other sectors. Such spillovers give rise to the possibility that coordination of investment across sectors – which the government can promote – is essential for industrialization. (1989a, pp. 1003–1004)

Note, however, the important caveat with regard to trade. If firms are able to take advantage of world markets, they are freed from dependence on demand spillovers from other sectors in the same economy; they can instead rely on a much larger world market. While it is possible to think of market-size externalities that are local rather than global – e.g. when geographical proximity matters or there are non-tradeable inputs[25] – the possibility of foreign trade greatly reduces the applicability of Murphy et al.'s argument.[26] Indeed, since government policy is often the greatest impediment to trade, the argument can even be read as one in favor of free trade rather than government intervention.

This objection is a general problem with the idea of promoting increasing-returns industries. If exporting is an option and transport costs low, firms can be expected to take advantage of it to reduce their costs and become competitive. Consider, for example, the case of an import-competing firm with strong scale economies (and assume the country in question is small in world markets). Trade protection would allow the firm to increase its output and reduce its unit costs. Is this a good idea? If the alternative is to close down the firm at no cost, the condition for such a policy to make sense is that the firm be able to reduce its average cost *below* the world price. Otherwise, we can save resources by shutting down the firm and importing what was locally produced before. But if the firm can reduce its average cost below its competitors' by expanding its scale of output sufficiently, it needs no inducement from the government to undertake what is a profitable strategy in any case.[27] The (necessary but not sufficient) condition for local welfare improvement due to a *small* increase in protection is less stringent, namely that the domestic *marginal* cost lie below the world price [Rodrik (1988)]. But of course the latter may still be an inferior strategy to letting the firm go bust.

Allowance for free entry generally weakens the case for trade protection even further. Entry in the presence of scale economies tends to crowd firms

---

[25] On the case with non-traded inputs, see Rodriguez (1993) and Rodrik (1994).

[26] Pack and Westphal (1986) make a similar argument in the presence of trade, but they critically assume that the import price of the relevant final good exceeds its export price (i.e. there exists transport costs).

[27] For a large-country the situation may be different. Trade protection may raise the marginal cost of the foreign firms, because it reduces their sales. This in turn makes the domestic firm achieve a larger market share even in foreign markets. This is Krugman's (1984) idea of import protection as export promotion.

and lead to duplication of fixed costs; protection leads to further entry, and aggravates the duplication. Harris (1984) has shown, in the context of a computable general equilibrium model for Canada, how the reversal of this process can lead to an "industry rationalization" effect that significantly enhances the welfare gains from trade liberalization. The basic mechanism can be understood by considering the equality between price and average cost in a model with free entry. In the aftermath of trade liberalization, the domestic price in import-competing industries has to be lower, which implies a lower level of average costs in the new equilibrium. What allows this new equilibrium to exist is the exit of some of the incumbent firms, which provides room for the remaining firms to expand their production lines and reduce their unit costs. The quantitative importance of this rationalization effect has been confirmed in simulation exercises carried out in partial equilibrium for several Turkish industries [Rodrik (1988)] and in a general equilibrium exercise for Korea [Gunasekera and Tyers (1991)]. The latter study estimates welfare gains of the order of 7 percent of GDP arising from lengthened production runs and increased labor productivity, a number that greatly exceeds anything that comes out of models with constant returns. However, a rather similar model calibrated to Cameroonian data yields negligible effects from industry rationalization [Devarajan and Rodrik (1991)].

Note that the potential for excessive entry creates a role for entry restrictions, especially when entry has been artifically spurred by trade restrictions. This point is rarely recognized in industrial-policy discussions, which too often assume the worst about the effects of such restrictions [e.g. Frischtak (1989)]. Whatever deleterious consequences entry barriers in countries like India and Argentina may have had, they may have at least prevented even greater departures from minimum efficient scale.

## 6.3. Policies to promote learning and growth

Recent models of endogenous growth have stressed how learning and purposive R&D activity drive economic growth through the creation of new products and the improvement in the quality of existing ones. Unlike in the neo-classical models of the Solow-type, long-run growth rates in these models are not pinned down by a forever-diminishing marginal productivity of capital, and can be affected by government policy [Lucas (1988), Romer (1986)]. Endogenous growth is obtained by allowing non-decreasing returns to reproducible assets, such as knowledge and human capital. A question of particular interest has been how international trade and trade policy influence growth in models of this kind. The answer is: it depends.

To see the different channels at work, consider a simple endogenous growth model of the type considered by Grossman and Helpman (1991) and Rivera-Batiz and Romer (1991). We distinguish between three sectors, which we call agriculture, manufacturing, and R&D. The agriculture sector is intensive in unskilled labor, while manufacturing is intensive in skilled labor. We suppose they trade at exogenously given world prices. The R&D sector also uses skilled labor and specializes in inventing intermediate goods, which are produced under monopolistically competitive conditions. The wider the range of intermediate goods, the lower are the costs in the manufacturing sector [as in Ethier (1982)]. (Alternatively, this cost effect could arise from knowledge spillovers produced in the R&D sector.) The profitability of producing these intermediate goods determines the rate at which new goods are produced, and therefore the rate at which manufacturing costs decline. The R&D sector is therefore the economy's growth sector: activity in this sector directly determines the economy's growth rate.

International trade has three main consequences in a model of this type.[28] Following Grossman and Helpman (1991, Chapter 9) and Rivera-Batiz and Romer (1991), we can list them as follows:

(1) The comparative-advantage or allocation effect. Static comparative advantage determines the instantaneous resource-pulls in an economy opening up to trade. If the effect of these is to direct resources towards the "growth sector" of the economy, the effect of trade is to speed up economic growth; otherwise, opening up to trade may lead to reduced growth. In the context of the model sketched out above, a country that is poorly endowed in human capital would experience a reduction in the relative wages of skilled labor, and therefore a decrease in the cost of doing R&D. The consequence would be an increase in that country's growth rate. The opposite is true for an economy that is well endowed with skilled labor [Grossman and Helpman (1991, Chapter 6)]. More broadly, trade is likely to enhance growth to the extent that innovative activity is more closely linked to the exporting sector than the import-competing sector, and diminish it otherwise.

(2) The market size or integration effect. International trade expands the size of the market which the R&D sector services; but it also increases the competition faced by the home R&D sector. The first of these effects generally increases growth, as long as there is some increasing returns built into the R&D sector. For example, when intermediate goods are traded and used in the R&D sector, the enlarged market size allows a wider range of inputs, lower costs, and therefore a boost in R&D activity and growth. Alternatively, when there is learning-by-doing, the larger market size speed up the rate of learning [Davis (1991)]. The second effect is generally detrimental to growth because

---

[28] A fourth, more direct, consequence arises from the enhanced contact with foreigners and with foreign technologies that trade often stimulates.

the smaller market share implied by each of the innovating domestic firms reduces the incentive to innovate. Feenstra (1990) provides a model of two countries with unequal sizes in which intermediate goods are not traded. The latter property implies that the smaller country has a cost disadvantage in producing these goods, and its firms lose market share when trade is opened up. Consequently, trade unambiguously reduces the smaller country's growth rate.

(3) The redundancy effect. In the absence of trade, some innovative activity is necessarily duplicated in different countries. That is, resources are devoted to developing identical products. With trade, such duplication can be avoided.

Hence, only the last of these effects is unambiguously favorable to trade. In view of this, it is possible to come up with models of trade and growth to satisfy any type of priors or to rationalize any conventional wisdom.[29] Complicating the analysis further, growth and welfare do not always go hand in hand in these models: it is possible for growth-enhancing policies to reduce welfare, and for welfare-enhancing opening up to reduce growth.

Are there any generalizations that can be drawn for developing countries in particular? There is one robust feature in the type of models considered here, and that is the following: the more asymmetric the trading countries are – in terms of size, extent of a head start, or static comparative advantage – the more likely that growth effects will be asymmetric also. This raises the danger that developing countries may end up with the short end of the stick, as could happen when comparative-advantage and/or market-size effects lead to a crowding out of their innovative sectors. For countries that are similar, the danger is less real.[30] Somewhat paradoxically, this resuscitates the theoretical case for regional integration schemes *among* developing countries, even though such schemes have long gone out of academic fashion.

A particularly noteworthy paper in this research tradition that has served to clarify the links among agricultural productivity, openness and growth is Matsuyama (1992). This paper shows how the effect of agricultural productivity on growth is mediated through the openness of an economy. Matsuyama considers a model with the following key features: (i) there are two sectors, agriculture and manufacturing; (ii) there is learning-by-doing in the manufac-

---

[29] Krugman (1987) and Young (1991) provide additional examples where trade is detrimental to growth. De Melo and Robinson (1990) present an imaginative CGE application to "explain" Korea's growth performance in terms of externalities arising from exports and from the acquisition of technology via imported goods. Buffie (1992) and Taylor (1992) explore models with yet additional channels of ambiguity. In Taylor's model, growth is driven by profitability, and the effect of commercial policy depends on how much it depresses the profitability of the export sector relative to the increase in the import-competing sector's profitability.

[30] As Rivera-Batiz and Romer (1991, p. 974) put it, "there is a strong presumption that trade restrictions between similar regions like North America and Europe will reduce worldwide rates of growth".

turing sector, which drives growth; and (iii) the income elasticity of demand for agricultural output is less than unity. In a closed economy, the model predicts that agricultural productivity is positively related to growth: the more productive is agriculture, the higher the resources that can be devoted to manufacturing, and the faster the rate of learning and growth. In an open economy, by contrast, this result is reversed: a more productive agriculture leads the economy to specialize in agriculture and therefore to withdraw resources from manufacturing, which is the engine of growth. Turning Matsuyama's results on their head, one can then argue that the optimal trade strategy for a developing country depends on its level of agricultural productivity. Countries that are poorly endowed in arable land have little to fear from openness; indeed they should encourage it. But countries that have a comparative advantage in agriculture should worry about the consequences of crowding out manufactures if they rely on trade too much.[31]

The focus on ideas and on learning in many of these papers is a useful counterweight to the traditional focus on the accumulation of physical and human capital (i.e. investment and schooling) as the engine of growth. It requires attention to be devoted to the microeconomics of how ideas are generated and transferred. As Romer has emphasized, the focus on ideas places openness to the outside world at the center of the analysis, but in a different way than one usually thinks of openness in trade models:

> When one considers the economic opportunities afforded by ideas, openness is central to the analysis, but not necessarily in the sense articulated by the classical theory of trade. In terms of the effect on the rate of growth (and even on the overall effects on consumer welfare), it probably matters little whether the consumers of a developing country have access to cigarettes and citrus products made in the US.
>
> What does matter is whether investors from the rest of the world have an incentive to put ideas to use in that nation. By creating the right incentives, any country in the world can follow the first of the two strategies mentioned in the title [of Romer's paper]: using ideas. But it also matters whether producers in a nation receive the right signals about the ideas that can be sold on world markets, whether they have access to the right inputs, and whether they receive the right rewards for generating such ideas. This is what is required for the second strategy, producing ideas. (p. 5)

Romer goes on to discuss the cases of Mauritius and Taiwan as archetypal examples of these two respective strategies. See also Amsden and Hikino

---

[31] For example, Lucas (1990) simulates a macro − econometric model of the Indian economy to find that real value added in manufacturing (at world prices) would fall in the aftermath of complete trade liberalization.

(1991) for historical examples on the two strategies, and Young (1992) for a parallel account on the divergent industrial strategies in Hong Kong and Singapore. These case studies illustrate that a government's commitment to provide the right incentives for the transfer and generation of new technologies (i.e. adequate property rights and policy stability) is of significantly greater importance than the extent of policy intervention per se.

Informal case studies like these aside, there are as yet practically no direct empirical tests of the specific trade-growth linkages identified above. We need such tests to close the large gap that presently exists between the empirical work described in Section 4.2.3 and the theoretical models discussed here. The former is informative but largely devoid of policy content, while the latter are stimulating, but remain empirically untested.

## 7. How to reform? Issues in the strategy of reform

The recognition that trade and industrial regimes in developing countries are sorely in need of reform, as well as the growing experience with reform, has led to an expanding literature on appropriate strategies for reform. Some of the issues involved – such as piecemeal reform – have a relatively long tradition of analysis within economics. Others – such as the analysis of policy credibility and of interaction with stabilization – are of more recent origin, and owe their genesis to the special circumstances of the 1980s. My review will stress the more recent analytical contributions. For broad discussions of reform strategy on various aspects of trade and industry, see Takacs (1989), Nellis and Kikeri (1989), Thomas, Nash et al. (1991), Michaely, Papageorgiou and Choksi (1991), Johnson (1991), Krause and Kihwan (1991) and Atiyas, Dutz, and Frischtak (1992). Evans (1991, 1992) provides a more heterodox perspective on reform strategy. On cost-benefit analysis of privatization in second-best environments, see Jones, Vogelsang and Tandon (1990).

### 7.1. The theory of piecemeal reform

The theory of piecemeal reform is a natural extension of the theory of the second best. The question it poses is the following: Suppose all policy distortions cannot be removed at once; what partial reforms can we undertake and be certain that we have increased (rather than reduced) aggregate real income? See Dixit (1985, Section 4) for a review of the literature and references. Two results stand out in this literature: (i) an equal percentage reduction in all distortions increases aggregate income (the "radial" method); and (ii) reducing the distortion on the most highly-taxed good increases aggregate income provided that good is a substitute to all others (the "concertina" method).

Two notable recent extensions of this literature are Falvey (1988) and Lopez and Panagariya (1992). Falvey shows that the presence of quantitative trade barriers does not affect these conclusions, provided "distortions" in the above is read as applying to tariff-ridden goods only: that is, the radial and concertina methods still work as long as they are applied to tariff-ridden goods only. Further, since the presence of quantitative restrictions cuts off spillovers, a loosening or removal of any quota distortion is beneficial if quotas are the only distortion. Lopez and Panagariya show that in the presence of a "pure" intermediate input (i.e. one that is not produced at home), the substitutability assumption of the concertina method will normally fail; in reasonable models, such an input has to be complement to at least one final good. Therefore, when pure intermediate goods have high tariffs, the concertina method cannot be relied on to reduce the overall tariff structure in a gradual manner.

## 7.2. Is tax or tariff uniformity a good idea?

Provided the substitutability condition holds at every step along the way, the logic of the concertina approach to reducing distortions leads us at the end of the road to a uniform tax or tariff system. Indeed, ruling out complementarities like those discussed by Lopez and Panagariya (1992), any move towards uniformity from above – that is, the reduction of the most extreme distortions – will necessarily be an improvement over the status quo ante.

This is occasionally interpreted as a justification for recommending uniform tariffs or, at least, reduced dispersion in rates. However, the theorems just stated are derived under the assumption that the tariffs in existence do not serve an economic or non-economic purpose in the first place. Once the stated goal of having taxes and/or tariffs is made explicit, we can almost always find a *non*-uniform tariff structure that will do better than any uniform one.[32] For revenue-raising purposes, for example, a differentiated tariff structure along Ramsey principles would be called for. For providing import-competing goods with a given amount of protection, a differentiated structure would be called for also, unless we do not care about consumption distortions. With pre-existing market distortions, the optimal tariff structure will be similarly non-uniform in general. A uniform tariff is optimal only when the objective of policy is to reduce aggregate imports to a certain level. For a transparent

[32] It goes without saying that tariffs are rarely first-best policies. The only exceptions are the presence of market power in world trade, and a non-economic objective that targets the volume of imports directly [see Dixit (1985)]. So considerations in the present paragraph apply to instances where the first-best policies are not available for some reason.

discussion of these issues, see Panagariya (1990). For a real-world application that shows how second-best tariff can significantly diverge from uniformity, see Devarajan and Lewis (1990). On the design of optimal tariffs for distributional or revenue reasons, see Heady and Mitra (1987). On how export taxes can be justified in the presence of revenue constraints and market distortions, see Roumasset and Setboonsarng (1988).

Tariff uniformity is sometimes recommended on the basis of administrative simplicity and political economy, rather than economic efficiency. However, such arguments are not always subjected to careful scrutiny. When they are, they turn out to have a number of limitations [see Panagariya and Rodrik (1993)].

## 7.3. Timing and sequencing of reform

A different set of second-best issues arises when we consider the time path of liberalization, possibly in connection with liberalization in other areas. Two questions in particular have dominated the analysis in this area: (i) how quickly should reform be introduced? and (ii) how should reform in different areas be sequenced?

On the speed of reform, the classic, but too-often neglected contribution is Mussa (1986). Mussa considers the optimal timing of trade reform in a model where domestic factors of production face adjustment costs when they relocate from one sector to another. Contrary to the widely-held belief that adjustment costs call for gradualism in policy reform, he shows that the optimal policy consists of an immediate jump to free trade unless there exists specific market distortions; adjustment costs by themselves are not an argument for gradual introduction of reform. To understand this conclusion, we have to draw a distinction between the rate at which the reform itself is introduced and the rate at which the private sector finds it optimal to adjust to the reform. In the presence of adjustment costs, it is true that agents may find it optimal to spread out over time their sectoral reallocation. However, it does not follow that reform itself should be spread out over time also. Mussa shows that, as long as individuals have rational expectations regarding the future path of factor rewards and there are no market distortions, they will in fact adjust at a socially optimal rate when the reform is introduced all at once. Departures from these assumptions may call for gradualism (or indeed overshooting). If, for example, individuals have static expectations regarding future factor prices, they may adjust too quickly, and then it may be beneficial to slow down the reform. Other complications arise when there are distortions in the adjustment process, or when the government wishes to moderate (for distributional reasons) the losses incurred by individuals in the previously-protected sectors.

On the issue of sequencing, most of the analytical work has focussed on the question of whether trade liberalization should precede or follow capital-account liberalization. Studies by Edwards (1984), Edwards and van Wijnbergen (1986), and Rodrik (1987b) generally come out in favor of a trade-first strategy. The transition to markets in Eastern Europe and the former Soviet Union has given rise to broad-ranging discussions of alternative sequencing options with regards to reforms in the areas of prices, trade, finance and privatization; see, for example, Genberg (1990), Hinds (1990), Kornai (1990), Lipton and Sachs (1990), Portes (1990) and Williamson (1991).

## 7.4. Credibility in policy reform

Policy reforms in the Southern Cone of Latin America during the 1970s and throughout the world during the 1980s were frequently met with skepticism on the part of the private sector, who had been deceived in the past by promises of reform and by aborted efforts. Calvo (1989) has shown how the lack of credibility that a reform will last introduces a distortion that could easily render the (incredible) reform harmful rather than beneficial. See Rodrik (1991) for an application of this idea to structural adjustment programs.

To see the basic idea, consider a trade reform that is put in place today, but is widely expected to be temporary. This temporariness introduces a distortion in the intertemporal structure of prices, the effect of which may outweigh the temporary elimination of the static distortion. In Calvo's (1989) model, the distortion exhibits itself in the form of over-borrowing while the reform lasts: since imported goods are perceived to be cheap only temporarily, the private sector goes into debt for usual reasons of intertemporal susbtitution. In a model where foreign borrowing is ruled out, the same intertemporal distortion would exhibit itself in the form of a sub-optimally low level of investment, thanks to a reduced saving rate (Rodrik, 1989a).

In view of the adverse incentives created for private-sector behavior, credibility problems can be self-fulfilling: the reversal of reform may come about for no other apparent reason than the belief that it will be aborted (Rodrik, 1991). In addition, credibility problems can arise because of dynamic inconsistencies in government policy. In an interesting paper, Matsuyama (1990) analyzes the extent to which a government can credibly threaten to liberalize so as to induce domestic firms to undertake appropriate investments. He shows that such threats are unlikely to be credible. As long as firms realize that the government's best option is not to liberalize in the absence of such investments, the firms' best strategy in turn is not to yield. Since liberalization "threats" are incredible, they are never carried out. Similarly, Hardy (1992) models the soft-budget constraint that is inherent in government policy, notably but not exclusively in Eastern European countries, as a form of dynamic inconsistency. As long as the government cares about unemployment, its commitment not to bail failing enterprises is not entirely credible. Hardy suggests that the creation of a "social safety net" may render such a commitment more credible, by reducing the income loss to unemployed workers.

As these examples show, depending on the precise source of the credibility problem and how it is modeled, the policy prescriptions vary. Froot (1988) suggests going slow on liberalization, while Rodrik (1989a) argues for going over-board to signal the government's true intentions. Engel and Kletzer (1991) show how credibility can be enhanced over time by optimal policy choice when individuals are Bayesian learners. For a broad, informal discussion of government strategies, including external commitments (e.g. accession to GATT), reputation-building, signalling, increasing the costs of policy reversal, and institutional design, see Rodrik (1989b).

## 7.5. The fallacy of composition

The simultaneous implementation of outward-oriented policies in countries producing the same commodity exports (e.g. coffee or cocoa) has raised the worry that a fallacy of composition may be the end result. Even if the terms-of-trade consequences can be judged minor for exporters taken one at a time, the same need not be the case for the group as a whole. Such considerations have been given increased salience by the exceptionally low level of real commodity prices in the 1980s. Over the longer horizon, there is evidence that the terms of trade for primary commodities have experienced a small, but statistically significant negative trend during the present century [Grilli and Yang (1988), Diakosavvas and Scandizzo (1991)]. These considerations give rise to the possibility that export taxes (whether administered singly or jointly) remain part of the optimal policy package for certain commodity exporters [Panagariya and Schiff (1990, 1992), Evans et al. (1992)]. However, in view of the extremely restrictive import policies already in place in these countries, it is likely that such considerations would not come into play short of drastic liberalizations. In other words, the existing restrictions are much too high to justify on the basis of terms-of-trade arguments.

Ever since Bhagwati (1968), it is known that a country with market power in trade cannot experience immiserizing growth as long as it has in place optimal export taxes. Bandyopadhyay (1992) has shown that this logic need not hold when there is more than a single exporter of the same commodity, unless exporters select their export tax cooperatively. As the qualifier in the previous sentence indicates, the reason is that export taxes that are selected, say, in a

Nash fashion cannot adequately cope with the externality generated by each country's growth. Even when countries impose their individually optimal export taxes, they can still be immiserized when they grow.

## 7.6. Political economy issues

One of the most important puzzles in understanding economic reform is the following: if reform is such a great idea, why are governments typically so reluctant to undertake it? There has been increased attention paid by economists to this question recently, for the simple reason that it is impossible to design sensible reform packages without understanding what keeps governments from embracing reform in the first place. Attempts to resolve the puzzle usually revolve around distributional issues: losers from reform, it is assumed, tend to be politically-powerful groups, such as urban industrialists and organized labor, while the gainers, such as agricultural workers and small industrialists, are disenfranchised and powerless.

Two recent papers have gone beyond this simple, almost tautological explanation. Alesina and Drazen (1991) focus on the question of why reforms are delayed, even though all groups lose as a consequence. While their reference point is a stabilization (i.e. macro) crisis, their basic argument is relevant to all distortions whose costs increase over time. Their answer relies on asymmetric information: when groups are uncertain about the costs incurred by their rivals, they may choose to enter a war of attrition in the hope that somebody else will give in first and agree to pay a disproportionately large share of the costs (or, more to the point, receive a disproportionately small share of the reform's benefits). What this argument shows is that reforms may be delayed even when all groups stand to benefit from it.

In Fernandez and Rodrik (1991), a different form of uncertainty is introduced. It is assumed that individuals do not know precisely how they will fare under reform, even though the aggregate consequences may be well known. This is motivated by the evidence that large trade reforms bring into existence new activities that could not have been predicted ex ante. The paper shows that under these circumstances, reforms that would have been accepted ex post (i.e. once the uncertainty is resolved) may fail to be adopted ex ante, even if individuals are risk neutral and completely rational. Political systems have a status-quo bias in the sense that many beneficial reforms are passed up, even though they would have been popular if introduced by a dictator.

The concern with distributional and other political-economy issues has led to their introduction into analyses that are otherwise quite conventional. For example, in their analysis of the Marshall Plan (which they call "history's most successful structural adjustment plan"), de Long and Eichengreen (1991) identify the Plan's major contribution as follows: it "facilitated the negotiation of a pro-growth 'social contract' that provided the political stability and climate necessary to support the postwar boom" (p. 6). Levy and van Wijnbergen (1992) pay special attention to distributional issues in their CGE analysis of agricultural liberalization in Mexico, focusing on poor farmers in particular, and recommend measures that would alleviate adverse consequences. De Janvry et al. (1992) construct an index of political feasibility of policy outcomes, based on a number of arguments drawn from the political-economy literature, and introduce it in a CGE model.

## 7.7. Interaction with stabilization policy

Perhaps the hallmark of the reforms of the 1980s has been their implementation in the context macroeconomic instability. Indeed, the most significant trade and price reforms often have been in reality mere appendages to stabilization programs (as in Bolivia in 1985, Mexico at end-1987, Brazil and Peru in 1990, Argentina in 1991). This despite the broad professional consensus, emerging largely from the failures in the Southern Cone of Latin America during the late 1970s, that a stable macroeconomic environment is a key prerequisite to the success of microeconomic reform [Corbo and de Melo (1987), Cavallo (1991) Hachette (1991)]. This consensus has received dramatic confirmation in research undertaken by Kaufmann (1991) at the World Bank. Kaufmann re-estimated rates of return from 1200 World Bank projects in 58 countries. He found that the overall quality of macroeconomic management – as measured by the extent of fiscal deficits, exchange-rate overvaluation, and negative real interest rates – made a significant difference to the productivity of investment projects. It is self-evident that triple-digit inflation can negate the benefits of structural reform: entrepreneurs are unlikely to take full advantage of relative-price changes when there is a high degree of uncertainty about the overall price level.

Hence, there can be little dissent from the view that macroeconomic stability is essential to the success of structural reform. Much of the debate on the wisdom of undertaking structural reform in the context of stabilization policies has focussed instead on whether the former can assist in the disinflation process. Three channels in particular have been addressed:

(1) Exchange-rate management. Trade liberalization typically calls for a compensating exchange rate depreciation, in view of the likely downward nominal rigidity of wages and other non-tradeables prices. Stabilization of the price level, by contrast, requires avoiding such jumps in the exchange rate. Hence liberalization in the midst of stabilization exerts conflicting pressures on exchange rate policy (Sachs, 1987). Usually, the conflict is resolved in favor of

stabilization, leading to a prolonged overvaluation and large trade deficits (as in Mexico after 1987 and Poland in 1991).

(2) *Importing price discipline from abroad.* Trade liberalization, and the removal of quantitative restrictions, in particular, may help disinflation by forcing convergence between domestic inflation in tradeables prices and external inflation. This strategy was tried in Chile during the 1970s, but has been judged a failure thanks to the backward-looking nature of wage contracting [Corbo and de Melo (1987)]. In the context of Eastern European stabilizations of the early 1990s, the strongest advocate of this strategy has been Jeffrey Sachs – somewhat paradoxically in light of his earlier predilections in favor of delaying liberalization [Sachs (1987)]. Sachs has argued that precious effort neeed not be wasted on breaking up monopolistic enterprises, as long as the trade regime is freed up in the initial stages of the program [Berg and Sachs (1991)].

(3) *Fiscal revenues.* Shoring up fiscal revenues is a primary goal of stabilization programs. Certain types of trade liberalization may go in the opposite direction, when they involve substantial cuts in export and import taxes. In practice, however, the typical trade liberalization package is as likely to increase fiscal revenues as to reduce them. Transforming quotas into tariffs is an unambiguously revenue-enhancing measure. So is reducing the scope of tariff exemptions, or reducing prohibitively high tariffs that encourage smuggling and squeeze out offical trade. A preliminary review of the evidence from countries undertaking SALs indicates the absence of any clear patterns with respect to fiscal consequences of trade reform [Greenaway and Milner (1991)].

In addition, structural reform can interact with stabilization in more subtle ways. One reason that so many Latin American governments have jumped on the free trade bandwagon is their desire to enhance the credibility of their stabilization efforts. What better way to signal that these governments now really mean business than to disavow their entire complex of import-substitution policies [Rodrik (1992c)]? A paper by Diwan (1990) makes this notion more precise in the context of bargaining with external creditors. He argues that a shift towards export-promoting policies increases the cost to a debtor government of repudiating its debt, because the trade penalties that would be incurred – such as the loss of trade credits – are proportional to the volume of trade. This renders the government's promise to honor its debt more credible, and thereby relaxes its credit ceiling.[33]

---

[33] As Diwan (1990) points out, however, a government may also choose to turn inward precisely because this reduces the cost of a future debt repudiation: "The choice between export promotion (EP) and import substitution (IS) depends on whether it is more profitable to increase the credit ceiling above inherited debt in order to borrow more, or to reduce it below inherited debt in order to repay less" (p. 306).

## 8. What has been achieved? Evidence on consequences of policy reform

Since the reforms of the 1980s are recent and still largely under way, a section evaluating the results of these reforms has to be necessarily briefer than one would wish. In addition, the results of structural reforms are likely to have been delayed by the environment of macroeconomic instability in which they have been typically carried out. For the same reason, the consequences of microeconomic reforms are hard to disentangle from the effects of stabilization policies. Available studies are too often sloppy in identifying precise cause-and-effect relationships.

For obvious reasons, the World Bank itself is the primary source for information on the extent of policy reform that has taken place – see, for example, Thomas et al. (1991) and Corbo et al. (1992) for detailed overviews (as well as evaluations). Webb and Shariff (1992) is a particularly useful source, describing the policy content of SALs and the evidence on their implementation. Table 45.1 summarizes some of their findings, and shows how wide-ranging the reforms have been, with sectoral and trade reforms dominating the agenda. Sixty-one countries have submitted themselves to the conditionality of at least one SAL (or SECAL – sector adjustment loan) over the period 1979–1989, and on average more than three-quarters of all conditions have

Table 45.1
Summary Information on SALs and SECALs, FY 1979–1989

|  | conditionality (%) | | implementation (%) | |
|---|---|---|---|---|
|  | dist'n of all actions | share of loans w/action | full | at least substantial |
| **A. Structural reforms** | 84 | n.a. | n.a. | n.a. |
| trade | 16 | 79 | 56 | 82 |
| sectoral | 28 | n.a. | n.a. | n.a. |
| industry | 5 | 44 | 53 | 65 |
| energy | 5 | 27 | 72 | 80 |
| agriculture | 17 | 62 | 49 | 74 |
| financial sector | 10 | 51 | 79 | 92 |
| govt. administ. | 9 | 72 | 54 | 68 |
| SOE reform | 14 | 65 | 67 | 77 |
| social policy | 3 | 24 | 55 | 82 |
| others | 5 | 49 | n.a. | n.a. |
| **B. Macro policies** | 16 | n.a. | n.a. | n.a. |
| fiscal | 8 | 67 | 72 | 89 |
| monetary | 3 | 42 | 61 | 89 |
| exchange rate | 3 | 45 | 71 | 81 |
| wage | 2 | 22 | 50 | 50 |
| All | 100 | n.a. | 60 | 79 |

*Source*: Adapted from Webb and Shariff (1992).

been substantially implemented. For other, less comprehensive accounts, see Whalley (1989), Rodrik (1992c), and Helleiner (1992b) on trade reforms, Williamson (1990) for a progress report which focuses on Latin America, and World Bank 1994) on Africa. See Lardy (1992) on the important case of China, and Pryor (1991) for an account of agricultural and other reforms in Marxist developing countries. Trade and industrial policy reforms in Eastern Europe are reviewed in Blanchard et al. (forthcoming). On privatization, World Bank (1992) is a comprehensive survey of developments over the last decade; it reports that more than 80 countries have launched ambitious efforts to privatize their public enterprises and that more than 2,000 enterprises (including 805 in Eastern Europe, however) have been privatized in developing countries since 1980.

## 8.1. The supply response and restructuring

World Bank staff has also been at the forefront of evaluating the consequences of policy reform. One strand of analysis has focused on whether countries that have received SALs have outperformed others, once other circumstances are controlled for to the extent that they can. Faini et al. (1991) and Corbo and Rojas (1992) have undertaken large-scale econometric studies addressing this question. The answer seems to be that, once external shocks are controlled for, SAL recipients tend to do better than comparator countries in exports and economic growth but worse in investment. These findings are broadly confirmed by the work of Mosley et al. (1991). The reduction in investment is puzzling, and suggests that the increase in growth may be largely due to the impact of additional imports made possible by external financing. However, there are important interpretational problems that attach to these studies. In particular, the links between specific policies and outcomes are not examined. And policy reform is measured simply by a dummy variable that takes the value of unity when a country has received a SAL.

The argument for getting prices right is predicated on the existence of a non-negligible supply response to price changes. With respect to exports, the evidence would appear to be clear: a credible, and lasting effort to increase the supply-price of exportables is rewarded by a large, often very quick export response. The export performance of Korea and Taiwan during the 1960s had already turned elasticity pessimism on its head. More recent experience has given additional reason to be confident about the presence of a strong supply response in exports. In countries where export profitability has been increased in a sustained fashion, export miracles have soon followed: see, for example, Hachette (1991) on Chile, Krueger and Aktan (1992) on Turkey, and Lardy (1992) on China. Even in Eastern Europe, where low-quality manufactures were long judged unmarketable in Western markets, a turn to undervalued exchange rates in 1990–1991 (alongside the collapse of domestic demand) has yielded a large increase in exports to the West (see Rodrik, forthcoming).

However, as this last example indicates, export booms have generally been associated with sharp currency devaluations and, occasionally, export subsidies. Export processing zones have also played a critical role in some other, more narrowly-based cases: electronic components in Malaysia, garments in Bangladesh and Sri Lanka, and the maquiladora in Mexico [Helleiner (1992b)]. It is more difficult to identify cases where import liberalization itself was causally implicated; Chile may be the only significant exception, but even here the effects were delayed well until the exchange rate began to play a supportive role in the mid-1980s. The Lerner symmetry theorem is a poor guide for the short-run, especially when the economy is mired in macroeconomic instability.

One of the striking regularities in the export performance of these countries has been that, once a decisive increase in exports is achieved, the process tends to be self-perpetuating even when the originally advantageous circumstances reverse themselves somewhat. In Korea and Turkey, exports have been affected during periods of prolonged real appreciation, but have not come crashing down. This suggests that export performance is subject to strong hysteresis effects: it may take a big push (i.e. sizable change in incentives) to get exports out, but by the same token, once the transition is made, not much may be required to keep them going. A rare glimpse into the microeconomics of the exporting decision is provided in a paper by Roberts and Tybout (1992). The authors carry out a statistical analysis of plant-level data from Colombia, and look for evidence of sunk costs and hysteresis in the decision of plants to export. They find strong persistence, in the sense that the exporting status of a firm exerts an inordinate influence on the future decision to export.

In poorer, agricultural countries such as those in Africa, the supply response may be considerably more limited than in Latin American or Asian countries. For one thing, agricultural supply elasticities are necessarily low in the short run. A survey of the aggregate supply response in agriculture suggests that long-run price elasticites of supply may be in the range of 0.3–0.9, with poorer countries at the lower end of this range [Chhibber (1990)]. Infrastructure constraints appear to be a key bottleneck. The sharp increase in cocoa output in Ghana following the price reforms of 1983 would seem to belie this conclusion. However, a significant (perhaps a third) of the increase in output can be attributed to previously smuggled exports now showing in offcial statistics [Green (1989)]. This example suggests that the true supply elasticity can be overstated when the presence of unoffical markets prior to reform are not taken into account. Also in Ghana, Steel and Webster (1991) have found some limited evidence of industrial restructuring at the firm level (mainly in product mix), but further adjustment has apparently beeen blocked by inadequate demand and lack of credit.

A healthy export response can be entirely consistent with sluggish industrial restructuring, if firms simply choose (and have the incentive) to substitute foreign markets for domestic markets. In Eastern Europe, where structural change is badly needed to get away from Soviet-style industrialization, the early evidence is that reform policies have not been able to foster much restructuring. There is some evidence that the much-repressed services sector has revived somewhat [Berg and Sachs (1991)]. But, as of the middle of 1992, there was scant evidence of restructuring within manufacturing industry [Estrin, Schaffer, and Singh (1992), Commander and Coricelli (1992), Borensztein, Demekas, and Ostry (1992)]. The reasons appear to be labor-hoarding by enterprises and the governments' reluctance to let large firms go bankrupt. In addition, the increase in exports to the West has ameliorated, but not entirely offset, the huge fall in industrial output that followed reform efforts. Hughes and Hare (1992) report, moreover, that the shift towards exports in the Eastern European countries has not noticeably pulled resources into the more competitive industries (as measured by domestic resource costs).

## 8.2. Consequences for static and dynamic efficiency

Evaluating the efficiency consequences of policy reforms is a difficult task, and one that differs considerably from model-based analyses of *prospective* reform. One needs a counterfactual regarding what would have happened in the absence of reform, and to disentangle the effects of the reform under consideration from the effects of other changes in the environment. To render a welfare judgement, one needs in addition a set of shadow prices to value the change in the quantities of outputs and inputs. Even if all these obstacles are surmounted, there is the difficulty of figuring out exactly what has happened. Here is Leroy Jones (1991) on evaluating divestiture:

> An all too typical story of divestiture runs as follows: visit country X and be told that enterprise Y is a divestiture success story with vastly enhanced profitability; visit company Y and be shown how costs have been reduced and demand increased by a variety of impressive management reforms; visit the political opposition and be told that profits were turned around primarily because of a side-condition of divestiture that competing imports be banned for five years. (p. 129)

Such difficulties have not stopped Jones and his colleagues from evaluating the welfare consequences recent privatization efforts [Galal et al. (1992)]. Their study is a rare and exemplary effort to apply a common methodology to reforms in different countries. Their analysis of twelve cases from Chile, Malaysia, Mexcio, and the U.K. reveals that 10 of them improved national welfare and 11 improved world welfare. Moreover, the welfare gains appear quantitatively significant.

The productivity consequences of China's reforms since the late 1970s have been the subject of a series of papers by Dollar (1990), Jefferson (1990), and Jefferson, Rawski, and Zheng (1992). Dollar (1990) finds that China's incentive reforms have led to rapid TFP growth and a reduction in TFP differentials across firms. Moreover, he finds that TFP growth was positively correlated with the share of profits that firms were allowed to retain. Jefferson (1990) draws attention to the pronounced increase in TFP in the iron and steel industry during the reform years, while Jefferson et al. (1992) argue that factor accumulation – mainly in material inputs – was still the principal contributor to aggregate growth in the state and collective sector.

The most systematic evidence to date on the efficiency consequences of trade reform comes from a research project led by James Tybout at the World Bank.[34] Tybout and his collaborators have assembled panel data sets from several developing countries, and have subjected them to statistical analysis, paying close attention to conceptual and econometric issues. Tybout (1992) provides a progress report, and links this research to antecedents. Three questions have been addressed in particular: (i) has trade liberalization led to reduced price-cost margins in import-competing sectors? (ii) has it resulted in firms taking better advantage of scale economies through industry rationalization? (iii) has it led to improvements in technical efficiency?

On the first question, Foroutan (1992), Levinsohn (1993), Harrison (1990), and Grether (1992) provide an affirmative answer. The first two authors analyze the Turkish case, where a substantial trade reform took place during the 1980s. In a three-digit industry-level analysis with panel data, Foroutan finds that higher import penetration is correlated with lower price-cost markups (controlling for capital-output ratios and fixed effects). Levinsohn undertakes a plant-level version of Foroutan's exercise. Also, instead of using import penetration as the independent variable, he looks at the change after 1984, the year that major trade reform was implemented. His finding is that price-cost gaps decreased in imperfectly competitive industries which experienced a decrease in protection, while they increased or stayed the same in others. Harrison undertakes an analysis very much like Levinsohn's for Côte d'Ivoire, and reaches broadly similar conclusions. Finally, Grether looks at both plant- and industry-level panel data from Mexico, and concludes that price-cost margins were reduced by the trade reforms of the 1980s; the relaxation of

---

[34] On the more recent evidence, see also Helleiner (1992b, p. 44) who summarizes the results of seventeen country studies he directed in the following terms: "The case studies in this volume offer very weak, if any, support for the proposition that either import liberalization or export expansion are particularly associated with overall productivity growth".

quantitative restrictions was apparently particularly effective, as trade theory would predict.

With regard to industry rationalization, the results are less encouraging. Tybout (1989) carries out an analysis of plant level data from Chile for the 1979–1985 period, and finds no relationship between import competition and exit rates. Roberts and Tybout (1991) examine annual plant-level data from Chile and Colombia, and find that, controlling for industry and country effects, higher trade exposure is positively correlated with *smaller* plant sizes over the long run. Further, the mix of high and low productivity plants is not strongly associated with trade exposure. As Roberts and Tybout indicate, "both of these findings cast doubt on the mechanisms linking trade, plant size, and productivity in a number of recent analytical and simulation studies" (1991, p. 2). Similar results are obtained in Tybout and Westbrook's (1992b) study on the Mexican liberalization: "We find that scale effects were only significant for a minority of industries during the sample period (1984–1989), and that improvements in scale efficiency were *not* associated with heightened foreign competition" (p. 1). A possibly dissenting conclusion is reached in Dutz's (1991) study on Morocco. Dutz finds that the probability of exit in response to an increase in imports is significantly higher among small firms than among large firms; together with his evidence that large firms are more efficient, this may suggest an improvement in average technical efficiency following liberalization. This conclusion needs to be tentative, however, since the focus should be on *net* rather than *gross* exit rates.

Finally, the available studies are generally favorable to the hypothesis that trade reform is conducive to gains in technical efficiency. Foroutan (1992) reports that growth in import penetration is correlated with growth in TFP in Turkey. Tybout et al. (1991) find in Chile that performance in TFP was better in industries that experienced the largest declines in protection. Similarly, industries undergoing the most dramatic reductions in protection in Mexico improved their efficiency the most (Tybout and Westbrook, 1992b; but see also the mixed results obtained by Grether, 1992). On the other hand, Harrison's (1990) results on Côte d'Ivoire fail to uncover a similar link once imperfect competition is explicitly allowed for: "our data suggest that when we incorporate imperfect competition into the productivity estimates [which are biased if perfect competition is assumed], there is no apparent relationship between productivity and trade reform" (p. 25).

## 9. Conclusions: What we know and what we don't

Few would disagree with the proposition that getting prices systematically and significantly wrong in the way that import-substituting countries have done in the past has been a costly mistake. But few would also disagree that getting prices right, in and of itself, will be insuffficient to make Bolivia or Ghana grow at Korean rates. A cautious conclusion from the literature surveyed here would be as follows: the benefits of price reform remain small in relation to developmental objectives, and tend to be linked to economic growth through uncertain and unreliable channels. Furthermore, the East Asian experience indicates that relative-price distortions, and the analysis thereof, are vastly over-emphasized relative to the institutional dimensions of reform. It bears repeating that the South Korean and Taiwanese economies have prospered in policy environments characterized by quantitative trade restrictions, selective subsidies, and discretionary incentives bearing more than a passing superficial resemblance to those in other developing countries. What has differed, of course, is the discipline exerted by the East Asian state over private-sector groups. It also bears repeating that countries like Mexico, Argentina, Chile, and Bolivia have travelled recently much faster and further on the road to price reform and trade liberalization than South Korea, Taiwan, and Japan before them ever did.

So a minimal conclusion for policy makers from the available evidence would be: get prices right if you can, but don't be deluded into thinking that reform ends there. Genuine reform requires the creation of a new set of interactions between government and the private sector, one that provides for an environment of policy stability and predictability, that discourages rent-seeking activities, and that improves on the governments' ability to discipline the private sector. In other words, the change that is needed is not only in policy, but also in policy *making*. The East Asian experience is full of clues as to what the end-product should look like. But we know much less about how to get there. Economists' comparative advantage may lie in analyzing price distortions; but it is research on issues of governance and institutional design that promises to yield the larger marginal social product.

## References

Aitken, B. and Harrison, A. (1992) 'Does proximity to foreign firms induce technology spillovers? Evidence from panel data', mimeo.

Alam, M.S. (1987) 'Trade orientation and macroeconomic performance in LDCs: An empirical study', *Economic Development and Cultural Change*, 39:839–848.

Alesina, A. and Drazen, A. (1991) 'Why are stabilizations delayed?' *American Economic Review*, 81:1170–1188.

Amsden, A. (1989) *Asia's next giant: South Korea and late industrialization.* New York and Oxford: Oxford University Press.

Amsden, A. and Hikino, T. (1991) 'Borrowing technology or innovating: An exploration of two paths to industrial development', New School for Social Research, mimeo.

Atiyas, I., Dutz, M. and Frischtak, C. (1992) *Fundamental issues and policy approaches in industrial restructuring.* Industry and Energy Department Working Paper, The World Bank, April.

Aw, B.Y. and Batra, G. (1993) 'Linking exports, technology, and productivity – A new approach', The Pennsylvania State University, mimeo.

Aw, B.Y. and Hwang, A. (1994) 'Productivity and the export market: A firm-level analysis', The Pennsylvania State University, mimeo.

Bagwell, K. and Staiger, R. (1989) 'The role of export subsidies when product quality is unknown', *Journal of International Economics*, 27:69–89.

Balassa, B. et al. (1971) *The structure of protection in developing countries.* Baltimore: Johns Hopkins University Press.

Balassa, B. (1978) 'Exports and economic growth: Further evidence', *Journal of Development Economics*, 5:181–190.

Balassa, B. (1981) *The newly industrializing countries in the world economy.* New York: Pergamon Press.

Balassa, B. (1981) 'Adjustment to external shocks in developing economies', World Bank Staff Working Paper No. 472.

Balassa, B. (1988) 'Interest of developing countries in the Uruguay Round', *The World Economy*, 11:39–54.

Balassa, B. and McCarthy, F.D. (1984) 'Adjustment policies in developing countries', World Bank Staff Working Paper No. 675.

Baldwin, R. (1992) 'High technology exports and strategic trade policy in developing countries: The case of Brazilian aircraft', in: G.K. Helleiner, ed., *Trade policy, industrialization and development.* Oxford: Clarendon Press.

Bandyopadhyay, S. (1992) 'Immiserizing growth in a multicountry framework in the presence of optimal export taxes', University of Maryland, mimeo.

Banuri, T., ed. (1991) *Economic liberalization: No panacea: The experiences of Latin America and Asia.* Oxford: Clarendon Press.

Bardhan, P. (1990) 'Symposium on the state and economic development', *Journal of Economic Perspectives*, 4:3–7.

Barro, R. (1991) 'Economic growth in a cross section of countries', *Quarterly Journal of Economics*, 407–443.

Bell, M., Ross-Larson, B. and Westphal, L. (1984) 'Assesssing the performance of infant industries', *Journal of Development Economics*, 16:101–128.

Berg, A. and Sachs, J. (1991) 'Structural adjustment and international trade in Eastern Europe: The case of Poland', mimeo.

Bhagwati, J. (1968) 'Distortions and immiserizing growth: A generalization', *Review of Economic Studies*, 35:481–485.

Bhagwati, J. (1978) *Foreign trade regimes and economic development: Anatomy and consequences of exchange control regimes.* Lexington, MA: Ballinger.

Bhagwati, J. (1982) 'Directly unproductive, profit-seeking (DUP) activities', *Journal of Political Economy*, 90:988–1002.

Bhagwati, J. (1993) *India's economy: The shackled giant.* Oxford: Clarendon Press.

Bhagwati, J. and Srinivasan, T.N. (1980) 'Revenue seeking: A generalization of the theory of tariffs', *Journal of Political Economy*, 88:1069–1087.

Biddle, W.J. and Milor, V. (1992) 'The quality of state intervention: A comparative analysis of Korea, Turkey and Brazil', Research proposal, Brown University, mimeo.

Biggs, T. and Levy, B. (1990) 'Strategic interventions and the political economy of industrial policy in developing countries', in: D.H. Perkins and M. Roemer, eds., *Reforming economic systems in developing countries.* Cambridge, MA: Harvard University Press.

Blanchard, O.J., Froot, K. and Sachs, J., eds., *The transition in Eastern Europe.* Chicago and London: University of Chicago Press, (forthcoming).

Borensztein, E.R., Demekas, D.G. and Ostry, J.D. (1992) 'The output decline in the aftermath of reform: The cases of Bulgaria, Czechoslovakia and Romania', mimeo.

Brander, J. and Spencer, B. (1985) 'Export subsidies and market-share rivalry', *Journal of International Economics*, 18:83–100.

Bruton, H. (1989) 'Import substitution', in: H. Chenery and T.N. Srinivasan, eds., *Handbook of development economics*, Vol. 2. Amsterdam: North-Holland.

Buffie, E.F. (1992) 'Commercial policy, growth and the distribution of income in a dynamic trade model', *Journal of Development Economics*, 37:1–30.

Calvo, G. (1989) 'Incredible reforms', in: G. Calvo et al., eds., *Debt, stabilization and development: Essays in honor of Carlos-Diaz-Alejandro*. New York: Basil Blackwell.

Cavallo, D. (1991) 'Argentina: Trade reform, 1976–82', in: G. Shepherd and C.G. Langoni, eds., *Trade reform: Lessons from eighteen countries*. San Francisco: ICS Press for International Center for Economic Growth.

Chen, T.-J, and Tang, D. (1987) 'Comparing technical efficiency between import-substituting and export-oriented foreign firms in a developing country', *Journal of Development Economics*, 26:277–289.

Chhibber, A. (1989) 'The aggregate supply response: A survey', in: S. Commander, ed., *Structural adjustment in agriculture: Theory and practice*. London: Overseas Development Institute.

Commander, S., ed. (1989) *Structural adjustment in agriculture: Theory and practice*. London: Overseas Development Institute.

Commander, S. and Coricelli, F. (1992) 'Output decline in Hungary and Poland in 1990/91: Structural change and aggregate shocks', mimeo.

Corbo, V., Fischer, S. and Webb, S., eds. (1992) *Adjustment lending revisited: Policies to restore growth*. Washington, DC: The World Bank.

Corbo, V. and de Melo, J. (1987) 'Lessons from the Southern Cone policy reforms', *The World Bank Research Observer*, 2:111–142.

Corbo, V. and Rojas, P. (1992) 'World Bank-supported adjustment programs: Country performance and effectiveness', in: V. Corbo, S. Fischer and S.B. Webb, eds., *Adjustment lending revisited: Policies to restore growth*. Washington DC: The World Bank.

Corbo, V., Goldstein, M. and Khan, M., eds. (1989) *Growth-oriented adjustment programs*. Washington, DC: IMF and The World Bank.

Corden, W.M. (1974) *Trade policy and economic welfare*. Oxford: Oxford University Press.

Corden, W.M. (1990) 'Strategic trade policy: How new? How sensible?' World Bank PPR Working Paper 396, April.

Dailami, M. (1991) 'Korea: Successful adjustment', in: V. Thomas et al. eds., *Restructuring economies in distress: Policy reform and the World Bank*. Oxford and New York: Oxford University Press.

Davis, D.R. (1991) 'Mutual dynamic gains from trade due to specialization in learning', mimeo.

de Janvry, A., Fargeix, A. and Sadoulet, E. (1992) 'The political feasibility of rural poverty reduction', *Journal of Development Economics*, 37:351–367.

de Long, J.B. and Eichengreen, B. (1991) 'The Marshall Plan: History's most successful structural adjustment plan', NBER Working Paper No. 3899, November.

de Long, J.B. and Summers, L. (1991) 'Equipment investment and economic growth', *Quarterly Journal of Economics*, 106:445–502.

de Melo, J. and Robinson, S. (1990) 'Productivity and externalities: Models of export-led growth', CEPR Discussion Paper No. 400, April.

de Soto, H. (1989) *The Other Path*. New York: Harper & Row.

Dervis, K. and Page, Jr., J.M. (1984) 'Industrial policy in developing countries', *Journal of Comparative Economics*, 8:436–451.

Devarajan, S. and Lewis, J.D. (1990) 'Structural adjustment and economic reform in Indonesia: Model-based policies vs. rules of thumb', in: D.H. Perkins and M. Roemer, eds., *Reforming economic systems in developing countries*. Cambridge, MA: Harvard University Press.

Devarajan, S. and Rodrik, D. (1991) 'Pro-competitive effects of trade reform: Results from a CGE model of Cameroon', *European Economic Review*, 35:1159–1186.

Diakosavvas, D. and Scandizzo, P.L. (1991) 'Trends in the terms of trade of primary commodities, 1900–1982: The controversy and its origins', *Economic Development and Cultural Change*, 39:231–264.

Diwan, I. (1990) 'Linking trade and external debt strategies', *Journal of International Economics*, 29:293–310.

Dixit, A.K. (1985) 'Tax policy in open economies', in: A.J. Auerbach and M. Feldstein, eds., *Handbook of public economics*, Vol. I. Amsterdam: North-Holland.

Dollar, D. (1990) 'Economic reform and allocative efficiency in China's state-owned industry', *Economic Development and Cultural Change*, 39:89–105.

Dollar, D. (1992) 'Outward-oriented developing economies really do grow more rapidly: Evidence from 95 LDCs, 1976–1985', *Economic Development and Cultural Change*, 40:523–544.

Dollar, D. and Sokoloff, K. (1990) 'Patterns of productivity growth in South Korean manufacturing industries, 1963–1979', *Journal of Development Economics*, 33:309–327.

Dutz, M.A. (1991) 'Firm output adjustment to trade liberalization: Theory with application to the Moroccan experience', World Bank WPS 602, February.

Easterly, W. (1992) 'Endogenous growth in developing countries with government-induced distortions', in: V. Corbo et al., eds., *Adjustment lending revisited*. Washington, DC: The World Bank.

Easterly, W. (1993) 'How much do distortions affect growth?' *Journal of Monetary Economics*, 32:187–212.

Eaton, J. and Grossman, G. (1986) 'Optimal trade and industrial policy under oligopoly', *Quarterly Journal of Economics*, 101:383–406.

Edwards, S. (1984) *The order of liberalization of the external sector in developing countries*. Princeton, NJ: Princeton Essays in International Finance No. 156.

Edwards, S. (1992) 'Trade orientation, distortions and growth in developing countries', *Journal of Development Economics*, 39(1):31–57.

Edwards, S. and van Wijnbergen, S. (1986) 'The welfare effects of trade and capital-market liberalization', *International Economic Review*, 27:141–148.

Edwards, S. and van Wijnbergen, S. (1989) 'Disequilibrium and structural adjustment', in: H. Chenery and T.N. Srinivasan, eds., *Handbook of development economics*, Vol. II. Amsterdam: North-Holland.

Engel, C. and Kletzer, K.M. (1991) 'Trade policy under endogenous credibility', *Journal of Development Economics*, 36:213–228.

Erzan, R., Kuwahara, K., Marchese, S. and Vossenaar, R. (1989) 'The profile of protection in developing countries', *UNCTAD Review*, 1(1):29–49.

Esfahani, H.S. (1991) 'Exports, imports, and economic growth in semi-industrialized countries', *Journal of Development Economics*, 35(1):93–116.

Estrin, S., Schaffer, M.E. and Singh, I. (1992) ' Enterprise adjustment in transition economies: Czechoslovakia, Hungary and Poland', mimeo.

Ethier, W. (1982) 'National and international returns to scale in the modern theory of international trade', *American Economic Review*, 72:389–405.

Evans, D. (1991) 'Visible and invisible hands in trade policy reform', in: C. Colclough and J. Manor, eds., *States or markets: Neo-liberalism and the development policy debate*. Oxford: Clarendon Press.

Evans, D. (1992) 'Institutions, sequencing and trade policy reform', University of Sussex, mimeo.

Evans, D., Goldin, I. and van der Mensbrugghe, D. (1992) 'Trade reform and the small country assumption', in: I. Goldin and L.A. Winters, eds., *Open economies: Structural adjustment and agriculture*. New York and London: Cambridge University Press.

Faini, R., de Melo, J., Senhadji-Semlali, A. and Stanton, J. (1991) 'Macro performance under adjustment lending', in: V. Thomas et al. eds., *Restructuring economies in distress*. Washington, DC: The World Bank.

Feder, G. (1983) 'On exports and economic growth', *Journal of Development Economics*, 12:59–74.

Feenstra, R. (1990) 'Trade and uneven growth', NBER Working Paper No. 3276, March.

Fernandez, R. and Rodrik, D. (1991) 'Resistance to reform: Status-quo bias in the presence of individual-specific uncertainty', *American Economic Review*, 81:1146–1155.

Fishlow, A. (1991) 'Some reflections on comparative Latin American economic performance and policy', in: T. Banuri, ed., *Economic liberalization: No panacea: The experiences of Latin America and Asia*. Oxford: Clarendon Press.

Foroutan, F. (1992) 'Foreign trade and its relation to competition and productivity in Turkish industry', June, The World Bank.

Frischtak, C. (1989) *Competition policies for industrializing countries*. Washington, DC: The World Bank.

Froot, K. (1988) 'Credibility, real interest rates, and the optimal speed of trade liberalization', *Journal of International Economics*, 25:71–93.

Galal, A., Jones, L., Tandon, P. and Vogelsang, I. (1992) *Welfare consequences of selling public enterprises: Case studies from Chile, Malaysia, Mexico, and the U.K.* Washington, DC: The World Bank, forthcoming.

Gallagher, M. (1991) *Rent-seeking and economic growth in Africa*. Boulder and Oxford: Westview Press.

Genberg, H. (1990) 'On the sequencing of reforms in Eastern Europe', Geneva: Graduate Institute of International Studies, mimeo.

Gereffi, G. and Wyman, D.L., eds. (1990) *Manufacturing miracles: Paths of industrialization in Latin America and East Asia*. Princeton, NJ: Princeton University Press, Princeton.

Green, R.H. (1989) 'Articulating stabilisation programmes and structural adjustment', in: Commander (1989).

Greenaway, D. and Milner, C. (1991) 'Fiscal dependence on trade taxes and trade policy reform', *Journal of Development Studies*, 27:96–132.

Grether, J.-M. (1992) 'Trade liberalization, market structure and performance in Mexican manufacturing: 1984–1989', mimeo.

Grilli, E. and Yang, M.C. (1988) 'Primary commodity prices, manufactured goods prices and the terms of trade of developing countries: What the long run shows', *The World Bank Economic Review*, 2:1–47.

Grossman, G. (1990) 'Promoting new industrial activities: A survey of recent arguments and evidence', *OECD Economic Studies*, 14(Spring):87–125.

Grossman, G. and Helpman, E. (1991) *Innovation and growth in the global economy*. Cambridge, MA: MIT Press.

Grossman, G. and Horn, H. (1988) 'Infant industry protection reconsidered: The case of informational barriers to entry', *Quarterly Journal of Economics*, CIII: 767–787.

Gunasekera, H.D.B.H. and Tyers, R. (1991) 'Imperfect competition and resturns to scale in a newly-industrializing economy: A general equilibrium analysis of Korean trade policy', *Journal of Development Economics*, 34:223–247.

Hachette, D. (1991) 'Chile: Trade liberalization since 1974', in: G. Shepherd and C.G. Langoni, eds., *Trade reform: Lessons from eighteen countries*. San Francisco: ICS Press for International Center for Economic Growth.

Hardy, D.C. (1992) 'Soft budget constraints, firm commitments, and the social safety net', *IMF Staff Papers*, 39:310–329.

Harris, R. (1984) 'Applied general equilibrium analysis of small open economies with scale economies and imperfect competition', *American Economic Review*, 74:1016–1033.

Harrison, A. (1990) 'Productivity, imperfect competition and trade liberalization in Côte d'Ivoire', World Bank Working Paper WPS 451, July.

Harrison, A. (1991) 'Openness and growth: A time-series, cross-country analysis for developing countries', The World Bank, mimeo.

Hart, O. (1983) 'The market mechanism as an incentive scheme', *Bell Journal of Economics*, 14:366–382.

Heady, C. and Mitra, P.K. (1987) 'Distributional and revenue raising arguments for tariffs', *Journal of Development Economics*, 26:77–101.

Helleiner, G.K. (1990) 'Trade strategy in medium-term adjustment', *World Development*, 18(6):879–897.

Helleiner, G.K., ed. (1992a) *Trade policy, industrialization and development*. Oxford: Clarendon Press.

Helleiner, G.K. (1992b) 'Trade policy and industrialization in turbulent times', mimeo.

Hinds, M. (1990) 'Issues in the introduction of market forces in Eastern European socialist economies', Washington, DC: The World Bank.

Hirschman, A.O (1958) *The strategy of economic development*. New Haven, CT: Yale University Press.

Hong, W. (1991) 'Import restriction and liberalization', in: L. Krause and K. Kihwan, eds.,

*Liberalization in the process of economic development.* Berkeley and Oxford: University of California Press.

Hughes, A. and Singh, A. (1991) 'The world economic slowdown and the Asian and Latin American economies: A comparative analysis of economic structure, policy, and performance', in: T. Banuri, ed., *Economic liberalization: No panacea: The experiences of Latin America and Asia.* Oxford: Clarendon Press.

Hughes, G. and Hare, P. (1992) 'Industrial policy and restructuring in Eastern Europe'. London: CEPR Discussion Paper No. 653.

Jefferson, G. (1990) 'China's iron and steel industry: Sources of enterprise efficiency and the impact of reform', *Journal of Development Economics,* 33:329–355.

Jefferson, G., Rawski, T. and Zheng, Y. (1992) 'Growth, efficiency, and convergence in China's state and collective industry', *Economic Development and Cultural Change,* 40:239–266.

Johnson, C. (1982) *MITI and the Japanese miracle.* Stanford: Stanford University Press.

Johnson, C. (1987) 'Political institutions and economic performance: A comparative analysis of the business-government relationship in Japan, South Korea and Taiwan', in: F. Deyo, ed., *The political economy of the new Asian industrialism.* Ithaca: Cornell University Press.

Johnson, D.G. (1991) 'Agriculture in the liberalization process', in: L. Krause and K. Kihwan, eds., *Liberalization in the process of economic development.* Berkeley and Oxford: Unversity of California Press.

Jones, L. (1991) 'Comment on reform of public enterprises', in: V. Thomas et al., eds., *Restructuring economies in distress.* Washington, DC: The World Bank.

Jones, L. and Sakong, I. (1980) *Government, business, and entrepreneurship in economic development: The Korean case.* Cambridge, MA: Harvard University Press.

Jones, L., Tandon, P. and Vogelsang, I. (1990) *Selling public enterprises: A cost-benefit methodology.* Cambridge, MA: MIT Press.

Jung, W.S. and Marshall, P.J. (1985) 'Exports, growth, and causality in developing countries', *Journal of Development Economics,* 18:1–12.

Katrak, H. (1989) 'Imported technologies and R&D in a newly-industrializing country: The experience of Indian enterprises', *Journal of Development Economics,* 31:123–139.

Katz, J.M., ed. (1987) *Technology generation in Latin American manufacturing industries.* London: Macmillan.

Kaufmann, D. (1991) 'The forgotten rationale for policy reform: The productivity of investment projects', April, The World Bank, mimeo.

Kornai, J. (1990) *The road to a free economy – Shifting from a socialist system: The example of Hungary.* New York: W.W. Norton.

Kostecki, M.M. and Tymowski, M.J. (1985) 'Customs duties versus other import charges in the developing countries', *Journal of World Trade Law,* 19:269–286.

Krause, L.B. and Kihwan, K., eds. (1991) *Liberalization in the process of economic development.* Berkeley and Oxford: Unversity of California Press.

Krueger, A.O. (1974) 'The political economy of the rent-seeking society', *American Economic Review,* 64:291–303.

Krueger, A.O. (1978) *Foreign trade regimes and economic development: Liberalization attempts and consequences.* Lexington, MA: Ballinger.

Krueger, A.O. (1983) *Trade and employment in developing countries: Synthesis and conclusions.* Chicago: University of Chicago Press.

Krueger, A.O. (1990) 'Government failures in development', NBER Working Paper No. 3340, April.

Krueger, A.O. and Aktan, O.H. (1992) *Swimming against the tide: Turkish trade reform in the 1980s.* San Francisco: ICS Press.

Krueger, A.O., Schiff, M. and Valdes, A., eds. (1991) *The political economy of agricultural pricing policy.* Baltimore and London: Johns Hopkins University Press.

Krueger, A.O., Schiff, M., and Valdes, A. (1988) 'Agricultural incentives in developing countries: Measuring the effects of sectoral and economy-wide policies', *World Bank Economic Review,* September:255–271.

Krueger, A.O. and Tuncer, B. (1982a) 'Growth of factor productivity in Turkish manufacturing industries', *Journal of Development Economics,* 11:307–326.

Krueger, A.O. and Tuncer, B. (1982b) 'An empirical test of the infant-industry argument', *American Economic Review*, 72:1142–1152.

Krugman, P. (1984) 'Import protection as export promotion', in: H. Kierzkowski, ed., *Monopolistic competition and international trade*. Oxford: Oxford University Press.

Krugman, P. (1986) *Strategic trade policy and the new international economics*. Cambridge, MA: MIT Press.

Krugman, P. (1987) 'The narrow moving band, the Dutch disease, and the competitive consequences of Mrs. Thatcher: Notes on trade in the presence of dynamic scale economies', *Journal of Development Economics*, 27:41–55.

Krugman, P. (1989) 'New trade theories and the less-developed countries', in: G. Calvo et al., eds., *Debt, stabilization, and development: Essays in honor of Carlos-Diaz-Alejandro*. New York: Basil Blackwell.

Krugman, P. (1991) 'History vs. expectations', *Quarterly Journal of Economics*, 106:651–667.

Krugman, P. (1992) 'Does the new trade theory require a new trade policy?' mimeo.

Lal, D. (1990) 'Political economy and public policy', International Center for Economic Growth, Occasional Paper No. 19.

Lall, S. (1987) *Learning to industrialize: The acquisition of technological capability in India*. Basingstoke and London: Macmillan.

Lardy, N.R. (1992) *Foreign trade and economic reform in China*. New York: Cambridge University Press.

Leamer, E. (1988) 'Measures of openness', in: R. Baldwin, ed., *Trade policy issues and empirical analysis*. Chicago: University of Chicago Press.

Lee, C.H. (1992) 'The government, financial system and large private enterprise in the economic development of South Korea', *World Development*, 20:187–192.

Lee, J.-W. (1992) 'Government intervention and productivity growth in Korean manufacturing industries', International Monetary Fund, mimeo.

Lee, N. (1992) 'Market structure and trade in developing countries', in: G.K. Helleiner, ed., *Trade policy, industrialization and development*. Oxford: Clarendon Press.

Levine, R. and Renelt, D. (1992) 'A sensitivity analysis of cross-country growth regressions', *American Economic Review*, 82(4):942–963.

Levinsohn, J. (1993) 'Testing the imports-as-market-discipline hypothesis', *Journal of International Economics*, 35:1–22.

Levy, B. (1991) 'Transactions costs, the size of firms and industrial policy: Lessons from a comparative case study of the footwear industry in Korea and Taiwan', *Journal of Development Economics*, 34:151–178.

Levy, S. and van Wijnbergen, S. (1992) 'Mexican agriculture in the Free Trade Agreement: Transition problems in economic reform', OECD Development Centre Technical Papers No. 63, May.

Levy, S. and Nolan, S. (1992) 'Trade and foreign investment policies under imperfect competition: Lessons for developing countries', *Journal of Development Economics*, 37:31–62.

Lipton, D. and Sachs, J. (1990) 'Creating a market economy in Eastern Europe: The case of Poland', *Brookings Papers on Economic Activity*, 1:75–133.

Little, I.M.D. (1987) 'Small manufacturing enterprise in developing countries', *The World Bank Economic Review*, 1:203–235.

Little, I., Scitovsky, T. and Scott, M. (1970) *Industry and trade in some developing countries*. London: Oxford University Press.

Lopez, R. and Panagariya, A. (1992) 'On the theory of piecemeal tariff reform: The case of pure imported intermediate inputs', *American Economic Review*, 82:615–625.

Lucas. R. (1988) 'On the mechanics of economic development', *Journal of Monetary Economics*, 22:3–42.

Lucas, R.E.B. (1989) 'Liberalization of Indian trade and industrial licensing: A disaggregated econometric model with simulations', *Journal of Development Economics*, 31:141–175.

Matsuyama, K. (1990) 'Perfect equilibria in a trade liberalization game', *American Economic Review*, 80:480–492.

Matsuyama, K. (1992) 'Agricultural productivity, comparative advantage and economic growth', *Journal of Economic Theory*, 58:317–334.

Michaely, M. (1977) 'Exports and economic growth: An empirical investigation', *Journal of Development Economics*, 4:49–54.

Michaely, M., Papageorgiou, D. and Choksi, A.M. (1991) *Liberalizing foreign trade – Lessons of experience in the developing world*. Cambridge, MA: Basil Blackwell.

Mitra, P. (1986) 'A description of adjustment to external shocks: Country groups', in: D. Lal and M. Wolf, eds., *Stagflation, savings and the state: Perspectives on the global economy*. New York: Oxford University Press.

Meier, G.M. and Steel, W.F., eds. (1989) *Industrial adjustment in sub-Saharan Africa*. Washington, DC: The World Bank.

Moran, C. (1991) 'Chile: economic crisis and recovery', in: V. Thomas et al., eds., *Restructuring economies in distress*. Oxford: Oxford University Press.

Mosley, P., Harrigan, J. and Toye, J. (1991) *Aid and power: The World Bank and policy-based lending*. London and New York: Routledge.

Murphy, K.M., Shleifer, A. and Vishny, R. (1989) 'Income distribution, market size and industrialization', *Quarterly Journal of Economics*, 104:537–564.

Murphy, K.M., Shleifer, A. and Vishny, R. (1989) 'Industrialization and the big push', *Journal of Political Economy*, 97:1003–1026.

Murphy, K.M., Shleifer, A. and Vishny, R. (1991) 'Allocation of talent and economic growth', *Quarterly Journal of Economics*, 106:503–530.

Mussa, M. (1986) 'The adjustment process and the timing of trade liberalization', in: A.M. Choksi and D. Papageorgiou, eds., *Economic liberalization in developing countries*. Oxford and New York: Basil Blackwell.

Nalebuff, B. and Stiglitz, J. (1983) 'Information, competition, and markets', *American Economic Review*, 73:278–283.

Nellis, J.R. and Kikeri, S. (1989) 'Public enterprise reform: Privatization and the World Bank', *World Development*, 17:659–672.

Neary, J.P. (1993) 'External shocks, policy response and economic performance', University College, Dublin, mimeo.

Nishimizu, M. and Robinson, S. (1984) 'Trade policies and productivity change in semi-industrialized countries', *Journal of Development Economics*, 16:177–206.

Nishimizu, M. and Page, J. (1991) 'Trade policy, market orientation and productivity change in industry', in: J. de Melo and A. Sapir, eds., *Trade theory and economic reform: Essays in honor of Bela Balassa*. Cambridge, MA: Basil Blackwell.

Nurkse, R. (1953) *Problems of capital formation in underdeveloped countries*. New York: Oxford University Press.

Onis, Z. (1991) 'Organization of export-oriented industrialization: The Turkish foreign trade companies in comparative perspective', in: T. Nas and M. Odekon, eds., *Politics and Economics of Turkish Liberalization*. London and Toronto: Associated Universities Press.

Pack, H. (1987) *Productivity, technology and industrial development*. New York: Oxford University Press.

Pack, H. (1988) 'Industrialization and trade', in: H.B. Chenery and T.N. Srinivasan, eds., *Handbook of development economics*, Vol. I. Amsterdam: North-Holland.

Pack, H. (1992) 'Learning and productivity change in developing countries', in: G.K. Helleiner, ed., *Trade policy, industrialization and development*. Oxford: Clarendon Press.

Pack, H. and Westphal. L. (1986) 'Industrial strategy and technological change: Theory versus reality', *Journal of Development Economics*, 22:87–128.

Panagariya, A. (1990) 'How should tariffs be structured', Country Economics Department WPS 353, World Bank, Washington, DC, February.

Panagariya, A. and Rodrik, D. (1993) 'Political economy arguments for a uniform tariff', *International Economic Review*, 34:685–703.

Panagariya, A. and Schiff, M. (1990) 'Commodity exports and real incomes in Africa: A preliminary analysis', mimeo.

Panagariya, A. and Schiff, M. (1992) 'Taxes versus quotas: The case of cocoa exports', in: I. Goldin and L.A. Winters, eds., *Open economies: Structural adjustment and agriculture*. New York and London: Cambridge University Press.

Pearson, R. (1987) 'Transfer of technology and domestic innovation in the cement industry', in:

J.M. Katz, ed., *Technology generation in Latin American manufacturing industries*. London: Macmillan.

Perez, L.A.P. and y Peniche, J.J.P. (1987) 'A summary of the principal findings of the case study on technological behavior of the Mexican steel firm, Altos Hornos de Mexico', in: J.M. Katz, ed., *Technology generation in Latin American manufacturing industries*. London: Macmillan Press.

Portes, R. (1990) 'The transition to convertibility for Eastern Europe and the USSR', CEPR Discussion Paper No. 500. London: Centre for Economic Policy Research.

Prasnikar, J., Svejnar, J. and Klinedinst, M. (1992) 'Structural adjustment policies and productive efficiency of socialist enterprises', *European Economic Review*, 36:179–199.

Pritchett, L. (1991) 'Measuring outward orientation in developing countries: Can it be done?' World Bank, mimeo.

Pryor, F.L. (1991) 'Economic reform in Third-World Marxist nations', Hoover Institution, Stanford University.

Pursell, G. (1990) 'Industrial sickness, primary and secondary: The effects of exit constraints on industrial performance', *The World Bank Economic Review*, 4:103–114.

Rivera-Batiz, L.A. and Romer, P.M. (1991) 'International trade with endogenous technological change', *European Economic Review*, 35:971–1004.

Roberts, M.J. and Tybout, J.R. (1991) 'Size rationalization and trade exposure in developing countries', World Bank WPS 594, February.

Roberts, M.J. and Tybout, J.R. (1992) 'Sunk costs and the decision to export in Colombia', Unpublished paper, January.

Rodriguez, A. (1993) 'The division of labor and economic development', Stanford University, mimeo.

Rodrik, D. (1987a) 'The economics of export-performance requirements', *Quarterly Journal of Economics*, 102:633–650.

Rodrik, D. (1987b) 'Trade and capital-account liberalization in a Keynesian economy', *Journal of International Economics*, 23:113–129.

Rodrik, D. (1988) 'Imperfect competition, scale economies, and trade policy in developing countries', in: R. Baldwin, ed., *Trade policy issues and empirical analysis*. Chicago and London: University of Chicago Press.

Rodrik, D. (1989a) 'Promises, promises: Credible policy reform via signalling', *The Economic Journal*, 99:756–772.

Rodrik, D. (1989b) 'Credibility of trade reform: A policy maker's guide', *The World Economy*.

Rodrik, D. (1991) 'Policy uncertainty and private investment in developing countries', *Journal of Development Economics*, 36:229–242.

Rodrik, D. (1992a) 'The rush to free trade in the developing world: Why so late? Why now? Will it last?' NBER Working Paper No. 3947, January.

Rodrik, D. (1992b) 'Closing the productivity gap: Does trade liberalization really help?' in: G. Helleiner, ed., *Trade policy, industrialization and development*. Oxford: Clarendon Press.

Rodrik, D. (1992c) 'The limits of trade policy reform in developing countries', *Journal of Economic Perspectives*, 6:87–105.

Rodrik, D. (1992d) 'Political economy and development policy', *European Economic Review*, 36:329–336.

Rodrik, D. (1993) 'Taking trade policy seriously: Export subsidization as a case study in policy effectiveness', National Bureau of Economic Research Working Paper No. 4567.

Rodrik, D. (1994) 'Coordination failures and government policy: A model with applications to East Asia and Eastern Europe', Columbia University, mimeo.

Rodrik, D., 'Foreign trade in Eastern Europe's transition: Early results', in: O.J. Blanchard et al., eds., *The transition in Eastern Europe*. Chicago and New York: University of Chicago Press, forthcoming.

Roemer, M. and Jones, C., eds. (1991) *Markets in developing countries: Parallel, fragmented and black*. San Francisco: ICS Press.

Romer, P. (1986) 'Increasing returns and long-run growth', *Journal of Political Economy*, 94:1002–1037.

Romer. P. (1992) 'Two strategies for economic development: Using ideas and producing ideas'.

Proceedings of the World Bank Annual Conference on Development Economics (Supplement to the World Bank Economic Review and the World Bank Research Observer).

Rosenstein-Rodan, P.N. (1943) 'Problems of industrialization of Eastern and South-eastern Europe', *Economic Journal*, 53:202–211.

Roumasset, J. and Setboonsarng, S. (1988) 'Second-best agricultural policy: Getting the price of Thai rice right', *Journal of Development Economics*, 28:323–340.

Sachs, J. (1985) 'External debt and macroeconomic performance in Latin America and East Asia', *Brookings Papers on Economic Activity*, 2:565–573.

Sachs, J. (1987) 'Trade and exchange rate policies in growth-oriented adjustment programs', in: V. Corbo, M. Goldstein, and M. Khan, eds., *Growth-oriented adjustment programs*. Washington, DC: IMF and The World Bank.

Scharfstein, D. (1988) 'Product-market competition and managerial slack', *Rand Journal of Economics*, 19:147–155.

Scherer, F.M. and Ross, D. (1990) *Industrial market structure and economic performance*: 3rd. ed. Boston: Houghton Mifflin.

Snape, R. (1991) 'East Asia: Trade reform in Korea and Singapore', in: G. Shepherd and C.G. Langoni, eds., *Trade reform: Lessons from eighteen countries*, San Francisco: ICS Press for International Center for Economic Growth.

Srinivasan, T.N. (1988) 'International trade and factor movements in development theory, policy, and experience', in: G. Ranis and T.N. Srinivasan, eds., *The state of development economics*. Cambridge, MA: Basil Blackwell.

Srinivasan, T.N. (1989) 'Recent theories of imperfect competition and international trade: Any implications for development strategy?' *Indian Economic Review*, 24:1–23.

Srinivasan, T.N. and Whalley, J., eds. (1986) *General equilibrium trade policy modeling*. Cambridge, MA: MIT Press.

Steel, W.F. and Webster, L.M. (1991) *Small enterprises under adjustment in Ghana*, World Bank Technical Paper Number 138, Washington, DC.

Stern, E. (1991) 'Evolution and lessons of adjustment lending', in: V. Thomas et al. eds., *Restructuring economies in distress: Policy reform and the World Bank*. Oxford and New York: Oxford University Press.

Stewart, F. and Ghani, E. (1992) 'Externalities, development, and trade', in: G.K. Helleiner, ed., *Trade policy, industrialization and development*. Oxford: Clarendon Press.

Streeten, P. (1989) 'A survey of the issues and options', in: S. Commander, ed., *Structural adjustment in agriculture*. London: Overseas Development Institute.

Summers, R. and Heston, A. (1988) 'A new set of international comparisons of real product and price levels: Estimates for 130 countries', *Review of Income and Wealth*, 34:1–25.

Svedberg, P. (1991) 'The export performance of sub-Saharan Africa', *Economic Development and Cultural Change*, 39:549–566.

Syrquin, M. and Chenery, H. (1989) 'Three decades of industrialization', *The World Bank Economic Review*, 3:145–181.

Takacs, W. (1989) 'Options for dismantling trade restrictions in developing countries', *The World Bank Research Observer*, 5:25–46.

Tanzi, V. and Shome, P. (1992) 'The role of taxation in the development of East Asian economies', in: T. Ito and A.O. Krueger, eds., *The political economy of tax reform*. Chicago and London: The University of Chicago Press.

Tarr, D. (1992) 'Rent-seeking and the benefits of price and trade reform in Poland: The automobile and color television cases', The World Bank, mimeo.

Taylor, L. (1991) 'Economic openness: Problems to the century's end', in: T. Banuri, ed., *Economic liberalization: No panacea: The experiences of Latin America and Asia*, Oxford: Clarendon Press.

Thomas, V., Nash, J. et al. (1991) *Best practices in trade policy reform*. Washington, DC: The World Bank.

Thomas, V. et al., eds. (1991) *Restructuring economies in distress: Policy reform and the World Bank*. Oxford and New York: Oxford University Press.

Tybout, J., de Melo, J. and Corbo, V. (1991) 'The effects of trade reforms on scale and technical efficiency: New evidence from Chile', *Journal of International Economics*, 31:231–250.

Tybout, J.R. (1992) 'Linking trade and productivity', *The World Bank Economic Review*, 6:189–211.

Tybout, J.R., with appendix by L. Liu (1989) 'Entry. exit, competition and productivity in the Chilean industrial sector', World Bank, unpublished paper, May.

Tybout J.R. and Westbrook, M.D. (1992a) 'Estimating returns to scale with large imperfect panels: An application to Chilean manufacturing industries', Georgetown University, unpublished paper, May.

Tybout J.R. and Westbrook, M.D. (1992b) 'Trade liberalization and the dimensions of efficiency change in Mexican manufacturing industries', Georgetown University, unpublished paper, July.

Wade, R. (1990) *Governing the market: Economic theory and the role of government in East Asian industrialization*. Princeton, NJ: Princeton University Press.

Waverman, L. and Murphy, S. (1992) 'Total factor productivity in automobile production in Argentina, Mexico, Korea, and Canada: The impacts of protection', in: G.K. Helleiner, ed., *Trade policy, industrialization and development*. Oxford: Clarendon Press.

Webb, S. and Shariff, K. (1992) 'Designing and implementing adjustment programs', in: V. Corbo, S. Fischer, and S.B. Webb, eds., *Adjustment lending revisited: Policies to restore growth*. Washington DC: The World Bank.

Westphal, L.E. (1982) 'Fostering technological mastery by means of selective infant-industry protection', in: M. Syrquin and S. Teitel, eds., *Trade, stability, technology, and equity in Latin America*. New York: Academic Press.

Westphal, L.E. (1990) 'Industrial policy in an export-propelled economy: Lessons from South Korea's experience', *Journal of Economic Perspectives*, 4:41–59.

Westphal, L.E. (1991) 'Comments on Korea: Structural adjustment', in: V. Thomas et al., eds., *Restructuring economies in distress*. Oxford: Oxford University Press.

Whalley, J. (1989) 'Recent trade liberalization in the developing world: What is behind it, and where is it headed?' Cambridge, MA: National Bureau of Economic Research Working Paper No. 3057.

Williamson, J. (1990) *The progress of policy reform in Latin America*. Washington, DC: Institute for International Economics, Policy Analyses in International Economics: 28.

Williamson, J. (1991) *The economic opening of Eastern Europe*. Washington, DC: Institute for International Economics.

Williamson, J. (1992) Comments on 'Adjustment programs and bank support', in: V. Corbo et al., eds., *Adjustment lending revisited*. Washington, DC: The World Bank.

World Bank (1987) *World development report*. Washington, DC: The World Bank.

World Bank (1992) *Privatization: The lessons of experience*, Country Economics Department, Washington, DC.

World Bank (1993) *The East Asian miracle: Economic growth and public policy*. New York: Oxford University Press.

World Bank (1994) *Adjustment in Africa: Reforms, results and the road ahead*. New York: Oxford University Press.

Yoon, C.-H. (1992) 'International competitiuon and market penetration: A model of the growth strategy of the Korean semiconductor industry', in: G.K. Helleiner, ed., *Trade policy, industrialization and development*. Oxford: Clarendon Press.

Young, A. (1991) 'Learning-by-doing and the dynamic effects of international trade', *Quarterly Journal of Economics*, 106:369–405.

*Chapter 46*

# THE CONTRIBUTIONS OF ENDOGENOUS GROWTH THEORY TO THE ANALYSIS OF DEVELOPMENT PROBLEMS: AN ASSESSMENT*

PRANAB BARDHAN

*University of California, Berkeley*

## Contents

*I am grateful to the Editors of this volume and to Paul Romer for their valuable comments.

*Handbook of Development Economics, Volume III, Edited by J. Behrman and T.N. Srinivasan*
© *Elsevier Science B.V., 1995*

## 1. Introduction

The "old" growth theory influenced the theory of economic development in several ways. Starting with the basic Harrod–Domar structure of capacity growth, development economists paid attention to the constraints posed by savings and the efficiency with which savings are utilized. The basic model was extended to incorporate structural rigidities constraining the capacity to convert exportables into imports of capital and intermediate goods (leading to the foreign exchange gap as an additional constraint) and the capacity to shift once-installed capital intersectorally (leading to a growth premium on investment allocation in favor of machine-making as in the Fel'dman–Mahalanobis planning model). The optimum growth literature led to a sophisticated discussion of terminal capacity constraints and social time discount rates in the context of development planning. The "turnpike" feature of optimum growth models, derived from the earlier model of von Neumann (1945), showed a useful convergence property of optimal paths in planning models. Given the persistence of unemployment and underemployment and the precapitalist organization of production in some sectors (like agriculture), the classical growth model of Smith, Ricardo and Marx (to which Arthur Lewis had drawn attention) was often considered more appropriate for studying development problems than the Solow–Swan neoclassical growth model.

Contrary to the claim sometimes made in the literature on the "new" growth theory, many of the growth models of the 1950's and the 1960's endogenized technical progress in significant ways: apart from Arrow's (1962) celebrated learning-by-doing model where learning emanated from the dynamic externalities of cumulated gross investment, the earlier related learning model of Haavelmo (1956), and Uzawa's (1965) model of investment in human capital generating technical change, there are several Kaldor models culminating in the Kaldor–Mirrlees model (1962) where investment is the vehicle of technical progress and Shell's (1967) model of inventive activity. Learning by doing particularly in the form of acquisition of tacit knowledge and inter-firm spillover effects of cumulated gross output influenced development theory by providing a formal rationale for an old argument for support of "infant" industry producing import-substitutes (or new exports), as in the models of Bardhan (1970) and Clemhout and Wan (1970). The acquired and sometimes policy-driven nature of dynamic comparative advantage, to which the East Asian challenge has awakened many developed-country trade theorists, has been a persistent theme in the trade and development literature for decades. In general the old literature on the microeconomics of technological progress has always emphasized the pervasiveness of externalities in the innovation process, in the transfer, absorption, development and adaptation of new technologies and the discussion in development economics on the problems posed by the catching-up process in the developing countries reflected this. Thus the models of Romer (1986) and Lucas (1988), while helping in the formalization of these ideas of dynamic externalities in a perfect competition framework, do not provide any substantial breakthrough in development theory as such.[1]

Where then are the distinctive contributions of the "new" growth theory that may be particularly useful for understanding development problems? They certainly do not lie in the so-called convergence controversy which has spawned a large part of published output in the literature.[2] The main result, reached on the basis of dubious cross-country regressions and even more dubious data quality, that the lack of convergence in per capita income growth rates across countries belies the standard presumption of the availability of the same technological opportunities in all countries of the world is not particularly earth-shaking from the point of view of development economics. As Solow (1994) comments on this body of empirical work: "I do not find this a confidence-inspiring project. It seems altogether too vulnerable to bias from omitted variables, to reverse causation, and above all to the recurrent suspicion that the experiences of various national economies are not to be explained as if they represent different 'points' on some well-defined surface". In any case a development economist plowing through this literature gets hardly any clue (and a lot of red herrings) about the factors determining the crucial international differences in factor productivity growth.

A much more substantive contribution of the "new" growth theory is to formalize endogenous technical progress in terms of a tractable imperfect-competition framework in which temporary monopoly power acts as a motivating force for private innovators. The leading work in this area of what has been called neo-Schumpeterian growth theory is by Romer (1987, 1990), Grossman and Helpman (1991), Segerstrom, Anant and Dinopoulos (1990), and Aghion and Howitt (1992). Growth theory has now been liberated from the confines of the competitive market framework of earlier endogenous growth models in which dynamic externalities played the central role (even considering the

---

[1] In fact as Srinivasan (1993) points out, human capital and the process of its accumulation play somewhat the same role in the Lucas (1988) model as the capital goods sector in the two-sector model of Mahalanobis (1955).

Development theory has even less to learn from the strand of new growth theory which shows that substantial growth is possible even in the absence of technical progress or increasing returns as long as the marginal product of capital has a positive lower bound, a result the old growth theorists were already aware of.

[2] For an evaluation of the empirical literature see Levine and Renelt (1992), Levine and Zervos (1993), Pack (1994) and Section 3 of Srinivasan (forthcoming). For an examination of the data quality see the symposium on Database for Development Analysis in the *Journal of Development Economics*, June 1994 issue.

models of Kaldor who repeatedly emphasized the importance of imperfect competition in the context of endogenous technical progress, the current models drawing upon the advances in industrial organization theory are more satisfactory). In particular, the emphasis on new goods and the fixed costs in introducing them provides valuable new insights. The major impact of this literature on development theory has been in the area of trade and technological diffusion in an international economy, which we discuss in the next section.

## 2. Trade and technological diffusion

The East Asian success stories have given credence[3] to the belief of many economists in a positive relationship between "outward-orientation" and economic development (although a rigorous empirical demonstration of the *causal* relationship between some satisfactory measure of outward-orientation and the rate of growth is rather scarce). Standard neoclassical growth theory did not provide any such general theorem on the effect of trade on the long-run growth rate.

A major result in the new literature is to show how economic integration in the world market, compared to isolation, helps long-run growth by avoiding unnecessary duplication of research and thus increases aggregate productivity of resources employed in the R & D sector (characterized by economies of scale). World market competition gives incentives to entrepreneurs in each of these countries to invent products that are unique in the world economy – see the models of Rivera-Batiz and Romer (1991) and Grossman and Helpman (1991), Chapter 9. One has, of course, to keep in mind the fact that sometimes these unique products are unique in the sense of product differentiation but not in the sense of any genuine technological advance (it is well-known, for example, that in the pharmaceutical industry a majority of the so-called new products are really recombinations of existing ingredients with an eye to prolonging patent protection, and that they are new, not therapeutically, but from the marketability point of view). Of course trade often helps transmission of useful ideas in production engineering and information about changing product patterns. But the presumption in many of the models of a common pool of knowledge capital created by international spillovers of technical information is sometimes not relevant for a poor country.

When knowledge accumulation is localized largely in the rich country and the poor country is also smaller in (economic) size, particularly in the size of its

---

[3] It should, however, be noted that the export boom in manufactures for Korea and Taiwan in the 1960's came *before* any significant trade liberalization. As Rodrik (1992) suggests, a realistic exchange rate policy and a generous program of export subsidies, rather than trade liberalization per se, may be the key ingredients for successful export performance.

already accumulated knowledge capital (which determines research effectiveness), the rich country captures a growing market share in the total number of differentiated varieties, and the entrepreneurs in the poor country foreseeing capital losses may innovate less rapidly in long-run equilibrium with international trade than it does under autarky, as shown by Feenstra (1990) and Grossman and Helpman (1991), Chapter 9. Trade reduces the profitability of R and D in the poor country as it places local entrepreneurs in competition with a rapidly expanding set of imported, differentiated products and may drive the country to specialize in production rather than research, and within production from high-tech products to traditional, possibly stagnant, industries which use its relatively plentiful supply of unskilled workers – thus slowing innovation and growth. For the lagging country isolation would have been more advantageous for the pace of innovation.[4]

These growth results are quite consistent with atemporal comparative advantage considerations except for the effect of the initial conditions of accumulated knowledge capital and country size. Much depends on the general-equilibrium effects on the intersectoral allocation of labor. For example, suppose output of finished goods depends on labor and a composite intermediate input $H$, where

$$H = \left[ \int_0^n x^\alpha(j)\, dj \right]^{1/\alpha}, \quad 1 > \alpha > 0 \tag{1}$$

with $x(j)$ as the intermediate input of type $j$ – all symmetric but imperfect substitutes aggregated in the standard Dixit-Stiglitz way – and $n$ as the measure of continually augmented inputs as well as the stock of cumulative knowledge capital. The blueprints for intermediate inputs are generated by research. Then the innovation output of the R and D sector is

$$\dot{n} = \frac{l}{a/n}, \tag{2}$$

where $l$ is the labor devoted to the R and D sector, $a$ is the fixed labor coefficient in the R and D sector, and research effectiveness of labor improves with the cumulative stock of knowledge capital. Thus the rate of growth $\dot{n}/n$ depends directly on what happens (say, as a result of trade expansion or restriction) to $l$: a trade-induced movement of labor away from the R and D sector toward the production sector will reduce the rate of growth in this case. Of course, slower growth does not necessarily mean that the consumer loses

---

[4] This is at least consistent with the view in the historical studies of Japan's innovation system that restrictions on imports and foreign direct investment may have played a major positive role in regard to R and D effort until the early 1970's. See Odagiri and Goto (1993).

from trade: apart from usual static gains from trade, consumers may have access to more varieties innovated abroad. But trade may sometimes cause a net welfare loss, since in the poorer country it accelerates a market failure (underinvestment in research in the initial situation) by allocating resources further away from research.

One should note that the relevant R and D for a poor country is, of course, more in technological adaptation of products and processes invented abroad and in imitation. But even this kind of a R and D sector is usually so small that major changes in aggregate productivity and growth on the basis of the trade-induced general-equilibrium type reallocation of fully employed resources into or away from the R and D sector, as emphasized by Grossman and Helpman, seems a little overdrawn if applied in the context of poor countries. In any case the ambiguity in the relationship between trade expansion and productivity growth in these general-equilibrium models only confirms similar conclusions in careful partial-equilibrium models, particularly when entry and exit from industries are not frictionless [see, for example, Rodrik (1992)].

In the Grossman–Helpman model of the innovating North and the imitating South with all firms in Bertrand competition with one another, imitation has two opposing effects on the incentive to innovate in the North: on the one hand, imitation reduces the duration of monopoly profits of the innovator; on the other hand, it frees up Northern labor to produce more of the as yet unimitated products and to conduct more R and D.[5] In these models labor costs form the only component of the cost of entry into the imitative-adaptive R and D activity in the South. So, armed with cheaper labor the Southern firms can relentlessly keep on targeting Northern products for imitation, unhampered by many of the formidable real-world non-labor constraints on entry (for example, those posed by the lack of a viable physical, social and educational infrastructure or that of organizational knowhow in a poor country).

In general most of the new models of trade and growth, by adopting the Dixit–Stiglitz-style consumer preferences, assume a uniform price elasticity and a unitary expenditure elasticity for each of the differentiated products which enter symmetrically in the utility function. This, of course, immediately rules out what has been a major preoccupation of the trade and development literature: to explore the implications of sectoral demand asymmetries for trade relationships between rich and poor countries. The Dixit–Stiglitz functional form also narrows the operation of scale economies to take the form of expansion of variety, not in the scale of output. The assumption of monopolistic competition and contestable markets in the models also precludes any

---

[5] It may also be noted that in the Grossman–Helpman (1991, Chapter 11) model of imitation, where the poor country grows faster with imitation and trade than without them, it is the process of imitation rather than the integration of product markets per se that contributes to a more rapid pace of innovation in the poor country.

serious examination of the impact of trade on growth through the lowering of entry barriers in oligopolistic industries, industry rationalization and reduction of the gap between actual and best practice international technology that foreign competitive pressure may induce. This gap between actual and best practice partly depends on the degree of modernization of the capital stock aggregated over different vintages. The "quality ladder" models, for example that of Grossman and Helpman (1991, Chapter 4), ignore this aspect by assuming that older inputs are instantaneously rendered obsolete by new inputs. The old "putty-clay" vintage models of capital, however, had old and new inputs co-existing and there was an endogenous determination of the economic life of capital in each industry. Bardhan and Kletzer (1984) develop such a vintage-capital model of endogenous growth with learning by doing, where they trace the impact of trade policy on the time-path of productivity.

The slow diffusion of technology from rich to poor countries is often interpreted in the literature as reflecting the frequent laxity in the enforcement of patents in poor countries and innovators in rich countries thus compelled to protect their ideas through secrecy. This brings us to the controversial issue of intellectual property rights (IPR), which has sometimes divided the rich and poor countries, as notably in the recent Uruguay Round discussions. Rich countries often claim that a tighter IPR regime encourages innovations (by expanding the duration of the innovator's monopoly) from which all countries benefit. Poor countries often counter this by pointing to their losses following upon increased monopoly power of the larger companies of rich countries. Since the poor countries provide a very small market for many industrial products, the disincentive effects of lax patent protection in those countries may be marginal on the rate of innovation in rich countries, and as such attempts at free riding by the poor countries may make sense, as Chin and Grossman (1990) suggest. To this Diwan and Rodrik (1991) add the qualification that the disincentive effects may be very significant in the case of innovation in technologies or products that are particularly appropriate for poor countries (for example, drugs against tropical diseases). But both of these theoretical models use a static partial-equilibrium framework. Helpman (1993) recently constructed a dynamic general-equilibrium model of innovation and imitation to discuss the question of IPR. In the long-run equilibrium of his model, a tighter IPR (reducing the rate of imitation by the lower-wage poor country) increases the fraction of the total number of products produced (unchallenged) in the rich country, but *lowers* the long-run rate of innovation of new products[6] (this works through the rise in the price-earning ratio of the R and D firm in the rich country, consequent upon the general-equilibrium

---

[6] This result may not be robust for the case where direct foreign investment as well as imitation acts as a channel of technology transfer, as Lai (1993) shows.

labor reallocation effect of a larger range of manufactured products produced in the rich country).[7] Even apart from this effect on the rate of innovation, a tighter IPR, by shifting production from the lower-wage (and therefore lower-price) country to the higher-wage country makes consumers in both countries worse off.

The discussion advocating a tighter IPR regime also ignores the cases of restrictive business practices of many multinational companies (like pre-emptive patenting and "sleeping" patents where new patents are taken out in poor countries simply to ward off competitors but seldom actually used in local production).[8] Furthermore, the flow of technology through direct investments by multinational enterprises to a poor country is often constrained not so much by restrictive government policy in the host country as by its lack of infrastructure (the development of which in turn is constrained by the difficulty of raising large loans in a severely imperfect international credit market).

In fact while the new models of trade and growth bring into sharp focus the features of monopolistic competition particularly in the sector producing intermediate products and, in some models, the Schumpeterian process of costly R and D races with the prospect of temporary monopoly power for the winner – aspects which were missing in most of the earlier macroeconomic growth models – there are other important aspects of imperfect competition (like the case of "sleeping" patents above or how international credit market imperfections shape the pattern of comparative advantage)[9] which need formalizing in the literature on trade and development. In general the growth literature that stresses the importance of capital market imperfections as the source of endogenous generation and persistence of wealth inequalities in the process of development is still in its infancy.[10]

In another respect the new literature marks a substantial advance over the old. This relates to the dynamic economies of scale associated with learning by doing. An important extension of the models of Bardhan (1970) and Clemhout and Wan (1970) has been carried out by Krugman (1987) and Boldrin and Scheinkman (1988), where the learning effects (emanating from production

---

[7] In a different context Mookherjee and Ray (1991) have shown that when a dominant firm decides on the adoption of a sequence of potential cost-reducing innovations with Bertrand competition in the product market, a faster rate of diffusion of the latest technology to a competitive fringe may, over some range, increase the competitive pressure on the leader, quickening the latter's pace of innovations.

[8] Some estimates by UNCTAD (1975) suggest that 90 to 95 percent of foreign-owned patents in developing countries are not used in those countries.

[9] Kletzer and Bardhan (1987) show how more costly credit under imperfect information may drive a poor country away from specializing in sophisticated manufactured products which require more selling and distribution costs than traditional primary products.

[10] For a brief review of this literature see Aghion and Bolton (1992).

experience measured by cumulated industry output) enhance over time the existing sectoral patterns of comparative advantage; this may call for a deliberate trade policy that can orchestrate a breakout from such a historical "lock-in".[11] An explanation of the reverse flow of capital and human skills from poor to rich countries in terms of the external effects of the higher average stock of human capital in rich countries, as suggested by Lucas (1990), is also an important corollary of these models of dynamic externalities and learning.

But these models of learning share with the earlier ones the unrealistic feature of continued learning at a given rate on a fixed set of goods. As Lucas (1993) comments, evidence on learning on narrowly defined product lines often shows high initial learning rates, declining over time as production cumulates, and for on-the-job learning to occur in an economy on a sustained basis it is necessary that workers and managers continue to take on tasks that are new to them, to continue to move up the quality ladder in goods. The major formulations that try to capture this in the context of an open economy are those of Young (1991) and Stokey (1991). On the basis of learning by doing that spills over across industries, although bounded in each industry, Young's model endogenizes the movement of goods out of the learning sector into a mature sector in which learning no longer occurs and thus gives a plausible account of an evolving trade structure. Stokey has a model of North-South trade, based on vertical product differentiation and international differences in labor quality; the South produces a low-quality spectrum of goods and the North a high-quality spectrum. If human capital is acquired through learning by doing and so is stimulated by the production of high-quality goods, free trade (as opposed to autarky) will speed up human capital accumulation in the North and slow it down in the South. A similar result is obtained by Young. The country that begins with a technological lead tends to widen that lead over time. (It, of course, does not follow that the South would be better off under autarky.) It also indicates why a policy of subsidizing infant export industries is sometimes more growth-promoting in the long run than that of protecting infant import-substitute industries, since in the former case the opportunities for learning spillover into newer and more sophisticated goods are wider than when one is restricted to the home market. Export growth encourages accumulation of technological capability not only in the producer firms but also in the specialized supplier firms through vertical linkage. A high level of skills in the labor force as in some of the East Asian cases facilitates this process. The rapid growth of exports also enabled these countries, as Pack (1992) points

---

[11] A similar model of hysteresis, based on self-reinforcing advantages not of learning but of headstarts in R and D, is developed in Grossman and Helpman (1991), Chapter 8.

out, to overcome imperfections in technology markets, such as monopolistic licensing fees, that limit the diffusion of proprietary knowledge and hinder a move toward international best practice.

Going beyond these learning models, one can generalize and say that probably the most important contribution of the new growth theory is to formally draw our attention to the process of introduction of an ever-expanding set of new goods and technologies (in the case of developing countries, often imports of new types of produced inputs) and the large fixed costs usually associated with it. These fixed costs underline the fundamental importance of nonconvexities and imperfect competition in economic analysis. As Romer (1994) shows, the welfare costs of restrictions on the process of introduction of new goods (as, for example, in the case of trade or foreign investment restrictions in developing countries) are substantially larger than the static misallocation effects in the case when we deal with a fixed set of goods. I agree with Romer (1994) when he says: "New growth theory may not be *new*, but it is *about* newness. And newness, like history, matters". The new literature in some ways diverts our attention from the abiding concern of development economists with the problems of structural transformation and with those of reallocation of resources from traditional sectors to other sectors with different organizational and technological dynamics. But it does serve a purpose in focusing attention on the serious nonconvexities involved in the process of diffusion and adoption of new goods and technologies in a developing country.

## 3. Strategic complementarities and increasing returns

While the emphasis in the new growth theory is to search for the factors that perpetuate growth, it is not directly concerned with an older question of development theory: how underdevelopment often tends to persist and how does a poor country get out of a poverty trap? Yet a fallout of the recent formalizations and explorations of dynamic externalities has been to revive interest in the older question. In the immediate postwar florescence of development economics one idea that was particularly prominent was that of how coordination of investments across sectors is essential for industrialization. The literature that grew out of the famous paper of Rosenstein-Rodan (1943) emphasized that when domestic markets are small (and foreign trade is costly), simultaneous expansion of many sectors can be self-sustaining through mutual demand support, even if by itself no sector can break even (primarily because firms in a sector may not by themselves be able to generate enough sales to render adoption of modern increasing-returns technologies with large fixed costs profitable). There was a presumption in this literature of multiple equilibria and the essential problem was posed as one of escaping a "low-level equilibrium trap" to a higher-income equilibrium with industrialization.

To capture the full flavor of this problem of strategic complementarity of industries in terms of market size, one needs a full-scale model of plant-level economies of scale in production (with the associated imperfections in market competition) which can be tapped with large demand spillovers. This formalization was done in a recent model by Murphy, Shleifer and Vishny (1989). One common objection to such models is that in an open economy where an industry faces the world market, the size of the domestic market cannot plausibly limit the adoption of increasing returns technologies. Such objections usually underestimate how the size of the domestic market matters even in an open-economy. In any case the idea of intersectoral complementarities in investment can be reformulated for an open economy with tradeable final outputs, but where jointly used infrastructure (like roads, railways, power stations or training facilities) and other non-traded support services and specialized inputs (like repair and maintenance, some ancillary parts and components, and financial, communication or distribution services) are indispensable for the production and distribution of the final goods. One variant of the models in Murphy, Shleifer and Vishny (1989) shows how in the case of shared infrastructure each industrializing firm that uses it contributes to the large fixed cost of building it and thus indirectly helps other users and hence makes their industrialization more likely. In one of the equilibria of the model the infrastructure will make money on its first-period investment if the economy industrializes, but will incur a large loss if no industrialization takes place and there are no users of its services. Thus the infrastructure is not built lest an insufficient number of firms industrialize and this in turn ensures that firms do not make the large-scale investments needed to industrialize. This is an underdevelopment trap caused by a coordination failure.

Alternatively, Rodríguez (1993) has a model of multiple equilibria arising from sectoral complementarity and cumulative processes generated by increasing returns in the production of support services and inputs. The tradeable final goods require these non-traded intermediate inputs and services readily available in close proximity. The domestic availability of a wide variety of such specialized inputs enhances the productive efficiency of the manufacturing sector, but the extent of input specialization (or division of labor in their production) is limited by the extent of the market. In such a situation the economy may get stuck in an equilibrium where the division of labor in the input producing sector is shallow and the final goods production remains confined to the use of low-productivity techniques that do not require a wide variety of inputs.[12] The task of development policy here is to compensate for an historical handicap (in the form of a trap of low-productivity specialization), either by trade policy or a policy of subsidization of fixed costs or of other ways of encouraging appropriate linkages between the finals goods sector and the intermediate inputs sector. In the model of the preceding paragraph, on the other hand, coordination of investments between sectors is the key, and the role of expectations (about investment by other firms) and self-fulfilling prophecy become more important. The task of development policy is to coordinate expectations around high investment. This "history versus expectations" dichotomy in the dynamic processes of how a particular equilibrium gets established has been further analyzed by Krugman (1991) and Matsuyama (1991) and the relative importance of the past and expected future is shown to depend on some parameters of the economy (like the discount rate and the speed of adjustment).

The idea of strategic complementarities between sectors generated by increasing returns must be one of the early examples in the flowering of the general literature on coordination failures in economics. It was so central to the development economics of the 1950's. Yet it lost much of its intellectual force in the subsequent decades, not so much because it lacked, until recently, a firm anchoring in a formal model using tools of imperfect markets equilibrium analysis, as Krugman (1992) suggests, but more because at the policy level the difficulties of aggregate coordination were underestimated (particularly at the existing levels of administrative capacity and political coherence in the developing countries), and the incentive and organizational issues of micro-management of capital were underappreciated. The resulting government failures diverted the profession's attention from what nevertheless remains an important source of market failure discovered by early development economics. From the policy point of view the new literature on learning and strategic complementaries, like the earlier development literature on externalities, underestimates the difficulty of identifying the few sectors and locations where the spillover effects may be large and particularly difficult to internalize. It is sometimes overlooked that learning is often highly localized and project-specific. Evenson and Westphal in Chapter 37 of this volume have pointed to the related policy problems arising from "tacitness and circumstantial sensitivity" of technology. In addition, the extent of spillovers depends crucially on the nature of competition that the policy environment promotes

---

[12] A low initial average level of human capital plays a similar trapping role in the model of Ciccone (1994), where the interdependence between individual human capital accumulation and the supply of specialized physical capital goods may lead to equilibria with no potential for technical progress or growth. Earlier Azariadis and Drazen (1990) had emphasized the threshold effects of human capital and the multiple balanced growth paths induced by the externalities in the technologies of human capital accumulation.

and its interaction with the nature of the physical, social and organizational infrastructure in the country.

Another by-product of the recent formalizations of market size, increasing returns and imperfect competition has been in the area of economic geography, which throws some light on the problem of urban concentration and uneven regional development in the developing countries. Krugman (1994) has a model of the endogenous determination of agglomeration economies out of the interaction among economies of scale at the plant level, transportation costs and factor mobility. (These economies may be particularly important in poor countries where basic manufacturing using the transport system is still more important than the new footloose service industries and where the small market size makes the issue of scale economies significant.) The pattern of urban growth and regional inequality are shaped by a tension between centripetal forces that tend to pull population and production into agglomerations and the centrifugal forces that tend to break up such agglomerations. On the one hand, firms want to locate close to the large market provided by other firms' workers, and workers want to live close to the supply of goods provided by other firms; on the other hand, commuting costs and urban land rent (not to speak of congestion and pollution) tend to generate diseconomies of city size. While this is no doubt a promising line of enquiry and opening the door for more sophisticated formalization, here as in other aspects of the new growth theory, the theoretical models have a long way to go before they can catch up with the complexity of the empirical reality, particularly in developing countries.

Robert Lucas (1988), pondering over the questions of differential development performance of poor countries and what can be done about it, says: "The consequences for human welfare involved in questions like these are simply staggering: Once one starts to think about them, it is hard to think about anything else". Coming from a leading economist in the mainstream, which has long marginalized development economics, this is indeed reassuring. But notwithstanding popular impressions to the contrary, the advances made so far in the new literature on growth theory (over and above its rediscovery, with great fanfare, of some of the insights of the old development literature)[13] have barely scratched the surface. The new emphasis on fixed costs and nonconvexities in the process of introduction of new goods and technologies is important. But these fixed costs actually go much beyond the ordinary set-up costs in starting new economic activities: particularly in a developing country they encompass massive costs of collective action in building new economic institutions and political coalitions and in breaking the deadlock of incumbent interests threatened by new technologies. While the new interest in model-

---

[13] See on this Bardhan (1993).

building will be helpful in sharpening our analytical tools and in critically examining our implicit assumptions, let us hope that it will not divert our attention from the organizational-institutional issues and distributive conflicts in the development process which are less amenable to neat formalization.

## References

Aghion, P. and Howitt, P. (1992) 'A model of growth through creative destruction', *Econometrica*, 60:322–352.
Aghion, P. and Bolton, P. (1992) 'Distribution and growth in models of imperfect capital markets', *European Economic Review*, 36:603–611.
Arrow, K.J.(1962) 'The economic implications of learning by doing', *Review of Economic Studies*, 29:155–173.
Azariadis, C. and Drazen, A. (1990) 'Threshold externalities in economic development', *Quarterly Journal of Economics*, 105:501–526.
Bardhan, P. (1970) *Economic growth, development and foreign trade: A study in pure theory*. New York: Wiley-Interscience.
Bardhan, P. (1993) 'Economics of development and the development of economics', *Journal of Economic Perspectives*, 7:129–142.
Bardhan, P. and Kletzer, K. (1984) 'Dynamic effects of protection on productivity', *Journal of International Economics*, 16:45–57.
Boldrin, M. and Scheinkman, J.A. (1988) 'Learning by doing, international trade and growth: A note', in: P.W. Anderson, K.J. Arrow and D. Pines, eds., *The Economy as an evolving complex system*. Reading: Addison-Wesley.
Chin, J.C. and Grossman, G.M. (1990) 'Intellectual property rights and North-South trade', in: R.W. Jones and A.O. Krueger, eds., *The political economy of international trade: Essays in honor of Robert E. Baldwin*. Cambridge: Blackwell.
Ciccone, A. (1994) 'Human capital and technical progress: Stagnation, transition, and growth', Stanford University, mimeo.
Clemhout, S. and Wan, H. (1970) 'Learning by doing and infant industry protection', *Review of Economic Studies*, 37:33–56.
Diwan, I. and Rodrik, R. (1991) 'Patents, appropriate technology, and north-south trade', *Journal of International Economics*, 30:27–47.
Feenstra, R.C. (1990) 'Trade and uneven growth', NBER Working Paper No. 3276.
Grossman, G.M. and Helpman, E. (1991) *Innovation and growth in the global economy*. Cambridge: MIT Press.
Haavelmo, T. (1956) *A study in the theory of economic evolution*. Amsterdam: North-Holland.
Helpman, E. (1993) 'Innovation, imitation, and intellectual property rights', *Econometrica*, 61:1247–1280.
Kaldor, N. and Mirrlees, J.A. (1962) 'A new model of economic growth', *Review of Economic Studies*, 29:174–192.
Kletzer, K. and Bardhan, P. (1987) 'Credit markets and patterns of international trade', *Journal of Development Economics*, 27:57–70.
Krugman, P. (1987) 'The narrow moving band, the Dutch disease, and the competitive consequences of Mrs. Thatcher: Notes on trade in the presence of dynamic scale economies', *Journal of Development Economics*, 27:41–55.
Krugman, P. (1991) 'History versus expectations', *Quarterly Journal of Economics*, 106:651–667.
Krugman, P. (1992) 'Toward a counter-counter revolution in development theory', *Proceedings of the World Bank Annual Conference on Development Economics*, 1992:15–38.
Krugman, P. (1994) 'Urban concentration: The role of increasing returns and transport costs', *Proceedings of the World Bank Annual Conference on Development Economics*, 1994.

Lai, E.L.C. (1993) 'International intellectual property rights protection and the rate of product innovation', unpublished.

Levine, R. and Renelt, D. (1992) 'A sensitivity analysis of cross-country growth regressions', *American Economic Review*, 82:942–963.

Levine, R. and Zervos, S. (1993) 'What we have learned about policy and growth from cross-country regressions', *American Economic Review*, 84:426–430.

Lucas, R.E. (1988) 'On the mechanics of economic development', *Journal of Monetary Economics*, 22:3–42.

Lucas, R.E. (1990) 'Why doesn't capital flow from rich to poor countries?', *American Economic Review*, 80:92–96

Lucas, R.E. (1993) 'Making a miracle', *Econometrica*, 61:251–272.

Mahalanobis, P.C. (1955) 'The approach of operational research to planning in India', *Sankhya: The Indian Journal of Statistics*, 16:3–62.

Matsuyama, K. (1991) 'Increasing returns, industrialization and indeterminacy of equilibrium', *Quarterly Journal of Economics*, 106:616–650.

Mookherjee, D. and Ray, D. (1991) 'On the competitive pressure created by the diffusion of innovations', *Journal of Economic Theory*, 54:124–147.

Murphy, K., Shleifer, A. and Vishny, R. (1989) 'Industrialization and the big push', *Journal of Political Economy*, 97:1003–1026.

Odagiri, H. and Goto, A. (1993) 'The Japanese system of innovation: Past, present and future', in: R.R. Nelson, ed., *National innovation systems: A comparative analysis*. New York: Oxford University Press.

Pack, H. (1992) 'Technology gaps between industrial and developing countries: Are there dividends for latecomers', *Proceedings of the World Bank Annual Conference on Development Economics*, 1992:283–302.

Pack, H. (1994) 'Endogenous growth theory: Intellectual appeal and empirical shortcomings', *Journal of Economic Perspectives*, 8:55–72.

Quah, D. and Rauch, J.E. (1990) 'Openness and the rate of economic growth', U.C. San Diego, mimeo.

Rivera-Batiz, L.A. and Romer, P.M. (1991) 'Economic integration and endogenous growth', *Quarterly Journal of Economics*, 106:531–555.

Rodríguez, A. (1993) 'The division of labor and economic development', Stanford University, mimeo.

Rodrik, D. (1992) 'Closing the productivity gap: Does trade liberalization really help?', in: G. Helleiner, ed., *Trade policy, industrialization and development: New perspectives*, Oxford: Clarendon Press.

Romer, P.M. (1986) 'Increasing returns and long-run growth', *Journal of Political Economy*, 94:1002–1037.

Romer, P.M. (1987) 'Growth based on increasing returns due to specialization', *American Economic Review*, 77:56–62.

Romer, P.M. (1990) 'Endogenous technological change', *Journal of Political Economy*, 98:S71–S102.

Romer, P.M. (1994) 'New goods, old theory, and the welfare costs of trade restrictions', *Journal of Development Economics*, 43(1):5–38.

Rosenstein-Rodan, P. (1943) 'Problems of industrialization of Eastern and Southeastern Europe', *Economic Journal*, 53:202–211.

Segerstrom, P.S., Anant, T.C.A. and Dinopoulos, E. (1990) 'A Schumpeterian model of the product life cycle', *American Economic Review*, 80:1077–1091.

Shell, K. (1967) 'A model of inventive activity and capital accumulation', in: K. Shell, ed., *Essays in the theory of optimal economic growth*. Cambridge: MIT Press.

Solow, R.M. (1994) 'Perspectives on growth theory', *Journal of Economic Perspectives*, 8:45–54.

Srinivasan, T.N. (1993) 'Comments on Paul Romer: Two strategies for economic development: Using ideas vs. producing ideas', *Proceedings of the World Bank Annual Conference on Development Economics*, 1992:103–109.

Srinivasan, T.N. (forthcoming) 'Long-run growth theories and empirics: Anything new?', in: T. Ito and A. Krueger, eds., *Lessons from East Asian growth*. Chicago: University of Chicago Press.

Stokey, N. (1991) 'The volume and composition of trade between rich and poor countries', *Review of Economic Studies*, 58:63–80.

Tybout, J.R. (1992) 'Linking trade and productivity: New research directions', *World Bank Economic Review*, 6:189–211.

United Nations Conference on Trade and Development (1975) 'The role of the patent system in the transfer of technology to developing countries', New York: United Nations.

Uzawa, H. (1965) 'Optimal technical change in an aggregative model of economic growth', *International Economic Review*, 6:18–31.

von Neumann, J. (1945) 'A model of general equilibrium', *Review of Economic Studies*, 13:1–9.

Young, A. (1991) 'Learning by doing and the dynamic effects of international trade', *Quarterly Journal of Economics*, 106:369–405.

# INDEX

Note: linked page numbers are often used as a space-saver so entries on these pages may not necessarily be continuous.